Adventuring with Books

NCTE Bibliography Series

Adventuring with Books

A Booklist for Pre-K–Grade 6

Tenth Edition

Edited by

Julie M. Jensen
The University of Texas at Austin

Nancy L. Roser
The University of Texas at Austin

National Council of Teachers of English
1111 W. Kenyon Road, Urbana, Illinois 61801-1096

Manuscript Editor: Jane M. Curran

Production Editor: Rona S. Smith

Interior Design: Doug Burnett

Cover Design: R. Maul

Cover Illustration: Wayne Anderson. From *Dragon* © 1992 by Wayne Anderson. Used by permission of Green Tiger Press, an imprint of the Simon & Schuster Children's Book Division.

NCTE Stock Number 00791-3050

Permissions acknowledgements for photographs appear on p. 594.

Eve Merriam quote, p. 339, excerpted from " 'I' Says the Poem" from *A Sky Full of Poems* by Eve Merriam. © 1964, 1970, 1973 by Eve Merriam. Reprinted by permission of Marian Reiner.

It is the policy of NCTE in its journals and other publications to provide a forum for the open discussion of ideas concerning the content and the teaching of English and the language arts. Publicity accorded to any particular point of view does not imply endorsement by the Executive Committee, the Board of Directors, or the membership at large, except in announcements of policy, where such endorsement is clearly specified.

Library of Congress Cataloging-in-Publication Data

National Council of Teachers of English. Committee to Revise the
    Elementary School Booklist.
        Adventuring with books : a booklist for pre-K–grade 6 / National
    Council of Teachers of English, Committee to Revise the Elementary
    School Booklist ; edited by Julie M. Jensen, Nancy L. Roser. — 10th
    ed.
            p.   cm. — (NCTE bibliography series, ISSN 1051-4740)
        Rev. ed. of: Adventuring with books / Mary Jett-Simpson, editor,
    and the Committee on the Elementary School Booklist of the National
    Council of Teachers of English. 9th ed. c1989.
        Includes index.
        ISBN 0-8141-0079-1 : $19.95
        1. Bibliography—United States—Best books—Children's literature.
    2. Children's literature—Bibliography. I. Jensen, Julie M. II. Roser, Nancy.
    III. National Council of Teachers of English. Committee on the Elementary
    School Booklist. Adventuring with books (9th ed. c 1989). IV. Title. V. Series.
    Z1037.N346 1993
    [PN1009.A1]
    011.62—dc20
                                                                        93-30112
                                                                        CIP

Contents

Acknowledgments

We are grateful to the College of Education at The University of Texas at Austin and to Dr. JoAnn Sweeney for the allocation of space, equipment, and supplies, and for providing the assistance of five exceedingly competent and pleasant people: Nona Brown, our secretary, and graduate student assistants Cynthia Farest, Priscilla Myers, Rasma Strautmanis, and Judy Abbott.

Were it not for the cooperation of publishers, we would have had neither books to review nor incentives for reviewers to persevere.

Thirty Austin, Texas, area teachers, librarians, bookstore owners, college faculty, and graduate students helped us to compose reviews. Collectively they are known as the Committee to Revise the Elementary School Booklist: Judy Abbott, Rasma Barbee, Jennifer Battle, Lowell J. Bethel, Anne Bustard, Mark Dressman, Bonnie M. Elliott, Colleen M. Fairbanks, Cynthia Farest, Edmund J. Farrell, Angela Ferree, Carolyn Foote, Cyndy Hoffman, Barbara Immroth, Kenneth Kidd, Shirley Lukenbill, Jane Manaster, Miriam Martinez, Sarah McCarthey, Priscilla Myers, Tim Myers, Connie Nutt, Sharon O'Neal, Sheila Pederson, Stuart Reifel, Joan M. Shiring, William Teale, Barbara Thomas, Jane Townsend, and Georgene Wilson.

To a publisher who shipped a last-minute book overnight in order to avoid a glaring omission, and to a committee member who on deadline day arrived in the rain with a review of a book too good to overlook, and to a graduate student who never measured her time, and. . . . Thank you for caring.

Introduction

The purpose of the tenth edition of *Adventuring with Books* is exactly that of its nine predecessors: to help teachers, librarians, parents, and others introduce books of exceptional literary and artistic merit, accuracy, and appeal to preschoolers through sixth graders. As children's books increase in numbers and as their significance grows in homes and schools, so too does the importance of informed adult guides who can bring together books and children. Literature for children is emerging as not only the heart of the language arts curriculum, but as a singularly important contributor to learning in all subject areas. We hope the larger, illustrated format of this edition attracts the attention of an audience of book selectors that is as numerous and diverse as the literature itself.

Because the editorship of *Adventuring with Books* offers a vantage point on the state of the literary art, we begin with a few observations, each offered with due regard for certain limitations. First, we did not receive books from all publishers of books for children, particularly small presses, and we received only those titles that publishers chose to send. Second, even if we had received all the books published between 1988 and 1992, time and space would have set limitations. Of 20,000 or so books that might have been reviewed, we have included nearly 1,800 annotations of approximately 2,000 books (two or more books in a series appear in a single review). Some of the following observations derive from the books that we have reviewed here, others from the thousands of other books that complete the set.

The Children's Literary Art, 1988–1992: A Few Observations

A future audience of historians could use *Adventuring* as a window on the times. Such an audience might conclude that American society and the world of children's books in the late 1980s and early 1990s was profoundly affected by emerging high technologies, showed interest in and concern for the environment, demonstrated the effects of economic stress, liked the sameness of related books, was more than a little nostalgic, took a great interest in the preschool child, honored poetry, struggled to acknowledge diversity within society, and tried to give children the best possible reading materials in their schools.

Technology. The imaginations of today's authors and illustrators are less constrained than previously by the processes of book production. Books come in all sizes: miniature versions of timeless tales and "big books," which are proving to be valuable resources in classrooms and libraries. Books today are not just a feast for the eyes, but sometimes for the nose, ears, and fingertips as well. Thanks to microchips, books make sounds and play music. They can be scratched and sniffed. They glow in the dark. Their parts pop up by themselves or can be pushed and pulled, removed and replaced. They may reflect the shape of their subject matter, or through a series of overlays may reveal layers of an object or living thing. The formerly functional, such as an endpaper, is often an interest-capturing contributor to a book's total effect. Variations in format are wide and accomplished in their sophistication.

As with innovations in format, light years have passed since printing with woodcuts was the means of reproducing art. Joining woodcuts today is a vast array of media, not just wood and linoleum prints, or watercolor, oil, and acrylic paintings, or pencil and ink drawings, but paper collages, cloth tapestries, photographs, clay and paper sculptures, mosaics, crayons, defraction foil, and holograms. Furthermore, these media, alone and in combination, are used in the full range of styles seen in art for any audience. Technological advancements have reduced many of the tedious aspects of creating book illustrations, such as preparing color separations for a printer by hand. New equipment can reproduce art in any medium. Because technology invites and allows experimentation, the result is ever more varied and interesting visual experiences for children.

Interest in the Environment. Books related to environmental issues are but one small slice of the world of nonfiction literature now available to young readers. This edition of *Adventuring* features a large selection of books pertaining to sciences and mathematics, including aeronautics and space, the animal kingdom, archeology, conservation and ecology, earth science, meteorology, oceanography, energy, human health and development, machines, plants, prehistoric life, and other subjects. An equally lengthy section relates to aspects of the social sciences: careers; communication; community life; ethnic, racial, and religious groups; food, clothing, and shelter; geography; government; history; human relationships; religion; social issues and family relationships; transportation; and more. The opportunity both to learn about and to enjoy a great range of subject-matter fields is provided by numerous prominent authors: Patricia Lauber, Millicent Selsam, Seymour

Simon, Brent Ashabranner, Aliki, Mitsumasa Anno, Franklyn Branley, Milton Meltzer, Alice Provensen, Laurence Pringle, and others.

Yet, one unmistakable observation within that world of nonfiction is that children in the late eighties and early nineties are growing up with a concern for the future of the Earth. Perhaps triggered by events like the 1989 Alaskan oil spill and the 1990 celebration of the twentieth anniversary of Earth Day, a wave of books was published which promote environmental causes like recycling, forest preservation, and pesticide-free food. Some of these books are subtle in their messages, some are overt. Selected titles, such as those involving oil slicks, threatened wildlife, and sanctions on whaling and logging, have encountered industry claims of manipulation and one-sidedness. Even the Teenage Mutant Ninja Turtles got into the environmental act with an ABC book, featuring *Acid* rain, *Global* warming, and *Ozone* depletion. Books about the environment are not only a way to influence young minds; they are also a way to make money. The fact that 750,000 copies of the 1990 book *50 Simple Things Kids Can Do to Save the Planet* were sold was not lost on publishers, our next topic.

The Economics of Publishing Children's Books. Within today's publishing world, children's books are a notable success story. Sales now top a billion dollars a year for the first time in history. The children's literature business is financially healthy, and, more than ever, it is market-driven. A couple of facts: Few independently owned publishing companies remain; most have merged with big business conglomerates. Library sales have shrunk, so publishers are placing their focus on marketing directly to consumers. Shoppers with limited time and limited knowledge make different kinds of selection decisions than do professionals. Author Kathryn Lasky has sounded a warning:

> There is a dark side to the current boom in juvenile publishing that has me concerned. The dark side is that trade publishers are starting to behave like business people—in the worst sense of the word. . . . What does the market want? You never heard that question ten years ago. You only heard people speaking in terms of criteria for excellence. . . . In the past, the children's book industry has been very tolerant of risk takers. It is not so now. They have found some formulas that work—The Baby-sitters Club and Waldo, for instance—that have had a huge impact on juvenile publishing. (Lasky 1991)

We have noticed several additional formulas for catching the buyer's eye, among them a) "celebrity authors," including Fergie, Carly Simon, Judy Collins, Dom Deluise, Jimmy Buffett, Leontyne Price, Margot Fonteyn, and Paul Simon; b) best-selling adult authors as authors of books for children, including Mark Helprin, Ken Follett, Danielle Steel, Ken Kesey, James Herriot, and James Michener; c) lavishly illustrated reissues of books, especially those likely read during the childhoods of current buyers; d) eye-catching toy books and book-toy combinations, including inflatable globes, banks, stuffed animals, lapel buttons, football cards, lockets, skateboard stickers, and lunch bags; e) spin-offs from other media, including Nintendo, Garfield, Indiana Jones, and others; and f) spin-offs from just-published successful books, most prominently series books. The Baby-sitters Club, for example, had sold over forty-one million copies by 1991. Indeed, if child appeal were our only criterion for book selection, this volume would be overflowing with reviews of series books. We do include numerous reviews of reillustrated editions of older works. Flashy books were as irresistible to our committee members as they are to the buying public, and flash does not necessarily preclude enduring literary and artistic merit.

Series Books. Perhaps one-third of the books that we received from publishers were sets of two or more titles with a unifying characteristic: the same characters or similar subject matter. Paperbacks in which readers meet the same characters in book after book—sometimes a new book every month—are a phenomenon of the times. Their success, from the standpoint of sales, is testimony that many young readers enjoy contemporary realistic fiction in which they can find comfort and security in sameness. Although none is reviewed here, familiar series like The Bobbsey Twins ("revised and reissued") and The Hardy Boys and Nancy Drew ("with new modernized characters") are ubiquitous, as are series that have become popular in recent years. Here are just a dozen: *The Saddle Club, Sweet Valley Kids, Sweet Valley Twins, Fifth Grade Stars, The Treehouse Times, Camp Sunnyside Friends, Sleepover Friends, Ballet One, The Baby-sitters Club, The Gymnasts, Bad News Ballet,* and *New Kids on the Block.*

Nonfiction series, unified by topic and format, are remarkable for their numbers and for their range in quality. Several series are reviewed here, with a single review pertaining to the series as a whole, classified by topic, usually social studies, or sciences and mathematics. Rest assured that even if it is not included here, a series of books can be found on almost any topic imaginable. These we know for sure: sports figures, sports, holidays, natural disasters, insects, mammals, reptiles, cities, states, countries, planets, occupations, famous writers, presidents, ancient civilizations, breeds of dogs, explorers, women artists, and thirteen books about thirteen different types of beans.

Nostalgia. Although contemporary issues and efforts toward social relevance—nontraditional families, family violence, homelessness, chemical dependence, AIDS—figure prominently in today's books, interest in the past is substantial. One can look backward (or homeward) through retellings, reissues, and new issues in a variety of genres— historical fiction, poetry, biography, and information books. Those who contend that the route to learning and loving history is to make it come alive can feel encouraged by the range of choices.

Authors seem eager to celebrate anniversaries through children's books. Most prominently and voluminously celebrated during this period was the 500th anniversary of Columbus's voyage of l492. From the numerous reviews of books about Columbus, readers will immediately recognize diverse historical perspectives and viewpoints, some celebratory and some calling into question the humanity of the "discoverers."

Titles published between 1988 and 1992 reflect not only a looking back to earlier times, but to earlier books. A fierce devotion to the tried-and-true may be nostalgia or simply good business. Whether it's revolving pictures from another century or reissues with or without new illustrations, many of today's new books are old books. They speak to buyers dependent on the familiar. So many elaborately illustrated old tales have appeared in recent years that children can enjoy comparing multiple versions of the same tale; for example, Gail Haley's, Fred Marcellino's, and Alain Vaës's versions of Perrault's *Puss in Boots,* or Jan Brett's, Helen Cooper's, and Louise Voce's renditions of Lear's *The Owl and the Pussycat.*

Books for the Early Years. As evidence mounts about the value of reading aloud to children during the preschool years, publishers have responded to parent and educator interest in securing children's futures. Joining *Good Night Moon* and *Pat the Bunny* are books in abundance for looking at and handling by the three-and-under set, especially concept books and toy books in cloth or glossy board format. Also reviewed in the chapter entitled "Books for Young Children" is a large variety of counting books, alphabet books, nursery rhyme collections, color books, song books, and concept books through which young children can solve a puzzle, have an adventure, learn, and enjoy.

Poetry in Abundance. Anthologies, collections by a single poet, and individual poems in picture-book form are liberally represented in this edition, often with illustrations attractive enough to challenge the words for attention. Familiar names from present and past appear in the Author Index: Prelutsky, Schwartz, Adoff, Ciardi, de la Mare, Dickinson, Fisher, Kennedy, Lear, Merriam, Nash, Stafford, Whittier. Both new collections and reissues address a range of topics and feelings, and they do so in a range of forms. Just two of the ways in which the importance of poetry for children was affirmed during this period were through the ongoing NCTE Award for Excellence in Poetry for Children and by bestowing the 1989 John Newbery Medal on Paul Fleischman for *Joyful Noise: Poems for Two Voices*. Because poetry is flourishing, those who wish to share it with children have more to choose from; today it is easy to build a collection of old and new poems, to demonstrate the variety of poetry, and to share poetry that children are likely to enjoy.

Quest to Reflect Cultural Diversity. The availability of books that authentically portray a range of cultures remains low, although one can find between these covers an outstanding collection of books written or illustrated by or about members of varied cultures. The annotations reflect not only African Americans, Hispanics, Asians, Native Americans, and other cultural groups within American society, but also describe books from and about other countries, some in translation. Writers of great promise from several cultures have emerged during the past few years, who, with nurturing, may allow the editor of the next edition of *Adventuring* a greater representation of multicultural titles.

Literature in the Classroom. Consensus continues to grow that literature plays a critical role in children's literacy and subject-matter learning, as does support for teachers who believe that children should not only learn how to read, but should become readers. One notable example is the Teachers as Readers project of the Association of American Publishers, which helps classroom teachers establish teacher reading groups on the theory that teachers who read and talk about books with their peers create rich literate environments in their classrooms. Evidence that literature is coming to classrooms can be seen in the many classroom trade-book collections which now augment central school libraries. It can also be seen in instructional materials, some of which are drawing heavily on trade books. A question to be answered by informed teachers is whether a particular resource preserves literature as an aesthetic and imaginative experience or diminishes it.

Users of *Adventuring* will find it easy to bring literature into the school curriculum. Books are classified into subject-matter fields like sciences and mathematics, social studies, and fine arts. For those who know the pleasure and learning associated with reading aloud, some especially fine choices are included: *Morning Girl* (Dorris), *Monkey Island* (Fox), *Nothing but the Truth* (Avi), *Flight: The Journey of Charles Lindbergh* (Burleigh), *Chicken Sunday* (Polacco), *Shiloh* (Naylor), *Amazing Grace* (Hoffman), *Seven Blind Mice* (Young), and *The Stinky Cheese Man, and Other Fairly Stupid Tales* (Scieszka), among dozens of others. Still other books ease the transition to independence in reading because of their predictable elements. Finally, many books are about school itself, about reading and writing, and about authors and illustrators.

The children's literary art from 1988 to 1992 is flourishing. Those who select books for children have more titles from which to choose with each passing year; examples of excellence exist in goodly numbers; and children's literature is being accorded ever greater importance by those who find themselves in the company of preschoolers through sixth graders. Our excitement about new and talented faces who have burst upon the scene is tempered, however, by the loss during these years of Isaac Asimov, Patricia Beatty, Roald Dahl, Carolyn Haywood, Arnold Lobel, James Marshall, Eve Merriam, Scott O'Dell, Peggy Parrish, Alvin Schwartz, Theodor Seuss Geisel, and Isaac Bashevis Singer. Children's reading experiences will be enriched forever by their gifts.

How to Read an Annotation

Bringing order to thousands of books is a daunting task. In the end we sorted them into thirteen imperfect categories, most with numerous subcategories, then subcategories of subcategories. The thirteen appear as "chapter" divisions, each one introduced with a quote from a distinguished contributor to that particular facet of literature for children. Some divisions are based on the age of the reader ("Books for Young Children"), some on genre ("Fantasy"), and some on content ("Fine Arts"). So much for parallelism. Classifying books is fraught with problems; solid arguments can be made for assigning a number of books to many different places. To illustrate, Joanna Cole and Bruce Degen's *The Magic School Bus inside the Human Body*, a field trip through the circulatory system, is a fantasy filled with scientific information. It is intriguing fiction and also a fine content-area resource which provokes discussion and makes learning memorable.

Each annotation has been assigned an interest level. The "interest age range" uses the publishers' designations of the youngest to oldest children who might be interested in either hearing the book read aloud or reading it on their own. Estimates are given in the absence of publisher information. We supply this designation with all due caution that for some books and some children it may be unduly restrictive.

We have tried to inform book-selection decisions by indicating honors and awards bestowed upon single books. We do this in two ways: as part of the annotation itself, and in an appendix which describes major awards and honor lists and which compiles the names of 1988–92 winners. Because of the proliferation of ways to honor books, we have generally not noted runners-up for awards, state awards, or foreign awards.

Except for the series books reviewed collectively, each bibliographical entry includes the International Standard Book Number (ISBN) for the library edition.

The annotations themselves range in length. Each includes a story summary or content statement and, when relevant, commentary on art and design. Occasionally the annotations suggest topically related books, books by the same author, or suggestions for responding to the book, such as storytelling, drama, reading aloud, readers' theatre, writing and art experiences, and possible connections with subject-matter units.

Adventuring closes with a Directory of Publishers for ordering purposes, the appendix of award-winning books, and four indexes: author, illustrator, subject, and title.

As we emerge from four years of floating on a sea of books, we have regrets, the major one being that we weren't able to include annotations for hundreds of additional titles as meritorious as many of those included here. We weren't finished; we simply had to quit. We hope that we have organized this collection in a way that is useful, but we learned in the process that the work of imaginative minds defies categorization. We have had the opportunity to see a great range of books—a range in quality, in subject matter, in format, and in artistic medium and style. Those who select books for children have an enviable "problem": choosing from among so many and varied literary offerings that can be recommended with enthusiasm and that will be read with pleasure.

In 1990, midway through our work on this project, *Publishers Weekly* reported on the ten best-selling paperback books for children. Eight of the ten featured Teenage Mutant Ninja Turtles, accounting for the sale of eight million copies. One of the two remaining best-sellers was about the New Kids on the Block, and the other was a selection from The Baby-sitters Club series. How to read an annotation? Read it voraciously and conscientiously, here and wherever book-selection advice can be found. The guidance of a teacher or librarian, parent or friend who is informed about the children's literary world is critical beyond question.

Work Cited

Lasky, Kathryn. 1991. "Creativity in a Boom Industry," *The Horn Book Magazine*, November/December.

Biography

Children look for clues to life.
They want the truth,
They need the truth,
and they deserve it.
So I try to present characters honestly
with their paradoxes and their complexities,
their strengths and their weaknesses.

Jean Fritz, "Making It Real,"
Children's Literature in Education

1 Biography

1.1 Adler, David A. **A Picture Book of Benjamin Franklin.** Illustrated by John and Alexandra Wallner. Holiday House, 1990. ISBN 0-8234-0792-6. 29p. 7–10 (est.).

A writer, an inventor, a scientist, a statesman—Benjamin Franklin was all of these and more. David Adler's historical account, a volume in the Picture Book Biography series, chronicles this founding father's life and accomplishments. Double-page illustrations colorfully depict the life and times of early America. This biography would complement other books about Franklin, such as Jean Fritz's *What's the Big Idea, Ben Franklin?*

1.2 Adler, David A. **A Picture Book of Christopher Columbus.** Illustrated by John and Alexandra Wallner. Holiday House, 1991. ISBN 0-8234-0857-4. 32p. 6–12 (est.).

Another in David Adler's Picture Book Biographies series, this account of Columbus's life from boyhood to death is told through simple, informative text and full-page illustrations.

1.3 Adler, David A. **A Picture Book of Eleanor Roosevelt.** Illustrated by Robert Casilla. Holiday House, 1991. ISBN 0-8234-0856-6. 29p. 8–12 (est.).

A shy child who learned to be independent at an early age, Eleanor Roosevelt grew up to become "first lady of the world." This easy-to-read Picture Book Biography offers a brief history of the life and accomplishments of this remarkable woman. Full-page watercolor paintings complement the text and capture the memorable events in her life.

1.4 Adler, David A. **A Picture Book of Harriet Tubman.** Illustrated by Samuel Byrd. Holiday House, 1992. ISBN 0-8234-0926-0. 28p. 6–9.

The eleventh book in David Adler's Picture Book Biography series depicts the life of a prominent African American woman in American history. In her more than ninety years, Harriet Tubman escaped slavery, used earnings from odd jobs to lead other slaves to freedom on the Underground Railroad, served as a nurse and a spy, fought for women's right to vote, and opened a home for the elderly poor. Dark, expressive watercolors portray the sorrow, mystery, and unfailing courage that marked her life.

1.5 Adler, David A. **A Picture Book of Helen Keller.** Illustrated by John and Alexandra Wallner. Holiday House, 1990. ISBN 0-8234-0818-3. 30p. 7–10 (est.).

Left deaf and blind by a childhood illness, Helen Keller grew to become an inspiration to others all over the world. This easy-to-understand book in the Picture Book Biography series chronicles the life story of this courageous woman and highlights the important aspects of her life, including her education with Anne Sullivan and her dedication to the American Federation for the Blind. Full-page, soft-colored illustrations help to explain the struggles and triumphs of a remarkable woman.

1.6 Adler, David A. **A Picture Book of Jesse Owens.** Illustrated by Robert Casilla. Holiday House, 1992. ISBN 0-8234-0966-X. 32p. 6–9 (est.).

Son of sharecroppers and grandson of slaves, Jesse Owens set three world records and tied a fourth at the 1936 Olympics. David Adler's Picture Book Biography of the child who could run and jump primarily traces Owens's development as an athlete, but it does not skirt the prejudice that he faced both at home and at the games. Hitler, for example, snubbed Owens at the Olympic Games in Berlin. Illustrations are reminiscent of softly tinted photographs.

1.7 Adler, David A. **A Picture Book of John F. Kennedy.** Illustrated by Robert Casilla. Holiday House, 1991. ISBN 0-8234-0884-1. 29p. 8–12 (est.).

Born into a rich and powerful family, John F. Kennedy carved his own identity through his achievements and career in government. This Picture Book Biography profiles Kennedy's life. Full-page, watercolor paintings, many from actual photographs, illustrate the significant events in his life, from his childhood to his assassination.

1.8 Adler, David A. **A Picture Book of Thomas Jefferson.** Illustrated by John and Alexandra Wallner. Holiday House, 1990. ISBN 0-8234-0791-8. 29p. 7–10 (est.).

He was eager to learn, loved to read and invent, and had ideas of his own—he was Thomas Jefferson. This Picture Book Biography presents a simple chronological account of Jefferson's private life as colonist and father, as well as his public life as legislator, statesman, and president—"father of our democracy." Colorful double-page watercolors illustrate the informative and straightforward text.

1.9   Aliki. **The King's Day: Louis XIV of France.** Illustrated by Aliki. Thomas Y. Crowell, 1989. ISBN 0-690-04590-5. 28p. 7–11.

King Louis XIV of France lived in the grandest of styles. His palaces were magnificent; his wigs, robes, and jewels were the finest; and his days were filled with ceremonial rituals and spectacular events. Detailed information can be gained both from the drawings and their captions, which together depict a day in the life of one of France's most extravagant and yet most brilliant kings.

1.10   Alper, Ann Fitzpatrick. **Forgotten Voyager: The Story of Amerigo Vespucci.** Carolrhoda Books, 1991. ISBN 0-87614-442-3. 80p. 8–12.

Amerigo Vespucci's accomplishments—and the slanders that contributed to his relative obscurity—are fleshed out in this readable account. From his Florentine childhood to his serious geographical scholarship and exploration, Vespucci is presented as an energetic, intelligent, and ambitious European discoverer. Historical illustrations and primary source material add power to the narrative.

1.11   Anderson, Joan. **Christopher Columbus: From Vision to Voyage.** Photographs by George Ancona. Dial Books for Young Readers, 1991. ISBN 0-8037-1042-9. 48p. 7–10 (est.).

Joan Anderson portrays Columbus as a man of "vivid imagination, great curiosity, tremendous energy, the courage to stand by his beliefs, and a willingness to take risks" in this account of the of the "inner" journey—the years 1459–92—that led to his first sailing. George Ancona's color photographs, set in Spain, feature members of the Spanish National Opera dressed in period costumes.

1.12   Banish, Roslyn, with Jennifer Jordan-Wong. **A Forever Family.** Photographs by Roslyn Banish. HarperCollins, 1992. ISBN 0-06-021674-3. 44p. 5–8.

After spending half of her life in foster homes, eight-year-old Jennifer Jordan-Wong tells the story of her adoption by a "forever family." With the help of black-and-white photographs of parents, extended family, foster parents, social workers, friends, pets, and important places and activities, a heartwarming and informative account emerges.

1.13   Bernheim, Mark. **Father of the Orphans: The Story of Janusz Korczak.** Lodestar Books, 1989. ISBN 0-525-67265-6. 160p. 11 and up (est.).

In this volume in the Jewish Biography series, Mark Bernheim weaves a poignant tale of dignity and love in Warsaw during the Nazi occupation. Janusz Korczak's story begins with his privileged childhood and moves through his adult life of poverty and sacrifice. Korczak was one of the first physicians in Europe to dedicate his career to the care of children, and his devotion to his orphanage resulted in the ultimate sacrifice of his life for these Jewish children. Middle-grade students will come away wanting to know more about how such atrocities could have occurred.

1.14   Bernstein, Joanne E., and Rose Blue, with Alan Jay Gerber. **Judith Resnik: Challenger Astronaut.** Lodestar Books, 1990. ISBN 0-525-67305-9. 100p. 10 and up (est.).

This biography traces Judith Resnik's life from young girl to engineer/scientist to space-shuttle astronaut. Although much of the book focuses on the *Discovery* mission and the *Challenger* tragedy that took Resnik's life, the authors also explore her reactions to her parents' bitter divorce, the influence of Judaism on her life, the breakup of her own marriage, and her struggle to become an astronaut. Black-and-white photos, a reading list, and an index complement the text.

1.15   Black, Sheila. **Sitting Bull and the Battle of the Little Bighorn.** Cwiklik, Robert. **King Philip and the War with the Colonists. Sequoyah and the Cherokee Alphabet.** McClard, Megan, and George Ypsilantis. **Hiawatha and the Iroquois League.** Shorto, Russell. **Geronimo and the Struggle for Apache Freedom. Tecumseh and the Dream of an American Indian Nation.** Illustrated by L. L. Cundiff; Ed Lee; T. Lewis; Frank Riccio; Tim Sisco; Robert L. Smith. Silver Burdett Press, 1989. Approx. 120p. 10–13.

Alvin Josephy's Biography Series of American Indians is characterized by its thoroughness, its accuracy, its sense of drama, and its emphasis on Native American perspectives. Each volume tells the story of a great Native American, with subjects ranging from Sitting Bull to Sequoyah to Hiawatha. The writing is clear and rich with historical detail, explanation, analysis, and narrative excitement. Line drawings and historical photographs accompany each text, along with a list of suggested readings.

1.16   Blos, Joan W. **The Heroine of the Titanic: A Tale Both True and Otherwise of the Life of Molly Brown.** Illustrated by Tennessee Dixon. Morrow Junior Books, 1991. ISBN 0-688-07547- 9. 40p. 6 and up.

Joan Blos pieces together the facts and legends surrounding the exuberant life of Margaret (Molly) Tobin Brown, focusing on her adventure-seeking derring-do and her courageous spirit as an "unsinkable" survivor of the *Titanic*. Brown's feats and foibles are recounted in lyrical prose, with text embedded in paintings that capture wistful hues of bygone elegance, but that give Molly Brown a vivacity undiminished by advancing age. As an added touch, a sprinkle of verse in Victorian frames works like a Greek chorus to comment on the saga.

1.17   Brighton, Catherine. **Nijinsky: Scenes from the Childhood of the Great Dancer.** Illustrated by Catherine Brighton. Doubleday, 1989. ISBN 0-385-24926-8. 26p. 4–8.

As a little boy, future great ballet dancer Vaslav Nijinsky traveled through Russia with his brother, sister, and theatrical parents and learned to dance. When the family fortunes changed and his father walked out, his mother taught dance, and Vaslav won a place at the Imperial Ballet School in St. Petersburg, propelling his legendary success. Bordered in dark green, evocative watercolor illustrations reveal not only the Nijinsky family, but a portrait of turn-of-the-century Russia as well.

1.18   Byars, Betsy. **The Moon and I.** Julian Messner, 1992. ISBN 0-671-74165-9. 96p. 10 and up (est.).

In lighthearted anecdotes woven together by a snake that she calls Moon, Betsy Byars describes her life and discusses her approach to writing in this slim, delightful memoir. Readers will learn how she associates her villains with the horrific Bubba of her youth, how she begins with title pages and keeps them long after she's forgotten their stories, and how she believes in the importance of characters and the need for authority in authoring. Black-and-white photographs show Byars with Moon throughout her life.

1.19 Carpenter, Angelica Shirley, and Jean Shirley. **L. Frank Baum: Royal Historian of Oz.** Lerner, 1992. ISBN 0-8225-4910-7. 144p. 10 and up.

Lyman Frank Baum was a fanciful child, imagining that scarecrows could run across the fields that they protected. Later, he dressed the window of his general store with pots and pans assembled to look like a man. Thus originated two of his characters in *The Wonderful Wizard of Oz.* Frank Baum's enterprises, his family life, and his determination to write despite ill health provide the framework for this responsible biography of an author who wrote his life into his stories for children.

1.20 Collins, David R. **Malcolm X: Black Rage.** Dillon Press, 1992. ISBN 0-87518-498-7. 104p. 10 and up.

Solutions to racial prejudice are complex and never easily discussed in the classroom. David Collins, however, portrays more than anger in this sensitive biography of Malcolm X, one of twenty-two books in the People in Focus series. Facts are presented, with the judgment of Malcolm's life left to the reader. Teachers and students alike will find the text, black-and-white photographs, bibliography, and index useful and informative.

1.21 Conrad, Pam. **Prairie Visions: The Life and Times of Solomon Butcher.** Photographs by Solomon Butcher. HarperCollins, 1991. ISBN 0-06-021375-2. 85p. 11 and up.

Solomon Butcher, an early Nebraska settler, was a man unable to decide which of his many talents and interests to pursue. He decided to record the settlement history of Custer County in photographs, a remarkably innovative project for the times. Captivated by his photographs while researching her novel *Prairie Songs,* Pam Conrad created a pictorial account of Butcher's eclectic life and of the courageous pioneer families that he immortalized more than a hundred years ago. *Notable 1991 Children's Trade Books in the Field of Social Studies.*

1.22 Crews, Donald. **Bigmama's.** Illustrated by Donald Crews. Greenwillow Books, 1991. ISBN 0-688-09951-3. 32p. 4–7 (est.).

Bigmama once told grandson Donald Crews, "Boy, you going to amount to something." This autobiographical picture book of author/illustrator Crews is further testimony to her faith. Recalling long-ago family train trips back to the farm in Cottondale, Florida, to see Bigmama and Bigpapa, Crews uses watercolor and color dyes to reassure that, in memory at least, nothing changes. From fishing hole to deep well to the peddle sewing machine in the hall and to the reunion with family, "everything is as it should be."

1.23 Darby, Jean. **Martin Luther King, Jr.** Lerner, 1990. ISBN 0-8225-4902-6. 144p. 10 and up.

This highly readable, concise biography of Martin Luther King, Jr., explores the charismatic man's life as a small child in segregated Atlanta, his early career as a Baptist minister in Montgomery, Alabama, and his subsequent emergence as leader of the American civil rights movement of the 1950s and 1960s. Accompanying the text are striking black-and-white photographs depicting King's family, the Montgomery bus boycott, Freedom Riders, and the famous March on Washington. Jean Darby concludes the book with a helpful bibliography, glossary, and index. *Notable 1990 Children's Trade Books in the Field of Social Studies.*

1.24 dePaola, Tomie. **Patrick: Patron Saint of Ireland.** Illustrated by Tomie dePaola. Holiday House, 1992. ISBN 0-8234-0924-4. 32p. 3–8 (est.).

The story of Saint Patrick begins with his boyhood in Britain, when he was kidnapped and enslaved in Ireland. Although he made his way home again, he returned to Ireland to found the first church there and to baptize thousands. Facts about Patrick's life are separated from the legends that surround him, including driving the snakes from Ireland. Tomie dePaola interprets both life and legends with earth-tone static forms that are uniquely his, but they are also reminiscent of early religious paintings.

1.25 Emmert, Michelle. **I'm the Big Sister Now.** Illustrated by Gail Owens. Albert Whitman, 1989. ISBN 0-8075-3458-7. 28p. 7–11 (est.).

Even though nine-year-old Michelle Emmert is younger than her sister Amy, Michelle plays the role of big sister because Amy has cerebral palsy and cannot walk or talk or sit unsupported. Nevertheless, Amy brings unmitigated joy to those who love her. In a straightforward description, Michelle tells Amy's story: her needs, her care, her gifts, and her responses to her world. A photograph of the sisters and illustrations in pencil and watercolor provide sensitive accompaniment to the narrative.

1.26 Fleischman, Paul. **Townsend's Warbler.** HarperCollins/Charlotte Zolotow Books, 1992. ISBN 0-06-021875-4. 52p. 9–12.

The story of naturalist John Kirk Townsend's exploration of the American Northwest in 1834 is interwoven with the story of a previously unknown warbler's migration from South America to North America. After an arduous journey and encounters with storms, wild rivers, and Native American war parties, Townsend discovered the warbler, which was later named for him. The text, which draws on Townsend's journal, is interspersed with black-and-white photos, paintings of period scenes, and portraits.

1.27   Ford, Barbara. **Walt Disney.** Walker, 1989. ISBN 0-8027-6865-2. 156p. 9–12.

This clearly narrated biography, generously illustrated with black-and-white photographs, provides fascinating insight into the creator of beloved characters for children. In spite of monetary hardships and the negativism of friends and family, Walt Disney's determination and perseverance enabled him to fulfill his dreams. Although there are references to Disney's personality quirks, the author leaves readers with an understanding of and admiration for a creative genius who revolutionized the entertainment world.

1.28   Foreman, Michael. **War Boy: A Country Childhood.** Illustrated by Michael Foreman. Little, Brown/Arcade, 1990. ISBN 1-55970-049-1. 92p. 8 and up (est.).

In a memoir of World War II from the perspective of a very young English boy, illustrator Michael Foreman re-creates a time when his village was crowded with soldiers, when barbed wire lined the beaches against invasion, and when incendiary bombs lit the night sky, one just missing young Michael's bed. But there are also memories of the respite of his mother's tea shop, boyhood games, and fatherly soldiers. The narration is dispassionate, and Foreman's watercolor illustrations are accompanied by line drawings, war posters, and diagrams.

1.29   Freedman, Russell. **The Wright Brothers: How They Invented the Airplane.** Illustrated by Wilbur and Orville Wright. Holiday House, 1991. ISBN 0-8234-0875-2. 124p. 8 and up.

Amazingly, Wilbur and Orville Wright, inventors of the airplane, never had any special training in science or engineering. Readers might also be interested to learn that when the brothers tested their first "full-size, man-carrying glider" in Kitty Hawk, North Carolina, in the fall of 1900, they lived in a tent, and that when the Wrights offered their successful airplane idea to the U.S. military, they were "turned down without a hearing." This photographic account of the Wrights' most famous invention is clearly written and well documented by their own words and photographs. *Notable 1991 Children's Trade Books in the Field of Social Studies.*

1.30   Fritz, Jean. **Bully for You, Teddy Roosevelt!** Illustrated by Mike Wimmer. G. P. Putnam's Sons, 1991. ISBN 0-399-21769-X. 128p. 10 and up.

Both adults and children will find this biography of Theodore Roosevelt by award-winning author Jean Fritz entertaining and may encounter some new facts about our twenty-sixth president. For example, Teddy Roosevelt once owned land in the Dakotas and wanted to become a rancher; he ran for mayor of New York City and was elected governor of New York before being nominated as vice-president under William McKinley; and he was the first person inaugurated to the Conservation Hall of Fame. *Notable 1991 Children's Trade Books in the Field of Social Studies.*

1.31   Fritz, Jean. **George Washington's Mother.** Illustrated by Dy-Anne DiSalvo-Ryan. Grosset and Dunlap, 1992. ISBN 0-448-40385-4. 48p. 7–9.

Not a great deal is known about George Washington's mother, Mary Ball Washington. But in her impeccable research style, Jean Fritz must have ferreted deeds, ledgers, and letters to add to published accounts. In the seamless result for beginning readers, Mary Washington is revealed as both strong and weak, dependent and independent, and always a bit impecunious. On tinted paper, the illustrations have both colonial flair and humor.

1.32   Fritz, Jean. **The Great Little Madison.** G. P. Putnam's Sons, 1989. ISBN 0-399-21768-1. 160p. 10 and up (est.).

Just as Jean Fritz skillfully sculpts the dimensions of "a pale, sickly boy with a weak voice" who became the fourth U.S. president, so does she tell of his times. Madison is revealed as a quiet but articulate spokesman and meticulous recordkeeper at the constitutional convention, as a student of government, as a friend and admirer of Jefferson, and, finally, as a president passionately devoted to the preservation of the union. Political crossfire is made comprehensible and intriguing. Dolley Madison's humor, courage, and vanity also shine through. *Boston Globe–Horn Book Nonfiction Award, 1990.*

1.33 Golenbock, Peter. **Teammates.** Illustrated by Paul Bacon. Harcourt Brace Jovanovich/Gulliver Books, 1990. ISBN 0-15-200603-6. 32p. 5–12 (est.).

Drawings, photographs, and baseball cards help tell an important story in baseball history. When Jackie Robinson joined the Brooklyn Dodgers in 1947, he became the first African American to play on a major-league baseball team, and also became a victim of slurs, slights, affronts, and threats from his teammates and others. The focal event of this account is when Pee Wee Reese crossed the field in Cincinnati, stood next to Robinson, put an arm around him, and silenced the taunting crowds by stating, "This man is my teammate." *Notable 1990 Children's Trade Books in the Field of Social Studies.*

1.34 Harrison, Barbara, and Daniel Terris. **A Twilight Struggle: The Life of John Fitzgerald Kennedy.** Lothrop, Lee and Shepard Books, 1992. ISBN 0-688-08830-9. 159p. 10 and up.

This balanced portrait of John F. Kennedy incorporates current historical information, family influences, and a cogent analysis of President Kennedy's political life. Based upon the Home Box Office documentary *JFK: In His Own Words,* the biography details both the president's personal life and his political career, revealing the president as a complex, even flawed, political leader. Photographs, a selected bibliography, a chronology of important events, and an index provide useful resources for the reader.

1.35 Haskins, Jim. **Outward Dreams: Black Inventors and Their Inventions.** Walker, 1991. ISBN 0-8027-6999-2. 128p. 12 and up.

If history is the living record of a society, its ideas, codes, laws, and achievements, then significant groups of people have been omitted from the record. Nowhere is this more true than with African American inventors and their inventions. Now the reader can learn who built the first steam engine, the first shoemaking machine, the first clock in the United States and the first traffic light. Jim Haskins offers a refreshing look at the contributions of African Americans, thus helping to correct some significant oversights. A comprehensive index of black inventors between 1834 and 1900 is included.

1.36   Houston, Gloria. **My Great-Aunt Arizona.** Illustrated by Susan Condie Lamb. HarperCollins, 1992. ISBN 0-06-022607-2. 32p. 6–10 (est.).

Arizona Houston Hughes was a singer, a reader, a dancer, a dreamer, and, most of all, a teacher. In this realistic yet fictional account of her life, Arizona touches generations of her Appalachian fourth-grade students and helps them aspire to visit those faraway places that she had only visited in her mind, through her voracious reading of books. Young teachers-to-be will delight in Susan Condie Lamb's expressive illustrations of a woman who perserved to achieve her dream and to help dreams emerge for others.

1.37   Hurwitz, Johanna. **Astrid Lindgren: Storyteller to the World.** Illustrated by Michael Dooling. Puffin Books, 1991. ISBN 0-14-032692-8. 54p. 7–11.

Astrid Lindgren enjoyed childhood on a farm in southern Sweden before moving to Stockholm, marrying, and raising a family. Her memories and adventures, some of which she told to her own children, were woven into more than forty books and were delightfully exaggerated in the tales of Pippi Longstocking. This affectionate biography in the Women of Our Time series attributes Lindgren's international success to her appealing interpretation of family life. Although the book is aimed toward seven- to eleven-year-old readers, it is sufficiently researched and detailed to appeal to teenagers.

1.38   Ireland, Karin. **Albert Einstein.** Silver Burdett Press, 1989. ISBN 0-382-09523-5. 144p. 10 and up.

The details of Einstein's daily life and personality presented in this biography help the reader appreciate him as a man rather than a superman. Einstein is portrayed as a single-minded, very private individual who was first considered a slow learner and who came to define the word *scientist.* Consistent with the format of the Pioneers in Change series, black-and-white photographs clarify the meaty text, and a time-line chronicles the scientist's major accomplishments.

1.39   Jaspersohn, William. **Senator: A Profile of Bill Bradley in the U.S. Senate.** Harcourt Brace Jovanovich, 1992. ISBN 0-15-272880-5. 224p. 12 and up.

Richly illustrated with both black-and-white and colored photographs, this lucid biography, somewhat breezy in tone, first sketches Bill Bradley's days as an All-American basketball player at Princeton, Rhodes scholar, and star with the New York Knickerbockers. Concentrating thereafter on Bradley's life as U.S. Senator from New Jersey, the volume presents the legislator in a variety of roles—author of major bills, envoy to the Soviet Union, campaigner for reelection. Bradley emerges throughout as industrious, highly intelligent, sensitive, and sensible.

1.40   Johnson, Rick L. **Bo Jackson: Baseball/Football Superstar.** Dillon Press, 1991. ISBN 0-87518-489-8. 64p. 7–10 (est.).

Superstar sports figure Bo Jackson was already a football, track, and baseball star back home in McAdory High School in McCalla, Alabama. At Auburn University, he won the Heisman Trophy as the best college football athlete in the nation, and after college he became both a professional baseball and football player. Yet, this Taking Part biography for younger readers, illustrated with photographs, makes Jackson a real person, an African American child of poverty with imperfect school behavior and serious youthful offenses, and in need of help in growing up.

1.41   Levinson, Nancy Smiler. **Christopher Columbus: Voyager to the Unknown.** Lodestar Books, 1990. ISBN 0-525-67292-3. 128p. 9–12.

This well-documented discussion of Columbus's voyages includes archival documents, black-and-white reproductions of portraits, and photographs of artifacts, charts, and maps. In chapter format, Nancy Smiler Levinson's oversize volume sets the historical stage, describes each of the voyages, and addresses the place of Christopher Columbus in history. In large print with lots of white space, information is presented in a straightforward way, without dodging the admiral's frailties. A chronology of events and even the crew list for the first voyage are included.

1.42   Little, Jean. **Stars Come Out Within.** Viking Penguin, 1990. ISBN 0-670-82965-X. 263p. 10 and up (est.).

Award-winning Canadian children's author Jean Little continues her memoirs first begun in *Little by Little*, this time focusing on her adult life. Little recounts episodes about her own writing, her short but meaningful teaching career, her remarkable mother, her significant friends, her Seeing-Eye dog, Zephyr, and SAM, her talking computer. Candid about her experiences with depression and the adjustments that she makes as her sight decreases, this determined woman of strength tells a moving story. *ALA Notable Children's Books, 1992.*

1.43   Livingston, Myra Cohn. **Let Freedom Ring: A Ballad of Martin Luther King, Jr.** Illustrated by Samuel Byrd. Holiday House, 1992. ISBN 0-8234-0957-0. 32p. 6–10 (est.).

The life work and mission of Martin Luther King, Jr., are told in ballad form, borrowing words and phrases from King's own sermons and speeches and embedding them within rhythmic text. Paintings are large, powerful, color interpretations of actual photographs and scenes from King's life. A reference page identifies the scenes and sources of quotations. The ballad concludes with a variation on its repeated chorus: "From every mountainside, let freedom ring. / Your dream is our dream, Martin Luther King."

1.44   Marrin, Albert. **Napoleon and the Napoleonic Wars.** Viking Penguin, 1991. ISBN 0-670-83480-7. 276p. 10 and up.

This biography thoughtfully presents the turmoil and triumphs of the Napoleonic era of the late seventeenth and early eighteenth centuries. Historian Albert Marrin traces Napoleon's life from his birth on Corsica to his early military successes as the "Little Corporal" to his victorious coronation as European Emperor to his ultimate defeat at Waterloo and imprisonment on Elba. Black-and-white illustrations (paintings, portraits, cartoons) and a helpful bibliography supplement the text. *National Council of Social Studies Notable Children's Trade Books, 1992.*

1.45   McKissack, Patricia C. **Jesse Jackson: A Biography.** Scholastic, 1989. ISBN 0-590-43181-1. 108p. 8–12.

Patricia McKissack's biography of African American leader Jesse Louis Jackson follows his many trails: from the dusty roads of Greenville, South Carolina, in 1941 to the difficult campaigns for the presidency in 1984 and 1988; from his leadership of SCLC's Operation Breadbasket in Chicago to his organization of the Rainbow Coalition in Washington, D.C.; from "country preacher" to eloquent orator; from commitment to America's poor to audiences with foreign dignitaries. Whatever Jackson's path, McKissack's words, along with dozens of black-and-white photographs, make clear Jackson's impact upon the course of history. *Notable 1989 Children's Trade Books in the Field of Social Studies.*

1.46   Neimark, Anne E. **Diego Rivera: Artist of the People.** Harper-Collins, 1992. ISBN 0-06-021784-7. 116p. 8–12.

In a fictionalized biography based partly on Diego Rivera's own autobiography and writings, Anne Neimark first creates a portrait of the Mexican artist as boy, round and curious and full of mischief and art. Then, against the political turmoil of his times, Rivera becomes a man, determined to record the stories around him and to be a participant as well. His records are his famous murals, testifying to his people in the places where his people would see them. Neimark includes reproductions of the artist's work, beginning with a drawing by three-year-old Diego.

1.47   Nichols, Janet. **American Music Makers: An Introduction to American Composers.** Walker, 1990. ISBN 0-8027-6958-6. 209p. 12 and up.

Janet Nichols offers ten fascinating portraits of talented American composers, from the nineteenth-century pianist Louis Gottschalk to the internationally acclaimed George Gershwin to the contemporary innovator Philip Glass. Presented in chronological order, the mini-biographies explore the musicians' personal lives, professional successes and failures, and specific contributions to the musical field. Black-and-white photos of the nine men and one woman accompany the text, along with bibliographies of recommended books and recordings, a glossary, and an index.

1.48   Osborne, Mary Pope. **The Many Lives of Benjamin Franklin.** Dial Books for Young Readers, 1990. ISBN 0-8037-0680-4. 144p. 9–12.

A scientist, statesman, diplomat, and inventor—Benjamin Franklin was all of these and more. The "many lives" of one of America's founding fathers are sequentially explored in Mary Pope Osborne's account of Franklin's life from childhood until death. A list of his accomplishments and a time-line of important events in his life help to organize the information presented in this book. Historical black-and-white photographs of early America further authenticate a well-researched biography. *Notable 1990 Children's Trade Books in the Field of Social Studies.*

1.49   Parks, Rosa, with Jim Haskins. **Rosa Parks: My Story.** Dial Books, 1992. ISBN 0-8037-0673-1. 192p. 12 and up (est.).

Rosa Parks's quiet defiance on a bus in Montgomery, Alabama, in 1955 is often cited as a pivotal moment in the struggle for civil rights in the United States. Here, with family photos and great modesty, Parks tells the story of her ancestry, her marriage, and the events that led to and affected her decision not to abandon her seat that day. Her arrest and her life subsequent to the ensuing societal changes are also documented.

1.50   Peet, Bill. **Bill Peet: An Autobiography.** Illustrated by Bill Peet. Houghton Mifflin, 1989. ISBN 0-395-50932-7. 90p. 6–12 (est.).

In a book filled with charcoal drawings of his beloved characters and true-life experiences on every page, popular and prolific author/illustrator Bill Peet tells the story of his life. As a young boy, he loved to draw. Hired at Walt Disney Studios upon graduation from art school, he remained for nearly thirty years and became one of Disney's top artists. At the same time, Peet began to write and illustrate the stories that he originally told to his own children. Now he works full-time creating books. *Caldecott Honor Medal, 1990.*

1.51   Porter, A. P. **Jump at de Sun: The Story of Zora Neale Hurston.** Carolrhoda Books, 1992. ISBN 0-87614-667-1. 96p. 8–12.

Folklorist/novelist Zora Neale Hurston celebrated a distinctively African cultural point of view at a time when the American part of her heritage was celebrated by many of her contemporaries. Her unorthodox views and eccentric personality prevented her from achieving in her lifetime the recognition or financial stability that she deserved. Author A. P. Porter recounts Hurston's triumphs and failures in honest and engaging terms; abundant photographs and clear prose combine to make an entertaining biography of this African American writer.

1.52   Rappaport, Doreen. **Living Dangerously: American Women Who Risked Their Lives for Adventure.** HarperCollins, 1991. ISBN 0-06-025109-3. 117p. 9–13.

Riding over Niagara Falls in a barrel, heading out on safari, and scaling Mount Huascarán in Peru are but three of the adventures recounted in this text. The reader learns about six women who, like their male counterparts Charles Lindbergh and Robert Perry, sought to accomplish feats of daring. Each portrayal includes black-and-white photographs and biographical data. The bibliography and list of other women adventurers provide suggestions for further reading.

A.

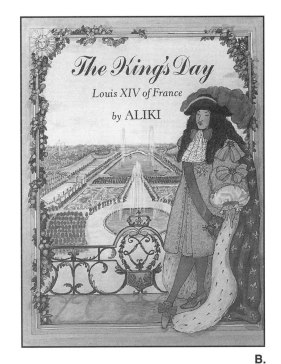

B.

C.

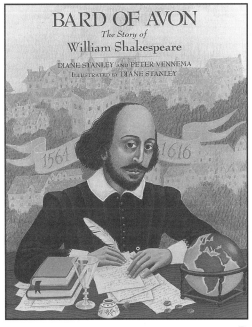

D.

A. *Dear Dr. Bell . . . Your friend, Helen Keller* by Judith St. George; cover illustration by Ellen Thompson (see 1.58). **B.** *The King's Day: Louis XIV of France* by Aliki (see 1.9). **C.** *Jump at de Sun: The Story of Zora Neale Hurston* by A. P. Porter (see 1.51). **D.** *Bard of Avon: The Story of William Shakespeare* by Diane Stanley and Peter Vennema; illustrated by Diane Stanley (see 1.61).

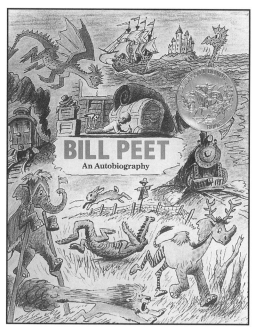

A.

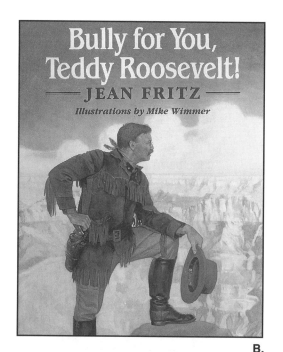

B.

C.

D.

A. *Bill Peet: An Autobiography* by Bill Peet (see 1.50). **B.** *Bully for You, Teddy Roosevelt!* by Jean Fritz; illustrations by Mike Wimmer (see 1.30). **C.** *Celia's Island Journal* by Celia Thaxter; adapted and illustrated by Loretta Krupinski (see 1.66). **D.** *Townsend's Warbler* by Paul Fleischman (see 1.26).

1.53 Richmond, Robin. **Introducing Michelangelo.** Little, Brown, 1991. ISBN 0-316-74440-9. 32p. 10–12.

This visually captivating account conveys both the sensory power of Michelangelo's work and the fascination of his life and era. Reproductions of the artist's friezes, statues, and portraits of Christian and mythic figures are augmented with works by his contemporaries, offered as further explanation of the historical period. For example, paintings of Florence, of Medici merchant princes, and of an artist's studio are included. Insets add practical information about how Michelangelo painted the Sistine Chapel and how its original luminescence has been restored.

1.54 Roth, Susan L. **Marco Polo: His Notebook.** Doubleday, 1991. ISBN 0-385-26555-7. 32p. 8–12 (est.).

This fictionalized version of Marco Polo's notebook, written on "parchment," records the thirteenth-century travels originally described in Polo's own *Travels of Marco Polo.* Maps, paintings, and drawings help to tell the tale of visiting Mount Ararat, Persian fire-eaters, the Great Khan, and China with its coal, postal service, and paper money. Visually splendid, the format invites close examination.

1.55 Rowland, Della. **The Story of Sacajawea, Guide to Lewis and Clark.** Illustrated by Richard Leonard. Dell/Yearling Books, 1989. ISBN 0-440-40215-8. 92p. 8–11.

Della Rowland dramatically relates the harrowing, exciting exploits of Sacajawea, the Shoshone guide to Lewis and Clark as they explored America's Northwest Territory. Stolen from her family as a young girl, enslaved by a rival Indian tribe, and then sold to a rough fur trapper, this young woman nevertheless revealed courage and wisdom far beyond her years. Boys and girls alike will enjoy reading about the expedition's encounters with hostile Native Americans, wild animals, and nature's harsh elements.

1.56 Ryan, Nolan, and Harvey Frommer. **Throwing Heat: The Autobiography of Nolan Ryan.** Avon Books, 1990. ISBN 0-380-70826-4. 249p. 12 and up (est.).

Nolan Ryan tells his story of growing up in a small Texas town, being drafted into the major leagues after high school, marrying his childhood sweetheart, and ultimately becoming the greatest pitcher in baseball history. Interspersed throughout the narrative are the voices of family, scouts, coaches, teammates, and competitors who have known Ryan over the years. The highly readable, interesting prose is complemented by black-and-white photographs of Ryan at different stages of his life.

1.57   Rylant, Cynthia. **But I'll Be Back Again: An Album.** Orchard Books/Richard Jackson Books, 1989. ISBN 0-531-08406-X. 80p. 10–12.

When Cynthia Rylant was a little girl in West Virginia, her father left her mother, and then her mother left her to go to nursing school. So Rylant lived with her grandparents and sought solace in music and her friends. Supplemented with quotes from Beatles songs and black-and-white photographs that create the appearance of a personal album, this honest, introspective autobiography documents Rylant's childhood and adolescence and includes her memories of thoughts and boyfriends, with which early adolescents can identify.

1.58   St. George, Judith. **Dear Dr. Bell . . . Your friend, Helen Keller.** G. P. Putnam's Sons, 1992. ISBN 0-399-2237-1. 96p. 10–12 (est.).

The lives of two inspirational contemporaries, Alexander Graham Bell and Helen Keller, crossed repeatedly. It was Bell who recommended to Keller's father that a tutor be secured for the girl, and so Annie Sullivan came into Keller's life. From the age of seven and for almost thirty-five years, Helen Keller corresponded with Dr. Bell. Judith St. George explains the inventor's early work for the deaf, but she primarily chronicles Keller's life and Keller and Bell's correspondence and meetings. Numerous black-and-white photographs accompany the text.

1.59   Senna, Carl. **Colin Powell: A Man of War and Peace.** Walker, 1992. ISBN 0-8027-8181-0. 176p. 8–12.

Of eleven chapters, Carl Senna devotes nine to Colin Powell's military career, tracing Powell's early service in Vietnam, where the young officer served two tours and was wounded, to his recent service as the first African American chair of the Joint Chiefs of Staff. Although Powell is presented as beloved son, able student, and caring husband and father, the author concentrates on the general's exceptional abilities as military tactician and diplomat. Clustered black-and-white photographs show Powell in various roles.

1.60   Simon, Sheridan. **Stephen Hawking: Unlocking the Universe.** Dillon Press, 1991. ISBN 0-87518-455-3. 115p. 10–12 (est.).

The personal and professional life of Stephen W. Hawking, who is sometimes called the greatest scientific thinker of the twentieth century, is described in this People in Focus book, from his early childhood and schooling to his scientific work. Hawking's contributions to cosmology—the study of the origin, evolution, and fate of the universe—are made comprehensible without loss of his moving personal story, for Hawking is a victim of ALS, or motor neuron disease, and is unable to walk or talk.

1.61   Stanley, Diane, and Peter Vennema. **Bard of Avon: The Story of William Shakespeare.** Illustrated by Diane Stanley. Morrow Junior Books, 1992. ISBN 0-688-09109-1. 48p. 7 and up.

The team of Diane Stanley and Peter Vennema has produced the backdrop for William Shakespeare's time and brought cohesion to the skimpy bits of information, documentation, and transactions still in existence. The narrative is storylike, with the authors cautious about filling in details for which there is no evidence. Full-page paintings offer brilliantly colored portrayals of sixteenth-century England, executed in blended gouache watercolors that yield, according to Stanley, "a somewhat naive, folk-art style."

1.62   Stanley, Fay. **The Last Princess: The Story of Princess Ka'iulani of Hawai'i.** Illustrated by Diane Stanley. Four Winds Press, 1991. ISBN 0-02-786785-4. 40p. 6–12 (est.).

Radiant gouache paintings illustrate the story of Princess Ka'iulani, born into the Hawaiian royal family but destined never to reign. While the princess attended school in England, American traders wrested political power from her aunt, the queen. Despite her courageous protests, and appeals to President Cleveland, Princess Ka'iulani won only the hearts of her people, not the return of her kingdom. She died at age twenty-three, many say of despair. An explanation of the Hawaiian language and a bibliography are included.

1.63   Stevens, Bryna. **Handel and the Famous Sword Swallower of Halle.** Illustrated by Ruth Tietjen Councell. Philomel Books, 1990. ISBN 0-399-21548-4. 32p. 4–8.

George Handel, Senior, the rich barber-surgeon of Halle, hated music. In fact, if it had not been for Aunt Anna, young George Frederick Handel might not have learned to play the clavichord at all, for some say that she kept a clavichord hidden in the attic. When a boy swallowed a knife, it was George the Elder's surgical talents that got him summoned to court, where the duke recognized George Frederick's musical gifts and pressured the father to let the boy study music. The dusty-toned pencil drawings are as spirited as the tellings; the author's notes offer sources for the anecdotal history.

1.64   Stevenson, James. **Don't You Know There's a War On?** Illustrated by James Stevenson. Greenwillow Books, 1992. ISBN 0-688-11384-2. 32p. 5 and up.

In 1942 the war was on, and the ten-year-old child narrator recalls daily efforts made on the home front while his father was away: ration books, blackouts, Spam, victory gardens, war stamps, stalking a suspected spy, collecting tinfoil, and waiting. The blend of child perspective and humor opens an important topic for discussion. Imaginative and minimal watercolor images capture the rarifed spirit of memory.

1.65   Teeters, Peggy. **Jules Verne: The Man Who Invented Tomorrow.** Walker, 1992. ISBN 0-8027-8191-8. 128p. 10 and up.

Author Peggy Teeters clearly presents the scope of Jules Verne's career, which was highly diverse before he fathered what is now known as science fiction. Of the nearly one hundred books that Verne wrote, sixty-five featured extraordinary voyages on, into, around, above, and below the earth. Teeters rightfully pays tribute to her subject's remarkable prescience: technological and scientific wonders that he foretold over a century ago have become or are emerging as today's commonplaces. Black-and-white photographs and sketches complement the text.

1.66   Thaxter, Celia (adapted by Loretta Krupinski). **Celia's Island Journal.** Illustrated by Loretta Krupinski. Little, Brown, 1992. ISBN 0-316-83921-3. 32p. 6–8 (est.).

When nineteenth-century poet Celia Thaxter was a child, she lived on an island off the coast of New Hampshire, where her father was the lighthouse keeper. There, with her young brother, she explored the rocky surfaces, watched the tidal pools, relished the seasons, and became an astute observer of nature. Thaxter kept her childhood impressions in a journal, describing her days so keenly that other children can share them today. The journal excerpts are bordered by island birds and plants; facing pages interpret the isolation and beauty in the family's life.

A.

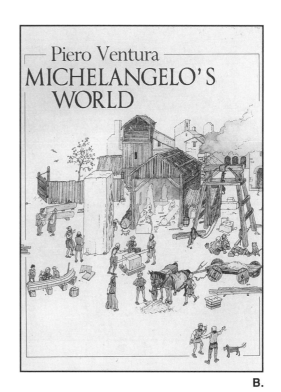

B.

C.

A. *Rosa Parks: My Story* by Rosa Parks with Jim Haskins (see 1.49).   **B.** *Michelangelo's World* by Piero Ventura (see 1.69).   **C.** *Prairie Visions: The Life and Times of Solomon Butcher* by Pam Conrad; jacket design by David Saylor (see 1.21).

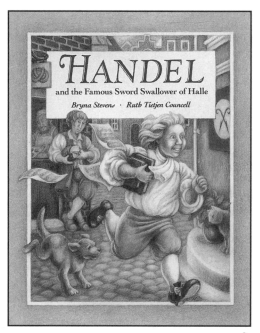

A.

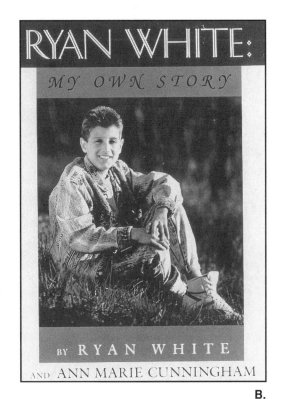

B.

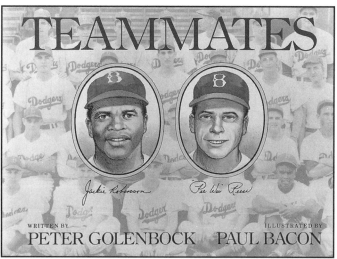

C.

A. *Handel and the Famous Sword Swallower of Halle* by Bryna Stevens; illustrated by Ruth Tietjen Councell (see 1.63). **B.** *Ryan White: My Own Story* by Ryan White and Ann Marie Cunningham (see 1.71). **C.** *Teammates* by Peter Golenbock; illustrated by Paul Bacon (see 1.33).

1.67 Turner, Robyn Montana. **Georgia O'Keeffe. Mary Cassatt. Rosa Bonheur.** Little, Brown, 1991–92. 32p. 6–10.

Women who became accomplished artists against the obstacles of little encouragement or praise for their efforts are the subjects of these picture-book biographies in the Portraits of Women Artists for Children series. Portraits of the artists and important landmarks in their lives are included, but most important are the radiant, full-color, captioned reproductions of their artwork that spill across the pages, subordinating the significance of gender to the supremacy of their art. *Notable 1991 Children's Trade Books in the Field of Social Studies.*

1.68 Ventura, Piero. **Great Composers.** Illustrated by Piero Ventura. G. P. Putnam's Sons, 1989. ISBN 0-399-21746-0. 124p. All ages.

From prehistoric cultures to the Beatles, *Great Composers* presents information on the role of music over the centuries. The book's profiles of selected composers present the history behind some of the world's most celebrated pieces of music. Piero Ventura's artwork includes lifelike portraits of composers and colorful sketches of their stages, theaters, and communities. Blackline sketches of various instruments and brief biographies of each composer can be used to supplement the text.

1.69 Ventura, Piero. **Michelangelo's World.** Illustrated by Piero Ventura. G. P. Putnam's Sons, 1989. ISBN 0-399-21593-X. 44p. 8 and up (est.).

Piero Ventura tells Michelangelo's story in first person, vividly recounting his experiences, his times, and both his triumphs and setbacks as painter and sculptor. Ventura's detailed and attractive color illustrations create the daily realities of a distant time. A time-line of the artist's life and a photographic glossary of his greatest works round out the text.

1.70 Weil, Lisl. **Wolferl: The First Six Years in the Life of Wolfgang Amadeus Mozart, 1756–1762.** Illustrated by Lisl Weil. Holiday House, 1991. ISBN 0-8234-0876-0. 30p. 6–9.

The early childhood of Mozart is recounted, from his birth to his first command performance for the Empress Maria Theresa of Austria at age six. Lisl Weil's cartoon-like illustrations in ink, crayon, and watercolor provide a charming view of life in eighteenth-century Vienna. A glossary helps explain the more difficult terms and place-names.

1.71   White, Ryan, and Ann Marie Cunningham. **Ryan White: My Own Story.** Dial Books, 1991. ISBN 0-8037-0977-3. 277p. 10 and up (est.).

Ryan White contracted AIDS at age thirteen from tainted blood used to treat his hemophilia. Before his death at age eighteen, he triumphed over the abuse of his community and became a cultural hero who championed all victims of discrimination. Despite lifelong illness, White was a normal kid from a working-class home. He and coauthor Ann Marie Cunningham write engagingly in unvarnished terms about the social and physical ravages of his disease. This very literate account will be an important book long after White's media celebrity has faded.

1.72   Wormser, Richard. **Pinkerton: America's First Private Eye.** Walker, 1990. ISBN 0-8027-6965-9. 120p. 10 and up (est.).

From humble roots in the nineteenth-century slums of Glasgow, Scotland, Allan Pinkerton struggled against slavery, made barrels, did police work, and eventually founded a detective agency that developed an international reputation for solving difficult crimes. Today that agency is a modern corporation with 50,000 employees devoted to preventing, rather than solving, crimes. Interested readers will appreciate the original photographs and drawings, the index, and the list of related books. *Notable 1990 Children's Trade Books in the Field of Social Studies.*

1.73   Zheng Zhensun and Alice Low. **A Young Painter: The Life and Paintings of Wang Yani—China's Extraordinary Young Artist.** Photographs by Zheng Zhensun. Scholastic Hardcover Books/Byron Preiss–New China Pictures Books, 1991. ISBN 0-590-44906-0. 80p. All ages.

Wang Yani, a precocious Chinese painter, began producing charming, energetic works at age three and soon won international attention. Readers will be fascinated by this lavishly illustrated account of her early life. Although the word *genius* doesn't appear in the text, it is evident in Wang Yani's free-flowing and sophisticated depictions of monkeys, cranes, cats, trees, and flowers. The text recounts her childhood, her relationship with her father, her artistic growth, and her personal development. Color photographs showcase the artist at work and reproduce her paintings. An index, map, and glossary of Chinese terms round out this introduction to a still-young artist.

Books for Young Children

The content of a children's book is basically unimportant. The sole purpose of that book is to convince the child that reading is great fun. The book must be so exciting and funny and wonderful that the child falls in love with it. Then the battle is won and the realization that books are easy and lovely and enthralling begins to dawn on the young reader. There need be no message in the book, no moral, just sheer entertainment.

Roald Dahl, *CBC Features*

2 Books for Young Children

Alphabet Books

2.1 Agard, John. **The Calypso Alphabet.** Illustrated by Jennifer Bent. Henry Holt, 1989. ISBN 0-8050-1177-3. 30p. 5–8.

Through a combination of scratchboard and bright watercolor inks, Jennifer Bent adds to the lively Caribbean flavor of this rhythmic alphabet book. In calypso beat and rhyming text, alphabet letters are matched with the island lexicon—"*h* for hurry-hurry. Hurry-hurry make bad curry." Children past alphabet learning will experience cultural snapshots through the pages. *Notable 1989 Children's Trade Books in the Field of Social Studies.*

2.2 Argent, Kerry. **Animal Capers.** Illustrated by Kerry Argent. Dial Books for Young Readers, 1989. ISBN 0-8037-0752-5. 40p. 3–7.

With a bright-eyed bird as "mascot," animals from anteaters to kookaburras to wombats and zebras follow one another across the pages of this alphabet book. Only on the final page does the reader discover where this cheery parade of animals is headed. Lively and humorous animals are rendered in chalk and colored pencil, spread engagingly across white backgrounds and involved in playful "capers" along the route.

2.3 Aylesworth, Jim. **The Folks in the Valley: A Pennsylvania Dutch ABC.** Illustrated by Stefano Vitale. HarperCollins, 1992. ISBN 0-06-021929-7. 32p. 3 and up.

"Alarm clocks ring / It's almost dawn / The folks in the valley / Stretch and yawn." From morning alarm-clock yawns to evening yawns over candlesticks, the Pennsylvania Dutch go about their busy days—harvesting wheat, splitting oaks, plowing fields, and milking cows—all described through an alphabet rhyming book. Stefano Vitale's primitive-style folk-art paintings, executed on textured wood and framed with stencils of Pennsylvania Dutch motifs, reflect the serenity and order of the lives of these "folks in the valley."

A.

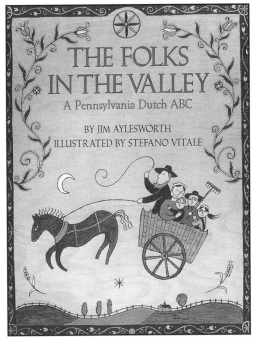

B.

C.

A. *Alison's Zinnia* by Anita Lobel (see 2.16). **B.** *The Folks in the Valley: A Pennsylvania Dutch ABC* by Jim Aylesworth; illustrated by Stefano Vitale (see 2.3). **C.** *Aardvarks, Disembark!* by Ann Jonas (see 2.13).

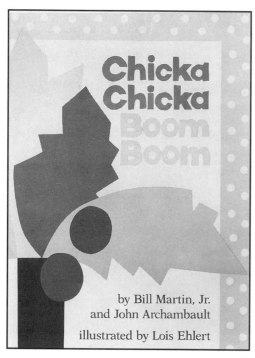

A.

B.

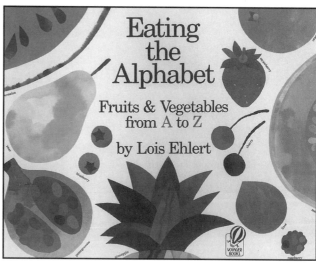

C.

A. *Chicka Chicka Boom Boom* by Bill Martin, Jr. and John Archambault; illustrated by Lois Ehlert (see 2.19). **B.** *Antler, Bear, Canoe: A Northwoods Alphabet Year* by Betsy Bowen (see 2.6). **C.** *Eating the Alphabet: Fruits & Vegetables from A to Z* by Lois Ehlert (see 2.10).

2.4   Aylesworth, Jim. **Old Black Fly.** Illustrated by Stephen Gammell. Henry Holt, 1992. ISBN 0-8050-1401-2. 32p. 2–6.

In this exuberant, rapping rhyme, Old Black Fly goes buzzing around having a very busy bad day. With bulging scarlet eyes and trailing multicolored paint splatters, Old Black Fly annoys his way through the alphabet and the house: "He ate on the crust / of the Apple pie. / He bothered the Baby and made her cry. Shoo fly! / Shoo fly! / Shoo." Stephen Gammell's paintings create the most buoyant havoc imaginable—messy patches and splotches of brilliant color—until *swat!*

2.5   Blake, Quentin. **Quentin Blake's ABC.** Illustrated by Quentin Blake. Alfred A. Knopf/Borzoi Books, 1989. ISBN 0-394-94149-7. 32p. 4–6.

Quentin Blake's energetic and humorous cartoon-like drawings feature individual alphabet letters in large print along with a rhyming line. Letters *C* and *D* work like this: "C is for Cockatoos / learning to scream; D is for Ducks / upside down in a stream." Screaming cockatoos deafen an old man and his grandchildren, but spark the interest of an old woman with an earhorn. Ducks take an underwater inspection of an upside-down diver. The whole effect is wacky fun.

2.6   Bowen, Betsy. **Antler, Bear, Canoe: A Northwoods Alphabet Year.** Illustrated by Betsy Bowen. Little, Brown/Joy Street Books, 1991. ISBN 0-316-10376-4. 28p. 4–8.

This alphabet/seasons/information book, inspired by the northwoods of Minnesota, features a moose Antler, a black Bear, and a snow-covered Canoe for January. February brings a Dogsled, Evenings spent reading or waxing skis by a wood stove, and ice Fishing. The illustrations were produced by carving the designs and letters backward into wood blocks, rolling black ink onto the white pine blocks, making prints of the designs and letters, and then applying paint to each print. The effect is one of visual strength and mood perfection, from loons on the lake to quiet on the pond.

2.7   Brown, Ruth. **Alphabet Times Four: An International ABC.** Illustrated by Ruth Brown. Dutton Children's Books, 1991. ISBN 0-525-44831-4. 32p. 4 and up.

This unusual alphabet book showcases the richly detailed and textured paintings of Ruth Brown against word labels for the subjects of the paintings printed in English, Spanish, French, and

German. Younger children may have difficulty identifying the focal object in some paintings, so an older reader might help them relish the pictures and might point out some of the subtle details of the illustrations and the arched frames in which they are displayed.

2.8   Cox, Lynn. **Crazy Alphabet.** Illustrated by Rodney McRae. Orchard Books, 1990. ISBN 0-531-08566-X. 32p. 3–6.

"A is for Apple. Everyone knows that." Less obvious, though, is "B is for Bird that ate the apple," and "C is for Cat that caught the bird that ate the apple." In cumulative story line, the alphabet sentences build on this repetitive pattern until, at last, a huge tongue-wagging "Yowie" eats everything and bursts, leaving only "Z for Zero." Each colorful page offers a crazy-quilt collage of shapes and patterns that cohere in the letter/sound illustrations.

2.9   Edwards, Michelle. **Alef-Bet: A Hebrew Alphabet Book.** Illustrated by Michelle Edwards. Lothrop, Lee and Shepard Books, 1992. ISBN 0-688-09725-1. 32p. 4 and up.

In a comfortably chaotic Israeli household, the *alef-bet,* or the Hebrew alphabet, is presented along with a selection of household words, translations, and pronunciations. Illustrations are so brimming with life that one could forget the book's mission and simply want to join the family. The older son rides in a wheelchair without fanfare, while the younger is a welcome baby. Gabi, the daughter, dresses in one costume after another as the pages turn.

2.10   Ehlert, Lois. **Eating the Alphabet: Fruits and Vegetables from A to Z.** Illustrated by Lois Ehlert. Harcourt Brace Jovanovich, 1989. ISBN 0-15-224435-2. 28p. 3–8.

From apples to zucchini, bright watercolor collages of fruits and vegetables spread across the pages of this alphabet book. In a style that is unique to Lois Ehlert, familiar and less familiar edibles are colorfully displayed, clearly labeled, and served up for inspection. Interesting histories of each of the fruits and vegetables appear in the book's glossary. As a follow-up, children might make collages of their favorite fruits and vegetables or put together their own "edible" alphabet book.

2.11   Elliott, David. **An Alphabet of Rotten Kids!** Illustrated by Oscar de Mejo. Philomel Books, 1991. ISBN 0-399-22260-X. 25p. 4–8.

Ernestine, who painted her poodle green, is just one of the rotten kids in this distinctive alphabet book. Each child, from Agatha to Zazu, is involved in mischief: Georgina cuts holes in her underwear because "no one ever saw her there," Ursula teaches kids to curse, and Vincent drinks finger paint. Primitive, elemental illustrations, markedly direct, are reminiscent of early cautionary tales and add to the harmless fun.

2.12   Hepworth, Cathi. *Antics: An Alphabetical Anthology.* Illustrated by Cathi Hepworth. G. P. Putnam's Sons, 1992. ISBN 0-399-21862-9. 32p. All ages.

Here's an ench*ant*ing alphabet book, with each letter represented by a single word that contains an "ant." For *A*, there's *ant*ique, a very old woman ant knitting in her rocker. For *B*, there's Brilli*ant*, a mad scientist ant wearing a laboratory coat, his legs at work with beakers and test tube. For *D*, it's a Devi*ant*, a punk antenna head with jam box, green mohawk, and shades. The ant portraits are adult funny at times (K*ant*? Nonchal*ant*?), but may inspire some classroom f*ant*asy writing.

2.13   Jonas, Ann. **Aardvarks, Disembark!** Illustrated by Ann Jonas. Greenwillow Books, 1990. ISBN 0-688-07207-0. 40p. 4–7.

After forty days and forty nights of rain, Noah invites the animal refugees to disembark—in alphabetical order! Surprisingly, when Noah gets to letter *Z* and "zebras," the ark is still full of animals—Noah hadn't called the zebus nor the youyous, the xerus nor the wapiti. Readers must rotate the book to follow the trail of exotic animals, many of which are either extinct or endangered, making their way down the mountain. A glossary is provided describing the animals' characteristics and habitats. *ALA Notable Children's Books, 1991.*

2.14   Lear, Edward. **A Was Once an Apple Pie.** Illustrated by Julie Lacome. Candlewick Press, 1992. ISBN 1-56402-000-2. 32p. 4–6.

Julie Lacome has given Edward Lear's nineteenth-century nonsense alphabet rhyme bright new images. Admitting the influence of her studies of American folk and craft design, the Scottish artist has used torn-paper and cut-paper shapes with painted details that sometimes float about the pages and that are sometimes tucked into frames bordered by folk-art motifs. For example, in the verse for *N*, "N was once a little needle," hexagons of calico are stitched together amid stylized spools and a pincushion.

2.15   Linscott, Jody. **Once Upon A to Z: An Alphabet Odyssey.** Illustrated by Claudia Porges Holland. Doubleday, 1991. ISBN 0-385-41907-4. 64p. 4–8.

"Andy always ate an astounding amount. Artichokes, apples, avocados and apricots. . . ." So begins the saga of Andy of the amazing appetite and his friend Daisy, who daily dispatched the "dozens of delicious delicacies" that Andy required. Each letter page signals a new alliterative pattern, and each is illustrated with brightly colored layers of cut paper, inspired, according to the artist, by the colors of the Caribbean Islands. Children and teachers may want to try their own alliterative stories.

2.16   Lobel, Anita. **Alison's Zinnia.** Illustrated by Anita Lobel. Greenwillow Books, 1990. ISBN 0-688-08866-X. 32p. 3 and up.

This elegant alphabet book is a garden of literacy. Each letter is represented by an expansive, full-color painting of a flower beginning with that initial—amaryllis to begonia to chrysanthemum to daffodil, and so on. Each page also includes a sentence linking a girl's name, a verb, and a flower's name in alphabetical rhythms: "Alison acquired an Amaryllis for Beryl," "Beryl bought a Begonia for Crystal," and so on through the alphabet. The pleasure of flowers, the chain of generosity as one child gives to the next, and the clever sentences all make this a warm and delightful work.

2.17   Lyon, George Ella. **A B Cedar: An Alphabet of Trees.** Illustrated by Tom Parker. Orchard Books, 1989. ISBN 0-531-08395-0. 32p. 3–7.

A row of shadowed alphabet letters bands the top border of each double-page spread of this alphabet book. From a narrow black foreground strip, the shapes of trees from aspen to zebrawood rise in silhouette against crisp white pages, given scale by ant-sized people. Dramatically, dark and light adult hands hold actual-size leaves of each tree for close inspection. In a flurry of autumn leaves at the book's end, readers are reminded of what trees provide—including this alphabet book!

2.18   Magee, Doug, and Robert Newman. **Let's Fly from A to Z.** Photographs by Doug Magee and Robert Newman. Cobblehill Books, 1992. ISBN 0-525-65105-5. 32p. 8 and up.

Beginning with *A* for airplanes that fly in the sky, and for airports where airplanes land and take off, a panoply of color photographs offers a range of perspectives on aircraft, equipment, and services. Organized by letters of the alphabet, some pages seem ideally suited: *F*, for example, is for fuselage and flaps, while *L* is for landing and landing lights. As with many topical alphabet books, some letters must stretch: *O* is for the opening on a jet engine.

2.19 Martin, Bill, Jr., and John Archambault. **Chicka Chicka Boom Boom.** Illustrated by Lois Ehlert. Simon and Schuster Books for Young Readers, 1989. ISBN 0-617-67949-X. 32p. 2–6.

"*A* told *B* and *B* told *C*, I'll meet you at the top of the coconut tree." In rhythmic, chant-like text that is sure to encourage children's instant participation, letters of the alphabet race to the top of the coconut tree. "Will there be enough room?" No! With a "Chicka chicka BOOM BOOM!" Lois Ehlert's bright and tropical-colored letters topple the tree and must untangle and wiggle-jiggle free. *ALA Notable Children's Books, 1989; Boston Globe–Horn Book Picture Honor Book, 1990; New Books of Merit, Winter 1990—The Five Owls.*

2.20 Merriam, Eve. **Goodnight to Annie: An Alphabet Lullaby.** Illustrated by Carol Schwartz. Hyperion Books for Children, 1992. ISBN 1-56282-206-3. 32p. 3–7.

After enjoying twenty-six bordered illustrations in gouache, colored pencil, and ink, each with a dominating uppercase letter, the young reader sees that Annie has joined in sleep such objects as *N*ightingales "nodding in their nest," *Q*ueens "doffing their crowns and drowsing under downy quilts," and *R*ainbows "fading from their rush of bright colors to rose and russet and deep indigo."

2.21 Merriam, Eve. **Where Is Everybody? An Animal Alphabet.** Illustrated by Diane de Groat. Simon and Schuster Books for Young Readers, 1989. ISBN 0-671-64964-7. 40p. 3–6.

Where is everybody? "Alligator is in the attic," "Bear is in the bakery," . . . and "Zebra is at the zoo." This alliterative phrase alphabet book offers hidden surprises on every page as Mole the photographer tracks down animal pals from A to Z. Bustling watercolor illustrations contain lots of additional items beginning with the featured letters: "Sheep is in the stroller," but he's riding past a store window displaying a Santa, a sale sign, skates, and a shovel.

2.22   Owens, Mary Beth. **A Caribou Alphabet.** Illustrated by Mary Beth Owens. Farrar, Straus and Giroux/Sunburst Books, 1990. ISBN 0-374-41043-7. 32p. 3–6.

This unique rhyming alphabet book focuses on caribou and their habits from A to Z. Detailed and delicately rendered caribou weave in and out of large-scaled alphabet letters, while a single line of a couplet describes the action in each scene. For example, wrapped with the letter *C*, and with a lowercase *c* forming a crescent moon, a caribou cow watches over the calf: "Caribou cows protect calves as they grow. . . ." A compendium of interesting caribou facts is provided at the book's end.

2.23   Phillips, Tamara. **Day Care ABC.** Illustrated by Dora Leder. Albert Whitman, 1989. ISBN 0-8075-1483-7. 32p. 2–7.

Each letter of the alphabet is used in an alliterative sentence that describes children's morning preparations for day care or preschool and the school activities that follow ("Sam shares a swing"). Large capital and lowercase letters mark each page, and classroom scenes are filled with objects that begin with the focus letter or sound. An index of the pictured objects is included at the book's end. The usefulness of the book reaches beyond a preschool/day-care audience.

2.24   Rubin, Cynthia Elyce, selected by. **ABC Americana from the National Gallery of Art.** Harcourt Brace Jovanovich/Gulliver Books, 1989. ISBN 0-15-200660-5. 32p. All ages.

The National Gallery of Art's *Index of American Design* lists 17,000 watercolor paintings which were commissioned during the Great Depression. Together they create a visual record of "representative objects of American design and folk art." For each letter of the alphabet, one object is featured against a white background, bound by a color border and captioned, such as "W is for Weather vane." A final page identifies the original object and its artist.

2.25   Shelby, Anne. **Potluck.** Illustrated by Irene Trivas. Orchard Books, 1991. ISBN 0-531-08519-8. 32p. 3–6.

Alpha and Betty invite all their friends, from Acton to Zelda, to a potluck, and brimming dishes from around the world are brought—alphabetically—to the table: "Edmund entered with enchiladas. . . ." From asparagus soup and bagels to yogurt and zucchini casserole, the colorful pages show a scrumptious feast.

Beyond the exuberance of the party, the book is a splendid example of the cultural variety that feeds the American palate.

2.26 Simpson, Gretchen Dow. **Gretchen's abc.** Illustrated by Gretchen Dow Simpson. HarperCollins/Laura Geringer Books, 1991. ISBN 0-06-025646-X. 27p. 3–6.

In this vibrant alphabet book, each letter is represented by a bright, bold, closeup depiction of a familiar object. Letter *F,* for example, is a striking red, white, and blue furl of cloth; children will delight in identifying it as "flag." Answers are provided at the end of the book. Illustrations for several of the letters were taken from covers of *The New Yorker* painted by illustrator Gretchen Dow Simpson.

2.27 Snow, Alan. **The Monster Book of A B C Sounds.** Illustrated by Alan Snow. Dial Books for Young Readers, 1991. ISBN 0-8037-0935. 28p. 2–10.

In this unconventional alphabet book, a parade of comical monsters plays hide-and-seek with a bunch of grinning, goofy rats. For each letter, a sound word beginning with that letter balloons across the oversize pages. For example, for the letter *U,* a pudgy blue monster wails "Uuugh!" when he finds the rats in his cabinet. And so it goes throughout Alan Snow's lively rendition of letter and sound correspondences. Borders are filled with letters and such not-so-often-seen objects and animals as emus, harmonicas, javelins, and kimonos in this visual treat.

2.28 Stock, Catherine. **Alexander's Midnight Snack: A Little Elephant's ABC.** Illustrated by Catherine Stock. Clarion Books, 1988. ISBN 0-89919-512-1. 31p. 3–6.

When Alexander gets thirsty in the middle of the night, he heads downstairs to the kitchen. But the little elephant's midnight snack turns into an alphabetically arranged feast that begins with apple pie, buns, and cinnamon cookies. In the end, Alexander returns to bed to catch some "Z's," and Alexander's mother wakes to find an awful big mess in the kitchen. Alliterative captions beneath amusing bordered watercolors feature the letter-of-the-page in bright red.

2.29 Wilner, Isabel. **A Garden Alphabet.** Illustrated by Ashley Wolff. Dutton Children's Books, 1991. ISBN 0-525-44731-8. 28p. 4–6.

From planning to harvesting, two gardeners—one an ambitious black-and-white border collie and the other her able assistant, a frog with a cowboy hat—make a step-by-step production of tending and protecting their backyard plot. Bright, bursting-with-color illustrations interpret each letter's rhyming verse.

Color Books

2.30   Ehlert, Lois. **Color Zoo.** Illustrated by Lois Ehlert. J. B. Lippin-cott, 1989. ISBN 0-397-32260-7. 32p. 3–5.

Lois Ehlert's characteristic vivid colors (as in *Growing Vegetable Soup*) surround cutout shapes, turning those shapes into animals. As each page is turned, a new shape is embellished into a different animal. Some of the images are fascinating, although a few are far-fetched. Color and shape concepts are clear, as are written labels identifying animals and shapes. Three glossaries at the end review ten shapes, sixteen colors, and nine animals. *Caldecott Honor Book, 1990.*

2.31   Fleming, Denise. **Lunch.** Illustrated by Denise Fleming. Henry Holt, 1992. ISBN 0-8050-1636-8. 32p. 2–6.

Never has lunch been so appreciated, sought out, gobbled, spilled, slurped, or chomped. Created out of handmade paper, a cunningly hungry mouse sniffs lunch. Like Eric Carle's *The Very Hungry Caterpillar*, he eats through larger-than-life-size vegetables and fruits, spewing the colors of their juices all about and splashing himself with the colors of lunch. Minimal text and exuberant appetite combine to make a manageable book for beginning readers and an invitation to write about still other hungry creatures.

2.32   Goennel, Heidi. **Colors.** Illustrated by Heidi Goennel. Little, Brown, 1990. ISBN 0-316-31843-4. 32p. 3–6.

In a brightly colored concept book for young children, round-faced, featureless children compare the colors of objects in their world with objects found in nature: "The bright sun is the color of my beach bucket." "Cotton candy is the color of summer roses." Heidi Goennel's simple forms yield pleasing page designs.

2.33   Kunhardt, Edith. **Red Day, Green Day.** Illustrated by Marylin Hafner. Greenwillow Books, 1992. ISBN 0-688-09400-7. 32p. 3 and up.

Kindergarten springs to life in full color as children celebrate the color days. Andrew wears his favorite pants on Red Day, brings orange gelatin for Orange Day, daffodils for Yellow Day, a toy tractor for Green Day, blueberries for Blue Day, and purple socks for Purple Day. When the color days are over, a rainy day stretches a huge rainbow across the sky, making "all the color days at once." Bright rainbow colors border the cheery school-day illustrations.

2.34 Rikys, Bodel. **Red Bear.** Illustrated by Bodel Rikys. Dial Books for Young Readers, 1992. ISBN 0-8037-1048-8. 24p. 1–5.

This color-concept book offers single color words juxtaposed against simple line drawings of a bear getting dressed and then visiting a circus. Each color word is printed in enlarged type on a matching color page. Red Bear pulls on blue pants, and the text reads simply "Blue." A yellow shirt, brown shoes, purple socks, and black cat all help to introduce crayon-box colors.

2.35 Williams, Sue. **I Went Walking.** Illustrated by Julie Vivas. Harcourt Brace Jovanovich/Gulliver Books, 1990. ISBN 0-15-200471-8. 32p. 3–7.

"I went walking. / What did you see? / I saw a black cat / Looking at me." An assortment of animals follow a young boy on his walk. Rhythmic, instantly readable text and large, whimsical paintings bring this simple story to life in a style very similar to *Brown Bear, Brown Bear, What Do You See?* by Bill Martin, Jr. *ALA Notable Children's Books, 1991.*

Concept Books

2.36 Anholt, Catherine, and Laurence Anholt. **All about You.** Illustrated by Catherine and Laurence Anholt. Viking Penguin, 1992. ISBN 0-670-84488-8. 32p. 3–6.

In a book perfect for laptime, the story rug, or an "All about Me" unit, young children are invited to talk about themselves, their feelings, their preferences, and their uniqueness. Each spread poses a question and follows it with small pictures to stimulate discussion: "When you wake up in the morning, how do you feel?" "Feeling" words appear beneath huggable children—*happy, tired, sad, noisy, quiet,* and *glad.* There are questions about clothes, toys, family, homes, friends, animals, and more.

2.37 Anholt, Catherine, and Laurence Anholt. **Kids.** Illustrated by Catherine and Laurence Anholt. Candlewick Press, 1992. ISBN 1-56402-097-5. 32p. 4–6.

In a book where kids seem to speak for themselves, the Anholts give them license to strut. Across double-page spreads, a bold "kid question" marches: "What's in a kid's pocket?" "What do kids look like?" or "What are nasty kids like?" The answers are jolly, rhyming, and perfectly matched to their illustrations. Anholt-drawn kids are scary and hairy, tall and small, grumpy and dumpy, and thoroughly charming.

2.38   Anholt, Catherine, and Laurence Anholt. **What I Like.** Illustrated by Catherine and Laurence Anholt. G. P. Putnam's Sons, 1991. ISBN 0-399-21863-7. 32p. 3–6.

Six active children do what children are especially good at—saying what they like and don't like. On facing pages, the bold, patterned text sets the stage: "What I like is . . ." or "What I don't like is . . . ," while small pictures aligned on the facing pages finish the sentences with rhyming phrases, such as "time to play" and "a holiday." A pair of twins also offers their likes and dislikes about being twins. What all six children like is being friends. The book prompts patterned writing with young children.

2.39   Anno, Mitsumasa. **Anno's Masks.** Illustrated by Mitsumasa Anno. Philomel Books, 1990. ISBN 0-399-21860-2. 22p. 3–6.

Each page of Anno's simple picture book offers a colored animal mask, including a dog, koala bear, lion, and cheetah. Small eye-holes are punched so young children can peek through the whole book or "wear" a special face. The only text is the label for the animal.

2.40   Bang, Molly. **Yellow Ball.** Illustrated by Molly Bang. Morrow Junior Books, 1991. ISBN 0-688-06315-2. 24p. 2 and up.

Cut-out figures with warm-brown skin tones toss a big yellow ball. The text reads "Catch," "Throw," and then "Uh-oh," as the yellow ball floats out to the big, wide-rolling sea. Its path is under a high bridge, above a fish, and below a winging gull. "Wind blowing / Storm growing." After a swirling storm, the yellow ball forms a perfect reflection of the full moon. And with the dawn, the yellow ball washes ashore and is found. Minimal rhyming text and expressive paintings combine in the simplest of story lines.

2.41   Blos, Joan W. **A Seed, a Flower, a Minute, an Hour.** Illustrated by Hans Poppel. Simon and Schuster Books for Young Readers, 1992. ISBN 0-671-73214-5. 24p. 2–5.

Newbery Medal-winner Joan Blos observes changes: a seed changing into a flower, a minute changing into an hour. "A cloud, a storm. A bee, a swarm"—changes affect many things. The growth concept as well as the rhyming text should provide young children with ample discussion opportunities. Hans Poppel's pastel-colored watercolor washes create a dream-like atmosphere for this sparsely worded poem.

2.42   Borden, Louise. **Caps, Hats, Socks, and Mittens: A Book about the Four Seasons.** Illustrated by Lillian Hoban. Scholastic Hardcover Books, 1989. ISBN 0-590-41257-4. 32p. 2–6.

"Winter is caps, hats, socks, and mittens." It's also sleds, hot mugs, and snug beds. Spring is "grass, grass, grass," and mud to dig. Summer is a ball game and a jar full of bugs. Fall is soccer and frost on the grass. Lillian Hoban's apple-cheeked children frolic across all four seasons.

2.43   Brown, Craig. **My Barn.** Illustrated by Craig Brown. Greenwillow Books, 1991. ISBN 0-688-08786-8. 24p. 3–6.

A farmer with a drooping hat and a large red barn rejoices in the sounds that his animals make. In highly repetitive text, the farmer announces each love: "I like the sound GOBBLE GOBBLE GOBBLLE GOBBLE GOBBLE . . . the sound a turkey makes," and "I like the sound HEE HAWWW HEEE HAWW HEE HAW . . . the sound a donkey makes." Each page substitutes only the animal name and the sound, making this a manageable early text for an emergent reader. Watercolor paintings are flecked with ink dots, giving a soil-like quality to the impressions.

2.44   Brown, Margaret Wise. **Baby Animals.** Illustrated by Susan Jeffers. Random House, 1989. ISBN 0-394-92040-6. 32p. 3–6.

Margaret Wise Brown's lyrical text, written in 1941, has been reissued, this time partnered with all new illustrations by Susan Jeffers. Young children can once again follow a little girl and baby animals through a day on the farm.

2.45   Brown, Margaret Wise. **Big Red Barn.** Illustrated by Felicia Bond. Harper and Row, 1989. ISBN 0-06-020749-3. 30p. 4–6.

A big red barn and the surrounding field are home for families of animals. Told in rhyme, this story is a simple tale of life on a farm from sunrise to moonlight. The bold, stylized drawings created for this newly illustrated edition by Felicia Bond complement the rich and rhythmic text cherished by children since 1956.

2.46   Brown, Margaret Wise. **Red Light, Green Light.** Illustrated by Leonard Weisgard. Scholastic Hardcover Books, 1992. ISBN 0-590-44558-8. 40p. 5–8.

First published in 1945, *Red Light, Green Light* has been re-created by Leonard Weisgard to "fix some of the things that bothered him over the years." Using casein, watercolor, crayon, and ink, Weisgard offers illustrations in nearly primitive style. Farm vehicles and animals in grays, tans, and olives contrast with touches of brilliant red and green—sun, leaves, steeples, and hydrants. But most important of all, the red and green of the traffic signal regulate the daytime traffic and work throughout the night.

2.47   Browne, Anthony. **Things I Like.** Illustrated by Anthony Browne. Alfred A. Knopf/Dragonfly Books, 1989. ISBN 0-394-94192-6. 32p. 3–6.

In this companion to Anthony Browne's *I Like Books*, the same moppet chimpanzee announces the other things that he really likes—such as "painting," "riding my bike," "climbing trees," and "kicking a ball." The minimal text and background-free illustrations are edged with thin-line frames, with an element from each picture giving a special touch to each corner. Throughout, the chimpanzee's expressions register perfect contentment with his favorite pursuits. Young children may want to try their own "things I like" book or list.

2.48   Butler, Dorothy. **My Brown Bear Barney.** Illustrated by Elizabeth Fuller. Greenwillow Books, 1989. ISBN 0-688-08568-7. 24p. 2–5.

A little girl may go many places and take many different things, but she must always take her most special friend. In Dorothy Butler's simple story, the special friend is "my brown bear Barney." The story is told in first person and accompanied by framed illustrations. Youngsters will be able to "read along" with the litany of things that you must take to the store, to the beach, to grandmother's, and to bed. And they will readily predict that no matter where you go, you simply must take "my brown bear Barney."

2.49   Calhoun, Mary. **While I Sleep.** Illustrated by Ed Young. Morrow Junior Books, 1992. ISBN 0-688-08201-7. 32p. 1–6.

Soothing pastels set the perfect tone for this bedtime lullaby conversation. A child asks where animals sleep; her parents' answers are accompanied by full-page depictions of each animal, active in the daylight and asleep in an ink-dyed insert. The contrast, for example, between the repeated form of the squirrel that represents leaping and the nighttime squirrel curled in sleep provides an effective representation of the rhythms of night and day. The questions end with the child snuggling into her blankets for sleep.

2.50   Carlstrom, Nancy White. **How Do You Say It Today, Jesse Bear?** Illustrated by Bruce Degen. Macmillan, 1992. ISBN 0-02-717276-7. 32p. 2–8.

Jesse Bear, now the hero of four of Nancy White Carlstrom's creations, is back to answer a special question in every month of the year. In January, Jesse says it "with whistles and cheers / It's a happy new year"; in February, Jesse will say it "with squiggles and lines / On my valentines." All through the year, Jesse and his family celebrate the months, seasons, and holidays, saying "it" in special ways. Bordered paintings are calendar-like, with the rhyming text blocked from the festivities.

2.51   Caseley, Judith. **Annie's Potty.** Illustrated by Judith Caseley. Greenwillow Books, 1990. ISBN 0-688-09066-4. 32p. 2 and up.

Annie's new potty is a place to be avoided. She prefers diapers to underpants, even if the underpants have bunnies on them. "I know you want to be a big girl," Mama tells Annie. "No, I don't. I'm a baby," Annie replies. But explanations, demonstrations, a toilet-trained friend, time, and patience help. Even when Annie is so busy playing that she forgets to use the potty, Mama understands, and together they clean up. Judith Caseley's drawings rely on simple lines, bold patterns, and white backdrops.

2.52   Cummings, Phil. **Goodness Gracious!** Illustrated by Craig Smith. Orchard Books, 1989. ISBN 0-531-08567-8. 32p. 3–6.

Take a look at every inch of her—her face, her hair, her peepers, and her toeses! Along with a group of imaginary creatures, a little girl has fun describing all the ways in which her body parts can look and work—in a near festival of adjectives. Bold, energetic drawings give high action to the rhyming text, which may encourage children to think of new ways to describe other familiar things.

2.53 Demi. **Find Demi's Baby Animals.** Illustrated by Demi. Grosset and Dunlap, 1990. ISBN 0-448-19169-5. 32p. 4–8.

In a hide-and-seek format book, children are invited to find the animal on the page that matches one in a small circle. Against backgrounds that are like pages from a wallpaper sample book—flower sprays, delicate vines, and abstract fronds—large outline shapes of animals are sprinkled with smaller pictures of the same animal at play. Even very young children will be able to find within the array the animal that exactly matches the one in the circle.

2.54 Demi. **Find Demi's Dinosaurs: An Animal Game Book.** Illustrated by Demi. Grosset and Dunlap, 1989. ISBN 0-448-19020-6. 39p. 4–8.

Learning the names of dinosaurs turns into a game with this brightly patterned artwork requiring foldout pages to contain it. While attending to the detail of finding such creatures as the quetzalcoatlus tucked among look-alikes within the gigantic rhamphorynchus, children can identify the names of their favorite dinosaurs at their fanciful best. Bold colors, finely drawn details, and a game format combine to provide information and entertainment for young children.

2.55 Demi. **Find Demi's Sea Creatures: An Animal Game Book.** Illustrated by Demi. Putnam and Grosset, 1991. ISBN 0-399-22122-3. 50p. 4–8.

A brilliantly colored gallery of sea animals features a large drawing of a species—octopus, oarfish, lobster, manatee—and many smaller versions of the same animal. Children view the animal in detail and also hunt through various natural poses in foldout pages to answer questions placed within superimposed insets.

2.56 Dodds, Dayle Ann. **The Color Box.** Illustrated by Giles Laroche. Little, Brown, 1992. ISBN 0-316-18820-4. 28p. 2–6.

In a color and shape concept book, a cut-paper monkey crawls through a box into an all-black world, totally black except for one yellow oval. The yellow oval is actually a cut-out shape, allowing the monkey a peek-a-boo preview of the yellow page beyond. Only cut-paper textures distinguish the yellow objects on the next page: yellow daisies, bees, and bananas, with one orange circle to lead on through a series of shapes to a succession of monochromatic worlds.

B.

A.

C.

A. *How Do You Say It Today, Jesse Bear?* by Nancy White Carlstrom; illustrated by Bruce Degen (see 2.50). **B.** *Pig in a Barrow* by Bert Kitchen (see 2.71). **C.** *Kids* written and illustrated by Catherine and Laurence Anholt (see 2.37).

A.

B.

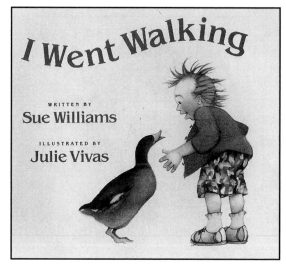

C.

A. *Color Farm* by Lois Ehlert (see 2.57).   **B.** *Lunch* by Denise Fleming (see 2.31).
C. *I Went Walking* by Sue Williams; illustrated by Julia Vivas (see 2.35).

2.57 Ehlert, Lois. **Color Farm.** Illustrated by Lois Ehlert. J. B. Lippincott, 1990. ISBN 0-397-32441-3. 15p. 3–6.

In this clever book, cutout shapes surrounded by bright, fluorescent-colored designs are layered upon each other to form common farm animals. As the pages are turned, the shapes are peeled away to reveal each new animal on the right page, with the removed shape clearly labeled and on view on the left. Lois Ehlert's *Color Zoo* follows the same unique format. *Outstanding Science Trade Books for Children in 1990.*

2.58 Finzel, Julia. **Large as Life.** Illustrated by Julia Finzel. Lothrop, Lee and Shepard Books, 1991. ISBN 0-688-10653-6. 32p. 3 and up.

Julia Finzel builds the concept of relative size by posing a simple question in poetic form: "Ladybug, ladybug where are you going / On the back of a butterfly, hardly showing?" In this nearly wordless book, however, it is the bold, textured paintings that will capture young children's attention as they look for the tiny ladybug on the foot of an elephant, the ear of a tiger, the nose of an owl, or the feather of a peacock. The paintings have a postmodern flair, presenting exaggerated parts of animals in a kaleidoscope of color and design.

2.59 Florian, Douglas. **Turtle Day.** Illustrated by Douglas Florian. Thomas Y. Crowell, 1989. ISBN 0-690-04745-2. 32p. 3–6.

Rich, childlike drawings illustrate the necessary daily activities that fill Turtle's life (and our lives, too): hunger leads to eating, friends lead to play, and fatigue leads to rest. Each page offers the reader an opportunity to predict what Turtle may do. Large and bold print will benefit the youngest readers. Basic information can be used to introduce concepts about the biological needs of turtles and of all animals. *Notable Children's Trade Books in Science, 1989.*

2.60 Florian, Douglas. **A Year in the Country.** Illustrated by Douglas Florian. Greenwillow Books, 1989. ISBN 0-688-08187-8. 32p. 2–6.

A scene from a farm, spreading edge to edge across the pages, reflects the seasonal changes that each month brings during a year in the country—from melting snow patches through buds and blossoms to golden harvest and winter's snows. The muted watercolor illustrations are labeled with the name of each month in large bold type.

2.61   George, Lonnie. **Star, Little Star.** Lewison, Wendy. **Nighty-Night.** Illustrated by Antonella Abbatiello; Giulia Orecchia. Grosset and Dunlap, 1991. 24p. 2–6.

Each of these board books in the Poke and Look series has a cutout shape (a star and crescent moon) on the cover and directly beneath on each right-hand page throughout the book. The shape regularly decreases in size, producing a textured tunnel through the book. In *Star, Little Star*, a rhyming text describes a curious baby fox that wanders out at night to assure himself that the world is asleep. In *Nighty-Night*, a pajama-clad reluctant sleeper cavorts in an imaginary adventure with the moon.

2.62   Goennel, Heidi. **My Dog.** Illustrated by Heidi Goennel. Orchard Books, 1989. ISBN 0-531-08434-5. 32p. 3–6.

Each of us has our trait preferences for dogs. The round-faced, featureless children on each page of Heidi Goennel's book indicate in spare text that they prefer their dogs with such features as floppy ears like bassets, soft noses like pugs, loud barks like German shepherds, or tall, tall legs like Great Danes. Bright primary colors, simple shapes, and flat backgounds lend a "flannel board" feel to Goennel's easily distinguishable style.

2.63   Gomboli, Mario. **What Else Could It Be? What Will It Be? What's Hiding? What's Missing?** Illustrated by Mario Gomboli. Boyds Mills/Bell Books, 1991. 12p. 2–5.

These riddle and puzzle board books are designed to involve the youngest listeners. *What's Missing?* has holes for little fingers, so that children provide the missing parts—legs for a crab, a trunk for an elephant, or ears for a rabbit. *What's Hiding?* camouflages a cutout shape within a design; turning the page reveals the answer. *What Will It Be?* and *What Else Could It Be?* ask children to imagine what other forms cutout shapes could represent. Illustrations are whimsical and warm.

2.64   Hartman, Gail. **For Strawberry Jam or Fireflies.** Illustrated by Ellen Weiss. Bradbury Press, 1989. ISBN 0-02-742990-3. 22p. 1–4.

Mason jars are for strawberry jam or fireflies. And what can you do with a wooden spoon? You can mix cookies or tap a tune. This concept book explores alternative uses for eleven items, such as a big tire, a ball of string, and chewy raisins. Full-page watercolor and colored-pencil illustrations will elicit children's suggestions for various uses for everyday objects around them.

2.65   Hoban, Julia. **Amy Loves the Snow.** Illustrated by Lillian Hoban. Harper and Row, 1989. ISBN 0-06-022395-2. 20p. 2–5.

Small hands will enjoy turning the pages of this little book about Amy, in her red mittens and scarf, who goes out with Daddy, in his blue mittens and scarf, to play in the snow. They have fun making footprints, catching snowflakes, and building a snowman. After Mommy contributes a carrot nose for the snowman, the three go inside for some hot chocolate. Lillian Hoban captures winter's essence in full-page illustrations with pastel shades of snowy blues and violets.

2.66   Hoban, Tana. **All about Where.** Photographs by Tana Hoban. Greenwillow Books, 1991. ISBN 0-688-09698-0. 28p. 2–7.

Photographer Tana Hoban has a special talent for developing learning opportunities from everyday situations. Here Hoban explores how objects relate to each other by providing a list of fifteen common prepositions from which children can choose words to describe the action in the brightly colored photographs: a baby rides *on* a bicycle, *behind* her mother, her head *under* her mother's shirt, and her thumb *in* her mouth. Hoban's photographs supply possibilities for many open-ended learning experiences.

2.67   Hoban, Tana. **Exactly the Opposite.** Photographs by Tana Hoban. Greenwillow Books, 1990. ISBN 0-688-08862-7. 32p. 2–5.

From fire and ice to whole and broken eggs to the front and back ends of sheep, a variety of unconventional subjects illustrates the concept of opposites in this wordless book. Yet, look again—you may find that the baskets holding the whole eggs are upright, while the baskets with the broken eggs are tipped over. Readers will discover that there are as many opposites in these vivid photographs as there are in the world around us. *Outstanding Science Trade Books for Children in 1990.*

2.68   Hoban, Tana. **Spirals, Curves, Fanshapes and Lines.** Photographs by Tana Hoban. Greenwillow Books, 1992. ISBN 0-688-11229-3. 32p. 2 and up.

Tana Hoban's glorious photographs reveal the lines, details, and textures of the world around us—fan-shaped radiants of the cockatoo's plume, spiral shadows of a wire wastebasket, the curl of a fossilized nautilus shell, and the graceful turn of a ram's horn. Inspired by this wordless book of photos to talk about and trace with fingers, readers will see their surroundings in new ways.

2.69   Jeunesse, Gallimard, and Pascale de Bourgoing. **Colors. Fruit. The Ladybug and Other Insects. Weather.** Illustrated by Sophie Kniffke; Sylvaine Perols; P. M. Valet. Scholastic/Cartwheel Books, 1989. 24p. 3–6.

This colorful, informative series of First Discovery Books uses simple text, big illustrations, and transparencies to teach basic topics like weather, insects, colors, and fruits. Each volume is small; the pages are stiff and plastic-coated; and the brightly painted, cheery illustrations will attract children. In the volume on weather, transparencies allow the reader to superimpose rain storms, clouds, and rainbows onto various landscapes. In the insect book, the insect transparencies show various parts of insect anatomy; teachers may want to pair it with Eric Carle's *The Grouchy Ladybug.*

2.70   Jonas, Ann. **Color Dance.** Illustrated by Ann Jonas. Greenwillow Books, 1989. ISBN 0-688-05991-0. 27p. 3–7.

Three young dancers with translucent red, yellow, and blue scarves demonstrate how colors combine to create more colors. Against a stark white background, the children use their scarves to make fourteen different colors before a fourth dancer introduces white, gray, and black. The simple text complements the bold watercolor illustrations. Each time a color is written in the text, its name is printed in ink of that color. A color wheel and a description of the relationship among colors appears on the final pages.

2.71   Kitchen, Bert. **Pig in a Barrow.** Illustrated by Bert Kitchen. Dial Books for Young Readers, 1991. ISBN 0-8037-0943-9. 25p. 4–8.

A happy pig in a barrow, a puppy crouching on a scale, and field mice in a parsley pot are a few of the farm animals beautifully illustrated in this collection of humorous verses. In a realistic style similar to John James Audubon's paintings, Bert Kitchen has drawn colorful and detailed portraits from the animal kingdom. The four-line rhyming verses that accompany each illustration offer an explanation of the drawing and occasionally extend readers' understanding of nature.

2.72   Koch, Michelle. **Hoot, Howl, Hiss.** Illustrated by Michelle Koch. Greenwillow Books, 1991. ISBN 0-688-09652-2. 24p. 2–5.

Woods, ponds, mountains, farms, and jungles have their own animals with their own special sounds. From these five habitats, each of three animals fills a full page against a plain white background. Washes and light shading give texture to the child-like depictions of animals that cluck, bleat, or chirp, as well as those that hoot, howl, or hiss.

2.73 Kuskin, Karla. **Roar and More.** Illustrated by Karla Kuskin. Harper and Row/Harper Trophy Books, 1990. ISBN 0-06-023619-1. 46p. 3–6.

Karla Kuskin, winner of the NCTE Award for Excellence in Poetry for Children in 1979, first published *Roar and More* in 1956. This reissue adds bright color to the original illustrations that accompany her animal rhymes. Following each rhyme, the animal's sounds blast or slither or bounce or roll across the pages in perfect mesh with the sound's originator. For example, dog sounds fill a double-paged spread in a cacophony of barks, growls, and yaps, while the bee's buzz quietly follows a meandering trail.

2.74 Leonard, Marcia. **Alphabet Bandits: An ABC Book. Bear's Busy Year: A Book about Seasons. Counting Kangaroos: A Book about Numbers. The Kitten Twins: A Book about Opposites. Noisy Neighbors: A Book about Animal Sounds. Paintbox Penguins: A Book about Colors.** Illustrated by Maryann Cocca-Leffler; Diane Palmisciano; Bari Weissman. Troll Associates, 1990. 24p. 2–6.

In a series of books covered by polka-dots and illustrated with jolly cartoons, young children are introduced to a parade of concepts through the antics of busy animals whose activities form a simple story line. For example, two kangaroo kids bring their pouches full of toys to Grandma's house. They carefully count out their booty, page by page, until Grandma announces that she can count, too. Grandma counts one big mess and two little kangaroos to clean it up.

2.75 MacDonald, Amy. **Let's Do It. Let's Make a Noise. Let's Play. Let's Try.** Illustrated by Maureen Roffey. Candlewick Press, 1992. 14p. 2–6.

These Let's Explore board books for the youngest child offer bright, simple, page-filling illustrations and large, high-contrast text. *Let's Make a Noise* invites children to make pet, train, truck, and baby sounds. *Let's Play* and *Let's Do It* ask for responses to simple questions, each beginning with "Can you..." ("Can you knock down the blocks?"). *Let's Try* depicts children attempting child-manageable skills: "Let's try to wash your tummy."

2.76   McMillan, Bruce. **Eating Fractions.** Photographs by Bruce McMillan. Scholastic Hardcover Books, 1991. ISBN 0-590-43770-4. 32p. 4–8.

First, you take one whole pizza pie. Then you cut it into four pieces, making fourths. When you eat a piece (1/4), you are "eating fractions." The mathematical concept of how halves, thirds, and fourths are a part of a whole is illustrated through full-page color photographs of nutritious snacks being shared among two friends and a dog. Recipes for the foods make it even easier to reinforce fractional concepts in the home or classroom.

2.77   Miller, Jane. **Farm Noises.** Photographs by Jane Miller. Simon and Schuster Books for Young Readers, 1989. ISBN 0-671-67450-1. 32p. 4–8.

On a trip around a country farm, the reader meets farm animals (and farm machinery) in striking photographs. Each of the photos is accompanied by appropriate animal sounds. Kindergarten teachers will find value for farm units and for the predictable text.

2.78   Miller, Margaret. **Who Uses This?** Photographs by Margaret Miller. Greenwillow Books, 1990. ISBN 0-688-08279-3. 40p. 3–6.

On a double-page spread, the simple bold question runs opposite a color photograph of a tool: "Who uses this?" Turn the page to find two more brilliant photographs, one of an adult, the other of a child, at work with the tool. Following the photograph of a rolling pin, a baker rolls dough and a child rolls modeling clay. The word *Baker* labels the pages. Tools in this concept book include a conductor's baton, a barber's scissors, a carpenter's hammer, and a gardener's watering can.

2.79   Morris, Ann. **Loving.** Photographs by Ken Heyman. Lothrop, Lee and Shepard Books, 1990. ISBN 0-688-06341-1. 32p. 3–7.

"Mommies and daddies take care of you for a long time." Parallels of the universality of human relationships can easily be drawn by young children when they read the simple, but expressive, text and see families from many lands engaged in similar nurturing activities. Color photographs depict how parents, siblings, and even pets love and take care of each other all around the world. An index and world map give additional information about the traditions and locations of the represented cultures.

2.80 Ormerod, Jan. **Come Back, Kittens. Come Back, Puppies.** Illustrated by Jan Ormerod. Lothrop, Lee and Shepard Books, 1992. 32p. 4–6.

Painted on transparent overlays, Jan Ormerod's kittens and puppies nearly disappear against backgrounds of the same color. So, when their parents call, "Come back, kittens" or "Come back, puppies," wandering babies can be brought home by young children who turn the overlay, placing the little animals against the left-hand page and their parents' protection. One tiny spotted puppy stays nearly hidden throughout, a thin line defining his shape against the floor. The text is large, repetitive, and instantly readable.

2.81 Paterson, Bettina. **In My House. In My Yard. My Clothes. My Toys.** Illustrated by Bettina Paterson. Henry Holt, 1992. 12p. 1–5.

In a series of board books, babies and toddlers can point to favorite toys, articles of clothing, familiar household items, and outdoor things. Torn-paper collages in clear colors make for textured effects against equally bright backgrounds. In addition, each page has a print label. Pictured toddlers are multiracial.

2.82 Ryder, Joanne. **Under the Moon.** Illustrated by Cheryl Harness. Random House/Just Right Books, 1989. ISBN 0-394-91960-2. 32p. 3–5.

Mama Mouse teaches her young one "special things," such as where to find the fattest seeds and how to hide from the owl. When it is time to go home, Mama uses gentle questioning to encourage her offspring to rely on memories of smells and sounds and textures to locate their meadow. Even though Little Mouse is sure their home is under the moon, Mama helps to sharpen the observations. At times, the guidance occurs in an inset box, wrapped by the meadow home.

2.83 Shapiro, Arnold. **Circles. Squares. Triangles.** Illustrated by Bari Weissman. Dial Books for Young Readers, 1992. 10p. 1–5.

Each double-page spread of these three sturdy board books opens into a circular-, square-, or triangular-shaped object in electric primary colors. The triangle book opens into a pine tree, a tent, and a mountain, while the circle becomes a ball, a moon, and a clock face. A natural extension activity for these Play-shapes Books would be for young authors to make similar books in the classroom or at home.

2.84   Shapiro, Arnold L. **Who Says That?** Illustrated by Monica Wellington. Dutton Children's Books, 1991. ISBN 0-525-44698-2. 32p. 2–5.

In simple rhyming text, the voices of animals are heard: "Monkeys chatter. Cats purr. Lions roar. Hummingbirds whir." Unlike animals, "girls and boys make different noise." As that refrain repeats, girls and boys whisper, giggle, shout, holler, whistle, and talk. Colorful, cartoon-like drawings match each text line, accompanied by print depictions of sounds, ranging from rolling moos to long purrs, from tiny squeaks to loud shrieks.

2.85   Sharratt, Nick. **The Green Queen. Monday Run-Day.** Illustrated by Nick Sharratt. Candlewick Press/Toddler Books, 1992. 20p. 1–6.

Two books by the same author have fun with language. In the first, Nick Sharratt combines color words with colorful illustrations to provide the fodder for wordplay. A "green queen" sleeps in a "red bed" and wears "blue shoes," but she wants to make her "gray day" a little more colorful. In the second book, the days of the week spark rhyming fun for a brown-and-white beagle and his friends. If Monday is "run-day," then Tuesday is "snooze-day." Each day makes for a crazy-day poem, with Sunday "bun-day" culminating the week.

2.86   Singer, Marilyn. **Nine O'Clock Lullaby.** Illustrated by Frané Lessac. HarperCollins, 1991. ISBN 0-06-025648-6. 27p. 4–8.

When it's 9 p.m. in Brooklyn, New York, and Mama reads a bedtime story, it's 2 a.m. in England and a little girl is up for a snack. It's 11 a.m. in Japan and a grandfather watches carp swimming in a pond, and it's 5 p.m. in Nome, Alaska, where children play a circle game. On this lullaby trip around the world readers view detailed and colorful folk-art illustrations of children living in twenty-four time zones.

2.87   Sis, Peter. **Beach Ball.** Illustrated by Peter Sis. Greenwillow Books, 1990. ISBN 0-688-09182-2. 32p. 4–6.

A long, thin stretch of speckled sand separates sky and shore on Peter Sis's title spread, as Mary and her mother spread their blanket on a seemingly isolated beach. And then . . . "the wind blew Mary's ball away." As Mary chases the beachball downwind, readers discover that the beach was not isolated at all, but rather populated with all sorts of fanciful activity. Each busy spread offers opportunity to discover colors, numbers, shapes, animals, or opposites, all the while following Mary's ball through a nearly wordless book.

2.88   Voce, Louise, Rosalinda Kightley, Tony Wells, Charlotte Knox, and Julie Lacome. **My First Book: Words and Pictures for the Very Young.** ISBN 1-56402-034-7. 62p. 2–6.

In an oversize book that can be read in any direction, stand-alone couplets stretch across double-page spreads that are covered with the bright paintings of contributing artists. Objects on the page are frequently labeled in bold, black print. One toy-covered page reads: "Do you have a teddy bear, yo-yo, or ball? / Which is your favorite toy of all?" Other pages ask for interaction. Young readers are to help baby animals find their mothers; count picnic founds; or name foods that animals like to eat.

2.89   Weiss, Nicki. **An Egg Is an Egg.** Illustrated by Nicki Weiss. G. P. Putman's Sons, 1990. ISBN 0-399-22182-4. 32p. 2–6.

"An egg is an egg until it hatches. And then it is a chick. A branch is a branch until it breaks. And then it is a stick." Through rhyming text and repetitive refrain, Nicki Weiss's theme is replayed: "Nothing stays the same. Everything can change." Everything changes, that is, except love—depicted as constant between a mother and young son. Large, chalky illustrations are filled with texture and pattern. A good companion book is Raffi's *Everything Grows.*

2.90   Williams, Vera B. **"More, More, More," Said the Baby: Three Love Stories.** Illustrated by Vera B. Williams. Greenwillow Books, 1990. ISBN 0-688-09174-1. 30p. 3–9 (est.).

These charming full-page paintings highlight three stories of babies and the grownups who love them. All three babies— Little Guy, Little Pumpkin, and Little Bird—are so fast that their daddy, grandma, and mama can barely catch them up! Each of the gouache paintings is a brightly colored depiction of the love and tenderness between baby and adult, and the happiness that they bring to each other through gentle play. *Caldecott Honor Book, 1991.*

2.91   Yorke, Jane, editor. **My First Look at Colors. My First Look at Home. My First Look at Numbers. My First Look at Opposites. My First Look at Seasons. My First Look at Shapes. My First Look at Sizes. My First Look at Touch.** Random House/Dorling Kindersley Books, 1990. 16p. 2–5.

What enormous fun! Preschoolers learn vocabulary and concepts through a brilliant array of three-dimensional color photographs. Unlikely, but singularly appropriate, objects are chosen to illustrate the concepts of home, seasons, sizes, opposites, touch, shapes, colors, and numbers. For example, in *My First Look at Touch,* readers are treated to a rough pineapple, a soft powder puff, and squishy marshmallows.

Counting Books

2.92   Aker, Suzanne. **What Comes in 2's, 3's, and 4's?** Illustrated by Bernie Karlin. Simon and Schuster Books for Young Readers, 1990. ISBN 0-671-67173-1. 32p. 2–5.

This variation on a counting book presents objects that normally come in twos, threes, and fours. Twos are hands and eyes and feet, handles on sinks, and wings on birds. Threes are tricycle wheels, meals in a day, and leaves on poison ivy. Fours are legs on tables, chairs, and dogs, seasons of the year, and corners on a book. Large illustrations make for easy counting. Teachers of young children can make good use of the concepts.

2.93   Archambault, John. **Counting Sheep.** Illustrated by John Rombola. Henry Holt, 1989. ISBN 0-8050-1135-8. 28p. 4–7.

Even after counting sheep, the narrator of this counting book still can't sleep, so he begins counting some rather imaginative animals to lift him off to dreamland—cotton-candy-spinning cats, orange giraffes, and pink raccoons. Brilliant full-page illustrations splash blazing colors on a baby-blue background.

2.94   Ashton, Elizabeth Allen. **An Old-Fashioned 1 2 3 Book.** Illustrated by Jessie Willcox Smith. Viking Penguin, 1991. ISBN 0-670-83499-8. 32p. 3–8.

Elizabeth Allen Ashton has selected works of artist Jessie Willcox Smith to produce a Victorian counting book filled with cherub-like children at play and accompanied by counting rhymes that retrofit the paintings. The paper is creamy and smooth; the numerals are aswirl with detail; and the paintings are bordered with the same flourish to yield the intended "old-fashioned" feel. Willcox Smith was well known for her covers for *Good Housekeeping* magazine during the early twentieth century.

2.95 Astley, Judy. **When One Cat Woke Up: A Cat Counting Book.** Illustrated by Judy Astley. Dial Books for Young Readers, 1990. ISBN 0-8037-0782-7. 32p. 3–7.

When one cat wakes up from its nap, it begins a romp through the house that results in increasing mischief. That one cat steals two fish, fights with three teddy bears, crumples four shirts, and on and on until ten muddy pawprints mark the cat's trail back to bed. Brightly colored drawings enhance the predictable progression of a cat having fun from one to ten.

2.96 Bennett, David. **One Cow, Moo, Moo!** Illustrated by Andy Cooke. Henry Holt, 1990. ISBN 0-8050-1416-0. 30p. 4–7.

When a young boy sees one cow go running by, he wonders why. His curiosity increases as he sees that the cow is chased by two horses that are, in turn, chased by three donkeys. The excitement grows as more and more different animals (all the way up to ten mice) pass by. The boy finds a surprising answer at the end of this cumulative counting book.

2.97 Chouinard, Roger, and Mariko Chouinard. **One Magic Box.** Illustrated by Roger Chouinard. Doubleday, 1989. ISBN 0-385-26204-3. 28p. 3–8.

When one magic box, locked with two locks, falls to the Earth one night, three socks, four policemen, and five monsters come to inspect it. The rhyming tale continues in this counting pattern, until, culminating at fifteen magic stars, the magic box swallows up all of the counting objects and characters who had previously made an appearance. Roger Chouinard creates a surrealistic atmosphere using brilliant colors and odd perspectives against starry, purple, pink, and black backgrounds.

2.98 Christelow, Eileen, retold by. **Five Little Monkeys Jumping on the Bed.** Illustrated by Eileen Christelow. Clarion Books, 1989. ISBN 0-89919-769-8. 30p. 3–7.

Once again those five little monkeys are jumping on the bed. In this familiar jingle, one little monkey at a time falls off and bumps his or her head. For each bump, Mama must call the doctor. And, of course, the doctor said, "No more monkeys jumping on the bed!" The delightful surprise in Eileen Christelow's illustrations is that once those monkey children are tucked in bed again, Mama Monkey jumps on her bed! Crayon-like drawings add whimsy to the monkeys' bedtime preparations.

2.99   Clements, Andrew. **Mother Earth's Counting Book.** Illustrated by Lonni Sue Johnson. Picture Book Studio, 1992. ISBN 0-88708-138-X. 44p. 3 and up.

One Earth takes center stage in this creative counting book. The world's wildlife, climate, oceans, deserts, people, and more are pictured in graceful pastel shades as the countable objects increase to the number ten, then return to one, emphasizing the Earth's uniqueness.

2.100   Crossley-Holland, Kevin. **Under the Sun and over the Moon.** Illustrated by Ian Penney. G. P. Putnam's Sons, 1989. ISBN 0-399-21946-3. 32p. All ages.

A boy wanders through ten gardens that serve as the organizing framework for this unconventional counting book. The first garden contains one sundial, one folded wing, one unicorn—one of everything. Pairs, of course, are found in the second garden, three of a kind in the next garden, and so on up to ten. The rhyming couplets that accompany each illustration guide the viewers in their search for sometimes-obscure items.

2.101   Dunrea, Olivier. **Deep Down Underground.** Illustrated by Olivier Dunrea. Macmillan, 1989. ISBN 0-02-732861-9. 32p. 3–7.

Insects, mice, toads, and other underground creatures "wriggle and wrangle," "scurry and scamper," "scooch and scrunch," "dance and prance," "patter and chatter," and "slide and glide" when they hear "1 wee moudiewort [Scottish for *mole*] digging, digging deep down underground." Regrettably, cadence-breaking ants merely "march and stamp," while toads "burrow and scrape." Earth-tone illustrations invite searching and counting to ten and back in this tongue-tangling, cumulative counting book. *Notable Children's Trade Books in Science, 1989.*

2.102   Fleming, Denise. **Count!** Illustrated by Denise Fleming. Henry Holt, 1992. ISBN 0-8050-1595-7. 32p. 2–6.

Okay, you counters, get ready: Count one gnu of the orange-and-yellow-speckled variety on a lavender backdrop that is bordered by smears from the gnu's pallette. Next, count two zebras of impossible stripe and energy. "Jump, zebras!" reads the big, bold text. Children can keep counting until they reach ten—all the while performing the antics of bouncing kangaroos, wiggling worms, and lizards that line up. Finally, it's counting by tens to reach fifty bees. "Count again, please."

2.103 French, Vivian. **One Ballerina Two.** Illustrated by Jan Ormerod. Lothrop, Lee and Shepard Books, 1991. ISBN 0-688-10334-0. 32p. 3–6.

A young ballerina ties her shoes and then gracefully checks those of her admirer, a rumpled younger ballerina "wannabe." With perfect form, in a continuous-motion illustration, the ballerina performs ten pliés. The words "10 Ten pliés" appear in crisp print to match the crispness of her leotard. Hair and skirt akimbo, the child does nine knee bends, and the words are printed in her own ragged crayon script. In warmly comic mime, the countdown continues—from pirouettes to gallops, from pas de chat to pony trots.

2.104 Geisert, Arthur. **Pigs from 1 to 10.** Illustrated by Arthur Geisert. Houghton Mifflin, 1992. ISBN 0-395-58519-8. 32p. 2–6.

During a bedtime story read by Mother Pig about a lost place with huge stone configurations, ten little pigs decide to go on a quest. With courage and resourcefulness, the pigs bridge an abyss and drill through a mountain to their goal. They copy the "stone configurations"—numerals from zero to nine—and bring the copies home. Every intricate black-and-white, double-page etching offers a quest for the reader as well: the numerals zero to nine (and the ten pigs) are embedded within each illustration for young readers to find.

2.105 Giganti, Paul, Jr. **Each Orange Had 8 Slices: A Counting Book.** Illustrated by Donald Crews. Greenwillow Books, 1992. ISBN 0-688-10429-0. 32p. 3 and up.

Although it *could* be a counting book for young children, this book could also serve as an introduction to multiplication. On each patterned page, an unseen narrator presents a set of objects (with related subsets) and three questions: "On my way to lunch I ate 2 juicy oranges. Each orange had 8 slices. Each slice had 2 small seeds." How many juicy oranges were there? How many slices? How many seeds? Donald Crews's illustrations are characteristically crisp, colorful, and countable.

2.106 Grossman, Virginia. **Ten Little Rabbits.** Illustrated by Sylvia Long. Chronicle Books, 1991. ISBN 0-87701-552-X. 25p. 2–6.

Vivid and whimsical illustrations, reminiscent of Beatrix Potter, accompany a counting rhyme in which rabbits portray Native Americans. Ten two-page paintings depict rabbits, attired in traditional Native American garments, who are engaged in such customs as performing a rain dance or sending a smoke signal. From the Sioux to the Navajo, each tribe is described in a glossary at the back of the book. *IRA Children's Book Award, 1992.*

2.107 Hayes, Sarah. **Nine Ducks Nine.** Illustrated by Sarah Hayes. Lothrop, Lee and Shepard Books, 1990. ISBN 0-688-09535-6. 32p. 3–6.

When nine ducks go out for a stroll in the meadow, a hungry but stupid fox follows closely and watches. One by one, the ducks run away, "down to the rickety-bridge." "I'm off," the departing duck always says. Finding one lone duck in the nest built on the rickety-bridge, Mr. Fox pounces, only to splash into the pond as the rickety-bridge gives way. Full-page watercolor paintings humorously illustrate this tale of nine clever ducks and their plan to spoil Mr. Fox's day. Rhyming phrases, a counting sequence, and repetitive lines are sure to invite young children's participation.

2.108 Linden, Ann Marie. **One Smiling Grandma: A Caribbean Counting Book.** Illustrated by Lynne Russell. Dial Books for Young Readers, 1992. ISBN 0-8037-1132-8. 24p. 2–6.

Besides "one smiling grandma in a rocking chair," the characteristic fare included in this joyful Caribbean counting rhyme are the marketplace, hummingbirds, flying fish, conch shells, sugar apples, hairy coconuts, and sleeping mongooses. Memories of Barbados and a special grandmother influenced the author's choice of set and characters. One bright-eyed girl experiences the bounty and color of her island interpreted by the artist in sun-bathed chalks.

2.109 MacCarthy, Patricia. **Ocean Parade: A Counting Book.** Illustrated by Patricia MacCarthy. Dial Books for Young Readers, 1990. ISBN 0-8037-0780-0. 32p. 2–6.

In an ocean parade, one big glimmering fish and two little fish swim across a blue silk page—batik gills, scales, and seafloor edged with white-frosting-like trim. Then come three flat fish, four thin fish, and five fat fish until patterned and rainbow fish of all sizes fill the pages, swimming among the sea plants. After nineteen transparent fish, the fish parade advances by tens to fifty; finally, one hundred silver fish swim about a sunken treasure chest.

2.110 Merriam, Eve. **Train Leaves the Station.** Illustrated by Dale Gottlieb. Henry Holt/Bill Martin Books,1992. ISBN 0-8050-1934-0. 32p. 3–6.

Dale Gottlieb's broad-lined, boldly colored illustrations for Eve Merriam's counting verse are as simple in form as the predictable text that they accompany. A toy train chugs past other nursery toys to rhythmic announcement: "Snake in the grass, angel in heaven, train leaves the station at seven-o-seven." When it's time for the ten-o-ten, the train is stuck in the station again, and toys are piled high in the toy box.

2.111 O'Keefe, Susan Heyboer. **One Hungry Monster: A Counting Book in Rhyme.** Illustrated by Lynn Munsinger. Little, Brown/Joy Street Books, 1989. ISBN 0-316-63385-2. 32p. 3–7.

One by one, ten hungry monsters appear in a little boy's bedroom and spill out into his home, where they wreak havoc upon the entire household, especially the kitchen, in search of food. After politely serving the ten monsters ten different foods and receiving only tricks and shenanigans in return, the boy finally orders them out of his house: "You are so bad / it makes me mad!" Busy watercolored pen-and-ink illustrations portray the chubby, green-eyed monsters as harmless rascals.

2.112 Pacovská, Květa. **One, Five, Many.** Illustrated by Květa Pacovská. Clarion Books, 1990. ISBN 0-395-54997-3. 28p. 4–6.

This unique number book, with its punch-outs, paper doors, peek windows, mirrors, and ingenious design, is a marvel of learning made pleasurable. It covers only the numbers one through ten, but presents them so thoroughly and imaginatively that young readers will return with delight, reinforcing the lessons. The illustrations are brilliantly colored, often of whimsical creatures, and delightful enough in themselves to bring readers to the book again and again.

2.113 Reiser, Lynn. **Christmas Counting.** Illustrated by Lynn Reiser. Greenwillow Books, 1992. ISBN 0-688-10677-3. 32p. 4 and up.

More than just for counting, this book, filled with colorful stylized paintings, provides a wealth of opportunities for fun and learning. Through a cumulative patterned story about a young fir tree and a family, young children can celebrate growth, new life, and family traditions. The predictable text and well-matched illustrations will have even the youngest joining in the fun.

2.114   Scott, Ann Herbert. **One Good Horse: A Cowpuncher's Counting Book.** Illustrated by Lynn Sweat. Greenwillow Books, 1990. ISBN 0-688-09147-4. 29p. 2 and up.

As a young boy accompanies his cowboy father on his ranch rounds, they describe the wide-open landscape numerically from one to ten, to fifty, and to one hundred before heading back home on their horse. Burnt orange, forest green, and teal hues dominate the realistic pencil and oil paintings by Lynn Sweat. The simple text is framed by thin orange and teal borders in Native American style.

2.115   Sheppard, Jeff. **The Right Number of Elephants.** Illustrated by Felicia Bond. Harper and Row, 1990. ISBN 0-06-025616-8. 32p. 4–7.

In a counting book featuring elephants, a young girl tells the exact number of elephants needed for various tasks. For example, if you need to paint the ceiling "and there isn't a ladder to be found, then the right number of elephants is . . . 9." While nine exuberant elephants slap paint everywhere, causing a riotous mess, there's a new problem: "When you go to the beach on a very warm day, the right number of elephants for shade is . . . 8." Felicia Bond's countdown watercolors make even one elephant special.

2.116   Sloat, Teri. **From One to One Hundred.** Illustrated by Teri Sloat. Dutton Children's Books, 1991. ISBN 0-525-44764-4. 32p. 3–7.

Here's a counting book that contextualizes the counting opportunities—even the numerals are embedded in the artwork. Objects to count are pictured at the bottom of each page. Simple to find is one princess roasting one marshmallow on the breath of one dragon. But how about fifty huskies pulling dogsleds past fifty spectators and headed toward a finish line of fifty frankfurters under fifty flags? Double-page spreads invite counting from one to ten, and then by tens to one hundred.

2.117   Thaler, Mike. **Seven Little Hippos.** Illustrated by Jerry Smath. Simon and Schuster Books for Young Readers, 1991. ISBN 0-671-72964-0. 28p. 4–8.

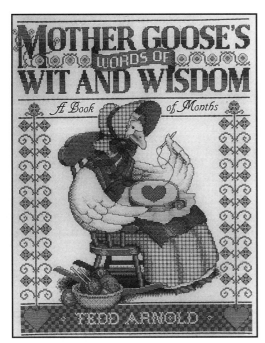

A.

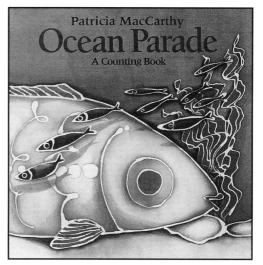

B.

C.

A. *Mother Goose's Words of Wit and Wisdom: A Book of Months* by Tedd Arnold (see 2.121).   **B.** *Ocean Parade: A Counting Book* by Patricia MacCarthy (see 2.109). **C.** *What Comes in 2's, 3's & 4's?* by Suzanne Aker; illustrated by Bernie Karlin (see 2.92).

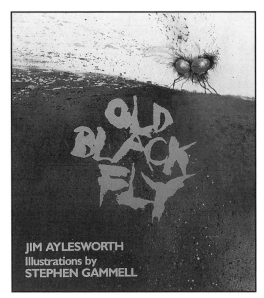

A.

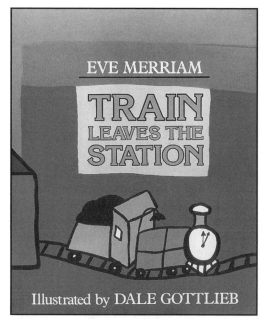

B.

C.

A. *Old Black Fly* by Jim Aylesworth; illustration by Stephen Gammell (see 2.4).
B. *Train Leaves the Station* by Eve Merriam; illustrated by Dale Gottlieb (see 2.110).
C. *Each Orange Had 8 Slices: A Counting Book* by Paul Giganti, Jr.; illustrated by Donald Crews (see 2.105).

In this familiar chant, pajama-clad hippos (instead of monkeys) are jumping on the bed until, one by one, each bounces off and bumps a hippo head. Youngsters instantly will be reading along with the hippo doctor, who warns, "No more little hippos jumping on the bed," as he wraps yards and yards of bandages around each swollen noggin. Jerry Smath's hippos are exuberant, so they crack the walls, shatter the floor, and burst through the ceiling, eventually demolishing the house.

2.118   Thornhill, Jan. **The Wildlife 1 2 3: A Nature Counting Book.** Illustrated by Jan Thornhill. Simon and Schuster Books for Young Readers, 1989. ISBN 0-671-67926-0. 32p. 4–8.

Wild animals from around the world accompany the numerals 1 to 20 as well as 25, 50, 100, and 1,000. Animals in natural settings and in striking compositions are framed by detailed designs. Some are camouflaged to provide readers with a bit of a counting challenge. Readers can count the animals in the illustrations as well as in the borders. Information about each animal appears on the final two pages entitled "Nature Notes." *Notable Children's Trade Books in Science, 1989.*

2.119   Van Fleet, Matthew. **One Yellow Lion.** Illustrated by Matthew Van Fleet. Dial Books for Young Readers, 1992. ISBN 0-8037-1099-2. 24p. 2–6.

In a simple concept book, two bold words appear on the left-hand side of the page: "One" and "Yellow." Opposite is a huge yellow numeral 1. Open the flap and half of that numeral becomes the tail of a cheerful lion cub. On the next page, the numeral 2 opens to become the neck of a graceful swan. After counting to ten, children can open a final five-fold page on which all the animals reprise their roles in an animal pyramid.

2.120   Wood, Jakki. **One Bear with Bees in His Hair.** Illustrated by Jakki Wood. Dutton Children's Books, 1990. ISBN 0-525-44695-8. 32p. 3–6.

In rhyming text that spreads one line at a time across the pages, the story cumulates: One bright orange honey-eating bear whose hair is populated by bees meets another bear, this one with purple fur. "Two bears—that's more fun. Oh, look! Another one!" Bears continue to meet others until they number ten and their mass crams and overflows the pages (making counting them a bit difficult). When all are assembled, they disperse for a game of hide-and-seek, laughably spottable by their incongruous fur colors.

Nursery Rhymes

2.121   Arnold, Tedd. **Mother Goose's Words of Wit and Wisdom: A Book of Months.** Dial Books for Young Readers, 1990. ISBN 0-8037-0826-2. 32p. 4 and up.

Many, many hands "pulled miles and miles of thread through what seemed to be acres of cloth" to produce a year-round Mother Goose illustrated with samplers. The counted cross-stitch and embroidered designs are bordered with raw linen, making handsome, framable compositions on each page. A final section explains the origin and history of traditional samplers, children's role in producing them, and a bibliography of historical needlework sources.

2.122   Brown, Ruth. **The World That Jack Built.** Illustrated by Ruth Brown. Dutton Children's Books, 1991. ISBN 0-525-44735-4. 26p. 4–7.

Although based on the traditional cumulative tale, Ruth Brown's message—that we must protect the environment—is up-to-the-minute. "This is the stream that flows past the trees that grow by the house that Jack built." Rich and sensitive paintings portray a love for animals and nature's beauty. Each scene also shows increasing human pollution as it is astutely observed through the eyes of a black cat.

2.123   Bullock, Kathleen. **It Chanced to Rain.** Illustrated by Kathleen Bullock. Simon and Schuster Books for Young Readers, 1989. ISBN 0-671-66005-5. 32p. 4–6.

In a whimsically illustrated adaptation of a nursery rhyme in which it rains on a variety of animal friends out for a walk, cats, dogs, rats, and pigs hurry home for dry clothes and a hot lunch, only to discover that the ducks are missing. Fearing the worst, the friends trek back out in the rain and find the ducks swimming in the river. At the close of the day, most of the animals end up in bed with sniffles, except for the ducks, who must wash all the lunch dishes.

2.124   Butterworth, Nick. **Nick Butterworth's Book of Nursery Rhymes.** Illustrated by Nick Butterworth. Viking Penguin, 1991. ISBN 0-670-83551-X. 52p. 2–7.

Through whimsical illustrations, Nick Butterworth creates witty, literal interpretations of twenty-two nursery rhymes. We see Mary's lamb eagerly raising its "hoof" from behind a school desk and Jack (the mouse) pole-vaulting over a candlestick. A few of the nursery rhymes in this American edition of a book first published in Great Britain are unfamiliar, but the distinctive illustrations make them all delightful.

2.125   Cauley, Lorinda Bryan. **Three Blind Mice: The Classic Nursery Rhyme.** Illustrated by Lorinda Bryan Cauley. G. P. Putnam's Sons, 1991. ISBN 0-399-21775-4. 28p. 4–8.

The complete adventure underlying this classic nursery rhyme is revitalized by Lorinda Bryan Cauley's uniquely individual mice in tiny hats, suspenders, or checked pants. The colorfully detailed paintings give a mouse's view of a treacherous world, evoking sympathy, horror, and then satisfaction when the mice finally recover their sight and their tails.

2.126   Cole, Joanna, and Stephanie Calmenson, compilers. **Pat-a-Cake, and Other Play Rhymes.** Illustrated by Alan Tiegreen. Morrow Junior Books, 1992. ISBN 0-688-11039-8. 48p. 1–4.

"For every mood and time of day," there are rhymes for babies' and toddlers' fingers, hands, toes, feet, and faces; there are rhymes for tickling, for knee riding, and for dancing. Text of the rhymes appears beneath demonstrations of adults and children at play. A gentle reminder cautions parents that a little stimulation goes a long way, and supports them as partners in language learning. A bibliography sends the interested reader to other sources.

2.127   Jones, Carol, compiler. **Hickory Dickory Dock, and Other Nursery Rhymes.** Illustrated by Carol Jones. Houghton Mifflin, 1992. ISBN 0-395-60834-1. 32p. 2–8.

Each of the eleven rhymes in this collection is printed on a bordered interleafed page with a cut-out hole that allows readers to preview a detail in the next full-page painting or to peek back at a portion of the prior illustration. The mouse who ran up the clock appears in each period-set watercolor and ink illustration.

2.128   Kemp, Moira, compiler. **Baa, Baa, Black Sheep. Hey Diddle Diddle. Hickory, Dickory, Dock. This Little Piggy.** Illustrated by Moira Kemp. Lodestar Books, 1991. 12p. 2–6.

The front covers of this nursery rhyme series are shaped to the main character's ears, so the heads of a mouse, pig, black sheep, and cat with a fiddle are discernible on each page of these simple board books. Throughout, the cheerful characters wear just the right clothing. For example, Baa Baa Black Sheep wears a bright patchwork shawl and peers over her glasses at the counter of her general store as she answers requests for wool.

2.129   Knight, Joan. **Tickle-Toe Rhymes.** Illustrated by John Wallner. Orchard Books, 1989. ISBN 0-531-05773-X. 32p. 2–5.

A variety of animals, including tigers, skunks, and pandas, engage in activities that stimulate counting rhymes, all based on "This Little Pig Went to Market." Some rhymes are clever and use atypical vocabulary in a fun way. The watercolor and ink illustrations are amusing, detailed, and certain to prompt discussion. The animals themselves, however, are small enough and integral enough to make counting a challenge for the very young.

2.130   Langley, Jonathan. **Rain, Rain, Go Away! A Book of Nursery Rhymes.** Illustrated by Jonathan Langley. Dial Books for Young Readers, 1991. ISBN 0-8037-0762-2. 93p. 2–6.

With bustling energy and detail-packed pages, ninety-two favorite nursery rhymes are illustrated in bright colors with rosy-cheeked, whimsical lads and lasses. Curly Locks has a sprinkling of freckles across her cherubic face; Yankee Doodle, wearing a cowboy hat, rides a wheeled horse. Page layouts group rhymes with common elements. For example, rainy-day rhymes are combined into a two-page spread that features a baker in a windmill, April showers, the Eency Weency spider, and rain, rain that won't let Johnny go out to play.

2.131   Lawson, Carol. **Teddy Bear, Teddy Bear.** Illustrated by Carol Lawson. Dial Books for Young Readers, 1991. ISBN 0-8037-0970-6. 32p. 2–6.

The familiar jump-rope rhyme is turned, line by line, into a cheery picture book that invites instant reading and enactment of the movements of a smiling yellow Teddy. Blue-crayon borders wrap Teddy in action—dancing on toes, touching his nose, turning around, and touching the ground. Smears of paint muss the edges of the pages, as though touched before it dried by a mischievous Teddy.

2.132   Opie, Iona, and Peter Opie. **The Little Dog Laughed.** Illustrated by Lucy Cousins. E. P. Dutton, 1990. ISBN 0-525-44573-0. 64p. 2–5.

Sixty-four Mother Goose rhymes, printed in a large, bold typeface, are presented with the characteristic simplicity of Lucy Cousins's art. Heavy black outlines and crayon-box primary colors accompany captions that are primitively scrawled in paint across each illustration. The result is a joyful, albeit unusual, interpretation of these classic rhymes. *ALA Notable Children's Books, 1991.*

2.133   Sutherland, Zena, compiler. **The Orchard Book of Nursery Rhymes.** Illustrated by Faith Jaques. Orchard Books, 1990. ISBN 0-531-05903-0. 96p. All ages.

Seventy-seven classic nursery rhymes, illustrated with period watercolors, are gathered into this beautifully designed edition with the feel and look of what a nursery rhyme collection should be. Faith Jaques has done meticulous research on the houses, domestic detail, and gardens of the Georgian period. In a palette of soft pinks, lilacs, blues, and greens, each of the scenes and characters is perfectly matched to its verse—and each verse is a favorite. Zena Sutherland reports the origins of some of the rhymes in "Selector's Notes."

2.134   Wadsworth, Olive A. **Over in the Meadow: An Old Counting Rhyme.** Illustrated by David A. Carter. Scholastic Hardcover Books, 1992. ISBN 0-590-44498-0. 32p. 2–6.

This traditional counting rhyme/song is enlivened with meadow dwellers executed in cut-paper collage. Animal textures and details are sponge-painted or stamped. The effect is lush springtime color, simplicity of line, and interesting detail (such as eight yellow lizards dotted with tiny orange stars). The entire rhyme is reprinted at the book's end, with the number words in boldface type.

2.135   Watson, Wendy. **Wendy Watson's Mother Goose.** Illustrated by Wendy Watson. Lothrop, Lee and Shepard Books, 1989. ISBN 0-688-05708-X. 160p. 4–8.

Wendy Watson's collection of over two hundred nursery rhymes is illustrated with simple, cheery scenes and characters— ranging from tucked-in cameos to two-page spreads. Although only the cover flap gives the clue, the rhymes are "art-organized" seasonally to cover the full year.

2.136   Yolen, Jane, editor. **The Lap-Time Song and Play Book.** Illustrated by Margot Tomes. Harcourt Brace Jovanovich, 1989. ISBN 0-15-243588-3. 32p. All ages.

Sixteen nursery games and rhymes are period-set by Margot Tomes's gouache paintings and then offered to those with children in their care along with directions for enacting the verses. Jane Yolen has also provided interesting background information for each entry. For example, the Baker's Man in "Patty-Cake, Patty Cake" may refer to *Beker's man,* an old Saxon term for priest. To "mark it with T" (as in older versions) meant to make the sign of the cross over the communion wafer. Adam Stemple, Yolen's son has provided musical arrangements for the piano, and Yolen offers an afterword, "About Lap Songs."

Paper Engineering

Lift-the-Flap

2.137   Angel, Marie. **Marie Angel's Exotic Alphabet: A Lift-the-Flap Alphabetic Safari.** Illustrated by Marie Angel. Dial Books for Young Readers, 1992. ISBN 0-8037-1247-2. 32p. 2–6.

Untie a red ribbon to unfold a nine-foot frieze printed on stiff board. Each fold frames a different wild animal habitat—an African coastal jungle, waterhole, and grasslands, as well as South and Central American jungles. Readers can open small flaps to discover an alphabet zoo—from a graceful antelope to a skunk-like zorilla. On the opposite side of the frieze, the names of all the exotic animals are printed on identical habitat backgrounds.

2.138   Argent, Kerry. **Happy Birthday, Wombat!** Illustrated by Kerry Argent. Little, Brown/Joy Street Books, 1991. ISBN 0-316-05097-0. 20p. 1–5.

While Wombat searches high and low for his birthday present, his assorted Australian animal friends—bandicoots, kangaroos, and koala bears—sneak past the lovable lumberer to gather for his surprise birthday party. Children will delight in lifting flaps to discover telltale streamers, banners, and gifts that Wombat, in his fervor, has overlooked. Charming illustrations offer memorable details, such as Wombat's palm-tree patterned Bermuda shorts and a multicolored patchwork quilt.

2.139 Bradman, Tony, and Margaret Chamberlain. **Who's Afraid of the Big Bad Wolf?** Illustrated by Margaret Chamberlain. Macmillan/Aladdin Books, 1989. ISBN 0-689-71291-X. 20p. 3–6.

Three comical pigs and a big bad wolf cavort across the pages of this lift-the-flap picture book. While the wolf threatens, bug-eyed forest animals ask in speech balloons, "Who's afraid of the big bad wolf?" Just lift a log or move a bush to discover the answer: "We are!" Readers must look under flying house parts to find the first two pigs. But with his assault on the brick house, the wolf is foiled by a wily girl pig. "Who's afraid of the boiling water?"

2.140 Coleridge, Sara. **January Brings the Snow: A Seasonal Hide-and-Seek.** Illustrated by Elizabeth Falconer. Orchard Books, 1989. ISBN 0-531-05824-7. 28p. 3–8.

The couplets of Sara Coleridge's nineteenth-century poem announce nature's offerings during each month of the year ("January brings the snow; / Makes the toes and fingers glow"). The lines of the poem appear beneath twelve windowpane borders that focus on two children at work or at play in seasonal activities. Lift the tabs to uncover the activities of a tiny family of field mice who are also frolicking through the seasons.

2.141 Cousins, Lucy. **What Can Rabbit Hear? What Can Rabbit See?** Illustrated by Lucy Cousins. Tambourine Books, 1991. 16p. 2 and up.

Sporting a red and white striped shirt, bespectacled Rabbit sees and hears the world around him: "What can Rabbit see in the pond?" Lift the flap to find a large goldfish. "What can Rabbit hear in the tree?" Lift the flap to reveal a chirping bird. Young children will discover ways to identify objects and learn common sounds, all the while delighting in illustrations that are bold, primary colored, and childlike.

2.142 Grindley, Sally. **Shhh!** Illustrated by Peter Utton. Little, Brown/Joy Street Books, 1992. ISBN 0-316-32899-5. 22p. 4–8.

Two tiny but unseen creatures approach the giant's castle—is it the reader and the listener? Fold out a door for an intruder's-eye view of the giant's dining room, and the adventure begins. On this tiptoe journey, readers can peek back through small doors to see if the cat, the hen, and then the wife are undisturbed. At last—the giant! Peek back. Awake! The giant is so menacing that readers are warned: "SHUT THE BOOK!" Illustrations are un-controlled strokes of exuberance.

2.143   Hill, Eric. **Spot Goes to the Park. Spot Sleeps Over.** Illustrated by Eric Hill. G. P. Putnam's Sons, 1990–91. 11p. 1–5.

Spot the amiable puppy has adventures with his assorted animal friends in this series of twelve books for young children. When Spot sleeps overnight at his monkey friend Steve's house, he brings a wagonload of toys, but forgets his teddy bear. When Spot is at the park, a friendly duck retrieves his ball from a pond. On each heavy page, the response to large, bold text is hidden under flaps. Simple line drawings in primary colors promote the elemental mood.

2.144   Pelham, David. **Sam's Sandwich.** Illustrated by David Pelham and Harry Willock. Dutton Children's Books, 1991. ISBN 0-525-44751-2. 22p. 5 and up.

No child would want to eat *Sam's Sandwich,* but some may want to read it and lift its flaps. Within sandwich dimensions, and between covers of laminated styrofoam "bread," a demonic looking brother-sister duo, Sam and Samantha, decide to make a sandwich, to which Samantha adds lettuce, tomatoes, cheese, watercress, cucumbers, salami, onions, and ketchup, while Sam slips in worms, snails, ants, flies, spiders, tadpoles, and centipedes.

2.145   Potter, Beatrix. **Beatrix Potter's Peter Rabbit: A Lift-the-Flap Rebus Book.** Illustrated by Colin Twinn. Frederick Warne, 1991. ISBN 0-7232-3798-0. 16p. 4–8.

Beatrix Potter's complete, original text is enlarged in this reissued rebus book. Tiny picture flaps mask selected story words that are revealed by lifting the flaps. In addition, there are some pop-up features, including a final peep into the underground rabbit hole. The artwork is Potter's original, but page layouts differ to accommodate the enlarged text.

2.146   Smith, Mavis. **"Fred, Is That You?" A Lift-the-Flap Book.** Illustrated by Mavis Smith. Little, Brown, 1992. ISBN 0-316-80241-7. 20p. 2–5.

A concerned duck follows different sets of tracks to find his friend, Fred, asking repeatedly: "Fred, is that you?" Beneath each variantly shaped flap (including a beach umbrella, a bedsheet on the clothesline, and even a refrigerator door), the duck finds the animal who really made the tracks and who points out the mistake in a rhyming couplet: "No, dude, no. Can't you see I'm a crow?" Bright colors, bold lines, and minimal backgrounds contribute to this surprise-ending book for beginners.

2.147   Varekamp, Marjolein. **Little Sam Takes a Bath.** Illustrated by Marjolein Varekamp. Orchard Books, 1991. ISBN 0-531-05944-8. 24p. 2–6.

In a "special effects" book, Little Sam, a roly-poly pig, gets dirty playing in the mud and must be coaxed into the bath by a patient mother. Children can participate by turning Little Sam over in the mudhole, peeking into cutout windows and doors, and sympathizing with Sam's reluctance to bathe. Most fun of all, though, is pulling the tab that makes Sam jump into the tub with a mighty splash, joining his pop-up seal and elephant.

Pop-ups

2.148   Carter, David A. **Surprise Party: A Lift-up Pop-up Book.** Illustrated by David A. Carter. Grosset and Dunlap, 1990. ISBN 0-488-40062-6. 16p. 4–6.

An alligator couple attends a surprise party and encounters "silly snakes," "beautiful birds," and "fabulous frogs" on full-color, pop-up pages. This birthday fun honors a surprise baby not yet hatched from a red polka-dot egg.

2.149   Dijs, Carla. **Who Sees You? At the Pond. Who Sees You? In the Jungle.** Illustrated by Carla Dijs. Grosset and Dunlap, 1992. 12p. 2–5.

"Who Sees You?" is the question posed in these two Little Pop-and-Peek Books. In every habitat, pop-up animals in vivid colors against stark white backgrounds answer the question. *At the Pond* features such creatures as a kelly-green frog with pop-up legs, a face-to-face view of a turtle with a wrinkly neck, and a shimmery blue fish with a flipping fin, while *In the Jungle* features brightly colored scenes with jungle animal pop-ups. The series also includes animals from the farm, ocean, zoo, and forest.

2.150   Fritz, Jean. **The Great Adventure of Christopher Columbus: A Pop-up Book.** Illustrated by Tomie dePaola. Putnam and Grosset, 1992. ISBN 0-399-22113-1. 12p. 5–9.

In Jean Fritz's inimitable clarity, accuracy, and simplicity of style, the Columbus adventure is retold along the side panels of six pop-up scenes designed by Tomie dePaola. Columbus bows to Ferdinand and Isabella, a ship skims the waves, Columbus plants the flag of Spain, the *Santa Maria* runs aground, and Columbus returns at the head of a procession. This is a pop-up book that bears reading aloud: "Too much! Much too much. The queen said no and sent Christopher Columbus on his way."

2.151   Moseley, Keith. **It Was a Dark and Stormy Night: A Pop-Up Mystery Whodunit.** Illustrated by Linda Birkinshaw. Dial Books, 1991. ISBN 0-8037-1021-6. 14p. 8–10.

Even though it was a dark and stormy night, Lady Penelope Pig wasn't going to let weather spoil her dinner party, an evening for showing off her newest diamond. As the storm rages, Victorian-clad animal guests are served by maid and butler in pop-up English drawing-room scenes. Then a blinding flash, the lights go out, and the diamond is stolen. Inspector Dog and careful readers must solve the crime. A tiny sealed envelope holds the solution at the book's end.

2.152   Rojany, Lisa. **The Hands-on Book of Big Machines.** Illustrated by Joel Snyder. Little, Brown, 1992. ISBN 0-316-41904-4. 14p. 6–10.

On construction sites, roadways, factories, and farms, big machines lift, dig, carry, and tear down. Paper engineering enables the monster machines in this book to move, scoop, or lift. Readers can even peek into some of these gigantic machines. The final page offers a robot arm in an auto factory as well as a dinosaur automated by machinery. The narrative is mindful of children's interests ("A backhoe can dig holes deep enough for a giraffe to stand in") and not overwhelmingly lengthy.

2.153   Stevenson, Robert Louis. **A Child's Garden of Verses: A Pop-up Book.** Illustrated by Jannat Messenger. Dutton Children's Books, 1992. ISBN 0-525-44997-3. 12p. 2–6.

Jannat Messenger has selected twelve of Stevenson's best-loved poems and given six of them a pop-up interpretation and/or movable features. For "The Wind," a butterfly kite spins upward; by pulling a tab, two other kites are launched skyward on curly strings. A small cadre of neighborhood children in dress-up costumes moves to "The Marching Song." One enthusiastic marcher claps the cymbals; another beats a drum.

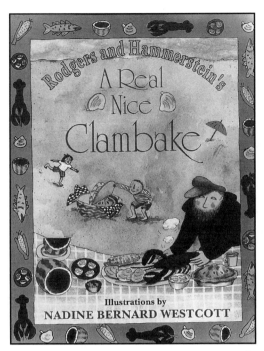

A.

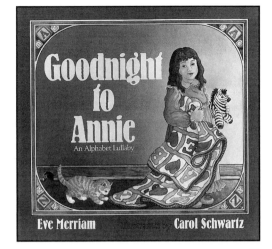

B.

C.

A. *A Real Nice Clambake* by Oscar Hammerstein; illustrated by Nadine Bernard Westcott (see 2.158). **B.** *Goodnight to Annie: An Alphabet Lullaby* by Eve Merriam; illustrated by Carol Schwartz (see 2.20). **C.** *The Pop-Up, Pull-Tab, Playtime House That Jack Built* by Nadine Bernard Westcott (see 2.154).

A.

B.

C.

A. *Fox Outfoxed* by James Marshall (see 9.12). **B.** *An Ocean World* by Peter Sis (see 2.174). **C.** *Twinkle, Twinkle, Little Star* by Jane Taylor, illustrated by Michael Hague (see 2.163).

2.154   Westcott, Nadine Bernard. **The Pop-Up, Pull-Tab, Playtime House That Jack Built.** Illustrated by Nadine Bernard Westcott. Little, Brown/Joy Street Books, 1991. ISBN 0-316-93138-1. 18p. 6–8.

Open the first flap to find the pop-up rat that ate the cheese in the house that Jack built. In this action-packed version of the best-known cumulative tale, Jack sleeps through it all. He misses the dog-cat-rat chase, the cow with the crumpled horn kicking over the milkpail, and even the wedding officiated by the shaven and shorn priest. On each page, the rat who started it all keeps popping up in unusual places, such as pockets or trousers. With all in disarray, Jack wakens to ask, "What are you all doing in my house?"

Pull-Tabs

2.155   Zelinsky, Paul O. **The Wheels on the Bus.** Illustrated by Paul O. Zelinsky. Dutton Books, 1990. ISBN 0-525-44644-3. 12p. 3–6.

Vivid colors, unusual typefaces, and double-page layouts make this an exuberant rendition of the familiar children's song. Each verse is accompanied not only by bustling illustrations rich with subtle details, but also with movable parts related to the repetitive line (such as wipers on the bus that *really* go swish, swish, swish). Though young readers may have difficulty manipulating pull-tabs, an older reader can help them want to take this trip again and again. *ALA Notable Children's Books, 1991.*

Songs and Music

2.156   Cauley, Lorinda Bryan, reteller. **Old MacDonald Had a Farm.** Illustrated by Lorinda Bryan Cauley. G. P. Putnam's Sons, 1989. ISBN 0-399-21628-6. 32p. 4–8.

Poor Old MacDonald! The chubby, cheerful farmer with round, wire-rimmed glasses is awakened by roosters early in the morning, and is surrounded by frolicking animals that follow him "here," "there," and "everywhere" until he sits down to have a piece of pie at night. The animated illustrations, in bright colors with comedic details, extend this simple folk song by showing the many duties on Old MacDonald's farm, all of which are continuously interrupted by the boisterous animals.

2.157 Guthrie, Woody, with Marjorie Mazia Guthrie. **Woody's 20 Grow Big Songs.** Illustrated by Woody Guthrie. HarperCollins, 1992. ISBN 0-06-020283-1. 48p. All ages.

Lost for over forty years, the manuscript for this collection of songs, composed by the Guthries for their daughter, has been replicated complete with Woody Guthrie's own original scratchy watercolors. An arrangement and accompanying chords for each song are included, as well as the variations provided by additional verses. Occasionally readers are invited to provide their own extrapolations. For "Dance Around," children wave, tiptoe, march, hop, run, jump, and fly.

2.158 Hammerstein, Oscar, II. **A Real Nice Clambake.** Illustrated by Nadine Bernard Westcott. Little, Brown/Joy Street Books, 1992. ISBN 0-316-75422-6. 32p. 4–8.

Baskets and buckets of ingredients arrive early on the beach in preparation for clam chowder, steamed lobsters, corn on the cob, blueberrry pie, and watermelon. Both lyrics and music are included for this song from Rodgers and Hammerstein's *Carousel,* illustrated here as a family celebration on the beach. Spread across the pages, the festivities include games and songs and, of course, eating. Illustrations are filled with details for revisiting, and pages are bordered in motifs from each spread.

2.159 Jones, Carol, compiler. **Old MacDonald Had a Farm.** Illustrated by Carol Jones. Houghton Mifflin, 1989. ISBN 0-395-49212-2. 30p. 4–8.

Full-page watercolor illustrations in warm earth tones have peepholes in the middle of the facing pages, allowing children to guess the identity of the next animal that they will meet on the farm and then to catch a backward glimpse of Farmer Mac-Donald at work. Jam-packed details in the illustrations offer children opportunities to notice and talk about other animals and things of interest found on Old MacDonald's farm.

2.160 Larrick, Nancy, compiler. **Songs from Mother Goose: With the Traditional Melody for Each.** Illustrated by Robin Spowart. Harper and Row, 1989. ISBN 0-06-023714-7. 60p. 2–6.

This hardcover collection features musical arrangements for fifty-six Mother Goose rhymes, from the most popular to the less familiar. The arrangements are simple and based on traditional melodies. Appendixes include notes on Mother Goose, notes on particular rhymes, and an index to first lines. Brightly colored illustrations—some decorative, some depicting the action of the rhymes—add to the overall attractiveness of the book.

2.161 Medearis, Angela Shelf. **The Zebra-Riding Cowboy: A Folk Song from the Old West.** Illustrated by Maria Christina Brusca. Henry Holt, 1992. ISBN 0-8050-1712-7. 32p. 4–8.

When a scholarly looking greenhorn shows up at the Z-Bar Ranch, the cowboys give him the zebra dun to ride, the orneriest horse of all. But the city fellow keeps his seat, proving his worth as a cowhand. In an afterword, Angela Shelf Medearis speculates about this cowboy (portrayed here as a genial African American with a twinkle in his eye), and documents the contributions of ethnically diverse cowboys in the Old West. The musical score for this cowboy ballad is also included.

2.162 Raffi. **Five Little Ducks.** Illustrated by Jose Aruego and Ariane Dewey. Crown, 1989. ISBN 0-517-56945-0. 32p. 3–7.

Five little ducks go out to play, swimming in their pond and peeking from behind lily pads. But when Mother Duck sounds her "Quack, quack, quack, quack, . . . only four little ducks came back." The text of this singable countdown book in the Raffi Songs to Read series follows the steady disappearance of the Easter-egg-colored ducklings, who play in dirt, swing off grasses, and slide down hills. When none remain and the seasons turn round again, the ducks return, bringing their own duck families.

2.163 Taylor, Jane. **Twinkle, Twinkle, Little Star.** Illustrated by Michael Hague. Morrow Junior Books, 1992. ISBN 0-688-11168-8. 24p. 2–6.

This 1806 nursery song is reenchanted by Michael Hague's fanciful watercolor-and-ink illustrations. From an English nursery, two young children view the nighttime sky, as revealed by fairies releasing a trail of twinkling stars. The star path guides them upward into a cloud-borne sailing ship past magical beasts and angelic hosts. With the arrival of the Pegasus-like dawn, the children return to the nursery. Readers will find (before *they* sleep) a fold-out page with glow-in-the-dark stars.

2.164 Titherington, Jeanne. **Baby's Boat.** Illustrated by Jeanne Titherington. Greenwillow Books, 1992. ISBN 0-688-08556-3. 24p. 3–5.

In the spirit of Wynken, Blynken, and Nod, a lifelike baby sails to dreamland in a silver moon boat. Jeanne Titherington's layers of blurred colored pencils seem to glow with starlight, creating a gentle accompaniment to the simple, comforting lullaby: "Sail, baby, sail / Out upon that sea, / Only don't forget to sail / Back again to me." A palette of lavender creates a quiet mood; the simple lines of verse are each bordered with a lavender frame.

2.165   Young, Ruth. **Golden Bear.** Illustrated by Rachel Isadora. Viking Penguin, 1992. ISBN 0-670-82577-8. 28p. 2–6.

"Golden Bear, Golden Bear, I have seen him everywhere." In rhyming text, this tender book tells about the playtime adventures of a stuffed bear and his nameless African American friend. From quiet rocking to skating and snowman making, the soft pastel drawings of Caldecott Honor-winner Rachel Isadora evoke the gentleness of the relationship between the boy and his bear. Endpapers feature music specially composed by the author for the book.

Wordless Books

2.166   Brown, Craig. **The Patchwork Farmer.** Illustrated by Craig Brown. Greenwillow Books, 1989. ISBN 0-688-07736-6. 22p. 4–6.

In a wordless text, a cheerful farmer rises with each dawn and pulls on his overalls, ready for his day. Workaday chores besiege the farmer's overalls, and after each mishap, he must reach into his scrapbasket to repair the damage with a bright patch. At last, the basket is empty of patches, the overalls full of them, and both the farmer and his sunlit fields are a patchwork of festive color. Pastels are freckled with ink to give texture and grit.

2.167   Butterworth, Nick. **Amanda's Butterfly.** Illustrated by Nick Butterworth. Delacorte Press, 1991. ISBN 0-385-30434-X. 40p. 3–6.

In a wordless picture book, perky Amanda goes on a butterfly hunt. Delayed by a rain shower, she ducks into a storage shed where she discovers a tiny fairy with a torn, unusable wing. Although Molly considers using the tools in the shed to make the repair, none suits the delicate fairy. So Molly races to her house for the tool that works perfectly on fairy wings—tape. Nick Butterworth's cheerful paintings are framed squares against glossy-white backgrounds.

2.168   Day, Alexandra. **Carl Goes Shopping.** Illustrated by Alexandra Day. Farrar, Straus and Giroux, 1989. ISBN 0-374-31110-2. 27p. 3–7.

Carl the dog is back, and this time he is instructed to take care of Baby in a department store while Mother runs an errand. Baby immediately gets out of the buggy and onto Carl's back for adventures throughout the store. Carl and Baby make it back to their buggy just in time for Mother's praise. This book of few words should elicit extensive elaborations as readers react to the duo's escapades.

2.169 Geisert, Arthur. **Oink.** Illustrated by Arthur Geisert. Houghton Mifflin, 1991. ISBN 0-395-55329-6. 32p. All ages.

In a nearly wordless book, Arthur Geisert achieves maximum impact with pink-tinted pigs, black-and-white backgrounds, and large and small "oinks." Piglets follow their mother's oinks through the pasture to the wallow spot. When Mother naps, they wander away, tempted by an apple tree. One by one, they make the leap from haystack to tree, with the letter *O*'s of their oinks trailing behind them. The boisterous oinking wakes the alarmed sow, who scolds with the loudest oink of all, putting her piggies back in a row.

2.170 Graham, Alastair. **Full Moon Soup; or, The Fall of the Hotel Splendide.** Illustrated by Alastair Graham. Dial Books for Young Readers, 1991. ISBN 0-8037-1045-3. 28p. 4–7.

In only a few pages of illustrations, and without a single word, Alastair Graham tells a myriad of detailed and hilarious stories in a cartoon-like feast. In a matter of minutes, the lunatic influence of the rising moon reduces a splendid hotel to rubble; a series of progressive cutaway views lets us watch the hotel's inhabitants—ordinary humans, extraterrestrials, sixteenth-century ghosts, and a rambunctious gorilla—deal with an untold number of zany mishaps. Guests are surprised, bumped, haunted, and even vacuumed.

2.171 Hoban, Tana. **Look Up, Look Down.** Photographs by Tana Hoban. Greenwillow Books, 1992. ISBN 0-688-10578-5. 32p. 2–7.

Just because you have looked up at skyscrapers, hot-air balloons, and tall trees or looked down at puddles and shadows doesn't mean that you have seen "ups and downs" as Tana Hoban has. In beautiful color photographs, readers view the upside of bleachers, birds perched on criss-cross wires, and the rib patterns of an open umbrella; by looking down, Hoban offers perspectives on foraging ants, a sunlit feather, and the inside of a spray of metal-spokes on a trash receptacle.

2.172   Hoban, Tana. **Shadows and Reflections.** Photographs by Tana Hoban. Greenwillow Books, 1990. ISBN 0-688-07090-6. 32p. 2 and up.

In this wordless picture book, full-page color photographs depict shadows or reflections of real objects, people, and animals. The shadow of a nearby fence is reflected on the side of a yellow car. The upside-down reflection of a brown bear is captured in a pool, perhaps at the zoo. Some photographs are easily recognizable; others must be studied to decipher distortions in the reflections or shadows. *Boston Globe–Horn Book Nonfiction Honor Book, 1990; Outstanding Science Trade Books for Children in 1990; ALA Notable Children's Books, 1991.*

2.173   Sara. **Across Town.** Illustrated by Sara. Orchard Books, 1991. ISBN 0-531-08532-5. 32p. 3–7.

In this wordless book, the lone figure of a man moves down a dark and ominous city street. Only when the man encounters a cat that is clearly his friend does the aura of menace vanish. The simple but dramatic artwork consists of torn, cardboard-colored paper shapes against a black background.

2.174   Sis, Peter. **An Ocean World.** Illustrated by Peter Sis. Greenwillow Books, 1992. ISBN 0-688-09068-0. 24p. 3 and up.

This near-wordless book follows a whale raised in captivity once she is released into the ocean. Through watercolor and ink drawings, Peter Sis interprets the whale's search for companionship. Across expanses of blue-green sea, she encounters whale-like shapes—a fishing boat, a blimp, a submarine, even a littering garbage scow—but no whale. In a satisfying conclusion, the lonely whale takes a deep dive and finds a mate.

2.175   Tafuri, Nancy. **Follow Me!** Illustrated by Nancy Tafuri. Greenwillow Books, 1990. ISBN 0-688-08774-4. 32p. 2 and up.

In a wordless picture book, a young seal peeks from beneath the flipper of its napping mother to observe the movements of a bright red crab. As the crab moves away, the baby seal follows, and Mama Seal follows her offspring. Up and over rocks, past gulls, sea urchins, starfish, prawns, and sea lions, the seal wanders. When the crab finds its group and dances off into the sea, the baby seal discovers that a watchful eye was never far away.

2.176   Wouters, Anne. **This Book Is for Us. This Book Is Too Small.**
Illustrated by Anne Wouters. Dutton Children's Books, 1991.
22p. 2–5.

In companion wordless books, a cheerful polar bear and a tiny
mole experience unusual adventures. In *This Book Is for Us*, Mole
is frightened by encroaching "blueness" on the pages. Try as he
might, Bear cannot stave it off. At last, frightened Mole and his
protector spot a hole in the blue and widen it to provide moonlight. In *This Book Is Too Small*, Bear grows too big for the boundaries of the pages. Little Mole finds a solution by pulling Bear to
a double-page spread.

Celebrations

Sing, Creatures, sing,
Angels and Men and Birds and everything.

Christina G. Rossetti

3 Celebrations

Birthdays

3.1   Anholt, Catherine. **The Snow Fairy and the Spaceman.** Illustrated by Catherine Anholt. Delacorte Press, 1991. ISBN 0-385-30422-6. 24p. 5–8. Fiction.

A boisterous little girl welcomes a lion, a king, and several other costumed guests to her birthday party. But her rudeness makes a timid and unhappy spaceman wish that he could go home. It takes a game of hide-and-seek and a surprise rescue to prompt an unlikely friendship between the shy spaceman and his snow-fairy hostess. Lively watercolors augment the text.

3.2   Brown, Marc. **Arthur's Birthday.** Illustrated by Marc Brown. Little, Brown/Joy Street Books, 1989. ISBN 0-316-11073-6. 30p. 4–7 (est.). Fiction.

In this thirteenth Arthur book, Arthur can't wait for his eighth birthday. When he hands out his invitations at school he discovers that his classmate Muffy has scheduled her birthday party for the same day. The class divides into two groups—the boys decide to attend Arthur's party, and the girls, Muffy's party. But Arthur comes up with a better plan. In the end, everyone arrives at Arthur's house to celebrate his birthday and to give Muffy a surprise party.

3.3   Jonas, Ann. **The 13th Clue.** Illustrated by Ann Jonas. Greenwillow Books, 1992. ISBN 0-688-09743-X. 32p. 4 and up. Fiction.

An open diary lies on the attic floor with an unfinished entry, its unseen writer bemoaning a day in which "nobody mentioned anything at breakfast" and "now no one is even home." But attached to the attic light is a note: "Find more clues." So the diarist does. There are clues spelled out by an extension cord, cut into the lawn, and marked by sticks. Even clues in pond moss help to lead further toward the surprise and the best birthday ever.

3.4   Mora, Pat. **A Birthday Basket for Tia.** Illustrated by Cecily Lang. Macmillan, 1992. ISBN 0-02-767400-2. 32p. 3–8 (est.). Fiction.

It is Cecilia's great-aunt's birthday. Her special Tia is ninety years old. ¡Noventa anos! As a present for Tia, Cecilia fills a basket with all the special things that she and Tia do together. There's their favorite book, their special cookie-mixing bowl, their teacup, the red ball that they throw, and the flowers that Tia loves. Brightly colored collages and a Mexican American girl with a childlike knack for perfect gift giving make for a warm, family book. ¡Feliz cumpleaños!

3.5 Polacco, Patricia. **Some Birthday!** Illustrated by Patricia Polacco. Simon and Schuster Books for Young Readers, 1991. ISBN 0-671-72750-8. 32p. 4–7 (est.). Fiction.

Patricia's birthday-to-remember starts out looking as though Dad has forgotten the day completely. Instead, that night he hatches a plan to photograph the monster of Clay Pit Bottoms—the meanest, ugliest monster of all. So Patricia, Dad, her brother, and her cousin gather supplies and set out. Suspense builds, and the monster they meet is not the one they expect. When things settle down and dry off, there's a real birthday. The drawings are family-warm, tousled, and rounded.

3.6 Samuels, Barbara. **Happy Birthday, Dolores.** Illustrated by Barbara Samuels. Orchard Books, 1989. ISBN 0-531-08391-8. 32p. 3–6. Fiction.

It's Dolores's birthday, and the whole family, including Duncan the cat, is awakened by her drum and vocal tribute to herself. Everyone knows someone like Dolores, who prefers helmet and boots to her party dress, who refuses to sit next to Stevie, and who locks the cat in a closet because "little children can be very rough with animals." When Duncan escapes and splats into the cake, it's just another in a series of silly situations that are augmented by the understated text and comical illustrations.

3.7 West, Colin. **Go Tell It to the Toucan.** Illustrated by Colin West. Bantam/Little Rooster Books, 1990. ISBN 0-553-05889-4. 24p. 4–8 (est.). Fiction.

When Jumbo the Elephant wants a jamboree to celebrate his birthday, he looks for the toucan to spread the word. Not finding the colorful bird, Jumbo tells the tiger, who in turn tells the zebra. So begins a series of conversations which end with a monkey finally telling "it to the toucan." Bright watercolor illustrations complement this cumulative tale filled with humor and surprise.

Christmas

3.8   Ahlberg, Janet, and Allan Ahlberg. **The Jolly Christmas Post-
         man.** Illustrated by Janet and Allan Ahlberg. Little, Brown, 1991.
         ISBN 0-316-02033-8. 34p. 3–8 (est.). Fiction.

Like the original *Jolly Postman*, this irresistible book describes the
postman's rounds and includes the mail he delivers—inserted in
envelope-like pages. Its rhymes are quiet and agreeable, the
illustrations homey and seasonal. But its greatest charm lies in
the cards and letters that are written by and to famous nursery-
rhyme characters. Children will be attracted by the story and
thrilled to examine the contents of each envelope.

3.9   Aliki. **Christmas Tree Memories.** Illustrated by Aliki. Harper-
         Collins, 1991. ISBN 0-06-020008-1. 24p. 4–8. Fiction.

"Tinng. Tinng." When a bell sounds for Christmas Eve, two
children and their parents nestle by their candle-lit tree, drink
hot cocoa, and reminisce about Christmases past. Each homemade ornament sparks a family recollection. Aliki's watercolor
and ink illustrations offer full-page memories, rich with the
warm details of family life. This intimate story will prompt
many readers' own holiday memories of relatives and friends.
Notable 1991 Children's Trade Books in the Field of Social Studies.

3.10 Bassett, Lisa. **Koala Christmas.** Illustrated by Jeni Bassett. Cob-
         blehill Books, 1991. ISBN 0-525-65065-2. 32p. 3–7 (est.). Fiction.

An argument between Wally Koala and his sister Carrie causes
a pre-Christmas disaster—the destruction of the family Christmas tree decorations. But through cooperation, determination,
and a flock of brightly colored lorikeets, not only is the day
saved, but a magically decorated house becomes the envy of the
koala neighborhood. Watercolor illustrations of furred and
feathered creatures are irresistible.

3.11 Branley, Franklyn M. **The Christmas Sky, rev. ed.** Illustrated by
         Stephen Fieser. Thomas Y. Crowell, 1990. ISBN 0-690-04772-X.
         47p. 8–12. Nonfiction.

A bright star appeared in the sky and led three Wise Men to a
stable in Bethlehem. Never to be seen again,this star has puzzled
astronomers through time. In this award-winning book first
published in 1966, noted astronomer and science writer
Franklyn Branley presents several theories explaining the mysterious light. Interwoven with Biblical accounts, a revised, fact-

filled text offers readers a thought-provoking look at an event that has "deep meaning to people around the world." New full-page, dark-shaded illustrations capture the mystery and drama. *School Library Journal Best Books, 1966; Outstanding Science Trade Books for Children in 1990.*

3.12 Breathed, Berkeley. **A Wish for Wings That Work: An Opus Christmas Story.** Illustrated by Berkeley Breathed. Little, Brown, 1991. ISBN 0-316-10758-1. 300p. 4–8 (est.). Fiction.

Poor Opus! He so wants to fly, but he can't because he is a penguin. After wistfully watching snow ducks soar, Opus writes Santa, asking for "wings that will go." On Christmas Eve, when Santa and his sleigh plunge into icy waters, it is Opus who swims to the rescue, using previously unappreciated strengths. Grateful, the snow ducks give Opus a very special Christmas gift. Berkeley Breathed's background as a cartoonist is apparent in the clean, crisp illustrations which extend the text with humor and sensitivity.

3.13 Brett, Jan. **The Wild Christmas Reindeer.** Illustrated by Jan Brett. G. P. Putnam's Sons, 1990. ISBN 0-399-22192-1. 29p. 4–8. Fiction.

Santa asked Teeka, a young neighbor, to get his reindeer ready to fly for Christmas Eve. As the days until Christmas tick by, marked by Jan Brett's glorious side panels of elves at work, Teeka is frustrated by her efforts to manage the wild reindeer. After a particularly difficult session that results in a jumble of antlers and a new understanding, Teeka finds that gentle ways can accomplish what force and fury cannot.

3.14 Bulla, Clyde Robert. **The Christmas Coat.** Illustrated by Sylvie Wickstrom. Alfred A. Knopf/Borzoi Books, 1989. ISBN 0-394-99385-3. 36p. 6–9. Fiction.

Brothers Hans and Otto tire their widowed mother with their persistent quarreling until, in despair, she draws a chalk line on the cottage floor to mark exclusive territory. But when Hans discovers a wrapped Christmas present on his side, the two brothers fight so bitterly that the beautiful coat inside is badly ripped. The common plight requires cooperative problem solving and sacrifice to ensure a Christmas for the coat's intended recipient. Smudged line drawings filled with pastel shades reflect the understated lessons of old-fashioned Christmas giving.

3.15   Bunting, Eve. **The Day before Christmas.** Illustrated by Beth Peck. Clarion Books, 1992. ISBN 0-89919-866-X. 32p. 4–8 (est.). Fiction.

"Seven is a good age for your first Nutcracker." That's what Grandpa thinks, so as a special gift he is taking Allie to the city for the Christmas Eve performance. Even though Dad is afraid that Grandpa may be saddened by memories of another little girl and another performance long ago, Grandpa says, "A loving memory is happy, not sad." It pleases Allie to know that the mother whom she can barely remember made the same trip at seven and loved the snow fairies best, too. Oil paintings translate California scenes and delicate costumes.

3.16   Cole, Joanna. **A Gift from Saint Francis: The First Crèche.** Illustrated by Michèle Lemieux. Morrow Junior Books, 1989. ISBN 0-688-06503-1. 28p. 6 and up (est.). Nonfiction.

Joanna Cole connects gentle St. Francis of Assisi with the first celebration of Christmas almost 800 years ago. Near Greccio, Italy, as a gift to the people, St. Francis staged a re-creation of the scene of the Christ Child's birth, with Mary, Joseph, shepherds, stable beasts, and the infant himself. Little children sang a lullaby, perhaps the world's first Christmas carol. The period paintings are in Renaissance style, golden-toned, and illuminated with medallions.

3.17   Collington, Peter. **On Christmas Eve.** Illustrated by Peter Collington. Alfred A. Knopf/Borzoi Books, 1990. ISBN 0-679-90830-7. 32p. 3–7. Fiction.

Peter Collington's *On Christmas Eve,* dedicated to "chimneyless children everywhere," will satisfy any child's curiosity about how Santa enters a home when there is no fireplace. Story frames on each page depict dainty fairies with tiny Christmas tree candles guiding Santa on his appointed rounds. Collington's use of earth tones, from the gray snow on the dappled endpapers to the warm gray-browns of the neighborhoods that Santa visits, creates a cozy wintry mood that permeates this wordless book.

3.18   Cutting, Michael. **The Little Crooked Christmas Tree.** Illustrated by Ron Broda. Scholastic Hardcover Books, 1991. ISBN 0-590-45204-5. 24p. 4–8. Fiction.

A combination of theme, intricate paper sculptures, and simple story line will likely attract young readers to this Christmas tale.

A little tree's sacrifice to shelter a family of doves causes its trunk to grow crooked, making it unsuitable for a Christmas tree. Although the plot is familiar, the design and texture of the illustrations—from springtime on the tree farm to the glittering outdoor Christmas tree—may inspire responsive paper art productions.

3.19   Delacre, Lulu, compiler. **Las Navidades: Popular Christmas Songs from Latin America.** Illustrated by Lulu Delacre. Scholastic Hardcover Books/Lucas Evans Books, 1990. ISBN 0-590-43548-5. 32p. 5–11. Nonfiction.

In this collection of seasonal songs, presented in both Spanish and English, the Christmas customs and celebrations of Latin America, from Christmas Eve through Epiphany, are described and explained. Lulu Delacre's paintings in the colors of her native Puerto Rico illustrate a variety of holiday activities. Detailed information about each custom, musical scores at the end of the book, and even the recipe for "Rosca de Reyes" may help other children participate in the customs of Latin America.

3.20   dePaola, Tomie. **Jingle the Christmas Clown.** Illustrated by Tomie dePaola. G. P. Putnam's Sons, 1992. ISBN 0-399-22338-X. 32p. 4–8. Fiction.

In a sentimental Christmas tale set in Italy, Jingle, the youngest clown of the circus and keeper of the baby animals, is left behind by the other performers in a village where the people are too poor for circuses. Jingle appreciates the wisdom and perspectives of the villagers, especially Donna Chiara. His Christmas gift for the village is a baby animal circus performed on a snowy village street under diamond stars. In this large-scale picture book, Tomie dePaola has painted background sets edge to edge.

3.21   Fleetwood, Jenni. **While Shepherds Watched.** Illustrated by Peter Melnyczuk. Lothrop, Lee and Shepard Books, 1992. ISBN 0-688-11599-3. 32p. 5 and up. Fiction.

Matthias is eager to celebrate his eighth birthday by spending the night with the other shepherds. While watching the birth of a lamb, he barely notices the brilliant light of an angel who has come to herald the birth of Jesus. With the shepherds and newborn lamb, he follows the star to the Bethlehem stable to see the baby. Paintings, scratched for texture and contrast, glowingly show the wonder and serenity of the dark night.

3.22   Goode, Diane, compiler. **Diane Goode's American Christmas.** Illustrated by Diane Goode. Dutton Children's Books, 1990. ISBN 0-525-44620-6. 80p. All ages. Fiction.

From Laura Ingalls Wilder's "Christmas on the Banks of Plum Creek" to Carson McCullers's "Christmas Eve Rhyme," this collection of poems, songs, traditional tales, and short stories captures the spirit of Christmas. Drawing upon the richness in American culture, Diane Goode has selected entries from various parts of the country, from different ethnic groups, and from the works of some of America's finest authors. Framed with decorative designs, the pages of this collection hold memorable and traditional selections lovingly illustrated with soft-colored paintings.

3.23   Guback, Georgia. **The Carolers.** Illustrated by Georgia Guback. Greenwillow Books, 1992. ISBN 0-688-09773-1. 34p. All ages. Fiction.

Five colorful carolers travel from house to house singing eleven songs of the Christmas season. As the villagers hear them, they put aside their holiday preparations and join the singing, causing the happy group to grow with every turn of the page. Lower borders of words and music enable readers to join the celebration. Cut-paper collage in vivid colors adds to the joy of the season.

3.24   Kneen, Maggie, compiler. **The Twelve Days of Christmas: A Revolving Picture Book.** Illustrated by Maggie Kneen. Dutton Children's Books, 1992. ISBN 0-525-44654-0. 12p. 4 and up. Nonfiction.

The verses of this centuries-old carol are illustrated in muted medieval tones within circular frames. Pull a ribboned tab, and six picture segments revolve to illustrate the next verse. For example, seven silky swans swim in a clear stream in sight of a distant castle until the picture revolves to reveal eight serene milkmaids gathered in a woven enclosure where sheep, chickens, and rabbits frolic. The verses themselves are bounded by holly, pears, bells, and packages.

3.25   Moore, Clement Clarke. **The Night before Christmas; or, A Visit of St. Nicholas: An Antique Reproduction.** Philomel Books, 1989. ISBN 0-399-21614-6. 24p. 4–8. Fiction.

This reproduction of an antique picture book dating to about 1870 will appeal to those whose Christmas memories echo with the sounds of Clement Moore's traditional poem: "Merry Christmas to all and to all a good night." The book is composed of ornate full-page illustrations of traditional Christmas scenes interspersed with the text of the poem. The illustrations, created from lithographs in soft Victorian colors, have been supplemented by hand-painted borders and introductory material consistent with the spirit of the original.

3.26 Neville, Mary. **The Christmas Tree Ride.** Illustrated by Megan Lloyd. Holiday House, 1992. ISBN 0-8234-0956-2. 32p. 4–8 (est.). Fiction.

"This Christmas," Dad says, "will you help me cut the tree?" And two eager children bundle into the station wagon for a ride far into the country to Mr. Pennyman's Christmas Tree Farm. Over icy streams, past houses with silver ribbons of smoke, and up a steep, ice-covered hill is the tree of choice. Mr. Pennyman chops it with his axe. Then it's a speedy downhill slide, followed by wonderful paper-chain decorations, and Mr. Pennyman himself invited to Christmas dinner.

3.27 Niland, Kilmeny. **A Bellbird in a Flame Tree: The Twelve Days of Christmas.** Illustrated by Kilmeny Niland. Tambourine Books, 1991. ISBN 0-688-10798-2. 32p. 3 and up. Fiction.

If "The Twelve Days of Christmas" had originated in Australia, one's true love may have expected to receive such delights as lorikeets, wallabies, and a bellbird in a flame tree. In celebration, there are quokkas cooking, numbats knitting, dingoes dancing, and koalas clowning. The panorama of Australian fauna seems a very merry setting for the holidays.

3.28 Nixon, Joan Lowery. **That's the Spirit, Claude.** Illustrated by Tracey Campbell Pearson. Viking Penguin, 1992. ISBN 0-670-83434-3. 32p. 6–10 (est.). Fiction.

Claude and Shirley's adopted kids, Bessie and Tom, anticipate the arrival of Sandy Claus, although he's never before been to frontier Texas. Bessie knits a Texas-sized stocking, writes a letter, and waits. So that the children won't be disappointed on Christmas Eve, roly-poly Claude dons red flannel underwear, flours his beard, and smacks right into the real Sandy (also wearing cowboy boots) on the roof. The dialect isn't quite Texan, but the spirit is. Pen and watercolor are used for lighthearted results.

3.29   Nordqvist, Sven. **Merry Christmas, Festus and Mercury.** Illustrated by Sven Nordqvist. Carolrhoda Books, 1989. ISBN 0-87614-383-4. 22p. 4–6 (est.). Fiction.

In the past, Farmer Festus and his zany cat, Mercury, have spent the day before Christmas Eve trimming the tree, shopping for food, and baking gingerbread. This year Festus injures his foot, so they can't proceed with their holiday plans. Their Christmas looks bleak until the neighbors help out, and Festus and Mercury end up having the merriest of times. Full-color cartoon-like illustrations, bursting with additional story detail and humor, enliven each page.

3.30   Pilkington, Brian. **Grandpa Claus.** Illustrated by Brian Pilkington. Carolrhoda Books, 1990. ISBN 0-87614-436-9. 28p. 4–8. Fiction.

Grandpa Harry loves to dress up as Santa Claus; in fact, he may be the best Santa impersonator in the world. Harry's beard—long, white, and real—ensures his job for the weeks before Christmas each year. But the worst times for Harry are the days after Christmas, when there is nothing to do but groom his beard and look for work. How Harry mismanages a series of part-time jobs between Christmases is the heart of the book. Lively, cartoon-like drawings add to the silliness.

3.31   Ray, Jane, compiler. **The Story of Christmas/La Historia de Navidad.** Illustrated by Jane Ray. Dutton Children's Books, 1991. ISBN 0-525-44768-7 (English); 0-525-44830-6 (Spanish). 32p. 6 and up. Nonfiction.

The story of Christmas—beginning with the angel Gabriel's tidings and ending with the safe return of Jesus, Mary, and Joseph to Nazareth—is told in the words of the Gospels of Matthew and Luke in the Authorized King James Version of the Bible. It is also told through Jane Ray's bordered folk-art paintings, highlighted with gold. Companion editions are available in English and Spanish.

3.32   Rogers, Jacqueline. **The Christmas Pageant.** Illustrated by Jacqueline Rogers. Grosset and Dunlap, 1989. ISBN 0-448-40151-7. 32p. 3–7. Fiction.

As the children in a snowy New England village prepare for the annual Christmas pageant in a barn by painting the flats, getting fitted for costumes, and rehearsing their roles, the Biblical story of Christmas serves as text. "Baby Jesus" squirms in a snowsuit, awaiting his entrance. Traditional Christmas hymns with piano arrangements are set into the illustrations. The dress rehearsal melts into the performance, as the "wise men" hurry through snow drifts, carrying their cutout camel. At the pageant's end, "Baby Jesus," fast asleep, is bundled home.

3.33 San Souci, Robert D. **The Christmas Ark.** Illustrated by Daniel San Souci. Doubleday, 1991. ISBN 0-385-24837-7. 30p. 6–10. Fiction.

Two girls, bound for San Francisco with their mother, are frustrated when their clipper ship is becalmed near the city on Christmas Eve. Missing their father and fearful that St. Nicholas will be unable to find them, they're reassured when a flying ark—piloted by the old saint himself—carries them around the world in search of the perfect place to spend Christmas. Full-page watercolors resplendent with the blues of sky and sea support each page of text, adding a sense of dreamy satisfaction to this warm story of family love.

3.34 Sharmat, Marjorie Weinman. **I'm Santa Claus and I'm Famous.** Illustrated by Marylin Hafner. Holiday House, 1990. ISBN 0-8234-0826-4. 30p. 4–8 (est.). Fiction.

It's Career Day at school, and Santa Claus is invited. Santa indicates that he will retire some day and will need a replacement. Now everyone wants to be Santa when they grow up! Santa solves the problem by asking those interested in the position to "try out" by showing love and by giving special presents like caring, listening, or laughing. Told in cartoon-like blocks, this story provides a starting point for discussion of intangible gifts.

3.35 Slate, Joseph. **Who Is Coming to Our House?** Illustrated by Ashley Wolff. G. P. Putnam's Sons/Sandcastle Books, 1991. ISBN 0-399-21790-8. 32p. 4–8. Fiction.

Stable animals prepare for the Christ child, all doing their part: "'We must clean,' says Lamb. 'Dust the beams,' says Ram." Woodcut-like animals emerge from heavily bordered stable scenes. Through rhyming text distributed one line per page, young children will soon be reading along. The repeated chorus is a question-answer from a soft-eyed cow and a tiny mouse: "'Who is coming to our house?' 'Someone, someone,' says Mouse." In the well-known final scene, the refrain varies: "Welcome, welcome to our house."

3.36   Solotareff, Grégoire. **Noël's Christmas Secret.** Illustrations by
            Grégoire Solotareff. Farrar, Straus and Giroux, 1989. ISBN 0-374-
            35544-4. 30p. 6–8 (est.). Fiction.

            When a boy named Noël discovers a huge sack in the forest with
            written instructions, he is drawn into the world of the dwarf
            magician toy makers, Apple, Piggy, and Thumb. If Noël follows
            their instructions and keeps the secret that they whisper, who
            knows what he may become? Bright primary colors and bold
            lines enhance the simple tale of the origin of Santa Claus.

3.37   Stevenson, James. **The Worst Person's Christmas.** Illustrated by
            James Stevenson. Greenwillow Books, 1991. ISBN 0-688-10211-5.
            32p. 4–10 (est.). Fiction.

            The "worst person in the world" doesn't like anything—espe-
            cially Christmas. Thinking "the worst" just needs to be shown
            kindness, the neighborhood children leave a fruitcake on his
            front step. But on his way to deposit the fruitcake in the garbage
            can, "the worst" trips, flops onto a sled, races through town out
            of control, and finally arrives at a neighborhood holiday party, a
            fruitcake gift in hand. In the face of genuine welcome, "the
            worst" has a change of heart (however momentary) and takes on
            a more "Christmas-like" disposition.

3.38   Taylor, Theodore. **Maria: A Christmas Story.** Harcourt Brace
            Jovanovich, 1992. ISBN 0-15-217763-9. 84p. 8–12. Fiction.

            Without thinking, eleven-year-old Maria, tired of hearing her
            two gringo friends brag about their families' elaborate floats for
            the San Lazaro, California, Christmas parade, blurts out that her
            family is entering this year. With no money and no help, save a
            picture Maria found in an old Spanish Bible, Father builds a
            simple nativity scene. After a stubborn ox sits down on the job,
            twenty Mexican American men rally to pull their people's first
            float. The humble scene silences the crowd and starts a tradition.

3.39   Tyler, Linda Wagner. **The After-Christmas Tree.** Illustrated by
            Susan Davis. Viking Penguin, 1990. ISBN 0-670-83045-3. 32p.
            4–7. Fiction.

            Linda Wagner Tyler and Susan Davis help children transform
            their sadness about the end of the holidays into the joy of creat-
            ing the "after-Christmas tree." The tree, which the narrator and
            her family redecorate as part of their after-Christmas party, is
            symbolic of life continuing beyond the holiday season. Davis's
            bright watercolors, reminiscent of folk art, capture the winter

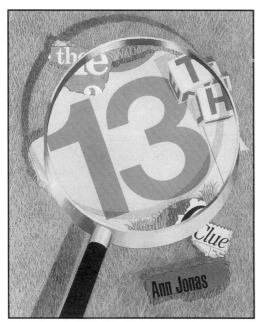

A.

B.

C.

A. *The 13th Clue* by Ann Jonas (see 3.3).   **B.** *A Birthday Basket for Tía* by Pat Mora; illustrated by Cecily Lang (see 3.4).   **C.** *The Jolly Christmas Postman* by Janet and Allan Ahlberg (see 3.8).

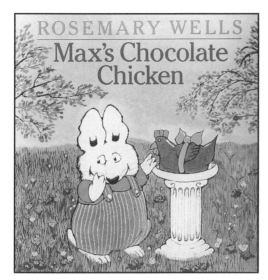

A.

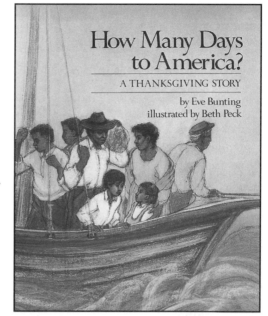

B.

C.

A. *Max's Chocolate Chicken* by Rosemary Wells (see 3.48). **B.** *How Many Days to America? A Thanksgiving Story* by Eve Bunting; illustrated by Beth Peck (see 3.75). **C.** *Big Pumpkin* by Erica Silverman; illustrated by S. D. Schindler (see 3.57).

wonderland of the outdoors. After reading the book, many children will want to set up their own "after-Christmas tree." The book would lend itself well to a January nature lesson in a primary classroom.

3.40 Wildsmith, Brian. **A Christmas Story.** Illustrated by Brian Wildsmith. Alfred A. Knopf/Borzoi Books, 1989. ISBN 0-679-90074-8. 24p. 5–10. Fiction.

Brian Wildsmith tells the Christmas story from the point of view of a little donkey who sets out after his mother on the road to Bethlehem. Along the way, the little donkey and his child companion ask travelers to point the way, until they see the glorious star. Luminous landscapes in golds, silvers, and royal blues establish the union of the ordinary and the miraculous.

3.41 Wilhelm, Hans. **Schnitzel's First Christmas.** Illustrated by Hans Wilhelm. Simon and Schuster Books for Young Readers, 1989. ISBN 0-671-67977-5. 26p. 4–7 (est.). Fiction.

Schnitzel is a puppy who has everything. When Gruff the cat explains that Santa is coming, Schnitzel learns that he must make a Christmas wish. But what is a pampered puppy to wish for? Even as Schnitzel meets Santa, he still has no wish. But wise Santa knows that a friend is the best Christmas present any puppy could wish for. Wintery watercolors bring on smiles.

3.42 Worth, Valerie. **At Christmas Time.** Illustrated by Antonio Frasconi. HarperCollins/Michael di Capua Books, 1992. ISBN 0-06-205020-6. 32p. All ages (est.). Nonfiction.

All the warmth, sights, sounds, and tastes of Christmas are entrapped in this collection of poems for an audience not bound by age. In "Wrappings," the poet declares: "The plainest / Underwear the / Homeliest socks, / Parceled in / golden foil and / Silver string, / Or even in flimsy / Red-and-green poinsettias, / Become the / Sumptuous offerings / Of a king." Light strings are likened to "a luminous vine, / Lush with the fruits / Of paradise." Fat woodcuts enhanced with paint, cut-paper collage, and reliefs give folk flavor.

3.43 Yolen, Jane. **Hark! A Christmas Sampler.** Illustrated by Tomie dePaola. G. P. Putnam's Sons, 1991. ISBN 0-399-21853-X. 128p. All ages (est.). Fiction/Nonfiction.

Jane Yolen and Tomi dePaola pair up to offer an oversized edition of stories, history, carols, poems, and legends of Christmas, set apart with the reverence and whimsy of dePaola's distinctive illustrations and designs. Beautiful original carols include the "Stable Hymn" and "The North Pole Express," both with words by Yolen and musical arrangement by her son, Adam Stemple. Also fun and sure to be performed is "The Foolish Shepherd: A Play in Verse."

Easter

3.44   **Easter: The King James Version.** Illustrated by Jan Pieńkowski. Alfred A. Knopf/Borzoi Books, 1989. ISBN 0-394-82455-5. 32p. All ages. Nonfiction.

In dramatic silhouettes against dappled backgrounds, the story of Easter unfolds from selected scripture verses taken from the King James Bible. Illuminated manuscript, gilded borders, and gold-outlined vines reach symbolically across the spreads. Grape, poppy, ivy, and holly vines are variantly spiked with thorns.

3.45   Kunhardt, Edith. **Danny and the Easter Egg.** Illustrated by Edith Kunhardt. Greenwillow Books, 1989. ISBN 0-688-08036-7. 21p. 3–6. Fiction.

In her fourth Danny book, Edith Kunhardt offers childlike drawings of the alligator preparing for Easter with his animal friends. Danny dyes one special egg with a *D* for Danny. The Easter morning egg hunt yields many treats, including Danny's special egg. Later that day, when the family visits Granny, Danny gives her his egg as an Easter present.

3.46   Polacco, Patricia. **Rechenka's Eggs.** Illustrated by Patricia Polacco. Philomel Books, 1988. ISBN 0-399-21501-8. 30p. 4–9 (est.). Fiction.

For many years Old Babushka has painted eggs in her beautiful Ukrainian style to take to the Easter Festival to be judged. One year, just before the festival, she discovers an injured goose. She names the goose Rechenka and decides to nurse her back to health. When Rechenka accidentally breaks all of Babushka's wonderfully painted eggs, what happens next is a miracle: Rechenka begins to lay stunningly colored eggs, one a morning, to replace the broken ones. The bright, detailed paintings authentically reproduce the Ukrainian style of egg painting and the spires of famed Russian cities. *IRA Children's Book Award (Illustration), 1989.*

3.47 Tarlow, Nora. **An Easter Alphabet: From a Poem by Nora Tarlow.** G. P. Putnam's Sons, 1991. ISBN 0-399-22194-8. 32p. 3–7 (est.). Fiction.

In an Easter-time rhyme, each letter of the alphabet is matched with a springtime symbol or action and is accompanied by a sentimental painting dating from the late nineteenth through the early twentieth centuries. Twenty-six artists are represented, their works selected predominately from German, English, and American postcards. Although many artists are anonymous, some classic Kate Greenaway is included.

3.48 Wells, Rosemary. **Max's Chocolate Chicken.** Illustrated by Rosemary Wells. Dial Books for Young Readers, 1989. ISBN 0-8037-0586-7. 32p. 3–7. Fiction.

On Easter morning Max is delighted to find a chocolate chicken in the birdbath, but his bossy sister Ruby insists that the one who finds the most Easter eggs is the one who gets the chicken. While Ruby finds a basketful of eggs, Max finds mud, acorns, a spoon, and ants, but no eggs. Yet despite his inability to stick to the task, Max scuttles away with the prize chicken, leaving Ruby ranting, bargaining, and bluffing. Luckily, the Easter Bunny drops a chocolate duck into the birdbath, leaving Ruby puzzled and the ending open for speculation.

Halloween

3.49 Bauer, Caroline Feller, editor. **Halloween: Stories and Poems.** Illustrated by Peter Sis. J. B. Lippincott, 1989. ISBN 0-397-32301-8. 82p. 6–12 (est.). Fiction/Nonfiction.

Creepy short stories and poems, both sprightly and gloomy, comprise this Halloween collection by Caroline Fetter Bauer. Along with works by Lilian Moore, Paul Galdone, Eleanor Farjeon, X. J. Kennedy, Jack Prelutsky, and Judith Viorst appear holiday recipes, a lengthy bibliography of Halloween books, and Peter Sis's understated black-and-white illustrations.

3.50 Bunting, Eve. **In the Haunted House.** Illustrated by Susan Meddaugh. Clarion Books, 1990. ISBN 0-395-51589-0. 28p. 5–8 (est.). Fiction.

Large and small sneakers enter a house "where the scary things hide." Creatures of all sorts—witches, mummies, and skeletons—menace the unseen visitors. Finally, big sneakers ahead of small, the visitors race outside, revealing a small daughter, ready to take her panting father through the Halloween House again. Accompanying Eve Bunting's rhyming text are Susan Meddaugh's scratchy illustrations, which are not-so-scary when examined closely: a red paint can sits behind a "blood-stained" coffin, the skeleton is on a stick, and the horned creature has a zipper.

3.51   Cassedy, Sylvia. **The Best Cat Suit of All.** Illustrated by Rosekrans Hoffman. Dial Books for Young Readers, 1991. ISBN 0-8037-0517-4. 48p. 5–7 (est.). Fiction.

Matthew is having a very bad Halloween day. With a runny nose and in a heap of self-pity, he must wear his cat suit indoors and just watch the parade of trick-or-treaters. Back where I used to live, Matthew grumps, Halloween wouldn't be cold, and kids wouldn't have to wear snowsuits under their costumes. Even the cat suits that other kids wear are judged by their failures—until the very best cat suit of all arrives. Rosekrans Hoffman's witty pencil and ink illustrations for this Easy-to-Read Book can't be contained by their frames.

3.52   Christelow, Eileen. **Jerome and the Witchcraft Kids.** Illustrated by Eileen Christelow. Clarion Books, 1988. ISBN 0-89919-742-6. 29p. 4–8 (est.). Fiction.

Jerome Alligator thinks that he is a terrific baby-sitter, much better than his sister Winifred. "No job is too difficult," his posters proclaim. "Don't let it go to your head," warns Winifred's friend, Lulu. Then Jerome gets a baby-sitting request from a Mrs. Witchcraft on Halloween night. Not only do the Witchcrafts live in a haunted house, but their refrigerator is full of eyeball sandwiches, vampire blood, and worms. When Jerome finally discovers that Winifred and Lulu have played a joke on him, he retaliates. Zany crayon illustrations add to the silliness.

3.53   Cohen, Miriam. **The Real-Skin Rubber Monster Mask.** Illustrated by Lillian Hoban. Greenwillow Books, 1990. ISBN 0-688-09123-7. 28p. 6–10 (est.). Fiction.

From the author/illustrator team that produced *When Will I Read?* and *First Grade Takes a Test* comes another warm and sensitive portrayal of childhood concerns. Jim's carefully chosen rubber monster mask is so frightening that on Halloween night it scares even him. But second-grade friends rally to ensure that Jim gets to share half of Willy's spaghetti and meatball costume.

Fear of scary things is the natural book talk that will emerge from young readers and listeners.

3.54 Howe, James. **Harold and Chester in Scared Silly: A Halloween Treat.** Illustrated by Leslie Morrill. Morrow Junior Books, 1989. ISBN 0-688-07667-X. 42p. 4–9 (est.). Fiction.

The house is dark and the Monroe family absent when Harold, the family's shaggy dog, begins his story. Harold and his friends, Howie, a timid puppy, Chester, a bossy cat, and Bunnicula, an unusual rabbit, are "scared silly" when a witch enters their house and concocts a witch's brew. Even when the mystery is resolved, Harold and his friends remain suspicious. Boys and girls will enjoy speculating about whether or not the witch is really Grandma in a costume.

3.55 Limburg, Peter R. **Weird! The Complete Book of Halloween Words.** Illustrated by Betsy Lewin. Bradbury Press, 1989. ISBN 0-02-759050-X. 122p. 8 and up (est.). Nonfiction.

Here's a one-stop, fun-filled reference book for Halloween, a compendium that traces the history of the symbols and the words most associated with the most shivery of holidays. Readers will learn, for example, that it was Shakespeare in *Macbeth* who first used the word *weird* and that souls of the dead took the form of bats. But unlike a strict etymological source, the text is stuffed with intriguing facts and humorous asides. Sections titled "Do You Know" offer child-appealing background related to Halloween traditions.

3.56 Martin, Bill, Jr., and John Archambault. **The Magic Pumpkin.** Illustrated by Robert J. Lee. Henry Holt, 1989. ISBN 0-8050-1134-X. 28p. 4–7 (est.). Fiction.

Halloween magic and mishap occur when the narrator of this ballad-like story, told in rhyming prose, chooses the wrong pumpkin from the pumpkin patch to guard his door on Halloween. The seemingly innocent pumpkin is really the leader of a gang of mischief-makers. However, all returns to normal when the jack-o'-lantern's candle is extinguished. Robert Lee's curly line drawings and wispy watercolor washes add an eerie touch to the tale.

3.57 Silverman, Erica. **Big Pumpkin.** Illustrated by S. D. Schindler. Macmillan, 1992. ISBN 0-02-782683-X. 32p. 4–8 (est.). Fiction.

In this variant of "The Great Big Enormous Turnip," a green-faced witch raises a pumpkin that is too large to harvest: "It's big and it's mine, but it's stuck on the vine." So, a series of her monstrous friends—ghost, vampire, and mummy—lends a hand. Even so, it takes the wit of a tiny bat to propose a cooperative plan that yields Halloween pumpkin pie for all. Full-page, spirited illustrations for this cumulative tale are done in gouache on colored papers.

3.58   Van Leeuwen, Jean. **Oliver and Amanda's Halloween.** Illustrated by Ann Schweninger. Dial Books for Young Readers, 1992. ISBN 0-8037-1238-3. 48p. 4–8 (est.). Fiction.

In an Easy-to-Read Book for beginning chapter-book readers, Oliver and Amanda Pig's sibling relationship is realistic, but cast with just the right degree of tolerance to make for a warm, family book. Oliver prefers scary costumes to Amanda's benign ones; Dad knows how to achieve compromise in carving a jack-o'-lantern to please both; Mom accepts that little pigs climb on things to reach donuts; and Amanda spots monsters on Halloween night. Illustrations are done in watercolor-washed colored pencils.

3.59   Watson, Wendy. **Boo! It's Halloween.** Illustrated by Wendy Watson. Clarion Books, 1992. ISBN 0-395-53628-6. 32p. 4–8 (est.). Fiction.

The whole family is preparing for Halloween. There are costumes to make, jack-o'-lanterns to cut, cookies to bake, and faces to paint. Then it's off to the school's haunted house for supper and games. But the fun is not over yet. The whole village pours onto the winding streets for trick-or-treating, and the reader is given a bat's eye view of the festivities. Wendy Watson has wound riddles, rhymes, and knock-knock jokes in speech balloons around the characters.

3.60   Yolen, Jane. **Best Witches: Poems for Halloween.** Illustrated by Elise Primavera. G. P. Putnam's Sons, 1989. ISBN 0-399-21539. 47p. 5–9 (est.). Fiction.

Did you know that the modern witch does aerobic exercise and flies on a vacuum cleaner? Or that witches participate in "witchy" game shows and usually put a little extra poison ivy on their pizzas? These surprising revelations and many others can be found in this collection of Jane Yolen's witch poems. The humorous verses and Elise Primavera's appealing illustrations should attract any Halloween enthusiast.

Jewish Holidays

3.61 Gross, Judith. **Celebrate: A Book of Jewish Holidays.** Illustrated by Bari Weissman. Platt and Munk/All Aboard Books, 1992. ISBN 0-448-40303-X. 30p. 5–8. Nonfiction.

Family and food take center stage on Jewish holidays, and Judith Gross emphasizes both. Joyous celebrations and the traditional demands of each occasion are colorfully illustrated. With smiling cartoon faces, the somber Day of Atonement loses its bleakness. The legends of Purim, Hanukkah, and Passover are deftly outlined, blending early origins and modern interpretation.

3.62 Kimmel, Eric A. **The Chanukkah Guest.** Illustrated by Giora Carmi. Holiday House, 1990. ISBN 0-8234-0788-8. 26p. 4–8 (est.). Fiction.

Bubba Brayna fixes potato latkes for Hanukkah, with extras for the rabbi, who is expected to visit. When a hungry, marauding bear comes to the cottage in the forest, Bubba, with her failing eyesight and hearing, believes that he is her bearded guest, and feeds him the treat. Giora Carmi's illustrations capture the humor of Eric Kimmel's mischievous tale so that children, like Bubba herself, can laugh at the absurd mistake.

3.63 Kimmel, Eric. **Hershel and the Hanukkah Goblins.** Illustrated by Trina Schart Hyman. Holiday House, 1989. ISBN 0-8234-0769-1. 32p. 4–9 (est.). Fiction.

The old synagogue is haunted by goblins who won't let the villagers celebrate Hanukkah, so Hershel volunteers to trick the goblins into lifting their evil curse. He must spend eight nights in the synagogue, lighting Hanukkah candles each night (without letting the goblins blow them out) and tricking the goblin king into lighting the last night's candles himself. This book includes full-color yet shadow-filled paintings of the monstrous goblins and concludes with a description of the Jewish traditions detailed in Hershel's adventure. *Caldecott Honor Book, 1990.*

3.64 Koralek, Jenny. **Hanukkah: The Festival of Lights.** Illustrated by Juan Wijngaard. Lothrop, Lee and Shepard Books, 1990. ISBN 0-888-09330-2. 32p. All ages. Nonfiction.

When the Romans sacked Jerusalem and caused havoc in the Temple, a vigilant family of Jewish brothers led the resistance. Against all odds, the eternal light continued to burn while a new supply of oil was found. The legend is celebrated as the Jewish festival of Hanukkah. This story, simply told, is illustrated with classic-style paintings set off in Roman-arched frames.

3.65   Manushkin, Fran. **Latkes and Applesauce: A Hanukkah Story.** Illustrated by Robin Spowart. Scholastic Hardcover Books, 1990. ISBN 0-590-42261-8. 32p. 6–10 (est.). Fiction.

Through the voice of the Jewish storyteller comes the story of a special Hanukkah—"perhaps a miracle. Maybe yes, maybe no." The Menashe family, isolated by a blizzard, fears that there will be no traditional Hanukkah feast of latkes and applesauce, and perhaps no food at all. Nevertheless, the family takes in a stray dog and kitten who come to their door. On the eighth night, the dog and cat become part of the miracle, ensuring the feast and earning new names for themselves—Latke and Applesauce. Scenes are softly blurred impressions in muted tones.

3.66   Modesitt, Jeanne, compiler. **Songs of Chanukah.** Illustrated by Robin Spowart. Little, Brown, 1992. ISBN 0-316-57739-1. 32p. 6–12 (est.). Nonfiction.

Fourteen songs for the eight-day holiday of Hanukkah are offered in both Hebrew and English, arranged for piano, guitar, and voice. Along with the musical scores are descriptions of the traditions of the candle lighting and its accompanying ceremonies. Rabbits and mice in human guise act out the religious and cultural patterns, recounting the tale of Maccabean heroism which is remembered through the lighting of candles, in games and dance, and through special recipes.

3.67   Youdovin, Susan Schaalman. **Why Does It Always Rain on Sukkot?** Illustrated by Miriam Nerlove. Albert Whitman, 1990. ISBN 0-8075-9079-7. 30p. 4–8. Fiction.

The chief angel is handing out special gifts to all the "Holidays." Among them, Passover, with a cohort of boisterous Israelites, receives the Seder plate, and a bespectacled Simchat Torah is given the scroll of the Law. Finally, little Sukkot, believing himself forgotten, sobs when presented with a *sukkah*. His tears are remembered each year when it rains through the branches of homemade *sukkahs*. Framed ink and watercolor paintings and a concluding description of the holidays on the Jewish calendar add charm and interest to each annual celebration. *Notable 1990 Children's Trade Books in the Field of Social Studies.*

3.68 Zalben, Jane Breskin. **Leo and Blossom's Sukkah.** Illustrated by Jane Breskin Zalben. Henry Holt, 1990. ISBN 0-8050-1226-5. 16p. 4–8 (est.). Fiction.

When brother and sister bears Leo and Blossom and their friends decide to build a *sukkah* to celebrate the harvest festival of Sukkot, they get carried away and hang too many fruits, vegetables, popcorn, and paper chains from the flimsy roof of the booth. When everything starts to fall, they welcome their parents' help and enjoy hearing their father tell the story of the Jewish festival. One of Jane Breskin Zalben's three books on Jewish holidays, this book might serve as an introduction to celebrations enjoyed by different religions.

Kwanzaa

3.69 Walter, Mildred Pitts. **Have a Happy . . . : A Novel.** Illustrated by Carole Byard. Lothrop, Lee and Shepard Books, 1989. ISBN 0-688-06923-1. 106p. 7–10. Fiction.

Besides the confusion of his birthday falling on Christmas, eleven-year-old Chris knows that his chances for getting a bicycle for either Christmas or his birthday are slim. His father has been out of work for a long time. Furthermore, nobody seems to take a Christmas birthday seriously. "They could just say, Have a happy. Then I could add anything I want: happy birthday, happy Christmas, happy Kwanzaa." It is the spirit of the African American holiday of Kwanzaa that draws his family together in celebration of their heritage, and problems find resolution. *Notable 1989 Children's Trade Books in the Field of Social Studies.*

Multiple Holidays

3.70 Baker, James W. **April Fools' Day Magic. New Year's Magic. Thanksgiving Magic.** Illustrated by George Overlie. Lerner, 1989. 48p. 6–12 (est.). Nonfiction.

Three in a series of Holiday Magic Books offer directions for holiday magic tricks. For New Year's, magicians can tell fortunes with a gravity-defying ring or can make a selected playing card show up at the end of the spelling of "Happy New Year." For Thanksgiving, magicians can perform a trick to demonstrate the never-ending nature of leftovers. At the end of each book, performers are shown tricks for doing better magic. Step-by-step directions are accompanied with two-color illustrations.

3.71   dePaola, Tomie. **My First Chanukah. My First Easter. My First Halloween. My First Passover. My First Thanksgiving.** Illustrated by Tomie dePaola. G. P. Putnam's Sons, 1989–92. 12p. 1–5. Nonfiction.

Young children are introduced to the basic concepts and symbols of five holidays—Hanukkah, Easter, Halloween, Passover, and Thanksgiving—with characteristic Tomie dePaola simplicity and charm in the My First Holidays series. The Halloween book tells readers that "Halloween colors are black and orange," while the Hanukkah book informs us that the middle candle in a menorah is "the shamash, or 'helper candle.' We use it to light the other candles." Watercolored ink drawings depict the most important details of each holiday.

3.72   Low, Alice, compiler. **The Family Read-Aloud Holiday Treasury.** Illustrated by Marc Brown. Little, Brown/Joy Street Books, 1991. ISBN 0-316-53368-8. 154p. All ages. Fiction/Nonfiction.

Suitable as a resource for classrooms, this collection offers choice stories, excerpts, songs, and poems in celebration of holidays great and small. Children can celebrate Grandparents' Day, Earth Day, Book Week, and even the First Day of School with literature read aloud. Included are works by Beverly Cleary, Jack Prelutsky, Ann Cameron, and Jean Fritz. Throughout the book, lively illustrations spill from Marc Brown's crayon-bordered frames.

3.73   Seuss, Dr. (Theodor S. Geisel). **Oh, the Places You'll Go!** Illustrated by Dr. Seuss. Random House, 1990. ISBN 0-679-90527-8. 32p. 6 and up. Fiction.

As a lasting legacy from Dr. Seuss, *Oh, the Places You'll Go!* is destined to be placed into the hands of those at the launch points, crossroads, and milestones of life. Although the "Seussian" pathways are pleasant, colorful nonsense, the good doctor acknowledges life's challenges, pitfalls, and stumbling blocks. Even so, the message is full of confidence and reassurance for the traveler: "Today is your day! / Your mountain is waiting. / So . . . *get on your way!*"

St. Patrick's Day

3.74 Kroll, Steven. **Mary McLean and the St. Patrick's Day Parade.** Illustrated by Michael Dooling. Scholastic Hardcover Books, 1991. ISBN 0-590-43701-1. 32p. 3–10 (est.). Fiction.

On the cover, an exuberant Irish-American lass of the nineteenth century, wearing a perfect shamrock, rides triumphantly in Mr. Finnegan's green-trimmed cart in the St. Patrick's Day Parade. The story tells how (with a bit of leprechaun magic) she gets there. Mary McLean, a refugee of the Irish potato famine, lives with her family in a cramped basement room in lower Manhattan. She is determined to ride in the parade, but Mr. Finnegan insists that she must do something special first—like find a perfect shamrock in the middle of the winter.

Thanksgiving

3.75 Bunting, Eve. **How Many Days to America? A Thanksgiving Story.** Illustrated by Beth Peck. Clarion Books, 1988. ISBN 0-89919-521-0. 30p. 5–9. Fiction.

"How many days to America?" asks the little girl as the small, overcrowded fishing boat pulls away from all that is familiar and dear to this Caribbean refugee family. Hope is the watchword as mother, father, son, and daughter, among others, make their way to a new life amid much adversity. This present-day Thanksgiving story reflects the multiculturalism that was embraced at the original table.

3.76 Hoban, Lillian. **Silly Tilly's Thanksgiving Dinner.** Illustrated by Lillian Hoban. Harper and Row, 1990. ISBN 0-06-022423-1. 63p. 4–8. Fiction.

In another adventure with Silly Tilly to amuse young readers, Silly Tilly tackles Thanksgiving dinner. Although her plans go awry, the dinner turns out to be a success when her guests show up with the food. Lillian Hoban's characterization of Tilly Mole in both word and illustration adds appeal, as does the text-to-illustrations ratio of this I Can Read Book.

3.77 Leedy, Loreen. **The Dragon Thanksgiving Feast: Things to Make and Do.** Illustrated by Loreen Leedy. Holiday House, 1990. ISBN 0-8234-0828-0. 28p. 4–8. Nonfiction.

"The dragons howl at the harvest moon, 'Thanksgiving Day is coming soon!'" And so, ten blue dragons with red scales, purple wings, and bulging green eyes begin their preparations. The busy dragons teach readers how to make such crafts as a wild bird feeder and an edible necklace and such recipe items as Munch & Crunch Salad. When the big day arrives, so do green and purple guests, a parade, games, a feast, and, finally, a nap. Dragon fans will also enjoy Loreen Leedy's *A Dragon Christmas*.

Valentine's Day

3.78   Buckley, Kate. **Love Notes.** Illustrated by Kate Buckley. Albert Whitman, 1989. ISBN 0-8075-4780-8. 32p. 7–10 (est.). Fiction.

Katy gets the first love note from Joe. She writes back that she loves him too, and tells her mother that she'll marry him. But Katy's note falls into the hands of Joe's friends, and a flurry of teasing erupts. As second graders work from "love" to "like," the playground is filled with familiar chants and taunts. Strips of pictures surrounding the text offer other playground lore— jump-rope jingles and clapping games. The satisfactory outcome is worth talking about in classrooms.

3.79   Hoban, Lillian. **Arthur's Great Big Valentine.** Illustrated by Lillian Hoban. Harper and Row, 1989. ISBN 0-06-022407-X. 64p. 5–8. Fiction.

In this latest addition to Lillian Hoban's series, Arthur and his best friend Norman have had a disagreement and are not speaking to each other. Arthur even stubbornly refuses to participate in Valentine's Day festivities. It takes a secret from Norman's little brother to finally get the two friends to admit that they miss each other. This warm story, supplemented with animated illustrations, is an I Can Read Book.

Classics

The classics should not be exempted from reevaluation by virtue of their past veneration. They should be able to compete favorably with contemporary books. Unimpressed by vintage or lineage, children seldom read a book because they think they should. They read more for enjoyment than edification.

Charlotte Huck, *Children's Literature in the Elementary School*

4 Classics

4.1 Barrie, J. M. **Peter Pan: The Complete and Unabridged Text.** Illustrated by Scott Gustafson. Viking Penguin/Ariel Books, 1991. ISBN 0-670-83608-7. 184p. All ages. Fiction.

Richer, darker, and more moving than other reissues of this classic, Scott Gustafson's powerful, lavish, full-color oil paintings set a superb frame for the magic and charm of the tale and the dramatic depictions of pirates, Indians, children, and lost boys. Worth a close look is the artist's rendition of the underground world of the lost boys.

4.2 Carroll, Lewis (compiled by Cooper Edens). **Alice's Adventures in Wonderland: The Ultimate Illustrated Edition.** Bantam Books, 1989. ISBN 0-553-05385-X. 208p. 4 and up (est.). Fiction.

This edition of Lewis Carroll's unabridged text features selected illustrations from more than twenty-five classic "Alice" editions, ranging from the original in 1865 through editions of the 1930s. Included in this visual chronicle are the artwork of John Tenniel, Margaret Tarrant, Millicent Sowerby, Milo Winter, and Harry Rountree, among others. The illustrations vary in color, style, and line from shadowy, black-and-white sketches to pale, soft-edged pastels to vibrant, bright-hued plates. This combination of strikingly different artistic interpretations will surprise and delight readers of all ages.

4.3 Chekhov, Anton (translated by Richard Pevear). **Kashtanka.** Illustrated by Barry Moser. G. P. Putnam's Sons, 1991. ISBN 0-399-21905-6. 47p. All ages. Fiction.

Russian children love this story of the foxlike Kashtanka, the lost dog who is found by a kindly animal trainer. In his new home, Kashtanka lives with a trained goose, pig, and cat. Eventually he, too, must practice to become part of their circus act. But when Kashtanka makes his debut at the circus, he is recognized by his former owners and races from the ring. Barry Moser's paintings of animals are formal portraits, while his street scenes are snowy postcards.

4.4 Dickens, Charles. **A Christmas Carol.** Illustrated by Scott Cook. Random House, 1990. ISBN 0-394-92239-5. 60p. 8–12. Fiction.

Charles Dickens's own abridgment of his nineteenth-century Christmas classic was created especially for reading aloud. Scott Cook's twenty-one amber-toned oil paintings manage to evoke both the warmth of the season's traditional festivities and the sparse trappings of the miserly Scrooge.

4.5   Hale, Lucretia (adapted by Amy Schwartz). **The Lady Who Put Salt in Her Coffee.** Illustrated by Amy Schwartz. Harcourt Brace Jovanovich, 1989. ISBN 0-15-243475-5. 32p. 4–8. Fiction.

Poor Mrs. Peterkin adds salt instead of sugar to her coffee. Her sympathetic family tries to help by seeking advice from the dotty local chemist, the village herb woman, and the matter-of-fact lady from Philadelphia. In this adaptation of Lucretia Hale's century-old tales in "The Peterkin Papers," Amy Schwartz's stylized illustrations allow Mrs. Peterkin to be lovably scatter-brained.

4.6   Hodges, Margaret, adapter. **Don Quixote and Sancho Panza.** Illustrated by Stephen Marchesi. Charles Scribner's Sons, 1992. ISBN 0-684-19235-7. 72p. 8–12 (est.). Fiction.

In her introduction, Margaret Hodges quotes the axiom that Don Quixote should be read at least three times—once as a youth, again in middle age, and finally in old age. If so, readers might want to begin with this abridged edition. Here, the Spanish knight errant sets off to defend kingdoms, protect damsels, punish the proud, and reward the humble. With a mix of idealism, slapstick, pathos, and kindness, he tilts at windmills and earnestly displays his bravery. Black-and-white illustrations are sensitive to the times and temperaments of the heroes.

4.7   Irving, Washington. **Rip Van Winkle.** Illustrations by Arthur Rackham. Dial Books, 1992. ISBN 0-8037-1264-2. 124p. All ages (est.). Fiction.

Washington Irving's classic tale of Rip Van Winkle, the amiable ne'er-do-well who sleeps for twenty years in the Catskill Mountains and misses the Revoluntionary War, has been reissued with celebrated artist Arthur Rackham's original 1905 illustrations. The publishers have reproduced the first edition of Irving's story using the original type and layout. The illustrations have been "enhanced by complementary colored backgrounds," resulting in a beautifully bound edition, printed on quality paper in a way that emphasizes the detail and care of Rackham's illustrations.

4.8   Irving, Washington (retold by John Howe). **Rip Van Winkle.** Illustrated by John Howe. Little, Brown, 1988. ISBN 0-316-37578-0. 30p. 4–8. Fiction.

This exquisitely illustrated version of Washington Irving's classic story of a twenty-year nap in the Catskill Mountains is a choice example of the role that children's books can play in introducing young readers to adult fiction. The text, adapted from the original, retains both color and reasonable complexity. John Howe's luminous and realistic full-color paintings make the story easy to follow and hold the reader's interest. The wizened and gnomish faces of Howe's men are especially engaging.

4.9   Kipling, Rudyard. **Just So Stories.** Illustrated by David Frampton. HarperCollins, 1991. ISBN 0-06-023296-X. 122p. 5 and up (est.). Fiction.

David Frampton's traditional woodcuts accompany twelve of Kipling's most-beloved pourquoi tales, including "The Elephant's Child," "How the Camel Got His Hump," and "How the Leopard Got His Spots." A full-page woodcut sets off the opening of each story; each major character is stylized and tinted in ochres, blues, and golden tans; and each story is dramatically bordered by black frames etched with the story motif.

4.10 Melville, Herman. **Catskill Eagle.** Illustrated by Thomas Locker. Philomel Books, 1991. ISBN 0-399-21857-2. 28p. 5 and up. Fiction.

These short, powerful lines from *Moby Dick,* set to sweeping illustrations of the Hudson Valley by painter Thomas Locker, make an excellent children's book. Melville's description of the Catskill eagle, which he compares to far-seeing, deep-minded individuals, is broad enough to be accessible to children. The paintings portray the eagle against a breathtaking natural background; the natural affinity that children feel for animals will draw them to these stirring depictions of eagles in flight, with their young at the nest, and lifting fish from icy streams.

4.11 Salten, Felix. **Bambi: A Life in the Woods.** Illustrated by Michael J. Woods. Simon and Schuster Books for Young Readers, 1992. ISBN 0-671-73937-9. 158p. 8–12 (est.). Fiction.

Over sixty-five years ago, John Galsworthy wrote in the foreword to *Bambi* that the book is "delicious not only for children but for those who are no longer so fortunate." For children

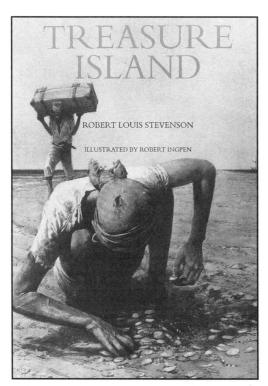

A.

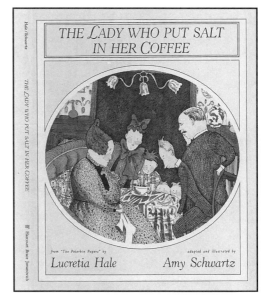

B.

C.

A. *Treasure Island* by Robert Louis Stevenson; illustrated by Robert Ingpen (see 4.13).
B. *The Lady Who Put Salt in Her Coffee* by Lucretia Hale; adapted and illustrated by Amy Schwartz (see 4.5). **C.** *The Antique Store Cat* by Leslie Baker (see 5.12).

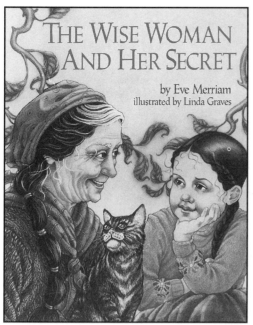

A.

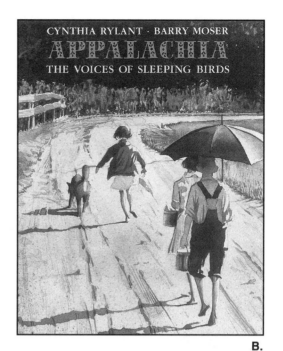

B.

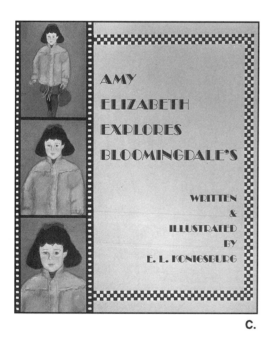

C.

D.

A. *The Wise Woman and Her Secret* by Eve Merriam; illustrated by Linda Graves (see 5.58). **B.** *Appalachia: The Voices of Sleeping Birds* by Cynthia Rylant and Barry Moser (see 5.63). **C.** *Amy Elizabeth Explores Bloomingdale's* by E. L. Konigsburg (see 5.56). **D.** *The Leaving* by Budge Wilson (see 5.64).

familiar only with the animated film, the text of the original Bambi may be a welcome read-aloud. Felix Salten knew the forest and its inhabitants well. Michael Woods's double-page watercolors in pale forest shades capture the buck's action and fear as truthfully as the fawn's idyllic glades.

4.12   Spyri, Johanna (translated by Helen B. Dole, with revisions by John Githens). **Tomi Ungerer's Heidi.** Illustrated by Tomi Ungerer. Delacorte Press, 1990. ISBN 0-385-30244-4. 310p. 8–12. Fiction.

Illustrator Tomi Ungerer has added depth and charm to the timeless *Heidi* by Johanna Spyri. Both black-and-white and color illustrations feature characters and incidents that are at once humorous and moving—from the delicate warm colors depicting a quiet moment shared by Grandmamma and Heidi reading by lamplight, to a black-ink sketch of an indignant Fraulein Rottenmeier that is framed by shadows and that emphasizes the witchlike characteristics of her profile. Ungerer's flair for capturing both sentiment and fancy in illustrations make this unabridged version of the classic unique.

4.13   Stevenson, Robert Louis. **Treasure Island.** Illustrated by Robert Ingpen. Viking Penguin, 1992. ISBN 0-670-84685-6. 176p. 8 and up. Fiction.

Opposite the list of color plates in Robert Ingpen's version of this classic tale is a realistic, carefully inked map of Treasure Island, dated 1750, ragged-edged and aged, but with its scale and lettering so perfectly rendered that it well serves the upcoming adventure. In this large-scale edition, chapter openings are double-page paintings, offering portrait-like character interpretations. Other paintings vary from a light-bathed view of Jim Hawkins to darkly menacing scenes. Penciled details add richness to each chapter.

4.14   Thoreau, Henry David (text selections by Steve Lowe). **Walden.** Illustrated by Robert Sabuda. Philomel Books, 1990. ISBN 0-399-22153-0. 30p. 4 –12. Nonfiction.

In 1845, Henry David Thoreau spent two years living alone in a cabin he built himself on the banks of Walden Pond near Concord, Massachusetts. Selected passages from *Walden* focus on experiences meaningful for children to create this celebration of Thoreau's masterpiece about life amid nature's quiet. Double-page linoleum-print illustrations, with text inset, create a warm tone of nineteenth-century America. This book can motivate younger readers to explore the adult version of *Walden* in later years. *Notable 1990 Children's Trade Books in the Field of Social Studies.*

4.15   Thurber, James. **Many Moons.** Illustrated by Marc Simont. Harcourt Brace Jovanovich/HBJ Contemporary Classics, 1990. ISBN 0-15-251872-X. 48p. 4–8. Fiction.

Originally illustrated by Louis Slobodkin and awarded the Caldecott Medal in 1944, James Thurber's story of the princess who wanted the moon—and got it—has been redesigned and reillustrated. Artist Marc Simont uses whimsical watercolor illustrations enveloped by areas of white space to bring to life the antics of the spoiled Princess Lenore.

4.16   Ushinsky, Konstantin (adapted by Marguerita Rudolph). **How a Shirt Grew in the Field.** Illustrations by Erika Weihs. Clarion Books, 1992. ISBN 0-395-59761-7. 32p. 6–9 (est.). Fiction.

When Vasya was promised a new shirt made of the flax seeds that his father sowed, he wondered how it was possible. Vasya observes the development of the seeds into silky grass, sheaves, woven cloth, and finally an embroidered linen shirt. New illustrations of a hundred-year-old tale feature rounded figures against a Ukrainian landscape.

Contemporary Realistic Fiction

If a children's writer presents . . . characters honestly and is truthful about their thoughts and their feelings, he [or she] is giving . . . readers "a means to gain a hold on fate" by showing them that they can trust their thoughts and their feelings, that they can have faith in themselves. He [or she] can also show them a bit of the world, the beginning of the path they have to tread; but the most important thing he [or she] has to offer is a little hope, and courage for the journey.

Nina Bawden, "Emotional Realism in Books
for Young People," *The Horn Book Magazine*

5 Contemporary Realistic Fiction

Adventure Stories

5.1   Albert, Burton. **Where Does the Trail Lead?** Illustrated by Brian Pinkney. Simon and Schuster Books for Young Readers, 1991. ISBN 0-671-73409-1. 30p. 4–8 (est.).

Detailed scratchboard illustrations create the feel of Massachusetts' Nantucket Island, ripe for exploration. And where *does* the trail lead? An African American boy follows it "over hills and hollows . . . past three limbs bent by the wind, and tide-pools of periwinkles." Through text that rises and falls as the tides, the child moves past derelict vestiges of the built landscape, a railroad track, shanties, and a fence, before returning to picnic with his family by the water's edge at twilight.

5.2   Crews, Donald. **Shortcut.** Illustrated by Donald Crews. Greenwillow Books, 1992. ISBN 0-688-06437-X. 32p. 4–7 (est.).

It's getting dark, so seven children decide to take the shortcut home—a shortcut that follows a train track along a narrow mound, surrounded by briers and water "full of snakes." The possibility of an oncoming train is not a concern for the frolicking friends, until . . . "Whoo-whoo!! Klackity-klak! Klackity-klak!" The close call sends them diving for safety. Donald Crews portrays his frightening memory in closeup perspectives, using watercolor and gouache paints in the shadowy colors of dusk.

5.3   George, Jean Craighead. **On the Far Side of the Mountain.** Illustrated by Jean Craighead George. Dutton Children's Books, 1990. ISBN 0-525-44563-3. 170p. 8–12.

Sequel to the 1959 classic *My Side of the Mountain*, Jean Craighead George's novel continues the adventures of Sam Gribley as he carves out a life for himself on his mountain. When Sam's sister suddenly disappears and his favorite pet, a peregrine falcon, is taken from him, Sam treks across the New York wilderness to rescue both. The award-winning author's prose, maps, and illustrations provide specific information for wilderness survival (such as the methods for constructing a water pump, twig compass, water bag, and tree house).

5.4   George, Jean Craighead. **Shark beneath the Reef.** ISBN 0-06-021993-9. 182p. 9 and up (est.).

Tomas, a ninth grader on the Island of Coronado, dreams of becoming the town's hero by catching the whale shark that rips his family's nets. Equal to his desire for helping his family as a great fisherman, though, is Tomas's hope of becoming a marine biologist. The choice is a difficult one in this coming-of-age novel about a Mexican boy. It is a good companion to Scott O'Dell's *The Black Pearl* and Hemingway's *The Old Man and the Sea*. *Notable 1989 Children's Trade Books in the Field of Social Studies.*

5.5   Helldorfer, Mary Claire. **Sailing to the Sea.** Illustrated by Loretta Krupinski. Viking Penguin, 1991. ISBN 0-670-83520-X. 32p. 5–8 (est.).

A young narrator describes in poetic prose his first sailing trip down the river to the sea: "Straight ahead are double bridges; steel spans cut the sky into puzzle pieces." Together, the boy and his aunt and uncle swim, pick flowers on shore, have dinner in a waterfront restaurant, and weather a hard storm. Finally, they reach the sea and reunite with family members who drive to meet them. A wide range of sea colors, perspectives, and moods show the joyous activities of sailing.

5.6   Lyon, George Ella. **Come a Tide.** Illustrated by Stephen Gammell. Orchard Books/Richard Jackson Books, 1990. ISBN 0-531-08454-X. 32p. 4–7.

Snows in March, coupled with rain, cause Grandma to predict: "It'll come a tide." As the flood-warning whistle blows, kinfolk and neighbors begin leaving their homes, checking on each other as they make their way to Grandma's house on higher ground. The waters subside and families begin to dig in the mud, searching for the buried treasure of their belongings, feeling safe until next spring. Stephen Gammell's cool-toned paintings are water-drenched and neighbor-friendly. *ALA Notable Children's Books, 1991.*

5.7   Radin, Ruth Yaffe. **High in the Mountains.** Illustrated by Ed Young. Macmillan, 1989. ISBN 0-02-775650-5. 30p. 5–10 (est.).

A child describes in warm and simple words the beauty of life in the mountains with Grandpa. Ed Young's impressionistic paintings in bright pastels help evoke the flavor of life in the high country. A companion book for comparison could be Cynthia Rylant's *When I Was Young in the Mountains*. *Notable Children's Trade Books in Science, 1989*.

5.8   Rand, Gloria. **Salty Dog.** Illustrated by Ted Rand. Henry Holt, 1989. ISBN 0-8050-0837-3. 30p. 9–11 (est.).

Zack is building a boat to sail around the world, and Salty Dog intends to stay by his side throughout the entire process. Salty soon learns to escape his snug, fenced-in home and ride the ferry to see Zack at the boatyard. Ted Rand's watercolors are so filled with movement that readers will think they, too, feel the sea spray when Zack and Salty finally embark on their maiden voyage.

5.9   Taylor, Theodore. **Sniper.** Harcourt Brace Jovanovich, 1989. ISBN 0-15-276420-8. 227p. 10–13 (est.).

Ben Jepson's parents own and operate a private big-cat preserve in Southern California. But only ten days after his parents leave for a research trip to Africa, everything at Los Coyotes seems to be going wrong—the chief animal handler is hospitalized, an elusive sniper shoots at the cats night after night, and a fire threatens the property. The local authorities are mystified. Unable to contact his parents, fifteen-year-old Ben and his friend Sandy find clues to the past that bring this adventure story to a thrilling conclusion. *ALA Best Books for Young Adults, 1990*.

Animal Stories

5.10   Aylesworth, Jim. **Mother Halverson's New Cat.** Illustrated by Toni Goffe. Atheneum, 1989. ISBN 0-689-31465-5. 26p. 5–8.

When Mother Halverson needs a new mouser for her pantry, she sends her husband to "look over the cats in the barn and bring in the best of the lot." Yet despite Farmer Halverson's efforts, none of the crabby, flabby, nor blabby cats meet Mother Halverson's expectations, and all are unceremoniously deposed. Finally, a shy tabby named Abby fulfills the job description to perfection. Humorous full-page drawings illustrate this cat tale with a lesson: "The nice shall inherit the mice."

5.11   Baker, Alan. **Two Tiny Mice.** Illustrated by Alan Baker. Dial Books for Young Readers, 1991. ISBN 0-8037-0973-0. 25p. 3–8 (est.).

When two tiny field mice investigate the world around them, they discover the many wonders of their woodland home. Written in rhythmic and descriptive verse, the book invites children to view nature from a "mouse's point of view." Full-color pencil sketches silhouetted against watercolor panoramas capture the beauty of various animals in their natural habitats.

5.12 Baker, Leslie. **The Antique Store Cat.** Illustrated by Leslie Baker. Little, Brown, 1992. ISBN 0-316-07837-9. 28p. 5–8 (est.).

On her birthday, Alice, a calico cat who lives in a third-story apartment, escapes to the city streets below. But Alice has trouble finding her way home and eventually finds shelter and company in an antique store. After her mischievous nature helps the store owner spot a fake statue, Alice is reunited with her owner and returns home. Soft, impressionistic watercolor paintings illustrate this sequel to *Third Story Cat*.

5.13 Barracca, Debra, and Sal Barracca. **The Adventures of Taxi Dog.** Illustrated by Mark Buehner. Dial Books for Young Readers, 1990. ISBN 0-8037-0672-3. 32p. 4–8.

Through rhyming verses, Maxi, a homeless dog, tells how he survived in the city until Jim the taxi driver adopts him and they begin to share the front seat of Jim's yellow cab. Together, man and dog rush a mother-to-be to the hospital, bring clowns from the airport, and enjoy each other's company. Brightly colored paintings (such as one of Maxi donning a Groucho Marx disguise to entertain passengers) add detail and wit. A cat and often a rabbit hide on each spread.

5.14 Calhoun, Mary. **High-Wire Henry.** Illustrated by Erick Ingraham. Morrow Junior Books, 1991. ISBN 0-688-08984-4. 40p. 5–10 (est.).

When a new puppy comes home, Henry, the Siamese cat from *Hot-Air Henry* and *Cross-Country Cat*, is no longer the center of attention. Determined to regain his place, Henry tries to impress his family by tightrope walking on branches and fences. Later, when the puppy is stranded on a window ledge, Henry uses his high-wire skills to turn rescuer. Full-page, realistic watercolors complement this humorous story of a cat that saves the day.

5.15 Carle, Eric. **The Very Quiet Cricket.** Illustrated by Eric Carle. Philomel Books, 1990. ISBN 0-399-21885-8. 24p. 3–6.

One warm day a tiny cricket is born and begins his encounters with other insects in his world. Yet when trying to answer their greetings, the little cricket can produce no sound—until he meets a female cricket and discovers his song. The rhythmic and repetitive text is illustrated with brightly colored, tissue-textured collage paintings. A microchip at the book's end treats readers to a cricket's chirp, "the most beautiful sound that she had ever heard."

5.16   Carlstrom, Nancy White. **Moose in the Garden.** Illustrated by Lisa Desimini. Harper and Row, 1990. ISBN 0-06-021014-1. 32p. 3–8 (est.).

When a hungry moose visits the garden, Mother and Father are none too pleased to see the intruder eat up all their broccoli, cabbage, and cauliflower. Their son, however, has a different perspective on the garden visitor. After all, he maintains, there are certain vegetables that no one should have to eat—like broccoli, cabbage, and cauliflower. Cumulative, rhythmic text and vibrant stylized paintings fill the pages to make this an inviting story.

5.17   Carter, Margaret. **Go Away, William.** Illustrated by Carol Wright. Macmillan, 1989. ISBN 0-02-717791-2. 25p. 4–8 (est.).

William the cat likes to be near his family. The trouble is that he gets in the middle of things—in the middle of Granny's sewing basket, Father's typing, and Rose's garden. The response of each family member is, "Oh, do go away, William!" But where should a cat who likes people go? The family devises a delightful solution. Brightly colored, cartoon-like illustrations support the book's simple and predictable text.

5.18   Cleveland-Peck, Patricia. **City Cat, Country Cat.** Illustrated by Gilly Marklew. Morrow Junior Books, 1992. ISBN 0-688-11645-0. 30p. 5–9 (est.).

Freckle is a very mysterious country cat. His owner, David, worries when Freckle leaves the farm for days on end, even though Freckle always returns. Sarah owns a city cat named Charlie, a cat with very similar characteristics. Like Freckle, Charlie disappears for days and causes Sarah to worry dreadfully. When Sarah decides to follow Charlie, she discovers that this cat leads a city life as "Charlie" and a country life as "Freckle." All ends happily when David and Sarah negotiate dual ownership of this city-country cat.

5.19 George, William T. **Box Turtle at Long Pond.** Illustrated by Lindsay Barrett George. Greenwillow Books, 1989. ISBN 0-688-08185-1. 25p. 5–8.

It has been a long day at Long Pond. The box turtle must find food, water, and shelter as well as defend itself from a hungry raccoon—all before the sun sets. Full-page, magnificently painted illustrations bring out the details of animal lives woven together in a simple setting. With its turtle's-eye view of the world, this book could enrich studies of turtles and habitat sharing. *Notable Children's Trade Books in Science, 1989.*

5.20 Gordon, Gaelyn. **Duckat.** Illustrated by Chris Gaskin. Scholastic Hardcover Books, 1992. ISBN 0-590-45455-2. 24p. 2–6.

Imagine a duck that says *meow,* hates the water, drinks milk from a bowl, catches mice, and chases balls of yarn. Mild little Mabel finds such a duck to be "Odd. Very odd." Despite her efforts to teach her "duckat" his identity, Mabel is unsuccessful until the duck escapes from a dog by flying to the top of a lamp post. "If you are a cat, you'll just have to stay up there," says Mabel. "Quack," says the duck, and flies down. It was only joking, you see.

5.21 Gottlieb, Dale. **Big Dog.** Illustrated by Dale Gottlieb. Morrow Junior Books, 1989. ISBN 0-688-07382-4. 32p. 3–7.

Lilly, a city child, is afraid of things—of the dark, of elevators, and of walking to the store. Her parents think a dog might help. But like the puppy in Norman Bridwell's *Clifford the Big Red Dog,* Lilly's beloved pet grows and grows and grows until Lilly must decide where her dog can live best. She acts with her growing-up head and heart to make the best decision. Stylized illustrations emphasize the size differences between the little girl and the Big Dog, whose needs she considers as well as her own.

5.22 Hindley, Judy. **Mrs. Mary Malarky's Seven Cats.** Illustrated by Denise Teasdale. Orchard Books, 1990. ISBN 0-531-08422-1. 32p. 4–7.

Each one is unique and each one is special; all together they are Mrs. Mary Malarky's seven cats. A baby-sitter by trade, Mrs. Malarky tells her own "bedtime" story about how seven cats came to live with her and how all but one found a new home. Watercolor-washed drawings illustrate this humorous tale of seven cats and a special baby-sitter.

5.23   Lindenbaum, Pija (retold by Gabrielle Charbonnet). **Boodil My Dog.** Illustrated by Pija Lindenbaum. Henry Holt, 1992. ISBN 0-8050-2444-1. 47p. 5–9 (est.).

In this English adaptation of a Swedish story, Boodil is described by her dog-loving owner as brilliant, strong, and brave. However, Pija Lindenbaum's whimsical pictures of Boodil the bull-terrier cause the reader to question such a description. Would a brilliant guard dog sleep in an overstuffed chair with her "blankee"? Would she be suspicious of rain puddles? Would she think the vacuum cleaner was a dangerous enemy? Children and adults alike will agree that regardless of Boodil's shortcomings, she is the perfect pet.

5.24   MacLachlan, Patricia. **Three Names.** Illustrated by Alexander Pertzoff. HarperCollins/Charlotte Zolotow Books, 1991. ISBN 0-06-024036-9. 32p. 5–9.

In Patricia MacLachlan's poetic prose, Great-grandfather tells of his youth, when boys wore overalls with buckles and rode to school in wagons. He describes a loyal dog with three names—called something different by each member of the family. Images of the prairie are offered in full-page, sun-kissed watercolor impressions of life that "stretch out like a quilt all around." Sensory impressions—smells of harness leather, of wood, and of hay—pervade. A likely companion book is Cynthia Rylant's *When I Was Young in the Mountains.*

5.25   McDonald, Megan. **Is This a House for Hermit Crab?** Illustrated by S. D. Schindler. Orchard Books/Richard Jackson Books, 1990. ISBN 0-531-08455-8. 26p. 3–7 (est.).

Hermit Crab is not happy with his old house—the shell on his back—so he sets out in search of a new house before the hungry pricklepine fish finds him and eats him. So he walks "along the shore, by sea, in the sand . . . *scritch-scratch, scritch-scratch*" in search of a new home. But every possible home that he finds is too dark or too deep or has too many holes or is already someone else's home. Is there *any* house for Hermit Crab? Pastel double-page spreads realistically depect the hermit crabs, pricklepine fish, and fiddler crabs of the story. *IRA Children's Book Award, 1991.*

5.26   Moore, Inga. **Six-Dinner Sid.** Illustrated by Inga Moore. Simon and Schuster Books for Young Readers, 1991. ISBN 0-671-73199-8. 28p. 6–10 (est.).

Sid the cat has six homes and six owners; consequently, he eats six dinners each day. But when he comes down with a cold and is taken to the vet six times, Sid's secret is discovered, and his six-meal-a-day life comes to an end—that is, until Sid finds new owners who feel that he is a six-dinner-deserving cat. Full-color sketches illustrate this humorous tale of a sociable and industrious cat with a mind of his own.

5.27 Naylor, Phyllis Reynolds. **Shiloh.** Atheneum, 1991. ISBN 0-689-31614-3. 144p. 8–13 (est.).

When a bedraggled, uncertain beagle follows eleven-year-old Marty home from near the Shiloh schoolhouse, Marty falls in love with the dog and calls him Shiloh. Marty learns that the dog is being abused by its owner, and he faces a dilemma between social and moral responsibilities. When he decides to hide Shiloh in a pen beyond his family's West Virginia home, he disobeys his parents, endangers the dog, and jeopardizes his family's trust. Marty's determination and monumental effort to gain Shiloh's freedom make for a lasting story. *Newbery Medal, 1992.*

5.28 Ormerod, Jan. **Kitten Day.** Illustrated by Jan Ormerod. Lothrop, Lee and Shepard Books, 1989. ISBN 0-688-08537-7. 32p. 3–6 (est.).

When a shy little, clever little, cheeky little kitten enters a young child's life, she must be patient and gentle and calm to win the kitten's confidence. And so she is. One line of simple, rhythmic text runs along the bottom of the page beneath Jan Ormerod's trademark divided-page illustrations of a child giving loving attention to her new pet.

5.29 Pedersen, Judy. **The Tiny Patient.** Illustrated by Judy Pedersen. Alfred A. Knopf/Borzoi Books, 1989. ISBN 0-394-90170-3. 32p. 4–8.

Simple human compassion for a wounded wild bird warms this story. The straightforward narrative relates the way a young girl and her grandmother care for a sparrow with a broken wing. The nature theme is carried into the soft illustrations and even the endpapers, colored in mellow earth-tones.

5.30 Pryor, Bonnie. **Greenbrook Farm.** Illustrated by Mark Graham. Simon and Schuster Books for Young Readers, 1991. ISBN 0-671-69205-4. 26p. 6–10 (est.).

Springtime at Greenbrook Farm means the smell of apple blossoms and the arrival of baby animals. Seen through the eyes of a young girl narrator going about her morning chores, life on the farm is filled with the excitement and activity of a spring day. Full-page impressionistic paintings help capture the wonder of new beginnings and the warmth of family tradition.

5.31   Ryder, Joanne. **Catching the Wind. Lizard in the Sun. Winter Whale.** Illustrated by Michael Rothman. Morrow Junior Books, 1989–91. 32p. 4–7.

The Just for a Day series invites readers to "become" a member of a flock of Canada geese, or a chameleon, or a humpback whale in a tropical sea. Joanne Ryder's lyrical descriptions read almost like poetry, while Michael Rothman's naturalistic, double-page paintings serve as background. Additional contributors to the series are zoologists, who have ensured that children read accurate portrayals of living animals at the same time as they enjoy imagining the world from alternative points of view.

5.32   Rylant, Cynthia. **Henry and Mudge Get the Cold Shivers: The Seventh Book of Their Adventures.** Illustrated by Suçie Stevenson. Bradbury Press, 1989. ISBN 0-02-778011-2. 48p. 5–7 (est.).

Two special friends, Henry and his huge, lovable dog, Mudge, are both sick. While Henry is confined to his bed, Mudge faithfully stays at his side. When Henry finally recovers, Mudge won't get up, so Mom decides Mudge must go to the vet. Now it's Henry's turn to be the devoted bedside companion while Mudge recuperates. This easy-to-read chapter book is the seventh in a series about Henry and his dog. Children who love dogs or who fantasize about owning a Mudge might try their hands at writing Henry and Mudge stories or other pet adventures of their own.

5.33   Schoenherr, John. **Bear.** Illustrated by John Schoenherr. Philomel Books, 1991. ISBN 0-399-22177-8. 28p. 4–8.

All alone, a young bear confronts the unforgiving wilderness. Fearful and hungry, he faces an angry moose, an old bear, and a stream of salmon that elude his grasp. But, with practice, he learns to fish and to survive on his own. Double-page spreads in realistic watercolors heighten the drama of the cub's search for his mother. Using browns, blues, and greys, Caldecott-winning artist John Schoenherr invites the reader into the Alaskan landscape.

5.34   Sharmat, Marjorie Weinman. **I'm the Best!** Illustrated by Will Hillenbrand. Holiday House, 1991. ISBN 0-8234-0859-0. 29p. 6–9 (est.).

Dudley the dog is called Sparky, Fluffy, Mopsy, Cedric, and Fritz as he is shuffled from owner to owner with varying degrees of love and affection. His most recent home, however, may be the best of all. Robert's loss of his dog, Fritz, who looked remarkably like Dudley, causes him to select Dudley from the many choices at the local pound. As Robert and Dudley become acquainted, each begins to love the other for his own unique qualities. Teachers may wish to use this book for a discussion about learning to love and get along with new members of a family or community.

5.35   Taylor, Theodore. **Tuck Triumphant.** Doubleday, 1991. ISBN 0-385-41480-3. 150p. 9 and up (est.).

In this sequel to *The Trouble with Tuck*, Helen's family discovers that Chok-Do, the Korean orphan whom they are adopting, is deaf. Believing themselves unable to cope with his disability, they search for a practical but loving solution. As the title suggests, Tuck provides the answer. A roller coaster of emotions results when Tuck, a blind golden Lab, and her own guide-dog, Daisy, become the the thread which binds this story into one of compassion and understanding for families and classrooms.

5.36   Vyner, Sue. **The Stolen Egg.** Illustrated by Tim Vyner. Viking Penguin, 1992. ISBN 0-670-84460-8. 32p. 4–6 (est.).

"Something was coming. . . ." With each successive invasion, an egg is transported to the habitat of the thief, who compares it with her own eggs. First, an albatross swoops down upon it, but before long the egg is carried away, in turn, by the snake, the crocodile, the ostrich, and the tortoise. Finally, the albatross reappears to carry the egg far across the seas to the place where she found it—at the feet of a father penguin. In a patterned tale with large-scale, realistic animals, the end is a joyous family reunion.

Ethnic, Racial, and Religious Groups

5.37   Crew, Linda. **Children of the River.** Delacorte Press, 1989. ISBN 0-385-29690-8. 213p. 12 and up (est.).

Sundara escapes war-torn Cambodia only one step ahead of the Khmer Rouge army, but as she flees to America she is forced to leave behind her family. In America, she finds herself struggling to keep alive her Cambodian heritage—which demands that she wait for her missing family to arrange her marriage to a Cambodian boy—while resisting the strong affection that she feels for Jonathan, an American high school boy. She cannot help but wonder: is she disloyal to her heritage if she feels love for this American? *IRA Children's Book Award, 1990.*

5.38   Dooley, Norah. **Everybody Cooks Rice.** Illustrated by Peter J. Thornton. Carolrhoda Books, 1991. ISBN 0-87614-412-1. 30p. 4–9.

As Carrie goes from house to house searching for her brother, she discovers that each family from a different country is making a rice dish. The full-page paintings support cultural diversity through the depictions of realistic family settings and characters. The use of solid figures, bright colors, and specific cultural characteristics by illustrator Peter Thornton produces an ideal, culturally diverse neighborhood. The recipes for rice included in the back provide a useful means for encouraging respect for diversity in the classroom.

5.39   Guy, Rosa. **The Ups and Downs of Carl Davis III.** Delacorte Press, 1989. ISBN 0-385-29724-6. 115p. 10 and up.

For a New York boy of twelve possessing "intellectual ability transcend[ing] that of most children my age," going to live with his grandmother in rural South Carolina is akin to exile. Carl's puffery sets him apart from the community; kids at school consider him a show-off, prattling on about black history. Grandma is patient; she has lived the history and suffered the racism that Carl experiences through a teacher. Grandma knows how to speak from the heart. In a story told entirely through letters home, Carl's frustration and confusion are replaced by growing acceptance of others and himself. *Notable 1989 Children's Trade Books in the Field of Social Studies.*

5.40   Levin, Ellen. **I Hate English!** Illustrated by Steve Björkman. Scholastic, 1989. ISBN 0-590-42305-3. 32p. 6–9.

Mei Mei hates English. In a heartwarming story of one child's determined resistance to learning English and her real, recognizable fears that she will lose her own identity in the midst of this new language, Ellen Levine succeeds in translating an important theme. At the Chinatown Learning Center in New York, bright Mei Mei, a newcomer from Hong Kong, works happily—in Chinese. But an inspired teacher with clever methods makes English irresistible. Now, Mei Mei speaks in whichever language she chooses.

5.41   Myers, Walter Dean. **The Mouse Rap.** Harper and Row, 1990. ISBN 0-06-024344-9. 186p. 8–12 (est.).

A busy summer is in store for Mouse, a fourteen-year-old boy in Harlem. Over a period of twelve weeks, he battles a bully, falls in and out of love, learns to dance, improves his basketball game, and grapples with his father's possible return to the family. Along the way, he discovers a gangster's fortune. The award-winning author's style includes African American dialect, playful slang, and a rap-lyric introduction to each chapter.

5.42   Polacco, Patricia. **Just Plain Fancy.** Illustrated by Patricia Polacco. Bantam/Little Rooster Books, 1990. ISBN 0-553-07062-2. 32p. 4–8.

Naomi longs to have something fancy, even though it's not the way of her Amish community. So when she discovers a fancy egg while out gathering hen eggs, Naomi decides to keep it. She is delighted with the peacock that hatches from the egg, until she discovers that the Amish shun people who dress too fancy. Though Naomi fears the worst, the outcome of this conflict is rewarding for everyone in this Amish community.

Human Relationships

Everyday Life

5.43   Brillhart, Julie. **Story Hour—Starring Megan!** Illustrated by Julie Brillhart. Albert Whitman, 1992. ISBN 0-8075-7628-X. 28p. 4–7.

On days when the baby-sitter can't come, Megan's mother, a librarian, takes Megan and her baby brother Nathan to work. Megan is her mother's assistant—watering plants and decorating the bulletin board. But best of all about the library, Megan likes to read books. She can't wait to read them, and she reads everyplace she goes—at home, at school, and in between. Then one day, right during story hour, baby Nathan howls, and guess who substitutes as story reader?

5.44   Bunting, Eve. **No Nap.** Illustrated by Susan Meddaugh. Clarion Books, 1989. ISBN 0-89919-813-9. 32p. 2–6 (est.).

"Daddy promised Mommy that Susie would take a nap." But try as he might, Susie is resistant. Dad's every plan and indulgence—snacking, walking, dancing, reading sleepy books, gathering favorite toys—result in Susie's refrain: "No nap." Finally, while coaxing Susie to pretend to be a sleepy little mouse who doesn't talk or move, Dad falls asleep in the midst of the strewn nap offerings. Light-touch illustrations translate the humor to small children.

5.45   Byars, Betsy. **Bingo Brown's Guide to Romance.** Viking Penguin, 1992. ISBN 0-670-84491-8. 115p. 10–13 (est.).

Bingo Brown is writing a guide to romance, dedicated to his baby brother. At least, Bingo is *planning* the guide—as a question-answer treatise, such as what if you send your true love a photocopied love letter because it was so good that you decided to keep a copy? Without warning, Bingo's girlfriend Melissa is back in town, acting strangely and causing Bingo to doubt himself and to behave weirdly. In Bingo's fourth adventure, his crush is funny, real, and painful.

5.46   Byars, Betsy. **Wanted . . . Mud Blossom.** Illustrated by Jacqueline Rogers. Delacorte Press, 1991. ISBN 0-385-30428-5. 148p. 8–12.

Everything has turned upside down at the Blossom household. Mom's new beau has canceled his weekend visit. Mad Mary, a local homeless person who is feared by some and loved by others, is missing. And young Junior Blossom has accused his grandfather's dog, Mud, of eating the class hamster that he brought home from school for the weekend. As usual, Betsy Byars creatively brings each story to a happy conclusion while managing to capture the absurdities of situations and the feelings of each member of the Blossom family.

5.47   Carlstrom, Nancy White. **The Snow Speaks.** Illustrated by Jane Dyer. Little, Brown, 1992. ISBN 0-316-12861-9. 30p. 6–10.

Alliterative language in a simple verse-like style reveals the sights and sounds of the first snow as two children watch for the snowplow, go down to the mailbox, make snow angels, and wait for the coming of Christmas. Their bright snow suits, along with the colors of the holiday, contrast with soft hues of the seasonal snowfall.

5.48   Coats, Laura Jane. **Mr. Jordan in the Park.** Illustrated by Laura Jane Coats. Macmillan, 1989. ISBN 0-02-719053-6. 27p. 4–8 (est.).

Mr. Jordan has always loved the park. As a baby, he rode in his carriage through the park, and as a toddler, he fed the birds. Still later, he played games and rode his bicycle through the park, and in time he married and shared activities in the park with his family. Although Mr. Jordan is now old, the park is still very much a part of his life. The simple narrative and pale tints of the illustrations reveal the richness of a life as it passes through different phases. *Notable 1989 Children's Trade Books in the Field of Social Studies.*

5.49　Cole, Barbara Hancock. **Texas Star.** Illustrated by Barbara Minton. Orchard Books/Richard Jackson Books, 1990. ISBN 0-531-08420-5. 32p. 4–7.

With the first frost, Mama brings in the begonias and the family begins preparations for winter—including preparing the house for a quilting party to finish Mama's Texas star quilt. Even though Papa grumbles that no new quilt is needed, he participates in scrubbing, polishing, baking, and setting up the quilt frame in the front room. Illustrations in luminous pastel shades offer varying perspectives on the cozy scenes. The book could be grouped with Valerie Flournoy's *The Patchwork Quilt*, Patricia Polacco's *The Keeping Quilt*, and others.

5.50　Downing, Julie. **White Snow, Blue Feather.** Illustrated by Julie Downing. Bradbury Press, 1989. ISBN 0-02-732530-X. 32p. 2–6.

A little boy marvels at the wonders of a wintry landscape after a deep snow. But of all the joys of nature that he discovers, it is the blue jay's feather, "a piece of the sky," that he carries home to his mother. Pastel winter scenes here contrast with the vivid images in Jack Keats's *Snowy Day*. But like Keats's classic, simple text reflects the exhilaration of snow play.

5.51　Hoban, Russell. **Monsters.** Illustrated by Quentin Blake. Scholastic Hardcover Books, 1989. ISBN 0-590-43422-5. 32p. 6–9.

John incessantly draws monsters. Parents and teachers of young children will recognize the behavior and the drawings themselves—a child's scrap-paper renderings of toothed and armed creatures jutting firepower. Urged by his mother to draw something else—something real—John complies. As his drawing of a really big, really serious, really threatening "something" begins to take shape over several days and several papers, a kindly therapist invites John to finish it. But finishing something real means an uncertain future for the grownups in John's life.

5.52   Jackson, Alison. **Crane's Rebound.** Illustrated by Diane Dawson Hearn. Dutton Children's Books, 1991. ISBN 0-535-44722-9. 122p. 8 and up.

Away from home for the first time at basketball camp, Leslie Crane must learn to deal with his attraction to a girl at the camp, a bully who seems never to miss a shot on the court, and his little brother, who calls almost every day. But can he also make it through his first double-date movie with the Girl of His Dreams? This is truly light, fun reading for kids, with no message beyond "Enjoy yourself."

5.53   Johnson, Angela. **Do Like Kyla.** Illustrated by James E. Ransome. Orchard Books/Richard Jackson Books, 1990. ISBN 0-531-08452-3. 32p. 4–7.

All day Kyla's younger sister follows her, imitating her every move, whether it is braiding her hair, putting honey on all her food, or crunching in the snow. Then something different happens between follower and leader—the roles shift. Full-page oil paintings in bold colors depict two African American sisters as they experience everyday life. Engaging illustrations extend the simple account narrated by the little sister.

5.54   Khalsa, Dayal Kaur. **How Pizza Came to Queens.** Illustrated by Dayal Kaur Khalsa. Clarkson N. Potter, 1989. ISBN 0-517-57126-9. 32p. 6–9.

When Mrs. Pelligrino comes to visit from Italy, she seems sad and lonely most of the time. It's evident that she misses pizza, but no one knows who or what pizza is, and Mrs. Pelligrino doesn't know enough English to explain. Then, after Penny and May do their "homework" at the library, they buy pizza ingredients for Mrs. Pelligrino, and everyone is a winner. Mrs. Pelligrino is happy to cook her favorite food, and an entire American neighborhood discovers a new and exciting dish. Paintings are brilliantly colored, folk-art simple, and 1950s-innocent.

5.55   Kimmelman, Leslie. **Frannie's Fruits.** Illustrated by Petra Mathers. Harper and Row, 1989. ISBN 0-06-023164-5. 32p. 5–7 (est.).

A rural summertime fruit, vegetable, and flower stand near the beach serves as the setting for a day-in-the-life story of an elementary-school girl and her dog. The girl helps her family by doing chores at the stand, where she learns about a range of shoppers and their preferences. Playful, childlike paintings match the story. *Notable 1989 Children's Trade Books in the Field of Social Studies.*

5.56   Konigsburg, E. L. **Amy Elizabeth Explores Bloomingdale's.** Illustrated by E. L. Konigsburg. Atheneum/Jean Karl Books, 1992. ISBN 0-689-31766-2. 32p. 4–8 (est.).

On pages as yellow as New York taxis, and border-checked to boot, Amy Elizabeth from Houston visits her grandmother in New York. With straight-faced charm, Amy Elizabeth makes observations on the Big Apple, comparing its attributes with her home town: "In Houston, people who have pets don't have pooper-scoopers because they have lawns." All during their event-packed visit, Grandmother promises a trip to Bloomingdale's, but they never quite make it. It was, according to Amy, "an excellent time not getting there."

5.57   Maestro, Betsy. **Snow Day.** Illustrated by Giulio Maestro. Scholastic Hardcover Books, 1989. ISBN 0-590-41283-3. 32p. 4–8 (est.).

Gray snow skies and snow smells signal the approaching storm. Dry brush strokes spread the snowfall across the pages. After the storm, the town is "white and still . . . , buried in deep drifts that cover the roads and sidewalks." Even though the children get to sled and build snowpeople, there is plenty of work for adults as the community digs out. Snow colors juxtapose against the orange-reds and yellow-greens of snow-removal equipment turning quiet stillness into action.

5.58   Merriam, Eve. **The Wise Woman and Her Secret.** Illustrated by Linda Graves. Simon and Schuster Books for Young Readers, 1991. ISBN 0-671-72603-X. 32p. 6–10 (est.).

When villagers seek an explanation for the wisdom of the old woman who lives in the hills, she invites them to discover the secret for themselves. They search her barn, test her well, and pull at the branches of her tree—all except Jenny, who gathers pebbles on the pathway, delights in a spider's web, and examines a penny drawn from the well. When Jenny shares the penny with the old woman and asks a string of questions, the secret of wisdom is revealed—to be curious, "to keep on wandering and wondering."

5.59   Miller, Jim Wayne. **Newfound.** Orchard Books/Richard Jackson Books, 1989. ISBN 0-531-05845-X. 256p. 12 and up.

Newfound chronicles the adolescence of Robert Wells in rural Tennessee. After his parents peacefully separate, Robert begins exploring his family history as well as the Appalachian countryside. He becomes closer to both sets of grandparents (who coexist on the same farm), watches his mother become more independent, goes coon hunting, and finds a girlfriend. An honest account of the pain and tension, as well as the love, which characterize a rather unusual extended family.

5.60   Nabb, Magdalen. **Josie Smith.** Illustrated by Pirkko Vainio. Margaret K. McElderry Books, 1989. ISBN 0-689-50485-3. 72p. 6–8 (est.).

First published in England, this book presents three misadventures of an enterprising young child, Josie Smith, who lives alone with her mother. In the first chapter, Josie must find a way to buy her mother birthday flowers with no money. Other story chapters find Josie painting a chalkboard but forgetting to protect her room from splatters, and adopting a cat who doesn't need a home. Child characters are direct with one another, and Briticisms add interest to the discourse.

5.61   Paulsen, Gary. **The Winter Room.** Orchard Books, 1989. ISBN 0-531-08439-6. 103p. 11 and up.

Gary Paulsen's earthy description of sights, sounds, and smells guide a tour through the seasons on a remote northern Minnesota farm during the 1930s. Eldon, the narrator, lives and works with his older brother Wayne, an eighth grader, his parents, and two elderly Norwegians, Nels and Uncle David. Their home's "winter room" is the setting for woodcarving, knitting, tobacco chewing, and, especially, storytelling during bitter cold and dark months. *Newbery Honor Book, 1990.*

5.62   Pfeffer, Susan Beth. **Dear Dad, Love Laurie.** Illustrated by Susan Beth Pfeffer. Scholastic Hardcover Books, 1989. ISBN 0-590-41681-2. 120p. 8–12 (est.).

This book, written entirely in the form of weekly letters from Laurie to her divorced father in Missouri, describes a young girl's highs and lows during sixth grade. In the course of one year, Laurie encounters new friends, disastrous birthday parties, fights with her mother, and loving reconciliations. The book is a good companion piece to Beverly Cleary's Newbery award-winning *Dear Mr. Henshaw.*

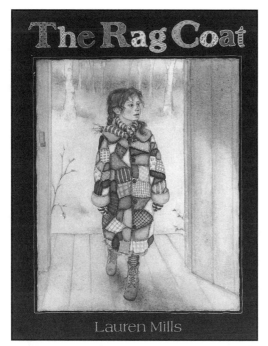

A.

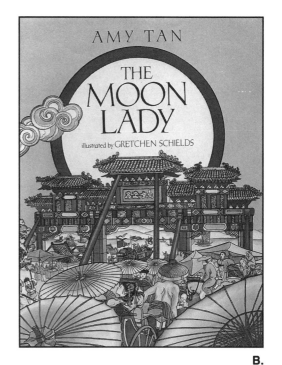

B.

C.

D.

A. *The Rag Coat* by Lauren Mills (see 5.123). **B.** *The Moon Lady* by Amy Tan; illustrated by Gretchen Schields (see 5.140). **C.** *Weird Parents* by Audrey Wood (see 5.146). **D.** *The Grandpa Days* by Joan W. Blos; illustrated by Emily Arnold McCully (see 5.75).

A.

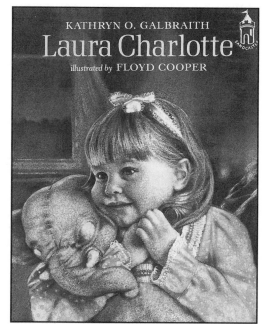

B.

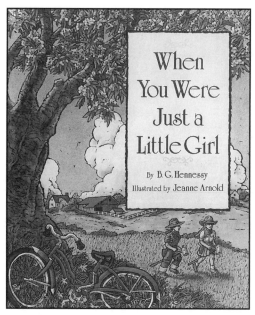

C.

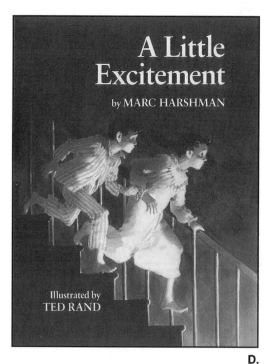

D.

A. *Go Fish* by Mary Stoltz; illustrated by Pat Cummings (see 5.139). **B.** *Laura Charlotte* by Kathryn O. Galbraith; illustrated by Floyd Cooper (see 5.93). **C.** *When You Were Just a Little Girl* by B. G. Hennessy; illustrated by Jeanne Arnold (see 5.102). **D.** *A Little Excitement* by Marc Harshman; illustrated by Ted Rand (see 5.99).

5.63 Rylant, Cynthia. **Appalachia: The Voices of Sleeping Birds.** Illustrated by Barry Moser. Harcourt Brace Jovanovich, 1991. ISBN 0-15-201605-8. 32p. 5 and up.

Through Cynthia Rylant, a native of West Virginia, and Barry Moser, of Tennessee, readers gain "from the inside" a sense of place and the people who live there. Lines from James Agee— "All my people are larger bodies than mine, quiet, with voices gentle and meaningless like the voices of sleeping birds"—inspire the title. Broad margins surround double-page spreads, with blocks of text facing transparent watercolors. *Boston Globe– Horn Book Nonfiction Award, 1991.*

5.64 Wilson, Budge. **The Leaving, and Other Stories.** Philomel Books, 1990. ISBN 0-399-21878-5. 207p. 11 and up.

In this collection of short stories, nine young women come of age in the Canadian province of Nova Scotia. Told with sensitivity, the stories delve into the conflicts that help mold each young woman. In the title story, a young narrator accompanies her mother on a brief journey to Halifax. The mother's temporary escape from husband and home changes the relations between the girl's parents, making home life more palatable. These are graceful tales marked by their subtlety. *Canadian Library Association's Young Adult Book Award, 1991.*

Family Life

5.65 Ackerman, Karen. **Just like Max.** Illustrated by George Schmidt. Alfred A. Knopf/Borzoi Books, 1990. ISBN 0-394-90176-2. 32p. 4–8 (est.).

All day long, Great-Uncle Max works on suits and dresses "for the fancy folk," while seven-year-old Aaron watches. When Max has a stroke and can no longer work, Aaron brings him cheer by making a dress, using the skills that he has learned from observing Max. Years later, it is Uncle Aaron, living in the same brownstone above his sister's family, who shows his nephew *his* craft— writing. Soft, pastel illustrations create a quiet mood for this tender story of an extended family.

5.66 Ackerman, Karen. **Song and Dance Man.** Illustrated by Stephen Gammell. Alfred A. Knopf/Dragonfly Books, 1992. ISBN 0-679-81995-9. 32p. All ages (est.).

The "good old days, the song and dance days" were when Grandpa appeared on the vaudeville stage. But the present is good, too, as Grandpa takes his three grandchildren to the attic, opens an old trunk, dons hat and cane, and joyfully reenacts his younger days. Stephen Gammell's award-winning colored-pencil illustrations—a blaze of light and color—keep readers mindful of advancing years. *Caldecott Medal, 1989; ALA Notable Children's Books, 1988.*

5.67   Addy, Sharon Hart. **A Visit with Great-Grandma.** Illustrated by Lydia Halverson. Albert Whitman, 1989. ISBN 0-8075-8497-5. 32p. 4–8 (est.).

A little girl visits her great-grandmother who came to America from Czechoslovakia. Even though Great-Grandma speaks little English, her relationship with Barbara is full of communication—especially when they make kolaches together. The two agree that they listen with their hearts. From the photographs and mementos in her apartment, Great-Grandma shares words from stories of long ago. Illustrations are quiet and loving, traveling across space and time when Great-Grandma remembers. A recipe for kolaches is included.

5.68   Adler, C. S. **One Sister Too Many.** Macmillan, 1989. ISBN 0-02-700271-3. 162p. 10–12 (est.).

While trying to adjust to a new family and approaching adolescence, the outspoken, impulsive twelve-year-old Case tries everyone's patience. When a new sitter begins to take care of her baby sister, Meredith, only Case is suspicious. Why does this sitter let people believe that Meredith is her own baby? Why does the sitter insist that Case can't love her new baby sister? When baby Meredith is missing one afternoon, the answers become clear. Middle-grade readers will cheer when Case solves the mystery and saves the day in this sequel to *Split Sisters.*

5.69   Anderson, Lena. **Stina.** Illustrated by Lena Anderson. Greenwillow Books, 1989. ISBN 0-688-08881-3. 32p. 4–8 (est.).

Stina loves her summer visits with her grandfather, who lives by the seashore. While Grandpa fishes for perch and flounder, Stina finds feathers, smooth sticks, and other cherished collectibles. Then, during a "real blow," Stina's curiosity leads her outside to see the storm. Rescued by Grandpa, Stina observes the storm with her grandfather and relishes the treasures that it brings. Lena Anderson's gentle characters are softly portrayed in watercolor.

5.70   Anderson, Lena. **Stina's Visit.** Illustrated by Lena Anderson. Greenwillow Books, 1991. ISBN 0-688-09666-2. 32p. 4–8 (est.).

The summer that Stina spends with her grandfather on his tiny island is the kind that feeds the warmest of memories. But the most interesting of all Lena's experiences is a birthday visit to meet her grandfather's somewhat eccentric friend, who has a wonderfully vivid imagination.

5.71   Auch, Mary Jane. **Mom Is Dating Weird Wayne.** Bantam/Skylark Books, 1991. ISBN 0-553-15916-X. 146p. 8–12.

Things haven't been the same at Jenna's house since Dad left and married Gladys, "the Vanna White of the recreational vehicle industry." Jenna's artistic, creative mom can't seem to keep a normal job. And six-year-old Corey has become fearful and shy. Jenna's best friend, Molly, is certain that everything could be solved if Mrs. Bartholomew would just marry the new math teacher. Instead, Mom meets the television weatherman—Wacky Wayne. Would things be in such a state if Dad were home?

5.72   Barrett, Joyce Durham. **Willie's Not the Hugging Kind.** Illustrated by Pat Cummings. Harper and Row, 1989. ISBN 0-06-020417-6. 32p. 5–8.

Willie liked hugging until his best friend told him that hugging was silly. Now it seems that hugging is everywhere— his teacher hugs the children; his sister hugs her bear; his daddy hugs his mother—but no one hugs Willie anymore. "Willie," says his sister, "you're just not the hugging kind. . . ," but Willie misses hugs, and hugging trees and bath towels doesn't really work because those things don't hug back. Pat Cummings's brightly colored details and caramel-perfect faces translate the story's warmth and security.

5.73   Bawden, Nina. **The Outside Child.** Lothrop, Lee and Shepard Books. ISBN 0-688-08965-8. 232p. 9–12 (est.).

In this novel set in England, thirteen-year-old Jane lives with her two eccentric and loving aunts, Sophie and Bill, short for Wilhemina. Her mother died when Jane was young, and her father is a sailor. After discovering that her father remarried ten years earlier, Jane, with the help of her best friend, Plato, learns more about her half-brother and half-sister, who live only a bus ride away. She wins their friendship before revealing her identity and comes to the realization that her place is with her aunts.

5.74   Blake, Robert J. **The Perfect Spot.** Illustrated by Robert J. Blake. Philomel Books, 1992. ISBN 0-399-22132-8. 32p. 4 and up.

For the artist father, the perfect spot is where light and shadows, trees and rocks inspire a painting. For the naturalist son, a perfect spot is where frogs, crickets, beetles, and salamanders beg to be caught. Together, each with his own equipment, father and son hike the woods looking for the perfect spot. Also together, and quite by accident, they find the perfect spot for both their pursuits. Robert Blake's watercolor paintings capture the forest trek.

5.75   Blos, Joan W. **The Grandpa Days.** Illustrated by Emily Arnold McCully. Simon and Schuster Books for Young Readers, 1989. ISBN 0-671-64640-0. 22p. 3–7.

When Philip visits his grandfather for a week, he discovers that Grandpa once built a treehouse from special drawings. Philip then draws his own plans, but learns that it's not possible to make his requested rocket ships and racing cars with Grandpa's carpenter tools. Finally, Philip designs something they *can* make, and together they hammer, paint, and drill to build a new sled. Pastel watercolors add warmth and detail to the pen-and-ink line drawings, which capture subtle gesture.

5.76   Bonners, Susan. **The Wooden Doll.** Illustrated by Susan Bonners. Lothrop, Lee and Shepard Books, 1991. ISBN 0-688-08282-3. 32p. 5–8.

Although Stephanie enjoys visiting her grandparents, she is disappointed that her immigrant grandfather keeps his wooden doll out of reach. When the chance arises, she brings it down from the top of the china cabinet and finds a family of smaller dolls nested inside and the name "Stephania" written underneath. Stephanie learns that the doll belonged to her great-grandmother in Poland and that her grandfather has been keeping the doll until Stephanie is old enough to treasure it herself. Homey, warm paintings portray family love.

5.77   Booth, Barbara D. **Mandy.** Illustrated by Jim LaMarche. Lothrop, Lee and Shepard Books, 1991. ISBN 0-688-10339-1. 32p. 6 and up.

Overcoming her fear of the dark, Mandy sets out to find her grandmother's treasured pin that was lost during their earlier walk. Barbara Booth's text deals knowledgeably and sensitively with issues related to deafness, while portraying Mandy as a strong, determined character. The full-page illustrations express the deep relationship between Mandy and her grandmother by focusing on the unspoken understanding between them. Rich pinks and purples dramatize the events and show the world from Mandy's point of view.

5.78 Bourgeois, Paulette. **Big Sarah's Little Boots.** Illustrated by Brenda Clark. Scholastic Hardcover Books, 1989. ISBN 0-590-42622-2. 32p. 3–6.

One rainy day Sarah discovers that her favorite boots no longer fit. Her mother explains that Sarah has grown, an explanation that Sarah rejects. Convinced that the boots have shrunk, Sarah tries every possible way to stretch them. Eventually, though, with the help of her understanding mother, Sarah realizes that new and bigger boots may actually be better than her favorite old ones. Sarah's expressions from total frustration to pure joy are perfectly childlike.

5.79 Brandenberg, Franz. **Aunt Nina, Good Night.** Illustrated by Aliki. Greenwillow Books, 1989. ISBN 0-688-07464-2. 32p. 2–6 (est.).

Husband and wife team Franz Brandenberg and Aliki continue the Aunt Nina series with a colorful and appealing story. Reminiscent of Frances's antics in Russell Hoban's *Bedtime for Frances,* Nina's nephews and nieces devise a series of excuses for not going to bed, excuses that their Aunt Nina handles adeptly. Bright, distinctive watercolor illustrations capture the energy of the characters and make the book perfect for younger readers and listeners.

5.80 Brooks, Bruce. **What Hearts.** HarperCollins/Laura Geringer Books, 1992. ISBN 0-06-021132-6. 194p. 10 and up.

Bruce Brooks presents a young boy at four junctures in his life, each of which requires that he be smart and forgiving in order to survive his changed world. At age seven, Asa is suddenly uprooted because of divorce, moves with his mother to a new state, and meets Dave, his mother's future husband. At age nine, he faces difficult decisions at school; at eleven, challenges involve baseball; and at twelve, love. In all, he survives tests of both head and heart. *Newbery Honor Book, 1993; ALA Notable Children's Books, 1993.*

5.81 Bunting, Eve. **Sharing Susan.** HarperCollins, 1991. ISBN 0-06-021694-8. 122p. 10–12 (est.).

Susan Moretti and her best friend Clemmie call it the "Big Worry." Something is definitely wrong in Susan's normally secure home. Her parents stop talking when she enters the room, her mom is constantly teary, and her dad is strained. The truth, when it emerges, is devastating: because of a hospital mix-up when she was born, Susan may not be her parents' child. Eve Bunting effectively captures Susan's horror and overwhelming confusion as two families pick through emotions to share the sole surviving daughter—Susan.

5.82   Bunting, Eve. **The Wednesday Surprise.** Illustrated by Donald Carrick. Clarion Books, 1989. ISBN 0-89919-721-3. 32p. 5–8 (est.).

When Grandmother comes to sit on Wednesdays, she always brings a big bag of books. Then she and seven-year-old Anna huddle over the books, heads together on the sofa, preparing for Papa's birthday surprise. Touchingly warm, but unsentimental, the story's surprise is withheld from the reader until the end, where it guarantees meaty discussion. Donald Carrick's illustrations are softly rendered in diffused light and shadows.

5.83   Carson, Jo. **Pulling My Leg.** Illustrated by Julie Downing. Orchard Books/Richard Jackson Books, 1990. ISBN 0-531-08417-5. 32p. 4–8 (est.).

When a little girl's loose tooth interferes with eating a pork chop, Uncle Tom declares it's time for an "ex-trac-tion." As Uncle Tom sends for the necessary implements—pliers, hammer, screwdriver, crowbar—the little girl isn't sure whether her uncle is trying to pull her tooth or her leg. The cheerful colored-pencil drawings add just the right touches of energy and humor to this delightful story.

5.84   Caseley, Judith. **The Cousins.** Illustrated by Judith Caseley. Greenwillow Books, 1990. ISBN 0-688-08434-6. 24p. 4 and up.

Jenny and Jessica are first cousins. They don't look a bit alike, and they don't act a bit alike. When they were toddlers, Jenny liked to finger-paint; Jessica liked to knock down block houses. Later, Jessica loved ballet lessons; Jenny preferred arts-and-crafts class. The girls are as opposite as can be—chalk and cheese, night and day. This is a celebration of individuality enriched by humorously stylized watercolor and colored-pencil art.

5.85   Caseley, Judith. **Dear Annie.** Illustrated by Judith Caseley. Greenwillow Books, 1991. ISBN 0-688-10011-2. 32p. 4 and up.

In a book to inspire classroom correspondence, Judith Caseley tells of Annie, whose correspondence with her grandpa began with her birth, when she would ride to the mailbox in a baby carrier. Now in school and able to reach the box herself, Annie has a shoe box with over one hundred treasured cards and notes from Grandpa for show-and-tell, all simple testaments to their affection. The text is composed almost entirely of Annie's correspondence to and from Grandpa, and the illustrations are rendered in watercolors and colored pencils.

5.86   Caseley, Judith. **The Noisemakers.** Illustrated by Judith Caseley. Greenwillow Books, 1992. ISBN 0-688-09395-7. 24p. 4 and up.

Young Sam and Laura love to growl, roar, and be boisterous. On an outing, the two friends cause trouble at a library, a restaurant, and a shopping mall, much to the chagrin of their mothers. The outing finally ends at a spot where noisemakers can do what they do best, and their mothers will think they are wonderful. Vivid watercolor and colored-pencil illustrations offer interesting patterns and details and depict quite typical children.

5.87   Cohen, Barbara. **The Long Way Home.** Illustrated by Diane de Groat. Lothrop, Lee and Shepard Books, 1990. ISBN 0-688-09674-3. 160p. 10 and up.

Because of their mother's chemotherapy, big changes have occurred in the lives of ten-year-old twins Sally and Emily. Instead of vacationing at the beach, they must attend day camp, where they are separated. Of the two, Sally has the most trouble feeling positive about anything, until she gains the friendship of the lovable but flaky bus driver, Claire. With Claire's help, Sally learns to confront her true feelings and conflicting emotions regarding her mother's illness.

5.88   Collier, James Lincoln. **The Winchesters.** Avon/Flare Books, 1989. ISBN 0-380-70808-6. 169p. 10 and up (est.).

Chris Winchester and his family are the "poor relatives" in the wealthy Winchester clan of New England. Chris's grandfather owns the town's major business, the mill, where dissatisfied workers are ready to go on strike. Chris is never really accepted by either his rich relatives or the town's blue-collar families. Ultimately, the teenager learns that happiness comes with being true to oneself, rather than trying to comply with the dictates of others. *Oklahoma Sequoyah Young Adult Book Award.*

5.89   Collins, Pat Lowery. **Taking Care of Tucker.** Illustrated by Maxie Chambliss. G. P. Putnam's Sons, 1989. ISBN 0-399-21586-7. 26p. 2–7.

Millie's aunt and uncle are taking a trip, and three-year-old cousin Tucker is coming to stay with Millie's family. Millie knows that she'll do a great job caring for Tucker, but homesick little Tucker does not cooperate. He cries, he kicks, he bites, he spits, and he screams. Finally, as Millie begins to despair, she discovers just the way to handle Tucker. Cartoon-like ink drawings filled in with bright watercolors add to the delight that readers will take in Tucker's mischief.

5.90   DeClements, Barthe. **Breaking Out.** Delacorte Press, 1991. ISBN 0-385-30503-6. 130p. 9–12.

It's not easy having your dad in prison, and it's even worse if some of your friends watched him get arrested. In this third book in a series, Bart DeClements deals with thirteen-year-old Jerry's simultaneous struggles to be accepted and to be true to his own unique strengths. While he comes to terms with his dad's talents and the judgments of friends, next-door neighbor Grace wrestles for her own kind of independence in this sequel to *Five-Finger Discount* and *Monkey See, Monkey Do.*

5.91   Delaney, Molly. **My Sister.** Illustrated by Molly Delaney. Atheneum, 1989. ISBN 0-689-31460-4. 32p. 4–8 (est.).

A little girl knows all too well what it means to be the younger sister—hand-me-downs, teasing, and a chance to lick the spoon (only when it's been used for mud pies). But that's only part of the story. This little sister also admits that when push comes to shove, it's mighty nice to have a big sister.

5.92   Dionetti, Michelle. **Coal Mine Peaches.** Illustrated by Anita Riggio. Orchard Books, 1991. ISBN 0-531-08548-1. 32p. 4–7.

Hard work was always part of Grandfather's life, but so was storytelling. As a boy in the coal mines, Grandfather entertained his brothers with stories. As a young man in New York City, he told stories to the men with whom he worked building the Brooklyn Bridge and to the young woman who was to become his wife. As Grandfather moved through life, in Italy and in America, he continued to enrich the lives of his children and grandchildren telling his stories and theirs. Muted watercolors capture the warmth of Grandfather's storytelling tradition.

5.93   Galbraith, Kathryn O. **Laura Charlotte.** Illustrations by Floyd Cooper. Philomel Books, 1990. ISBN 0-399-21613-8. 32p. 4–8.

Laura Charlotte can't sleep, so she asks her mother for her favorite bedtime story—the tale of how Charlotte the elephant came to be hers. Long ago when Laura's mother turned five, her grandmother sent her a gray flannel elephant, stitched from scraps. Laura's mother lovingly tells of Charlotte's importance in her own life and how she packed the elephant away to await her own little girl. Full-color paintings provide nostalgic impressions of the mother's childhood.

5.94   Garland, Sarah. **Polly's Puffin.** Illustrated by Sarah Garland. Greenwillow Books, 1989. ISBN 0-688-08749-3. 24p. 3–6.

Having a baby brother, one who tosses everything from his stroller, can be a real problem—especially if you're the big sister, Polly, and the baby has tossed your very own toy puffin into the coat hood of a stranger sitting nearby. But with an understanding mom and a hectic chase, things are put in order. The baby's antics in the cheerful illustrations offset the anxiety of a lost favorite possession.

5.95   Gauch, Patricia Lee. **Dance, Tanya.** Illustrated by Satomi Ichikawa. Philomel Books, 1989. ISBN 0-399-21521-2. 28p. 4–8.

The soft pink and yellow casts of the watercolors convey the warm, loving sentiment of a little girl's wish to be a ballet dancer like her sister. Tanya's toddler-like dance is performed in her underwear, as she trips and sprawls in her attempts to mime both her sister's costume and graceful ballet positions. More than anything, Tanya wants to take ballet lessons, too. After her sister's recital, sleepy Tanya rouses herself to dance exuberantly for the family. Soon, there are lessons for Tanya, too.

5.96   Godden, Rumer. **Listen to the Nightingale.** Viking Penguin, 1992. ISBN 0-670-84517-5. 198p. 7–11.

The rarified world of a London ballet school surrounds ten-year-old Lottie, an orphan reared by the school's costume mistress. When not in class, Lottie copes with an unusually humble home life, friends and adversaries, her adored puppy, Prince, and the exotic Italian family who adopt the dog when Lottie must give him up. Mindful of Noel Streatfeild's classic, *Ballet Shoes*, and with the same unhurried detail, the story winds through numerous challenges before reaching a comforting finale.

5.97   Greenwald, Sheila. **Rosy Cole Discovers America!** Illustrated by Sheila Greenwald. Little, Brown/Joy Street Books, 1992. ISBN 0-316-32721-2. 96p. 7–11 (est.).

Rosy is ashamed of her humdrum family background so she invents a more interesting past for the Columbus Day class project. Everyone must dress as one of their great-grandparents, and only last-minute honesty brings the truth tumbling out, as Rosy finds pride in ancestors who boasted neither riches nor suffering.

5.98   Halak, Glenn. **A Grandmother's Story.** Illustrated by Glenn Halak. Simon and Schuster/Green Tiger Press, 1992. ISBN 0-671-74953-6. 32p. 3–8 (est.).

"There was an old woman who rowed out to sea. / Her neighbors all thought she was mad as could be." In rhythmic verse, a grandmother inexplicably keeps rowing until she "arrived where she knew she must be," and rescues her grandson from drowning. Paintings are as economical as the verse, rendered in primitive style and bold colors, with only the grandmother's broad back visible to the onlooker. Testifying to the bonds of the heart and to miracles, the message of this rhyming story may be best suited for late primary graders.

5.99   Harshman, Marc. **A Little Excitement.** Illustrated by Ted Rand. Cobblehill Books, 1989. ISBN 0-525-65001-6. 32p. 4–8 (est.).

In dramatic testimony to the theme of being careful about making wishes, a farm family battles a chimney fire soon after bored young Willie wishes for a little excitement in his life. Ted Rand achieves dramatic contrasts in scenes of blazing heat against a snow-covered world. Family and neighbors band together toward a common end, and narrator Willie gains appreciation for some new friends—his brave sisters.

5.100   Haynes, Mary. **Catch the Sea.** Bradbury Press, 1989. ISBN 0-02-743451-6. 172p. 9 and up.

Thirteen-year-old Lily wishes she had as much artistic talent as either of her divorced parents. After her father is called away unexpectedly, Lily remains at their family beach house trying out her own artwork on one of her father's patrons. Learning to cope on her own and the heady acceptance of her art make Lily more confident to begin the next year.

5.101   Henkes, Kevin. **Shhhh.** Illustrated by Kevin Henkes. Greenwillow Books, 1989. ISBN 0-688-07986-5. 32p. 3–6 (est.).

Every family needs an alarm clock. In this family, a tousled child serves well. When "Everything is quiet. / Everyone is sleeping,"—Bear, Bunny, cat, dog, baby, and Mama and Papa—then "SHHHH," it's time for the early-rising child to reach for her horn and "WAKE THEM ALL UP!" Kevin Henke's acrylics allow the canvas to give texture to the warm-colored, full-paged scenes.

5.102   Hennessy, B. G. **When You Were Just a Little Girl.** Illustrated by Jeanne Arnold. Viking Penguin, 1991. ISBN 0-670-82998-6. 32p. 3–8.

When Grandma was a little girl, birthday cakes were just as sweet, the same moon shone in the sky at night, and Christmas was the best time of the year. In a nostalgic view of a simpler time, Grandma, in rhyming text, shares her memories of childhood with two grandchildren who ask that she sit and talk for a while. Wooden blocks, cookie cutters, and paper chains are art elements that border old-fashioned images.

5.103   Hoban, Julia. **Amy Loves the Rain.** Illustrated by Lillian Hoban. Harper and Row, 1989. ISBN 0-06-022358-8. 20p. 3–5 (est.).

In one of four "Amy" stories, Julia Hoban offers preschoolers the comfort of the familiar—a ride in the carseat on a rainy day to pick up Daddy. Amy notices the sounds and colors of a rainy day, the "swish swak of the wipers," the "splash, plash of puddles," and the "black and shiny streets." Best of all, Amy has brought an umbrella to share with Daddy, who has forgotten his. Pastel chalks offer the muted tones of a rainy day.

5.104   Hughes, Dean. **Family Pose.** Atheneum, 1989. ISBN 0-689-31396-9. 184p. 9 and up.

Eleven-year-old David, in search of a new life and a new beginning in the warmth and promise of California, abandons his unhappy home life. Trying to survive on the street, David—cold, hungry, and friendless—meets Paul, a hotel bellboy who risks his job by letting David sleep in a vacant room. Paul sees something of himself in David, and, in time, they discover together the meaning of human commitment. *Notable 1989 Children's Trade Books in the Field of Social Studies.*

5.105   Hughes, Shirley. **Angel Mae: A Tale of Trotter Street.** Illustrated by Shirley Hughes. Mulberry Books, 1992. ISBN 0-688-11847-X. 32p. 4 and up.

Anticipating the birth of a new baby at home, Mae has another source of excitement at school—the upcoming Christmas pageant. Even though she's a little out of sorts with her mother's weariness, Mae lands the part of the Angel Gabriel (which she pronounces "Gave-you"). New baby and the pageant occur simultaneously, but Dad attends both debuts. Mae is pixie perfect, with strands of loose hair escaping her pig tails, tiny wire glasses, and expressive face.

5.106   Hughes, Shirley. **The Big Alfie Out of Doors Storybook.** Illustrated by Shirley Hughes. Lothrop, Lee and Shepard Books, 1992. ISBN 0-688-11428-8. 64p. 3 and up.

In yet another book featuring the lively and inquisitive preschooler named Alfie, four stories are told. Each describes a warm and loving family outing, and each is followed by a poem about everyday experience. The book glows from beginning to end with its irresistible paintings of children in their natural surroundings.

5.107   Hurwitz, Johanna. **Aldo Peanut Butter.** Illustrated by Diane de Groat. Morrow Junior Books, 1990. ISBN 0-688-09751-0. 113p. 8–11 (est.).

In this sequel to *Aldo Applesauce*, eleven-year-old Aldo's new puppies, Peanut and Butter, are the catalysts for the hilarious jams in which Aldo and his sisters find themselves: nocturnal destruction of a neighbor's lawn, lobsters on the loose, and even green hair. Short paragraphs, full of true-to-life dialogue, make the text exceptionally readable.

5.108   Hurwitz, Johanna. **"E" Is for Elisa.** Illustrated by Lillian Hoban. Morrow Junior Books, 1991. ISBN 0-688-10440-1. 86p. 8–12 (est.).

Four-year-old Elisa wants more than anything else to be as grown-up as her brother, eight-year-old Russell. There are snags along the way. Elisa still cries a lot and about a lot of things, but she does manage some giant steps toward growing up. For instance, she learns to keep a secret and knows that the letters of her name (Elisa M) spell: "A Smile." Lillian Hoban's illustrations for this fifth in a series about Russell, Elisa, and their family are warm and appealing.

5.109   Hurwitz, Johanna. **Roz and Ozzie.** Illustrated by Eileen McKeating. Morrow Junior Books, 1992. ISBN 0-688-10945-4. 128p. 7–10 (est.).

At eight going on nine and the new girl in school, Rosalind Sasser thinks that the last person she needs following her around is her second-grade neighbor, Ozzie. Worse still, Ozzie is her uncle, and he doesn't keep that information to himself. Although he is a nuisance and a bit of an embarrassment with his puppy-like traits, Ozzie's fierce loyalty and devotion win Roz's acceptance, and compromise is achieved in this chapter book for young readers.

5.110 Hurwitz, Johanna. **Russell and Elisa.** Illustrated by Lillian Hoban. Morrow Junior Books, 1989. ISBN 0-688-08793-0. 88p. 8–13 (est.).

Little sister Elisa, now nearly four years old, comes to the forefront in this fourth book about Russell and his family. Each of the six stand-alone chapters, peppered with Lillian Hoban's doe-eyed sketches of the children's predicaments, makes for an effective read-aloud. Elisa, for example, gets trapped under the dining table during a dinner party. Russell typically meets the events of Elisa's day with "Big deal" and "So What," but he pitches in like a pro to comfort Elisa when her doll Airmail is left overnight in the library.

5.111 Hutchins, Pat. **Tidy Titch.** Illustrated by Pat Hutchins. Greenwillow Books, 1991. ISBN 0-688-09964-5. 32p. 4–7 (est.).

Youngest child Titch keeps his room tidiest of all. Says Mother to Peter and Mary, "How tidy Titch's room is . . . and how messy your rooms are. I think you should tidy them up." So Peter and Mary dig in, and Titch offers to help. Soon castoff games, toys, books, costumes, and hats are adopted by Titch, resulting in two tidy rooms and one very satisfied Titch at play in a cascading jumble. The repetitive phrase for reading along is, "I'll have them."

5.112 Johnson, Angela. **The Leaving Morning.** Illustrated by David Soman. Orchard Books/Richard Jackson Books, 1992. ISBN 0-531-08592-9. 32p. 4–7.

"Leavings" happen. A young African American narrator and his sister say wistful good-byes to the familiar in their lives and then leave "lips" on the windows of their apartment on moving day. Through one of childhood's unsettling experiences, the narrator recalls the comfort and warmth of his neighborhood and building, but also his daddy's promise that "in a little while we'd be someplace we'd love." David Soman's watercolors are both bustling impressions of urban life and reflections of quiet faces.

5.113   Johnson, Angela. **One of Three.** Illustrated by David Soman. Orchard Books, 1991. ISBN 0-531-08555-4. 32p. 3–6.

They are three together—Eva, Nikki, and "me," the youngest sister and the narrator. They walk to school together, sit together outside the bakery to look and smell, and on snowy days they squeeze into a taxi together with Mama, Grandma, and Aunt Sara. But sometimes, Nikki and Eva go alone, and "I'm left behind. Not one of three, just one." It's then that the youngest child turns to someone else—Daddy and Mama—"and that's fine, too." David Soman provides an urban background for a loving African American family.

5.114   Johnson, Angela. **Tell Me a Story, Mama.** Illustrated by David Soman. Orchard Books/Richard Jackson Books, 1989. ISBN 0-531-08394-2. 28p. 3–6.

A five-year-old African American girl asks her mother to tell her stories of the mother's childhood. The girl knows the stories so well, however, that she actually ends up telling them to the mother. The words form a dialogue between mother and child, while the watercolor art depicts various family members involved in the stories. This gentle tale about parent-child relations illustrates how the culture and stories of the family are passed from generation to generation.

5.115   Johnson, Angela. **When I Am Old with You.** Illustrated by David Soman. Orchard Books/Richard Jackson Books, 1990. ISBN 0-531-08484-1. 32p. 4–7.

A young African American child spends the day with his loving grandfather. As they talk and rock together on the porch, the boy promises that "when I am old with you, Grandaddy," the two of them will do all their favorite things together—fishing, walking, playing cards, riding the tractor, and having bacon, just bacon, for breakfast. Soft watercolors create tranquil scenes and quiet moments. *Coretta Scott King Honor Book (Illustration), 1991.*

5.116   Kherdian, David. **A Song for Uncle Harry.** Illustrated by Nonny Hogrogian. Philomel Books, 1989. ISBN 0-399-21895-5. 76p. 8–12.

To Petey, no one in the whole world is like Uncle Harry. For as long as the twelve-year-old boy can remember, their relationship has grown in mutual love and respect. Whether enjoying each other's company while fishing or collecting things, the bonds seem unchangeable. Then Petey discovers that Uncle Harry's heart holds some unshared plans. David Kherdian's Armenian characters understand one another in this 1930s story, and Petey comes to understand change and its relationship to love.

5.117 Lasky, Kathryn. **I Have an Aunt on Marlborough Street.** Illustrated by Susan Guevara. Macmillan, 1992. ISBN 0-02-751701-2. 31p. 6–10 (est.).

Phoebe visits her aunt, who is also named Phoebe, on Marlborough Street in Boston, where the sidewalks are brick and the houses touch shoulders. Together they make the everyday things about city life become opportunities for fantasy and enjoyment. The subtleties of the language and the softness and warmth of the watercolors provide a glimpse of their relationship as they experience all of the seasons together.

5.118 Lehrman, Robert. **Separations.** Viking Penguin, 1990. ISBN 0-670-81646-9. 224p. 10 and up.

An aspiring tennis player, Kim feels her comfortable life torn apart when her parents' divorce requires a move to Manhattan. Changes! New apartment . . . city school . . . Dad's fiancée . . . Mom's career . . . even a new tennis coach! But it is the mix of anger and love that Kim feels toward her dad that spurs a series of events which reunite the family emotionally, if not physically. All stages of grief over this family crisis are experienced through Kim's eyes.

5.119 Lyon, George Ella. **Basket.** Illustrated by Mary Szilagyi. Orchard Books/Richard Jackson Books, 1990. ISBN 0-531-08486-8. 32p. 4–7.

Grandmother's oak basket holds all the necessities of her family's life, when it is not full of plums or Christmas holly. But when Grandmother moves to the city, her basket becomes lost. From then on, the basket takes on the disproportionate capacity of memory. Whatever is missing, Grandmother is sure that it is in her basket. Colored-pencil and watercolor illustrations create a "yesterday" feel for this family history, told in a first-person account by the granddaughter.

5.120 Martin, Ann M. **Eleven Kids, One Summer.** Holiday House, 1991. ISBN 0-8234-0912-0. 152p. 8–12.

All thirteen members of the Rosso family—eleven children and two parents, plus a cat—rent a beach house on Fire Island for the summer. Alphabetically named, from fifteen-year-old Abigail to baby Keegan, the children each assume the central role in one chapter. Island adventures range from solving mysteries to meeting new kids to playing pranks to becoming movie extras. Sibling rivalry and birth order contribute to the conflicts and solutions.

5.121   Mazer, Norma Fox. **C, My Name Is Cal.** Scholastic Hardcover Books, 1990. ISBN 0-590-41833-5. 160p. 9–12.

Two adolescent boys, Garo without a mother and Cal without a father, are part of the unique "family" in this story. Cal's mother works as a housekeeper for Garo's father, whose job as an airline pilot often keeps him away from home. Cal, serious and hardworking, is the direct opposite of Garo, yet over the course of several years the boys forge a strong friendship, and together they unravel some of the mysteries and challenges of adolescence.

5.122   McKay, Hilary. **The Exiles.** Margaret K. McElderry Books, 1992. ISBN 0-689-50555-8. 217p. 10 and up (est.).

Four sisters—Ruth, Naomi, Rachel, and Phoebe—find themselves "exiles" when their parents decide to use an inheritance to remodel the kitchen. The summer of exile for the girls, whose ages range from six to thirteen, is spent with Big Grandma, who is as determined about child rearing as she is tall. First, Big Grandma believes in discipline, chores, and exercise. Second, she believes that the girls read too much, so she locks her books away. The girls' humor, despair, letters home, and country adventures are hilarious. *Guardian Children's Fiction Award, 1992.*

5.123   Mills, Lauren. **The Rag Coat.** Illustrated by Lauren Mills. Little, Brown, 1991. ISBN 0-316-57407-4. 28p. 4–8.

Inspired by the stories, songs, and crafts of the Appalachian region, and remembering a quilted coat that she herself wore, Lauren Mills uses watercolor and pencil drawings to tell the story of a child named Minna, daughter of a miner and a quiltmaker, who has no coat of her own. Even though it was her dying father's wish that Minna go to school, she can't go without a coat. Kindly neighbors, scrapbags, and stories of quilt pieces make for the warmest coat of all.

5.124   Murphy, Jill. **Worlds Apart.** G. P. Putnam's Sons, 1988. ISBN 0-399-21566-2. 127p. 10–13 (est.).

Although life in London with her mother is happy, eleven-year-old Susan launches a daring and secret quest to meet her natural father, whose life is "worlds apart" from her own. The plot is almost a cliché, yet Susan's lively narration and loving description of the adults in her life make the book enjoyable.

5.125   Oppenheim, Shulamith Levey. **Waiting for Noah.** Illustrated by Lillian Hoban. Harper and Row/Charlotte Zolotow Books, 1990. ISBN 0-06-024634-0. 32p. 4–7.

Noah loves to hear Nana tell the story of the day when he was born. On that day, Noah's daddy called to say Noah was about to be born, so Nana spent all day clipping raspberry bushes and shining pots, trying to keep busy as she waited for Noah. Bright, colorful pastel drawings depict Noah and Nana in their warm relationship, picking berries and reminiscing together.

5.126   Patterson, Nancy Ruth. **The Christmas Cup.** Illustrated by Leslie Bowman. Orchard Books, 1989. ISBN 0-531-08421-3. 80p. 8–10.

When eight-year-old Ann Megan McCallie spends her hard-earned money to buy a worthless old milkshake cup, her grandmother helps her understand its value. Using the cup as a bank during the year, Megan and Nannie decide the benefactor of the Christmas cup contents should be someone who has meant the most to them during the year. As Christmas approaches, Megan makes her decision and learns the true meaning of the season. Full-page black-and-white sketches capture the mood and spirit of this true-to-life story about family and giving. *Notable 1989 Children's Trade Books in the Field of Social Studies.*

5.127   Polacco, Patricia. **Thunder Cake.** Illustrated by Patricia Polacco. Philomel Books, 1990. ISBN 0-399-22231-6. 30p. 4–8.

Patricia Polacco reveals the magical way in which her Russian grandmother helped her lose her fear of thunder as a little girl. When a storm threatens on the horizon, Grandma observes that it's "Thunder Cake baking weather" and hastens to find ingredients as each clap of thunder and strike of lightning draws closer and closer. By the time the storm arrives, a delicious Thunder Cake is baked and a troublesome fear tamed. Colorful folk-art drawings lend the story an old-world mood.

5.128   Porte, Barbara Ann. **Taxicab Tales.** Illustrated by Yossi Abolafia. Greenwillow Books, 1992. ISBN 0-688-09908-4. 54p. 5 and up.

Abigail's father drives a taxi. After work, he tells Abigail and her brother Sam stories about his day, and their mother paints pictures of the stories. Sometimes Abigail thinks the stories are really true. In a warm, family-centered chapter book for young readers, Daddy tells of a famous actress who rode in his cab in disguise, of Wendell Wertzweiler who brought his goose for show-and-tell, and of the man with a donkey head. Black-and-white shaded sketches add to the fun.

5.129   Rice, Eve. **Peter's Pockets.** Illustrated by Nancy Winslow Parker. Greenwillow Books, 1989. ISBN 0-688-07242-9. 30p. 3–6 (est.).

One Saturday morning Peter and Uncle Nick go to the boat pond. Peter finds numerous things to collect, but his brand-new pants have no pockets, so the feather, ball, marble, and other objects must go into Uncle Nick's pockets. When they arrive home, Peter's mother sews six colorful pockets onto Peter's pants—one for each new treasure. Watercolor paints and colored pencils illustrate this satisfying story.

5.130   Richardson, John. **The Hiding Beast.** Illustrated by John Richardson. Houghton Mifflin, 1988. ISBN 0-395-49213-0. 29p. 5–8 (est.).

Rodney lives with his aunt in a very grand house, and every time poor Rodney tries to have some fun, Aunt Jacosta is nearby saying, "Don't, dear!" When Rodney is sent to the family library to "read a nice quiet book," he discovers instead a "brilliant" book about wild, hairy things. As Rodney's beast comes to life, John Richardson leaves the reader guessing. Is the beast real? Is it only Rodney's imagination? Is Aunt Jocasta playing a game with Rodney? Will the real hiding beast please stand up?

5.131   Roe, Eileen. **Staying with Grandma.** Illustrated by Jacqueline Rogers. Bradbury Press, 1989. ISBN 0-02-777371-X. 29p. 1–6.

A child describes a visit to Grandma's country house and all the fun to be had there. Favorite activities include running in the sprinkler, catching frogs, and using Grandma's bubble bath. The expressive watercolor and colored-pencil illustrations dominate the brief text and convey the special bond that can exist between the very young and the elderly. This is a book to reassure any small child who is left behind at Grandma's house when parents go out of town.

5.132 Russo, Marisabina. **A Visit to Oma.** Illustrated by Marisabina Russo. Greenwillow Books, 1991. ISBN 0-688-09624-7. 32p. 4 and up.

Every Sunday Celeste goes to visit her great-grandmother Oma. While Oma always tells Celeste stories in a language that she doesn't understand, this doesn't bother Celeste, who simply makes up a story to fit Oma's gestures and expressions. This Sunday the story that Celeste makes up is about Oma's bravery and independence in the face of an unwanted marriage arranged by her parents. In a story filled with warmth, Celeste's love for Oma easily overcomes the language barrier. Bold-colored illustrations are in folk-art style.

5.133 Russo, Marisabina. **Waiting for Hannah.** Illustrated by Marisabina Russo. Greenwillow Books, 1989. ISBN 0-688-08016-2. 32p. 4–7 (est.).

A little girl named Hannah asks her mother what she did while she waited for Hannah to be born. The answer to that question is the story of a long hot summer during which her mother went about her daily activities impatiently dreaming of the big day. The wait and the birth are documented in bordered, gouache folk-art illustrations.

5.134 Russo, Marisabina. **Where Is Ben?** Illustrated by Marisabina Russo. Greenwillow Books, 1990. ISBN 0-688-08013-8. 32p. 3 and up.

Although Ben's mother is busy rolling dough, peeling apples, and making crust for a pie, Ben keeps interrupting her work. "Mama, come find me," he says, and Ben's mother answers, "Where is Ben?" She then follows telltale clues—an upside-down laundry basket, a jumble of boots—to locate her hiding son. The repetitive lines in Mama and Ben's hide-and-seek game will encourage young children to read along. Marisabina Russo's chunky gouache paintings fill right-hand pages; bold text appears on the left.

5.135 Rylant, Cynthia. **Henry and Mudge and the Forever Sea: The Sixth Book of Their Adventures.** Illustrated by Suçie Stevenson. Bradbury Press, 1989. ISBN 0-02-778007-4. 48p. 6–8.

When Henry and his father take Henry's dog, Mudge, to the beach for the first time, they spend a perfect day splashing in the water, building a sand castle, eating hot dogs, discovering crabs, and eating snowcones. As with the other five Henry and Mudge books, beginning readers can handle this one on their own.

5.136   Shefelman, Janice. **Victoria House.** Illustrated by Tom Shefelman. Harcourt Brace Jovanovich/Gulliver Books, 1988. ISBN 0-15-200630-3. 26p. 5–8 (est.).

When architect Sarah falls in love with a vacant and long-neglected Victorian house, she and husband Jess decide to move the house to the city to make it their family home and office and to fill it with "talk and laughter." The technical aspects of planning and executing such a move are scrupulously described, right down to the architectural blueprints. Ink-line and watercolor illustrations allow for a detailed depiction of Victoria House's authentic gazebo and gingerbread trim.

5.137   Sheldon, Dyan. **The Whales' Song.** Illustrated by Gary Blythe. Dial Books for Young Readers, 1990. ISBN 0-8037-0972-2. 25p. 4–8 (est.).

Lilly's grandmother tells her about the whales that she loved as a child and about their special gift of song to those who are patient and who bring something perfect to the water's edge. Despite her great-uncle's dismissal of the whales' songs, Lilly dreams of hearing the whales and is rewarded for both her gift of a perfect flower and her faith. Gary Blythe's large oil paintings rely on texture, light, and color to create the dream-like quality of Lilly's experiences.

5.138   Smalls-Hector, Irene. **Jonathan and His Mommy.** Illustrations by Michael Hays. Little, Brown, 1992. ISBN 0-316-79870-3. 32p. 5–8 (est.).

When Jonathan's mother ties on his shoes, it's time for a walk in the city. Past neighbors, apartments, shops, and construction, Jonathan and his mother have special ways of walking and talking. They take big giant steps and talk in giant voices. They take bunny hops and baby steps, running steps and slow-motion steps, ballet steps and crazy crisscross steps. When it's time for walking home again, they take Jonathan-and-Mommy steps, a loving relationship evident on each sunny page in this story about an African American boy and his mother.

5.139   Stolz, Mary. **Go Fish.** Illustrated by Pat Cummings. HarperCollins, 1991. ISBN 0-06-025822-5. 74p. 7–10 (est.).

Mary Stolz captures a day in the life of Grandfather, young Thomas, and their ever-hungry cat, Ringo. Purposeful literacy events and an African American family's love of reading, writing, and storytelling are skillfully woven into the story. The loving conversations between Grandfather and Thomas will sound familiar to many. Pat Cummings's black-and-white multiple-perspective drawings are alternately blocked or stretched across the pages of this chapter book for young readers.

5.140 Tan, Amy. **The Moon Lady.** Illustrated by Gretchen Schields. Macmillan, 1992. ISBN 0-02-788830-4. 32p. 6–10 (est.).

Best-selling novelist Amy Tan offers her first book for children, a story within a story told by Nai-nai to her three restless granddaughters held captive by rain. Nai-nai's tale is of her childhood in China, of her own restlessness, and of her desire to see the Moon Lady and to convey a secret wish from her heart. Today's children will understand the conflicting emotions, guilt, mischief, calamities, growing pains, and resolution. The watercolor paintings are brilliantly colored, detailed, and engaging Chinese folk art.

5.141 Temple, Charles. **On the Riverbank.** Illustrated by Melanie Hall. Houghton Mifflin, 1992. ISBN 0-395-61591-7. 32p. 6–10 (est.).

Charles Temple says that the words and the rhythms from this tribute to "fishin' on the riverbank" came to him as he was playing his banjo and daydreaming on the James River. The rhythms of memory plunk out the tune of a riverbank song that gets feet to tapping and catfish to biting: "Can't you hear those crickets going, 'Crick, crick, crick'?" The shades of June are peppered with black, and the whole scratchy effect gives a dancing exuberance to this African American family's fishing expedition.

5.142 Thomas, Elizabeth. **Green Beans.** Illustrated by Vicki Jo Redenbaugh. Carolrhoda Books, 1992. ISBN 0-87614-708-2. 32p. 5–8.

Gramma is the proper sort, a creature of habit, and the kind of person whom people obey. But her green bean plants are another story entirely. Despite Gramma's best efforts, they refuse to grow. Only when Gramma takes a trip, leaving Dorothea and her father in charge of the garden, does a miracle occur, and green beans reach skyward. Dorothea's success causes Gramma to relax her gardening routines, and some other staid rituals as well. Vicki Jo Redenbaugh's good-natured characters are lanky as bean poles.

5.143   Waddell, Martin. **Once There Were Giants.** Illustrated by Penny Dale. Delacorte Press, 1989. ISBN 0-385-29806-4. 24p. All ages.

To a baby, everyone larger seems to be a giant. From page to page the gentle first-person narrative and endearing illustrations show how over time the baby reaches childhood, then her teenage years, and then college. She eventually marries and has her own baby—who smiles up at surrounding giants. *Notable 1989 Children's Trade Books in the Field of Social Studies.*

5.144   Wallace-Brodeur, Ruth. **Home by Five.** Illustrations by Mark Graham. Margaret K. McElderry Books, 1992. ISBN 0-689-50509-4. 32p. 5–9.

Ruth Wallace-Brodeur gently and humorously portrays Rosie, a child who takes time to explore her city world—even it if means not getting home on time. Although Rosie earnestly tries to avoid distractions when given a deadline for being home, she is a child who notices things. The author's portrayal of Rosie's good intentions and of her parents' understanding of childhood adds to the sweetness of the story. Mark Graham's representational artwork relies on soft grays and browns to create wintry scenes in which Rosie's face stands out.

5.145   Williams, Sherley Anne. **Working Cotton.** Illustrated by Carole Byard. Harcourt Brace Jovanovich, 1992. ISBN 0-15-299624-9. 32p. 4–8.

In summer, Shelan is up before daybreak to pick cotton in the fields of central California with her African American family. The hard life and the transiency of people seen in one field but missing from the next is a rueful pattern, but not unpleasing to Shelan, who enjoys doing her share of work with the family. The simple text and vibrant acrylic paintings recapture the details of the migrant worker lifestyle. *Caldecott Honor Book, 1992.*

5.146   Wood, Audrey. **Weird Parents.** Illustrated by Audrey Wood. Dial Books for Young Readers, 1990. ISBN 0-8037-0649-9. 32p. 4–8.

"There once was a boy who had weird parents." Just how weird are they? Well, the weird mother engages in such embarrassments as blowing kisses from the bus stop, packing lunch surprises, and talking about the boy as though he isn't there. The weird father shakes hands with everyone, wears a weird hat, and walks like a chicken in crowds. Both of them laugh out loud in the movies. There are days when the boy wishes that they were like other parents, but then again. . . . Audrey Wood's flamboyant, lovingly depicted parents frolic across the pages.

5.147 Yarbrough, Camille. **The Shimmershine Queens.** G. P. Putnam's Sons, 1989. ISBN 0-399-21465-8. 142p. 10 and up (est.).

Fifth-grade Angie has the "get-up gift." Elderly Cousin Seatta tells her so. It's a gift of spirit traceable to slave days, a gift that gives dreamers the "shimmershine feeling"—optimism in the face of trouble. And Angie's troubles are many: her daddy has gone, her mother is sick, and the kids at her inner-city school tease her about her dark skin. Then comes a special drama teacher who reaches Angie and her friend Michelle with an African project in which they role-play eighteenth-century children, stolen into slavery, who dance their defiance.

5.148 Zolotow, Charlotte. **The Quiet Mother and the Noisy Little Boy.** Illustrated by Marc Simont. Harper and Row, 1989. ISBN 0-06-026979-0. 28p. 4–7 (est.).

A little boy named Sandy loves noise, but his mother does not. Not until Sandy leaves for a day's visit with relatives does his mother discover how much she misses him. And not until the wildest and noisiest relatives come for a visit does Sandy discover how noisy he has been. Both realize that noise and quiet are good at different times for different things. The lesson is shared through Charlotte Zolotow's gentle writing and Marc Simont's exuberant color.

5.149 Zolotow, Charlotte. **This Quiet Lady.** Illustrated by Anita Lobel. Greenwillow Books, 1992. ISBN 0-688-09306-X. 24p. 3–7 (est.).

Quiet text follows a young girl as she inspects photographs and snapshots of her mother at varying stages of her mother's life: "This curly-haired little girl with the doll drooping from her hand is my mother." Anita Lobel's French-set illustrations juxtapose large full-color portraits of the mother against muted-tone representations of the child-narrator. When the little girl turns to a picture of her mother holding her as an infant, the "life" story comes full cycle as she realizes that "here is where I begin."

Friendship

5.150   Aamundsen, Nina Ring. **Two Short and One Long.** Houghton Mifflin, 1990. ISBN 0-395-52434-2. 103p. 9–12 (est.).

As the summer holiday draws to a close, twelve-year-old Jonas and his somewhat mysterious best friend Einar observe a large Afghan family moving into their Oslo, Norway, neighborhood. When Jonas befriends Hewad, the Afghan boy, Einar becomes quiet and disapproving, causing Jonas to question the closeness of their friendship. This insightful story, translated by the author from the Norwegian, is about Einar conquering fears brought on by a tragic past and about all three boys growing to understand each other. *Mildred L. Batchelder Award, 1990.*

5.151   Aylesworth, Jim. **Mr. McGill Goes to Town.** Illustrated by Thomas Graham. Henry Holt, 1989. ISBN 0-8050-0772-5. 30p. 4–8 (est.).

Mr. McGill is repairing his mill, but it's too much work for one person. So he seeks Mr. McRae's help. Mr. McRae is cutting his hay, and the two friends join forces on that task, but it's too much work for two people. They must seek Mr. McCall's assistance. But Mr. McCall is building a wall, so the three friends pitch in on that job only to discover they need still more help. This cumulative tale, with embedded rhyming text, culminates with five friends working together to complete everyone's chores in no time at all.

5.152   Barbour, Karen. **Nancy.** Illustrated by Karen Barbour. Harcourt Brace Jovanovich, 1989. ISBN 0-15-256675-9. 32p. 4–7 (est.).

Nancy moves into a new neighborhood and is ignored by four best friends who decide not to play with her. However, once Nancy invites the girls to her wild and wacky birthday party, the girls become "five best friends." Modernistic gouache-and-watercolor illustrations are done with Picasso-esque flair.

5.153   Brisson, Pat. **Your Best Friend, Kate.** Illustrated by Rick Brown. Bradbury Press, 1989. ISBN 0-02-714350-3. 30p. 7–10 (est.).

In a book with text consisting entirely of notes, letters, and postcards, Kate stays in touch with her best friend, Lucy, as Kate travels with her family through eleven states. The flow of notes gives humorous, affectionate, and informative glimpses of the sights, as well as of the challenges of traveling with a smart-alecky younger brother. Tucked around the edges of the pages are state birds, flowers, and trees. Postcards from their own particular sites may inspire young students of geography.

5.154 Bunting, Eve. **Summer Wheels.** Illustrated by Thomas B. Allen. Harcourt Brace Jovanovich, 1992. ISBN 0-15-207000-1. 48p. 6–10.

The Bicycle Man's rules are simple: *Neighborhood kids can check out bicycles every day. For free. Just have them back by four. Fix them if they break.* Lawrence and Brady have their own favorite summer wheels that they borrow. When a big kid, nearly twelve, checks out Lawrence's bike, signing the book as "Abrehem Lincoln," the boys know that he has no intention of returning it. Themes of trust and second chances will give children something to talk over. Hazy charcoal and pastel drawings locate this neighborhood near your own.

5.155 Burns, Theresa. **You're Not My Cat.** Illustrated by Theresa Burns. J. B. Lippincott, 1989. ISBN 0-397-32341-7. 32p. 6–9 (est.).

A little girl spends her days with an alley cat named Gus, who she insists is *not* her cat. As their friendship grows, the little girl soon realizes that Gus is her pal and a part of her life forever. Cross-hatching and color pencil give texture and detail to this tale of an alley cat that finds a home.

5.156 Cave, Hugh B. **Conquering Kilmarnie.** Macmillan, 1989. ISBN 0-02-717781-5. 176p. 10 and up.

A wild pig and a mutual need for peer companionship bring together American-born Peter, who is still grieving over the death of his mother and brother, and Zackie, a Jamaican island boy. They grow to understand each other's cultures as they fight nature and endure family circumstances. With an action-filled plot, the story of their friendship is sure to entice the early adolescent reader. Set on a Jamaican coffee plantation, the story is also filled with information subtly folded into the plot.

5.157 Christopher, Matt. **Return of the Home Run Kid.** Illustrated by Paul Casale. Little, Brown, 1992. ISBN 0-316-14080-5. 168p. 9 and up (est.).

In this sequel to *The Kid Who Only Hit Homers*, Sylvester Coddmyer III experiences a baseball slump, making him question his success during the previous season. Helped by a stranger, Cheeko, Sylvester begins to play too aggressively and to take shortcuts. Cheeko bears an uncanny resemblance to Eddie Cicotte, a member of the notorious 1919 Black Sox team.

Sylvester learns that giving his best effort is the way to play the game. Pencil illustrations realistically depict some of the episodes.

5.158   Cleary, Beverly. **Strider.** Illustrated by Paul O. Zelinsky. Morrow Junior Books, 1991. ISBN 0-688-09901-7. 192p. 8 and up.

When Leigh Botts (a character in Beverly Cleary's *Dear Mr. Henshaw*) and his friend Barry find an abandoned dog on the beach, they develop a joint custody agreement for the dog, whom they name Strider. Strider's time with Leigh is spent in the no-pets-allowed cottage that he shares with his mother. Exercising the dog readies Leigh for the track team, but he grows in other ways as well—in his relation with his father, in his problem solving, and in his feelings for a dog who fills a need that children will understand. Leigh's account is written in a series of diary entries.

5.159   Clifton, Lucille. **Three Wishes.** Illustrated by Michael Hays. Doubleday Books for Young Readers, 1992. ISBN 0-385-30497-8. 32p. 5–8.

In this first-person account told in an African American dialect, narrator Zenobia attests to the truth of the saying that if you find a penny with your birthdate on New Year's Day, you can make three wishes. As in the folktale, Nobie is careless with her first two wishes and must use the third to right a wrong. Her wise mother helps her to understand that good friends are the fulfillment of one's greatest wish. Michael Hays's acrylic paintings show the texture of the linen canvas and seem to emit warmth and light.

5.160   Corcoran, Barbara. **The Potato Kid.** Atheneum/Jean Karl Books, 1989. ISBN 0-689-31589-9. 172p. 9 and up (est.).

Fourteen-year-old Ellis's plans to spend the summer on a horse ranch go awry when her mother is obliged to hostess a ten-year-old girl from a poverty-stricken potato-farming family. Disappointed, Ellis is charged with entertaining Lilac, with whom she has nothing in common except circumstance. The story of how they cope is told in a humorous, often-poignant narrative in which both girls and the reader learn to accept and appreciate differences in people.

5.161   Fosburgh, Lisa. **Afternoon Magic.** Macmillan, 1989. ISBN 0-02-735431-8. 211p. 10 and up (est.).

They were all latchkey kids in an upscale neighborhood who took comfort in meeting each other after school at Willie's house, where they shared television and snacks. Amid the uncertainties of Willie's life, including busy, bickering parents, an abusive friend of the family, and an interfering grandmother, they were a constant, even if no one knew they came. Then, into these predictable afternoons, comes new-neighbor Harold, who performs magic tricks, but also threatens, connives, blackmails, dominates, and vandalizes.

5.162 Gibbons, Faye. **King Shoes and Clown Pockets.** Morrow Junior Books, 1989. ISBN 0-688-06592-9. 231p. 9 and up (est.).

According to one fourth-grade reader, this book, set in Alabama, is a "modern *Tom Sawyer* with everything I like in a book: drama, comedy, and adventure." The unusual title nicknames the main characters, Raymond Brock, youngest child of neglectful, too-busy parents, and Bruce Manis, son of a frequently absent junk dealer and a runaway mom. Through a series of hilarious adventures, King Shoes and Clown Pockets come to understand their unhappy homes, cope with the unfairness of life, and mature as a result.

5.163 Gilson, Jamie. **Sticks and Stones and Skeleton Bones.** Illustrations by Dee deRosa. Lothrop, Lee and Shepard Books, 1991. ISBN 0-688-10098-8. 162p. 8–11.

Digging up a time capsule, falling down an escalator, and fist fighting at school turn fifth graders Hobie and Nick into former best friends. Because of a recent flood, their school meets in a shopping mall—complete with Santa Claus. It takes two student mediators and a not-so-jolly St. Nick to help the boys mend their differences. Jamie Gilson presents life in the fifth grade with smiles and hearty laughter.

5.164 Haywood, Carolyn. **Eddie's Friend Boodles.** Illustrated by Catherine Stock. Morrow Junior Books, 1990. ISBN 0-688-09028-1. 80p. 6 and up.

In Carolyn Haywood's last book for children, a manuscript completed shortly before her death, Eddie Wilson's friend Boodles assumes center stage. Intrigued by the circus performance that he and Eddie attend, Boodles attempts to teach his dog Poochie some tricks, with the usual sorts of calamities and chuckles. But Boodles remembers Turnip the Clown's advice: "You have to believe. . . . You have to love your dog, and your dog has to love you back." And love does the trick.

5.165   Henkes, Kevin. **Words of Stone.** Greenwillow Books, 1992. ISBN 0-688-11356-7. 152p. 10 and up (est.).

Ten-year-old Blaze Werla lives with his artist father and his grandmother, but mostly he is alone, apart, and afraid, trying to accept his mother's death. When brash Joselle Stark, abandoned by her mother, "the beautiful Vicki," moves into the neighborhood to live with her own grandmother, she learns details of Blaze's fears and begins to leave messages on the hillside—"words of stone"—that open the wounds of Blaze's past. Over time, the two meet and become friends, and each fills the other's needs. Blaze offers Joselle his sensitivity, and she gives him courage to face his past.

5.166   Holmes, Barbara Ware. **Charlotte Shakespeare and Annie the Great.** Illustrated by John Himmelman. Harper and Row, 1989. ISBN 0-06-022615-3. 152p. 9–12.

Partly because her sixth-grade teacher believes in her, Charlotte Cheetham writes a play for her class that is so funny and scary that her father calls her Charlotte Shakespeare. As director, Charlotte believes that her shy friend Annie should play the lead, but brash Tina covets the part. Through coaching by Charlotte's father, Annie wins the part—and a lot of attention as well. Charlotte learns some things about jealousy, about being in charge, and about collaboration. Bravo, Charlotte, for a witty and contemporary third-encore performance.

5.167   Jones, Rebecca C. **Matthew and Tilly.** Illustrated by Beth Peck. Dutton Children's Books, 1991. ISBN 0-525-44684-2. 32p. 3–6 (est.).

Matthew and Tilly are the best of friends, boy and girl, black and white. They ride bikes together, sell lemonade together, and play sidewalk games together. But one day, while coloring together, Matthew breaks Tilly's purple crayon, and the friendship crumbles, too, until each realizes how the best times depend on a best friend. Beth Peck's dark-tone paintings are impressions of her own childhood neighborhood of Washington Heights in New York City.

5.168   Kherdian, David. **The Great Fishing Contest.** Illustrated by Nonny Hogrogian. Philomel Books, 1991. ISBN 0-399-22263-4. 46p. 7–10 (est.).

Best friends Jason and Sammy enter the children's fishing contest at the zoo, a contest which has as its grand prize a complete spinning outfit. Painstakingly, the boys plan their strategies, their floats, and their position on the banks of the pond. They even plan how to earn a second fishing outfit should one of them win. In a slim book divided into chapters, Nonny Hogrogian uses pastels to produce edge-to-edge scenes of boys who fish smart, meet challenges, and know friendship.

5.169 Lillie, Patricia. **Jake and Rosie.** Illustrated by Patricia Lillie. Greenwillow Books, 1989. ISBN 0-688-07625-4. 24p. 6–8 (est.).

When friends are friends like Jake and Rosie—exactly the same size and with hair almost the same color—they do everything together. They play pirates, draw monsters, trade one shoe to be twins, and even get the chicken pox together. But when Rosie is gone one day, Jake suffers separation pain as only young children can until Rosie returns sporting new shoes just like Jake's. Simple illustrations show the warm friendship between sexes and races.

5.170 Lisle, Janet Taylor. **Afternoon of the Elves.** Orchard Books, 1989. ISBN 0-531-08437-X. 122p. 9–11.

Hillary befriends the mysterious Sara-Kate because of the miniature village in her backyard, which Sara-Kate claims was built by elves. Only through the strength of their friendship does Sara-Kate let Hillary know about her mother's mental illness and the resulting disintegration of her family. *Newbery Honor Book, 1990.*

5.171 Mazer, Norma Fox. **Babyface.** Morrow Junior Books, 1990. ISBN 0-688-08752-3. 165p. 12 and up.

Award-winning author Norma Fox Mazer recounts the story of two fourteen-year-old best friends, Toni and Julie, and the struggles that envelop their families. When Julie's family shatters and she moves away, Toni is left alone to deal with her own problems: sibling jealousy, family illness and dissension, the rollercoaster ride of first love, and the need to balance her growing sense of independence with an equally strong desire for family support. Regardless of the topic (puppy love, pending divorce, changing relationships), Mazer portrays situations realistically with clear, easily readable prose.

5.172 Mazer, Norma Fox. **Silver.** Avon Books/Flare Books, 1989. ISBN 0-380-75026-0. 202p. 10 and up.

Sarabeth Silver and her mother barely manage to survive financially in their house trailer. When Sarabeth suddenly has the opportunity to attend junior high school in a wealthy district, her mother jumps at this chance to improve her daughter's education. During the course of one year, Sarabeth learns that the pains and pleasures of preadolescence cross all economic levels. Topics sensitively portrayed include the changing family unit, single parenting, friendships, first love, and sexual abuse. *ALA Best Books for Young Adults.*

5.173 McKenna, Colleen O'Shaughnessy. **Fifth Grade: Here Comes Trouble.** Scholastic Hardcover Books, 1989. ISBN 0-590-41733-9. 137p. 8–12 (est.).

Collette Murphy, age ten, wants to find out why she's different from her friends, who consider her a party pooper and a fuddy duddy. In so doing, she decides, against her better judgment, to accept her friend Marsha's invitation to go shopping for teenage things and to attend her boy-girl "Signpost to Maturity" birthday party. Shopping at Boss's in the mall turns into a nightmare, but at the party Collette turns her attention to making sure that Marsha's eleventh-year celebration is her greatest.

5.174 Naylor, Phyllis Reynolds. **Alice in Rapture, Sort Of.** Atheneum/Jean Karl Books, 1989. ISBN 0-689-31466-3. 166p. 10–12 (est.).

This sequel to *The Agony of Alice* follows Alice, Elizabeth, and Pamela through the summer before they enter junior high. For Alice, it is also the summer of her first boyfriend. Her two best friends have boyfriends, too, since rumor has it that having a boyfriend is critical to seventh-grade success. Together they struggle through adolescent worries—sometimes funny, sometimes poignant—and Alice wishes that she had a mother to turn to. As fall arrives, Alice decides that for now she needs a "special friend" more than a boyfriend.

5.175 Orgel, Doris. **Nobodies and Somebodies.** ISBN 0-670-82754-1. 152p. 8–12.

In Ms. Tatum's fifth-grade class, the girls in the in-group dress alike and are members of an exclusive Super Stars Club. Almost anything can cause their classmates to feel like "nobodies" around the Supes—Laura, because she's the new girl, and Janet, because she stutters. Even Vero, who's a member, feels uncertain of herself and of the constancy of her family's love. In chapters titled with their names, these three girls tell their stories, and learn about themselves, each other, and friendship.

5.176 Pendergraft, Patricia. **Brushy Mountain.** Philomel Books, 1989. ISBN 0-399-21610-3. 207p. 10 and up.

Mountain dialect, an engrossing plot, and colorful characters make this book a wonderful read-aloud. The plot is driven by thirteen-year-old Arney's aborted and humorous attempts to put an end to crotchety old man Hooker. Inevitably his actions rescue the ungrateful old man instead. A pet turkey, fire, storms, and the birth of the old man's grandchild add excitement and humor to this warm story of a boy who learns that a thorny exterior frequently hides an unhappy person inside.

5.177 Polacco, Patricia. **Chicken Sunday.** Illustrated by Patricia Polacco. Philomel Books, 1992. ISBN 0-399-22133-6. 32p. 4–8.

Patricia Polacco's memories of childhood include Sunday's fried chicken with Miss Eula Mae Walker and her grandsons, Stewart and Winston. Miss Eula's African American family become like Polacco's own. Little wonder that she wants more than anything in the world to help her "brothers" get Miss Eula a special Easter bonnet. Line drawings are shaded with warm skin tones, vibrant colors, and even actual photographs tucked into cozy family scenes. By painting and selling Ukrainian eggs, the children earn money for the bonnet, and two cultures are blended.

5.178 Polacco, Patricia. **Picnic at Mudsock Meadow.** Illustrated by Patricia Polacco. G. P. Putnam's Sons, 1992. ISBN 0-399-21811-4. 32p. 4–8.

William is sure that the eerie lights hanging over Quicksand Bottoms are just swamp gas, and not the ghost of old Titus Dinworthy. "Peeeeeee youuuuuuu," retorts Hester Bledden, causing William to blush as "red as a Union City farm-fresh tomato," and she beats him in one contest after another. In a final attempt to better Hester, William braves the swamp. And Hester Bledden is proud as punch to share a plate-o'-cream with the swamp monster at Mudsock Meadow's annual Halloween picnic.

5.179 Rodowsky, Colby. **Dog Days.** Illustrated by Kathleen Collins Howell. Farrar, Straus and Giroux, 1990. ISBN 0-374-36342-0. 131p. 7–11 (est.).

Rosie Riggs's summer vacation couldn't be worse. Her best friend left for Minnesota, her mom left for work, and her favorite baby-sitter left for Cape Cod. Summer life takes a turn for the better, however, when "Sandy the Super Dog" and his owner, a famous children's author, move in next door. Exciting events turn the summer into one of important discoveries of both friendships and fantasies.

5.180   Ross, Tony. **A Fairy Tale.** Illustrated by Tony Ross. Little, Brown, 1991. ISBN 0-316-75750-0. 32p. 4–8 (est.).

Bessie doesn't believe in fairies or magic. But her elderly neighbor, Mrs. Leaf, does. Mrs. Leaf reminds Bessie of the magic of a perfect summer afternoon and the pure happiness of certain Christmas Eves. Mrs. Leaf admits that even she might be a fairy, which Bessie scoffs at since Mrs. Leaf is neither little nor pretty. As Bessie grows and changes, so does her relationship with Mrs. Leaf, and even Mrs. Leaf herself. Tony Ross's illustrations stroke grays and blue-violets into milltown skies and enhance the transformation of the characters.

5.181   Rylant, Cynthia. **An Angel for Solomon Singer.** Illustrated by Peter Catalanotto. Orchard Books/Richard Jackson Books, 1992. ISBN 0-531-08578-3. 32p. All ages.

Living in a hotel for men in New York City with no fireplace for sitting, no picture window for bird-watching, and no cat, Solomon Singer "loved where he lived not at all." So Solomon wanders the city as he wandered the fields of his native Indiana in his boyhood. When he finds the Westway Cafe, where a waiter named Angel smiles at him, Solomon's perceptions change. Peter Catalanotto's paintings capture the soul of the book, merging dreamy visions with puddly reflected city lights.

5.182   Sharmat, Marjorie Weinman, and Mitchell Sharmat. **The Pizza Monster.** Illustrated by Denise Brunkus. Delacorte Press, 1989. ISBN 0-385-29722-X. 48p. 5–8.

Because Olivia Sharp is good at solving problems and good at keeping secrets, she decides to become a secret agent. Her first call comes from Duncan, an eternal pessimist who has lost his best friend. The Eloise-like Olivia grabs her boa, enlists Willie her chauffeur, and enthusiastically embarks on her first assignment. Soon, though, she discovers that even fifty pizzas won't buy a friend, and that Duncan's case will require serious work on the fundamentals of friendship.

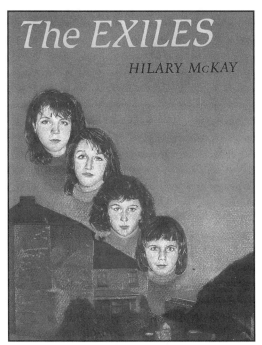

A.

B.

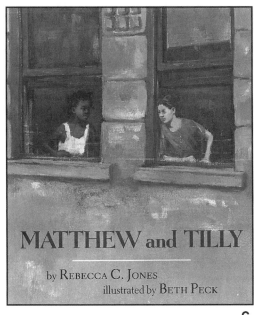

C.

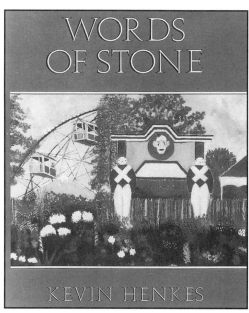

D.

A. *The Exiles* by Hilary McKay (see 5.122). **B.** *What Hearts* by Bruce Brooks (see 5.80). **C.** *Matthew and Tilly* by Rebecca C. Jones; illustrated by Beth Peck (see 5.167). **D.** *Words of Stone* by Kevin Henkes (see 5.165).

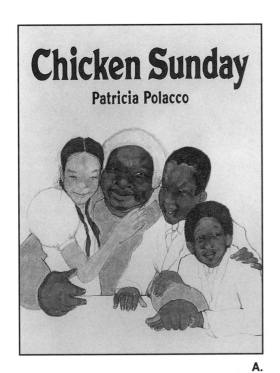

A.

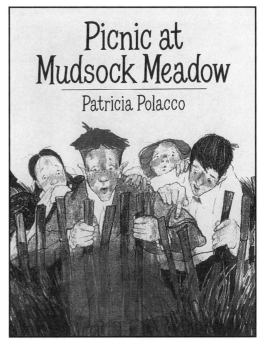

B.

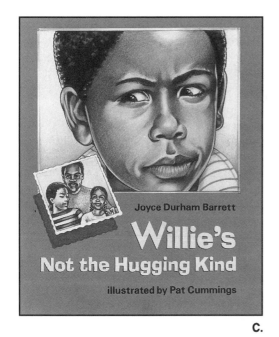

C.

D.

A. *Chicken Sunday* by Patricia Polacco (see 5.177).   **B.** *Picnic at Mudsock Meadow* by Patricia Polacco (see 5.178).   **C.** *Willie's Not the Hugging Kind* by Joyce Durham Barrett; illustrated by Pat Cummings (see 5.72).   **D.** *Loop the Loop* by Barbara Dugan; illustrated by James Stevenson (see 5.297).

5.183 Slepian, Jan. **The Broccoli Tapes.** Philomel Books, 1988. ISBN 0-399-21712-6. 157p. 8–12 (est.).

When Sara's family is temporarily relocated from Boston to Hawaii, she and her brother Sam feel cut off from their mainland friends and unaccepted in their new school. Then they must cope with their grandmother's hospitalization and death. Lonely Sara maintains ties with her old sixth-grade classroom by tape-recording her experiences and her feelings. Through the tapes, Sara tells of their discovery of a broccoli-eating cat, trapped in lava rocks, and of the wary Eddie, as mistrustful as the cat. The children's attempts to win the trust of both cat and boy move the story to a poignant ending. *ALA Notable Children's Books, 1989; School Library Journal's Best Books, 1989; ALA Booklist Children's Editors' Choices, 1989.*

5.184 Snyder, Zilpha Keatly. **Libby on Wednesday.** Dell/Yearling Books, 1991. ISBN 0-440-40498-3. 196p. 9–13 (est.).

Libby McCall feels more than a little different from the other students at Morrison Middle School. Libby's feelings stem mostly from the fact that she is attending school for the first time. Besides being younger (only eleven), she is smaller than the others, and initially she is too forthcoming with her intellect. After winning a writing contest, Libby is assigned to a Wednesday writing workshop with four other students, and the group members begin to reveal themselves through their writing and responses. *ALA Best Books for Young Adults.*

5.185 Spinelli, Jerry. **Fourth Grade Rats.** Illustrated by Paul Casale. Scholastic Hardcover Books, 1991. ISBN 0-590-44243-0. 84p. 7–9.

"First grade babies! Second grade cats! Third grade angels! Fourth grade . . . RATS!" Suds liked being a third-grade angel, but now his best friend Joey is after him to become a true fourth-grade rat—to push younger kids off swings, eat baloney (not peanut butter and jelly) sandwiches, and defy his mother—in order to take the first steps toward becoming a "man." However, Suds eventually learns that growing up is much more complex than impressing Joey Peterson.

5.186 Wallace, Bill. **The Biggest Klutz in Fifth Grade.** Holiday House, 1992. ISBN 0-8234-0984-8. 148p. 9 and up.

A bet between characters reminiscent of Thomas Rockwell's *How to Eat Fried Worms* drives the plot of this hilarious story. Pat is a klutz, and everyone knows it. He proves it by getting stuck under a chain-link fence during the greatest tackle of his ten-year-old life. But can he remain accident-free long enought to win the bet so that Neal (and not he) has to kiss Kristine, the Blimp, in front of the whole school? Fifth-grade jargon, short chapters, and "don't-stop-now!" chapter endings keep the reader engrossed all the way to the surprising ending.

5.187 Winthrop, Elizabeth. **The Best Friends Club: A Lizzie and Harold Story.** Illustrated by Martha Weston. Lothrop, Lee and Shepard Books, 1989. ISBN 0-688-07583-5. 28p. 4–7.

Because Lizzie and Harold are constant companions, they decide to establish the Best Friends Club. When Lizzie writes her own restrictive club rules, suddenly no one but the two friends can be admitted. Harold doesn't want to be in such an exclusive club, and when he finds a new friend, Lizzie is hurt. Soon Harold's diplomacy wins Lizzie over, and a new club, the No Rules Club, is formed. Children who are just beginning to test social relationships will find author Elizabeth Winthrop's perspectives both funny and informative.

Illness or Death

5.188 Ackerman, Karen. **The Broken Boy.** Philomel Books, 1991. ISBN 0-399-22254-5. 160p. 10 and up.

At the edge of puberty, twelve-year-old Solly must learn the limits of his responsibility for and friendship with Daniel, an emotionally disturbed boy who lives next door. Daniel's violent tantrums and his belief that he is connected spiritually to a polio victim who lived in the same house years before test and finally strengthen Solly's own belief in himself and his family. Karen Ackerman deftly combines a strong mystery with a coming-of-age tale.

5.189 Amadeo, Diana M. **There's a Little Bit of Me in Jamey.** Illustrated by Judith Friedman. Albert Whitman, 1989. ISBN 0-8075-7854-1. 29p. 6–9.

Brian is confused, afraid, and angry when his younger brother Jamey's leukemia becomes worse. Then Jamey comes home from the hospital, and Mom, Dad, and Grandma seem to forget about Brian, so consumed are they with concern for Jamey's health. Eventually, Brian's anger is assuaged, and he offers a "little bit of himself," his own bone marrow, to help save his brother's life. Written by a nurse, the book features characters that are composites of her patients and their families as they struggle with childhood cancer.

5.190 Brooks, Bruce. **Everywhere.** Harper and Row, 1990. ISBN 0-06-020729-9. 70p. 9 and up.

It is eleven-year-old Dooley who keeps a white boy's mind off his grandfather, a grandfather who lies dying upstairs, a victim of a weak heart. Dooley is Lucy's nephew, and he has accompanied his African American aunt on her nursing assignment. When Dooley suggests some soul switching between a turtle and the narrator's grandfather, there is soul searching about death, about life, about fear, and about trust. This is a book worth discussion with upper graders.

5.191 Bunting, Eve. **The Wall.** Illustrated by Ronald Himler. Clarion Books, 1990. ISBN 0-395-51588-2. 29p. 4–8.

This touching portrayal of a boy and his father searching for a name at the Vietnam Veterans Memorial speaks to both children and adults. Through the young boy's eyes, the reader meets other visitors to "The Wall"—a disabled veteran, a mourning couple, and young girls on an outing with little understanding of the memorial's significance. Eve Bunting artfully juxtaposes the young boy's longing for his fallen grandfather and his understanding that his grandfather's name is in a permanent place of honor. The paintings are quietly haunting.

5.192 Hamilton, Virginia. **Cousins.** Philomel Books, 1990. ISBN 0-399-22164-6. 125p. 10 and up.

Eleven-year-old Cammy is devoted to her frail ninety-four-year-old grandmother, now in a care home, and is reconciled to her eventual passing. Too busy with other things, her brother and cousins rarely visit their grandmother. When Cammy witnesses the accidental drowning of Patty Ann, a cousin her own age with a seemingly perfect life, Cammy leans on Gram and learns the process of recovery from such a dramatic event. *Notable 1990 Children's Trade Books in the Field of Social Studies; ALA Notable Children's Books, 1991.*

5.193 Johnston, Tony. **Grandpa's Song.** Illustrated by Brad Sneed. Dial Books for Young Readers, 1991. ISBN 0-8037-0802-5. 30p. 5–9.

Exaggerated caricatures captured in bold bright watercolors are a joyful addition to this poignant tale of a young girl and her aging grandpa. With the straightforward innocence and love that only a child possesses, she responds to her grandpa's growing forgetfulness by helping him to sing their favorite song, thereby taking away some of his fear and sadness.

5.194 Jordan, MaryKate. **Losing Uncle Tim.** Illustrated by Judith Friedman. Albert Whitman, 1989. ISBN 0-8075-4756-5. 32p. 7–11.

Daniel and his Uncle Tim enjoy spending time together—they go sledding, talk, and play with toys in Uncle Tim's antique shop. When Daniel asks why his "favorite grown-up" has been increasingly tired lately, he learns that Uncle Tim has AIDS and that he will probably die. Watercolor illustrations in subdued tones portray Daniel as he goes through a series of emotions—pity, fear, anger, and sadness—until he begins to cope with his uncle's disease and eventual death.

5.195 Keller, Holly. **The Best Present.** Illustrated by Holly Keller. Greenwillow Books, 1989. ISBN 0-688-07320-4. 28p. 4–7 (est.).

Eight-year-old Rosie wants to visit her grandmother in the hospital, but the rules state that visitors must be at least ten years old. With the help of her friend Kate, Rosie dresses up to look older, buys three carnations, and heads for the hospital. But the hospital guard is not fooled, and Rosie must send up the flowers for Grandmother with the elevator man. When Grandmother comes home, she shows Rosie all of her get-well cards and her favorite present—three carnations. *Notable 1989 Children's Books in the Field of Social Studies.*

5.196 Laird, Elizabeth. **Loving Ben.** Delacorte Press, 1989. ISBN 0-385-29810-2. 183p. 10 and up (est.).

Twelve-year-old Anna Peacock experiences troubles and triumphs with girlfriends and boyfriends, with school, and with popularity, but central to this novel is her love for her brother Ben. When Ben is born, Anna knows something is wrong. Anna and her family soon come to understand that their new baby is hydrocephalic and severely disabled. Then they must deal with Ben's death. Author Elizabeth Laird conveys to readers her understanding of the gifts that disabled children have to offer.

5.197 Madenski, Melissa. **Some of the Pieces.** Illustrated by Deborah Kogan Ray. Little, Brown, 1991. ISBN 0-316-54324-1. 30p. 4–8.

With words perfectly chosen, this bittersweet story carries the young reader from the pain of losing a parent, through the healing process, and out of that bleak tunnel to the other side, where memories once again bring smiles. During a day of sharing their memories, Dylan tells his mother, "it's like when Dad died, he split into a thousand pieces so he could be with all the people he loved. And I'm glad some of the pieces are with me." Easy and comforting, Deborah Kogan Ray's illustrations befit the story's mood and theme.

5.198 Mayne, William. **Gideon Ahoy!** Delacorte Press, 1989. ISBN 0-440-50126-1. 156p. Ages 10 and up.

Twelve-year-old Eva has always thought her family was a little overwhelming, especially her brother Gideon, who is both brain-damaged and deaf. But she never imagines that such a horrifying accident as befalls Gideon could occur in her family of strangers. Gideon's first job—opening and closing bridges on a canal barge—may be his last, but it may also bring the eccentric members of Eva's family closer together than they've ever been before. *Boston Globe–Horn Book Honor Book, 1989.*

5.199 Polacco, Patricia. **Uncle Vova's Tree.** Illustrated by Patricia Polacco. Philomel Books, 1989. ISBN 0-399-21617-0. 30p. 4–8.

A Christmas season with Uncle Vova is rich with love and his Russian homeland traditions of dancing, special ornaments, a sleigh ride, Russian foods, and decorating a tree for the animals. Then comes a sad time, the Christmas when Uncle Vova is gone. Yet through memories and the keeping of traditions, the children discover that their uncle's love will always be with them. Warmly colored folk-art patterns surround penciled faces, capturing a simple, joyous time. *Notable 1989 Children's Trade Books in the Field of Social Studies.*

5.200 Roth, Susan L. **We'll Ride Elephants through Brooklyn.** Illustrated by Susan L. Roth. Farrar, Straus and Giroux, 1989. ISBN 0-374-38258-1. 29p. 3–6 (est.).

A little girl anticipates the day when Grandpa will get better. That special day will feature a parade through Brooklyn complete with elephants, balloons, a band, dancing and cartwheels, and root beer and cupcakes. Brightly colored collage illustrations enhance this celebration of a child's love for her grandpa.

5.201 Rylant, Cynthia. **Missing May.** Orchard Books/Richard Jackson Books, 1992. ISBN 0-531-08596-1. 89p. 11 and up.

When May dies, life almost stops for Ob, her husband of many years, and for twelve-year-old Summer, the orphaned niece whom the couple has raised in their old age. May's life spirit had buoyed them, bringing them strength because "We had May to brag on us both." Summer, May said repeatedly, was the best little girl that she ever knew. And to May, arthritic Ob was the sun and the moon. So when Cletus, an odd neighbor boy with his own set of gifts, brings them an ad for a spiritual medium, Ob grasps at the chance to communicate with May once again. Cynthia Rylant's story, set in West Virginia, offers great love and achieves great healing. *Boston Globe–Horn Book Fiction Award, 1992; Newbery Medal, 1993.*

5.202   Rylant, Cynthia. **Mr. Griggs' Work.** Illustrated by Julie Downing. Orchard Books/Richard Jackson Books, 1989. ISBN 0-531-08369-1. 27p. 4–7.

With the sensitivity to which her readers are accustomed, Cynthia Rylant tells the story of Mr. Griggs, a man who loves his work in a small-town post office so much that he can't stop thinking about it. When he gets sick and must miss work for the first time ever, he is miserable. Upon recovery and return to work, he relishes being there even more, asking his first customer, "almost gleefully, 'First Class or Parcel Post?'" Colorful pastel illustrations show the pride and joy that Mr. Griggs has in his work.

5.203   Springer, Nancy. **Colt.** Dial Books for Young Readers, 1991. ISBN 0-8037-1022-4. 121p. 10 and up.

Participating in a horseback riding program for the disabled, Colt Vittorio, at first reluctant, comes to cherish his time in the saddle and out of his wheelchair. He gains needed physical strength and confidence. But when he develops a physical problem that prevents him from riding, his new stepfather finds the solution in a Paso Fino horse—a breed that does not trot. This warm story concludes with a harrowing ride that fosters Colt's inner strength and resources.

5.204   Stolz, Mary. **King Emmett the Second.** Illustrated by Garth Williams. Greenwillow Books, 1991. ISBN 0-688-09520-8. 56p. 7 and up.

In this sequel to *Emmett's Pig*, Emmett Murphy must deal simultaneously with two traumas in his life: news of the death of his beloved pet pig, King Emmett, and a pending family move from New York to Ohio. Emmett's initial refusal to be comforted or cajoled by his new porch or garden or neighbors or even a new bicycle seems perfectly reasonable and childlike. Eventually, Emmett comes to love both Ohio and a new pet. Garth Williams's intermittent sketches include a Wilbur-like remembrance of King Emmett the First.

5.205 Thomas, Jane Resh. **Saying Good-bye to Grandma.** Illustrated by Marcia Sewall. Clarion Books, 1988. ISBN 0-89919-645-4. 48p. 6–9.

At age seven, Suzie is faced with saying good-bye to Grandma. Suzie and her mother and father travel to Grandma's funeral, where they gather with other friends and relatives to grieve, to bid a final farewell, and to celebrate the love that they have for one another. From the cousins' whispered game of hide-and-seek in the casket display room of the funeral home to the tears that Grandpa sheds, it is both a touching and real story. Certainly this book will assist teachers, counselors, and parents as they help children understand the death of a loved one. *Joan Fassler Memorial Book Award, Association for the Care of Children's Health, 1989.*

5.206 Thurman, Chuck. **A Time for Remembering.** Illustrated by Elizabeth Sayles. Simon and Schuster Books for Young Readers, 1989. ISBN 0-671-68573-2. 25p. 4–8 (est.).

A boy's grandfather gave him many things, good times, and opportunities to learn and grow. After his grandfather's death, the boy sits in front of a fireplace and uses a flower that his grandfather gave him on their last visit together to open a well of memories that will keep his grandfather alive forever. Shadowy, expressionistic paintings are somber, yet comforting.

5.207 Wilson, Johnniece Marshall. **Robin on His Own.** Scholastic Hardcover Books, 1990. ISBN 0-590-41813-0. 144p. 8–12.

When Aunt Belle marries and moves out of town, Robin's widowed father decides that he and Robin must move to a smaller apartment, which means that Robin may lose his cat, his new parakeet, and his friends. Robin is also trying to come to terms with the death of his mother. Left alone one night, Robin sets out to visit Aunt Belle, with disastrous consequences. Johnniece Marshall Wilson's portrait of African American family life is warm and convincing.

5.208 Woodruff, Elvira. **Dear Napoleon, I Know You're Dead, But....** Illustrated by Noah and Jess Woodruff. Holiday House, 1992. ISBN 0-8234-0962-7. 220p. 10 and up (est.).

When Marty's fourth-grade teacher asks the class to write a letter to a famous person, Marty can think of no living hero—none, that is, except Gramps. For weeks, though, Gramps has been confined to a nursing home, too ill to live with Marty and his mother. On a whim, Marty writes to Napoleon. When Gramps hears of it, he hints of a way to get the letter across time. In the end, Gramps has taught Marty laughter, magic, mystery, and hope.

5.209   Ziefert, Harriet. **When Daddy Had the Chicken Pox.** Illustrated by Lionel Kalish. HarperCollins, 1991. ISBN 0-06-026907-3. 28p. 4–8 (est.).

Ellen is fearful when her father becomes so ill with the chicken pox that he can't go to work or attend her ballet recital. But after a few days, his lack of interest in everything turns to requests for food, the newspaper, and his briefcase. Stylized illustrations chronicle the return to health as pox fade and frowns turn to smiles.

School Life and Day Care

5.210   Baehr, Patricia. **School Isn't Fair!** Illustrated by R. W. Alley. Four Winds Press, 1989. ISBN 0-02-708130-3. 30p. 4–6 (est.).

Edward finds one grumble after another at school—the snack-time carrot with the stump left on, Donny who knocks him down, Linda who obstructs his view and splashes juice, and Mrs. Monroe who has no sense of justice. In the end, Edward's skill in zipping jackets brings a triumphant turn of events. Stylized drawings, highlighted with colored pencil and watercolor, complement a story of childhood that rings true. *Notable 1989 Children's Trade Books in the Field of Social Studies.*

5.211   Bunting, Eve. **Our Sixth-Grade Sugar Babies.** J. B. Lippincott, 1990. ISBN 0-397-32452-9. 146p. 9–12.

When Mrs. Oda gives her sixth-grade class an assignment in responsibility, each student becomes "parent" to a five-pound bag of sugar for one week. Even though their sugar babies are never to be left alone, Vicki becomes distracted by a seventh-grade boy and temporarily abandons her baby on the lawn. When she returns, both "baby" and an elderly neighbor have disappeared. Vicki must decide whether to own up to her responsibilities or to take an easier route.

5.212 Bunting, Eve. **Our Teacher's Having a Baby.** Illustrated by Diane de Groat. Clarion Books, 1992. ISBN 0-395-60470-2. 32p. 6–8 (est.).

The title page is crayoned in a child's hand and thumbtacked to a bulletin board. Diane de Groat's watercolors bring a classroom family to life as Mrs. Neal explains to her first graders that "Teachers can be mothers, too." Narrator Samantha and the other children engage in touching baby preparations such as putting stickers on their teacher's shirt, "right on the stretched-out part," writing letters, picking names, and cutting out baby things for the bulletin board. Their questions and concerns are childlike and honest, their teacher sensitive and open.

5.213 Carrick, Carol. **Left Behind.** Illustrated by Donald Carrick. Clarion Books, 1988. ISBN 0-89919-535-0. 29p. 5–8.

Manifesting many children's fears, Christopher becomes separated from his classmates on a trip to the aquarium. When he steps from the subway to let other passengers off, the train leaves without him. With all the worries and confusion of a lost child, Christopher tries to maintain his bearings, read signs, and look for help. A policeman who knows what to do and an understanding teacher make for a comforting conclusion. Watercolors bustle with city life.

5.214 Cleary, Beverly. **Muggie Maggie.** Illustrated by Kay Life. Morrow Junior Books, 1990. ISBN 0-688-08554-7. 70p. 8–12 (est.).

Third-grader Maggie Schultz decides that she has no use for cursive writing, with its imprecise squiggles so different from manuscript printing and writing with the computer. Her disposition gets worse when she tries writing her name in cursive at school and it comes out "Muggie," a name that sticks. Maggie stubbornly refuses to back down, and in the process she learns that there is a greater significance to cursive writing than just learning to close her loops.

5.215 Delton, Judy. **My Mom Made Me Go to School.** Illustrated by Lisa McCue. Delacorte Press, 1991. ISBN 0-385-30330-0. 32p. 5–8.

Summer over, Mom announces that it's time for preparations for school. For the kindergarten-bound narrator, Archie, that means such things as new corduroy pants (the color of peas) that hang over his shoes, won't bend, and smell awful. It means new shoes that pinch, a dental checkup, booster shots, and a haircut that makes his head feel like a toothbrush. No wonder Archie decides that he's not going to school. Lisa McCue's cheerful illustrations are suitably impish.

5.216 Hennessy, B. G. **School Days.** Illustrated by Tracey Campbell Pearson. Viking Penguin, 1990. ISBN 0-670-83025-9. 32p. 3–8.

Dedicated to "all the teachers who make school fun," this book is a visual treat—beginning with the arrival of the school bus, through circle time and show and tell, to the last good-bye. In watercolor washes, children are depicted alternately playing, listening to stories, painting a huge blue whale, tending classroom pets, or making letter games. Rhyming text is printed as a teacher's handwriting on writing lines along the bottom borders. The pictures are worth close inspection for humorous details.

5.217 Hoffman, Phyllis. **Meatball.** Illustrated by Emily Arnold McCully. HarperCollins/Charlotte Zolotow Books, 1991. ISBN 0-06-022564-5. 32p. 2–7.

Marilyn is called Meatball by her day-care teacher, Julia, because Marilyn is round and yummy. Marilyn relates in first person her day-care routine—from morning drop-off to evening pickup. Included are descriptions of work and play, friends and centers, naps and snacks. The tone is gentle and comforting, as are Emily Arnold McCully's warm, multicultural classroom scenes.

5.218 Hurwitz, Johanna. **Class President.** Illustrated by Sheila Hamanaka. Morrow Junior Books, 1990. ISBN 0-688-09114-8. 85p. 7 and up.

As the fifth grade begins, Julio Sanchez and his friends are assigned a new teacher who initiates some unusual activities. One is the election of a class president. Cricket Kaufman, the smartest girl in class, and Lucas Cott, the class clown, appear to be the only choices until Julio's surprising nomination. Unassuming Julio is nominated because of his kindness, generosity, and leadership abilities. Julio's eventual election is set against the background of normal fifth-grade turmoils. Black-and-white illustrations add to the story's realism.

5.219 Lowry, Lois. **Your Move, J. P.!** Dell/Yearling Books, 1991. ISBN 0-440-40497-5. 122p. 9–12 (est.).

J. P. Tate is twelve, a good student, a champion chess player, and in love. The object of his crush is Angela Patricia Galsworthy, newly arrived from England, with traits that make J. P. use deodorant and think in trite phrases: her hair is like spun gold, her teeth like pearls, her eyes like pools. To gain Angela's affection, J. P. falls into a "web of deception" that involves a fictitious disease and rich relatives. True friendship and gently guided self-inspection turn things around.

5.220 Martin, Ann. **Rachel Parker, Kindergarten Show-Off.** Illustrated by Nancy Poydar. Holiday House, 1992. ISBN 0-8234-0935-X. 32p. 4–7 (est.).

For the energetic, five-year-old African American narrator, Olivia, who is "very good at kindergarten," there is great expectation that the new neighbors may have a girl just her age. But when Rachel Elizabeth Parker moves in and can also read and write, has two first names, a puppet stage, a granddaddy who gives candy, *and* a baby sister, it may be too much for Olivia to bear. A sensitive teacher and a shared task help cement friendship.

5.221 McKenna, Colleen O'Shaughnessy. **Fourth Grade Is a Jinx.** Scholastic Hardcover Books, 1989. ISBN 0-590-41735-5. 168p. 8–12.

To Collette's horror and embarrassment, when her fourth-grade teacher breaks her leg, Collette's own mother is selected as the substitute! Although the class is pleased, Collette is not, because the happy routine of the Murphy's home life is destroyed by her mother's working. The familiar story problems, the somewhat exaggerated characters of snooty Marsha and pesky Roger, abundant conversation, and short paragraphs make this a sure favorite of intermediate children.

5.222 Morris, Judy K. **The Kid Who Ran for Principal.** J. B. Lippincott, 1989. ISBN 0-397-32360-3. 212p. 8–12.

Sixth graders have reasons to work hard on their class election project to change Daniel Webster Elementary from a "good little school" to a "great little school": good math, good teaching, fair rules, a soccer coach, workable equipment. Class member Bonnie Mann, chosen to run for interim principal, learns that more than her shy, "good-little-girl" reputation is necessary to effect changes. She must be assertive before the school community. Election night arrives, and parents are surprised to learn the depth of student commitment to the campaign.

5.223 Roe, Eliane Corbeil. **Circle of Light.** Harper and Row, 1989. ISBN 0-06-025079-8. 248p. 10 and up.

Lucy, a thirteen-year-old French Canadian, reluctantly agrees to represent her Catholic school in a regional scholastic competition. During the long months of hard study, Lucy grapples with isolation, teasing, grief over the deaths of her father and brother, and the pains of first love. Ultimately, her discipline and maturity bring honor to her school, pride and consolation to her family, and romance to her life.

5.224 Sharmat, Marjorie Weinman, and Mitchell Sharmat. **The Princess of the Fillmore Street School.** Illustrated by Denise Brunkus. Delacorte Press, 1989. ISBN 0-385-29811-0. 44p. 5–8.

In her second adventure as Agent for Secrets, Olivia Sharp, who is a cross between the pampered Eloise of the Ritz and the resourceful Encyclopedia Brown, is approached by neat-freak Desiree in her campaign to become Princess of Fillmore Street School. With chauffeur and boa, Olivia skirts disasters and wraps up a happy ending.

5.225 Waggoner, Karen. **The Lemonade Babysitter.** Illustrated by Dorothy Donohue. Little, Brown/Joy Street Books, 1992. ISBN 0-316-91711-7. 29p. 4–7 (est.).

Molly prefers tagging along to the office with her single mom rather than staying at home with a baby-sitter. In fact, when elderly neighbor Mr. Herbert shows up, Molly announces that she is too old for baby-sitters. When Molly realizes the inevitable, she makes plans to ensure his resignation. Yet Mr. Herbert remains good-natured, leading Molly to surprise him with her own brand of homemade lemonade. Expressive ink drawings will help readers to speculate on Mr. Herbert's return.

Humorous Stories

5.226 Blume, Judy. **Fudge-a-Mania.** Dutton Children's Books, 1990. ISBN 0-525-44672-9. 147p. 7–11 (est.).

"Blueberry Baby Feet," "Dizzy for Izzy," and "Turtle the Dog Meets Skunk": these are possible titles for chapters in the chaos that results when the families of Fudge Hatcher and Sheila Tubman spend three weeks together in the same vacation home. And at the center of most escapades is five-year-old Fudge. As more than half of the text consists of conversation, the book, or one of its many hilarious episodes, lends itself to classroom plays or amusing read-alouds.

5.227   Brittain, Bill. **My Buddy, the King.** Harper and Row, 1989. ISBN 0-06-020725-6. 135p. 9–12.

Tim Quilt just happens to be at the drug store on Saturday morning when the teenage king of Mokobway nearly chokes on a hot dog. It's Tim who saves his life, so interested government agents "encourage" Tim to become the king's buddy for the sake of rich oil reserves. But more trouble awaits the young ruler in a tussle for power among the people of Mokobway, and Tim's quick wits are needed again. Two friends who struggle to understand different cultures make for high-interest, funny episodes.

5.228   Busselle, Rebecca. **Bathing Ugly.** Orchard Books/Richard Jackson Books, 1988. ISBN 0-531-08401-9. 184p. 11 and up (est.).

When thirteen-year-old Betsy Sherman discovers that her mother sent her to camp to lose weight, Betsy is determined to turn her current image around and be selected this year's "Bathing Beauty." Instead, because of her good-natured personality and chubby figure, she is chosen to participate in the comical "Bathing Ugly" contest. Told in first person, Betsy's tale of designing and donning the most outrageous bathing costume in contest history is satisfying and giggle-producing.

5.229   Byars, Betsy. **The Seven Treasure Hunts.** Illustrated by Jennifer Barrett. HarperCollins, 1991. ISBN 0-06-020886-4. 74p. 7–11.

Fun and misadventure follow pals Jackson and Goat as the two boys set up a series of treasure hunts, determined to outsmart each other. During one of the hunts, Jackson inadvertently antagonizes Goat's bossy older sister, Rachel, by eating her Popsicle, so Rachel throws a kink into the boys' fun. Written by Newbery award-winning author Betsy Byars, this humorous book, enhanced by comical pen-and-ink drawings, is appropriate both for middle-grade readers or as a read-aloud book for primary-grade children.

5.230   Carris, Joan. **The Greatest Idea Ever.** Illustrated by Carol Newsom. J. B. Lippincott, 1990. ISBN 0-397-32379-4. 167p. 8–12.

Enterprising fourth-grader Gus Howard and his great ideas manage both to impress and to vex almost every significant other in his life—his mother; his saintly, patient teacher, Mr. Keene; and Nanny Vincent, his female counterpart and archnemesis. This time Gus tries to train a new dog and to organize a school art show. Joan Carris tells her innocent story in simple, plain English and weaves plot complications that are neatly tied in this fourth book about the Howard boys.

5.231   Conford, Ellen. **Dear Mom, Get Me Out of Here!** Little, Brown, 1992. ISBN 0-316-15370-2. 160p. 10–12 (est.).

For thirteen-year-old Paul Tanner, the boarding school that his parents chose, Burnside, is a cross between a medieval dungeon and a looney bin. Orson Autrey, Paul's self-proclaimed genius of a roommate (who tries to fly in his spare time), explains it this way: "You have to understand that there's something wrong with every kid here." Teachers, too, are unusual. Coach Waldrup, for example, schedules outdoor checkers tournaments in the snow. Then there's the malevolent Headmaster Pickles—Paul and friends suspect that he has a dark past and try to uncover his secrets.

5.232   Danziger, Paula. **Earth to Matthew.** Delacorte Press, 1991. ISBN 0-385-30453-6. 148p. 9–12.

Matthew Martin, lead character in two previous books by Paula Danziger, begins to experience some of the pangs of growing up: girls (in particular, one girl) are almost worth being teased about, some of his best retorts are being left unspoken, and a school project on the ecosystem is intriguing. In this adventure, Matthew and his class take a field trip to the Franklin Institute as part of their ecology study, an event that meshes story line with some didactic content.

5.233   Danziger, Paula. **Everyone Else's Parents Said Yes.** Delacorte Press, 1989. ISBN 0-385-29805-6. 115p. 9–12.

Matthew Martin can't wait until his eleventh-birthday sleep-over. He spends the time counting the days, tormenting girls, including his sister Amanda, and planning the list of junk food to serve. But just before the birthday, he has a fight with his best friend Joshua, the girls in his sixth-grade class organize to get their revenge, and Matthew finds his plans askew. In Paula Danziger's breezy style, Matthew's remorse, if not sincere, is at least funny in this first book about Matthew.

5.234   Danziger, Paula. **Make like a Tree and Leave.** Delacorte Press, 1990. ISBN 0-385-30151-0. 117p. 9–12.

Matthew Martin's adventure in this second book involves sibling rivalry and antics associated with serving as chair of the Mummy Committee on the Egypt Unit Project. From classmate

Brian Bruno's entrapment in a plaster mummy cast to a sudsy pet wash that is an altruistic effort to raise money for a class-mate's medical treatment, situations are fast-moving, making the book well suited as a read-aloud.

5.235 Gilson, Jamie. **Hobie Hanson: Greatest Hero of the Mall.** Illustrated by Anita Riggio. Lothrop, Lee and Shepard Books, 1989. ISBN 0-688-08968-2. 149p. 8–12 (est.).

Hobie's dreams of heroic deeds fade as he, the child whom he's baby-sitting, and Fido are rescued by know-it-all Molly during a town flood. Then, when classes for the fourth through sixth grades at Central School are forced to resume at the defunct "Bob's Togs for All the Family" in Wilhurst Mall, it is Molly who finds the bag of valuables that Hobie lost during his rescue. The bag is later stolen, and Hobie's laughable ordeals while retrieving his treasures from Larry Lion earn him the long-awaited title of "Greatest Hero of the Mall."

5.236 Goode, Diane. **Where's Our Mama?** Illustrated by Diane Goode. Dutton Children's Books, 1991. ISBN 0-525-44770-9. 28p. 3–7 (est.).

At the Gare d'Orsay, a Paris train station, Mama's hat blows off, and she chases it out of sight. With Mama lost, her children beg a gendarme's help in finding "the most beautiful woman in the world." Together, they search the city—visiting a school, a baker, a theater—but they see no one who looks or acts like Mama. Meantime, careful readers will spot Mama flitting in and out of scenes looking for her children. But weren't they supposed to wait at the station? Diane Goode's period costumes and scenes reflect the cluttered, elegant charm of the Parisian setting and a comforting ending as well.

5.237 Grossman, Bill. **The Guy Who Was Five Minutes Late.** Illustrations by Judy Glasser. Harper and Row, 1990. ISBN 0-06-022269-7. 32p. 3–6 (est.).

When a baby is born just five minutes late, this sets the pattern for his entire life. Ever after, "by night or by day, / at work or at play," he is always five minutes late. When he is late to his own wedding, the bride marries his brother instead. But things turn out just fine when he meets the Princess Carrie, who shares his late trait. Rhyming text, an identifiable theme, and stylized illustrations make for exaggerated fun.

5.238   Hutchins, Pat. **Rats!** Illustrated by Laurence Hutchins. Greenwillow Books, 1989. ISBN 0-688-07776-5. 96p. 6–10 (est.).

More than anything, Sam wants a rat. He wants a rat so badly that he buys one before asking his parents' permission. Nevertheless, after a full-tilt public relations campaign, Sam's parents acquiesce, and Nibbles is his. But one small rat wreaks giant havoc. Nibbles scares visitor Veronica into a faint, creates racket enough so that the police are notified, and ends up giving birth to nine new Nibbles. Laurence Hutchins's black-and-white drawings are wacky matches for the text.

5.239   Levine, Evan. **Not the Piano, Mrs. Medley!** Illustrated by S. D. Schindler. Orchard Books/Richard Jackson Books, 1991. ISBN 0-531-08556-2. 32p. 4–7.

Despite Max's impatience, his grandmother, Mrs. Medley, can't walk to the beach without packing half her belongings—including table, chairs, bongo drums, her Monopoly set, and an accordion. But once there, she's so smitten by the sand and the waves that she forgets all of the paraphernalia, and the two laugh together when they realize she has brought everything but the swimsuits! Illustrations are filled with the humorous clutter of Mrs. Medley's possessions and her infectious glee when she recognizes her silliness.

5.240   Lillie, Patricia. **When the Rooster Crowed.** Illustrated by Nancy Winslow Parker. Greenwillow Books, 1991. ISBN 0-688-09379-5. 32p. 3–6.

For a farmer awakened by the crow of the rooster at ten minutes to five, there is need for "ten more minutes." When his cow says "Mmmooo," and his rooster goes "Cock-a-doodle-doo" again, it's "five more minutes" that the farmer needs. Other barnyard animals add to the rooster's wake-up call, but it takes them all in chorus to make the farmer say, "ALL RIGHT!" and begin his morning chores. Colors are morning-cheerful, shapes are simple, and scenes are uncluttered.

5.241   Lowry, Lois. **Anastasia at This Address.** Houghton Mifflin, 1991. ISBN 0-395-56263-5. 130p. 8–12.

Eighth in the Anastasia series, this humorous novel explores Anastasia's misadventures in the world of romance. Responding to a personal ad written by a wealthy, sophisticated, twenty-eight-year-old bachelor, Anastasia begins a correspondence full of half-truths in order to spice up her lackluster love life. When a friend's wedding and fate intervene, Anastasia ends her "love-letters" escapade with a big sigh of relief.

5.242 Mahy, Margaret. **The Great White Man-Eating Shark: A Cautionary Tale.** Illustrated by Jonathan Allen. Dial Books for Young Readers, 1990. ISBN 0-8037-0749-5. 32p. 5–8.

It is not Norvin's fault that he is an actor who looks like a great white shark. But it *is* his fault that he is such a greedy boy that he doesn't want to share the cove with other swimmers. Through a combination of his looks, his swimming agility, his acting talent, and a strapped-on dorsal fin, Norvin terrorizes the summer crowd, sending people screeching to shore. His plot is foiled, however, by the appearance of a real shark who takes a fancy to Norvin.

5.243 Manes, Stephen. **Chocolate-Covered Ants.** Scholastic Hardcover Books, 1990. ISBN 0-590-40960-3. 103p. 8–12.

It all starts when Max's little brother Adam gets an ant farm for his birthday. That's when Max tells Adam about people eating chocolate-covered ants. Because Adam refuses to accept that contention, the bet is on. The taste of ants is eloquently described in a story that is reminiscent of Thomas Rockwell's *How to Eat Fried Worms*. Stephen Manes offers groaners for middle graders that include ants sneaked into ice cream, hidden in covers, and exploded in the microwave.

5.244 Manes, Stephen. **Make Four Million Dollar$ by Next Thur$day!** Illustrated by George Ulrich. Bantam/Skylark Books, 1991. ISBN 0-553-07050-9. 87p. 8–12 (est.).

Jason Nozzle wants to be a multimillionaire. Lucky for him, he finds a book by Dr. K. Pinkerton Silverfish titled *Make Four Million Dollar$ by Next Thur$day*. The book's instructions are to follow Dr. Silverfish's advice without deviation and definitely not to read ahead. So Jason buries money, pins thirty-seven dollar signs to his clothes for a day, chants a money mantra, and, in general, performs to code. Readers may recognize Dr. Silverfish as author of *Be a Perfect Person in Just Three Days*.

5.245 Paulsen, Gary. **The Boy Who Owned the School: A Comedy of Love.** Orchard Books/Richard Jackson Books, 1990. ISBN 0-531-08465-5. 85p. 11 and up.

Jacob Freisten does his best to slip through high school—and life—completely unnoticed. In order to avoid flunking English, he is forced by Mrs. Hilsak to help out as a stage-crew member for the school play. When his love for the play's star, Maria Tesser, goes unrequited, Jacob finally energizes himself, discovering both romance and his own potential. Gary Paulsen's dry humor and highly readable prose make this an easy read for less motivated students.

5.246 Peck, Robert Newton. **Higbee's Halloween.** Walker, 1990. ISBN 0-0827-6969-1. 101p. 10–12.

Halloween in Clod's Corner is unforgettable the year that the Striker gang moves in from Siberia. When Canker, Hernia, Zitt, and the other Strikers erect their torture-chamber fort in town, Higbee H. Higgenbottom knows he must counter the bullies. As told by his friend and reluctant accomplice, Quincy, the tale centers on revenge, pumpkin pies, and a cannon on the village green. Quincy's pompous language offsets Higbee's Huck Finn nonchalance, and the pieces fall together for the "smashing" climax.

5.247 Peck, Robert Newton. **Soup in Love.** Illustrated by Charles Robinson. Delacorte Press, 1992. ISBN 0-385-30563-X. 114p. 9–12.

Soup and Rob are up to new plans and pranks in their twelfth adventure in 1920s rural Vermont. This time the boys are aiming to win the prize for the most unusual valentine in the village in order to impress the town's prettiest girls. The valentine construction depends on Mrs. Spazzatura's new refrigerator box, a leftover toboggan, a white horse named Black Thunder, and a visitor named Ox. The results are as funny and as predictable as readers can imagine.

5.248 Pinkwater, Daniel. **Uncle Melvin.** Illustrated by Daniel Pinkwater. Macmillan, 1989. ISBN 0-02-774675-5. 27p. 5–8.

Charles's Uncle Melvin is different from other people. Some even say that he's crazy. Uncle Melvin says that he understands what the birds and animals say to him. He says that his old-fashioned derby keeps his thoughts from bouncing away. He even thinks that the president is an iguana. But Charles knows that Uncle Melvin has a special perception and understanding about the world. Daniel Pinkwater's scribbly backgrounds, bright colors, and mild faces give a lift to this warm tale for children.

5.249 Remkiewicz, Frank. **Greedyanna.** Illustrated by Frank Remkiewicz. Lothrop, Lee and Shepard Books, 1992. ISBN 0-688-10295-6. 32p. 4–8.

Little Anna is "going through a phase." For her, everything (except lima beans) is "Mine!" Brother Eddie renames her "Greedyanna," and the family indulges her totally, even moving to the garage so the greedy one does not have to share the house. But Greedyanna soon learns that being selfish is lonely and not much fun after all. Ink drawings painted with watercolor and gouache are as comical as the words.

5.250 Sachar, Louis. **Wayside School Is Falling Down.** Illustrated by Joel Schick. Lothrop, Lee and Shepard Books, 1989. ISBN 0-688-07868-0. 179p. 8–10.

The students from the looney thirty-story Wayside School are back in this sequel to *Sideways Stories from Wayside School.* Back is Mrs. Jewls, teacher on the thirtieth floor for a "class where nobody was strange because nobody was normal." Back are the three Erics (Fry, Bacon, and Ovens). Back is Todd, who always rides the kindergarten bus home at noon because his name is forever on the board. Back, too, are all the other students who dread Mrs. Mush's cafeteria concoctions, who avoid the basement at all costs, and who puzzle over the absence of a twenty-ninth floor.

5.251 Samuels, Barbara. **What's So Great about Cindy Snappleby?** Illustrated by Barbara Samuels. Orchard Books, 1992. ISBN 0-531-08579-1. 32p. 3–6.

Cool Cindy Snappleby is coming to play with Dolores's big sister, Faye. Cindy wears pink hair ribbons and pink-dotted dresses and thinks little children are usually messy and pesty. Self-assured Cindy shares the secret of how she always wins in jacks by saying, "steady as a rock and cool as a cucumber." It's up to Dolores to shake Cindy Snappleby's calm by sharing some secrets of her own—including a box of live frogs. Sisters align in this Dolores story filled with bright action.

5.252 Spinelli, Jerry. **The Bathwater Gang.** Illustrated by Meredith Johnson. Little, Brown/Springboard Books, 1990. ISBN 0-316-80720-6. 59p. 7–11 (est.).

When Granny suggests to bored Bertie that a good summer activity may be to start a gang, Granny had in mind a *good* gang—one that does projects. But "gangs" have a different connotation for Mrs. Pickwell, the mother of Bertie's best friend, and she refuses to let her daughter join. And it looks as though Mrs. Pickwell is right: a boys' gang forms to combat Bertie's, and balloon and egg fights break out. It takes Granny starting *her* own gang to settle the fracas.

5.253   Stevenson, Suçie. **Jessica the Blue Streak.** Illustrated by Suçie Stevenson. Orchard Books/Richard Jackson Books, 1989. ISBN 0-531-08398-5. 29p. 5–8 (est.).

Daddy brings home an energetic, six-month-old puppy named Jessica. The family dogs are not impressed with this "blue streak," and the children spend their day fetching things Jessica has snatched, keeping Jessica from chewing shoes and furniture, and cleaning up after her. Cartoon-like watercolors show rambunctious Jessica in action.

5.254   Tusa, Tricia. **Sherman and Pearl.** Illustrated by Tricia Tusa. Macmillan, 1989. ISBN 0-02-789542-4. 28p. 4–8 (est.).

Sherman and Pearl like to sit by their dirt road every day and wave to all the people who pass by. But when bulldozers come to build a freeway just beyond the old dirt road, being friendly becomes a lot harder. Unwilling to give up hope, they wait and wait until the people finally choose to leave the freeway behind and return to the old dirt road. Expressive watercolors make Sherman and Pearl a comical pair.

5.255   Wilson, Sarah. **The Day That Henry Cleaned His Room.** Illustrated by Sarah Wilson. Simon and Schuster Books for Young Readers, 1990. ISBN 0-671-69202-X. 32p. 4–8.

The cartoon-like figures bring an animated quality to this humorous account of Henry's room cleaning. Animals, scientists, the army, and his family all help Henry get rid of the clutter, the moss, and the mismatched socks that are lurking under his bed. But Henry isn't happy until his old friends return.

5.256   Woodruff, Elvira. **Show and Tell.** Illustrated by Denise Brunkus. Holiday House, 1991. ISBN 0-8234-0883-3. 32p. 4–8.

Andy has wild red hair, horn-rimmed glasses, huge front teeth, and the most boring show-and-tell ideas in the whole kindergarten—maybe even in the whole world. Once he brought a paperclip, another time a shoestring, and then a bent fork. Even Mrs. Applelarney yawned. But then Andy finds a bubble jar with a warning label attached and sets a new standard in zany show-and-tell history.

Mystery Stories

5.257 Alexander, Sue. **World Famous Muriel and the Magic Mystery.** Illustrated by Marla Frazee. Thomas Y. Crowell, 1990. ISBN 0-690-04789-4. 32p. 5–8 (est.).

When the Great Hokus Pokus disappears in the middle of an unsuccessful rehearsal for his magic show, Professor Ballyhoo enlists the help of the World Famous Muriel in finding him. Armed with a batch of peanut butter cookies (which help her do her best thinking), Muriel relies on her extraordinary powers of deduction to trace the Great Hokus Pokus to the place where a magician in difficulty would most likely go—the public library. Readers will find Marla Frazee's detailed illustrations as engaging as the story line.

5.258 Bunting, Eve. **Coffin on a Case.** HarperCollins, 1992. ISBN 0-06-020274-2. 106p. 10 and up (est.).

Like Sam Spade, Paul Coffin's dad is a private detective— trench coat, slouchy hat, and name on a frosted glass door. All Dad needs, Paul is sure, is either for Mom to come back or for a really gorgeous woman to ask them to take her case. Enter gorgeous Lily Larson, age sixteen, whose mother is missing and who needs a detective. The case falls circuitously to Paul, and before things settle, the mystery involves wooden storks, art thieves, and kidnapping.

5.259 DeClements, Barthe. **Wake Me at Midnight.** Viking Penguin, 1991. ISBN 0-670-84038-6. 154p. 8–12.

Caitlin LeBlanc's neighborhood bustles with nocturnal activity—and all of it seems inexplicable. For example, someone next door shovels in the backyard at midnight. Is it quiet, skinny, thirteen-year-old "Bones," who Caitlin suspects doesn't get enough to eat? And across the street, the Dorman's house has strange comings and goings at all hours. With her new neighbor, Missy, Caitlin is drawn into crime detection. Her own home life with a traveling father, work-weary mother, and unexpected baby brother offers other problems.

5.260 Dillon, Eilís. **The Island of Ghosts.** Charles Scribner's Sons/Books for Young Readers, 1989. ISBN 0-684-19107-5. 151p. 10 and up.

Dara and Brendan, twelve-year-old best friends, share the simple traditions of their Irish island village, often swimming, sailing, and storytelling with their younger sisters. Their lives are interrupted by an offer of tutoring for school entrance exams by an American engineer with a mysterious past. Under the guise of gaining the boys' friendship, the American darkly hints of interest in a nearby island, said to be haunted; then he kidnaps and questions the boys. As a read-aloud, this book offers much for talking over—loyalty, family, morality, and traditions.

5.261   Giff, Patricia Reilly. **Garbage Juice for Breakfast.** Illustrated by Blanche Sims. Dell/Young Yearling Books, 1989. ISBN 0-440-40207-7. 69p. 6–9.

Campers at Camp Wild-in-the-Woods agree that garbage juice any time tastes yucky, but solving Miss Perry's mysteries is definitelty thrilling—especially for competitors Dawn Bosco, the Polka Dot Private Eye, and Lizzie Lee, the Cool Cat Detective. When the announced mystery contest is "HELP TO FIND TREASURE," each girl is confident that she will find the treasure first. Searching for clues in the barn and through the trails, the two detectives, neck-in-neck, unravel the mystery of "Treasure" and unleash some of their personal problems along the way. Five other Polka Dot Private Eye books are available to interested readers.

5.262   Roennfeldt, Mary. **What's That Noise?** Illustrated by Robert Roennfeldt. Orchard Books, 1992. ISBN 0-531-08572-4. 32p. 3–6.

George hears a strange noise in the night and searches for its source. Readers will spot a chalky white cat bounding from page to page, but sleepy George misses it all. Green, shadowy beasts announce the cat's passage in the briefest of speech balloons: "screech" or "bray" or "growl." The next morning, when a very tired, confused George dons his zookeeper uniform, a fuzzy white cat peeks from under his bed. The zoo animals know who made that noise in the night. "Do you?"

5.263   Sharmat, Marjorie Weinman. **Nate the Great and the Halloween Hunt. Nate the Great and the Musical Note. Nate the Great and the Stolen Base. Nate the Great Goes Down in the Dumps.** Illustrated by Marc Simont. G. P. Putnam's Sons, 1989–92. 48p. 6–9.

In the spirit of the Encyclopedia Brown classics, detective Nate the Great hunts down clues and solves cases with the aid of his dog, Sludge, and his eccentric friend Rosamond. Each easy-to-read story in the Nate the Great series contains a mystery com-

A.

B.

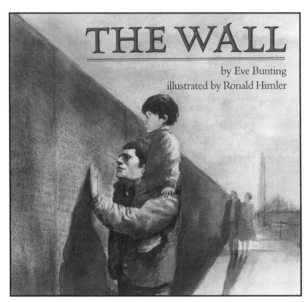

C.

A. *The Vandemark Mummy* by Cynthia Voigt (see 5.267).   **B.** *Nate the Great and the Stolen Base* by Marjorie Weinman Sharmat; illustrated by Marc Simont (see 5.263). **C.** *The Wall* by Eve Bunting; illustrated by Ronald Himler (see 5.191).

A.

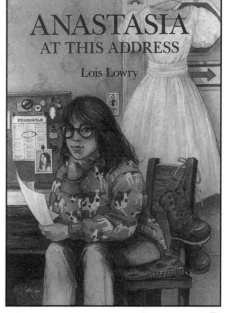

B.

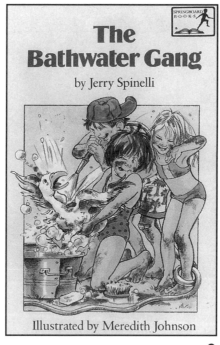

C.

D.

A. *Greedyanna* by Frank Remkiewicz (see 5.249). **B.** *Anastasia at This Address* by Lois Lowry (see 5.241). **C.** *The Bathwater Gang* by Jerry Spinelli; illustrated by Meredith Johnson (see 5.252). **D.** *Fudge-a-Mania* by Judy Blume (see 5.226).

plete with clues that the reader can use to think along with Nate. Simple illustrations in limited colors portray the action on a part of nearly every page.

5.264 Singer, Marilyn. **The Hoax on You.** Illustrated by Richard Williams. Harper and Row, 1989. ISBN 0-06-025851-9. 59p. 8–12 (est.).

In this sixth book of the Sam and Dave mystery series, identical twins Sam and Dave Bean find themselves tailing the new foreign exchange student in town. Jewelry has been stolen from the homes that she has visited, and the junior detectives are hot on her trail. The book's relatively short sentences, heavy reliance on dialogue to move the plot along, and black-and-white illustrations all make this an easy read for young mystery fans.

5.265 Sobol, Donald J. **Encyclopedia Brown and the Case of the Disgusting Sneakers.** Illustrated by Gail Owens. Morrow Junior Books, 1990. ISBN 0-688-09012-5. 92p. 7–12.

Untouched by inflation, ageless Encyclopedia Brown still charges twenty-five cents in each of these ten new cases. Smelly sneakers, pink and orange canoes, and strangely carved trees provide some of the clues. The stories, as always, are full of humorous similes and provide readers with a chance to apply their own knowledge of science and deduction to match wits with the boy genius.

5.266 Trease, Geoffrey. **A Flight of Angels.** Lerner, 1989. ISBN 0-8225-0731-5. 120p. 9–13.

A mysteriously marked cellar in historical Nottingham, England, intrigues Sheila and her three classmates into exploring underground caves and investigating a 400-year-old secret. Aided by a history-buff librarian, the resourceful detectives use clues and deductive reasoning to solve a mystery that involves a religious conflict of the Middle Ages and to resolve a present-day dilemma.

5.267 Voigt, Cynthia. **The Vandemark Mummy.** Fawcett Juniper Books, 1992. ISBN 0-449-70417-3. 209p. 10 and up (est.).

Moving with their college instructor father to Maine, Althea Hall and her brother Phineas try to adjust to life in a new place without Mom, who has a new job on the West Coast. Through the terms of a founder's family will, Mr. Hall unexpectedly becomes curator of a bequeathed Egyptian collection. Even though the Halls take the responsibility seriously, the collection's mummy is stolen. Then Althea is missing, too, and Phineas must do some clever sleuthing before a thief's greed endangers his sister's life. Characters are realistically and fully drawn.

Respect for Nature

5.268 Allen, Judy. **Tiger.** Illustrated by Tudor Humphries. Candlewick Press, 1992. ISBN 1-56402-083-5. 29p. 6–10 (est.).

When a rumor starts that there is a tiger in the woods, the villagers plan to kill it to become strong, brave, and wealthy. A famous hunter comes to track the tiger, and Young Lee, a boy who does not want the tiger to die, wishes the hunter bad luck. Through delicate earth-tone watercolors, the illustrator shares not only the secret of "shooting" the tiger without killing it, but the mountainous countryside and the beauty of the great South Chinese Tiger. A concluding Tiger Fact Sheet enlists readers' help in tiger-saving efforts.

5.269 Aschenbrenner, Gerald (adapted by Joanne Fink). **Jack, the Seal and the Sea.** Illustrated by Joanne Fink. Silver Burdett Press, 1988. ISBN 0-382-09735-1. 28p. 4–7 (est.).

Jack, a fisherman like his father, nets a seal dying from water pollution. After helping the seal, Jack is rewarded by a healthy catch and, through a dream, is alerted to the dangers of polluting the sea. Now Jack sails not to fish but to deliver his message that everyone must join in the effort to clean up our seas. Both Jack and the creatures of the sea are endearingly portrayed in realistic black, white, and sepia drawings.

5.270 Baker, Jeannie. **Window.** Illustrated by Jeannie Baker. Greenwillow Books, 1991. ISBN 0-688-08918-6. 24p. All ages (est.).

In a series of wordless, strikingly unusual double-page spreads, a boy's view through a windowpane changes from wilderness to city as he changes from infant to adult. Through the glass, readers see collage constructions depicting environmental change; on windowsill and frame they see objects depicting advancing age. A concluding author's note, extrapolating to humankind's destruction of wilderness and consequent extinction of species, urges each individual to protect the environment. *Notable 1991 Children's Trade Books in the Field of Social Studies.*

5.271 Björk, Christina (translated by Joan Sandin). **Linnea's Almanac.** Illustrated by Lena Anderson. R & S Books, 1989. ISBN 91-29-59176-7. 61p. 6–10 (est.).

An almanac that Linnea receives for Christmas inspires her to keep her own almanac, in which she records all her activities and reports on what's happening in the world around her. When the January snows come, she opens a bird restaurant; in February, she repots plants; and in March, Linnea spies the first spring flower and hears the blackbirds sing. From Linnea's month-by-month accounting of her discoveries, readers will learn scientifically verified information about their natural environment.

5.272 Blyler, Allison. **Finding Foxes.** Illustrated by Robert J. Blake. Philomel Books, 1991. ISBN 0-399-22264-2. 32p. 6–8 (est.).

In poetic text and double-page earth-tone paintings, the movement, mystery, and majesty of the red fox are illuminated for the not-so-young reader. The hunt and the kill are urgent—"The fox is cruelly red, in a knife of sun." Through metaphor and a tone that is hushed and respectful, Allison Blyler offers "the ways of the fox," while Robert Blake interprets those ways in dappled forest scenes in which the foxes are hiding from the reader. These gouache paintings in olives and browns show brush strokes against canvas-like page borders.

5.273 Carlstrom, Nancy White. **Goodbye Geese.** Illustrated by Ed Young. Philomel Books, 1991. ISBN 0-399-21832-7. 34p. 4–6.

On an outdoor walk toward the end of autumn, a father poetically describes winter in answer to his child's simple yet complex questions. Each metaphoric answer stimulates another question. The child wonders whether winter has hands, a voice, a shape. "Does winter have ears?" the child asks. "When geese spread their wings in the sky and fly honking south, winter hears and winter comes." Caldecott-medalist Ed Young brings a glowing stillness to the change in seasons.

5.274 Chall, Martha Wilson. **Up North at the Cabin.** Illustrated by Steve Johnson. Lothrop, Lee and Shepard Books, 1992. ISBN 0-688-09733-2. 32p. 5 and up.

A child recalls her family trips to a cabin in the north, where days were filled with swimming, canoeing, water skiing, and fishing with Grandpa, using peanut-butter-and-worm sandwiches for bait. As with Cynthia Rylant's *When I Was Young in the Mountains*, Martha Wilson Chall's poetic text testifies to the spirit and beauty of a special place etched in clear memories. Grandma's corn-on-the-cob is nibbled while "loons dance down the sun." Steve Johnson's paintings catch the light and mottled shadows of perfect summer days.

5.275   Cotler, Joanna. **Sky Above, Earth Below.** Illustrated by Joanna Cotler. Harper and Row/Charlotte Zolotow Books, 1990. ISBN 0-06-021366-3. 32p. 3–5.

Patterns of sky and earth look beautiful to a little girl viewing them through an airplane window. Joanna Cotler's simple cut-out pictures of clouds, stars, rivers, trees, houses, and animals are set against vividly contrasting backgrounds. Sparse text adds drama to the minimalist shapes and patterns of the illustrations.

5.276   Cowcher, Helen. **Antarctica.** Illustrated by Helen Cowcher. Farrar, Straus and Giroux, 1990. ISBN 0-374-30368-1. 36p. 4–8.

In this thought-provoking yet gentle tale, Helen Cowcher describes the life of Antarctic inhabitants—emperor and Adélie penguins and Weddell seals. Paralleling predictable hazards of natural enemies with the unknown threats of new arrivals—human beings—the author leaves the consequences of human intrusion upon the ancient Antarctic world an open-ended question. Watercolor washes effectively portray a pristine environment of mystery and ice. *Outstanding Science Trade Books for Children in 1990.*

5.277   Ehlert, Lois. **Feathers for Lunch.** Illustrated by Lois Ehlert. Harcourt Brace Jovanovich, 1990. ISBN 0-15-230550-5. 32p. 3–8.

When the cat slips out the door, he looks around for a special lunch. As the belled cat "jingles" his way through the garden, he and young readers meet twelve backyard birds, including mourning doves, a northern cardinal, and an American robin. But despite the cat's best sneaking and snooping, all this feline gets is "feathers for lunch." The humorous rhyming text is bountifully illustrated with brilliant and clearly labeled collages of birds and flowers. An illustrated listing of the birds and information about their size, food, and habitat complete the book. *Outstanding Science Trade Books for Children in 1990.*

5.278   Florian, Douglas. **Nature Walk.** Illustrated by Douglas Florian. Greenwillow Books, 1989. ISBN 0-688-08269-6. 29p. 3–7.

Two children and a guide go on a nature trail and discover pine cones, hidden lakes, swallowtails, and more. Captioned, earth-tone illustrations along with a seek-and-find activity help readers to conclude that discovering nature means seeing more than you expected to see. *ALA Notable Children's Trade Books in Science, 1989.*

5.279 Hamilton, Virginia. **Drylongso.** Illustrated by Jerry Pinkney. Harcourt Brace Jovanovich, 1992. ISBN 0-15-224241-4. 64p. 8–12.

West of the Mississippi in the 1970s, dust storms come. No matter that Mamalou covers the cracks with tatter cloths—dust gets in everyplace. To young Lindy's family, the dust also brings Drylongso, a quiet boy of mythic proportions whose name once meant "long-time drought." Drylongso knows about overplowing, what plants hold the soil, and how to use a divining rod. Virginia Hamilton's text sings as it teaches, and Jerry Pinkney's illustrations transport readers through the thirsty storm and its aftermath.

5.280 Heiligman, Deborah. **Into the Night.** Illustrated by Melissa Sweet. Harper and Row, 1990. ISBN 0-06-026382-2. 26p. 4–8 (est.).

As a little boy readies for bed, he questions his mother: "Do you think our day is over too soon?" Together, they recall their event-filled day. Told in rhyming couplets, the lyrical text recounts their play, their walk through the meadows, and their discoveries of nature's treasures. Large pastel watercolor illustrations capture mother and son's outdoor adventure and help to create a reassuring story of important life events as day passes "into the night."

5.281 Hol, Coby. **A Visit to the Farm.** Illustrated by Coby Hol. North-South Books, 1989. ISBN 1-55858-000-X. 24p. 4–8 (est.).

For the first time, Julie and Martin have permission to spend a day at the farm on their own. Visiting old and new friends, the children watch and feed many animals, including chickens, pigs, and rabbits. Leaving with an armload of farm-fresh treats, Julie and Martin look forward to their next visit. Torn-paper collages against great white spaces illustrate this simple, satisfying story of a day on the farm.

5.282 Ichikawa, Satomi. **Nora's Duck.** Illustrated by Satomi Ichikawa. Philomel Books, 1991. ISBN 0-399-21805-X. 32p. 4–8.

When Nora finds an injured duckling, she takes it to Doctor John. During her visit, Nora meets many once-injured animals that have come to live on this specialized farm under Doctor John's care. Watercolor illustrations accompany this story of the importance of all living creatures. The author's afterword provides readers with information about the real Doctor John and his animal sanctuary in Kent, England.

5.283   Johnson, Herschel. **A Visit to the Country.** Illustrated by Romare Bearden. Harper and Row, 1989. ISBN 0-06-022854-7. 32p. 2–8.

Even though people are always coming and going through the country on the *Mountain Express*, Mike and his grandparents are content to stay on their farm caring for Bessie, gathering eggs, and watching nature at play. When Mike finds a cardinal nestling, he and his grandparents nurture the bird until it learns to fly. Then a decision must be made about "comings and goings." The paintings by the late African American artist Romare Bearden, winner of the 1987 National Medal of Arts, add drama to this, his only children's book.

5.284   Lyon, George Ella. **Who Came Down That Road?** Illustrated by Peter Catalanotto. Orchard Books/Richard Jackson Books, 1992. ISBN 0-531-08587-2. 32p. 4–7.

When a boy asks a question about who came down the road, the mother responds in a reverie. She leads him back through history to her grandparents, the Civil War, the Native Americans, the mastodons—back to the beginning of time. Brilliant, impressionistic, full-page watercolors alternating light with shadow have a dream-like quality that hints at mysteries beyond those visible.

5.285   McDonald, Megan. **Whoo-oo Is It?** Illustrated by S. D. Schindler. Orchard Books/Richard Jackson Books, 1992. ISBN 0-531-08574-0. 32p. 2–6.

A lyrical narrative and soft, dark, naturalistic paintings mesh to form an owl's night world. From her barnloft nest, Mother Owl hears mysterious noises. She searches to find their source, encountering a snake, a dragonfly, and other night creatures, each with its distinctive sound. Just at dawn she realizes that the eggs she has guarded and warmed have begun to change. This book is both an onomatopoeic experience and an evocation of the wonder of living beings.

5.286 Murphy, Jim. **The Call of the Wolves.** Illustrated by Mark Alan Weatherby. Scholastic Hardcover Books, 1989. ISBN 0-590-41941-2. 32p. 4–8.

As a young Arctic wolf and his pack attack a herd of caribou, the young wolf is injured by a rifle shot from an airplane and must fight desperately through a blizzard to return to the safety of its pack. This magnificently and realistically illustrated book is useful in learning of the plight of the Arctic wolf, an endangered species. The author has added a factual account of the past, present, and future of the wolf and a bibliography.

5.287 Parnall, Peter. **Quiet.** Illustrated by Peter Parnall. Morrow Junior Books, 1989. ISBN 0-688-08205-X. 28p. 5–10 (est.).

A child waits in quiet for a raven, chipmunk, mouse, and chickadee to come close to him as he lies on the ground, "a quiet, wrinkled thing under a pile of seeds and apple cores." And quietly, quietly they come. Peter Parnall's detailed illustrations bring the forest to life. *Notable Children's Trade Books in Science, 1989.*

5.288 Rockwell, Anne. **Apples and Pumpkins.** Illustrated by Lizzy Rockwell. Macmillan, 1989. ISBN 0-02-777270-5. 22p. 4–8.

Fall brings red and yellow leaves and a trip to Comstock Farms, where a little girl and her family pick a bushel of red apples and the best pumpkin of all. On Halloween night, the pumpkin shines with its jack-o'-lantern light and the apples are a treat for costumed tricksters. Rich autumn-colored paintings help to illustrate one little girl's enjoyment of the fall season. *ALA Notable Children's Trade Books in Science, 1989.*

5.289 Rockwell, Anne. **My Spring Robin.** Illustrated by Harlow Rockwell and Lizzy Rockwell. Macmillan, 1989. ISBN 0-02-777611-5. 24p. 2–6.

Harlow and Lizzy Rockwell's large uncluttered illustrations follow a young girl's discovery of signs of spring as she searches for the special robin that flew away last fall. After such wonders as crocuses, tiny toads, daffodils, soft rain showers, and violets appear, the robin heralds spring's return with that special "Cheer-up, cheerilee!" song.

5.290 Schlein, Miriam. **The Year of the Panda.** Illustrated by Kam Mak. Thomas Y. Crowell, 1990. ISBN 0-690-04866-1. 83p. 8–12 (est.).

Lu Yi, a young farm boy in China, rescues an orphaned baby panda that has moved to lower slopes in search of food because the bamboo forests are dying. In the process of nursing the panda back to health, Lu Yi learns about a massive government relocation program for this endangered species. The boy accompanies the cub to the Panda Rescue Center and there learns even more about the animals and how they are being protected.

5.291   Tresselt, Alvin. **The Gift of the Tree.** Illustrated by Henri Sorensen. Lothrop, Lee and Shepard Books, 1992. ISBN 0-688-10685-4. 32p. 4–8 (est.).

First published in 1972 as *The Dead Tree*, this book depicts the normal life cycle of an oak tree. At first a healthy haven for wildlife, providing a "rich rain of acorns," the tree is slowly besieged by enemies. Over time, carpenter ants, grub beetles, and termites eat out "passageways in wondrous patterns." Felled by a storm, the oak continues to provide shelter and food, nourishing the earth as it rots. Oil paintings reflect the tree's majesty and the moods of the passing seasons.

5.292   Turner, Ann. **Heron Street.** Illustrated by Lisa Desimini. Harper and Row/Charlotte Zolotow Books, 1989. ISBN 0-06-026185-4. 32p. 6–9.

In this lyrical story, Ann Turner chronicles the changes wrought by human hands upon a seaside marsh. In particular, Turner's story focuses on how the sounds of this community change over time. Lisa Desimini's vivid illustrations in a folk-art style create a striking complement to the story. The book could be used in the classroom in an environment/ecology unit, or to illustrate onomatopoeia in writing. *Notable 1989 Children's Trade Books in the Field of Social Studies.*

5.293   Weller, Francis Ward. **I Wonder If I'll See a Whale.** Illustrated by Ted Lewin. Philomel Books, 1991. ISBN 0-399-21474-7. 32p. 4–8.

A young girl watches expectantly, even reverently, from the deck of a whale-watching boat, hoping for more than a brief glimpse of the humpbacks that migrate in spring to New England coasts. The crew knows the whales by their markings and have given them names. Suddenly, "To starboard!" someone calls, and the adventure begins. The child's sense of excitement and awe as the "giants" spout, breach, feed, dive, and simply register curiosity is handled expertly both through Francis Ward Weller's poetic text and Ted Lewin's immense, sea-splashed mammal "cousins."

5.294 Wellington, Monica. **Seasons of Swans.** Illustrated by Monica Wellington. Dutton Children's Books, 1990. ISBN 0-525-44621-4. 32p. 3–7.

This realistic story of two swans living on Willow Pond accurately describes the nesting behavior of swans, as well as how they train their cygnets to swim and protect them from would-be predators. After a summer of feeding on waterweeds and insects, the baby swans grow strong and independent, leaving their nest in early fall. Flat illustrations in dark outlines, showing a boy and girl observing the swans' development, add to the narrative feel of this informational text.

5.295 Williams, David. **Walking to the Creek.** Illustrated by Thomas B. Allen. Alfred A. Knopf/Borzoi Books, 1990. ISBN 0-394-90598-9. 32p. 5–8.

The love of family and the wonder of nature are central themes of *Walking to the Creek,* which describes twin boys visiting their grandparents' farm. As the boys hike to the creek near the farm, they delight in the beauty of the natural world. Thomas Allen's soft, earth-tone, chalk illustrations of the farm and creek complement David Williams's descriptive images. The book provides an excellent example of figurative language.

Social Issues

5.296 Avi. **Nothing but the Truth: A Documentary Novel.** Orchard Books/Richard Jackson Books, 1991. ISBN 0-531-08559-7. 177p. 9 and up.

In a collage of perspectives, accounts emerge of an incident that occurs in Margaret Narwin's ninth-grade homeroom: track-team hopeful Philip Mallory hums along during the taped playing of "The Star-Spangled Banner." Since students are to remain silent during the anthem, Miss Narwin sends him to the office. The situation escalates, and eventually Philip is suspended. Through memos, phone transcripts, letters, journals, and news accounts, the principles reveal their views of the incident as it grows, punishes, and creates a moratorium on rights and responsibilities. *Jane Addams Award, 1991; Newbery Honor Book, 1992.*

5.297   Dugan, Barbara. **Loop the Loop.** Illustrated by James Stevenson. Greenwillow Books, 1992. ISBN 0-688-09648-4. 32p. 5 and up (est.).

This captivating story follows the relationship between a shy girl and a passionate, life-loving old woman fighting the vicissitudes of age. Anne befriends Mrs. Simpson, who laughs, wisecracks, and performs fabulous yo-yo tricks—from her wheelchair. But Mrs. Simpson's declining health forces their relationship into new forms, a problem that the author presents honestly and resolves gracefully. In the end we see how much human beings can give each other. James Stevenson's whimsical watercolors harmonize perfectly with the warm-hearted realism of the story.

5.298   Durell, Ann, and Marilyn Sachs, editors. **The Big Book for Peace.** Dutton Children's Books, 1990. ISBN 0-525-44605-2. 128p. 7–12.

This anthology in many genres and graphic forms presents a stellar company of thirty-four well-known authors and illustrators, including Nancy Willard, Jean Fritz, Lloyd Alexander, Maurice Sendak, and Diane and Leo Dillon, all of whom speak eloquently and in their own ways for peace. Selections include histories, humor, poems, and a song. Proceeds from the book's sales aid five organizations that work for peace. *Jane Addams Award, 1991.*

5.299   Dygard, Thomas J. **Forward Pass.** Morrow Junior Books, 1989. ISBN 0-688-07961-X. 186p. 12 and up.

Coach Frank Gardner finds the perfect receiver for his top-notch quarterback in a girl basketball player, Jill Winston. Jill is eager to join the team, her parents (with reservations) give their consent, and the rules do not prohibit a girl player. But can Frank, Jill, and the team weather public opinion?

5.300   Fox, Paula. **Monkey Island.** Orchard Books/Richard Jackson Books, 1991. ISBN 0-531-08562-7. 160p. 10 and up.

Eleven-year-old Clay Garrity's father disappeared in the past, and now his mother has run away from their New York City hotel room. As Clay struggles with abandonment, homelessness, hunger, and threats, there are counterbalancing forces—friends on the street. There is Buddy, a young African American, complex with hope and despair, yet constant in caring, and there is philosophical Calvin, a former teacher whose tragedies include

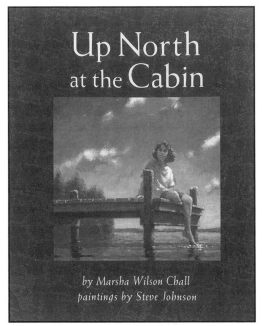

A.

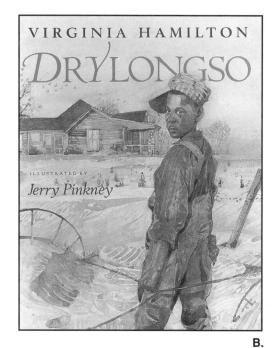

B.

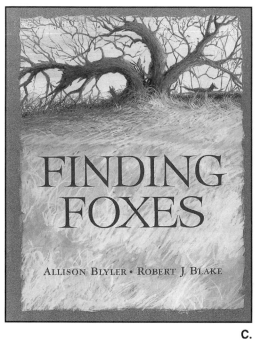

C.

D.

A. *Up North at the Cabin* by Marsha Wilson Chall; illustrated by Steve Johnson (see 5.274).   **B.** *Drylongso* by Virginia Hamilton; illustrated by Jerry Pinkney (see 5.279).
C. *Finding Foxes* by Allison Blyler; illustrated by Robert J. Blake (see 5.272).   **D.** *The Year of the Panda* by Miriam Schlein; illustrated by Kam Mak (see 5.290).

A.

B.

C.

D.

A. *The Big Book for Peace* by various authors (see 5.298). **B.** *Amazing Grace* by Mary Hoffman; illustrated by Caroline Binch (see 5.301). **C.** *Our Teacher's Having a Baby* by Eve Bunting; illustrated by Diane de Groat (see 5.212). **D.** *The Lemonade Babysitter* by Karen Waggoner; illustrated by Dorothy Donohue (see 5.225).

alcoholism. Clay hears their stories, receives the handouts, and works the garbage. The quiet resolution ties many of the plot strings. *Notable 1991 Children's Trade Books in the Field of Social Studies.*

5.301   Hoffman, Mary. **Amazing Grace.** Illustrated by Caroline Binch. Dial Books for Young Readers, 1991. ISBN 0-8037-1040-2. 25p. 4–8.

Because she is a girl who loves stories—from books, from movies, and from out of Nana's head—Grace acts them out. She is a peg-leg pirate, Aladdin of the lamp, Joan of Arc, Anansi the Spider, or Mowgli. But Raj says Grace can't play Peter Pan in the school play because Grace is black. Exquisitely detailed paintings, rich with expression, draw readers into the warmth of a female family in which Nana knows that if you put your mind to it, you can be anything you want to be. *Notable 1991 Children's Trade Books in the Field of Social Studies.*

5.302   Kraus, Joanna Halpert. **Tall Boy's Journey.** Illustrated by Karen Ritz. Carolrhoda Books, 1992. ISBN 0-87614-746-5. 48p. 7–10.

When eight-year-old Kim Moo Yong is adopted by kind American parents, he is lonely and scared. He has never slept alone for fear of tigers, nor seen long noses, nor eaten with a knife and fork. His new father's Korean colleague, who also came to America as a child, understands how it feels to be placed in a new culture and is able to help the family draw closer. This gentle, haunting book shows the universality of sensitivity and kindness.

5.303   Muldoon, Kathleen M. **Princess Pooh.** Illustrated by Linda Shute. Albert Whitman, 1989. ISBN 0-8075-6627-6. 26p. 7–10.

Princess Pooh is Patty Jean's nickname for her older sister, who uses a wheelchair. Resentful of the extra attention the "Princess" receives, Patty Jean finds out just how tricky and nasty the constraint can be. With a new respect she asks, "How can you smile all the time when you're in that yucky chair?" The illustrations capture the characters' feelings in this fine launching spot for a discussion on disabilities.

5.304   Osofsky, Audrey. **My Buddy.** Illustrated by Ted Rand. Henry Holt, 1992. ISBN 0-8050-1747-X. 32p. 4–8 (est.).

Buddy is a boy's best friend; he's a golden retriever who "looks like the sun is always shining on him." The narrator describes

Buddy not only as his friend but also as his arms and legs, helping him do things that he can't do for himself because of muscular dystrophy. The description of Buddy's selection, training, duties, and responsibilities is based on a real boy and his dog, as well as on research at the Canine Companions for Independence in Santa Rosa, California. Ted Rand's illustrations show the bond of buddies at school and home.

5.305   Pettepiece, Thomas, and Anatoly Aleksin, editors. **Face to Face: A Collection of Stories by Celebrated Soviet and American Writers.** Philomel Books, 1990. ISBN 0-399-21951-X. 233p. 12 and up (est.).

For the first time, nine Soviet and nine American authors for children and young adults share their insights about humanity in a single volume. Ranging in length from four to seventeen pages, the short stories delve into universal themes and issues, including taking responsibility for one's actions, understanding the importance of loyalty, grappling with the problem of evil, recognizing the value of family. Authors represented include Robert Cormier, Katherine Paterson, Walter Dean Myers, Jean Fritz, Yuri Yakovlev, and Vytaute Zilinskaite.

5.306   Shulevitz, Uri. **Toddlecreek Post Office.** Illustrated by Uri Shulevitz. Farrar, Straus and Giroux, 1990. ISBN 0-374-37635-2. 28p. 6 and up.

The village post office is the social hub of Toddlecreek. Each morning Vernon Stamps, the postmaster, shares his customers' lives and problems. But the postal inspector appears unexpectedly, announcing that the post office must close because of insufficient business. In vivid illustrations that are painted in glowing orange tempered with blue, Caldecott Medal-winner Uri Shulevitz shows how swiftly the comforting pattern of life in a small community can be changed.

5.307   Spinelli, Jerry. **Maniac Magee.** Harper Trophy Books, 1992. ISBN 0-06-440424-2. 184p. 8–12 (est.).

Twelve-year-old Jeffrey Lionel "Maniac" Magee's behavior is the stuff of legend: he scored forty-nine touchdowns in a single game, he kept an eight-inch cockroach on a leash, he ran faster and farther than anyone else. What's more, "Maniac" was orphaned at age three, fled uncaring relatives at age eight, and now lives on his own. What is known for certain is his legacy: kids from the East End and West End of Two Mills, Pennsylvania, may now be found holding opposite ends of the same jump rope chanting, "Ma-niac, Ma-niac / He's so cool...." *Boston Globe–Horn Book Fiction Award, 1990; Newbery Medal, 1991.*

5.308 Spinelli, Jerry. **There's a Girl in My Hammerlock.** Simon and Schuster Books for Young Readers, 1991. ISBN 0-671-74684-7. 199p. 9 and up (est.).

When eighth-grader Maisie Potter fails to make the cheerleading squad, she just *knows* it is because "Luscious" Liz Lampley didn't vote for her. So to spite Liz, who happens to be dating wrestler Eric Delong, athletic Maisie tries out for the boys' wrestling team—and makes it! Fighting the disapproval of coaches, schoolmates, and almost everyone in town, Maisie unexpectedly finds strength, heroism, and—most importantly—self-acceptance.

5.309 Wojciechowski, Susan. **Patty Dillman of Hot Dog Fame.** Orchard Books, 1989. ISBN 0-531-08410-8. 180p. 10 and up (est.).

Eighth-grader Patricia Dillman tells her humorously moving story about how she develops from "wienie head," who gets into trouble at school, to "Queen of the Hot Dogs." Volunteering to serve meals to the homeless at St. Luke's Soup Kitchen is neither her idea nor her "cup of tea." She's more concerned about keeping her first real boyfriend, Tim, interested in her. As Christmas nears, Patty finds herself willing to sacrifice fun with friends for the joy of giving.

5.310 Zheleznikov, Vladimir (translated by Antonina W. Bouis). **Scarecrow.** J. B. Lippincott, 1990. ISBN 0-397-32317-4. 148p. 10 and up.

Twelve-year-old Lena comes to live with her eccentric grandfather in small town, present-day Russia. On her first day of school she is confronted by unwelcoming classmates. A persistent soul, she tries to cover for Dimka, her new friend and crush, and takes the blame for causing the cancellation of a field trip to Moscow. This brings out the worst of middle-school cruelty and unkindness. In Antonina Bouis's splendid translation the spirit of the tale might be American, but the absence of a "happy ever after" ending is unfamiliar and unexpected.

Stories about Other Lands and People

5.311 Appiah, Sonia. **Amoko and Efua Bear.** Illustrated by Carol Easmon. Macmillan, 1989. ISBN 0-02-705591-4. 28p. 4–8 (est.).

Five-year-old Amoko and her family live in Ghana in West Africa. Like many American children, Amoko goes everywhere with her toy bear, Efua. But in her excitement over the gift of a new toy drum, Amoko accidentally leaves Efua outdoors overnight. When Amoko's father finds the damaged-but-repairable bear and returns it, she is overjoyed. Through text and full-page folk-art illustrations, readers will share a familiar experience while becoming acquainted with an unfamiliar culture.

5.312   Carlstrom, Nancy White. **Light: Stories of a Small Kindness.** Illustrated by Lisa Desimini. Little, Brown, 1990. ISBN 0-316-12857-0. 42p. 8–12.

Seven stories of children from Mexico, Haiti, Guatemala, and New York City share a theme. In each, some act of kindness or charity is extended: a young boy overcomes his fear in a dark cave, a busload of Down's syndrome children escape danger, an artist explains his inspiration for the painting of a blue parrot, and disabled children learn to rejoice in overcoming obstacles. An author's note indicates that one story, "Frederico's Fantastico Day," is based on her own experiences as a teacher. Lisa Desimini's black-and-white illustrations project strong images from each story. Proceeds from the book's sales aid Mexican and Haitian schools for disabled children.

5.313   Dorros, Arthur. **Tonight Is Carnaval.** Illustrated by the Club de Madres Virgen del Carmen of Lima, Peru. Dutton Children's Books, 1991. ISBN 0-525-44641-9. 32p. 5–8.

Once a year, the people of the Andes Mountains of South America get together with their friends from neighboring villages to dance, feast, and sing in celebration of Carnaval. A typical family prepares for the big event—Mama weaves cloth, Papa chops wood, and the entire family gathers potatoes. This book's unique illustrations are photographs of *arpilleras*, three-dimensional wall-hangings that depict Peruvian village life. An appendix includes labeled pictures showing how *arpilleras* are made, as well a glossary of unfamiliar terms. *Notable 1991 Children's Trade Books in the Field of Social Studies.*

5.314   Gackenbach, Dick. **With Love from Gran.** Illustrated by Dick Gackenbach. Clarion Books, 1989. ISBN 0-89919-842-2. 29p. 3–6.

When Gran goes off to see the world, her grandson is the recipient of gifts from around the globe, including a gypsy wagon from Budapest, a Cossack suit from Moscow, an African mask from Timbuktu, and a kangaroo from Adelaide. The best gift of all, though, is Gran's return. Young children may enjoy locating Gran's souvenir stops as a springboard to the study of cultures and countries around the world.

5.315 Heide, Florence Parry, and Judith Heide Gilliland. **The Day of Ahmed's Secret.** Illustrated by Ted Lewin. Lothrop, Lee and Shepard Books, 1990. ISBN 0-688-08895-3. 32p. 6–9.

All day long Ahmed holds tight to his secret as he delivers *butagaz* (butane gas) from his donkey cart. The streets of Cairo bustle with merchants and shoppers—colorful stalls vending brass, rugs, and vegetables, coops of chickens and rabbits, and even a string of camels. Despite the sights and sounds that clamor for attention, Ahmed concentrates on the secret that he will share with his family at the close of the day: he can write his name. Ted Lewin's paintings, both realistic and instructive, contrast the ancient and modern city. *ALA Notable Children's Books, 1991.*

5.316 Isadora, Rachel. **At the Crossroads.** Illustrated by Rachel Isadora. Greenwillow Books, 1991. ISBN 0-688-05271-1. 32p. 4–7 (est.).

"Today our fathers are coming home!" Singing and dancing children eagerly await the homecoming of their fathers, who for many months have been working in distant gold, diamond, and coal mines. Vibrant watercolor illustrations of expectant and joyous young faces shine through the sorrows of family separation typical in segregated South African townships. *Notable 1991 Children's Trade Books in the Field of Social Studies.*

5.317 Isadora, Rachel. **Over the Green Hills.** Illustrated by Rachel Isadora. Greenwillow Books, 1992. ISBN 0-688-10510-6. 32p. 4–8 (est.).

It is the day for Zolani, his mother, and his baby sister to take a long walk to visit Grandmother Zindzi in Transkei, an independent black state on the east coast of South Africa. They pack dried fish and *mielies* (ears of corn) for Grandmother, and Zolani loads mussels on the goat. Mother walks with dried fish, a pumpkin, and even a chicken on her head. The countryside is jungle-bright with a blue, washed sky. Along the way, neighbors send their greetings, and Zolani explores his beautiful world.

5.318   Jacobs, Shannon K. **Song of the Giraffe.** Illustrated by Pamela Johnson. Little, Brown/Springboard Books, 1991. ISBN 0-316-45555-5. 55p. 7–9 (est.).

Black-and-white pencil drawings help to tell the story of Kisana, a member of the Bokuru tribe in Africa. She has a universal problem—she feels ostracized because she is physically different from her tribe. Much smaller than the other girls, Kisana has both light skin and light hair. To gain acceptance from the dark-skinned tribe, she journeys to find a special gift for the tribal feast. The tribulations that she undergoes to find her gift make for a warm story of growing up, family relationships, and worthiness.

5.319   Major, Kevin. **Blood Red Ochre.** Delacorte Press, 1989. ISBN 0-385-29794-7. 147p. 12 and up.

In alternating chapters, this novel simultaneously offers two Canadian stories—one, a modern tale of fifteen-year-old David's relationship with his family and new girlfriend in Newfoundland; the second, a narrative by Dauvoodaset, one of the last Beothuk Indians, whose race became extinct approximately two hundred years ago. In the final chapters, the protagonists of both stories meet in a mystic encounter, blending past and present, with each defending the land and people that he loves.

5.320   Mennen, Ingrid, and Niki Daly. **Somewhere in Africa.** Illustrated by Nicolaas Maritz. Dutton Children's Books, 1992. ISBN 0-525-44848-9. 32p. 3–8 (est.).

In the Africa that Ashraf knows, no lions lie in the tall grass, no crocodiles glide through muddy rivers, and no zebras race across the plains. Instead, Ashraf lives in a city "in the very tip of the great African continent," where shops and traffic and noise and music fill his world. The other Africa is captured securely in his favorite library book—one he checks out again and again. Paintings are vivid, sun-drenched, perspective-free impressions of Cape Town.

5.321   Neville, Emily Cheney. **The China Year.** HarperCollins, 1991. ISBN 0-06-024384-8. 244p. 10 and up.

When thirteen-year-old Henrietta Rich's father has a year's appointment in Beijing, she and her mother go along, too. Living in cramped "Foreign Expert" quarters on the university campus, Henri is fascinated by her surroundings, but homesick for New York City. A young Chinese boy befriends her, and their unexpected cultural differences come to life as the two explore the city and meet each other's families. This is a lively, cleverly veiled introduction to China.

5.322 Pomerantz, Charlotte. **The Chalk Doll.** Illustrated by Frané Lessac. J. B. Lippincott, 1989. ISBN 0-397-32319-0. 30p. 3–7 (est.).

Rose loves the tales of her mother's humble Jamaican childhood. She envies the simple homemade rag doll that her mother would have traded for a store-bought "chalk doll." She hears how three pennies provided a wonderful birthday gift, and how as a little barefoot girl her mom made high heels with mango pits dipped in road tar. Primitive paintings in bold colors illustrate the shared memories. *Notable 1989 Children's Trade Books in the Field of Social Studies.*

5.323 Schami, Rafik (translated by Rika Lesser). **A Hand Full of Stars.** Dutton Children's Books, 1990. ISBN 0-525-44535-8. 195p. 12 and up (est.).

As a young boy in modern Damascus grows from a child to an adult, he begins to see the world around him in a different light. From his simpler observations about love and friendship, he begins to see the injustices of his government, the brutality of a system that is unconcerned about the poor or the helpless, and he pours his feelings of anger into his daily journal. At length he finds a dangerous outlet for his frustration—a forbidden underground newspaper. *Mildred L. Batchelder Award, 1991.*

5.324 Schermbrucker, Reviva. **Charlie's House.** Illustrated by Niki Daly. Viking Penguin, 1991. ISBN 0-670-84024-6. 28p. 3–8.

Watercolor washes help to tell the story of young Charlie, who lives in a corrugated iron and scrap shelter in Guguletu, South Africa. After the rains cause a leaky roof, a determined Charlie goes outside to build his own dream house in the mud beside the soggy shelter. He fashions big rooms, with a bedroom for his mother and granny and another all for himself. His imaginary world encroaches upon his reality, until one way or another, his dream comes true. *Notable 1992 Children's Trade Books in the Field of Social Studies.*

5.325 Staples, Suzanne Fisher. **Shabanu: Daughter of the Wind.** Alfred A. Knopf, 1989. ISBN 0-394-94815-7. 240p. 12 and up.

Eleven-year-old Shabanu finds herself torn between the traditions of her Pakistani culture—traditions that demand she marry the man of her beloved father's choosing—and her innermost desire to rebel against a marriage to a man for whom she feels nothing but contempt. How can she betray her father, Dadi, and the centuries-old ways of her people without giving up her own happiness? *Newbery Honor Book, 1990.*

5.326 Williams, Karen Lynn. **Galimoto.** Illustrated by Catherine Stock. Mulberry Books, 1991. ISBN 0-668-10991-8. 32p. 4–8.

Seven-year-old Kondi, who lives in a village in Malawi, Africa, treasures all the belongings that he keeps in an old shoebox. One day, when he decides to make a *galimoto,* a toy vehicle made from wire, Kondi goes about the village asking, begging, or offering to trade his keepsakes for pieces of wire for his project. Kondi's traditional push toy is a great success, and children will rejoice in his ingenuity. Watercolor paintings are awash with the patterns and bustle of village life.

Survival

5.327 Paulsen, Gary. **The Voyage of the Frog.** Orchard Books/Richard Jackson Books, 1989. ISBN 0-531-08405-1. 143p. 10 and up (est.).

Fourteen-year-old David is caught in a fierce storm when he goes out on his sailboat to scatter the ashes of his recently deceased uncle. For nine days he struggles against becalmed seas, sharks, killer whales, and more storms. By the end of his journey, David has learned important lessons about conquering fear, grieving for his uncle, and developing self-reliance. This book is a good companion piece to the author's *Hatchet.*

5.328 Wild, Margaret. **Let the Celebrations Begin!** Illustrated by Julie Vivas. Orchard Books, 1991. ISBN 0-531-08537-6. 32p. 3–6.

Miriam is helping the women with whom she lives to stitch a toy for each child so that they can celebrate when the soldiers come to liberate the concentration camp. Until then, home is Hut 18, the scene of remarkable hope. Heads shaved and gaunt from long hunger, the women transform inch after inch of tattered clothes into toys. Julie Vivas's illustrations create a luminous joy that extinguishes the macabre reality.

Fantasy

At heart, the issues raised in a work of fantasy are those we face in real life. In whatever guise—our own daily nightmares of war, intolerance, inhumanity; or the struggles of an Assistant Pig-Keeper against the Lord of Death—the problems are agonizingly familiar. And an openness to compassion, love, and mercy is as essential to us here and now as it is to any inhabitant of an imaginary kingdom.

Lloyd Alexander, Newbery Award
Acceptance Speech for *The High King*

6 Fantasy

Adventure and Magic

6.1 Alexander, Lloyd. **The Jedera Adventure.** E. P. Dutton, 1989. ISBN 0-525-44481-5. 152p. 8–12 (est.).

Returning a library book may be routine, but not when it involves the adventure-loving heroine Vesper Holly. Accompanied by her beloved guardian Brinnie and with the help of several Jedera inhabitants, including a blue-faced warrior, Vesper treks across the desert of Northern Africa to Bel Saaba and once again foils one of Dr. Helvitius's insidious plots to rule the world. Tribal feuds, ill-tempered camels, romance, and mysterious secrets help to create another action-packed adventure with Lloyd Alexander's dauntless heroine.

6.2 Alexander, Lloyd. **The Philadelphia Adventure.** Dutton Children's Books, 1990. ISBN 0-525-44564-1. 160p. 10 and up.

The year is 1876, and the Centennial Exposition is about to open in Philadelphia. But danger and political embarrassment threaten to mar the opening, and President Grant must seek the help of the city's most adventurous citizen, Vesper Holly. True to her nature, Vesper, with the help of her memorable friends, once again foils the evil Dr. Helvitius's scheme to conquer the world. Woven with bits of American history, this final novel in Lloyd Alexander's series of tales about the daring heroine is filled with adventure, humor, and action-packed surprises.

6.3 Alexander, Lloyd. **The Remarkable Journey of Prince Jen.** Dutton Children's Books, 1991. ISBN 0-545-44826-8. 273p. 10 and up (est.).

Bearing six unusual gifts, Prince Jen begins his journey to the kingdom of T'ienkuo. But the journey is filled with peril and misfortune, and the young prince must struggle with evil forces and also with himself to fulfill his destiny as king. Weaving details from the culture of ancient China, Lloyd Alexander once again creates an intriguing and suspenseful fantasy about the true meaning of "kingdom on earth."

6.4 Balian, Lorna. **Wilbur's Space Machine.** Illustrated by Lorna Balian. Holiday House, 1990. ISBN 0-8234-0836-1. 32p. 4–8 (est.).

Violet and Wilbur live alone in the middle of nowhere, and they like it that way. Gradually, though, people begin to move into their valley, until they find themselves with no room at all. In desperation Wilbur builds a "space machine" that enables them to find peace and quiet in a most unexpected way. Expressive and humorous watercolors show Wilbur's resourcefulness.

6.5 Ballard, Robin. **Cat and Alex and the Magic Flying Carpet.** Illustrated by Robin Ballard. HarperCollins, 1991. ISBN 0-06-020390-0. 32p. 3–7.

As Alex watches the rain fall outside his window, he sees his friend Cat arrive in a strange-looking cloak. Cat explains that his wrap is a magic flying carpet and tells Alex of his wondrous adventures around the world. Alex, longing for a trip to the moon, joins Cat on the carpet. Falling asleep, they take a magical ride together. Stylized watercolors illustrate this story of friendship.

6.6 Bentley, Nancy. **I've Got Your Nose!** Illustrated by Don Madden. Doubleday, 1991. ISBN 0-385-41296-7. 32p. 4–8.

Nahzella the witch conforms to witches' standards on most measures, except that her nose is a cute little button nose more suitable for a princess. No spell from her spell book can produce a just-right witch's nose. So Nahzella looks up a spell for "Steal," and tries to change her nose another way. Still, no matter for which nose she "exchanges" hers, there are always unanticipated problems: the farmer's nose is allergic, the dog's too sensitive. Eventually, of course, Nahzella settles happily for her button nose.

6.7 Berger, Barbara Helen. **Gwinna.** Illustrated by Barbara Helen Berger. Philomel Books, 1990. ISBN 0-399-21738-X. 128p. 6 and up (est.).

When a woodcutter and his wife wish for a child, the Mother of the Owls gives them Gwinna with the stipulation that at the age of twelve, she must return. As Gwinna grows up, she follows the owls back to their grotto, where Mother of the Owls shows Gwinna her wings. After learning to fly, Gwinna is drawn to the mountain where she meets a golden griffin and another friend who give her the secret of the wind's song. Luminescent, haunting illustrations embellish this magical tale of an enchanted young girl who fulfills her dream.

6.8   Bradshaw, Gillian. **The Dragon and the Thief.** Greenwillow Books, 1991. ISBN 0-688-10575-0. 154p. 10 and up.

Prahotep, the hapless son of a deceased ancient Egyptian farmer, discovers the lair of a she-dragon, Hathor. He persuades Hathor to travel with him up the Nile to Nubia, where other dragons are rumored to be alive. Their journey is one of danger and excitement as they are pursued by the evil priest/magician Nefersenet. Gillian Bradshaw brings ancient Egyptian society to life in this lively, very original historical fantasy.

6.9   Clément, Claude (translated by Lenny Hort). **The Voice of the Wood.** Illustrated by Frédéric Clément. Dial Books, 1989. ISBN 0-8037-0635-9. 22p. 8–12 (est.).

This short and simple tale expresses powerfully the fundamental mystery of music. Surrealistic illustrations depict a Venetian craftsman as he creates a cello from the wood of a beautiful tree, a tree in which wind and birds made captivating music long ago. But the famed musician who attempts to play the cello must first learn about the deeper harmonies of humanity and nature before he can draw sound from the instrument. The text is clear and spare, the illustrations quiet and haunting, and the overall tone one of reverence for the miracle of music.

6.10   Cole, Joanna. **The Magic School Bus Inside the Human Body.** Illustrated by Bruce Degen. Scholastic, 1989. ISBN 0-590-41427-5. 38p. 8–13.

This is one in a series of books that takes readers on magical science trips aboard a mysterious school bus. This time the class of strange Ms. Frizzle sets out on a field trip to the science museum, but they end up on a journey through the digestive and circulatory systems of a fellow classmate. Taking the philosophy of meaningful student involvement to its extreme, Ms. Frizzle, in wild science garb, cleverly teaches both children and adults about the wonderful workings of the human body.

6.11   Jacques, Brian. **Mariel of Redwall.** Illustrated by Gary Chalk. Philomel Books, 1992. ISBN 0-399-22144-1. 387p. 10 and up.

Against the backdrop of Redwall Abbey and Mossflower Woods, Brian Jacques offers the fourth in his series of medieval adventure tales, this one featuring an intrepid heroine, the mousemaid Mariel, in a mission of revenge against the vicious sea-rats of Terramort Island. Jolly hares, badger warriors, brave mice, and a host of moles, hedgehogs, and otters play support-

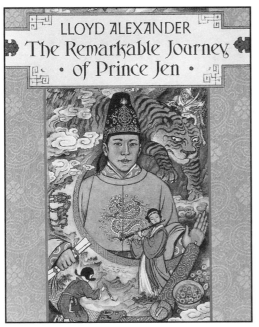

A.

B.

C.

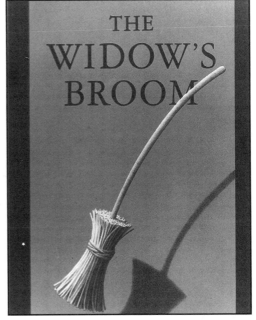

D.

A. *The Remarkable Journey of Prince Jen* by Lloyd Alexander (see 6.3). **B.** *The Jedera Adventure* by Lloyd Alexander (see 6.1). **C.** *Shiloh* by Phyllis Reynolds Naylor (see 5.27). **D.** *The Widow's Broom* by Chris Van Allsburg (see 6.21).

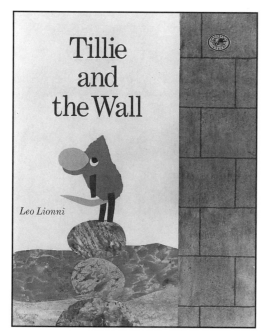

A.

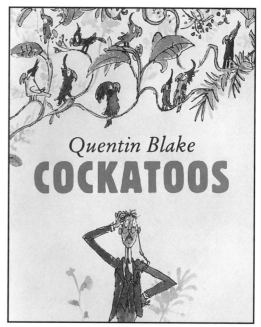

B.

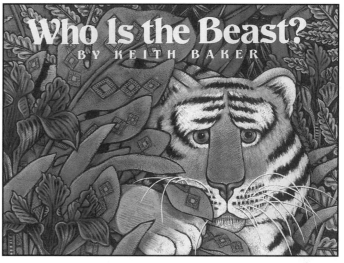

C.

A. *Tillie and the Wall* by Leo Lionni (see 6.88).   **B.** *Cockatoos* by Quentin Blake (see 6.198).   **C.** *Who Is the Beast?* by Keith Baker (see 6.26).

ing roles in this swashbuckling tale with enough scheming, swordplay, piracy, violence, and triumph to pique the interest of Redwall fans.

6.12   Kelleher, Victor. **The Red King.** Dial Books, 1990. ISBN 0-8037-0758-4. 176p. 11 and up.

The people of Forest Land fear the evil Red King, who rules his kingdom through fear and the threat of a feverish disease. His tyranny is unchallenged until a band of traveling tricksters, facing danger and death, puts an end to the reign of the mysterious and haunting ruler. Filled with suspense and intrigue, Victor Kelleher's well-written tale is sure to please fans of the supernatural.

6.13   Le Guin, Ursula K. **A Ride on the Red Mare's Back.** Illustrated by Julie Downing. Orchard Books/Richard Jackson Books, 1992. ISBN 0-531-08591-0. 48p. 4–7.

In a northern land where the winter days are short and snow is deep, the troll people have stolen a girl's little brother. With only her brave heart and her carved red wooden horse, the little girl sets out to rescue him. When the beloved toy becomes a real horse for one night, the girl has a champion that can travel over snow and distract the trolls. Julie Downing's paintings turn the traditional Swedish Dalarna Horse into a spirited steed.

6.14   Lindbergh, Anne. **Travel Far, Pay No Fare.** HarperCollins, 1992. ISBN 0-06-021776-6. 201p. 10 and up (est.).

Son of a famous children's book author, Owen Noonan prefers TV and their quiet Boston life to reading. But now his mother is marrying Uncle Jack in Vermont, and Owen is about to become big brother to an avid reader, nine-year-old Parsley. Parsley's plans for putting the wedding asunder include the use of a magical bookmark that delivers on its promise to "Travel far, pay no fare." Anne Lindbergh interweaves characters and pets across literary selections in thought-provoking ways.

6.15   Mahy, Margaret. **The Dragon of an Ordinary Family.** Illustrated by Helen Oxenbury. Dial Books for Young Readers, 1992. ISBN 0-8037-1062-3. 42p. 4–8.

The Belsakis are an ordinary family who live in an ordinary house on an ordinary street. Then, to prove he is *not* a fuddy-duddy, Mr. Belsaki buys an extraordinary pet for his son, Orlando. As in Steven Kellogg's *The Mysterious Tadpole*, the new pet quickly outgrows his surroundings. Luckily, though, dragons can fly, and so this pet takes all the Belsakis for a lovely vacation on the Isles of Magic. Bowlers, umbrellas, and British breakfast fare cue where the story was originally published.

6.16   Morgan, Helen. **The Witch Doll.** Viking Penguin, 1992. ISBN 0-670-84285-0. 143p. 8–12.

The curious work bag that bounces from the junkman's cart has a doll inside—a wooden doll with shiny black hair and a transfixing, evil gaze. For Linda, who finds the doll, it becomes the centerpiece of an unfolding story that moves between the present and the past to explain the origin of the doll and its powers to transform through witchcraft. Heroine Linda is a plucky sort who makes for effective contrast with the threats around her.

6.17   Pacovská, Květa (translated by Anthea Bell). **The Little Flower King.** Illustrated by Květa Pacovská. Picture Book Studio/Michael Neugebauer Books, 1992. ISBN 0-88708-221-1. 32p. 4–8 (est.).

Readers peering through a clear dust jacket and then through a colorfully framed cutout in the covers will see from the front a solitary king, but from the back they will see a king and queen. Between the covers is the tale of a princess who is found in a tulip that the king planted in his own palace garden. This modern, vibrantly colored, mixed-media, playful, humorous, and sometimes-puzzling fairy tale comes from the imagination of Czech artist Květa Pacovská, the 1992 Hans Christian Andersen medalist.

6.18   Pendergraft, Patricia. **The Legend of Daisy Flowerdew.** Philomel Books, 1990. ISBN 0-399-22176-X. 190p. 10 and up.

After Granny Henry passes away, Daisy goes to live with her real mother, Jesse. But Daisy is quiet and perceived as being different. She finds solace in two magical paper dolls. When Jesse and her husband arrange Daisy's marriage to money-seeking Elmer Goots, Daisy disappears with the help of her two magical friends. The town of Vineyard Flats searches for a way to explain the mysterious events surrounding the legend of Daisy Flowerdew.

6.19   Silverman, Maida. **The Magic Well.** Illustrated by Manuel Boix. Simon and Schuster Books for Young Readers, 1989. ISBN 0-617-67885-X. 32p. 4–8.

Meeting the fairy queen at a magic well, Janet willingly goes with her to the kingdom of the fairies, leaving behind only a single rose as a sign to her mother that she is well. When Janet asks to return to her mother, she finds herself a captive of the fairies. Only through her own clever efforts and her mother's love is Janet finally saved. Manuel Boix's delicate and detailed paintings complement the magic of a tale inspired by an ancient ballad.

6.20 Turner, Ann. **Rosemary's Witch.** Harper Collins/Charlotte Zolotow Books, 1991. ISBN 0-06-026128-5. 164p. 10–12.

When her family moves to an old New England farmhouse, nine-year-old Rosemary looks forward to making the house her home and establishing her own identity. But a 150-year-old witch who lived in the house as a young girl threatens Rosemary's plans, and the Morgenthau family faces the possiblity of forfeiting their dreams. In the end, Rosemary gives the witch the love she needs, and as a result, Rosemary brings peace to the New England countryside. Understanding and personal discovery are woven into this eerie tale filled with mystery and witchcraft.

6.21 Van Allsburg, Chris. **The Widow's Broom.** Illustrated by Chris Van Allsburg. Houghton Mifflin, 1992. ISBN 0-395-64051-2. 32p. 8 and up (est.).

A witch makes an unexpected stop when her broom loses its power to stay aloft right over Widow Shaw's garden. Under the widow's tender care, the witch recovers from the fall, but she leaves her broom behind. Not totally worn-out, the broom proves useful to the widow. It chops wood, mops floors, feeds chickens, and even plays the piano. But suspicious neighbor Spivey accuses the broom of devilment and says that it must go. Surrealistic images in textured sepia capture the magic, but the action sequence is never far from a smile.

6.22 Yolen, Jane. **The Dragon's Boy.** Harper and Row, 1990. ISBN 0-06-026790-9. 120p. 8–13 (est.).

In this original King Arthur story, the young orphan, Artos, has trouble becoming a part of castle life. Then he finds a dark cave, home of a wise old dragon, who helps him, with the aid of a magical sword, become friends with Lancelot and other young men at the castle. As Artos gains wisdom, he also learns that his real name is Artos Pendragon and that he is the son of Merlinnus, the old apothecary who is also the wise dragon in disguise. *Notable 1990 Children's Trade Books in the Field of Social Studies.*

Animal Fantasy

6.23   Anderson, Wayne. **Dragon.** Illustrated by Wayne Anderson. Simon and Schuster/Green Tiger Press, 1992. ISBN 0-671-78397-1. 32p. 6–10 (est.).

When a precious egg drops from the sky, the mother screams, but it is too late. And so, deep within the sea, comforted by fishes, a newborn creature hatches. "Where is my mother?" and "What am I?" he asks. In his search for his kind, the creature discovers that he shares traits with fish, dragonflies, birds, snakes, and crocodiles. But it takes a child who reads to know the creature's identity and to steer him safely home. Muted greens interpret the wrenching despair of a lost dragon.

6.24   Asch, Frank. **Dear Brother.** Illustrated by Vladimir Vagin. Scholastic Hardcover Books, 1992. ISBN 0-590-43107-2. 32p. 6–9.

Joey and Marvin discover a bundle of letters in the attic, illustrated with "interesting pictures." All night the two mice read the correspondence between their great-great-uncles, Timothy, who stayed in the country, and Henry, who settled in the city. Affectionate letters recount the milestones of the brothers' years apart and memories shared, and ingeniously record urban and rural lifestyles of the past. Paintings in dyes, gouache, and watercolors neatly frame the action opposite the actual letters.

6.25   Ashabranner, Brent. **I'm in the Zoo, Too!** Illustrated by Janet Stevens. Cobblehill Books, 1989. ISBN 0-525-65002-4. 28p. 4–8 (est.).

Burl the squirrel lives *at* the the zoo but not *in* the zoo. Curious about the difference, which his mother assures him is important, Burl sets out to find the answer. Although all his animal friends fail to explain the distinction, Burl discovers it when he unwarily decides to perform in a cage. Activity-filled, detailed watercolor paintings make the book "readable" by all ages.

6.26   Baker, Keith. **Who Is the Beast?** Illustrated by Keith Baker. Harcourt Brace Jovanovich, 1990. ISBN 0-15-296057-0. 32p. 3–7.

"The beast, the beast!" Smaller jungle animals flee the beastly tiger whose tiger parts are revealed one-by-one in lush Henri Rousseau-like paintings, set against chantable, rhyming text.

"The beast?" thinks the tiger. "I see no beast. I just see me." Gently, he matches each of his fearsome characteristics against those of the jungle creatures, helping everyone to discover the commonalities of nature.

6.27 Barasch, Marc Ian. **No Plain Pets.** Illustrated by Henrik Drescher. HarperCollins, 1991. ISBN 0-06-022473-8. 36p. 4–8.

In vibrantly illustrated rhyming text, a child muses about the pet he wants. "I don't want one that's plain—/ Some dumb Puff or Fluff / With a parakeet brain." Maybe a big, black gorilla, an electric eel, or a jungle snake. But the main thing is, as with all good pet owners, the pet will be loved. Illustrations are stylized, quirky, and crowded with figures, doodles, and textures.

6.28 Birchman, David F. **Brother Billy Bronto's Bygone Blues Band.** Illustrated by John O'Brien. Lothrop, Lee and Shepard Books, 1992. ISBN 0-688-10424-X. 32p. 5 and up.

"There was Rex the King Tyrone / on the slide trombone / and Brother Billy on the bass. / There was a mean / allosaurus saxophonist / nicknamed Lizard Lips Grace." Long ago, dinosaur Dixieland could be heard on Basin Street. But because of demand "from throughout the land," the beasts take an ill-fated train ride which lands the blues "in a pool of ooze." Dappled watercolors on ink drawings enliven the musical mood.

6.29 Blackwood, Mary. **Derek the Knitting Dinosaur.** Illustrated by Kerry Argent. Carolrhoda Books, 1990. ISBN 0-87614-400-8. 32p. 3–8 (est.).

Derek is more green and more gentle than his dinosaur brothers, Fang and Fearless. Although a part of Derek wants to look and act more like a *real* dinosaur, Derek prefers knitting to roaring about. Derek's knit products stockpile until brightly patterned sweaters, socks, vests, mittens, scarves, and pants overflow his stone house. And then something strange happens. The world becomes colder, and fierce dinosaurs need woolly things. Expansive watercolored figures accompany the rhyming text.

6.30 Breathed, Berkeley. **The Last Basselope: One Ferocious Story.** Illustrated by Berkeley Breathed. Little, Brown, 1992. ISBN 0-316-10761-1. 32p. 6–10 (est.).

Cartoonist Berkeley Breathed advises in his second book: "Best results will be obtained when read in an open, sunny meadow. . . . Under no conditions should a television be in the vicinity." Airbrushed backgrounds and vibrant surface colors add to the adventure of Opus, the Great and Famous Discoverer, who, with his team of "volunteers" (Milquetoast, Ronald-Ann, and Bill the Cat) searches for the Last Great Basselope—of razor horn and slobbery fang. But the Basselope is different from expected, and needs protection from thundering hordes of media.

6.31   Brett, Jan. **Berlioz the Bear.** Illustrated by Jan Brett. G. P. Putnam's Sons, 1991. ISBN 0-399-22248-0. 32p. 4–8.

Inspiration for Jan Brett's bass-playing bear came both from the nineteenth-century composer Hector Berlioz and from her own double-bass-playing husband who, like Berlioz the bear, once noticed a loud buzz in his bass. The buzzing so distracts Berlioz the bear that he drives the orchestra's bandwagon into a large hole in the road. The temperamental mule pulling the wagon refuses to budge until an angry bee persuades the mule to get moving. Elaborately detailed Bavarian scenes include embroidered costumes, painted carts and cottages, and Brett's trademark borders, foreshadowing the town in preparation for the gala ball at which Berlioz is to perform.

6.32   Brown, Marc. **Arthur Babysits.** Illustrated by Marc Brown. Little, Brown/Joy Street Books, 1992. ISBN 0-316-11293-3. 32p. 4–8 (est.).

Good-humoredly, Arthur agrees to baby-sit for the terrible Tibble twins while their grandmother is out. Everyone, especially his sister D. W., warns him that the Tibble twins are trouble. Dressed in cowboy suits and brandishing firearms, the twins torment Arthur with the stereotypic baby-sitter's initiation rites, including tying him to a chair. Despite D. W.'s continuing phone calls with advice, Arthur figures out for himself the best baby-sitting trick of all—a good storytime.

6.33   Brown, Marc. **Arthur Meets the President.** Illustrated by Marc Brown. Little, Brown/Joy Street Books, 1991. ISBN 0-316-11265-8. 30p. 4–8 (est.).

When Arthur's class enters a national essay contest on "How I Can Help to Make America Great," Arthur wins, and his entire class is invited to attend a special ceremony at the White House. Everyone is excited except Arthur, who must recite his speech from memory before the president. In the Rose Garden, his notecards scatter; Arthur panics and forgets his speech. But resourceful sister D. W. comes to his rescue with an innovative cue card.

6.34   Brown, Marc. **Arthur's Pet Business.** Illustrated by Marc Brown. Little, Brown/Joy Street Books, 1990. ISBN 0-316-11262-3. 30p. 4–8.

Wanting a new puppy, Arthur opens his own pet business to show his family his "responsible" side. But when business booms, Arthur finds himself baby-sitting a myriad of animals, one of which suddenly disappears. In the satisfying end, Arthur finds the missing pet and is rewarded with one of her new puppies. Fourteenth in the Arthur series, this adventure humorously invites readers both to laugh and to think about responsibility.

6.35   Browne, Anthony. **Bear Goes to Town.** Illustrated by Anthony Browne. Doubleday, 1989. ISBN 0-385-26525-5. 32p. 3–6.

Like Harold with his purple crayon, Bear has a magic pencil. Traveling to town, Bear meets a companionable cat and immediately draws Cat something to eat. But when Cat is captured by the animal patrol, Bear draws roller skates to chase the van, a ladder to reach Cat's "cell," and a saw to remove the bars. Bear can even draw a door to release all the animals, banana skins to aid their escape, and a rolling pastoral setting for their happy home.

6.36   Browne, Anthony. **I Like Books.** Illustrated by Anthony Browne. Alfred A. Knopf/Dragonfly Books, 1989. ISBN 0-394-94186-1. 18p. 3–7 (est.).

An adorable chimp announces the fact that he likes books. In ten simple sentences he lists his favorite kinds of books. They range from funny books to books about dinosaurs to strange books. With each declaration, the illustration reflects the book genre.

6.37   Bucknall, Caroline. **One Bear in the Hospital.** Illustrated by Caroline Bucknall. Dial Books for Young Readers, 1991. ISBN 0-8037-0847-5. 30p. 3–6.

Caroline Bucknall's bouncing bears and the rhyming, rhythmic text that accompanied them in two previous books return for more read-along fun. This time, Ted Bear has a bicycle accident, and although he is doubtful about a hospital stay, he receives tender care in the "cubs" wing. At home again, Ted is back in the races—this time in a wheelchair with his broken leg. Black ink and crayon-like shades give touchable texture to the bears.

6.38   Carlson, Nancy. **Take Time to Relax!** Illustrated by Nancy Carlson. Viking Penguin, 1991. ISBN 0-670-83287-1. 32p. 2–6 (est.).

The not-so-subtle message in Nancy Carlson's picture book is that families overschedule their lives. With computer classes, aerobics classes, cake decorating classes, and dance classes, the Beaver family is always on the go. "Until one morning . . . it was snowing like crazy." While snowbound, the family tells stories, sings, builds a fire, and pops corn. When the snowplow finally makes its way through, the family stays put. Paired with the rhyming text are warm home scenes that show Beavers in robes and pajamas taking some time to relax.

6.39   Carlson, Nancy. **A Visit to Grandma's.** Illustrated by Nancy Carlson. Viking Penguin, 1991. ISBN 0-0670-83288-X. 32p. 4–8 (est.).

As Tina and her parents plan a holiday visit to Grandma's new Florida condominium, they imagine her knitting by the fire and baking her special Thanksgiving pies. But Grandma has changed! Now she wears lavender pants, loud jewelry, and pink sunglasses. Grandma drives a sports car, takes aerobics classes, plays charades until midnight, buys her pies, and makes reservations for Thanksgiving dinner. At first wary, Tina and her parents begin to loosen up. Nancy Carlson's scenes are Florida-bright, and her beaver characters are amusing.

6.40   Cazet, Denys. **Daydreams.** Illustrated by Denys Cazet. Orchard Books/Richard Jackson Books, 1990. ISBN 0-531-08481-7. 32p. 4–7.

All the little animals in Miss Williams's class love her very dearly. Even so, on one blustery day, they can't stop the invasion of daydreams. Imaginations create desert heroes, threatening dinosaurs, and even giant snack foods. Miss Williams understands. She reads a story that feeds daydreams. "Wishes and hopes travel with daydreams," she says. By the close of day, Miss Williams has some daydreams of her own about the children's futures. Half-tone watercolors and placid faces give a sweet-dreams flavor.

6.41   Cazet, Denys. **Mother Night.** Illustrated by Denys Cazet. Orchard Books, 1989. ISBN 0-531-08430-2. 32p. 3–6.

With a simple, poetic story line that traces a cycle from dusk to dawn, animal parents put their children to bed following familiar routines, and then lovingly awaken them in the morning. Denys Cazet's watercolor and pencil illustrations in soft shades of blue, green, and pink create the enchanting world of animal dreams. This story may comfort young children who have nighttime fears.

6.42   Cazet, Denys. **Never Spit on Your Shoes.** Illustrated by Denys Cazet. Orchard Books/Richard Jackson Books, 1990. ISBN 0-531-08447-7. 26p. 4–6.

Mother listens as Arnie describes the hardships that he encountered during his first day in first grade: sitting at a desk, finding the "boys' room," and nostalgically watching the kindergarten bus pull away. But Arnie also explains the joys of making a new friend, determining classroom rules, drawing pictures with new crayons, and counting to sixteen. Told with cartoon-like style, this is a book for waylaying first-grade fears and preparing for the first day of school.

6.43   Chambless, Jane. **Tucker and the Bear.** Illustrated by Jane Chambless. Simon and Schuster Books for Young Readers, 1989. ISBN 0-671-67357-2. 36p. 4–8 (est.).

Tucker lives alone on the edge of the woods, reading, drawing, and enjoying his daydreams. When a bear joins Tucker for the winter in exchange for helping with the housework, Tucker soon finds that he has bargained for trouble along with the bear's companionship. But when the bear leaves, Tucker discovers the loneliness of a lost friendship, and he welcomes the bear's return with heartfelt gratitude. Detail-filled illustrations make this story even more endearing.

6.44   Charles, Donald. **Paddy Pig's Poems: A Story about an Amusing Fellow and His Friends.** Illustrated by Donald Charles. Simon and Schuster Books for Young Readers, 1989. ISBN 0-671-67081-6. 27p. 5–10 (est.).

Paddy Pig, a literary individualist, writes delightful and, at first glance, predictable verse. However, at the end of the final line of each poem, Paddy inserts a nonrhyming word. When Paddy's conventional friends criticize his unusual style, Paddy sends them home. Young readers and writers may want to try some unconventional writing of their own.

6.45   Cherry, Lynne. **Archie, Follow Me.** Illustrated by Lynne Cherry. Dutton Children's Books, 1990. ISBN 0-525-44647-8. 32p. 4–6.

Richly detailed pen-and-ink and watercolor illustrations of an adventuresome tabby cat, Archie, and his devoted mistress illuminate this first-person narrative. According to his young mistress, Archie is there at wake-up time, follows her around the house until she leaves for school, and is ready for their afternoon adventures in the woods after she returns from school. But after dark, the roles reverse, and Archie is the leader, offering a world where one can see the night "through a cat's eyes."

6.46   Chorao, Kay. **The Cherry Pie Baby.** Illustrated by Kay Chorao. E. P. Dutton, 1989. ISBN 0-525-4435-1. 27p. 4–7 (est.).

Annie, an only child, wants a baby brother in the worst way, so she strikes a bargain with a newfound friend. She offers young Beau five pies from her father's wagon in exchange for Beau's baby brother, Claude. After sneaking Claude home, Annie's fantasies about baby brothers begin to fade as an inconsolable Claude ruins her toys, breaks her tea set, and wails continuously. When Papa discovers this unexpected guest, Annie must return little Claude to his family. Kay Chorao's portrayal of an only child's desires, told with dog characters, rings true.

6.47   Conly, Jane Leslie. **R-T, Margaret, and the Rats of NIMH.** Illustrated by Leonard Lubin. Harper and Row, 1990. ISBN 0-06-021364-7. 260p. 9–12.

When Margaret and Artie (R-T) get lost in the woods, they stumble upon a secret colony of superintelligent rats. With the help of Christopher and the rest of the famous rats of NIMH, who first appeared in Robert O'Brien's Newbery Award-winning *Mrs. Frisby and the Rats of NIMH*, the two humans survive and learn a lot about life in the process. But home again, the children face difficulties in keeping their promise not to reveal the rats' whereabouts. Unpredictable events and disclosures of secrets help build to an exciting climax. The second sequel of superb fantasy novels by the daughter of the late O'Brien continues to capture children's hearts and imaginations.

6.48   Conover, Chris. **Mother Goose and the Sly Fox.** Illustrated by Chris Conover. Farrar, Straus and Giroux, 1989. ISBN 0-374-35072-8. 28p. 4–8.

In the rich Dutch decor of this retelling, the setting is detailed with fine lace, windmills, tulips, and Delft pottery and tiles. Rather than a preyed-upon passel of lambs, the innocents are adorable, lace-ruffed goslings and their caregiver mouse. Mother Goose, in fine winged cap, returns home to discover that six of her children have been flummoxed by the fox. But clever Mrs. Goose knows how to substitute stones for children in a sack. Chris Conover's version doesn't allow the goslings to get consumed, and the fox learns his lesson.

6.49 Cushman, Doug. **Camp Big Paw.** Illustrated by Doug Cushman. Harper and Row, 1990. ISBN 0-06-021368-X. 64p. 6–8.

It's summer, and the campers have arrived at Camp Big Paw. When the contests for camping badges begin, newcomer Cyril the Cat and his cabin mates, Ben and Obie, run into trouble with the camp bully, Nigel Snootbutter. In the end, Cyril, with Nigel's unsuspecting help, "uses his head" to win a very special badge. Colorful cartoon-like illustrations complement this I Can Read chapter book about a group of animals' misadventures at summer camp.

6.50 Cushman, Doug. **Possum Stew.** Illustrated by Doug Cushman. E. P. Dutton, 1990. ISBN 0-525-44566-8. 32p. 3–6.

Possum likes nothing better than tricking folks. Finally, though, he tricks Bear and Gator one time too many. Determined to have the last laugh, Bear and Gator invite Possum to dinner, and Possum himself almost ends up in the stew pot. Both the text, written in the tradition of the trickster tale, and the illustrations will keep children laughing.

6.51 Delacre, Lulu. **Time for School, Nathan!** Illustrated by Lulu Delacre. Scholastic Hardcover Books, 1989. ISBN 0-590-41942-0. 32p. 3–7.

Eager to start school, Nathan the elephant explains to his best friend Nicholas the mouse that school is something that he, Nathan, must do alone. But Nicholas, not easily dissuaded, stows away in Nathan's schoolbag. At school, Nicholas makes mischief—singing during storytime, upsetting things, and disrupting Nathan's budding friendships. When Nathan acts glum, Nicholas admits his fear of losing his best friend. Reassurances and rebuilding contribute to the gentle theme. In the muted-toned illustrations, Nathan's "elephantness" seems a perfectly normal classroom occurrence.

6.52 dePaola, Tomie. **Bonjour, Mr. Satie.** Illustrated by Tomie de-Paola. G. P. Putnam's Sons, 1991. ISBN 0-399-21782-7. 28p. 5–9.

Tomie dePaola slyly advises that if anyone in his story looks or sounds familiar, he's "not the least bit surprised." The range of players who appear in Gertrude's 1920 Paris salon will certainly be familiar to adults—Zelda Fitzgerald, Ernest Hemingway, Ezra Pound, and Isadora Duncan, to name only a few whose countenances are identified by first name on the book jacket. The debonaire cat, Uncle Satie, must judge an exhibition of the paintings of Henri (Matisse) and Pablo (Picasso), and his diplomacy ends the artists' feud. Vibrant teal, orange, and purple illustrations dominate the tale.

6.53 dePaola, Tomie. **Haircuts for the Woolseys. Too Many Hopkins.** Illustrated by Tomie dePaola. G. P. Putnam's Sons, 1989. 10p. 2–5.

Spring arrives at Fiddle-Dee-Dee Farms in two warm-hearted tales illustrated in characteristic Tomie dePaola style. In the first book, the Woolseys, a family of sheep, get their spring haircuts. However, when a cold north wind blows in, leaving the bare-headed Woolseys chilled, Granny saves the day with a special surprise. In the second book, when all fifteen rabbit children descend upon their garden to plant vegetables, the result is a muddy mess. So Mommy Hopkins takes charge and organizes her brood with efficiency.

6.54 dePaola, Tomie. **Little Grunt and the Big Egg: A Prehistoric Fairy Tale.** Illustrated by Tomie dePaola. Holiday House, 1990. ISBN 0-8234-0730-6. 30p. 4–8.

When Little Grunt finds a huge egg for a prehistoric omelet, no one in the family realizes that it will hatch into George, a lovable but fast-growing brontosaurus pet. But growing is what George seems to do best, and soon he is much too big for the cave. Little Grunt is distraught over turning his pet out into the wild. Then a powerful volcanic eruption proves how handy big friends can be. Tomie dePaola's recognizable flat, jughead characters wear furs and winsome expressions against softly watercolored settings.

6.55 Donnelly, Liza. **Dinosaur Beach.** Illustrated by Liza Donnelly. Scholastic/Lucas Evans Books, 1989. ISBN 0-590-42175-1. 32p. 3–7.

Take one dinosaur-loving boy and his dog, Bones, add the discovery of an elasmosaurus on their trip to the beach, and you have the ingredients for an adventure sure to please dinosaur fans. Although all the other beach visitors rush screeching away, the story hero simply slips onto the back of the elasmosaurus and is whisked away to Dinosaur Beach. There other friendly dinosaurs jam and play volleyball—and even build a sand sculpture of the boy and his dog.

6.56   Dumbleton, Mike. **Dial-a-Croc.** Illustrated by Ann James. Orchard Books, 1991. ISBN 0-531-08545-7. 30p. 4–8 (est.).

To become rich, Vanessa captures a crocodile in the Australian outback. "You have a choice," she tells him. "You can be ten handbags and five pairs of shoes, or you can help me make lots of money." So "Dial-a-Croc" works a variety of jobs, including Swim Team Scarer, Ice Crusher, and Ticket Puncher. But he misses home. "You have a choice," he says to Vanessa. "You can be my breakfast . . . or you can take me home." Humorous illustrations add levity to an exploitation that turns to friendship.

6.57   Dunbar, Joyce. **Four Fierce Kittens.** Illustrated by Jakki Wood. Scholastic Hardcover Books, 1992. ISBN 0-590-45535-4. 32p. 2–6.

Four mischievous kittens set out for some excitement on the farm. Pretending to be tigers, leopards, and lions, the kittens soon learn that a kitty "meow" is not nearly as frightening as a "cluck" or an "oink" or a "quack." But can a "meow" scare a puppy? Indeed. Four fierce kittens make a puppy "scat." Watercolor paintings illustrate this rhythmic, repetitive text.

6.58   Ehlert, Lois. **Circus.** Illustrated by Lois Ehlert. HarperCollins, 1992. ISBN 0-06-020252-1. 32p. 2–6 (est.).

A border of stars frames the circus-act pages, which are narrower than the book's covers. In collages bolder than even Lois Ehlert fans have come to expect, each vivid circus act is composed of shapes akin to a child's pegboard game. Electric-blue striped Samu the Tiger jumps wildly through a flaming hoop against glossy black, and grass-green goats tumble against fuschia. Fluorescent, geometric graphics make for an atypical circus of marching snakes, leaping lizards, and the flying Zucchinis.

6.59 Elzbieta. **Brave Babette and Sly Tom.** Illustrated by Elzbieta. Dial Books for Young Readers, 1989. ISBN 0-8037-0633-2. 36p. 4–8.

Almost immediately after the birth of Babette the mouse in a blackbird's nest in the Luxembourg Gardens, her mother is chased away by a nasty cat named Sly Tom. Fortunately, the blackbird adopts Babette, who grows up to be such a feisty little mouse that she is able to best Sly Tom. Illustrations are textured backdrops in earth-gray and brown overlaid with impressions of trees and the simply drawn animals.

6.60 Emberley, Michael. **Ruby.** Illustrated by Michael Emberley. Little, Brown, 1990. ISBN 0-316-23643-8. 32p. 3–7 (est.).

Ruby, a Red Riding Hood-like mouse, sets off in her red cloak to deliver triple-cheese pies to her granny. Although Ruby's mother warns her not to talk to strangers (especially cats), Ruby is defended on the street by a well-dressed, whiskered stranger when a grimy reptile accosts her. Like the wolf, the stranger races ahead to Granny's house—by taxi in this urban tale. But a clever Ruby makes a quick phone call to ensure a satisfying, surprise ending. *ALA Notable Children's Books, 1991.*

6.61 Engel, Diana. **Josephina Hates Her Name.** Illustrated by Diana Engel. Morrow Junior Books, 1989. ISBN 0-688-07796-X. 32p. 4–8 (est.).

Josephina the alligator hates her name—she thinks it's ugly, old-fashioned, and too unusual. When she plays with her friends, she even suggests that they trade names, but no one ever wants Josephina's name. Then, Grandma tells Josephina all about the remarkable great-aunt after whom she is named. When Josephina tells the story to her friends, they are more than ready to trade names, but Josephina won't hear of it.

6.62 Ernst, Lisa Campbell. **When Bluebell Sang.** Illustrated by Lisa Campbell Ernst. Bradbury Press, 1989. ISBN 0-02-733561-5. 32p. 5–7 (est.).

Farmer Swenson discovers that one of his dairy cows, Bluebell, can sing beautifully. After performing for the local community, Bluebell falls victim to a greedy talent agent, Big Eddie, who takes Swenson and Bluebell on tour in a scheme to make Bluebell famous and himself rich. Dressed in the latest fashion, Bluebell is indeed a success. Although she is a trendsetter wherever she goes, Bluebell and Swenson are homesick. Finally, they devise a clever plan to return home to the farm and resume a life of peace and anonymity.

6.63 Geraghty, Paul. **Over the Steamy Swamp.** Illustrated by Paul Geraghty. Harcourt Brace Jovanovich/Gulliver Books, 1989. ISBN 0-15-200561-7. 32p. 3–6.

A steamy swamp is the setting for this circular cumulative tale with a food chain theme. A mosquito is threatened by a dragonfly who is threatened by a frog who is threatened by . . . and on and on, until the greatest threat of all appears—a hunter, who falls prey to the mosquito! Exaggerated actions fill the swamp scenes with color and humor.

6.64 Giffard, Hannah. **Red Fox.** Illustrated by Hannah Giffard. Dial Books for Young Readers, 1991. ISBN 0-8037-0869-6. 25p. 4–8 (est.).

Hungry Red Fox sets out at night to find food for himself and his mate. But his typical hunting routine meets with unusual misfortune, and so Red Fox must brave the city to find something to eat. Returning home with a city-style meal, Red Fox finds that he now has a few more mouths to feed. Brightly colored stylized paintings, highlighted with white, illustrate this nocturnal adventure of a determined fox.

6.65 Grossman, Bill. **Tommy at the Grocery Store.** Illustrated by Victoria Chess. Harper and Row, 1989. ISBN 0-06-022409-6. 32p. 3–7.

Is Tommy the Pig a potato? Well, he does have eyes! Or maybe a ruler? After all, he has feet! After Tommy's mother inadvertently leaves him at the grocery store, customers mistakenly identify him as various grocery items and whisk him home. Though each case of mistaken identity is discovered before disasters occur, Tommy's predicaments and separation may be disconcerting for very young children. Victoria Chess's bright, detailed watercolor illustrations bring out the humor of Bill Grossman's rhyming text.

6.66 Guarino, Deborah. **Is Your Mama a Llama?** Illustrated by Steven Kellogg. Scholastic Hardcover Books, 1989. ISBN 0-590-41387-2. 32p. 4–7.

In a rhyming and patterned text, a curious baby llama named Lloyd asks each of his animal friends the same question: "Is your mama a llama?" The friends, in turn, give Lloyd clues to the identity of their mamas. In the end, with help from his friend Llyn, Lloyd gets the answer to his question and finds his own llama mama. Steven Kellogg's detail-rich watercolor illustrations capture the innocent beauty of animal mothers and their babies.

6.67   Hawkins, Colin, and Jacqui Hawkins. **Crocodile Creek: The Cry in the Night.** Illustrated by Colin Hawkins. Doubleday, 1989. ISBN 0-385-24980-2. 30p. 3–8 (est.).

On his houseboat, Baby Crocker wakes one morning out of sorts and feeling snappy. Besides crankiness, his teething pains make him bite off a table leg and chew up a life preserver. Baby even chews off the mooring rope of the houseboat, and he and the houseboat float off alone toward Fatal Falls. But it's Gran the windsurfer to the rescue. This humorous story follows Baby Crocker's family and frenzies in cartoon illustrations and dialogue.

6.68   Hayes, Sarah. **This Is the Bear and the Scary Night.** Illustrated by Helen Craig. Little, Brown/Joy Street Books, 1992. ISBN 0-316-35250-0. 24p. 3–6 (est.).

"This is the boy who forgot his bear and left him behind in the park on the chair." In rhyming text, the cumulative story unfolds. A boy's favorite bear is forgotten and must spend the night in the park. The poor bear is swept up by an owl, dropped into a pond, rescued by a trombone player, and eventually reunited with his young owner. Perky drawings are shaded with faded-jeans blues and park-bench greens.

6.69   Henkes, Kevin. **Julius, the Baby of the World.** Illustrated by Kevin Henkes. Greenwillow Books, 1990. ISBN 0-688-08944-5. 32p. 4–7 (est.).

Lilly's excitement about the new baby turns to jealousy when her brother arrives and gets lots of parental attention. Lilly alternates between ignoring Baby Julius and undermining his upbringing. Over his mouse crib, she scrambles the alphabet, whispers "you're ugly," and tries to make him disappear. But when a visiting cousin insults Baby Julius, Lilly rises to his defense and insists that Julius is "The Baby of the World." Lilly's mouse moods are hilarious, recognizable, and captivating. *ALA Notable Children's Books, 1991.*

6.70 Himmelman, John. **A Guest Is a Guest.** Illustrated by John Himmelman. Dutton Children's Books, 1991. ISBN 0-525-44720-2. 32p. 3–8 (est.).

"A guest is a guest and we must show them our best." So say the Beanbucket family when their pigs move into the farmhouse with them. Because the pigs are accepted, in come the chickens. With pigs taking over the kitchen, and hens on every cushion, the cows and horses move in. Finally, patient Farmer Beanbucket reaches his limit: "Enough is enough," he cries. So—the animals throw the Beanbuckets out! Charming animals make themselves at home in overstuffed watercolor comfort.

6.71 Howe, James. **Hot Fudge.** Illustrated by Leslie Morrill. Morrow Junior Books, 1990. ISBN 0-688-09701-4. 32p. 5 and up.

Harold, the Monroe family's large, loquacious, and chocolate-loving canine, is left at home on a Saturday morning along with a pan of homemade fudge. But Harold is not alone. Sharing the household are the Monroe's other pets: Chester, their arrogant cat, little Howie, the dachshund, and Bunnicula, the vampire bunny. Soon after Chester reads in the morning newspaper that there are robbers in the neighborhood, the fudge is missing. Harold, Chester, and Howie try to solve the crime.

6.72 Hurd, Thacher. **Blackberry Ramble.** Illustrated by Thacher Hurd. Crown, 1989. ISBN 0-517-57105-6. 29p. 3–8 (est.).

It is a beautiful day, and Mother and Father Mouse are trying to complete their spring cleaning. At first, Baby Mouse is "just noodling around," but she soon gets into mischief. The patient parents finally give up their cleaning project for a picnic with Baby. Mouse antics continue, including a wild ride with Baby Mouse at the wheel, and a splattering fall into the blackberry pie. Thacher Hurd's bright illustrations will make any reader long for a spring day on the farm.

6.73 Jacques, Brian. **Mattimeo.** Illustrated by Gary Chalk. Philomel Books, 1990. ISBN 0-399-21741-X. 446p. 10 and up.

When Slagar the Fox and his evil band of mercenaries kidnap the young of Redwall Abbey and enslave them in the kingdom of Malkariss, warrior mouse Mathias and his followers must rescue Redwall's future leaders. Those remaining at the abbey face an equally perilous threat from General Ironbeak and his gang of wicked birds. As the final battle begins, the warriors find new strength, and Mattimeo, son of Mathias, fulfills his destiny. This final episode in the Redwall trilogy finds human-like heroes triumphing over evil.

6.74 Jorgensen, Gail. **Crocodile Beat.** Illustrated by Patricia Mullins. Bradbury Press, 1989. ISBN 0-02-748010-0. 32p. 1–6.

Brilliant tissue-paper and paint collages across double-page spreads display hissing snakes, booming elephants, swishing birds, chattering monkeys, splashing ducks, and growling bears "dancing and playing and stomping their feet." Roaring King Lion, shouldered by two bears on his bright red throne, leads the noisy parade. When the crowd awakens a mean, snapping crocodile, King Lion steps in to save the day. Young children will enjoy the sing-song text and the subtle expressions on the faces of the abundant animals.

6.75 Joyce, William. **Bently and Egg.** Illustrated by William Joyce. HarperCollins/Laura Geringer Books, 1992. ISBN 0-06-020386-2. 28p. 3–8.

Artistic frog Bently Hopperton is entrusted with the single egg of his best friend, Kack Kack, when the duck is away. Unlike Horton, Bently is a less-than-faithful steward. Because the egg is bald and bare, Bently paints it in dazzling colors. The Easter-like egg then attracts the attention of a boy who promptly "eggnaps" it! Poor Bently must brave all sorts of hilarious challenges to retrieve the precious egg. Large-scale watercolors in a spring-green palette are perfect for the woodland characters.

6.76 Kalman, Maira. **Ooh-La-La (Max in Love).** Illustrated by Maira Kalman. Viking Penguin, 1991. ISBN 0-670-84163-3. 32p. 8 and up.

Max Stravinsky, the millionaire poet dog, takes a whirlwind tour of Paris, where he loses his heart to the beautiful Crêpes Suzette. In a satiric spoof on the salon, Maira Kalman gives wit, savoir faire, and a touch of the dramatic to his cast: Fritz from the Ritz, Madame Camembert, Charlotte Russe, Peach Melba, and Pierre Potpourri. A panoply of styles moderne (including a Blue Suite in salute to Picasso) and printing which flows across the illustrations give this picture book for older readers a lighthearted and energetic style.

6.77 Karlin, Nurit. **Little Big Mouse.** Illustrated by Nurit Karlin. HarperCollins, 1991. ISBN 0-06-021608-5. 32p. 3–6 (est.).

A tiny mouse is dissatisfied with his size. Everyone, it seems, is bigger than he. More than anything, he wants to be really BIG. With knapsack on his back, he sets out to discover how to get big. Out in the world, he meets a circus elephant, who explains, "I think I was big even when I was little." Then Mouse's nose tickles, and a tiny flea asks how Mouse got so big. Simple text and bold-stroke illustrations are good companions.

6.78   Keller, Holly. **The New Boy.** Illustrated by Holly Keller. Greenwillow Books, 1991. ISBN 0-688-09828-2. 22p. 4–7 (est.).

When Milton the mouse arrives in Miss Higgins's kindergarten class, chaos erupts. He puts caterpillars in lunch boxes, knocks over blocks, and eats all the cherries off the special cupcakes that Gregory brings for a snack. Even when Milton decides to be good, things don't work out much better. When a new boy arrives, readers will enjoy predicting how he will behave and how Milton will be affected. Holly Keller's simple illustrations have humor that will engage beginning readers.

6.79   Kettner, Christine. **An Ordinary Cat.** Illustrated by Christine Kettner. HarperCollins, 1991. ISBN 0-06-023173-4. 26p. 6–10 (est.).

To his family, William is an ordinary cat. But at night, William becomes "extraordinary" as he drives a cab, delivers important fares, and even plays in a band. At dawn, William returns home and resumes his ordinary existence. Bold-colored cartoon-like drawings illustrate the secret nighttime adventures of a proper daytime cat.

6.80   King-Smith, Dick. **Ace: The Very Important Pig.** Illustrated by Lynette Hemmant. Crown, 1990. ISBN 0-517-57833-6. 134p. 8–12 (est.).

Marked by an ace of clubs on his side, Ace is more than just an average pig. As Farmer Tubbs soon discovers, this unusual great-grandson of Babe, the sheepherding pig whose story is told in Dick King-Smith's *Babe: The Gallant Pig*, not only can understand human speech, but he also likes to watch television. After Ace appears on the BBC, he becomes a celebrity and a "very important pig." Set in the English countryside, this humorous animal fantasy is filled with colorful animal characters that children will enjoy getting to know.

6.81   King-Smith, Dick. **Martin's Mice.** Illustrated by Jez Alborough. Crown, 1989. ISBN 0-517-57113-7. 128p. 8–12.

Instead of hunting mice like other barn cats, Martin adopts them. In a bathtub-style cage, Martin keeps the mouse mother Drusilla and her children, caring for and protecting them. But the mice request their freedom. It is only when Martin himself is sold and kept as a pet in a city apartment that he comes to understand independence. After a daring escape, Martin returns to the farm to establish a true friendship with Drusilla.

6.82   King-Smith, Dick, compiler. **The Animal Parade: A Collection of Stories and Poems.** Illustrated by Jocelyn Wild. Tambourine Books, 1992. ISBN 0-688-11375-3. 93p. 6 and up.

Dick King-Smith indicates that he has collected his favorite animal tales—some comical, some dramatic, some frightening, and some even tragic. Along with fables by Aesop, there are excerpts from *Wind in the Willows, Alice in Wonderland, The Jungle Book, The Tale of Jeremy Fisher, Black Beauty,* and *White Fang.* Sprinkled throughout are selections from the author's own poems and stories. Illustrator Jocelyn Wild has given the animals in this collection both texture and feelings.

6.83   Kraus, Robert. **Phil the Ventriloquist.** Illustrated by Robert Kraus. Greenwillow Books, 1989. ISBN 0-688-07988-1. 32p. 3–7 (est.).

Phil the rabbit is a ventriloquist. He can make the scrambled eggs talk and the telephone ring. His parents beg him to use a ventriloquist's dummy instead of making chairs say, "Don't sit on me." But Phil won't listen. He'd rather make his father's shoes sing and his mother's hat tell jokes. Then one day a burglar breaks into Phil's house, and ventriloquism saves the day. As in his Spider and Daddy Long Ears books, Robert Kraus's drawings and text are big, bold, and simple.

6.84   Kwitz, Mary DeBall. **Shadow over Mousehaven Manor.** Illustrated by Stella Ormai. Scholastic Hardcover Books, 1989. ISBN 0-590-42034-8. 128p. 7–11.

When Minabell Mouse receives an urgent request to visit her gravely ill Aunt Pitty Pat in their ancestral home, Minabell must set out in a Christmas Eve snowstorm to Mousehaven Manor. Despite warnings from a secret agent and an encounter with an evil pack of rats, the courageous mouse continues on her journey, determined to rescue her aunt and her family home from the Prairie Pirates, a dangerous band of rodents. With the help of friends, Minabell and her aunt foil a treacherous plan and save the manor and the state of Illinois from destruction. Black-line sketches illustrate this animal adventure story.

6.85 Kyte, Dennis. **Zackary Raffles.** Illustrated by Dennis Kyte. Doubleday, 1989. ISBN 0-385-24653-6. 28p. 4–8 (est.).

Like all young mice who reach the age of six, Zackary Raffles is eligible to join the Mouse Soldiers, Brave and True. To do so, he must pass three tests: walk the Rope of Courage, solve the mysterious riddle, and spend the night standing guard on Lookout Rock. But Zackary is afraid of the dark—so afraid that he never sleeps at night and he carries a lantern in the daytime in case the sun goes behind a cloud. Humorous watercolor illustrations will allow comparisons of mouse- and human-scaled objects. Children who share Zackary's fear will take comfort in his triumph.

6.86 Le Guin, Ursula K. **Catwings Return.** Illustrated by S. D. Schindler. Orchard Books/Richard Jackson Books, 1989. ISBN 0-531-08403-5. 48p. 6–10 (est.).

In this sequel to *Catwings*, Ursula Le Guin continues her flying cat fantasy with this heartwarming family-reunion tale. Now living in safety, four winged tabby cats, perfectly detailed in ink with color washes, reminisce about their mother and their first home in the city. When two of the cats decide to visit their alley birthplace, they discover and rescue a tiny winged kitten from a building being demolished. Learning the kitten is their sister, they take her home to the country.

6.87 Lindbergh, Reeve. **The Day the Goose Got Loose.** Illustrated by Steven Kellogg. Dial Books for Young Readers, 1990. ISBN 0-8037-0409-7. 32p. 4–8.

When the goose gets loose, the havoc begins, and before it's all over both the farm and the town are in for a comical spree. The frolicking goose lets loose the chickens, the sheep, and the horses, and teases the bull into a charging mode. What got into that goose? The farm child dreams an enchanting answer. Reeve Lindbergh's rhyming text includes a repetitive phrase. Steven Kellogg's action-packed illustrations beg to be examined closely.

6.88 Lionni, Leo. **Tillie and the Wall.** Illustrated by Leo Lionni. Alfred A. Knopf/Borzoi Books, 1989. ISBN 0-394-92155-0. 27p. 4–8 (est.).

Tillie and her companion mice wonder about the other side of a wall that "had been there ever since the mice could remember."

It is too high to climb over, too thick to drill through, and too long to go around, but Tillie is inspired by earthworms to burrow underneath the wall. On the other side, she discovers mice like herself who receive her joyously and follow her back through the tunnel. Leo Lionni's familiar collage-style mice are in harmony with the simplicity of the message. *Notable 1989 Children's Trade Books in the Field of Social Studies.*

6.89   Marshall, James. **Fox Be Nimble.** Illustrated by James Marshall. Dial Books for Young Readers, 1990. ISBN 0-8037-0761-4. 48p. 4–8.

Fox is busy practicing to be a rock star, but his mom interrupts his starring role, sending him to baby-sit the mischievous Ling children. Discovering his baby-sitting duties to be more than he expected, Fox climbs new heights to get the job done. In the process he achieves stardom, albeit not the kind he wanted. This collection of three fun-filled stories, all humorously illustrated, is another book about lovable and trouble-finding Fox in the Easy-to-Read Books series. *ALA Notable Children's Books, 1991.*

6.90   Maxner, Joyce. **Lady Bugatti.** Illustrated by Kevin Hawkes. Lothrop, Lee and Shepard Books, 1991. ISBN 0-688-10341-3. 32p. 5 and up.

In lilting and clever poetry, this picture book tells the story of a chic and urbane ladybug hostess as she entertains insect guests. The text is amusing; the illustrations are irresistible. Lady Bugatti's friends are sophisticated urbanites, and we see them in lushly colored urban settings in art-deco paintings. Like Joyce Maxner's *Nicholas Cricket*, this book will charm young readers with its detailed and humorous depiction of insects and animals as glitterati from the Roaring Twenties.

6.91   Maxner, Joyce. **Nicholas Cricket.** Illustrated by William Joyce. HarperCollins/Harper Trophy Books, 1989. ISBN 0-06-024222-1. 20p. 3–8 (est.).

The soft, luminous paintings of William Joyce—in which insects and small animals dress and act like fashionable Americans of the 1920s—give an entrancing air to this picture book. The verse, clever and musical, describes the cricket banjo player's part in an all-night fest at his cabaret. The art-deco illustrations provide a perfect setting for the energetic re-creation of Nick's sophisticated chums, and no child will be able to resist this tantalizing glimpse of their night life.

6.92 McCully, Emily Arnold. **The Evil Spell.** Illustrated by Emily Arnold McCully. Harper and Row, 1990. ISBN 0-06-024154-3. 32p. 5–8.

In this sequel to *ZaZa's Big Break,* Emily Arnold McCully's droll illustrations tell yet another humorous tale of the loving, theatrical bear family. When Edwin at long last gets a leading role and a chance to deliver the lines that break the evil spell and save the day, he is overcome with stage fright and runs away, too embarrassed to face the theater again. However, his wise and loving parents convince him to return. Perhaps more important, Edwin is able to break his own "evil spell" and to believe in himself.

6.93 McCully, Emily Arnold. **Speak Up, Blanche!** Illustrated by Emily Arnold McCully. HarperCollins, 1991. ISBN 0-06-024228-0. 32p. 4–8 (est.).

When the benefactress of Farm Theater asks Bruno and the other actors to teach the craft of acting to her grandchild, Blanche, the animals cannot refuse. But Blanche is very shy and makes a challenging pupil. Her tiny lamb voice is printed in the smallest of type. She can't act, sell tickets, or collect props. But she is never without her sketchbooks, and eventually she gains the courage to convince the troupe that she would make a perfect set designer.

6.94 McPhail, David. **Pig Pig Gets a Job.** Illustrated by David McPhail. Dutton Children's Books, 1990. ISBN 0-525-44619-2. 24p. 4–8.

In Pig Pig's newest adventure, he learns an elementary lesson of economics: if one wants to buy something, one must work. Pig Pig's visions of what he can do to earn money are humorously exaggerated in David McPhail's illustrations—baker of mud pies, builder of tumbledown houses, and maniacal car mechanic. All wild plans are gently reproved by Mother Pig, who helps Pig Pig decide what tasks are sensible for a young pig.

6.95 Meddaugh, Susan. **Martha Speaks.** Illustrated by Susan Meddaugh. Houghton Mifflin, 1992. ISBN 0-395-63313-3. 32p. 4–8 (est.).

Martha is a perfectly ordinary dog until she eats alphabet soup and begins to talk. At first her family is delighted that Martha can speak, even though her words aren't always appropriate, such as "Why is that man so fat?" Finally, Martha talks so much that her words blanket the pages and the family yells, "Martha, please! SHUT UP!" But she redeems herself during a burglary, and children will appreciate her cleverness.

6.96   Minarik, Else Holmelund. **Am I Beautiful?** Illustrated by Yossi Abolafia. Greenwillow Books, 1992. ISBN 0-688-09912-2. 24p. 3 and up.

As Little Hippo walks through the jungle, he overhears parents exclaiming over their children's beauty and grace. In each instance, Little Hippo asks the parent, "Am I beautiful, too?" In no case—whether by lioness, heron, or human mother—is his beauty confirmed. So, Little Hippo does what all children learn to do—he asks his own mother, who answers: ". . . all hippos are beautiful. And you are the most beautiful of all, because you are mine!" Watercolor paints edged in black ink offer airy interpretations of an important question.

6.97   Minarik, Else Holmelund. **Percy and the Five Houses.** Illustrated by James Stevenson. Greenwillow Books, 1989. ISBN 0-688-08105-3. 20p. 4–10.

Creator of the Little Bear stories, Else Holmelund Minarik teams simple text with James Stevenson's breezy art to tell the story of Percy, a river beaver who finds a piece of real gold. Conned by Ferd the Fox, Percy uses the gold to join the House of the Month Club, a club that mails out new houses for each month of the year. But cardboard castles, crepe-paper trees, and igloos are no match for a beaver's natural habitat, and Percy discovers that his dam is the best house of all.

6.98   Modrell, Dolores. **Tales of Tiddly.** Illustrated by Ellen Eagle. Simon and Schuster Books for Young Readers, 1990. ISBN 0-671-69204-6. 36p. 5–7 (est.).

This is a set of three simple stories about Tiddly, a small homeless kitty, Mr. Bones, a very sophisticated and well-organized cat, and Uncle Meezo, a white terrier with the kindest face that Tiddly has ever seen. The two friends generously take in Tiddly, making him a part of their family. The resulting adventures may serve as a lead-in to classroom discussions about families' similarities and unique characteristics.

6.99   Norman, Philip Ross. **The Carrot War.** Illustrated by Philip Ross Norman. Little, Brown, 1992. ISBN 0-316-61200-6. 32p. 4–7 (est.).

Just before the Midsummer Feast, the Horrible Hares, carrot thieves of the first magnitude, pilfer every Rabbit carrot, and "bunnynap" Carbuncle, the Rabbits' Carrot Expert. In true Trojan style, the peaceful Rabbits build a giant bunny-filled carrot to gain access to the Hares' fort. The details of the fort and the plans for assault beg to be inspected. Revenge is funny and harmless in its effect. For example, Black Ear, the Horrible Hare Emperor, is doused with a flagon of carrot wine.

6.100 Norman, Philip Ross. **A Mammoth Imagination.** Illustrated by Philip Ross Norman. Little, Brown, 1992. ISBN 0-316-61201-4. 32p. 4–8 (est.).

Little Bonbon, a wild boar, has a wild imagination. He needs it because the grownup wild boars are boring. While the others just eat and look for mushrooms to eat again, Bonbon exercises his imagination. Then, following some huge footprints, he discovers a herd of friendly mammoths who have toys and paints and beds for jumping. There is even mammoth music for dancing. Back home again, Bonbon is certain that he will always have a playmate—because of his "mammoth imagination."

6.101 Novak, Matt. **While the Shepherd Slept.** Illustrated by Matt Novak. Orchard Books, 1991. ISBN 0-531-08515-5. 32p. 3–7 (est.).

A tired little shepherd nods off under a shady tree while his fat white sheep quietly sneak away, as they always do. They're off to the theater where each afternoon they don costumes and perform vaudeville routines, songs, and dances. When the matinee is over, they nibble their way back to the shepherd, ready for sleep in their warm barn. Then, in a surprising twist, the little shepherd goes to the theater, where, under the same spotlight, he dances until dawn.

6.102 Numeroff, Laura Joffe. **If You Give a Moose a Muffin.** Illustrated by Felicia Bond. HarperCollins/Laura Geringer Books, 1991. ISBN 0-06-024406-2. 28p. 6–11 (est.).

When a moose comes for a visit, a little boy tries to make it feel at home by offering a muffin. But it doesn't take long before the host conjectures that a moose may not be so easily satisfied, and that it may request other things to go with the muffin—jam, more muffins, and maybe a sweater. The moose may even want socks, then make a puppet show, and need to paint scenery.

Laura Joffe Numeroff's characters have just the right touch of whimsy when creating their jolly havoc.

6.103   Otto, Carolyn. **Dinosaur Chase.** Illustrated by Thacher Hurd. HarperCollins, 1991. ISBN 0-06-021614-X. 32p. 2–6 (est.).

When only dinosaurs populate the world, they swim and surf, fish and fly. But some masked dinosaurs are stealing jewels! Over the bridge they run, pursued by dinosaur police. Posing as dinosaur statues in the park, the robbers are unable to fool the police. With very little text and rhyming phrases ("Dinosaur chase, dinosaur race, hiding in a dinosaur place"), this bedtime dinosaur adventure will encourage young readers. Edge-to-edge paintings are in transparent watercolors, shaded, and outlined with India ink.

6.104   Patz, Nancy. **Sarah Bear and Sweet Sidney.** Illustrated by Nancy Patz. Four Winds Press, 1989. ISBN 0-02-770270-7. 28p. 6–10.

It is practically springtime, and Sweet Sidney is ready to awaken, but Sarah Bear is content to continue hibernating until spring really arrives. So, to pass the time, Sweet Sidney does the spring cleaning, prepares a picnic, and finally falls back to sleep. When spring does arrive, both bears awaken and prance off to the meadow to enjoy honey-nut rolls and laugh in the sunshine. The rhythmic text, occasionally expressed in rhyme, brings the bears' adventures to life. Dynamic illustrations, in pencil, watercolor, and inks, animate the text and capture the passing of winter.

6.105   Pearson, Susan. **Well, I Never!** Illustrated by James Warhola. Simon and Schuster Books for Young Readers, 1990. ISBN 0-671-69199-6. 32p. 4–8 (est.).

It is a strange Saturday on the farm. First Pa bales the sheep instead of the hay. Then Ma feeds the chickens popcorn, which pops inside their stomachs, causing them to bounce on the barn roof as Ma runs back and forth, trying to catch their eggs in the laundry basket. When the family finally discovers the cause of their outrageous problems, the challenge is to find a solution. Zany illustrations are the perfect complement to this tall tale.

6.106   Pfister, Marcus (translated by J. Alison James). **Rainbow Fish.** Illustrated by Marcus Pfister. North-South Books, 1992. ISBN 1-55858-010-7. 32p. 5–8.

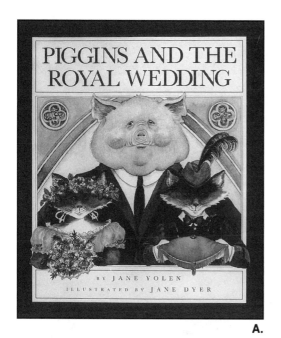

A.

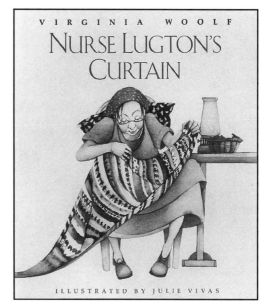

B.

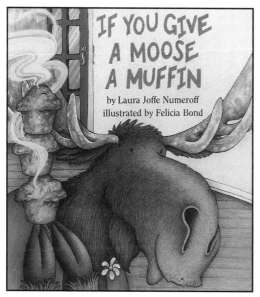

C.

D.

A. *Piggins and the Royal Wedding* by Jane Yolen; illustrated by Jane Dyer (see 6.165).
B. *Nurse Lugton's Curtain* by Virginia Woolf; illustrated by Julie Vivas (see 6.163).
C. *If You Give a Moose a Muffin* by Laura Joffe Numeroff; illustrated by Felicia Bond
(see 6.102).   **D.** *You Silly Goose* by Ellen Stoll Walsh (see 6.148).

A.

B.

C.

A. *Little Mouse's Painting* by Diane Wolkstein; illustrated by Maryjane Begin (see 6.160). **B.** *Tuesday* by David Wiesner (see 6.155). **C.** *Frog Odyssey* by Juliet and Charles Snape (see 6.125).

An extraordinary fish takes pride in his shimmering scales—scales of such beauty and reflected gleam that he is amazing to other fish. But pride leaves Rainbow Fish lonely until he learns the lesson of sacrifice and the rewards of generosity. The world of Rainbow Fish is washed in blues, greens, and lavenders. His scales are enhanced with defraction foil, an innovative holographic technique that creates depth, color change, and reflected geometric patterns as the pages are shifted in the light.

6.107 Pochocki, Ethel. **The Attic Mice.** Illustrated by David Catrow. Henry Holt, 1990. ISBN 0-8505-1298-2. 113p. 8–10 (est.).

Living in the attic of an old doll farmhouse in the middle of a linoleum yard, a family of mice share hair-raising adventures, growing pains, understanding, and love. The story of their everyday experiences and their acceptance of a "good-for-nothing" horse chestnut into the family is colorfully and humorously told. Pen-and-ink drawings detail this warmhearted tale.

6.108 Pomerantz, Charlotte. **Flap Your Wings and Try.** Illustrated by Nancy Tafuri. Greenwillow Books, 1989. ISBN 0-688-08020-0. 20p. 4–8.

With encouragement and patience, a baby seagull learns to fly. Once aloft in the sky, the bird then encourages others to "flap your wings and try." Nancy Tafuri's full-page illustrations, beautifully created with watercolor and black ink, capture the effort and the achievement. The rhyme and predictable pattern of Charlotte Pomerantz's text will encourage young children to try their own wings at reading.

6.109 Quackenbush, Robert. **Danger in Tibet. Evil under the Sea. Lost in the Amazon.** Illustrated by Robert Quackenbush. Pippin Press, 1989–92. 32p. 6–10.

Unabashed environmentalist Miss Mallard, the world famous "ducktective," solves ecological mysteries around the globe. In Australia, someone or something is destroying the Great Barrier Reef. In the Amazon, the rain forests are in danger. And in Tibet, it is Mr. Everest that could be destroyed. Miss Mallard (and young readers) pick up clues amid lots of information, eventually deducing the solutions. Full-page watercolors, humor, and thin volumes in the Miss Mallard Mystery series will invite young readers.

6.110 Ravilious, Robin. **Two in a Pocket.** Illustrated by Robin Ravilious. Little, Brown, 1991. ISBN 0-316-73449-7. 24p. 4–8.

With spring's arrival, Snippet the dormouse finds herself in new surroundings, sharing a coat-pocket home with Jenny the wren. When Jenny is hurt by a cat, Snippet nurses her back to health, and the two unlikely housemates develop a strong friendship. When summer comes, the coat is carried away by the farmer to make a scarecrow. Home again in her field, Snippet settles happily into one pocket, with Jenny in the other. Softly colored pencil sketches illustrate this heartwarming story of friendship.

6.111　Reeves, Mona Rabun. **I Had a Cat.** Illustrated by Julie Downing. Bradbury Press, 1989. ISBN 0-02-775731-5. 30p. 4–7 (est.).

In this fanciful story written in rhyme, a little girl's house is filled to overflowing with a rambunctious menagerie. To deal with the problem of too many animals, she visits the zookeeper, a farmer, and a boy; they all help her out by taking various animals. Then, beginning to feel somewhat lonely, the little girl returns home and is relieved to discover that she still has her cat. Bright, exuberant watercolors create a chaotic mood.

6.112　Robertus, Polly M. **The Dog Who Had Kittens.** Illustrated by Janet Stevens. Holiday House, 1991. ISBN 0-8234-0860-4. 28p. 6–10 (est.).

When Eloise has her kittens, Baxter the bassett hound feels like an outcast. But when he becomes a full-time baby-sitter for the kittens, Baxter understands the joy of fatherhood. Then the kittens are given away to new homes, and Baxter is lonely until he discovers a newfound friendship with Eloise. Watercolored black-crayon drawings capture the emotions of this heartwarming story about the need for companionship.

6.113　Ross, Christine. **Lily and the Bears.** Illustrated by Christine Ross. Houghton Mifflin, 1991. ISBN 0-395-55332-6. 24p. 4–8.

Lily wants to be "something big and brave . . . and tough." So every morning, instead of getting dressed up in children's clothes, she puts on a bear suit and acts like a wild bear, much to her mother's, father's, and grandmother's dismay. One day, Lily's class goes to the zoo, and Lily finds herself mistakenly locked into the bear cage. There she discovers what wild bears are *really* like. Delicately drawn wax pencil and watercolor illustrations enrich Lily's story with humorous details.

6.114　Ruch, Sandi Barrett. **Junkyard Dog.** Illustrated by Marjory Wunsch. Orchard Books, 1990. ISBN 0-531-08442-6. 89p. 8–11 (est.).

The widowed junkman, Zlotnick, obtains what he thinks is a fierce guard dog named Max. But little Huey, one of the junkman's four children, makes friends with Max without Zlotnick's knowledge. Zlotnick changes his mind about Max when Huey is accidentally trapped in an old refrigerator, and Max rescues him. Max then becomes a member of the family. Sandi Barrett Ruch tells her black-and-white illustrated story from the unique point of view of an observant toad, a longtime resident of the junkyard.

6.115 Ryder, Joanne. **The Bear on the Moon.** Illustrated by Carol Lacey. Morrow Junior Books, 1991. ISBN 0-688-08110-X. 32p. 6–10 (est.).

When "there was nothing at the top of the world but the sea where the white bears lived," one observant, curious bear climbed the northern lights to explore the moon. In a creation myth based on Joanne Ryder's own childhood wonderings and imagination, the polar bear tosses the moon's snowy, icy surface to the bears below, building the Arctic ice cap and accounting for the waning moon. Carol Lacey's furry, wet polar bears are realistic against expressionistic backdrops, her compositions balanced and peaceful.

6.116 Schotter, Roni. **Bunny's Night Out.** Illustrated by Margot Apple. Little, Brown/Joy Street Books, 1989. ISBN 0-316-77465-0. 29p. 4–8 (est.).

Bedtime is not Bunny's favorite time of the day. So one night, when the moon seems to call him out to play, Bunny crawls out of his rabbit home and begins a series of nighttime adventures, including sharing a leftover meal with a band of raccoons. But when the rain begins to fall, a cold and wet Bunny hops home and realizes that his bed is the best place to be. Soft, colored-pencil drawings illustrate this adventurous bedtime story.

6.117 Schwartz, Henry. **How I Captured a Dinosaur.** Illustrated by Amy Schwartz. Orchard Books/Richard Jackson Books, 1989. ISBN 0-531-08370-5. 28p. 4–7.

When dinosaurs are sighted along the Baja Peninsula of Mexico, Liz Bradford is determined to see one for herself. Luckily, her family is about to embark on a camping vacation, and she is able to convince them to set up camp near the sightings. Liz's first-person account of how she lures "Albert" (short for Albertosaurus) with a hamburger and how she domesticates him will stir the imagination of any young dinosaur lover.

6.118 Schwartz, Roslyn. **Rose and Dorothy.** Illustrated by Roslyn Schwartz. Orchard Books, 1991. ISBN 0-531-08518-X. 32p. 3–7.

Two very different creatures—Dorothy, a huge singing elephant, and Rose, a tiny mouse—transcend size differences to become the best of friends, in a story reminiscent of William Steig's *Amos and Boris*. But these two friends cohabitate, and Dorothy's size eventually drives delicate Rose to near collapse. Hurt feelings are resolved through a good talk, and buying the big house next door makes for a happy ending. Ink and crayon drawings provide hilarious detail. Watch for Dorothy at the art gallery!

6.119 Seligson, Susan, and Howie Schneider. **The Amazing Amos and the Greatest Couch on Earth.** Illustrated by Susan Seligson and Howie Schneider. Little, Brown/Joy Street Books, 1989. ISBN 0-316-78033-2. 30p. 4–8 (est.).

Varoom! Amos the dog is off on his second journey. With just a flick of his paw, Amos can make his favorite couch move. His owners, Mr. and Mrs. Bobson, rarely worry about him because they know he is a good driver. However, the Bobsons are unaware that this time Amos's adventure has taken him to a circus where he and his fantastic couch are a part of the show. Again, Amos's exploits are filled with fun, imagination, and lively animation.

6.120 Sharmat, Andrew. **Smedge.** Illustrated by Chris L. Demarest. Macmillan, 1989. ISBN 0-02-782261-3. 30p. 4–9 (est.).

What do pets do all day when their owners go to work? Well, one dog, Smedge, the Pettey's perfect pet, dons suit and briefcase to serve as topdog adviser to the president of the United States. The Petteys never suspect that Smedge is escorted each day, by limousine, to a posh Washington office to meet with high-level officials and to lunch at clubs. Even as insightful Smedge manages to save the country from a disastrous trade agreement, his owners continue to think of him as their lovable, lazy (but obedient) pet.

6.121 Silverman, Erica. **Warm in Winter.** Illustrated by Michael J. Deraney. Macmillan, 1989. ISBN 0-02-782661-9. 30p. 4–8 (est.).

It's summer, and new friends Rabbit and Badger enjoy lemonade, checkers, and each other's company. When winter comes, Badger is lonesome and decides to accept an invitation to visit her friend Rabbit. Trudging through an icy snowstorm, Badger, thinking that she will never be warm and dry again, finally arrives at Rabbit's house. Snuggling up by the fire in warm flannel, the two friends once again enjoy each other's company, and Badger discovers the true meaning of "warm in winter." Pencil and watercolor illustrations in earth-tone hues help to tell a story that is sure to warm children's hearts.

6.122   Simon, Carly. **Amy the Dancing Bear.** Illustrated by Margot Datz. Doubleday, 1989. ISBN 0-385-26721-5. 36p. 5–8 (est.).

It's bedtime, but try as she might, Amy's mother cannot persuade her daughter to stop dancing and get ready for bed. Only when Mother Bear falls asleep does Amy realize that it really is time to say goodnight. Though singer Carly Simon's text is written in florid Victorian-like prose that may be unusual for children, Margot Datz's illustrations convey the warmth of the mother-daughter relationship.

6.123   Singer, Marilyn. **Chester the Out-of-Work Dog.** Illustrated by Cat Bowman Smith. Henry Holt, 1992. ISBN 0-8050-1828-X. 30p. 5–8 (est.).

Chester is a happy, hard-working Border collie who protects and herds his family's sheep. But when Chester and his family move to the city, he feels displaced and at loose ends. He tries herding squirrels and pigeons, but it's not the same. Finally, after herding some lost children in costumes to Chester A. Arthur Elementary School, Chester lands a job as the school's ever-so-capable crossing guard. Although teachers and young readers will have to look beyond Marilyn Singer's all-too-traditional depiction of male and female roles, Chester's circumstances could stimulate discussions about change.

6.124   Smith, Wendy. **Think Hippo!** Illustrated by Wendy Smith. Carolrhoda Books, 1989. ISBN 0-87614-372-9. 24p. 4–8 (est.).

It's time for school to begin, and Desirée, the third of three hippo children, nervously thinks about her first day. Fearing that she will be neither as smart nor as tough as her brother and sister, Desirée seeks advice from her siblings and timidly swims away to school. When a "hippo-sized" problem at recess is surmounted by a "Desirée-style" solution, she becomes confident in herself and about school. Bright watercolor illustrations complement this humorous story of courage and individuality.

6.125   Snape, Juliet, and Charles Snape. **Frog Odyssey.** Illustrated by Juliet and Charles Snape. Simon and Schuster Books for Young Readers, 1991. ISBN 0-671-74741-X. 32p. 4–8 (est.).

Albert and the other frogs live in a polluted pond at the city's edge, now threatened by new construction. With a jar for transporting the tadpoles and carrying their favorite diving post, the frogs begin their odyssey to safety, eluding an alley cat, sewer rats, and traffic, and eventually reaching a perfect new home in the city park. The realism of these distinctive watercolor frogs and city scenes makes a fantasy adventure almost believable.

6.126   Stefanec-Ogren, Cathy. **Sly, P.I.: The Case of the Missing Shoes.** Illustrated by Priscilla Posey Circolo. Harper and Row, 1989. ISBN 0-06-024632-4. 48p. 6–9.

It's opening night at the ballet, and Sly, P.I., a self-made fox detective, visits his old friend Miss Lotta Oink, a renowned ballerina. When Lotta discovers that first her toe shoes and then her costumes are missing, Sly investigates the case and finally uncovers the culprit. Simple black-and-white drawings accompany this easy-to-read backstage whodunit.

6.127   Steig, William. **Dr. De Soto Goes to Africa.** Illustrated by William Steig. HarperCollins/Michael di Capua Books, 1992. ISBN 0-06-205003-6. 32p. 3–8 (est.).

More than a decade has passed since Dr. De Soto outfoxed the fox, so a whole new generation of children is ready for a sequel. The "one-in-a-million, hum-dinger of a dentist" is off to Africa in response to the plea of an elephant with an unbearable toothache. This time Dr. De Soto's nemesis is a rhesus monkey named Honkitonk, who kidnaps the doctor. Mrs. De Soto ably pinch-hits as a substitute dentist, and the happy ending hints that the mice duo may be bound for further adventures.

6.128   Sundgaard, Arnold. **The Bear Who Loved Puccini.** Illustrated by Dominic Catalano. Philomel Books, 1992. ISBN 0-399-22135-2. 32p. 6–10 (est.).

Robert Remsen "Barefoot" Rainfield is an extraordinary northern Minnesota bear. First, he falls in love with the music of Puccini, and then, encouraged by Chief Shorty John Sundown, Barefoot sets out to seek his fortune as an opera singer in St. Paul. When a famous La Scala maestro discovers Barefoot singing Puccini in a St. Paul café, the message is clear: the most unlikely dreams can come true. Pastel watercolors are shaded and hatched with black.

6.129 Talbott, Hudson, as told to. **Your Pet Dinosaur: An Owner's Manual by Dr. Rex.** Illustrated by Hudson Talbott. Morrow Junior Books, 1992. ISBN 0-688-11338-9. 32p. 7 and up.

Dr. Rex, a fellow at the Museum of Relatively Natural History, produces his third book about his own species—a pet owner's guide to choosing, caring for, training, and living with one's own dinosaur. The headings are right out of more traditional "guides"—"Bringing the Baby Home," "Housebreaking," and "Discipline"—but the scenes depict hysteria. Imagine, for example, housebreaking a brontosaurus, or territory wars between neighborhood pets. Other features of the guide include letters to Dr. Rex, fashions for dinosaurs, and photos of Show Dinos.

6.130 Taylor, Scott. **Dinosaur James.** Illustrated by Scott Taylor. Morrow Junior Books, 1990. ISBN 0-688-08577-6. 32p. 5 and up.

This book describes in rhyme a little boy who has dinosaurs on his clothes, on his lunchbox, and in his bedroom. At first James's obsession appears excessive: "'Will you come out to the playground to play?' 'No,' says James, 'I'd rather stay,'" as he builds a giant dinosaur with his toys. However, when a schoolyard bully picks on James, it turns out that dinosaurs can be quite helpful after all. Bordered ink and watercolor illustrations bring James's passion to life.

6.131 Teague, Mark. **The Trouble with the Johnsons.** Illustrated by Mark Teague. Scholastic Hardcover Books, 1989. ISBN 0-590-42394-0. 32p. 5–8.

Elmo and his cat Leon hate their new home in the city, so one night they hop a train to their old house in the country. Although the current occupants, the Johnsons, are receptive and kind, they are also dinosaurs. In time Elmo realizes that he misses his parents, and he decides that his real home is his new home. Alternating richly colored and black-and-white illustrations lend a surrealistic quality to this dream-like book.

6.132 Thomas, Patricia. **"Stand Back," Said the Elephant, "I'm Going to Sneeze!"** Illustrated by Wallace Tripp. Lothrop, Lee and Shepard Books, 1990. ISBN 0-688-09339-6. 32p. 4–7.

Stand back . . . the elephant is about to sneeze! Creatures remember how depleted they were after its last sneeze. The zebra lost stripes, the bees their stings, and the bear turned bare. In rhyme, all the animals beg the elephant, "Please don't sneeze!" When the tiny mouse scares away the sneeze, the elephant's great guffaws of delighted laughter are just as destructive as the sneeze! Wonderfully expressive animals draw sympathy as well as amusement in this newly illustrated reissue.

6.133 Tolhurst, Marilyn. **Somebody and the Three Blairs.** Illustrated by Simone Abel. Orchard Books, 1991. ISBN 0-531-08478-7. 32p. 3–6.

When Mr. and Mrs. Blair and Baby Blair go on an outing, somebody comes to explore their home. This somebody (who happens to be a bear) makes himself at home in the Blairs' house. He samples all the food, tries out everyone's chair, and even selects the best bed for a nap. This variant is the perfect companion volume for the original *Goldilocks and the Three Bears*.

6.134 Tompert, Ann. **Grandfather Tang's Story.** Illustrated by Robert Andrew Parker. Crown, 1990. ISBN 0-517-57272-9. 32p. 4 and up (est.).

Little Soo listens to Grandpa Tang tell the story of the two fox fairies, Wu Ling and Chou, and watches him illustrate his tale with seven-piece paper tangrams. He rearranges the pieces deftly to show the fox fairies change from one animal form to another as they compete and argue and chase each other. The traditional Chinese puzzle pieces share pages with watercolor illustrations, and a final note describes how children can invent their own designs and stories.

6.135 Turner, Ann. **Hedgehog for Breakfast.** Illustrated by Lisa McCue. Macmillan, 1989. ISBN 0-02-789241-7. 30p. 4–10 (est.).

For a young fox, "having a hedgehog for breakfast" can only mean one thing—a tasty meal. So when Papa Fox tells George and Charles to invite Mrs. Hedgehog for breakfast, the two set about their plans to cook their guest. Unaware of these plans, Mrs. Hedgehog enjoys her hot bath and drying time in the oven. When Papa and Mama return, the confusion is cleared up and all the foxes sit down with their guest to a breakfast of oatmeal and cream. Colorful drawings, rich in detail, help to tell this amusing tale of idiomatic confusion.

6.136 Turner, Charles. **The Turtle and the Moon.** Illustrated by Melissa Bay Mathis. Dutton Children's Books. ISBN 0-525-44659-1. 32p. 4–8 (est.).

A lonely turtle spends each day alone, napping, walking, and swimming. Then one night, he wakes and discovers the moon for the first time. Challenging the moon to a race in the lake, the turtle finds that the moon's luminous reflection is a perfect companion. As she follows the turtle through day and night, Melissa Bay Mathis captures, in beautiful pastels, the ever-changing lights and colors of nature.

6.137 Van Caster, Nancy. **An Alligator Lives in Benjamin's House.** Illustrated by Dale Gottlieb. Philomel Books, 1990. ISBN 0-399-21489-5. 28p. 3–7.

A variety of animals live in Benjamin's house. An alligator is hiding under his bed, waiting to pounce on his mother's feet when she's vacuuming. A snake winds down the stairs, a lion lurks under the kitchen table, and a monkey does tricks in the living room. Rabbits, puppies, kittens, whales, and bears take their turns as manifestations of a young boy's imagination, and each shares some trait with Benjamin. Colorful, offbeat paintings contribute to the whimsy.

6.138 Van Laan, Nancy. **Possum Come a-Knockin'.** Illustrated by George Booth. Alfred A. Knopf/Borzoi Books, 1990. ISBN 0-394-92206-9. 22p. 3–6 (est.).

Cartoon-like illustrations accompany the high-spirited rhyming text in this cumulative tale, making it a perfect read-aloud. An impish little possum decked out in a forest green stovepipe hat knocks continually at the door of a house, much to the irritation of its occupants: Pa, Granny, Pappy, Ma, Baby, Sis, Tom-cat, Coon-dawg, Brother, and Sister. The possum fools them all, gleefully hanging by his tail from a tree.

6.139 van Pallandt, Nicolas. **The Butterfly Night of Old Brown Bear.** Illustrated by Nicolas van Pallandt. Farrar, Straus and Giroux, 1992. ISBN 0-374-31009-2. 32p. 4–6 (est.).

Old Brown Bear collects butterflies and moths, some with names so long that "they reach from his door to the other side of the rivers." One day, while lolling about in his garden, he is teased by a brilliant blue moth—a tantalizing new species. With butterfly net a-whizzing, Brown Bear charges, but the elusive moth flutters higher and higher until Brown Bear is taking bouncy steps across lunar craters. One memorable painting shows Brown Bear teetering perilously from the topmost twig of an ancient elm.

6.140 Velthuijs, Max (translated by Anthea Bell). **Frog in Love.** Illustrated by Max Velthuijs. Farrar, Straus and Giroux, 1989. ISBN 0-374-32465-4. 23p. 4–10 (est.).

There can be only one reason why Frog feels funny and his heart goes "thump-thump": Frog is in love! Setting out to win his beloved Duck's affection, Frog paints pictures and picks flowers. But when Frog is injured as he attempts to show Duck his love by setting a high-jump record, it is Duck who comes to help. As Duck nurses Frog back to health, the two discover their love for one another. Bright watercolor paintings illustrate the simple message: "Love knows no boundaries."

6.141 Vincent, Gabrielle. **Ernest and Celestine at the Circus.** Illustrated by Gabrielle Vincent. Greenwillow Books, 1989. ISBN 0-688-08685-3. 24p. 3–6 (est.).

In softly watercolored browns and grays, Gabrielle Vincent creates a new "adventure" for her gentle characters: Ernest, the bear, and Celestine, the mouse. Ernest returns to his act as a circus clown, enlisting Celestine as his reluctantly shy, but proud, assistant. Loving and supportive friendship undergirds the story told exclusively through the characters' dialogue.

6.142 Waddell, Martin. **Farmer Duck.** Illustrated by Helen Oxenbury. Candlewick Press, 1992. ISBN 1-56402-009-6. 32p. 4–8 (est.).

A duck works day after day for a lazy old farmer who lounges in bed and calls repeatedly, "How goes the work?" All day long the duck fetches the cow, gathers the hens, saws the wood, and irons the clothes, eventually growing "so sleepy and weepy and tired" that the farm animals take pity. They band together, toss the lazy farmer out, take over the farm, and happily share the chores. Helen Oxenbury's animals are gentle and sympathetic, while the farmer is a burly, hairy lummox.

6.143 Waddell, Martin. **Owl Babies.** Illustrated by Patrick Benson. Candlewick Press, 1992. ISBN 1-56402-101-7. 32p. 4–7 (est.).

Three wide-eyed baby owls—Sarah, Percy, and Bill—stare out from their hole in the tree, a background created with black ink and watercolor cross-hatching. They have awakened to find that their mother is missing, so the babies wait and wait for her return. Although Sarah and Percy are reassuring, Bill's repeated chorus is recognizable: "I want my mommy!" As loneliness and worries get bigger, the babies climb onto one branch for comfort.

Closing their eyes, they wish their mother home. "AND SHE CAME."

6.144 Wagener, Gerda (translated by Nina Ignatowicz). **Leo the Lion.** Illustrated by Reinhard Michl. HarperCollins, 1991. ISBN 0-06-021657-3. 32p. 5–7 (est.).

Leo is the loneliest lion in the world. He wants to be loved and petted just like Mr. Brown's pet cat, Katrinka. But Leo is just too big, and everyone is afraid of him. So off goes Leo to find someone who will hold him on a lap and pet him. Leo encounters many different people with the same result: they don't understand that Leo is big "only on the outside," so they run. After a runaway locomotive crashes in the desert, Leo meets a female lion who returns his love.

6.145 Wagner, Karen. **Silly Fred.** Illustrated by Normand Chartier. Macmillan, 1989. ISBN 0-02-792280-4. 30p. 4–6 (est.).

Fred is a pig who loves to sing songs like "Leafity leafity leaf, loofity loofity loo, loo-hoo, loo-hoo, loo-hoo, loo, loo, loo" and to turn somersaults on the bed. He likes being silly and, in fact, doesn't know how to act any other way. But one day he meets a beaver who does not approve of silliness. Fred tries to be more serious, only to discover that life is not much fun without somersaults and songs. Pink-dominated pencil and watercolor illustrations depict expressive pigs.

6.146 Wahl, Jan. **The Sleepytime Book.** Illustrated by Arden Johnson. Tambourine Books, 1992. ISBN 0-688-10276-X. 32p. 3 and up.

In misty pastels, lovable anthropomorphic creatures go about their nighttime activities. A moose with a soft striped scarf around his neck settles down in a nest of tall grasses. Frogs in neckties croon together under a full moon, and thrushes perch with closed eyes and bowed heads. The text is simple, rhythmic, and alliterative. Everything culminates with a sleeping baby snuggled under a blue and white flowered quilt. Lullaby cadences and the appeal of familiar animals make this a soothing choice for sleepy-time reading.

6.147 Wallace, Bill. **Totally Disgusting!** Illustrated by Leslie Morrill. Holiday House, 1991. ISBN 0-8234-0873-6. 111p. 7–11 (est.).

Because a little kitten repeatedly mews and kisses his new owner, Jessica, she announces that his name will be "Mewkiss." Even though Mewkiss adores Jessica, he finds such a name to be totally disgusting! Through wise advice from an elderly neighborhood cat, Mewkiss learns to see his name in a different light and eventually saves Jessica from a fateful encounter with a local rat. As usual, Bill Wallace's fondness for and knowledge of animals shines through, complemented by Leslie Morrill's expressive black-and-white drawings.

6.148   Walsh, Ellen Stoll. **You Silly Goose.** Illustrated by Ellen Stoll Walsh. Harcourt Brace Jovanovich, 1992. ISBN 0-15-299865-9. 32p. 3–8.

Cut- and torn-paper collages shape George the responsible mouse, his friend Emily the goose, and Emily's newly hatched downy yellow goslings. When George announces that he has seen the fox "with his big ears, bright eyes, and sleek, shiny fur," nosy neighbor Lulu thinks that George himself fits that description, and flips him into the pond. When the real fox shows up, George must save Lulu, forcing Emily to ask, "Now who is the fox and who is the silly goose?"

6.149   Waters, Tony. **The Sailor's Bride.** Illustrated by Tony Waters. Doubleday, 1991. ISBN 0-345-41441-2. 28p. 6 and up (est.).

When Susanna marries Whitewhiskers, the sailor mouse, everyone warns her that her life will be lonely, for "Sailors love only the sea." When Whitewhiskers is presumably lost at sea, Susanna takes the children and sets out to find her beloved husband. Reunited once again, the two mice realize their special bond, and Whitewhiskers discovers the special qualities of his "sailor bride." Inspired by a famous painting and the work of Beatrix Potter, Tony Waters has created a heartwarming story of love and adventure.

6.150   Wellington, Monica. **The Sheep Follow.** Illustrated by Monica Wellington. Dutton Children's Books, 1992. ISBN 0-525-44837-3. 32p. 3–6 (est.).

At first the sheep follow the shepherd, but when the shepherd falls asleep, the sheep follow a butterfly, waddling geese, a cat, and then some pigs, rabbits, fish, and ducks. Finally, a dog barks and chases the sheep back to the shepherd. A rested shepherd is ready to go, but the tired sheep won't follow. Simple text with repetitive refrain ("And the sheep follow") ensures immediate success for an early reader. Bright, simple illustrations could easily become flannelboard retellings.

6.151 Wells, Rosemary. **Don't Spill It Again, James.** Illustrated by Rosemary Wells. Dial Books for Young Readers, 1991. ISBN 0-8037-2119-6. 48p. 3–7.

Having a big brother can sometimes be difficult. But as James discovers, older siblings can also be loving and caring. In this collection of three rhyming short stories, Rosemary Wells invites children to share in the special relationship between James and his older brother. The book's colorful and endearing drawings are sure to elicit laughter and will encourage children to offer their own ideas about growing up with brothers and sisters.

6.152 Wells, Rosemary. **First Tomato. The Island Light. Moss Pillows.** Illustrated by Rosemary Wells. Dial Books for Young Readers, 1992. 32p. 3–6 (est.).

"Far beyond the moon and stars, / Twenty light-years south of Mars, / Spins the gentle Bunny Planet / And the Bunny Queen is Janet." Each little bunny in Rosemary Wells's Voyage to the Bunny Planet series needs a place of escape when troubles stack up. Felix, for example, gets sick in front of his whole art class and has to take medicine that tastes like gasoline. Things are different on the Bunny Planet, where Queen Janet shows Felix the day that should have been. Other books show other rabbits having a bad day. In gentle rhyme, everything is made right on the Bunny Planet.

6.153 Wells, Rosemary. **Fritz and the Mess Fairy.** Illustrated by Rosemary Wells. Dial Books for Young Readers, 1991. ISBN 0-8037-0983-8. 29p. 4–8 (est.).

Everyone in the skunk family is fed up with Fritz. Wherever he goes, he leaves a big mess. When his science experiment goes awry, Fritz is visited by the Mess Fairy, who creates an even bigger mess in the house and helps Fritz realize the importance of being neat. Large colorful watercolors illustrate this humorous look at responsibility.

6.154 Wells, Rosemary. **Max's Dragon Shirt.** Illustrated by Rosemary Wells. Dial Books for Young Readers, 1991. ISBN 0-8037-0945-5. 22p. 3–7.

Even though Max loves his old blue pants, his sister Ruby has the task of shopping with Max for new clothes. But Max only wants to buy a dragon shirt, and Ruby gets sidetracked trying on dresses. Frantic when separated, the two rabbits are comfortingly reunited in another satisfying, simple story of attachment, responsibility, and an ice-cream-covered dragon shirt.

6.155 Wiesner, David. **Tuesday.** Illustrated by David Wiesner. Clarion Books, 1991. ISBN 0-395-55113-7. 32p. 4–10 (est.).

In David Wiesner's Caldecott Medal acceptance speech, he explained his choice of title: " . . . the more I said 'T-u-e-s-d-a-y,' the more I like the 'ooze' quality it had. It seemed to go with frogs." Flying lilly pads that send their riders aloft through the night sky, terrifying a turtle, causing a midnight snacker to mistrust his eyes, teasing a dog, and providing a surreal amphibian experience, make for a wonderful, wordless adventure. *Caldecott Medal, 1992.*

6.156 Wild, Margaret. **My Dearest Dinosaur.** Illustrated by Donna Rawlins. Orchard Books, 1992. ISBN 0-531-08603-8. 32p. 4–7.

Through a series of letters, a mother dinosaur lovingly tells her mate of the status and changes in their family while he has been away seeking a safer place for them to live. In sparse but poignant prose, she describes a Tyrannosaurus attack, hungry snakes, and the antics of their fearless offspring, The Cheeky One. Against Cretaceous landscapes, the saurolophus-like beast reflects loneliness, pride, hope, and fear for her absent mate.

6.157 Wilhelm, Hans. **More Bunny Trouble.** Illustrated by Hans Wilhelm. Scholastic Hardcover Books, 1989. ISBN 0-590-41589-1. 32p. 4–8.

It's the day before Easter, and Ralph the bunny is busy decorating eggs and watching his baby sister, Emily. But when Emily crawls away and becomes lost in tall grass, Ralph once again has "bunny trouble." With the sun setting and an uninvited red fox in pursuit, Ralph and the rest of the rabbits join paws and locate the little lost bunny. This sequel to *Bunny Trouble* offers children not only another adventure with Ralph, the soccer-playing rabbit, but a lesson in responsibility.

6.158 Wilkon, Piotr. **Rosie the Cool Cat.** Illustrated by Jozef Wilkon. Viking Penguin, 1991. ISBN 0-670-83707-5. 24p. 4–10 (est.).

Rosie the cat is not like anyone in her family—she has orange fur and she "did everything differently from her sisters and brothers." So Rosie sets out on her own, becomes a famous rock star, and eventually has her own kittens, one of which is different from all the rest. Full-color chalk illustrations of hairy, bright-eyed cats celebrate the importance of individual differences.

6.159 Winch, Madeleine. **Come by Chance.** Illustrated by Madeleine Winch. Crown, 1990. ISBN 0-517-57667-8. 31p. 5–8 (est.).

When Bertha discovers a tumble-down, abandoned house, she sweeps, mends, patches, and scrubs until she has a home. One evening, stormy weather brings cows, dogs, cats, and birds, among other animals, to her door seeking shelter. Bertha welcomes these new friends who found her "by chance." All but a cat depart when spring arrives, but chances are that next winter. . . . Colorful double-page spreads display an irresistible menagerie.

6.160 Wolkstein, Diane. **Little Mouse's Painting.** Illustrated by Maryjane Begin. Morrow Junior Books, 1992. ISBN 0-688-07610-6. 32p. 4 and up.

As Little Mouse paints at her easel, her friends disagree about the subject of her painting, for each sees himself in her art. Readers see the painting only at the end of the book, thereby understanding the ambiguity of art and the possibilities for expression. Maryjane Begin's layered watercolor and acrylic paintings are richly textured, glowing portraits.

6.161 Wood, Audrey. **Little Penguin's Tale.** Illustrated by Audrey Wood. Harcourt Brace Jovanovich, 1989. ISBN 0-15-246475-1. 32p. 3–6 (est.).

Grand Nanny Penguin tells her seven charges a tale from the past. The seventh penguin isn't listening and sneaks away into the snowy, polar world to have some fun, where his antics parallel Nanny's story: he dances with the gooney birds, cavorts at the Walrus Polar Club, and narrowly escapes being eaten by a whale. Vivid watercolor and colored-pencil illustrations bring this rollicking tale to life.

6.162 Wood, Audrey. **Oh My Baby Bear!** Illustrated by Audrey Wood. Harcourt Brace Jovanovich, 1990. ISBN 0-15-257698-3. 32p. 2–6.

Oversized, pastel-colored illustrations follow Mama and Papa Bear as they awaken Baby Bear, dress him, feed him, care for him all day, give him a bath, and then tuck him into bed with a story and a kiss. When Baby Bear tries to perform these tasks by himself, he makes quite a mess, to which his parents respond: "Oh my Baby Bear! Let me show you how." Eventually he learns to do these tasks, and then he is called Little Bear. But . . . there is still one thing he is not too big for.

6.163 Woolf, Virginia. **Nurse Lugton's Curtain.** Illustrated by Julie Vivas. Harcourt Brace Jovanovich/Gulliver Books, 1991. ISBN 0-15-200545-5. 32p. 7 and up.

In a tale of fancy that Virginia Woolf probably wrote in 1924, Nurse Lugton dozes over her stitches, "and on her knees, covering the whole of her apron, was a large piece of figured blue stuff." At her fifth snore, "the blue stuff" turns to blue air, and the wild animals on the drawing-room curtains come to life. From elephants to mongooses, an imaginatively painted menagerie gambol over the grassy, flower-strewn "curtain" to the lake near Millamarchmantopolis to drink.

6.164 Yektai, Niki. **Hi Bears, Bye Bears.** Illustrated by Diane deGroat. Orchard Books, 1990. ISBN 0-531-08458-2. 32p. 3–6.

Bears of all stripes—short, long, weak, strong—and in all sorts of costumes, roles, and situations cover the pages of this rhyming text for young children. Eventually, readers learn that all of the bears are for sale, and that young Sam must pick just one. After Sam makes his choice, the text asks, "Which bear would you choose?" It will mean some turning back, some thinking over, and some talk.

6.165 Yolen, Jane. **Piggins and the Royal Wedding.** Illustrated by Jane Dyer. Harcourt Brace Jovanovich, 1989. ISBN 0-15-261687-X. 32p. 4–8.

It's the day of the royal wedding, and Piggins, the mystery-solving porcine butler, is helping the Reynard family prepare for the festivities. When the royal wedding ring disappears before the ceremony, Piggins solves the mystery and clears young Rexy Reynard, the ring bearer, of the crime. Following in the tradition of *Piggins* and *Picnic with Piggins,* Jane Yolen and Jane Dyer once again team up to create an English-style mystery complete with humor and suspense. Colored pencils and dyes entertainingly capture the ceremony of nineteenth-century British aristocracy.

Folk Literature

6.166 Alexander, Lloyd. **The Fortune-Tellers.** Illustrated by Trina Schart Hyman. Dutton Children's Books, 1992. ISBN 0-525-44849-7. 32p. 6–10 (est.).

When a young carpenter seeks to have his fortune change, he asks a fortune-teller about his future. "Rich you will surely be," the old man assures him. "On one condition: that, you earn large sums of money." Each query for his future is similarly received. Returning to ask the fortune-teller further questions, the young carpenter is mistaken for the old man transfigured, and fortunes foretold come true. Ink, acrylic, and crayon illustrations are set in Cameroon in West Africa, and filled with the remarkable colors, patterns, and textures of marketplaces and villages.

6.167 Bernatová, Eva. **The Wonder Shoes.** Illustrated by Fiona Moodie. Farrar, Straus and Giroux, 1990. ISBN 0-374-38476-2. 24p. 6–8 (est.).

Emma, a new girl in the village, experiences isolation when the other children will not play with her. After seeing the circus come to town, Emma receives a new pair of shoes from a dancer and decides to involve the other children in creating their own circus. The stylized paintings add detail to the simple story, providing a medieval backdrop for the timeless themes of loneliness and connection.

6.168 Brown, Judith Gwyn. **The Mask of the Dancing Princess.** Illustrated by Judith Gwyn Brown. Atheneum, 1989. ISBN 0-689-31427-2. 46p. 5–8.

Petulant Princess Rosamond wishes only one thing for her tenth birthday: a child who looks exactly like herself. The kingdom is searched in vain for a child as beautiful as the spoiled princess until, at last, a child of wandering troubadors performs a masquerade in the princess's image. Through mistaken identity, Princess Rosamond is whisked away and held captive by the actors. Over time, she learns to dance and laugh and love. Full-page oils and charcoals translate the French court and gypsy fires.

6.169 Fleischman, Sid. **Here Comes McBroom! Three More Tall Tales. McBroom's Wonderful One-Acre Farm: Three Tall Tales.** Illustrated by Quentin Blake. Greenwillow Books, 1992. Approx. 70p. 6 and up.

Newbery-winner Sid Fleischman originally wrote these six tall tales about the adventurous McBroom family twenty-five years ago. The McBrooms—narrator Josh McBroom, his "dear wife, Melissa," and their eleven (or is it twelve?) children—own a farm in Iowa, where the soil is so rich that if you drop a nickel, it grows into a quarter. The individual stories are reprinted as an anniversary edition in a two-book set with large-type text and action-filled line drawings.

6.170 Goble, Paul. **Beyond the Ridge.** Illustrated by Paul Goble. Bradbury Press, 1989. ISBN 0-02-736581-6. 32p. All ages.

In this poignant Plains Indian tale of the spiritual journey of death, Paul Goble's paintings and graceful language are characteristically sensitive to tribal traditions. As an old woman lies dying, and the family prepares her body for burial, the woman's spirit walks in afterlife to a steep slope beyond the ridge—a place "from which we came and to which we shall return." Bright opaque and transparent watercolors are applied almost to the inked outlines, leaving thin white lines that give brilliance and clarity.

6.171 Gwynne, Fred. **Pondlarker.** Illustrated by Fred Gwynne. Simon and Schuster Books for Young Readers, 1990. ISBN 0-671-70846-5. 30p. 4–10.

It is no small wonder that after Pondlarker the frog hears his favorite story told over and over, his greatest ambition is to be kissed by a princess and become a handsome prince. When Pondlarker's lifelong dream almost becomes a reality, he finds that his expectations about the wonderful life of princes have been exaggerated. In the process, Pondlarker discovers that he prefers just being a frog. Fred Gwynne's quirky, double-page illustrations are drawn in froggy greens and blues.

6.172 Hazen, Barbara Shook. **The Knight Who Was Afraid of the Dark.** Illustrated by Tony Ross. Dial Books for Young Readers, 1989. ISBN 0-8037-0668-5. 32p. 4–8.

Sir Fred is a bold and brave knight—except when he must face the dark. When Melvin the Miffed, the castle bully, discovers this "crack in Sir Fred's armor," Melvin devises a scheme to expose Sir Fred and his fears. At Melvin's urgings, Lady Wendylyn invites Sir Fred to a midnight rendezvous, and so the brave knight faces a challenge and a decision. In the end, the knight and his lady reveal their fears and find love. Tony Ross's light and colorful cartoon-like drawings amusingly illustrate this medieval tale that ends happily ever after.

6.173 Kesey, Ken. **The Sea Lion.** Illustrated by Neil Waldman. Viking Penguin, 1991. ISBN 0-670-83916-7. 48p. All ages.

On pages the colors of sunsets and sea, dramatic graphics interpret the characters and sea-cliff setting of the text. Eemook (meaning "The Broken Gift"), an orphaned Native American boy with a crooked back and shriveled leg, is adopted by the ancient rootwoman and grows to be clever and insightful. Although Eemook is repudiated by the chief of the Sea Cliff People and scorned by all but Shoola, the chief's daughter, he alone recognizes the evil in a strange visitor, and his bravery and cleverness break the spell and save his tribe.

6.174 Kroll, Steven. **Princess Abigail and the Wonderful Hat.** Illustrated by Patience Brewster. Holiday House, 1991. ISBN 0-8234-0853-1. 30p. 4–8.

What's a princess to do? Her vain father has promised her hand to the designer of the most sumptuous hat—and to the princess's horror, the successful haberdasher is short, ugly, and long in the tooth. She runs away, only to encounter a large, beneficent green lizard, who helps her resolve her predicament. In the end, innocence triumphs, and vanity is left powerless. This original fairy tale has the whimsy, predictability, and happy ending of classic tales, and is humorous, too. Detail and expressiveness in the richly colored illustrations will intrigue readers.

6.175 Lattimore, Deborah Nourse. **The Dragon's Robe.** Illustrated by Deborah Nourse Lattimore. Harper Row, 1990. ISBN 0-06-023723-6. 30p. 6–11.

This original tale, an amalgam of Chinese historical material and motifs, centers on an orphaned weaver girl, Kwan Yin. When two of the emperor's nobles anger the rain dragon and thus bring drought and invasion to China, Kwan Yin begins to weave a robe to place before the shrine of the rain dragon. The two nobles try to prevent her from completing her task, as does the great Khan, leader of the invading army. Can she finish the robe in time to save her country? Like Deborah Nourse Lattimore's other picture books (*The Prince and the Golden Ax: A Minoan Tale* and *Why There Is No Arguing In Heaven: A Mayan Myth*), this book personalizes a distant culture through a young protagonist. It also imparts that culture's flavor through powerful, full-color paintings in imitation of classical works.

6.176 Levitin, Sonia. **The Man Who Kept His Heart in a Bucket.** Illustrated by Jerry Pinkney. Dial Books for Young Readers, 1991. ISBN 0-8037-1030-5. 28p. 5 and up (est.).

Hurt by his first love, Jack carries his heart in a bucket, determined never to lose it again. When a lovely maiden steals the heart, Jack must solve a riddle to get it back. But along the way, he discovers that his "heart is in the right place" after all. Richly illustrated in watercolors and colored pencil, Jack's village and its citizens are bustling with life. Cream paper enriches the warm earth tones of these village scenes.

6.177   Lobel, Anita. **The Dwarf Giant.** Illustrated by Anita Lobel. Holiday House, 1991. ISBN 0-8234-0852-3. 30p. 5–8.

Life in this Japanese kingdom is peaceful until a strange, magical dwarf—with European features and clothing—appears. Hoodwinking the prince with his tricks, the dwarf reveals his purpose: to destroy the prince and princess and usurp their power. Anita Lobel's full-color illustrations for this original Japanese story are imitations of Japanese art. Her wise princess makes an admirable and levelheaded heroine. Whether meant to be anti-imperialistic or not, the story ends happily—with a hint of more adventure to come. *Notable 1991 Children's Trade Books in the Field of Social Studies.*

6.178   Ludwig, Warren. **Good Morning, Granny Rose.** Illustrated by Warren Ludwig. G. P. Putnam's Sons/Whitebird Books, 1990. ISBN 0-399-21950-1. 32p. 3–8 (est.).

On a wintry Ozark morning, Granny Rose and her dog Henry go for a walk to watch the sunrise. When a sudden snowstorm hits, the two seek shelter in a cave, only to discover that the cave already has a furry, sleeping occupant. The restless bear stirs, and resourceful Granny applies a folk remedy: she stuffs the bear's paw right back into his mouth. Broadface Granny in tiny glasses and faithful Henry the beagle register perfect expressions throughout the story.

6.179   Mahy, Margaret. **The Queen's Goat.** Illustrated by Emma Chichester Clark. Dial Books for Young Readers, 1991. ISBN 0-8037-0938-2. 23p. 6–12 (est.).

When an invitation to a pet show arrives, the queen, who has no pets, decides to take Carmen, the royal gardener's goat. But Carmen gets loose and races pell-mell through the kingdom, leaving disaster in her wake and arriving at the pet show decorated with two tambourines, naval flags, a satin nightgown, a frilly lace petticoat, red long johns, and the royal petunias. Thus adorned, Carmen is awarded the prize for the best-dressed pet in the parade. Frenetic Carmen provides comic contrast with the staid park scenes.

6.180 Martin, Jacqueline Briggs. **Good Times on Grandfather Mountain.** Illustrated by Susan Gaber. Orchard Books, 1992. ISBN 0-531-08577-5. 30p. 6–10 (est.).

Old Washburn is an optimist. In the proportions and language of a folktale, Old Washburn meets his trials and turns them into triumphs. When his cow runs away, he just whittles her milk pail into a drum. When his cabin is destroyed by a storm, he whittles himself a fancy fiddle. The varied perspectives of illustrator Susan Gaber offer such surprises as an eyeball-to-eyeball inspection of the cow, the whittler's view of wood shavings spewing from deft strokes, and a roof-top, cabin-raising view of mountain dancing.

6.181 Paterson, Katherine. **The King's Equal.** Illustrated by Vladimir Vagin. HarperCollins, 1992. ISBN 0-06-022497-5. 64p. 6–10 (est.).

Katherine Paterson says that she wrote *The King's Equal,* a tale with a feminist slant, especially for the Russian artist Vladimir Vagin's crisp and elegant paintings. Arrogant Prince Raphael is charged by his dying father, the king, to find a princess as beautiful, intelligent, and wealthy as the prince believes himself to be. Although the prince's advisers search far and wide, hope wanes until a beautiful, wise, and good shepherdess proves that she is not only the future king's equal—but his superior.

6.182 Paterson, Katherine. **The Tale of the Mandarin Ducks.** Illustrated by Leo and Diane Dillon. Lodestar Books, 1990. ISBN 0-525-67283-4. 36p. 5–8.

This collaboration between a respected author and equally renowned artists has produced a colorful and engaging original Japanese folktale. When a cruel lord captures a beautiful mandarin duck for its plummage, kindly servants take pity and release it. The servants are then sentenced to death, but their kindness is magically repaid. Flat and spacious illustrations in Japanese *ukiyo-e* style match the mood in this tale of compassion and love. *Notable 1990 Children's Trade Books in the Field of Social Studies; ALA Notable Children's Books, 1991; Boston Globe–Horn Book Picture Book Award, 1991.*

6.183 Pattison, Darcy. **The River Dragon.** Illustrated by Jean and Mou-Sien Tseng. Lothrop, Lee and Shepard Books, 1991. ISBN 0-688-10427-4. 32p. 4–8 (est.).

Ying-Shao the blacksmith crosses a dragon-haunted river when he travels to the home of his betrothed. Her father disapproves of Ying-Shao's trade and tries to stir up the dragon's wrath against the young suitor. This modern tale, inspired by Chinese folklore, is based on the reassuring notion that the small can overcome the huge through cleverness. The watercolor and ink illustrations, particularly those of the dragon among the mists of the river gorge, are vibrant and riveting.

6.184   Polacco, Patricia. **Boat Ride with Lillian Two Blossom.** Illustrated by Patricia Polacco. Philomel Books, 1988. ISBN 0-399-21470-4. 32p. 4–7.

On a quiet summer day, two children are out fishing on the pond and wondering what makes the wind blow, the rain fall, and the sun, the moon, and the stars shine. Suddenly, old Lillian Two Blossom appears, offering to answer the children's questions. The three paddle off together on a mystical boat ride, exploring Native American interpretations of nature's wonders. Patricia Polacco's airy watercolor illustrations and remarkable perspectives create a dream-like effect, pulling the reader into the children's experience.

6.185   Rosen, Michael, editor. **South and North, East and West: The Oxfam Book of Children's Stories.** Candlewick Press, 1992. ISBN 1-56402-117-3. 95p. 6–12 (est.).

To honor the fiftieth year of the international charity organization Oxfam, which receives the book's proceeds, this collection of stories was gathered by Oxfam staff from the peoples of Africa, Asia, Latin America, and the Caribbean. To accompany the twenty-five diverse tales, twenty-two artists, largely from England, Canada, and New Zealand, were selected to represent the tales' cultural traditions and flavors. For example, David Sim's colored woodcuts dramatically interpret a Zimbabwe tale of a greedy father.

6.186   Sanderson, Ruth. **The Enchanted Wood: An Original Fairy Tale.** Illustrated by Ruth Sanderson. Little, Brown, 1991. ISBN 0-316-77018-3. 32p. 5–8.

This original fairy tale includes many traditional elements, including three noble princes who must enter the Enchanted Wood seeking the Heart of the World in order to save their father's drought-stricken kingdom. All who enter the Enchanted Wood are bewitched by images of that which they desire most.

A.

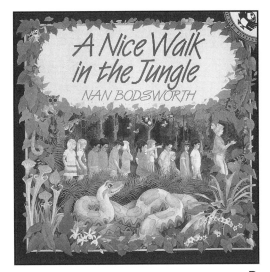

B.

C.

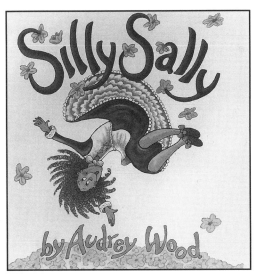

D.

A. *South and North, East and West: The Oxfam Book of Children's Stories* edited by Michael Rosen (see 6.185). **B.** *A Nice Walk in the Jungle* by Nan Bodsworth (see 6.200). **C.** *The Horrendous Hullabaloo* by Margaret Mahy; illustrated by Patricia MacCarthy (see 6.211). **D.** *Silly Sally* by Audrey Wood (see 6.223).

A.

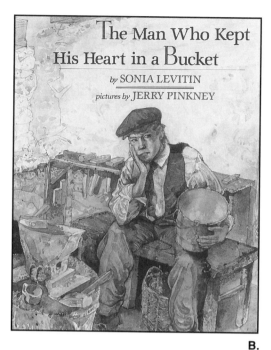

B.

C.

A. *Beyond the Ridge* written and illustrated by Paul Goble (see 6.170). **B.** *The Man Who Kept His Heart in a Bucket* by Sonia Levitin; illustrated by Jerry Pinkney (see 6.176). **C.** *The Fortune-Tellers* by Lloyd Alexander; illustrated by Trina Schart Hyman (see 6.166).

In the end, however, the good-hearted youngest prince and the gatekeeper's daughter are kept safe by the selflessness of their desires. Intricately detailed, romantic paintings accompany the story, combining realism and a medieval atmosphere in muted shades.

6.187   Scieszka, Jon. **The Frog Prince, Continued.** Illustrated by Steve Johnson. Viking Penguin, 1991. ISBN 0-670-83421-1. 30p. 5 and up.

Here's a story where they don't live happily ever after. After the frog has been soundly kissed by the princess and turned into a prince physically, his mannerisms remain quite froggish, and he and the princess are miserable together. So the prince sets off to find some magic that will transform him back into a frog. Steve Johnson's illustrations are captivatingly illogical caricatures. Although not all readers will appreciate the mild satire, modern children are sure to enjoy what eventually becomes, surprisingly enough, a fable about relationships. *ALA Notable Children's Books, 1992; ALA Recommended Books for Reluctant Readers, 1992.*

6.188   Segal, Jerry. **The Place Where Nobody Stopped.** Illustrated by Dav Pilkey. Orchard Books/Richard Jackson Books, 1991. ISBN 0-531-08497-3. 160p. 11 and up.

Contented but lonesome in his isolated Russian hamlet, Yosip the Baker cheerfully grants Mordechai ben Yahbahbai and his family temporary lodging. The nineteenth century draws to a close, the family multiplies, and the baker's joy increases as he protects his household from the czar's soldiers. The family is Jewish, but this is never mentioned, even though it is central to the plot. A lively tale of ethnic compatibility, the book is appropriate for readers and listeners across a broad age range.

6.189   Sherman, Josepha. **Child of Faerie, Child of Earth.** Illustrated by Rick Farley. Walker, 1992. ISBN 0-8027-8112-8. 159p. 12 and up.

Lovely Graciosa is raised by an unloving father whose jealous second wife, a sinister enchantress, punishes her stepdaughter severely. Graciosa is courted and protected by the dashing Prince Percinet, who is half mortal and half faerie. Graciosa must decide whether to give up the world she knows, admit to the magical powers that lie dormant within her, and live forever in the kingdom of Faerie. Her emotional struggles are with the issues of possessing "powers" and the potential godlessness of magic and those who possess it.

6.190   Singer, Marilyn. **The Golden Heart of Winter.** Illustrated by Robert Rayevsky. Morrow Junior Books, 1991. ISBN 0-688-07718-8. 40p. 6 and up.

To determine his heir, an aging father sends his three sons on a quest to find something of great value. It is his youngest son, Half, who recognizes beauty in the world around him and the value of living things. In an act of courage that revives the Golden Heart of Winter and prevents Death's triumph in the world, Half brings his father the object of greatest value—a good and faithful heart. Ink, watercolor, and acrylic paintings interpret the tale in a surrealistic style.

6.191   Threadgall, Colin. **Proud Rooster and the Fox.** Illustrated by Colin Threadgall. Tambourine Books, 1991. ISBN 0-688-11124-6. 32p. 4–8 (est.).

A tenacious Fox outwits a proud Rooster through a series of foxy attempts to invade the chicken coop. Because old Rooster's vision is keen, Fox's disguises don't work. So wily Fox proposes a game of hide-and-seek: Fox hides, and Rooster must crow when he spots Fox. All day long the game goes on until a weary Rooster with laryngitis can't even make a tiny croak when Fox steals the hens. But no matter—Fox only wanted fresh eggs for breakfast. Colin Threadgall's illustrations are perky.

6.192   Watts, Bernadette. **Tattercoats.** Illustrated by Bernadette Watts. North-South Books, 1989. ISBN 1-55858-002-6. 25p. 6–10 (est.).

When the children visit Tattercoats, a ragged scarecrow, they bring companionship as well as scarves and gloves. Yet in the fall and winter, Tattercoats feels abandoned and lonely because the children stay inside and do not visit him. With the coming of spring, he is restored to a place of honor, close by the house, looking after the garden. Full-page impressionistic illustrations enhance the themes of loneliness and caring. *Notable 1989 Children's Trade Books in the Field of Social Studies.*

6.193   Wood, Douglas. **Old Turtle.** Illustrated by Cheng-Khee Chee. Pfeifer-Hamilton, 1992. ISBN 0-938586-48-3. 43p. 3–6 (est.).

Old Turtle has the answer that all the other creatures do not: Old Turtle knows who and what God is. Filled with lifelike watercolors depicting nature in its most amazing glory, this book offers a charming tale of spiritual renewal and appreciation for the world around us. Old Turtle's message of hope is simple yet profound: God is, he says. And the beauty of the Earth is the proof. *IRA Children's Book Award, 1993.*

6.194 Yolen, Jane. **Dove Isabeau.** Illustrated by Dennis Nolan. Harcourt Brace Jovanovich, 1989. ISBN 0-15-224131-0. 29p. 7–11 (est.).

Haunting blue and gray watercolors touched with red illuminate this original fairy tale, complete with all of the traditional elements, in which a jealous stepmother turns the gentle and lovely Dove Isabeau into a fire-breathing dragon. The evil spell is broken by the king's son, Kemp Owain, with assistance from Dove's faithful white cat, but then Dove and the cat must undo a spell cast on the prince. Kemp and Dove marry and happily rule the kingdom together. Dennis Nolan's dragon is as fierce and ugly as his Dove is bewitchingly beautiful.

6.195 Yolen, Jane. **Sky Dogs.** Illustrated by Barry Moser. Harcourt Brace Jovanovich, 1990. ISBN 0-15-275480-6. 32p. 4–8.

From Blackfoot Indian legends, Jane Yolen creates a new story about a motherless young boy who is a member of the first band of Native Americans to see horses. Believing that they are large dogs sent from the sky, from the creator of all things, the people call the them "Sky Dogs." In first-person narration, He-who-loves-horses describes the strange beasts and how he overcomes his fear of them. Dramatic burnt-orange, yellow, and brown watercolors provide a reverent backdrop. *ALA Notable Children's Books, 1991.*

Humorous Fantasy

6.196 Agee, Jon. **The Return of Freddy Legrand.** Illustrated by Jon Agee. Farrar, Straus and Giroux, 1992. ISBN 0-374-36249-1. 32p. 4–7 (est.).

"Curses!" cries pilot Freddy LeGrand, as his airplane, *The Golden Gull*, plummets toward Earth. But all is well, and the famous pilot parachutes to safety, rescued by Sophie and Albert, farmers with a curiosity about flight. No farmer himself, Freddy returns to Paris and a hero's welcome. Even so, his second plane, *The Silver Swan*, meets disaster in the Alps, but look . . . up in the sky . . . it's Sophie and Albert and the refurbished *Golden Gull*. Heavy black outlines give Jon Agee's comical illustrations weight and panache.

6.197   Ball, Duncan. **Jeremy's Tail.** Illustrated by Donna Rawlins. Orchard Books, 1991. ISBN 0-531-08551-1. 32p. 3–6.

Jeremy is determined to pin the tail on the donkey. So with blindfold in place, he proceeds straight ahead, all the time thinking that he is in the living room. However, the reader knows otherwise. Donna Rawlins's humorous illustrations show Jeremy marching onto a bus, through the city, eventually around the world, and through space, as he perseveres in his quest to pin the tail on the donkey.

6.198   Blake, Quentin. **Cockatoos.** Illustrated by Quentin Blake. Little, Brown, 1992. ISBN 0-316-09951-1. 32p. 6–9 (est.).

A man of habit, the slightly stuffy, slightly daft Professor Dupont greets his ten prized cockatoos in the same way every day: "Good morning, my fine feathered friends!" Finally, the cockatoos, nearly crazed by the sameness of it all, escape through the conservatory window and hide. The baffled professor searches all about his house, but fails to find a single cockatoo. Yet, there among the characteristic scrawl of Quentin Blake's comic artistry, the reader can spot the birds in absurd camouflage poses.

6.199   Blundell, Tony. **Beware of Boys.** Illustrated by Tony Blundell. Greenwillow Books, 1992. ISBN 0-688-10925-X. 32p. 4 and up.

Readers will find a model of resourcefulness in this zany tale of a boy who is captured by a wolf. Convincing the wolf that boys taste better cooked, the hero dispatches the animal hither and yon to gather the unlikely ingredients for boy recipes. The drooling villain lugs barn doors, barrels of bricks, and a seashore of sand—as well as daffodils and a red bicycle. Finally, the exhausted wolf collapses. Poetic justice reigns as the boy peddles home on a red bicycle bringing flowers for his mother.

6.200   Bodsworth, Nan. **A Nice Walk in the Jungle.** Illustrated by Nan Bodsworth. Viking Penguin/Puffin Books, 1992. ISBN 0-14-054127-6. 32p. 4–8 (est.).

When Miss Jellaby's class goes on a nature walk in the "jungle," they spot all sorts of wildlife—spiders, crickets, and lizards. But only Tim spots the pink, purple, and green boa constrictor gobbling children at the back of the line. Spread within the tropical foliage are plenty of real jungle inhabitants for readers to discover. When the last child is swallowed, a now-alert teacher punches out the boa constrictor, rescues her children, and takes everyone to the Burger Bungalow.

6.201   Cecil, Laura, compiler. **Stuff and Nonsense.** Illustrated by Emma Chichester Clark. Greenwillow Books, 1989. ISBN 0-688-08898-8. 93p. All ages.

Laura Cecil explains in her introduction that she always loved the imaginative idea that objects have lives of their own. Here, she has collected a set of stories and rhymes in which objects ("inanimate stuff") come to life and live out their nonsensical dramas. Included in the collection is Joseph Jacobs's "Johnny-cake," a version of the gingerbread boy, Hans Christian Andersen's "The Shepherdess and the Chimney Sweep," and "The Sorcerer's Apprentice." Cecil's own tale of "The Voracious Vacuum Cleaner" plays on an early fear of many children.

6.202   Cole, Babette. **King Change-a-lot.** Illustrated by Babette Cole. G. P. Putnam's Sons, 1989. ISBN 0-399-21670-7. 29p. 4–8.

Things in the land of Spendfortune couldn't be worse, so baby Prince Change-a-lot decides that he can run the kingdom better than his mom and dad. With the help of a genie, the prince becomes king and makes a few changes that save the kingdom from ruin. In the tradition of her *Princess Smartypants* and *Prince Cinders,* Babette Cole tells a story with a royal touch that is sure to tickle the funny bone.

6.203   Cole, Babette. **Tarzanna!** Illustrated by Babette Cole. G. P. Putnam's Sons, 1992. ISBN 0-399-21837-8. 32p. 4–8.

Tarzanna has yellow straw-like hair, wears skimpy animal skins and red lipstick, and swings on vines with her friends, the animals. One day she captures a strange animal who happens to be a boy studying spiders in the jungle. Gerald teaches Tarzanna English and takes her home with him. In New York, Tarzanna misses the jungle, sets the zoo animals free, runs away with Gerald and the animals, and even saves the president—who gratefully pays everyone's airfare back to the jungle.

6.204   Coville, Bruce. **My Teacher Fried My Brains.** Illustrated by John Pierard. Pocket Books/Minstrel Books, 1991. ISBN 0-671-72710-9. 136p. 8–12.

In the sequel to *My Teacher Is an Alien,* seventh-grader Duncan Dougal discovers that the aliens that caused nerdy Peter Thompson's disappearance have not yet vacated planet Earth. Since Duncan has a reputation for being a troublemaker, no one is likely to believe him. No one, that is, except vulnerable Miss Karpou, the new home economics teacher. But is Miss Karpou really who she seems? Bruce Coville mixes realism with just the right elixir of fantasy, humor, and issues.

6.205 Cummings, Pat. **Petey Moroni's Camp Runamok Diary.** Illustrated by Pat Cummings. Bradbury Press, 1992. ISBN 0-02-725513. 32p. 5–8 (est.).

The kids at Camp Runamok have been losing their snacks—their cheese twists, their Puff 'n' Stuff pastries, and their Caramel Crunchies. But the clues are telling: furry hand, little footprints, good climber. Petey Moroni keeps track in his bright yellow diary. By "Day 5," readers get a good look at the robber raccoon, which continues to elude the campers. A final hilarious spread shows an overstuffed raccoon flat on its back awash in junk food wrappers and candy bits.

6.206 Dahl, Roald. **Esio Trot.** Illustrated by Quentin Blake. Viking Penguin, 1990. ISBN 0-670-83451-3. 64p. 6–9 (est.).

Mrs. Silver loves her tortoise, Alfie. Mr. Hoppy, her neighbor, loves his garden. But Mr. Hoppy also secretly loves Mrs. Silver. In this happy little tale, Mr. Hoppy devises a "magical" scheme to convince Mrs. Silver that Alfie is growing swiftly, all in the hope of winning her affection. Mrs. Silver offers to be his "slave for life" if murmuring "Esio Trot" (*tortoise* spelled backward) will help Alfie grow. Quentin Blake's familiar penned drawings reflect the whimsical plot.

6.207 Gilman, Phoebe. **Grandma and the Pirates.** Illustrated by Phoebe Gilman. Scholastic Hardcover Books, 1990. ISBN 0-590-43426-8. 32p. 5–8.

Grandma, Melissa, and Oliver the parrot are kidnapped by pirates. At first, life on board a pirate ship isn't so bad. Oliver learns to sing pirate songs, Grandma cooks lots of noodle pudding, and Melissa helps sail the ship. But the pirates are mean and nasty, so Grandma, Melissa, and Oliver repeatedly, though unsuccessfully, try to escape from the ship. Then, when Melissa realizes their tactics have been wrong all along, the tables are finally turned.

6.208 Henwood, Simon. **The Clock Shop.** Illustrated by Simon Henwood. Farrar, Straus and Giroux. ISBN 0-374-31380-6. 24p. 4–7 (est.).

The townspeople have all kinds of clocks, from the mundane to the somewhat fantastic, and the clockmaker is always ready with his tools to fix the broken ones. Sometimes the clockmaker worries about what would happen if every clock stopped at the same time, but he knows that could never happen. Zany, action-packed illustrations reflect the action-packed life of the town's most responsible citizen.

6.209 Lent, Blair. **Molasses Flood.** Illustrated by Blair Lent. Houghton Mifflin, 1992. ISBN 0-395-45314-3. 32p. 4–8 (est.).

Charley Owen Muldoon lives near a molasses tank by the Boston waterfront at the turn of the twentieth century. On one warm January day, the molasses tank expands and explodes, flooding Boston with a "heavy, sticky, slow-moving sea." Exaggerating from an actual historical event, the author has created a Boston of his mother's time, as well as an explanation for its configuration. Charley's house, along with trolleys, carts, and ferries, floats on molasses past identifiable landmarks.

6.210 Mahy, Margaret. **The Blood-and-Thunder Adventure on Hurricane Peak.** Illustrated by Wendy Smith. Margaret K. McElderry Books, 1989. ISBN 0-689-50488-8. 132p. 8–12 (est.).

In a zany tale of magic, mayhem, and mistaken identities, a wicked industrialist learns that crime does not pay, and a scientist and magician learn to respect each other's crafts. Besides all that, young Huxley and Zaza Hammond learn that Hurricane Peak School is a perfect place for writing and illustrating their blood-and-thunder stories—especially since hurricanes are a daily occurrence, the head prefect is a talking cat, and the head mistress has been missing for forty years.

6.211 Mahy, Margaret. **The Horrendous Hullabaloo.** Illustrated by Patricia MacCarthy. Viking Penguin/Vanessa Hamilton Books, 1992. ISBN 0-670-84547-7. 26p. 4–8 (est.).

Peregrine the Pirate is certain that his aunt and his parrot would not enjoy the horrendous hullabaloos at the pirate parties that he attends, so he leaves the two of them at home to cook and tidy up while he enjoys his pirate's life. But one day his auntie and parrot have had enough of abandonment; they join together to plan a hullabaloo of their own, one with plenty of rumplebumpkins and alliterative phrases. Patricia MacCarthy's trademark white-edged paintings contrast with the hullabaloo colors.

6.212 Mahy, Margaret. **The Pumpkin Man and the Crafty Creeper.** Illustrated by Helen Craig. Lothrop, Lee and Shepard Books, 1991. ISBN 0-688-10348-0. 32p. 5–8.

When a talking plant begs Mr. Parkin to save it from the cruel life that it leads in Lily Rose Willowherb's garden, he feels compelled to respond to its plight. Yet when the plant shows its true colors and becomes a conniving, demanding creeper, it is poor Mr. Parkin who needs rescuing. The plant gains increasing prominence illustration by illustration until Mr. Parkin's eventual rescue.

6.213 Marshall, James. **The Cut-Ups Crack Up.** Illustrated by James Marshall. Viking Penguin, 1992. ISBN 0-670-84486-1. 32p. 3–8 (est.).

Joe and Spuds, the cut-ups of all time, exaggerate just a bit too much to friends Charles Andrew Frothingham and Mary Frances Hooley. This time the boys claim that they have their own car. To prove it, they intend to video themselves "just sitting" in Principal Lamar J. Spurgle's fancy red sports car. But once in the car, Joe and Spuds are off for a wacky ride. As in all their adventures, the cut-ups are sassy and sly, but also good-humored, constantly surprised, and funny.

6.214 Patron, Susan. **Burgoo Stew.** Illustrated by Mike Shenon. Orchard Books/Richard Jackson Books, 1991. ISBN 0-531-08516-3. 32p. 3–6.

In this French folktale, five quarrelsome, rowdy boys set out to find Old Billy Que to see if he has some food that they can steal. The answer is burgoo stew—a version of the old favorite, "Stone Soup," with its "secret ingredient." The boys help out with potatoes, carrots, onions, and stew fixings as Old Billy requests. Illustrations are humorous watercolor scenes of good stew and a wise cook curing the crankies and the hungries. (At least "they were never, ever quite so bad or quite so hungry again.")

6.215 Provensen, Alice. **Punch in New York.** Illustrated by Alice Provensen. Viking Penguin, 1991. ISBN 0-670-82790-8. 32p. 3–8.

When the bag containing Punch, the brawling star of the Punch and Judy puppet show, is stolen from Professore Tucci-Piccini at the smoggy New York City airport, the city itself has much to fear. Punch rips off a hot dog vendor, foils a band of muggers, beats a nasty man, and becomes chauffeur for the richest man in the world before reuniting with his friends. While Punch's notorious escapades could benefit from an adult's explanation, Alice Provensen's comical oil paintings are rich with the characteristic energy of New York City. *New York Times Best-Illustrated Children's Books, 1991.*

6.216 Pulver, Robin. **Nobody's Mother Is in Second Grade.** Illustrated by G. Brian Karas. Dial Books for Young Readers, 1992. ISBN 0-8037-1211-1. 32p. 4–8 (est.).

Of course mothers don't go to second grade. "That would be ridiculous," Cassandra says. But what if Mother loved second grade and desperately wishes she could go back? The only solution is for Mother to visit second grade disguised as a plant (so as not to be ridiculous). "There is something peculiar about that plant," the children whisper—a plant that plays on the playground, eats lunch, and gives hugs. The cartoon-like plant mom is truly (and purposefully) ridiculous.

6.217 Remkiewicz, Frank. **The Last Time I Saw Harris.** Illustrated by Frank Remkiewicz. Lothrop, Lee and Shepard Books, 1991. ISBN 0-688-10292-1. 32p. 5 and up.

Little rich boy Edmund and his best friend, a talking parrot named Harris, like to play with color flash cards. When Harris gets blown out the window in a windstorm, Edmund and Higgins, the chauffeur, set out to find him. Traveling in a long limousine, they show color flash cards to many different birds until they find the one that knows the entire color wheel. Bordered watercolor line drawings supplement the text with their humorous portrayal of the trappings of wealth.

6.218 Sabraw, John. **I Wouldn't Be Scared.** Illustrated by John Sabraw. Orchard Books/Richard Jackson Books, 1989. ISBN 0-531-08418-3. 32p. 4–6.

John Sabraw's first book humorously explores the theme of confronting one's fears. A gallant boy hunts an imaginary beast through his neighborhood, imagining how he would defeat his foe at every turn. The hero is distinctively drawn, with large round eyes, pencil-thin arms, and coonskin cap. Sabraw's cartoon-like illustrations convey whimsy and humor. Elementary students could create their own drawings of monsters to defeat.

6.219 Smith, Lane. **Glasses (Who Needs 'em?).** Illustrated by Lane Smith. Viking Penguin, 1991. ISBN 0-670-84160-9. 30p. 5–8 (est.).

When the young narrator finds out from his optometrist that he needs glasses, the boy indignantly refuses. So, the slightly daffy doctor points out that "lots of folks wear glasses and love 'em." Beginning with the boy's mom and dad and moving on to potatoes, planets, and "short, fuzzy bunnies," the mad doctor becomes more and more agitated as he enumerates a bizarre list of eyeglass wearers. Lane Smith's characteristically surreal illustrations provide an added dimension of wackiness and fun. *ALA Notable Children's Books, 1992.*

6.220 Stevenson, James. **National Worm Day.** Illustrated by James Stevenson. Greenwillow Books, 1990. ISBN 0-688-08772-8. 40p. 5 and up.

A worm, snail, rhinoceros, and mole are the cast of characters in this collection of three witty vignettes. Together they celebrate National Worm Day, friendship, and the fact that being different is what makes each one special. The pithy text is primarily dialogue, supported by James Stevenson's watercolor and black-pen illustrations of the four friends in action.

6.221 Stevenson, James. **Rolling Rose.** Illustrated by James Stevenson. Greenwillow Books, 1992. ISBN 0-688-10675-7. 24p. 3 and up.

One day baby Rose rolls unnoticed out of the kitchen door in her baby stroller. She is soon joined by eighty-four other babies on wheels for a city tour and a cross-country jaunt. James Stevenson's light and cheery watercolors fit the mood of the story perfectly, right down to the cows' blank faces as the baby parade rolls past. This rollicking peripatetic adventure introduces a baby who knows how to get real mileage out of her baby stroller.

6.222 Willis, Val. **The Surprise in the Wardrobe.** Illustrated by John Shelley. Farrar, Straus and Giroux, 1990. ISBN 0-374-37309-4. 30p. 5–8 (est.).

In the second tale of Bobby Bell's unusual surprises, Bobby amazes his classmates with a witch who lives in his wardrobe. The children have a riotous time with a witch who can do loop-the-loops on her broom and turn cabbage and stew into french fries and hot dogs. But mean-spirited Jenny Wood gets fat green frogs on her plate, and defiant Peter Drew sets off a spell of bats and beetles. Detailed borders surround action-packed scenes and bear close inspection.

6.223 Wood, Audrey. **Silly Sally.** Illustrated by Audrey Wood. Harcourt Brace Jovanovich, 1992. ISBN 0-15-274428-2. 32p. 3–7.

When red-haired Silly Sally goes to town, she walks "backwards, upside down." Along the way, she meets a pig, a loon, and a sheep, with whom she dances, plays leapfrog, and finally falls asleep. It's forward-walking, right-side-up Neddy Buttercup that tickles Sally and thereby gets the gang up and active again. This rhyming tale is illustrated in big, bright pastel colors and contains lively characters with rosy cheeks and spirited expressions.

6.224   Yorinks, Arthur. **Oh, Brother.** Illustrated by Richard Egielski. Farrar, Straus and Giroux/Michael di Capua Books, 1989. ISBN 0-374-35599-1. 32p. 6–9.

In a tongue-in-cheek Horatio Alger story, two naughty brothers are shipwrecked, washed up in New York, and "not spared the harshness of life." Through all their depression-era travails, they never stop arguing. But fate turns when Nathan, the old tailor, makes them his sons and apprentices. At Nathan's death, the two boys disguise themselves as old men and continue to run the tailor shop. That, of course, is when they meet Mrs. Guggenheim, who takes them to the Queen. . . .

6.225   Yorinks, Arthur. **Ugh.** Illustrated by Richard Egielski. Farrar, Straus and Giroux/Michael di Capua Books, 1990. ISBN 0-374-38028-7. 32p. 4–8 (est.).

In a Cinderella-like spoof, a cave boy, Ugh, has a miserable life. His brothers and sisters command him: "Rub feet!" "Get grub!" "Mop floor!" When cave scientist Oy invents the wheel, the cave world is not impressed ("Wheel stink!" announces the hunter, Eh). But Ugh uses the wheel to make a bicycle. Amazed, the cave world looks high and low for the one who can ride this creation: "Whoever make this, he be king!" And so, with action aplenty, Ugh, "be big-shot boy."

Imagination and Dreams

6.226   Alcorn, Johnny. **Rembrandt's Beret; or, The Painter's Crown.** Illustrated by Stephen Alcorn. Tambourine Books, 1991. ISBN 0-688-10207-7. 32p. 6 and up.

The Alcorn brothers, author and illustrator, tell young readers to "seek out paintings by the Old Masters. . . . They will speak to you." The painter grandfather who narrates this tale is recounting a time in his youth when he was locked in the Uffizi Gallery of Florence, Italy. The paintings not only spoke to him but even contested the right to paint his portrait. Winner over Rubens, Caravaggio, Michelangelo, and Titian was Rembrandt, who loaned his beret and brushes to the painter-to-be. Thickly applied oils capture the Old Masters' styles.

6.227 Allison, Diane Worfolk. **This Is the Key to the Kingdom.** Illustrated by Diane Worfolk Allison. Little, Brown, 1992. ISBN 0-316-03432-0. 30p. 4–8 (est.).

Diane Worfolk Allison's full-page, subtle watercolors and familiar children's chant lead readers through the kingdom to the city, to the town, to the street, to the lane. . . . The reader follows a young African American child leaving a bleak urban environment behind as she travels through a splendid fantasy kingdom filled with beauty and love. But there's more at work here than imagination. In the end, she must retrace her travels. Still, other lives are enriched by her contact with imagined kingdoms, proving love is the real key.

6.228 Anderson, Joan. **Harry's Helicopter.** Photographs by George Ancona. Morrow Junior Books, 1990. ISBN 0-688-09187-3. 32p. 5 and up.

Harry Hopkins likes helicopters better than anything else. On Harry's birthday, his father makes him a bright red cardboard helicopter big enough for Harry to climb into. Steering with a plumber's friend, Harry pretends to fly his chopper, dreaming of a time when he and his helicopter will *really* fly. And then it happens. With George Ancona's sharp color photographs, young readers can fly with Harry over houses and steeples toward Central Park, skyscrapers, and even the Statue of Liberty.

6.229 Baillie, Allan. **Drac and the Gremlin.** Illustrated by Jane Tanner. Dial Books for Young Readers, 1989. ISBN 0-8037-0628-6. 32p. 4–8.

Drac, a sun-kissed Warrior Queen of Tirnol Two, must capture the Gremlin of the Groaning Grotto (sometimes known as her brother). There are really two stories here—one in text, the other in pictures. The children's imaginations elevate the text to high fantasy, much like Calvin in his adventures with Hobbes, while the realistic paintings are of two children playing with their pets. Because the planet is saved, the White Wizard (sometimes called Dad), rewards them with Twin Crimson Cones (sometimes called ice cream).

6.230 Bate, Lucy. **How Georgina Drove the Car Very Carefully from Boston to New York.** Illustrated by Tamar Taylor. Crown, 1989. ISBN 0-517-57142-0. 32p. 3–6.

One day while bouncing on her mother's knee, little Georgina announces, "I drive the car." So begins her imaginary family trip to visit grandparents in New York. There are sights to be seen along the way, but not for Georgina; she is too occupied with driving *very* carefully, although she does have time for a real kid-style meal en route. Through simple text and stylized drawings, being responsible is cast in a clearly positive light.

6.231 Bax, Martin. **Edmond Went Far Away.** Illustrated by Michael Foreman. Harcourt Brace Jovanovich, 1989. ISBN 0-15-22105-7. 48p. 4–8.

Edmond lives on a farm where he has many animal friends. After he tells each of his friends that he is going away, he follows the path over the hill to "far away," imagining that he is accompanied by them. When Edmond returns home the next morning, all of his friends are happy to see him, including the sow and her brand new piglets. Rich, descriptive language and Michael Foreman's watercolors evoke a warm, secure feeling. This story is a good example of the "home-adventure-home" pattern in literature.

6.232 Blos, Joan W. **Lottie's Circus.** Illustrated by Irene Trivas. Morrow Junior Books, 1989. ISBN 0-688-06747-6. 32p. 6–10 (est.).

For something special to happen, Lottie explains to her cat and her toys, "you make-believe." Storybooks help with Lottie's imagining. As readers turn the pages, Lottie's imagination creates the extravaganza of a circus from preparation to performance. Irene Trivas's paintings show an energetic child, her cat Famous, and her toys in their circus roles—as ringmaster, performers, and audience. The imaginative adventure is a big-top success. Later, snug on her father's lap for storytime, Lottie's adventure tucks itself in.

6.233 Burningham, John. **Hey! Get Off Our Train.** Illustrated by John Burningham. Crown, 1989. ISBN 0-517-57643-0. 32p. 2–6 (est.).

When a pajama-clad boy and a pajama-case dog are scooted to bed, they climb aboard a toy train and begin a dream journey through the habitats of endangered species. One by one, an elephant, seal, whooping crane, tiger, and polar bear board the train. Each is met with the shout: "Hey! Get off our train." Each in turn explains its plight and, in cumulative fashion, warns that "soon there will be none of us left." Sparse text and wispy line drawings of characters are juxtaposed against full-page impressions of lemon skies, frothy snows, and drenching rains.

6.234 Carlstrom, Nancy White. **Who Gets the Sun out of Bed?** Illustrated by David McPhail. Little, Brown, 1992. ISBN 0-316-12862-7. 32p. 6–10 (est.).

"IN THE COLD DARK WINTER, / who gets the sun out of bed?" Come the whispered replies: "Not the spruce tree...." "Not the stars...." As the turning Earth reveals the glowing four-poster bed of the rising sun, part of the answer is revealed: Moon! "Get the sun out of bed, Moon!" Bunny Midnight has a role to play as well, as does the boy, Nicholas. Moon nudges Midnight, who kisses the boy, who greets the sun. Peeking from beneath his covers, Sun opens one eye.

6.235 Cassedy, Sylvia. **Lucie Babbidge's House.** Thomas Y. Crowell, 1989. ISBN 0-690-04798-3. 243p. 9–12.

Lucie's unhappy life at the orphanage is changed when she finds a dollhouse with a family of dolls. Lucie, called Goosey-Loosey by her classmates, retreats to the perfect life of her new make-believe family, and this secret life becomes her reality.

6.236 Desaix, Frank. **Hilary and the Lions.** Illustrated by Debbi Durland Desaix. Farrar, Straus and Giroux, 1990. ISBN 0-374-33237-1. 30p. 4–8 (est.).

After losing her parents in the hubbub of New York City, Hilary falls asleep against one of the two great stone lions in front of the library steps. When the lions come alive for their one magic night a year, Hilary rides them through the streets of New York. Debbi Durland Desaix's use of muted browns, grays, and greens evokes a dream-like quality appropriate for the night's adventure and making new friends.

6.237 Dorros, Arthur. **Abuela.** Illustrated by Elisa Kleven. Dutton Children's Books, 1991. ISBN 0-525-44750-4. 40p. 4–8.

Abuela is the ideal melding of story and illustration. In Arthur Dorros's joyful, loving story, a young girl fantasizes flying over New York City with her beloved grandmother. The love between granddaughter and grandmother shines through the lyrical language and rich illustrations. Dorros's natural incorporation of Spanish words into the story and the folk-art style of Elisa Klevin's mixed-media illustrations give the book a unique multicultural flavor. *ALA Notable Children's Books, 1992.*

6.238 Farber, Norma. **Return of the Shadows.** Illustrated by Andrea Baruffi. HarperCollins/Laura Geringer Books, 1992. ISBN 0-06-020519-9. 38p. 4–8.

When Mimi falls asleep, her shadow slips out, leading other shadows to break free and roam in unlikely places. A camel's shadow rests under an iceberg, and a rhino's shadow leans on the Washington Monument. A skyscraper's shadow creeps into the jungle, and a bicycle's shadow rides on clouds beside a plane. At twilight, the shadows become bewildered and disoriented, "no longer sure of what they were." In darkness, shadows long for home and the shape that they know best. At sunrise, each rushes to find the place it had been born. The pictures are silent and surreal—like shadows.

6.239 Gilden, Mel. **Harry Newberry and the Raiders of the Red Drink.** Henry Holt, 1989. ISBN 0-8050-0698-2. 151p. 9–13 (est.).

Frequently comic-book characters come alive in a child's imagination. But what happens when the whole family (except unimaginative Dad) and the entire town start seeing the comic-book heroes invading their community? Harry Newberry has reason to believe that his own mother may be super hero Tuatara herself. A visit to Aunt Agnes provides an exciting adventure which helps unravel the mysterious goings-on. Fact is difficult to distinguish from fantasy throughout this fun and farfetched mystery.

6.240 Heine, Helme (translated by Ralph Manheim). **The Marvelous Journey through the Night.** Illustrated by Helme Heine. Farrar, Straus and Giroux, 1990. ISBN 0-374-38478-9. 26p. 5–10.

German author/illustrator Helme Heine has created an evocative and whimsical explanation for dreaming—a "marvelous journey" that one undertakes without hindrance from passport, money, or luggage. The text is simple and poetic, describing irresistible Sleep who, with his moon lantern, makes your eyelids droop and leads you to his sister, Dream, who can guide you to the land of Heart's Desire. Full-color surrealistic paintings are dream-touched, but comforting.

6.241 James, Betsy. **The Dream Stair.** Illustrated by Richard Jesse Watson. Harper and Row, 1990. ISBN 0-06-022788-5. 32p. 5–7 (est.).

At bedtime, a young Hispanic child receives a candle from her grandmother to keep her safe. As she dreams, Granny's candle leads her up the dream stairs to play in an attic room, then down the stairs to the cellar room for more play, then to bed. In the morning, Granny is there to hear about her dreams. Bold color splotches of a dream world where inanimate things have life contrast with the warm-toned realism of Granny's home.

6.242 Jones, Diana Wynne. **Yes, Dear.** Illustrated by Graham Philpot. Greenwillow Books, 1992. ISBN 0-688-11195-5. 28p. 4 and up.

Autumn leaves are falling, and Kay catches a magic one. Unfortunately, no one in her family has time to listen to stories about a golden leaf's wonderful talents. Then Kay approaches Grandmother, who understands because she, too, had a magic leaf as a child. The watercolored pen-and-ink drawings add humorous details and interesting perspectives.

6.243 Leverich, Kathleen. **Hilary and the Troublemakers.** Illustrated by Walter Lorraine. Greenwillow Books, 1992. ISBN 0-688-10857-1. 138p. 6–9 (est.).

For Hilary, troublemakers are just part of life. A huge, homework-eating owl waylays her on the way to school. Her piggy bank absolutely refuses to yield her savings when she truly intends to buy her family gifts. Even innocent-looking snow people, built when she was supposed to be baby-sitting indoors, become blackmailing terrorists at her bedroom window, demanding her crayons and her baby cousin. With straight-faced humor, Kathleen Leverich sketches Hilary's imaginative creatures so that they feel real to readers, too.

6.244 Lindbergh, Reeve. **Benjamin's Barn.** Illustrated by Susan Jeffers. Dial Books for Young Readers, 1990. ISBN 0-8037-0614-6. 24p. 3–8.

The talented author and illustrator of *Midnight Farm* team up again to produce in gentle verse and intricately detailed paintings the warmth and imaginative possibilities that an ordinary barn has for a small boy. For Benjamin's barn is so big, tall, wide, and soft that it can shelter such fantasies as elephants, pteradactyls, a pirate ship, an entire brass band, or a royal family. But since the barn is already full of its own standard residents, a satisfied Benjamin decides that he "won't let the rest in after all."

6.245 Martin, Rafe. **Will's Mammoth.** Illustrated by Stephen Gammell. G. P. Putnam's Sons, 1989. ISBN 0-399-21627-8. 29p. 4–8 (est.).

Even though no one else believes that mammoths exist, a very special one is still alive and well in Will's imagination. Stephen Gammell's beautiful illustrations depict a day in which Will has a wordless romp in the snow with his very own mammoth and several other beasts before his mother calls him to dinner. Children with an interest in prehistoric creatures will want this on their reading lists. *ALA Notable Children's Books, 1989; School Library Journal Best Books, 1989; Horn Book Fanfare, 1990.*

6.246 McLerran, Alice. **Roxaboxen.** Illustrated by Barbara Cooney. Lothrop, Lee and Shepard Books, 1991. ISBN 0-688-07593-3. 30p. 5–8.

To those who have not been to Roxaboxen, it looks like any hill in the desert—nothing but sand, cactus, rocks, and old discarded boxes. But to Marian and her friends, Roxaboxen is a special place with buried treasure, ice cream parlors, and houses of jewels. Barbara Cooney's pastels, shimmering with desert hues, take us to a multidimensional world of fantasy and play.

6.247 McPhail, David. **The Party.** Illustrated by David McPhail. Little, Brown/Joy Street Books, 1990. ISBN 0-316-56330-7. 32p. 4–8.

Beneath his bed light, a young boy and his stuffed animals plan a midnight party. When Dad comes to read the bedtime story, he falls sound asleep on the bed. But the party *must* go on. Stuffed friends become live friends, floating on balloons, riding the electric train, dancing, and then heading to the kitchen for snacks. Even sleeping Dad rides the elephant to the kitchen. David McPhail's pajama-clad host and his lovable menagerie are quietly raucous.

6.248 Minarik, Else Holmelund. **The Little Girl and the Dragon.** Illustrated by Martine Gourbault. Greenwillow Books, 1991. ISBN 0-688-09914-9. 24p. 3–7 (est.).

Once a little girl had a book about a dragon, and all was well. Then one day, the dragon gets out of the book, swallows the girl's toys, and refuses to give them back. It takes the girl's quick wits and intrepid spirit to entrap the dragon and regain what belongs to her. Outsized by the sprawling lavender-green monster, the child is more than a match for the creature's intellect. The dragon book is instantly recognizable as the one the reader holds, making the possibility of an escaping dragon ongoing.

6.249 Pfanner, Louise. **Louise Builds a House.** Illustrated by Louise Pfanner. Orchard Books, 1989. ISBN 0-531-08396-9. 32p. 3–6.

When Louise sets out to build her dream home, she imagines every conceivable detail—a flat roof for kite flying, big windows for reading, a tower for observing the stars, and even a moat for her boat. After seeing Louise's wonderful house, depicted with elemental line drawings and watercolor washes, children may want to create their own imaginary dream houses.

6.250 Polacco, Patricia. **Appelemando's Dreams.** Illustrated by Patricia Polacco. Philomel Books, 1991. ISBN 0-399-21800-9. 30p. 4–8.

Appelemando is a quiet, slow boy who lives in a very drab village but who dreams wondrously beautiful dreams for his friends. One day his dreams escape, exuding fantastic images into the lackluster village. At first, the elders don't believe in the existence or worth of Appelemando's special gift, but after a crisis, even the suspicious elders cannot deny the value of this gift. Patricia Polacco's detailed drawings evoke the sentiments of an ethnic village and the magic of believing.

6.251 Pringle, Laurence. **Jesse Builds a Road.** Illustrated by Leslie Holt Morrill. Macmillan, 1989. ISBN 0-02-775311-5. 30p. 3–6.

Acclaimed nonfiction author Laurence Pringle tries his hand at writing for younger children in this, his first picture book. While Jesse plays with his dog and his miniature construction machinery, his toys spring to life. A brief but factual description of the digging, scraping, and paving required to build a road evolves in the setting of Jesse's playtime. Watercolor illustrations are painted from perspectives which lend energy to the action.

6.252 Reed, Lynn Rowe. **Rattlesnake Stew.** Illustrated by Lynn Rowe Reed. Farrar, Straus and Giroux, 1990. ISBN 0-374-36190-8. 32p. 3–7 (est.).

A nighttime wind whirls and swirls Billy out of his bed; roaring and soaring, it transports him into a world of cowboys, cacti, and prairie dogs. Bright oil pastels depict the dream sequences in a closeup, surrealistic style, while lyrical text tells of Billy's adventures. As the winds return Billy to his own bed, his mother is calling him in to taste the rattlesnake stew that she has made for him.

6.253 Riddell, Chris. **The Trouble with Elephants.** Illustrated by Chris Riddell. Harper and Row/Harper Trophy Books, 1990. ISBN 0-397-32273-9. 22p. 3–7.

According to one little girl, the trouble with elephants is that they spill bathwater, leave a pink elephant ring around the tub, and slide down the bannister to breakfast. But as she as well as others who share this book soon discover, the real trouble with elephants is that "you can't help but love them." Humorous full-page illustrations that depict pachyderms in a variety of "troublesome" predicaments bring to life a little girl's imagination and adoration for a much-loved stuffed animal.

6.254 Ringgold, Faith. **Tar Beach.** Illustrated by Faith Ringgold. Crown, 1991. ISBN 0-517-58031-4. 32p. 4 and up (est.).

"Sleeping on Tar Beach was magical. Lying on the roof in the night, with stars and skyscraper buildings all around me, made me feel rich, like I owned all that I could see." As Cassie sleeps on the rooftop of her Harlem apartment building, she magically flies over the city, claiming ownership of a beautiful bridge and buildings as a means to fulfill her dreams. Text appears beneath each double-page acrylic folk-art painting, as does a reproduced segment of Faith Ringgold's story quilt, *Tar Beach*, one of five autobiographical works in the Women on the Bridge series hanging in New York City's Guggenheim Museum. *Caldecott Honor Book, 1992; Coretta Scott King Award (Illustration), 1992.*

6.255 Rodgers, Frank. **Doodle Dog.** Illustrated by Frank Rodgers. Dutton Children's Books, 1990. ISBN 0-525-44585-4. 32p. 3–7.

Little Sam wishes hard for a pet, a little dog that can fetch and catch and sleep on his bed. So Sam and his mother draw the dog that he wants—a kind of doodle picture that Sam names Doodle. Frank Rodgers's charming story captures a child who wants something so badly that the dream comes alive. Colorful, friendly illustrations give Sam, Mother, and Doodle appeal.

6.256 Rosenberg, Liz. **Adelaide and the Night Train.** Illustrated by Lisa Desimini. Harper and Row/Charlotte Zolotow Books, 1989. ISBN 0-06-025103-4. 30p. 3–7 (est.).

Late one night, Adelaide, lying wide awake, boards the whistling train that passes by her house. She watches nighttime happenings from its window—a waitress serving hamburgers at an all-night diner, an owl gliding noiselessly in search of food, and babies dreaming in their cribs. After this extraordinary trip, Adelaide *always* listens for the night train to lull her to sleep at bedtime. Poetic, rhythmic prose and surrealistic acrylic paintings supply a dreamy mystery to the night train's ride.

6.257 Rovetch, Lissa. **Trigwater Did It.** Illustrated by Lissa Rovetch. Morrow Junior Books/Seashore Books, 1989. ISBN 0-688-08058-8. 32p. 4–8 (est.).

Trouble seems to follow Arnie, and everyone assumes that he is the trouble-maker. No one believes that his green friend Trigwater is causing the difficulties; after all, no one else can even see Trigwater. Finally, when the principal gives Arnie an ultimatum, he knows that he must teach Trigwater some manners. The outcome of Arnie's campaign delights everyone. Stylized watercolors contribute to the mischievous mood.

6.258   Van Laan, Nancy. **A Mouse in My House.** Illustrated by Marjorie Priceman. Alfred A. Knopf/Borzoi Books, 1990. ISBN 0-679-90043. 32p. 3–7 (est.).

"A mouse is in my house—and it acts like me!" Just like a mouse, a small boy invades the cookie jar. ("It climbs and it wriggles as it nibbles and it giggles.") In rhyming, rhythmic text ideal for reading aloud, the boy becomes other creatures as well: he's a pouncing cat, a toy-scattering dog, and a slippery, bathtime fish. Whatever persona is adopted, the actions are guaranteed to be rambunctious. Splashes of watercolor spill over the ink line drawings, giving a hasty energy to the animal-like antics.

6.259   Weir, Alison. **Peter, Good Night.** Illustrated by Deborah Kogan Ray. E. P. Dutton, 1989. ISBN 0-525-44464-5. 24p. 2–6.

Peter snuggles in bed with his stuffed animals and looks out of the window. One by one, the stars, the moon, the clouds, the treetops, the night bird, the fog, the breeze, and the cat wish him good night. In this warm and gentle book, with colored-pencil illustrations in muted shades, the repetitive, lyrical prose will appeal for bedtime reading.

6.260   Wiesner, David. **Hurricane.** Illustrated by David Wiesner. Clarion Books, 1990. ISBN 0-395-54382-7. 32p. 4–8.

Delightful, detailed, and realistic watercolor paintings bring preparations for a hurricane to life. After the storm passes, two brothers' imaginations are kindled by a fallen tree. Their days are filled with forays into its branches, which become imaginary jungles, oceans, and even outer space: "The tree was a private place, big enough for secret dreams, small enough for shared adventure." The arrival of men with a chainsaw is a disaster, but the boys eye the remaining tree in the yard with childlike hope.

6.261   Willard, Nancy. **The High Rise Glorious Skittle Skat Roarious Sky Pie Angel Food Cake.** Illustrated by Richard Jesse Watson. Harcourt Brace Jovanovich, 1990. ISBN 0-15-234332-6. 64p. 6 and up.

To bake her mother the best birthday cake of all, a young girl must first find her great-grandmother's secret-ingredient recipe for a High Rise Glorious Skittle Skat Roarious Sky Pie Angel Food Cake. Luckily, Great-Grandmother left some clues in her ledger books. Well-timed heavenly intervention also helps to ensure that the cake is baked with both "evol" and a golden thimble. The heavenly "hosts" are a festival of color in their robes, feathers, ribbons, and flowers.

6.262 Wood, Don, and Audrey Wood. **Piggies.** Illustrated by Don Wood. Harcourt Brace Jovanovich, 1991. ISBN 0-15-256341-5. 32p. 3–6 (est.).

The narrator, whose chubby, childlike hands are in each double-page illustration of this wonder-filled book, has ten little imaginary piggies—fat piggies sit on the thumbs, smart piggies on the index fingers, long piggies stretch out on the middle fingers, silly piggies clown on the ring fingers, and wee piggies play on the little fingers. Together, they get hot, cold, clean, and dirty—and misbehave at bedtime. Pink- and golden-toned oil paintings depict the piggies' activities with closeup, whimsical detail.

6.263 Yolen, Jane, and Martin H. Greenberg, editors. **Things That Go Bump in the Night: A Collection of Original Stories.** Harper and Row, 1989. ISBN 0-06-026803-4. 280p. 10 and up.

This collection of eighteen eerie, fantastic stories by such popular writers as William Sleator, Dianna Wynne Jones, Anne Crompton, and Jane Yolen herself offers encounters with ghosts, wizards, living chairs, and talking rabbits. Readers learn that appearances can be deceiving, and that the devils within their own psyches can be the most terrifying of all.

6.264 Zolotow, Charlotte. **The Seashore Book.** Illustrated by Wendell Minor. HarperCollins, 1992. ISBN 0-06-020214-9. 32p. 4–9.

Close your eyes and imagine as a mother vividly paints with words the seashore that her young son has never seen. Then open your eyes and expand that vision with watercolored seascapes that invite you to step right onto the sand with birds and sea creatures among the lapping waves. The day ends with the satifying feeling that your imagination can take you anywhere.

Other Worlds

6.265   Le Guin, Ursula K. **Tehanu: The Last Book of Earthsea.**
Atheneum/Jean Karl Books, 1990. ISBN 0-689-31595-3. 226p. 11
and up (est.).

In the fourth book of the Earthsea fantasy series, Ged has lost his
powers as Archmage. Goha, now a middle-aged widow, has
taken under wing Therru, a small, severely abused little girl.
During the course of the novel, these three characters encounter
wicked wizards, good kings, fiery dragons, and powerful magic.
Due to several sensitive issues that are presented (rape, child
abuse, differences between the sexes, feminism), the novel is
recommended for advanced, mature readers.

6.266   Pinkwater, Daniel. **Guys from Space.** Illustrated by Daniel Pinkwater. Macmillan, 1989. ISBN 0-02-774672-0. 29p. 5–8.

If a spaceship landed in *your* yard and if the friendly "space
guys" inside asked if you could go for a ride in space, would
you? Wearing the dog's dish for a space helmet, the hero of
Daniel Pinkwater's farce gets permission from Mom ("That's
nice") to travel to a strange new planet with talking rocks and
with "space things" who serve root beer floats—all for the cost
of a plastic fish.

6.267   Rodda, Emily. **Finders Keepers.** Illustrated by Noela Young.
Greenwillow Books, 1991. ISBN 0-688-10516-5. 184p. 10 and up.

An Australian preteen, Patrick, is contacted by computer from a
parallel world on the other side of a time-space divider called
the Barrier. When the Barrier ruptures, objects from each side fall
through to the other side and are lost to their owners. Patrick
must find three objects on his side that individuals on the other
side desperately want returned. His search raises some interesting moral issues about ownership, loyalty, and trust. This is a
witty, well-constructed science fantasy.

6.268   Young, Ruth. **A Trip to Mars.** Illustrated by Maryann Cocca-Leffler. Orchard Books, 1990. ISBN 0-531-08492-2. 32p. 2–6.

Want to know how to plan for a trip to Mars? As a young girl
packs, we learn about appropriate clothing and necessary supplies for the Martian climate and topography. Four concluding
pages of facts from the young traveler's space journal, along
with brightly colored and humorous illustrations, round out this
introduction to the red planet.

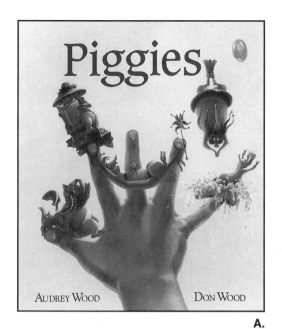

A.

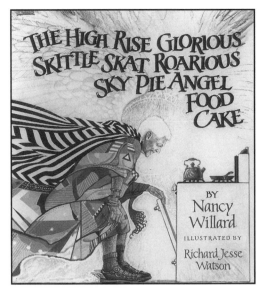

B.

C.

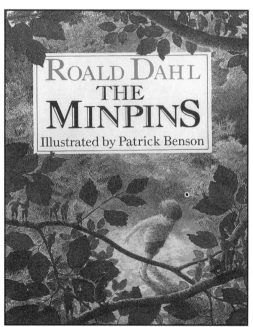

D.

A. *Piggies* by Audrey Wood and Don Wood (see 6.262). **B.** *The High Rise Glorious Skittle Skat Roarious Sky Pie Angel Food Cake* by Nancy Willard; illustrated by Richard Jesse Watson (see 6.261). **C.** *Tehanu: The Last Book of Earthsea* by Ursula K. Le Guin (see 6.265). **D.** *The Minpins* by Roald Dahl; illustrated by Patrick Benson (see 6.319).

A.

B.

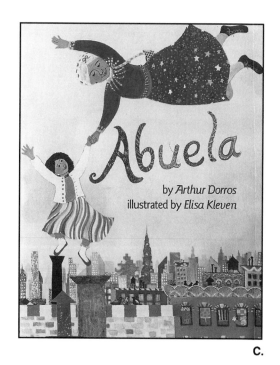

C.

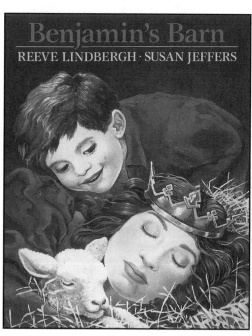

D.

A. *Will's Mammoth* by Rafe Martin; illustrated by Stephen Gammell (see 6.245).
B. *Tar Beach* by Faith Ringgold (see 6.254). **C.** *Abuela* by Arthur Dorros; illustrated by Elisa Kleven (see 6.237). **D.** *Benjamin's Barn* by Reeve Lindbergh; illustrated by Susan Jeffers (see 6.244).

Science Fiction

6.269 Asimov, Janet, and Isaac Asimov. **Norby and Yobo's Great Adventure.** Walker, 1989. ISBN 0-8027-6894-6. 100p. 9 and up (est.).

Like its seven predecessors in the Norby series, this latest adventure carries space-cadet Jeff and his teaching robot, Norby, into perilous situations. With Admiral Yobo, the trio travel back in time to prehistoric Earth to investigate the origins of a family relic. After being gored by a woolly mammoth and rescuing a young girl, Jeff realizes that they have altered the past and therefore the future. Danger awaits as they try to rectify their actions in Ice-Age Eurasia.

6.270 Barron, T. A. **Heartlight.** Philomel Books, 1990. ISBN 0-399-22180-8. 272p. 10 and up.

Cosmic forces are anchored in fundamental human experiences in this exciting, well-crafted science fantasy. With the aid of Pure Condensed Light (PCL), Kate Prancer follows her astrophysicist grandfather across the universe to the great star Trethoniel, which is mysteriously draining energy from the Earth's sun. She meets some extraordinary creatures from the planet Nel Sauria, and through confrontations with The Darkness, she helps save the universe. Elements of mysticism, mystery, and horror intertwine in this tale.

6.271 Chetwin, Grace. **The Starstone: From Tales of Gom in the Legends of Ulm.** Bradbury Press, 1989. ISBN 0-02-718315-7. 240p. 10 and up.

In this sequel to *The Riddle and the Rune,* Gom, the young boy from Windy Mountain, serves as apprentice to a wizard who isn't teaching him the magical arts fast enough. Katak, the Evil One, is becoming more aggressive in his attempts to climb the shelter-giving Crystal Stairs. Gom's innate senses and some new friends help him to protect the Crystal Stairs and recover the lost emerald seal, and Gom becomes a legendary wizard himself.

6.272 Gilden, Mel. **Outer Space and All That Junk.** J. B. Lippincott, 1989. ISBN 0-397-32307-7. 167p. 10 and up.

This sci-fi mystery would be a perfect read-aloud during an ecology unit. The plot hinges on the premise that those piles of junk littering our homes and countryside are really outer-space aliens waiting for the opportunity to go home. The main characters, Myron Duberville, eccentric Uncle Hugo, Letitia Reticuli, and Myron's cohort, Princess, the boss's niece, are brought to life through vivid description, abundant dialogue, and a rich variety of sentence structures.

6.273 Kitamura, Satoshi. **UFO Diary.** Illustrated by Satoshi Kitamura. Farrar, Straus and Giroux, 1989. ISBN 0-374-38026-0. 32p. 3–7 (est.).

When a strange flying object takes a wrong turn at the Milky Way, the navigator encounters the big, blue marble Earth. One innovative illustration demonstrates the spacecraft's approach through successive layers of the atmosphere on multiple strips across the page. The spacecraft descends until the alien/narrator spots a friendly looking Earth creature. Readers never see the alien, but view some of the action from its perspective. After a ride on the spacecraft, the earthling boy offers a gift from his planet—a growing thing.

Supernatural Tales

6.274 Ackerman, Karen. **The Banshee.** Illustrated by David Ray. Philomel Books, 1990. ISBN 0-399-21924-2. 32p. 4–8 (est.).

When night falls, the banshee, a legendary wailing Irish spirit, comes to the village seeking someone to share her loneliness. At each house, though, the banshee encounters love and warmth, which leave no room for her sad song. The contrasts between light and dark found in the illustrations serve as the perfect vehicle for contrasting the worlds of the banshee and the villagers.

6.275 Brighton, Catherine. **Dearest Grandmama.** Illustrated by Catherine Brighton. Doubleday, 1991. ISBN 0-385-41844-2. 32p. 4–8.

From the sailing ship *Meralda*, a young girl traveling with her father writes a series of letters to her grandmother, all dated in the closing months of 1830. The letters are the only text of this eerie account of Maudie-Ann's encounter with a silent boy who climbs from the sea to become her shipboard companion. Mysteriously, the boy carries a letter dated forty-two years into the future, makes no reflection in the mirror, and saves her life.

6.276 Brittain, Bill. **Professor Popkin's Prodigious Polish: A Tale of the Coven Tree.** Illustrated by Andrew Glass. Harper and Row, 1990. ISBN 0-06-020727-2. 152p. 8–12.

Fifteen-year-old Luther Gilpin decides to become a salesman, hoping to make his fortune and leave his family's farm. He orders a case of Professor Popkin's Prodigious Polish, unaware that the polish brings to life whatever objects on which it is applied. In this newest mystery in Bill Brittain's Coven Tree series, Luther's adventures selling and dealing with the polish teach him lessons about appreciating what he already has. Andrew Glass's illustrations add an eerie feel to the mystery.

6.277 Browne, Anthony. **The Tunnel.** Illustrated by Anthony Browne. Alfred A. Knopf/Borzoi Books, 1989. ISBN 0-394-94582-4. 24p. 4–8 (est.).

Jack and Rose, a brother and sister as different as can be, are always arguing. When they are sent outside by their mother, Jack discovers a tunnel. Rose refuses to explore it, so Jack goes alone. When he doesn't return, Rose must overcome her fear through courage and love, even enduring the threatening woods at the end of the tunnel to save her brother. Through surreal images, Anthony Browne manages to infuse a contemporary story with folktale menace; the heroine even wears a red cloak.

6.278 Cecil, Laura, compiler. **Boo! Stories to Make You Jump.** Illustrated by Emma Chichester Clark. Greenwillow Books, 1990. ISBN 0-688-09842-8. 93p. 4–8 (est.).

If not making readers jump, this collection of poems, traditional tales, and lore could at least give them delicious shivers. Included are funny, scary stories authored by Margaret Mahy and Diana Wynne Jones, and spooky rhymes by Ogden Nash, Jack Prelutsky, and Ben Jonson. There are ideal choices for reading or telling. In particular, watch for those selections that allow the ending to be shouted.

6.279 Cole, Joanna, and Stephanie Calmenson, compilers. **The Scary Book.** Illustrated by Chris Demarest, Marilyn Hirsh, Arnold Lobel, and Dirk Zimmer. Morrow Junior Books, 1991. ISBN 0-688-10654-4. 127p. 4 and up.

This compilation of stories, poems, tricks, riddles, and jokes offers easy reading for the middle-grader, who will also be most likely to appreciate the "tricks," including instructions for making "bloody finger in a box" and playing the dead man game. The story collection includes the benign "Strange Bumps" by Arnold Lobel, as well as the more threatening "Bony-Legs" by

Joanna Cole herself, a tale of a child-eating witch who is foiled by a young girl. Be warned: the jokes and riddles are groaners.

6.280   Conrad, Pam. **Stonewords: A Ghost Story.** Harper and Row, 1990. ISBN 0-06-021316-7. 130p. 10 and up.

Zoe Louise died in 1870 when she was eleven years old. Now a present-day Zoe discovers the ghost of Zoe Louise when she goes down an unused back staircase in her house. Two lives become intertwined as the two Zoes search for a way to travel back in time to save Zoe Louise from the fire that took her life. *Boston Globe–Horn Book Honor Book, 1990.*

6.281   Fleischman, Sid. **The Midnight Horse.** Illustrated by Peter Sis. Greenwillow Books, 1990. ISBN 0-688-09441-4. 96p. 8 and up.

Recently orphaned, young Touch arrives by stagecoach in Cricklewood to meet his grouchy and wicked great-uncle, Judge Wigglesforth, the kind Miss Sally who runs Red Raven Inn, and The Great Chaffalo, a ghostly magician who is said to turn straw into horses. With his own courage and a bit of magic, Touch outwits his villainous great-uncle, reclaims his rightful inheritance, and saves the Red Raven Inn for Miss Sally. Applause. *ALA Notable Children's Books, 1991.*

6.282   Hamilton, Virginia. **The All Jahdu Storybook.** Illustrated by Barry Moser. Harcourt Brace Jovanovich, 1991. ISBN 0-15-239498-2. 128p. 8 and up.

From a world where Trouble is a giant with a barrel for an earring, where magic can make Sweetdream or Nightmare, where Yin and Yang speak to a magical little being named Jahdu, Virginia Hamilton has fashioned tales in which folklore and contemporary life seamlessly coexist. In these strange, gripping stories, Jahdu, the child-trickster, meets dangers and opportunities, winning out in the end and allowing young readers to explore the dark and light of the world.

6.283   McKissack, Patricia C. **The Dark-Thirty: Southern Tales of the Supernatural.** Illustrated by Brian Pinkney. Alfred A. Knopf/Borzoi Books, 1992. ISBN 0-676-91863-9. 122p. 10 and up (est.).

The thirty minutes of twilight when it is neither day nor night are the best time to tell one of these spine-tingling tales rooted in African American history and its oral storytelling tradition from slavery to the civil rights era. Each of the ten original stories is accompanied by a dramatic black-and-white scratch-board illustration. *Coretta Scott King Award (Writing), 1993; Newbery Honor Book, 1993.*

6.284 Naylor, Phyllis Reynolds. **The Witch's Eye.** Illustrated by Joe Burleson. Delacorte Press, 1990. ISBN 0-385-30157-X. 179p. 9–12.

In Phyllis Reynolds Naylor's fourth tale of witch spells and magic, best friends Lynn and Mouse are plagued by a talisman of Witch Tuggle, who died in a fire. After Mrs. Tuggle's green glass eye is discovered in the ashes of the fire, mysterious behavioral changes overcome Lynn's family. Lynn and Mouse demonstrate remarkable pluck in their attempts to triumph over the eye's powers. The extraordinary occurrences are set against an ordinary family's pursuits, making the events feel even more chilling.

6.285 Robertson, Joanne. **Sea Witches.** Illustrated by László Gál. Dial Books for Young Readers, 1991. ISBN 0-8037-1070-4. 28p. 4–8.

Eerie and riveting full-color depictions of witches and shipwrecks, bordered by a surrealistic collage of sea creatures, provide a haunting glimpse into Scottish superstition. For example, a Scottish grandmother warns her grandson to crush his eggshells after meals, since witches use unbroken shells as boats and then go to sea to destroy ships by sorcery. The rhythmic haiku prose, though reminiscent of Old English poetry, is completely accessible to young readers.

6.286 Schertle, Alice. **Witch Hazel.** Illustrated by Margot Tomes. HarperCollins, 1991. ISBN 0-06-025141-7. 32p. 3–8 (est.).

Because Johnny is too little to help with the plowing, his older brothers give him a handful of pumpkin seeds to plant. Because Johnny needs a scarecrow to guard his pumpkin vines, his brothers cut a witch hazel branch, and Johnny dresses "Witch Hazel" in a gingham dress. Under the edge of her skirt, the largest pumpkin grows, full of magical promise and testimony to a young boy's faith. In earthen browns, grays, and greens, Margot Tomes's illustrations match the story's mood.

6.287 Shecter, Ben. **The Big Stew.** Illustrated by Ben Shecter. HarperCollins/Charlotte Zolotow Books, 1991. ISBN 0-06-025610-9. 32p. 2–6 (est.).

On a stew day, a cheery, rounded couple set about adding "a little of this, a little of that" to their stewpot. Their enthusiasm for adding more and still more transforms them into frenzied witches, dumping snakes, toads, rats, and bats into the stew. When the pot finally erupts into a scary goblin, the words "TOO MUCH" cover the pages, and the couple returns to normal to eat their stew, learning "enough is enough."

6.288   Shyer, Marlene Fanta. **Ruby, the Red-Hot Witch of Bloomingdale's.** Viking Penguin, 1991. ISBN 0-670-83473-4. 151p. 8–12.

Caught in a rainstorm on their way to visit their father, eight-year-old Thomas and his older sister Petra run into Bloomingdale's department store, where they encounter a friendly "witch" named Ruby. Ruby has cures for everything, including Thomas's idiosyncratic hiccups and Petra's longing for a reconcilliation of her parents. Marlene Fanta Shyer never admits that Ruby can actually work magic, so the reader is left uncertain. This is a book for libraries courageous enough to provide a playful, magical story for middle-grade students, even if it does include a witch's spell or two.

6.289   Wangerin, Walter, Jr. **Elisabeth and the Water-Troll.** Illustrated by Deborah Healy. HarperCollins, 1991. ISBN 0-6-026354-7. 64p. 7–12.

Written in an oral style, the tale of the water-troll tells of prejudicial fear. Grieving for the death of her mother, Elisabeth weeps tears into the well of a lonely water-troll and touches his heart. Intending to comfort her, he steals her from her bed. At first, the troll frightens Elisabeth, but soon she senses his gentleness. When the villagers discover her absence, they set a blazing fire around the troll's well, testing his allegiance to Elisabeth. Stylized paintings interpret the poignancy of the troll's sacrifice.

6.290   Wyllie, Stephen. **Ghost Train: A Spooky Hologram Book.** Illustations by Brian Lee. Dial Books, 1992. ISBN 0-8037-1163-8. 24p. 4–8 (est.).

Three spooky friends—Headless Hector, the Gray Lady, and the Silver Skeleton—happily haunt Ravenswick Castle for nearly four hundred years until the castle falls into ruin. In a saga narrated by the Silver Skeleton, the three friends wander aimlessly for a time until they find a perfect new home—the Ghost Train ride at the amusement park. The story seems secondary, however, to the book's execution: shivery holographic images spring from the pages, eyes following the reader, the skeleton even opening and closing its mouth.

6.291 Yolen, Jane. **The Faery Flag: Stories and Poems of Fantasy and the Supernatural.** Orchard Books, 1989. ISBN 0-531-08438-8. 120p. 10 and up.

Award-winning author Jane Yolen creates new worlds that blend traditional folktales and fairy tales with original modern fantasy. In these tales and poems, a young girl sprouts wings, unicorns heal abused children, and maligned storybook wolves tell their side of the story. Fairies, witches, dragons, and princesses abound, providing enjoyable reading for child and adult alike.

Time Fantasy

6.292 Bellairs, John. **The Trolley to Yesterday.** Illustrated by Edward Gorey. Dial Books for Young Readers, 1989. ISBN 0-8037-0582-4. 183p. 10 and up.

In this sixth Johnny Dixon adventure involving Professor Childermass, thirteen-year-old Johnny and his friend, Fergie, are worried by Professor Childermass's strange behavior. Then the professor proposes something even stranger—travel through time on a red and green trolley with faded gold paint. The professor's destination is Constantinople in 1453 during the Turkish invasion of the Byzantine Empire. Together, the three face great dangers from the battles and from trying to save from death or enslavement the people who seek refuge in the Church of the Holy Wisdom. But the professor knows the events of history.

6.293 Climo, Shirley. **T. J.'s Ghost.** Thomas Y. Crowell, 1989. ISBN 0-690-04691-X. 151p. 10 and up (est.).

T. J.'s boring vacation with Auntie Onion and Uncle Will at their California beach cabin takes a mysterious turn when eerie moans come from the foggy ocean. Only T. J. can hear the voice calling her by name. The mystery unfolds as she discovers an Australian ghost boy who stowed away on a ship which wrecked 120 years ago. As T. J. struggles to help him, she also learns to love and appreciate the eccentricities of her aunt and uncle.

6.294 Fleischman, Paul. **Time Train.** Illustrated by Claire Ewart. HarperCollins/Charlotte Zolotow Books, 1991. ISBN 0-06-021710-3. 32p. 5–9 (est.).

On a class trip, a group of students from New York board the *Rocky Mountain Unlimited* at the train station, and find themselves traveling not only across the country to Utah, but also back in time. At their destination, they ride a stegosaurus and eat scrambled pterodactyl eggs. The children's adventures are boldly depicted, with unusual perspectives and surreal watercolors.

6.295 L'Engle, Madeleine. **An Acceptable Time.** Farrar, Straus, and Giroux, 1989. ISBN 0-374-30027-5. 343p. 10 and up (est.).

Continuing the Murry family saga begun in *A Wrinkle in Time,* Madeleine L'Engle's newest novel recounts the adventures of Meg Murry's teenage daughter, Polly O'Keefe. While staying at her grandparents' New England farmhouse, Polly unexpectedly slips through a "time gate" and finds herself in a land and society that existed three thousand years ago. Thus begins a dangerous, exciting, time-travel escapade in which she learns about druids, Celtic customs, and the importance of love for every era and culture.

6.296 Lindbergh, Anne. **Three Lives to Live.** Little, Brown, 1992. ISBN 0-316-52628-2. 183p. 11 and up (est.).

When Garet Atkin's seventh-grade class is assigned the task of writing autobiographies, Garet begins her wry chronicles with the previous summer, when she met her "twin sister" Daisy for the first time. Daisy entered Garet's life suddenly and unexpectedly when she fell down the laundry chute in Grandmother Gratkin's old house. Notwithstanding her strange arrival, Daisy seemed different—completely at home in Grandmother's house, but fascinated by electronics. Because Grandmother won't answer questions, Garet must untangle the mysterious identity of Daisy, and eventually her grandmother, and even herself.

6.297 Murphy, Shirley Rousseau (with Welch Suggs). **Medallion of the Black Hound.** Harper and Row, 1989. ISBN 0-06-024369-4. 182p. 8–12.

Through the magical powers of the Medallion of the Black Hound, young David Shepard is transported back through time to the ancient land of Meryn and finds himself in the middle of a struggle of good versus evil. Using the powers of his medallion and his own courage, David helps to defeat the evil of Balcher, preserving the kingdom and his family's legacy. Woven with

Celtic lore, this well-written fantasy will carry the reader into a world of intrigue and suspense.

6.298 Peck, Richard. **Voices after Midnight.** Delacorte Press, 1989. ISBN 0-385-29779-3. 181p. 10 and up.

Fourteen-year-old Chad looks forward to his family's two-week vacation in New York City. The one-hundred-year-old town-house that his family rents, though, has an eerie quality about it. When Chad and his little brother try to track down the ghostly voices that they hear at night, they suddenly find themselves pulled back in time to the winter of 1888. Thus begins the boys' adventure as they frantically work to save the lives of the young people who lived in the house over a century ago.

6.299 Scieszka, Jon. **The Good, the Bad, and the Goofy. Knights of the Kitchen Table. The Not-So-Jolly Roger.** Illustrated by Lane Smith. Viking Penguin, 1991–92. Approx. 57p. 7–11.

The three adventurous heroes of the Time Warp Trio—Fred, Sam, and Joe—are up to rollicking fun in their escapades of the past. Whether escaping from mean and ugly pirates, from a skewer-bearing knight, or from cattle stampedes, finding "The Book" (a gift from Joe's magician uncle) in their new time zone is the only way to recross time barriers. Lane Smith's zany black-and-white drawings are action-packed.

Toys and Dolls

6.300 Adler, C. S. **Help, Pink Pig!** G. P. Putnam's Sons, 1990. ISBN 0-399-22183-2. 160p. 9–11 (est.).

Moving to Los Angeles to live with her single mother, latchkey child Amanda escapes boredom and the torment of the apartment bully by entering a fantasy world with her miniature rose quartz pig. Robbie, another lonely and unhappy young neighbor, and Amanda enter a magical world together and face a dragon and a cruel knight. These imaginary adventures help the children cope with life and assert themselves in contemporary, urban L.A.

6.301 Babbitt, Natalie. **Nellie: A Cat on Her Own.** Illustrated by Natalie Babbitt. Farrar, Straus and Giroux/Michael di Capua Books, 1989. ISBN 0-374-35506-1. 26p. 5–10 (est.).

Nellie is a cat marionette who loves to dance. When her mistress dies, she is left alone and fears she will never dance again. But

Nellie's friend Tom, a real cat, takes her to a special gathering of friends. There, in the moonlight, Nellie dances again—this time on her own.

6.302   Baker, Keith. **The Magic Fan.** Illustrated by Keith Baker. Harcourt Brace Jovanovich, 1989. ISBN 0-15-250750-7. 20p. 4–8 (est.).

Keith Baker's lushly illustrated picture book tells the story of Yoshi, a Japanese boy who loves to build things, but who has run out of ideas. When he finds a magic fan, which depicts illustrations of what to build next, his inspiration returns. It takes a near disaster for Yoshi to realize that the magic is not in the fan, but in himself. Alternate fan-shaped pages and rich jade tones contribute to the book's uniqueness and appeal. *Notable 1989 Children's Trade Books in the Field of Social Studies.*

6.303   Hissey, Jane. **Little Bear Lost.** Illustrated by Jane Hissey. Philomel Books, 1989. ISBN 0-399-21743-6. 32p. 3–6.

Soft-hued nostalgic drawings accompany the story of Little Bear, who gets lost from the other nursery animals during a game of hide-and-seek. After a thorough search, and even after painting a "lost bear" poster, the worried friends find a very full, napping Little Bear inside the picnic basket. The polite exchanges among the stuffed friends are reminiscent of A. A. Milne's writings.

6.304   Polacco, Patricia. **Babushka's Doll.** Illustrated by Patricia Polacco. Simon and Schuster Books for Young Readers, 1990. ISBN 0-671-68343-8. 28p. 6–10 (est.).

Natasha is a very demanding child. She only wants to play, and she doesn't like to wait for anything. When her grandmother, Babushka, goes to the store, she lets Natasha play with her own childhood doll. When the rambunctious and impatient doll comes to life, Natasha learns what being mischievous is all about and, as a result, becomes a "not so naughty little girl." Colorful pencil, marking pen, and acrylic illustrations help to tell this Russian tale. *Notable 1990 Children's Trade Books in the Field of Social Studies.*

6.305   Rendal, Justine. **The Dancing Cat.** Illustrated by Bernhard Oberdieck. Simon and Schuster Books for Young Readers, 1991. ISBN 0-671-72637-4. 28p. 6–10 (est.).

A toy cat believes that she's made to dance. But her dreams are shattered when her owner adds her to a collection of stuffed fighting cats. When the cat does not fulfill her owner's needs, she is given away to Ben, a gentle boy who names her Tasha because he too believes that she is a dancer. Adorned in a dancing costume and placed on a stage, Tasha realizes her dream and becomes the Dancing Cat. Soft-toned colored pencil drawings illustrate a spirited story.

Unique Beings

Humans with Special Powers

6.306 Ayres, Becky. **Victoria Flies High.** Illustrated by Robin Michal Koontz. Cobblehill Books, 1990. ISBN 0-525-65014-8. 32p. 4–8.

When her kite is destroyed, it looks as though there is no way for Victoria the pig to beat her arch-enemy Arnold in the kite-flying contest. Then Mr. Orsini, the magician, transforms Victoria herself into a kite, and she discovers the value of determination, courage, and a little magic.

6.307 Brittain, Bill. **Wings.** HarperCollins, 1991. ISBN 0-06-020649-7. 137p. 9–12 (est.).

Ian's back wrenches with agonizing pain as strange, tender protuberances grow larger at his shoulder blades. Meanwhile, he is increasingly isolated by family members who desperately seek conformity and acceptance. As in Susan Green's *Self-Portrait with Wings,* the images of sprouting wings are vivid in Bill Brittain's story. Readers not only can sense the strange awkwardness but can vicariously experience the spectacular feat of learning to fly. For Ian, flying is analogous to freeing himself from perceived limitations, both physical and emotional. A strong friendship develops with another class outcast.

6.308 Bursik, Rose. **Amelia's Fantastic Flight.** Illustrated by Rose Bursik. Henry Holt, 1992. ISBN 0-8050-1872-7. 32p. 4–6 (est.).

"Amelia loved airplanes. So she built one." Then "she took it for a little spin"—around the world. For each country Amelia visits, an alliterative phrase describes her reactions ("She got a kick out of Kenya"), while an inset map marks her journey, continent to continent. Each sharp-lined, detailed painting highlights geographical features, archeological sites, or natural history scenes. Then it's back home in time for dinner.

6.309 Carle, Eric. **Draw Me a Star.** Illustrated by Eric Carle. Philomel Books, 1992. ISBN 0-399-1877-7. 32p. 4 and up.

"Draw me a star. And the artist drew a star." Eric Carle's creation-like story begins with a young boy at work painting a five-pointed star. The star, which "was good," asks for the sun, so the artist draws that, too. Rendered in acrylic-splattered layered tissue, each creation asks for another until the aging artist has painted trees, people, animals, insects, and flowers. At last, the moon asks for a star. Having come full circle, the old artist and his star transcend the night sky.

6.310 Clément, Claude. **The Man Who Lit the Stars.** Illustrated by John Howe. Little, Brown, 1992. ISBN 0-316-14741-9. 32p. 6–10 (est.).

"He was a man with no belongings, no family, no hearth to welcome him home, a vagabond from nowhere with no destination." Yet the stranger's mission was worthy. When confronted by hulking, dice-throwing woodcutters, the vagabond explains, "I polish the stars." Intrigued, perhaps half-believing, a homeless ragged child watches the starlighter adjust his long ladder and begin the climb. From this allegorical tale with its silky, Rennaisance-era paintings comes fresh perspective on the streaking comets of a clear night sky.

6.311 Green, Susan. **Self-Portrait with Wings.** Little, Brown, 1989. ISBN 0-316-32677-1. 206p. 10–12 (est.).

Jennifer Rosen, almost twelve, loves to ice skate, but her twirls and leaps and arabesques never quite match those of the natural athlete Penelope, nor even those of the other girls at the rink. To skate to adulation, Jennifer imagines she needs the lift of wings. In a self-portrait she sketches the wings that she needs, and, miraculously, the wings appear. As in *Mail-Order Wings* by Beatrice Gormley, the wings cause both Jennifer and her friend Angela some embarrassments, some duplicity, and some grand adventure.

6.312 Heller, Nicholas. **A Troll Story.** Illustrated by Nicholas Heller. Greenwillow Books, 1990. ISBN 0-688-08971-2. 24p. 3–7 (est.).

Lewis can turn himself into a troll whenever he wants. Of course, his family would never approve, so he only turns himself into a troll late at night. Nicholas Heller's whimsical, lighthearted story allows readers and listeners to try on another personality. Flat, bold patterns are achieved with bright watercolor paints and black ink against stark white backgrounds,

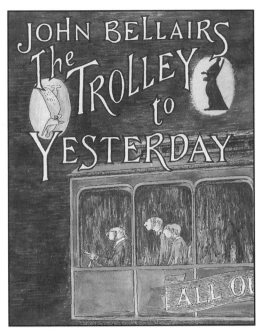

A.

B.

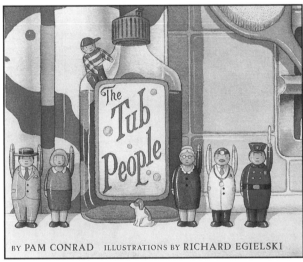

C.

A. *The Trolley to Yesterday* by John Bellairs (see 6.292). **B.** *June 29, 1999* by David Wiesner (see 6.328). **C.** *The Tub People* by Pam Conrad; illustrated by Richard Egielski (see 6.318).

A.

B.

C.

A. *Trouble with Trolls* by Jan Brett (see 6.317).   **B.** *The Dark-Thirty: Southern Tales of the Supernatural* by Patricia C. McKissack; illustrated by Brian Pinkney (see 6.283).
C. *The Rainbabies* by Laura Krauss Melmed; illustrated by Jim LaMarche (see 6.323).

adding childlike simplicity in art to the appealing humor of the story.

6.313 Kehret, Peg. **Sisters, Long Ago.** Cobblehill Books, 1990. ISBN 0-525-65021-0. 149p. 10 and up.

Willow Paige nearly drowns on her thirteenth birthday. Her near-death experience reveals a past life in ancient Egypt as well as special powers. As she struggles to understand these revelations, she tries to use her powers to help heal her sister, Sarah, who suffers from leukemia. Although the loving energy that Willow feels cannot save her sister, she comes to understand the importance of love, joy, and kindness in her own life.

6.314 Rawlins, Donna. **Digging to China.** Illustrated by Donna Rawlins. Orchard Books, 1989. ISBN 0-531-08414-0. 32p. 4–7.

Young Alexis learns a secret from her elderly neighbor Marj, who has learned the secret from *her* mother: if you dig deep enough into the earth, you will find yourself in China. Marj is sure that China is an exotic place, but feels that she is too old to go. So Alexis digs the hole alone to bring Marj a birthday surprise. Donna Rawlins illustrates her friendship story with warmly colored flat drawings bordered like well-framed photographs. A realistic counterpart is *How to Dig a Hole to the Other Side of the World* by Faith McNulty.

6.315 Woodruff, Elvira. **The Wing Shop.** Illustrated by Stephen Gammell. Holiday House, 1991. ISBN 0-8234-0825-6. 32p. 6–10 (est.).

Matthew's new house doesn't suit him as well as the one back on Main Street. If only he could fly, he would go back. A pigeon leads Matthew to Featherman's Wing Shop, where wings of all sizes, shapes, and colors can be taken for test flights. After some faulty starts, Matthew glides over his old house to discover changes. Stephen Gammell's feathery tones and billowy clouds lend just the right imaginative flair to the flight and comfort to the realization that home is wherever you live.

Make-Believe Characters

6.316 Barker, Cicely Mary. **The Fairy Necklaces.** Illustrated by Cicely Mary Barker. Frederick Warne, 1991. ISBN 0-7232-4000-0. 62p. All ages.

The delicate touch of Cicely Mary Barker's watercolor illustrations, most often seen in her once-popular "Flower Fairies" books, sends readers back to a time when fairies and elves used their magic to ease the burdens of poor children. In this tale, young Jenny, a poor country girl, wishes for a necklace for each day of the year. Much to her surprise, the fairies oblige. Now it's up to Jenny and her family to use her newfound riches wisely. This small reprint of Barker's 1946 tale has been faithfully and elegantly produced.

6.317 Brett, Jan. **Trouble with Trolls.** Illustrated by Jan Brett. G. P. Putnam's Sons, 1992. ISBN 0-399-22336-3. 32p. 4–8 (est.).

The trouble with trolls all begins when fearless Treva decides to visit her cousin across Mount Baldy. With her dog Tuffi, she sets off, leaving her chalet far below. Meantime, underground, frolicking trolls make preparations for a dog of their own, gathering collar and water bowl and making a basket bed. At each turn in her path, Treva must rely on her quick wits to meet challenges from these dognapping trolls. As usual, the details in Jan Brett's paintings make re-viewing a mandate.

6.318 Conrad, Pam. **The Tub People.** Illustrated by Richard Egielski. Harper and Row, 1989. ISBN 0-06-021341-X. 29p. 2–8.

For all children who have stared with a combination of wonder and terror at their disappearing bathwater and the swirling drain, this story may introduce a little comfort. Tub Child, one of a family of wooden tub toys, is pulled down the drain and must be rescued by a "big people" plumber. Richard Egielski manages to impart a static life to the rigid figures and a feeling of peaceful resolution.

6.319 Dahl, Roald. **The Minpins.** Illustrated by Patrick Benson. Viking Penguin, 1991. ISBN 0-670-84168-4. 42p. 3–8.

Bored little Billy disobeys his mother's warnings and ventures beyond the garden gate to explore the allegorical Forest of Sin. Chased by a terrible, smoke-blowing, fire-breathing Gruncher, Billy escapes by climbing a tall tree where he discovers the Lilliputian-like Minpins. The giant Billy devises a clever plan to save the Minpins and himself. Published posthumously, the story reflects Roald Dahl's glee in providing delicious scaries for the young and exquisite language for reading aloud. The illustrations contrast size and power and offer magic in perfect strokes.

6.320 Hutchins, Pat. **Silly Billy!** Illustrated by Pat Hutchins. Greenwillow Books, 1992. ISBN 0-688-10818-0. 32p. 3–6 (est.).

A green monster named Hazel has a typical problem: her little brother Billy constantly disrupts her toys and games. "SILLY BILLY! You've spoiled my game!" shouts Hazel each time. Finally, Hazel decides to sleep in the toy box, which Billy naturally wants to do, too. . . . Familiar subject matter, repetitive text, and lively watercolor illustrations of lime green monsters in orange vests and purple dresses make this a book which promises to join its companions, *The Very Worst Monster* and *Where's My Baby?*, as a favorite for young children.

6.321 Kehret, Peg. **Horror at the Haunted House.** Cobblehill Books, 1992. ISBN 0-525-65106-3. 132p. 8 and up (est.).

Near Halloween, Ellen Streater and her brother Corey act in a "haunted house" production to support the renovation of the Clayton mansion. Ellen, always sensitive to the vibrations of others, is visited by the ghost of Lydia Clayton, former mistress of the mansion. The ghost wants Ellen's help in protecting her Wedgwood china collection, but Ellen does not understand why the china is in need of protection. When Ellen decides to investigate, she exposes herself both to danger and to a crime.

6.322 Le Guin, Ursula K. **Fish Soup.** Illustrated by Patrick Wynne. Atheneum, 1992. ISBN 0-689-31733-6. 32p. 6–9 (est.).

The Thinking Man of Moha and the Writing Woman of Maho are best friends, although completely different. When one day the Thinking Man suggests that they need a child to run messages between them, the result is a magical tale of expectations too great and too small, as well as a parable on parenting and friendships. Patrick Wynne's detailed pen-and-ink illustrations are done on creamy paper, inhabited by flying mice and fish and revealing the eccentricities of opposite characteristics in friends.

6.323 Melmed, Laura Krauss. **The Rainbabies.** Illustrated by Jim La-Marche. Lothrop, Lee and Shepard Books, 1992. ISBN 0-688-10756-7. 32p. 6 and up.

The luminous surrealistic illustrations on front and back covers will draw readers into this magical tale of an old couple who have everything in life except the one thing that they want most—a child. Adventures abound after a magic moon shower delivers twelve tiny moonbabies. With a happy ending and folk-tale style, this story will be asked for again and again.

6.324 Nones, Eric Jon. **Wendell.** Illustrated by Eric Jon Nones. Farrar, Straus and Giroux, 1989. ISBN 0-374-38266-2. 32p. 4–8 (est.).

Wendell is a cat who shares his house with his owners and a troop of gnomic mischief-makers. Only Wendell can see the tiny gnomes so he gets blamed for all their deeds—from cracked plates to missing eyeglasses. Even when he is put outdoors, he is blamed for all that goes wrong. Fortunately, Wendell is a good mouser so he redeems himself and sends the gnomes packing. The fun of being "in" on the invisible trouble-makers and Wendell's innocence will appeal to anyone ever falsely accused. Illustrations depict muted 1950s-style home furnishings and characters spread edge to edge. Only the Muppet-like gnomes and Wendell are vivid.

6.325   Peck, Sylvia. **Seal Child.** Illustrated by Robert Andrew Parker. Morrow Junior Books, 1989. ISBN 0-688-08682-9. 200p. 8–12.

Molly is fascinated by the seals on Ambrose Island when her family takes a winter vacation to their Maine cottage. Although her father is a zoologist, it is Ruby, an elderly, full-time island resident, who teaches Molly about seals. After Molly has a deeply moving experience looking into the eyes of an orphaned seal pup, Ruby introduces her to Meara, a pale, odd girl who suddenly and mysteriously appears on the island. The story is inspired by the legends of selkies, seals in human form.

6.326   Steig, William. **Shrek!** Illustrated by William Steig. Farrar, Straus and Giroux/Michael di Capua Books, 1990. ISBN 0-374-36877-5. 28p. 5–10.

Unabashedly proving that beauty is indeed in the eye of the beholder, Shrek the monster, with his fumes, lice, repulsive manners, and occasional nasty temper, pursues his true love, Apple Streudel, "the most stunningly ugly princess on the surface of the planet." Sprinkled with rhyme and elevated with William Steig's lofty language, the tale will appeal more to middle graders and may even send them scrambling for dictionaries. Watercolor and ink illustrations are reminiscent of Steig's *Sylvester and the Magic Pebble.*

6.327   Teague, Mark. **Moog-Moog, Space Barber.** Illustrated by Mark Teague. Scholastic Hardcover Books, 1990. ISBN 0-590-43332-6. 32p. 6–9.

Elmo gets the most embarrassing, terrible haircut—it is so bad that he and his cat, Leon, travel to the wondrous outer-space barber, Moog-Moog, to have his hair fixed. The next day at school it is comforting for Elmo to see his friend Buford also wearing a baseball hat to cover his haircut (and for the same reason). Amicable space monsters and exhilarating full-color illustrations round out the story.

6.328 Wiesner, David. **June 29, 1999.** Illustrated by David Wiesner. Clarion Books, 1992. ISBN 0-395-59762-5. 32p. 6–12 (est.).

Holly Ever's science experiment is extraordinary indeed for a child of her age in 1999. To measure the effect of the ionosphere on plant growth, Holly uses weather balloons to launch her seedling cups. Not since Judith Barrett's *Cloudy with a Chance of Meatballs* has such giant food fallen from the sky. But are these vegetables really Holly's experiment gone awry? The fantasy is enhanced by the realism of the landing sites, the perspective shifts, and the incredulity of the observers—both earthbound and extraterrestrial.

Fine Arts

Art is universal.
The barriers of
language,
time,
and culture
crumble in a moment of looking.

Jan Greenberg and
Sandra Jordan
The Painter's Eye:
Learning to Look at
Contemporary American Art

7 Fine Arts

Performing Arts

7.1 Fonteyn, Margot, reteller. **Swan Lake.** Illustrated by Trina Schart Hyman. Harcourt Brace Jovanovich/Gulliver Books, 1989. ISBN 0-15-200600-1. 32p. All ages. Fiction.

Margot Fonteyn retells the story of Tchaikovsky's classic ballet as a fairy tale. Prince Siegfried's love for the swan queen, Odette, promises to break the spell that keeps her imprisoned as a bird. But tricked by the wizard, Siegfried pledges his true love to the disguised Odile, the wizard's daughter, and dooms his true love through his innocent act of betrayal. Despairing, Siegfried follows Odette in death. Trina Schart Hyman's acrylic and pastel paintings, edged with thin ink lines, are alternately romantic, threatening, and moon-splashed.

7.2 Greaves, Margaret, reteller. **The Magic Flute: The Story of Mozart's Opera.** Illustrated by Francesca Crespi. Henry Holt, 1989. ISBN 0-8050-0887-X. 32p. 5–8 (est.). Fiction.

The story of Prince Tamino and his rescue of the beautiful Princess Pamina is retold with rounded, childlike figures in Oriental costumes, and set against stage flats or, alternately, against plain white pages, each bordered and illuminated. The action of Mozart's last opera follows both Tamino and his magic flute, as well as the bird catcher, Papageno, with his magic bells. Scenes are posed to represent their drama, while Papageno's cavorting provides relief.

7.3 Haskins, James. **Black Dance in America: A History through Its People.** Thomas Y. Crowell, 1990. ISBN 0-690-04659-6. 232p. 12 and up. Nonfiction.

From jazz dancing to break dancing, many of the dances of today descended from African dances that have been performed for hundreds of years. This exploration of the evolution of black dance in America includes insightful stories of the lives of some of America's most famous African American dancers, such as Bill "Bojangles" Robinson and Michael Jackson. Filled with fascinating black-and-white photographs of African American dancers at work, this book offers a unique perspective on the

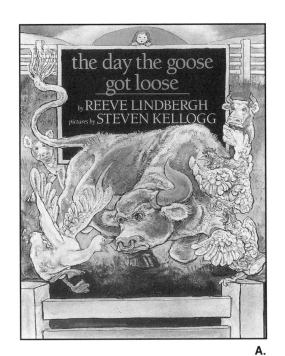

A.

B.

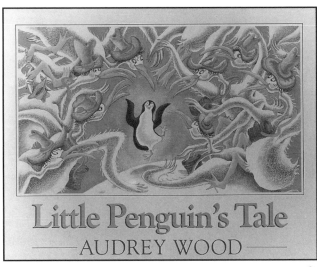

C.

A. *The Day the Goose Got Loose* by Reeve Lindbergh; illustrated by Steven Kellogg (see 6.87). **B.** *The Frog Prince Continued* story by Jon Scieszka; illustrations by Steve Johnson (see 6.187). **C.** *Little Penguin's Tale* by Audrey Wood (see 6.161).

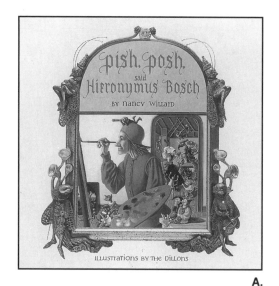

A.

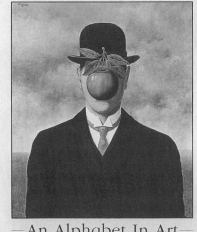

B.

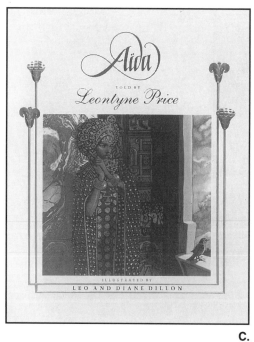

C.

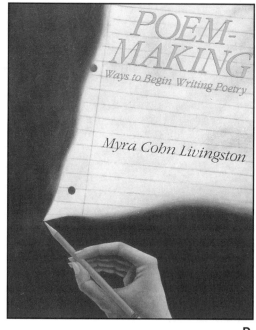

D.

A. *Pish, Posh, said Hieronymus Bosch* by Nancy Willard; illustrated by Diane Dillon and Leo Dillon (see 7.18). **B.** *I Spy: An Alphabet in Art* devised and selected by Lucy Micklethwait (see 7.14). **C.** *Aïda* told by Leontyne Price; illustrated by Leo Dillon and Diane Dillon (see 7.5). **D.** *Poem-Making: Ways to Begin Writing Poetry* by Myra Cohn Livingston (see 10.110).

roots of modern dance. *Coretta Scott King Honor Book (Writing), 1991.*

7.4 Isadora, Rachel, adapter. **Swan Lake.** Illustrated by Rachel Isadora. G. P. Putnam's Sons, 1991. ISBN 0-399-21730-4. 32p. 6–12 (est.). Fiction.

Rachel Isadora's adaptation of the transformation tale that is portrayed in Tchaikovsky's classical ballet about the prince who falls in love with the swan queen sets light-bathed ballerinas against watercolor-washed backdrops. Impressionistic scenes vary from murky, swirling night skies to airy onion-dome scenes. The illustrations beg for the music. Children may also enjoy comparing Isadora's dancers with those created by Chris Van Allsburg for Mark Helprin's version of *Swan Lake* or with Trina Schart Hyman's illustrations for Margot Fonteyn's version.

7.5 Price, Leontyne, reteller. **Aïda.** Illustrated by Leo and Diane Dillon. Harcourt Brace Jovanovich/Gulliver Books, 1990. ISBN 0-15-200405-X. 32p. 8 and up (est.). Fiction.

When her homeland is invaded, Princess Aïda of Ethiopia is captured and enslaved to the Egyptian Princess Amneris. When Aïda falls in love with Radames, a captain in Egypt's great army, she must choose between her love for country and her Egyptian captain. In this retelling by soprano Leontyne Price, Verdi's tragic opera is brought to life with rich prose and magnificent artwork. The Dillons' exquisite marbleized paintings, enriched with Egyptian architecture and gold-sculptured borders, help to dramatize the conflicts of courage and honor. *ALA Notable Children's Books, 1991; Coretta Scott King Award (Illustration), 1991.*

7.6 San Souci, Robert, reteller. **The Firebird.** Illustrated by Kris Waldherr. Dial Books for Young Readers, 1992. ISBN 0-8037-0800-9. 32p. 4–8. Fiction.

Robert San Souci retells the tale of Prince Ivan's love for the beautiful Princess Elena and his efforts to save her from her captor, an evil wizard. Using a magical talisman—a feather from a grateful Firebird whom Prince Ivan has set free—the prince and princess undertake a series of trials to bring about the wizard's demise. Oil paintings, applied over golden acrylic, offer stylized medieval landscapes and castle scenes in this adaptation of Stravinsky's ballet.

7.7 Verdy, Violette. **Of Swans, Sugarplums and Satin Slippers: Ballet Stories for Children.** Illustrated by Marcia Brown. Scholastic Hardcover Books, 1991. ISBN 0-590-43484-5. 80p. 7–11. Fiction.

Violette Verdy, a principal ballerina for the New York City Ballet between 1958 and 1976, tells the stories of six ballets, *The Firebird, Coppelia, Swan Lake, The Nutcracker, Giselle,* and *Sleeping Beauty.* Each story begins with background information on the ballet, including Verdy's response to her own role in the ballet. Some of Marcia Brown's full-page paintings of the sets are painted in a folk-art style, bright and flat; however, the Wilis of Giselle and the Sugar Plum Fairy are diaphanous images.

7.8 Werner, Vivian, reteller. **Petrouchka: The Story of the Ballet.** Illustrated by John Collier. Viking Penguin/Bryon Preiss Books, 1992. ISBN 0-670-83607-9. 32p. 8 and up (est.). Fiction.

Vivian Werner gently tells the story of Stravinsky's ballet about Petrouchka, the clown-puppet with a heart, who yearns for his freedom from the Old Magician so that he can both dance freely and love the beautiful Ballerina. Like Tomi dePaola's *Clown of God,* Petrouchka is transformed in the final tragic scene, freed at last to dance and to catch snowflakes on his tongue. John Collier's pastel and gouache illustrations forebode tragedy, even when the text describes festivity and color.

Visual Arts

7.9 Cummings, Pat, compiler and editor. **Talking with Artists: Conversations with Victoria Chess, Pat Cummings, Leo and Diane Dillon, Richard Egielski, Lois Ehlert, Lisa Campbell Ernst, Tom Feelings, Steven Kellogg, Jerry Pinkney, Amy Schwartz, Lane Smith, Chris Van Allsburg, and David Wiesner.** Bradbury Press, 1992. ISBN 0-02-724245-5. 96p. 9 and up. Nonfiction.

Preceding "conversations" with fourteen prominent, contemporary American illustrators of books for children is a page addressed "Dear Reader," intended to enlighten and inspire budding artists. Each artist profile features the artist's signature, photographs of the artist as child and adult, an autobiographical sketch, answers to eight standard questions frequently asked by children, and full-color reproductions of sample artwork. Concluding is a glossary and a booklist composed of the artists' five favorite books that they have illustrated. *Boston Globe–Horn Book Nonfiction Award, 1992.*

7.10 Day, David. **Aska's Animals.** Illustrated by Warabé Aska. Doubleday Books for Young Readers, 1991. ISBN 0-385-25315-X. 32p. All ages. Nonfiction.

Imagining the beginnings of animals from around the world—kangaroo, polar bear, musk ox, camel—Canadian artist Warabé Aska created fourteen oil paintings as intriguing to adult as to child. Each is large, brilliantly colored, and unique for its realistic depiction of groups of animals which, through subtle gradations, come to blend seamlessly into the landscape. For example, lifelike deer that were once "tree spirits" bound in a marshy foreground, and appear as a forest of antlers in the background. David Day's interpretive poems keep readers in the spell.

7.11 Garza, Carmen Lomas, as told to Harriet Rohmer (translated by Rosalma Zubizarreta). **Family Pictures/Cuadros de familia.** Illustrated by Carmen Lomas Garza. Children's Book Press, 1990. ISBN 0-89239-050-6. 32p. 4–8 (est.). Nonfiction.

Carmen Lomas Garza is a folk artist who painted more than a dozen pictures of her memories of growing up in a Texas border town. She was then interviewed to create the text which appears first in English, then in Spanish. Oils, acrylics, gouache, and paper cutouts are her media for depicting a trip to the fair, harvesting oranges, hitting a piñata at a birthday party, making tamales, and other important scenes of childhood. *ALA Notable Children's Books, 1990.*

7.12 Greenberg, Jan, and Sandra Jordan. **The Painter's Eye: Learning to Look at Contemporary American Art.** Delacorte Press, 1991. ISBN 0-385-30319-X. 96p. 10 and up. Nonfiction.

"*The Painter's Eye* provides the necessary tools for young readers to begin a lifetime appreciation of paintings and the work that painters do—as well as the magic they create." It fully achieves those objectives through conversations with the artists themselves, reproductions of postwar American paintings, photographs of the artists at work, interviews and quotes, an art glossary, museum lists, a bibliography, an index, and a readable, informative text.

7.13 Lattimore, Deborah Nourse. **The Sailor Who Captured the Sea: A Story of the Book of Kells.** Illustrated by Deborah Nourse Lattimore. HarperCollins, 1991. ISBN 0-06-023711-2. 30p. 7–10. Fiction.

Three Irish brothers find out, in turn, that circumstances call forth their hidden creativity. In the end, their creative struggle saves their monastery home. This fictive account of the making of the magnificent Book of Kells personalizes distant historical achievements; its theme concerns the individual's struggle to find fulfilling work. The compelling watercolor illustrations are lightly washed to simulate the look of ancient parchment, and each page is bordered with intricate designs reminiscent of manuscripts sumptuously illustrated by monks of old. *Notable 1991 Children's Trade Books in the Field of Social Studies.*

7.14   Micklethwait, Lucy. **I Spy: An Alphabet in Art.** Greenwillow Books, 1992. ISBN 0-688-116779-5. 64p. All ages. Nonfiction.

In this alphabet "I Spy" game, Lucy Micklethwait presents twenty-six well-known paintings and invites their close inspection. On one page, simple text announces: "I spy / with my little eye / something beginning with [a letter name]"; on the facing page is a beautifully reproduced print. Finding a "B" object is as simple as finding the ball in Henri Rousseau's *Football Players.* Among the other artists whose works are represented are Vermeer, Miró, Renoir, Chagall, Seurat, Matisse, Goya, Steen, Boticelli, and Picasso.

7.15   National Gallery of Canada and Anne Newlands. **Meet Edgar Degas.** J. B. Lippincott, 1989. ISBN 0-397-32369-7. 30p. 6 and up (est.). Nonfiction.

Letters, notebooks, and other archival records make possible a first-person narrative in which Edgar Degas leads readers on a tour through a gallery of his paintings, stopping before each to describe what it represents, his reasons for choosing the subject, and the technique that he has employed. Beautifully reproduced on quality paper, the paintings make a delightful introduction to Degas. Throughout the book the artist's times, attitudes, abilities, and interests are revealed.

7.16   Peppin, Anthea. **Nature in Art. People in Art. Places in Art.** Williams, Helen. **Stories in Art.** Millbrook Press, 1991–92. 48p. 7–12. Nonfiction.

Four companion volumes on people, places, nature, and stories in the visual arts reach over time and place to spell out how primitive and studied techniques combine with creativity to capture the magic of art. Not only does the large-format, full-color, profusely illustrated design of the Millbrook Arts Library introduce artists throughout history, but the specific questions and instructions help readers to think about art and to become involved in artistic experiences.

7.17 Roalf, Peggy. **Families: Looking at Paintings. Horses: Looking at Paintings. Landscapes: Looking at Paintings. Seascapes: Looking at Paintings.** Hyperion Books for Children, 1992. 48p. 8–12. Nonfiction.

Created to "inspire young readers to observe their world and to use their imaginations to see like a painter," these four paper-bound volumes in the Jacques Lowe Visual Arts Projects series, complete with glossary and index, demonstrate that great artists have viewed the same subject in varied ways. Double-page spreads feature an individual painting, with a color photograph on the right and text discussing period, artist, and artistic technique on the left.

7.18 Willard, Nancy. **Pish, Posh, Said Hieronymus Bosch.** Illustrated by the Dillons. Harcourt Brace Jovanovich, 1991. ISBN 0-15-262210-1. 32p. All ages (est.). Fiction.

In elegant, whimsical, and accessible verse, Nancy Willard tells of a housekeeper working for the famous Flemish painter Hieronymus Bosch. But the bizarre creatures of Bosch's paintings—including pickle-winged fish, three-legged thistles, and human drainpipes—give her no rest. Magnificent illustrations by Leo, Diane, and Lee Dillon include full-color paintings and monochrome line drawings in imitative homage to the classical painter. Readers of Willard's other books—such as *A Visit to William Blake's Inn*—as well as new readers will be thrilled with this masterpiece.

7.19 Yenawine, Philip. **Color. Lines. Shapes. Stories.** Museum of Modern Art and Delacorte Press, 1991. 22p. 4-8. Nonfiction.

The Art Books for Children series presents basic artistic concepts and vocabulary to young children through the use of full-color reproductions of works from the collections of the Museum of Modern Art in New York. Questions on each page invite readers to look closely at works of art. Each book ends with a two-page synopsis of the art presented, including the artist, the title, the media used, and a brief description.

Historical Fiction

The man without a past is fiction; even willful ignorance cannot erase our history. Only in eternal night will man be shadowless, and the past not follow the present into the future. . . . Knowledge of the past—of history—gives perspective to our world.

Erik Christian Haugaard, *The Rider and His Horse*

8 Historical Fiction

Prehistoric Times

8.1   Nolan, Dennis. **Wolf Child.** Illustrated by Dennis Nolan. Macmillan, 1989. ISBN 0-02-768141-6. 40p. 7–10 (est.).

Nine-year-old Teo lived 18,000 years ago when humans first used animals for companions. Though ill and weak, the boy experiences love through the friendship of an orphaned wolf cub and pride through his talent, learned as an apprentice, of crafting stone tools. Photorealistic watercolor paintings are remarkable in their detail and feeling. *Notable 1989 Children's Trade Books in the Field of Social Studies.*

Medieval Times

8.2   Dana, Barbara. **Young Joan.** HarperCollins/Charlotte Zolotow Books, 1991. ISBN 0-06-021423-6. 371p. 10–13 (est.).

Born in France during the Hundred Years' War, young Joan of Arc lives a simple life, surrounded by her loving family. But she soon discovers that her future involves the fulfillment of an old prophecy that tells of a young maiden who saves France. Guided by the voices of saints and strengthened by her faith in God, Joan faces danger and eventual death in her struggle to save her country in its battle with England. This fascinating novel describes how a French heroine grows to understand and fulfill her destiny.

Fifteenth and Sixteenth Centuries

8.3   Conrad, Pam. **Pedro's Journal: A Voyage with Christopher Columbus, August 3, 1492–February 14, 1493.** Illustrated by Peter Koeppen. Boyds Mills Press/Caroline House, 1991. ISBN 1-878093-17-7. 84p. 7–10 (est.).

Pedro de Salcedo was a cabin boy on the *Santa Maria,* not because he liked the sea or because he had nautical skills, but because he could read and write. At the captain's behest, Pedro kept a journal with dated entries which included not only descriptions of the events during Columbus's first trans-Atlantic voyage but also sketches of the sights. Pam Conrad's storytelling and Peter Koeppen's black-and-white line drawings are based on the best guesses of historians about events and sights on the journey.

8.4   Dorris, Michael. **Morning Girl.** Hyperion Books for Children, 1992. ISBN 1-56282-285-3. 74p. 8 and up.

In alternating chapters and from differing perspectives, twelve-year-old Morning Girl, who loves the day, and her younger brother, Star Boy, who loves the night, share imagery-filled incidents from everyday Taino life. The year is 1492. Crises like a tropical storm and their mother's miscarriage are surmounted. All is well on their Caribbean island until the closing pages when Morning Girl goes for a swim and encounters a canoeful of "visitors." The book ends with a disturbing passage from Columbus's diary. *Scott O'Dell Award for Historical Fiction, 1993.*

8.5   Foreman, Michael, and Richard Seaver. **The Boy Who Sailed with Columbus.** Illustrated by Michael Foreman. Little, Brown/Arcade, 1992 . ISBN 1-55970-178-1. 71p. 8–13 (est.).

The log of Christopher Columbus documents the wreck of one of his ships on Christmas Day, 1492, when a ship's boy, left in charge, fell asleep. In this fictionalized picture book in impressionistic watercolor, the full story of Leif, the ship's boy, is spun out—from his signing on through the historic voyage to the days and years after the voyage. Left behind by Columbus, Leif is captured by a native tribe and apprenticed to the tribal medicine man. Years later, fully acculturated and a grandfather, he once again sees European sailors, and in a telling gesture, he packs up his family and moves westward.

8.6   Locker, Thomas. **The Land of Gray Wolf.** Illustrated by Thomas Locker. Dial Books, 1991. ISBN 0-8037-0937-4. 32p. All ages.

Thomas Locker illustrates this account of contact between Europeans and Eastern Native Americans with oil paintings in a semi-primitive, sweeping style that evokes the luminous, open spaces of unsettled North America. Running Deer, an Indian boy, is approaching adulthood at a time when his tribe's very existence is threatened by the coming of the whites. In a straightforward style, the narrative presents the various problems that tribal Americans faced and leaves the reader with a mixed hope for a return to this natural way of life. *Notable 1991 Children's Trade Books in the Field of Social Studies.*

8.7   Smith, Barry. **The First Voyage of Christopher Columbus, 1492.**
Illustrated by Barry Smith. Viking Penguin, 1992. ISBN 0-670-
84051-3. 30p. 4–8 (est.).

A young sailor in need of a job signs on, unknowingly, with
Christopher Columbus. Simple text tells the sailor's version of
the voyage and safe return. In addition, map details on each
page allow readers to locate the ships' positions en route, while
a fold-out map at the back of the book tracks the entire voyage.
Bordered watercolors give a sense of the action and attitudes,
including strident gray waves and both Columbus and his sailor
with upside-down smiles.

8.8   Stolz, Mary. **Bartholomew Fair.** Greenwillow Books/Beech Tree
Books, 1990. ISBN 0-688-11501-2. 160p. 11 and up (est.).

Mary Stolz takes readers along to the "clamor and clatter and
color and confusion" of London's Bartholomew Fair in 1597.
Action follows six characters' ventures to the fair—two school-
boys of opposite social standing, a maligned apprentice, a
wealthy cloth merchant, a vegetable washer from the queen's
kitchens, and Queen Elizabeth herself. Each brings expectations,
all come together in logical ways, and each leaves with some
satisfaction. Stolz's text is beautifully crafted yet challenging,
with terms and speech reflective of the historical period.

8.9   Ventura, Piero. **1492: The Year of the New World.** Illustrated by
Piero Ventura. G. P. Putnam's Sons, 1992. ISBN 0-399-22332-0.
93p. All ages.

Piero Ventura provides "an imaginary journey through the
Europe of 1492" and a chance to sail with Columbus himself.
The time-frame is given social perspective by an imaginary citizen of each old-world country, while detailed sketches and maps
help to interpret the history and geography of the regions. Readers are also introduced to the civilizations of the New World—
the Tainos, Aztecs, Maya, Incas, and Buffalo Hunters. Succinct
concluding sections address "Europe After Columbus" and the
effect of the voyages on Native Americans.

8.10   Yolen, Jane. **Encounter.** Illustrated by David Shannon. Harcourt
Brace Jovanovich, 1992. ISBN 0-15-225962-7. 32p. 6–12.

A threatening dream of three great-winged birds with voices like
thunder disturbs the sleep of a child of the Taino tribe on the
island of San Salvador. From his wary perspective, the boy tells
in cadence-like speech of the arrival of "three great sailing ca-

noes" of Christopher Columbus: "We did not know them as human beings, for they hid their bodies in colors, like parrots." Despite the child's warnings, the tribe offers welcome, feasts, and gifts, and in return receives beads, bells, and extinction. Acrylic paintings, jungle-lush and eloquent, are based on written descriptions.

Seventeenth and Eighteenth Centuries

United States

8.11   Cooney, Barbara. **Island Boy.** Illustrated by Barbara Cooney. Viking Kestrel, 1988. ISBN 0-670-81749-X. 32p. 4–8 (est.).

Matthais's pa built the first house on Tibbets Island, and for the rest of his long life, Matthais would find himself coming back to that island again and again. This charming tale of a child's growth into a father (and a grandfather) is enhanced by colorful paintings in the tradition of old-world artists, paintings that reflect a time when life in New England was dedicated to family, community, and the land. Spanning Matthais's entire life, this book recalls a forgotten way of life. *Boston Globe–Horn Book Honor Book, 1989.*

8.12   Fleischman, Paul. **Saturnalia.** HarperKeypoint/Charlotte Zolotow Books, 1992. ISBN 0-06-021913-0. 112p. 10–12 (est.).

In 1681, the working populace of Boston is composed of masters and servants, journeymen and apprentices, shopkeepers and tithingmen. Paul Fleischman weaves their lives together through the story of William, a fourteen-year-old Narragansett Indian who has been apprenticed for six years to kindly Mr. Currie, the printer, after his tribe was slaughtered by the English. Although he has come to accept his new family, William does not repress his longing for the old. Each night, he slips through Boston's streets, playing his bone flute, desperately searching for his twin brother and his past. *Boston Globe–Horn Book Honor Book, 1990.*

8.13   Harness, Cheryl. **Three Young Pilgrims.** Illustrated by Cheryl Harness. Bradbury Press, 1992. ISBN 0-02-74643-2. 32p. 5–10.

Cheryl Harness tells the fictionalized tale of the Allerton family and their children, Mary, Remember, and Bartholomew, whose travels and travails were representative of other *Mayflower* Pilgrims who sailed for a new land. Although an author's note denies that the book is intended as a scholarly work, the water-color, gouache, and pencil illustrations inform through labeled maps, cutaways, time-lines, and both panoramic and detailed views of the family's struggles, leading to the first Thanksgiving.

8.14   Hudson, Jan. **Dawn Rider.** Philomel Books, 1990. ISBN 0-399-22178-6. 170p. 10 and up.

In syntax echoing the spirit of the Blackfoot, Jan Hudson tells the story of sixteen-year-old Kit Fox, who questions the values and traditions of her tribe, but who must nevertheless adhere to them. Women are not to hunt, yet Kit yearns to develop those skills. Only men may ride horses, yet Kit, with the help of her cousin Found Arrow, tames a wild stallion. These new abilities are tested when Kit must save her Blackfoot tribe from a raid by their traditional enemy, the Snakes.

8.15   Keehn, Sally M. **I Am Regina.** Philomel Books, 1991. ISBN 0-399-21797-5. 240p. 10 and up.

Regina, a ten-year-old Pennsylvania girl, is kidnapped by Native Americans in 1755 and is forced to live as a member of their tribe. Based on a true story, the novel realistically portrays both the cruelty and compassion that Regina experiences during her nine years of captivity. When the French and Indian War ceases and Regina is ultimately reunited with her mother, this mature, indomitable young woman empathizes with the victims of both sides of the war.

8.16   Luhrmann, Winifred Bruce. **Only Brave Tomorrows.** Houghton Mifflin, 1989. ISBN 0-395-47983-5. 190p. 10 and up.

Leaving her comfortable life in England behind, Faith Ralston comes to Massachusetts with her father to make a new home in the colonies. When she is left alone after surviving an Indian massacre, Faith's struggles lead to a discovery of her own strengths and her future. Set during King Philip's War in the late 1600s, this poignant story chronicles a young girl's efforts to find and establish her own place in the world.

8.17   Rinaldi, Ann. **A Break with Charity: A Story about the Salem Witch Trials.** Harcourt Brace Jovanovich/Gulliver Books, 1992. ISBN 0-15-200353-3. 256p. 10 and up.

Told in flashback, Ann Rinaldi's historically accurate novel re-counts the hysteria and terror surrounding the Salem witch tri-als of 1692. Fourteen-year-old Susanna English learns that ringleader Ann Putnam is faking her "bewitched" state. But if Susanna reveals Putnam's dissembling, she fears that her own family will assuredly be accused of witchcraft and condemned to death. Ultimately, the young teen's honesty and courage are rewarded.

8.18 Turner, Ann. **Katie's Trunk.** Illustrated by Ron Himler. Macmillan, 1992. ISBN 0-02-789512-2. 32p. 6–10 (est.).

Katie's Trunk is based on a true incident in the life of one of the author's ancestors at the beginning of the American Revolution. Young Katie and her Tory family flee to the woods when a group of colonists threatens their home. At the last minute, though, Katie boldly returns to protect their property. Realizing the futility of her resistance, she climbs into a trunk filled with clothing, and there discovers that goodness exists even in conflict. Watercolor paintings set graceful period scenes.

World

8.19 Garfield, Leon. **Young Nick and Jubilee.** Illustrated by Ted Lewin. Delacorte Press, 1989. ISBN 0-385-29777-7. 135p. 10 and up (est.).

Leon Garfield, award-winning British author of juvenile historical fiction, once again sets his tale in eighteenth-century London. Ten-year-old Nick and his younger sister, orphaned and destitute, hope to attend the city's charity school. Needing a "father" to sponsor them, they persuade Mr. Owen, bachelor and pickpocket extraordinaire, to perform the role. Thus begin the trio's adventures as a family. Ted Lewin's black-and-white illustrations provide readers with additional information about English life in the 1700s.

8.20 O'Dell, Scott. **My Name Is Not Angelica.** Dell/Yearling Books, 1990. ISBN 0-440-40379-0. 130p. 8–12.

In Scott O'Dell's tragic last novel, sixteen-year-old Raisha and her betrothed, Konje, an African tribal chief, are captured and sold into slavery by members of a neighboring village. Descriptive, fast-paced prose follows their arduous voyage on a stifling slave ship to the West Indies of 1733. On St. Johns, Konje escapes, becoming the leader of a band of runaway slaves who communicate with talking drums to plan revolt. Beautiful Raisha, called Angelica by her planter-owner, knows her fate still lies with Konje.

Nineteenth Century

United States

8.21   Avi. **The Man Who Was Poe.** Orchard Books, 1989. ISBN 0-531-08433-7. 208p. 11 and up.

When Edmund and his sister are seemingly abandoned in a strange hotel room in nineteenth-century Rhode Island, Edmund must finally disobey his aunt and leave to get food. But he returns to find that his sister has disappeared! This ghostly tale relates Edmund's search to unravel the mystery of his family's disappearance, aided by the reluctantly helpful Auguste Dupin (a.k.a. Edgar Allan Poe). Since fragments of the real Poe's personality and tragic life are interwoven into the plot, the book would enhance a literature unit on mysteries.

8.22   Beatty, Patricia. **Sarah and Me and the Lady from the Sea.** Morrow Junior Books, 1989. ISBN 0-688-08045-6. 182p. 9–12 (est.).

The Flood of 1894 bankrupts twelve-year-old Marcella Abbott's family. They are forced to sell their Portland, Oregon, home and to live year-round in their summer home on the coast of Washington. Their pampered and privileged world is gone, and Marcy has trouble adjusting to a new lifestyle. Through a shared loss and a mysterious woman, Marcy becomes friends with Sarah Kimball, whom Patricia Beatty's readers first met in *The Nickel-Plated Beauty*. Marcy and Sarah share presents, confidences, and the discovery of the identity of the lady from the sea—a shipwrecked Russian. Beatty offers another lively characterization in this suspenseful tale.

8.23   Beatty, Patricia. **Who Comes with Cannons?** Morrow Junior Books, 1992. ISBN 0-688-11028-2. 186p. 10 and up (est.).

Orphaned Tabitha Ruth (Truth) moves from Indiana to live with her Quaker relatives in North Carolina. At the dawn of the Civil War, Truth becomes part of her aunt and uncle's Underground Railroad station, sending slaves northward. Shy and uncertain of her place within her new family, Truth gains courage as story events unfold. Threats to her pacifist family from slaveholders and from the encroaching battlefront require courage. She must even petition Mrs. Lincoln to gain her cousin's freedom from a Yankee prison.

A.

B.

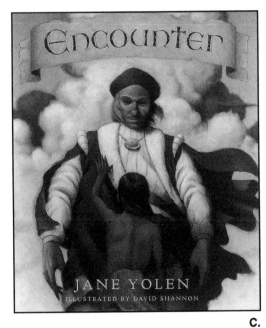

C.

A. *Morning Girl* by Michael Dorris (see 8.4).   **B.** *Young Joan* by Barbara Dana (see 8.2).   **C.** *Encounter* by Jane Yolen; illustrated by David Shannon (see 8.10).

A.

B.

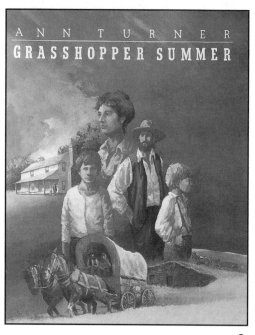

C.

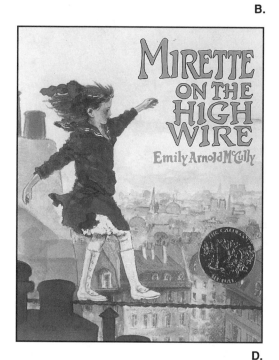

D.

A. *Three Young Pilgrims* by Cheryl Harness (see 8.13). **B.** *Katie's Trunk* by Ann Turner; illustrated by Ron Himler (see 8.18). **C.** *Grasshopper Summer* by Ann Turner (see 8.43). **D.** *Mirette on the High Wire* by Emily Arnold McCully (see 8.52).

8.24 Beatty, Patricia, and Phillip Robbins. **Eben Tyne, Powder-monkey.** Morrow Junior Books, 1990. ISBN 0-688-08884-8. 227p. 9–13 (est.).

Eben Tyne, almost fourteen, is separated from family and friends when he is selected to be a powdermonkey (the boy who scurries to the ship's hold and back to refill the powder supply for the cannons) on the crew of the *Merrimack,* renamed the *Virginia* by the Confederates during the Civil War. Through the ship's preparation and then a furious, smoking, clanging battle, Eben learns about loyalty and strength of purpose. The historical novel is so rampant with detail that diagrams and maps will be a necessary supplement.

8.25 Conrad, Pam. **My Daniel.** Harper and Row, 1989. ISBN 0-06-021314-0. 137p. 10 and up.

Julia Creath Summerwaite sits at last in the natural history museum looking at the dinosaur bones that her brother found long ago when they were children. The story that she begins to tell her grandchildren is of the harshness of her Nebraska childhood, and how young Daniel Creath discovered the bones in the river and lost his life trying to protect his find from dinosaur grave robbers. The plot moves between the present day and the memories of her brother's sacrifice. *Notable 1989 Children's Trade Books in the Field of Social Studies.*

8.26 Fleischman, Sid. **Jim Ugly.** Illustrated by Jos. A. Smith. Greenwillow Books, 1992. ISBN 0-688-10886-5. 144p. 8 and up.

Jim Ugly is a very loyal but very ornery dog who is part mongrel and part wolf. He belongs to an actor in the days of the California gold rush, and the owner's possession of forty pounds of diamonds gets him "buried." But is he really dead? His son, twelve-year-old Jake, and an irascible bounty hunter think not. Their race to find him, with Jim Ugly's sense of smell as Jake's only guide, takes the pair on a journey from Nevada to California and introduces a troupe of characters that enlivens the route.

8.27 Harvey, Brett. **My Prairie Christmas.** Illustrated by Deborah Kogan Ray. Holiday House, 1990. ISBN 0-8234-0827-2. 29p. 5–8.

This is the Plaisted family's first Christmas season on the prairie, away from their beloved Maine. When Christmas day arrives, Papa, caught in a blizzard, still has not returned home. But Mama, in true pioneer fashion, helps the children keep their hopes and Christmas spirit alive. Papa finally arrives, bearing a "goodie-filled" barrel from Maine. Earth-tone sketches capture the times and spirit of frontier America and help to set the tone of a heartwarming story of family and the true meaning of Christmas. *Notable 1990 Children's Trade Books in the Field of Social Studies.*

8.28   Holland, Isabelle. **The Journey Home.** Scholastic Hardcover Books, 1990. ISBN 0-590-43110-2. 192p. 8–12.

When their mother dies, sisters Maggie and Annie are sent west on the orphan train to be adopted by a pioneer family. Taken in by the Russells, the two girls struggle to make a new life, overcoming religious prejudice, illiteracy, and the fear of losing one another. Set in the late 1800s, this story of two Irish Catholic sisters' journey to find a new home captures the spirit of new beginnings.

8.29   Hoobler, Dorothy, Thomas Hoobler, and Carey-Greenberg Associates. **A Promise at the Alamo: The Story of a Texas Girl.** Illustrated by Jennifer Hewitson. Silver Burdett Press, 1992. ISBN 0-382-24147-9. 64p. 9–12.

As Santa Anna's troops gather outside the walls of the Alamo, Maria and her family prepare to defend the newly forming Republic of Texas. Set in 1836, this story of a girl's courage and determination to keep a promise brings to life the heroic battle of the Alamo. This book both recounts an important event and celebrates the Hispanic culture.

8.30   Hooks, William H. **The Ballad of Belle Dorcas.** Illustrated by Brian Pinkney. Alfred A. Knopf/Borzoi Books, 1990. ISBN 0-394-84645-1. 32p. 6–10 (est.).

In this conjure tale from North Carolina, the beautiful Belle Dorcas gives up her freedom to marry her true love, the slave Joshua. When the master forces them to be apart, Belle seeks a powerful spell from Granny Lizard, the conjurer. Brian Pinkney's colorful, etching-like illustrations highlight this haunting love story.

8.31   Karr, Kathleen. **It Ain't Always Easy.** Farrar, Straus and Giroux, 1990. ISBN 0-374-33645-8. 229p. 10 and up (est.).

Plucky orphans, eleven-year-old Jack and eight-year-old Mandy, travel from New York City to the Pennsylvania countryside in 1882, looking for love and a family. Eventually they find both, with help from Miss Blackman of the Children's Aid Society and a burly Nebraska rancher named Redbeard. With crisp dialogue and effective characterization, Kathleen Karr has produced an engrossing story of survival in a society which neglects and even abuses its homeless children, reminiscent of (but superior to) the "rags-to-respectability" novels of Horatio Alger, Jr.

8.32   Kimmel, Eric A. **Four Dollars and Fifty Cents.** Illustrated by Glen Rounds. Holiday House, 1990. ISBN 0-8234-0817-5. 32p. 6–10 (est.).

Here's a tale for reading aloud both for its cowboy lingo and its surprise ending. Although "it's a terrible thing to call a cowboy a deadbeat, . . . in Shorty Long's case it was true." Shorty owed Widow Macrae a walloping four dollars and fifty cents, and she was determined to collect—even if she had to "lay him out flatter 'n the bottom of a skillet." To escape his creditor, Shorty fakes his death, and the widow kindly offers to bury him. Line-and-crayon drawings are trail dust-spewing images of an unkempt West.

8.33   Levin, Betty. **Brother Moose.** Greenwillow Books, 1990. ISBN 0-688-09266-7. 210p. 10 and up (est.).

Nell and Louisa, two orphan girls being delivered to separate families in Canada in the late 1800s, have their plans disrupted. First Nell's prospective family suddenly leaves for Maine without her. Then Nell rescues Louisa from the abusive home in which she's been placed. Together they head for Maine to find Nell's new family. With Indian Joe and his grandson, the girls encounter blizzards, illness, a train wreck, and a friendly moose before reaching their new home.

8.34   Lyon, George Ella. **Cecil's Story.** Illustrated by Peter Catalanotto. Orchard Books, 1991. ISBN 0-531-08512-0. 32p. 4–8 (est.).

With great poignancy, a child's concerns and imaginings merge during the Civil War: "If your papa went off to war, / he might get hurt / and your mama might go to fetch him." As he stays with the neighbors, waiting, helping, hiding tears, time passes, beautifully illustrated across one spread by the development and hatching of a chick. The scene shifts to the campfires at the front and the child's imagining what life would be like "if . . . papa should not come home." Muted colors allow the merger of fears and hopes.

8.35   Lyons, Mary E. **Letters from a Slave Girl: The Story of Harriet Jacobs.** Charles Scribner's Sons, 1992. ISBN 0-684-19446-5. 146p. 10–13.

In a fictionalized account told entirely through letters "written" by Harriet Jacobs (1813–97), an African American child born into slavery, Mary Lyons portrays a life of courage, hope, and great injustice. As a twelve-year-old, Harriet writes to her dead Mama, describing her loneliness, expressing her grief, and confessing the sexual harassment that she is experiencing. As an adult, she chooses the life of a runaway, spending seven years in an attic crawlspace, separated from her two children. Although the content of the book is heartrending, Harriet's saucy spirit shines through.

8.36   Meyer, Carolyn. **Where the Broken Heart Still Beats: The Story of Cynthia Ann Parker.** Harcourt Brace Jovanovich/Gulliver Books, 1992. ISBN 0-15-200639-7. 192p. 8–12.

When Cynthia Ann Parker (1827?–1864) was "rescued" from her Comanche captors, the Texas legislature voted her a state hero. But "Sinty Ann" yearned to return to her Comanche husband and two sons, and she struggled throughout her captivity by her pioneer relatives to pass her Indian ways on to her young daughter. In finely wrought chapters that alternately tell the story from the points of view of Cynthia Ann and her cousin Lucy, the cultural conflict between Native Americans and pioneers is honestly and evenly discussed.

8.37   Myers, Walter Dean. **The Righteous Revenge of Artemis Bonner.** HarperCollins, 1992. ISBN 0-06-020846-5. 140p. 10 and up.

With rolling good humor masquerading in the cadences of formal speech, Artemis Bonner, a fifteen-year-old African American boy, writes his journal of planned revenge against Catfish Grimes: Catfish, it seems, shot dead Artemis's uncle, Ugly Ned, in the streets of Tombstone. As Catfish and his unladylike companion, Miss Lucy Featherdip, move from site to site in search of Uncle Ugly's stowed fortune, Artemis must skirmish repeatedly with his nemesis, dealing with such woes as cactus needles, ant beds, and hungry bears—"all for that treasure."

8.38   Paterson, Katherine. **Lyddie.** Lodestar Books, 1991. ISBN 0-525-67338-5. 182p. 9 and up (est.).

Set in New England in the mid 1840s, this novel depicts the life of Lyddie Worthen, a destitute Vermont farm girl who must leave her home and support herself as a factory worker in Lowell, Massachusetts. In the mill, she endures illness from exhaustion, unsanitary conditions, low pay, sexual advances from her manager, and isolation from her family. Like other young female protagonists in Katherine Paterson's award-winning novels, Lyddie not only survives but actually improves her lot in life through her resourcefulness, industry, and indomitable courage. *Notable 1991 Children's Trade Books in the Field of Social Studies; ALA Notable Children's Books, 1992.*

8.39 Reeder, Carolyn. **Shades of Gray.** Macmillan, 1989. ISBN 0-02-775810-9. 152p. 10–12 (est.).

Orphaned by the Civil War and its aftermath, twelve-year-old Will Page is forced to live with his uncle's family. Because Uncle Jed refused to fight the Yankees, Will considers him a traitor. But as Will works alongside his uncle on the farm, he learns to appreciate both the older man's strengths and the many faces of loss. Topics, themes, and style of this book easily blend into an intermediate curriculum. *ALA Notable Children's Books, 1990; Scott O'Dell Award for Historical Fiction, 1990; Virginia Library Association Children's Book Award.*

8.40 Rounds, Glen. **Cowboys.** Illustrated by Glen Rounds. Holiday House, 1991. ISBN 0-8234-0867-1. 32p. 3–7 (est.).

When a rancher hires a cowboy to ride the range, the work day is long and hard. Glen Rounds's brief text and scratchy illustrations take the cowboy from sunup to sundown in a kind of "bunkhouse to bunkhouse" saga that demonstrates saddling and breaking a horse, looking for strays, rescuing steers, meeting snakes and storms head on, and even conquering a stampede. Line and color work together for lanky, scruffy cowboy images.

8.41 Sanders, Scott Russell. **Aurora Means Dawn.** Illustrated by Jill Kastner. Bradbury Press, 1989. ISBN 0-02-778270-0. 30p. 6–9.

This picture-book account of early pioneer life in Ohio is based on fact, but it is embellished to help young readers imagine the difficult lives of American settlers. In this story, the Sheldons travel from Connecticut to Ohio in 1800 to join the settlement of Aurora, only to realize that they are the first settlers in the community. Watercolor paintings are accurately detailed, giving life to the print and suggesting strongly the beauty of this challenging new land. A short afterword explains the factual basis in this story of a real Mr. and Mrs. Sheldon and their seven children. *Notable 1989 Children's Trade Books in the Field of Social Studies.*

8.42   Sanders, Scott Russell. **Warm as Wool.** Illustrated by Helen Cogancherry. Bradbury Press, 1992. ISBN 0-02-778139-9. 32p. 6–10 (est.).

In an author's note, Scott Russell Sanders writes that "Children enter the past . . . not through names and dates, but through the feelings of those who lived in the past." Drawing from a nineteenth-century record book, he re-creates the story of the Ward family, focusing particularly on Betsy Ward, the first pioneer to own sheep in Randolph Township, Ohio. Because of her children's desperate need for warm wool clothes, Betsy purchased the sheep in 1805 with saved coins. Watercolor and pencil illustrations inform readers of time and place and convey the Wards' determination.

8.43   Turner, Ann. **Grasshopper Summer.** Macmillan, 1989. ISBN 0-02-789511-4. 166p. 9–12 (est.).

Eleven-year-old Sam White and his family move from bucolic Kentucky to the raw southern Dakota Territory of 1874. The journey itself is challenging, and the land that they settle is vast and harsh. Coupled with the external tension of the landscape is Sam's struggle to adjust, as compared with his younger brother Billy's natural optimism. After their sod house is built, crops are planted, only to be destroyed by a terrifying grasshopper plague. Determined to persevere, the family remains on the land. Ann Turner's dialogue-filled saga of a pioneer family that triumphs would make for a good read-aloud. *Notable 1989 Children's Trade Books in the Field of Social Studies.*

8.44   Van Leeuwen, Jean. **Going West.** Illustrated by Thomas B. Allen. Dial Books for Young Readers, 1992. ISBN 0-8037-1028-3. 32p. 5–9.

Illustrated with earth-tone chalks on roughly textured brown paper, the story of a pioneer family's westward journey and settlement is told through the eyes of seven-year-old Hannah. Hannah's voice is both childlike and lyrical: "Here is what was in our wagon . . ."; "Rebecca caught a cold. At night she coughed and coughed. Mama looked worried, but still we rode on. Going West." Brutal weather, deprivation, and isolation are evident, as are steadfastness, ingenuity, and hope.

8.45   Wisler, G. Clifton. **Piper's Ferry: A Tale of the Texas Revolution.** Lodestar Books, 1990. ISBN 0-525-67303-2. 144p. 10 and up.

Leaving his home in New Orleans, young Tim Piper heads to Texas to help his uncle run a ferry across the Brazos River. As Tim tries to find his place in this new land, he builds strong friendships and faces danger and personal conflict. Told through the eyes and voice of Tim, this historically based novel, rich with the characters and events of the Texas revolution, tells a story of a young teen's struggle to become a man.

8.46   Wisler, G. Clifton. **Red Cap.** Lodestar Books, 1991. ISBN 0-525-67337-7. 160p. 10-13 (est.).

Set during the Civil War and based on a real boy's exploits, this novel portrays thirteen-year-old Ransom Powell as he copes with his duties as a drummer boy in the Union army. Then Ransom is captured and sent to the notorious Andersonville prison camp. Ultimately, the young boy's wit, stoicism, and bravery make him a hero to his fellow prisoners and allow him to escape to the North.

World

8.47   Avi. **The True Confessions of Charlotte Doyle.** Avon/Flare Books, 1992. ISBN 0-380-71475-2. 232p. 10 and up.

"Not every thirteen-year-old girl is accused of murder, brought to trial, and found guilty. . . . For my part I intend to tell the truth as *I* lived it." So begins the unexpectedly terrifying tale told by Charlotte Doyle, the only female passenger aboard the *Seahawk* on a Liverpool-to-Providence voyage with vicious sailors and a tyrannical captain during the summer of 1832. Readers willing to tear themselves away from rapidly unfolding action will appreciate an appendix naming ship locations and equipment and explaining ship's time. *ALA Notable Book, 1990; Boston Globe–Horn Book Fiction Award, 1991; Newbery Honor Book, 1991.*

8.48   Crofford, Emily. **Born in the Year of Courage.** Carolrhoda Books, 1991. ISBN 0-87614-679-5. 160p. 10 and up.

Manjiro, a fifteen-year-old Japanese fisherman living in the mid nineteenth century, becomes shipwrecked and stranded on a deserted island. Based on actual events, the story describes Manjiro's rescue by American whalers, his subsequent training at sea and education in the United States, and his great success as a courageous, talented navigator. Since at that time Japan's policy of isolationism meant virtually no trade with Western countries, Manjiro became a key negotiator in opening up trade relations between the United States and Japan in the 1850s.

8.49   Hautzig, Esther. **Riches.** Illustrated by Donna Diamond. Harper-Collins/Charlotte Zolotow Books, 1992. ISBN 0-06-022260-3. 43p. 8 and up (est.).

Successful, hard-working shop owners Samuel and Chaya-Rivka grow old and desire a more restful life. Wanting most of all to find a way to please the Almighty, Samuel seeks guidance from a wise rabbi. In following his advice, the couple learns that the giving of oneself can be more important than the giving of material things. Black-and-white drawings capture devotion and humility.

8.50   Hudson, Jan. **Sweetgrass.** Philomel Books, 1989. ISBN 0-399-21721-5. 157p. 8–12.

This is a well-researched novel about Sweetgrass, a fifteen-year-old Blackfoot Indian girl living on the prairies of Alberta in western Canada in the nineteenth century. Told in first person, it chronicles the daily life, dreams, and courage of Sweetgrass as she experiences awakening emotions of love and battles a devastating smallpox epidemic which threatens to annihilate her tribe. Through a suspenseful plot and abundant dialogue, the book subtly but skillfully educates the young reader in the ways of the Blackfoot. *Canada Council Children's Literature Prize; CLA Book of the Year for Children; ALA Booklist Children's Editors' Choices, 1989; ALA Notable Children's Books, 1990.*

8.51   Lutzeier, Elizabeth. **The Coldest Winter.** Holiday House, 1991. ISBN 0-8234-0899-X. 153p. 10 and up.

In this fictional account of the Irish Potato Famine of the 1840s, Eamonn and his family are evicted from their farm in the dead of winter by British troops because their landlord wants more pasture land. They walk to a city in search of work and famine relief, then begin to die of starvation and yellow fever. Author Elizabeth Lutzeier does an exceptional job of dramatizing the political and economic dynamics of social disintegration.

8.52   McCully, Emily Arnold. **Mirette on the High Wire.** Illustrated by Emily Arnold McCully. G. P. Putnam's Sons, 1992. ISBN 0-399-22130-1. 32p. 4–8.

In 1890s Paris, the best place to stay if you are an acrobat, juggler, or mime is at the widow Gateau's boardinghouse. There, guests receive superb treatment from the widow and her daughter, Mirette. One retiring guest, though, fascinates Mirette above all others, and she begs the high-wire artist, the Great Bellini, for instruction. Mirette's determination both to learn tightrope walking and to help the Great Bellini, who has become fearful of the wire, is charmingly interpreted through Emily Arnold McCully's watercolors. *Caldecott Medal, 1993.*

Twentieth Century

United States: Early in the Century

8.53 Allen, Thomas B. **On Granddaddy's Farm.** Illustrated by Thomas B. Allen. Alfred A. Knopf/Borzoi Books, 1989. ISBN 0-394-99613-5. 32p. 4–7 (est.).

While Granddaddy works as a train brakeman on the Nashville to Montgomery run four days a week, three cousins help Granny run the farm. The children water the plants, tend the animals, haul coal and water from the well, as well as ride the mule and play in the haystacks. Soft, textured pastels depict pastoral scenes from a 1930s Tennessee farm.

8.54 Cooney, Barbara. **Hattie and the Wild Waves: A Story from Brooklyn.** Illustrated by Barbara Cooney. Viking Penguin, 1990. ISBN 0-670-83056-9. 40p. 3–8.

Growing up in Brooklyn at the turn of the century, Hattie, daughter of German immigrants, enjoys sketching river boats and ocean waves. As the years go by and Hattie's brother and sister make their way in the world, her family worries about what will become of their youngest daughter. But Hattie knows her own mind and, with the help of a fortune-teller, finally realizes her dream of becoming an artist. Barbara Cooney's primitive-style illustrations, painted with acrylics and accented with pencils, help to capture the story of an American era that was spirited with independence and strength of family.

8.55 Corcoran, Barbara. **The Private War of Lillian Adams.** Atheneum/Jean Karl Books, 1989. ISBN 0-689-31443-4. 166p. 9–12.

It's 1917, World War I is raging, and Lillian's family has just moved to a small New England town. The fifth grader, eager to be noticed and make friends, convinces her classmates that their town is harboring a spy. In the end, Lillian learns that rumors can be a dangerous thing.

8.56 Cross, Verda. **Great-Grandma Tells of Threshing Day.** Illustrated by Gail Owens. Albert Whitman, 1992. ISBN 0-8075-3042-5. 38p. 6–11.

"Threshing day is the best day of the year. . . . I'll remember it all the days of my life. . . . And I did just that. . . . " At age seventy-eight, Verda Cross, a.k.a. Great-Grandma, transports us to a June day in the early 1900s and reminisces about the winter wheat harvest on a Missouri farm. Through her words and through Gail Owens's masterful pastel illustrations, we are reminded of the sense of community, of pitching in to accomplish a task, so commonplace in an earlier day.

8.57 Fleischman, Paul. **Shadow Play.** Illustrated by Eric Beddows. Harper and Row/Charlotte Zolotow Books, 1990. ISBN 0-06-021865-7. 34p. 4–8.

At a county fair in the early 1900s, the silhouetted "LeGrand Family" introduces the shadow puppet play of "Beauty and the Beast." As the play progresses, the bull Stupendo from a neighboring tent crashes the stage and terrorizes the LeGrands. At last, Stupendo is tamed by the gentle, youngest LeGrand. When the audience is invited backstage, they are amazed to discover that the shadows, including the bull, were all made by a master puppeteer, echoing the moral of the fairy tale itself: "Appearances are as thin and deceptive—as shadows."

8.58 Gregory, Kristiana. **Earthquake at Dawn.** Harcourt Brace Jovanovich/Gulliver Books, 1992. ISBN 0-15-200446-7. 187p. 10 and up.

In a fictionalized account, two young women, photographer Edith Irvine and her assistant, witness the San Francisco earthquake of 1906. In the aftermath, the pair becomes involved with a family of Irish immigrants, meets Jack London, and, against the wishes of civic leaders, manages to photograph the dimensions of the disaster. This is first-rate historical fiction, and it would have been a real treat to have the text accompanied by surviving photographs by the real Edith Irvine.

8.59 Houston, Gloria. **Littlejim.** Illustrated by Thomas B. Allen. Philomel Books, 1990. ISBN 0-399-22222-0. 172p. 8–12.

Living in rural North Carolina in the early 1900s, twelve-year-old Littlejim Houston is happy being the best student in his class. But Papa thinks that Littlejim is wasting time on "book learning" and should instead be learning to live off the land. Through a newspaper's essay contest, Littlejim struggles with his need to become a scholar and his desire to please his father, and in the process he proves what it means to be a man. Full-page black-line sketches illustrate this sensitive story of a father's acceptance and a young boy's coming of age in Appalachia. *Notable 1990 Children's Trade Books in the Field of Social Studies.*

8.60   Leighton, Maxinne Rhea. **An Ellis Island Christmas.** Illustrated by Dennis Nolan. Viking Penguin, 1992. ISBN 0-670-83182-4. 32p. 3–8.

Six-year-old Krysia and her family leave Poland to join Papa in America. Although sad to leave behind friends and her doll, Yola, Krysia is excited about the reunion. Arriving in the forbidding immigration hall on Christmas Eve, Mama retrieves Yola from a wicker basket to ease the strangeness that surrounds Krysia. The story is told in detailed retrospect, with paintings adding a chimerical quality to remembered scenes from the Polish village to Ellis Island.

8.61   Leonard, Laura. **Saving Damaris.** Atheneum/Jean Karl Books, 1989. ISBN 0-689-31553-8. 198p. 8–12.

Through an engaging diary, twelve-year-old Abby tells how she, her brother Joel, and her sister Damaris struggle to hold their family together after the sudden death of their mother. It is early twentieth-century America, and sixteen-year-old Damaris goes to work at Mr. Buttchenbacher's emporium. Abby and Joel try to prevent their beautiful sister from trying to aid the family by accepting marriage to the wealthy but ill-tempered widower. The wedding seems unstoppable until the children discover that there is no room for them in Mr. B's plans.

8.62   McDonald, Megan. **The Great Pumpkin Switch.** Illustrated by Ted Lewin. Orchard Books/Richard Jackson Books, 1992. ISBN 0-531-08600-3. 32p. 4–7.

"Sit close now, and I'll tell you." In a chair by a window, a grandfather begins a tale about a time when he and his friend Otto were boys, and Grandpa's sister, Rosie, had grown Big Max—the biggest pumpkin ever—for her Sunflower Girls patches. But the boys inadvertently cut the pumpkin vine, and Big Max rolled, bounced, and smashed into the street below. Ted Lewin's knicker-clad characters with their Radio Flyer create nostalgia for a time past.

8.63   Precek, Katharine Wilson. **Penny in the Road.** Illustrated by Patricia Cullen-Clark. Macmillan, 1989. ISBN 0-02-774970-3. 32p. 4–8.

A sense of wonder and respect permeate Katharine Wilson Precek's story that a grandfather tells of himself as a country boy in 1913 who, after finding a 1793 penny, imagines what life must have been like for the boy who dropped it. In the present, the grandchildren can imagine the boyhood of the grandfather who wondered. Patricia Cullen-Clark's soft pastel illustrations add to the sense of a gently faded past which lingers.

8.64   Shefelman, Janice. **A Peddler's Dream.** Illustrated by Tom Shefelman. Houghton Mifflin, 1992. ISBN 0-395-60904-6. 32p. 6–10 (est.).

A Lebanese immigrant pursues his dream of becoming a merchant in the New World. The realistic historical tale, set at the turn of the century, tells of the hopes, frustrations, and eventual successes of Soloman Joseph Azar in his climb from peddler to clerk to partner and, finally, to owner of the clothing store of his dreams. The author-illustrator team capture both the feeling and setting of the Old World, as well as the fictionalized American town of Arcadia.

8.65   Wallace, Bill. **Buffalo Gal.** Holiday House, 1992. ISBN 0-8234-0943-0. 185p. 11 and up (est.).

In this romantic adventure story set in 1904, the Guthridge women participate in efforts to save the buffalo from extinction. Amanda Guthridge and her mother travel to Oklahoma and then Texas to help round up a herd of buffalo that will be sent to safety on a ranch. During the trip's adventures, Amanda meets David Talltree, a Native American soldier who escorts them on their journey. At first, Amanda and David have little use for each other, but their slowly developing respect turns to love.

8.66   Wyman, Andrea. **Red Sky at Morning.** Holiday House, 1991. ISBN 0-8234-0903-1. 225p. 10 and up.

While her father seeks a new farm in Oregon, Callie is left alone in Indiana with her Grandfather Opa to tend the farm and Callie's sick mother. Friendships, love, and the simple pleasures of early twentieth-century prairie life enable Callie and Opa to endure the disease and death that strike her family and town during her father's absence. An enriching novel to accompany a history unit, this book would also make a captivating read-aloud.

8.67   Yep, Laurence. **The Star Fisher.** Morrow Junior Books, 1991. ISBN 0-688-09365-5. 160p. 8 and up.

Loosely based on Laurence Yep's own family background, this novel examines the struggles and triumphs of a Chinese American family moving from Ohio to West Virginia in the 1920s. The protagonist, fifteen-year-old Joan Lee, is dismayed by the prejudice that her family encounters from several townspeople when her father tries to establish a laundry business. Aided by ancient Miss Lucy and her friend Bernice, Joan Lee and her mother's delicious apple pies ultimately win over the hearts of their small-town neighbors.

United States: World War I and Next Two Decades

8.68   Green, Connie Jordan. **Emmy.** Margaret K. McElderry Books, 1992. ISBN 0-689-50556-6. 152p. 10–13 (est.).

Nothing has been the same since Emmy's father was disabled in the mine accident. Pa has become reclusive; for Emmy, there is never-ending work to be done and no time for herself. Nonetheless, the family is determined to overcome the odds and stay together. Then Emmy's brother is in a mining accident, and even this resolve appears threatened. But the strength of family ties proves strong enough to hold the family together and to bring back the Pa that everyone loves.

8.69   Morris, Linda Lowe. **Morning Milking.** Illustrated by David DeRan. Picture Book Studio, 1991. ISBN 0-88708-173-8. 34p. 6–8 (est.).

This account of a farm girl helping her father with milking the cows, though simple, is entrancing and profound. The water-color illustrations are warm and serene, rendering farm life with loving care. The text, plain in language and rich in detail, resonates with the love between parent and child, the human yearning to freeze happiness in time, the beauty of land and animals, and the power of storytelling.

8.70   Skurzynski, Gloria. **Good-bye, Billy Radish.** Bradbury Press, 1992. ISBN 0-02-782921-9. 138p. 10 and up.

Against the backdrop of the United States entering World War I, two young boys entering adolescence develop a deep friendship. The characters of Hank Kerner, an "all-American" boy who aspires to be a doctor, and Bazyli Radichevych, a Ukrainian immigrant who accepts his destiny as a steel worker in the small Pennsylvania town, are complex and appealing. Within the context of several focal incidents, the characters face career decisions, crises of personal and cultural identity, and death. Black-and-white photos illuminate the era.

United States: World War II and Later

8.71   Avi. **"Who Was That Masked Man, Anyway?"** Orchard Books/Richard Jackson Books, 1992. ISBN 0-531-08607-0. 176p. 9 and up.

Franklin D. Wattleson and Mario Calvino are next-door neighbors and best friends, even though Frankie's radio adventure shows—the Green Hornet, the Lone Ranger, the Shadow—spill into his ordinary 1945 life and out through his imaginary persona, Chet Barker (with his faithful sidekick, Skipper O'Malley). Meanwhile, Frankie's brother Tom, wounded in the war, is uncommunicative; Miss Gomez isn't happy with Frankie's school behavior; and the roomer, Dr. Smerdlow, just *could* be a spy. Told entirely in dialogue, Avi's story and its characters are great fun.

8.72   Cormier, Robert. **Other Bells for Us to Ring.** Illustrated by Deborah Kogan Ray. Delacorte Press, 1990. ISBN 0-385-30245-2. 136p. 9–12.

Just prior to the outbreak of World War II, eleven-year-old Darcy Webster has at last found a friend in the irrepressible Kathleen Mary O'Hara. With her flaming orange hair, an adventurous soul, and a firm religious faith, Kathleen Mary's spirit lifts Darcy's own, even through Kathleen Mary must deal with an abusive father. But then the war begins, Darcy's father is shipped overseas, and her precious friend disappears. Darcy is left to consider the place of miracles in her life—and how promises are almost always kept.

8.73   Dillon, Eilís. **Children of Bach.** Charles Scribner's Sons, 1992. ISBN 0-684-19440-6. 164p. 10 and up (est.).

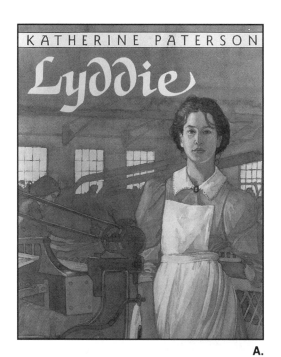

A.

B.

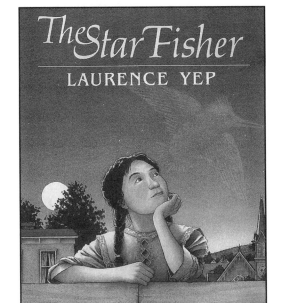

C.

D.

A. *Lyddie* by Katherine Paterson (see 8.38). **B.** *Shadow Play* by Paul Fleischman; illustrated by Eric Beddows (see 8.57). **C.** *The Star Fisher* by Laurence Yep (see 8.67). **D.** *No Star Nights* by Anna Egan Smucker; illustrated by Steve Johnson (see 8.84).

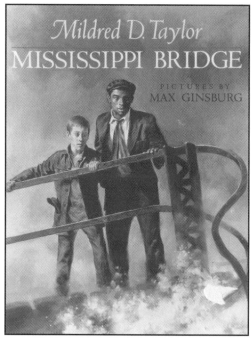

A.

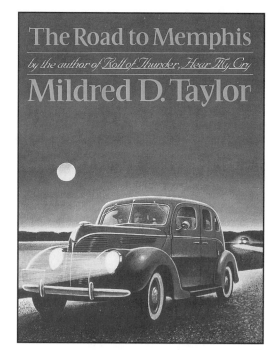

B.

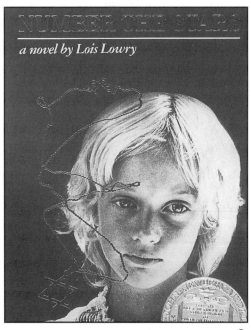

C.

D.

A. *Mississippi Bridge* by Mildred D. Taylor; illustrated by Max Ginsburg (see 8.85).
B. *The Road to Memphis* by Mildred Taylor (see 8.86). **C.** *Number the Stars* by Lois Lowry (see 8.93). **D.** *Stepping on the Cracks* by Mary Downing Hahn (see 8.74).

All of Pali's family are Jewish musicians living in Hungary during World War II. He comes home one day to find that his parents have been taken by the Nazis controlling their city. Smuggled in a van, Pali, his two siblings, his aunt, a neighbor, and a friend embark on a dangerous journey to Italy to escape their parents' fate. Along the way, the troupe receives the help of strangers and overcomes their sorrows with the power of music.

8.74   Hahn, Mary Downing. **Stepping on the Cracks.** Clarion Books, 1991. ISBN 0-395-58507-4. 216p. 10 and up (est.).

Eleven-year-old Margaret, the narrator, and Elizabeth are best friends. They are preoccupied with World War II, each having a brother in the military. But they have also had a war since kindergarten with the sixth-grade bully, mean Gordy Smith. In the process of getting even for his misdeeds, they discover that in a hut in the woods Gordy is hiding an army deserter—his own brother Stuart. The result is a questioning of their attitudes toward Gordy and toward war, but never their status as best friends. *Scott O'Dell Award for Historical Fiction, 1992.*

8.75   Härtling, Peter (translated by Elizabeth D. Crawford). **Crutches.** Lothrop, Lee and Shepard Books, 1988. ISBN 0-688-07991-1. 163p. 9 and up.

In the harrowing final days of World War II, Thomas finds himself alone in Vienna, his last hope of finding a living relative dashed in the rubble of his aunt's abandoned home. Then comes hope in the form of the one-legged man who calls himself Crutches. With Crutches, Thomas believes he can triumph over the tragedies that surround him and find his missing mother and the life he left behind. *Mildred L. Batchelder Award, 1989.*

8.76   Heide, Florence Parry, and Judith Heide Gilliland. **Sami and the Time of the Troubles.** Illustrated by Ted Lewin. Clarion Books, 1992. ISBN 0-395-55964-2. 32p. 8–12.

Sami, a ten-year-old Lebanese boy, "lives in the time of the troubles," a time of gunfire and bombs that has lasted all his life. Bombed-out Beruit is Sami's playground. When fighting occurs, Sami's family must live in a basement. Even so, his mother insists that there be things of beauty to remind them of days before the troubles. Through his grandfather's stories, Sami comes to understand that children must demand peace. Ted Lewin's watercolors reflect the light play and shadows of streets and cavern.

8.77   Hest, Amy. **Fancy Aunt Jess.** Illustrated by Amy Schwartz. Morrow Junior Books, 1990. ISBN 0-688-08097-9. 32p. 5–7 (est.).

Aunt Jess wears spiky high heels, dresses oh-so-stylishly, lives in New York City, and is single at a time when being single makes the butcher's wife grunt. She'll get married, she says, when she meets someone special. Amy Schwartz's paintings set a 1950s scene for a Jewish aunt and her glamorous lifestyle as viewed through the adoring eyes of her young niece. Then, through the efforts of two look-alike nieces, Aunt Jess meets Uncle Harry at Friday services and there's a "special wedding."

8.78   Houston, Gloria. **But No Candy.** Illustrated by Lloyd Bloom. Philomel Books, 1992. ISBN 0-399-22142-5. 32p. 4 and up.

Afternoons were the favorite part of Lee's day. With a chocolate bar from the candy counter in her daddy's store, she escaped to her special tree, where she slowly peeled the paper, savored each nibble, and made the chocolate last as long as possible. But when war came, there was no more chocolate. Despite all the sacrifices, and even while missing Uncle Ted, Lee desperately missed chocolate. At war's end, with Uncle Ted safely home, favorite things taste different, and little girls know when they have grown.

8.79   Kinsey-Warnock, Natalie. **The Canada Geese Quilt.** Illustrated by Leslie W. Bowman. Cobblehill Books, 1989. ISBN 0-525-65004-0. 60p. 9 and up.

Spring always brings the geese back to Vermont, but this spring brings changes to ten-year-old Ariel's life as well: her mother announces that she is expecting another baby, and her grandmother suffers a stroke. Ariel now faces uncertainty and must learn to give of herself. Later, a special quilt from her grandmother helps Ariel to feel safe and secure once again. Black-and-white sketches illustrate this touching story of family and personal growth set in the 1940s. *Notable 1989 Children's Trade Books in the Field of Social Studies.*

8.80   Levitin, Sonia. **Silver Days.** Atheneum, 1989. ISBN 0-689-31563-5. 186p. 10 and up (est.).

This sequel to *Journey to America* continues the Platt family's story of escape from Nazi Germany to freedom in the United States. Told through the eyes of fifteen-year-old Lisa Platt, the novel describes the hardships that Jewish immigrants encountered in the early 1940s as they struggled with the English language, American customs, and financial constraints. Readers will also enjoy the poignant portrayal of family love, sibling relationships, and a young girl's dream to dance. *Notable 1989 Children's Trade Books in the Field of Social Studies.*

8.81   Nelson, Theresa. **And One for All.** Orchard Books/Richard Jackson Books, 1989. ISBN 0-531-08404-3. 182p. 11 and up (est.).

Theresa Nelson's award-winning novel poignantly examines young Geraldine's loving relationships with her older brother Wing and his best friend, Sam, during the years 1966–68. Wing, a good athlete but poor student, drops out of high school to fight in Vietnam. In contrast, Sam becomes a conscientious objector and peace activist. Ultimately, Geraldine realizes that patriotism can take many different forms. Realistic characterizations and sensitive depictions of conflicting viewpoints make this a touching story. *Notable 1989 Children's Trade Books in the Field of Social Studies.*

8.82   Paulsen, Gary. **The Cookcamp.** Orchard Books/Richard Jackson Books, 1991. ISBN 0-531-08527-9. 128p. 10–12.

In 1944, a five-year-old boy living in Chicago is sent by his mother to join his Norwegian grandmother in northern Minnesota. His grandmother is a camp cook for a road-construction crew, and the men with whom she works fill the boy's summer days with good food, ample love, and helpful lessons about life. Lacking in fast-paced plot action, the novel nevertheless offers simple, straightforward prose, making the book a quick read.

8.83   Ray, Deborah Kogan. **My Daddy Was a Soldier: A World War II Story.** Illustrated by Deborah Kogan Ray. Holiday House, 1990. ISBN 0-8234-0795-0. 37p. 8–12 (est.).

In 1943, eight-year-old Jeannie's father leaves to fight in World War II. "You'll always be with me, Jeannie-O" are his last words as he departs for army camp. This is the story of victory gardens, scrap drives, food rations, Betty Grable hairdos, and families left behind. Through the shaded grays of pencil drawings and unadorned text, both children and adults will better understand the universality of feelings that accompany separation. *Notable 1990 Children's Trade Books in the Field of Social Studies.*

8.84   Smucker, Anna Egan. **No Star Nights.** Illustrated by Steve Johnson. Alfred A. Knopf/Borzoi Books, 1989. ISBN 0-394-99925-8. 38p. 7–10 (est.).

With great clarity and glowing color, the beauty and grit of ordinary daily life in a West Virginia steel-mill town are captured in Steve Johnson's paintings—family dinner, a baseball game, and millworkers against rust-colored skies and billowing stacks. In a text that reflects memories of the author's childhood, young readers will experience the powerful mood of 1950s America. *Notable 1989 Children's Trade Books in the Field of Social Studies; IRA Children's Book Award, 1990.*

8.85   Taylor, Mildred D. **Mississippi Bridge.** Illustrated by Max Ginsburg. Dial Books for Young Readers, 1990. ISBN 0-8037-0427-5. 64p. 8–12.

During a heavy rainstorm in 1930s rural Mississippi, an astonished Jeremy Simms—white, ten years old, and a neighbor of the Logan family—watches a bus driver order black passengers off the bus to make room for white riders. Just outside of town the bus crosses a raging creek at high speed, smashes through the railing of the old bridge, and tumbles into the water. Jeremy joins others in an attempt to rescue survivors, but there are none. Black-and-white pencil drawings heighten the drama of another Mildred Taylor retelling of tales from her father's boyhood. *Notable 1990 Children's Trade Books in the Field of Social Studies.*

8.86   Taylor, Mildred. **The Road to Memphis.** Dial Books, 1990. ISBN 0-8037-0340-6. 288p. 12 and up.

Mildred Taylor's story of the Logan family of rural Mississippi continues in this novel about three harrowing days in December 1941. Cassie, now sixteen, describes an action-packed road trip to Memphis incited by an African American friend who is fleeing white tormentors after an altercation. Prejudice, death, a touch of romance, and reconciliation all take center stage in this high drama. *Notable 1990 Children's Trade Books in the Field of Social Studies; Coretta Scott King Award (Writing), 1991.*

8.87   Yolen, Jane. **Letting Swift River Go.** Illustrated by Barbara Cooney. Little, Brown, 1992. ISBN 0-316-9689-4. 32p. 6–10 (est.).

Accompanied by Barbara Cooney's primitive watercolor, gouache, and pencil illustrations, Jane Yolen's poignant story tells of the flooding of the Swift River Valley of western Massachusetts to create the Quabbin Reservoir. As recalled by Sally Jane, a child of six when the changes began, trout fishing, graveyard picnics, and sugaring time were exchanged for "a long, gray wilderness" of concrete. Boston's "thirst" meant relocation of graves, deforestation, and demolition of houses. Visiting the beautiful waterway as an adult, Sally remembers and lets go.

World: World War I and Next Two Decades

8.88   Hesse, Karen. **Letters from Rifka.** Henry Holt, 1992. ISBN 0-8050-1964-2. 148p. 11 and up.

It is 1919 when twelve-year-old Rifka and her family flee the oppression against Jews in Russia. They are bound for America, where Rifka imagines that she will be safe from the Russian soldiers she so fears. Carrying only her treasured volume of poetry by Alexander Pushkin, Rifka begins an odyssey that will take her from the Polish border to Ellis Island, an odyssey of hope and courage detailed in her letters to Tovah, a cousin whom she has left behind. *IRA Children's Book Award, 1993.*

World: World War II and Later

8.89   Hill, Susan. **The Glass Angels.** Illustrated by Valerie Littlewood. Candlewick Press, 1991. ISBN 1-56402-111-4. 92p. 9 and up (est.).

In post–World War II London, Tillie lives with her widowed mother, who barely makes ends meet through her sewing. Near Christmas, Tillie's mother becomes ill, and the wedding dress that she has been making is ruined when the ceiling collapses. Tillie must take charge, learning that the meaning of Christmas is often revealed unexpectedly by a gift of glass angels or the help of friends. Valerie Littlewood's illustrations, including both ink drawings and color paintings, make this a beautifully crafted book.

8.90   Kordon, Klaus (translated by Elizabeth D. Crawford). **Brothers Like Friends.** Philomel Books, 1992. ISBN 0-399-22137-9. 206p. 10 and up.

Seven-year-old Frank idolizes Burkie, his fourteen-year-old half-brother, and shares his distress when their widowed mother marries a lazy bully. Set in 1950s East Germany, the daily hardships aggravate the family situation. All Frank's happiness rests in Burkie's friendship and sharing his success on the soccer team. When a secret confession, seemingly about a soccer injury, leads to Burkie's death, Frank senses his own responsibility, and his shattered life is hard to put together. *German Youth Literature Award, Runner-up.*

8.91   Laird, Christa. **Shadow of the Wall.** Greenwillow Books, 1990. ISBN 0-688-09336-1. 192p. 12 and up.

Misha lives with his sisters in an orphanage in the Warsaw ghetto in 1942 and begs for food for their widowed mother. Christa Laird writes with calculated restraint about the deprivation, the terror, and the bravery of thirteen-year-old Misha and the thousands like him who lost their childhoods or lives during the war. Central to this novel is one of Poland's true heroes of the war, Dr. Janusz Korczak.

8.92   Lingard, Joan. **Between Two Worlds.** Lodestar Books, 1991. ISBN 0-525-67360-1. 186p. 12 and up.

This sequel to *Tug of War* continues the saga of the Petersons, a family of Latvian refugees who immigrate to Toronto after World War II. Their story is told through the family's teenage daughter, Astra. Through hard work, the family struggles to make a new life in the postwar world. Joan Lingard simplifies and romanticizes the trials of immigrant life, uniting all her subplots with multiple happy endings. Late 1940s popular culture is well represented, however, as are the anachronisms of the Cold War.

8.93   Lowry, Lois. **Number the Stars.** Houghton Mifflin, 1989. ISBN 0-395-51060-0. 137p. 10 and up (est.).

"Halte!" The first encounter that Danish Annemarie and her Jewish friend Ellen have with German soldiers is while racing each other home from school. As the Nazis attempt to "relocate" all Jews from Copenhagen in 1943, Annemarie's family "adopts" Ellen as their daughter and through a clever scheme attempts to help her family to safety. As the plot builds to an exciting climax, Annemarie displays the extraordinary courage which became common in wartime Europe. *Notable 1989 Children's Trade Books in the Field of Social Studies; Newbery Medal, 1990.*

8.94   Morpurgo, Michael. **Waiting for Anya.** Viking Penguin, 1991. ISBN 0-670-83735-0. 172p. 10 and up.

Set in the French village of Lescun during World War II, the novel recounts the daring exploits of twelve-year-old Jo as he and his adult friend Benjamin plan the escape of twelve Jewish children into adjacent Spain. With the help of the village priest and a sympathetic German soldier, eleven of the children succeed. Although Benjamin, who also is Jewish, and one girl are captured and eventually die at Auschwitz, the story nonetheless offers a generally optimistic ending: Anya, the daughter for whom Benjamin was waiting, rather than fleeing to safety in Spain himself, arrives safely in Lescun at the end of the war. *ALA Best Books for Young Adults, 1992.*

8.95   Orlev, Uri (translated by Hillel Halkin). **The Man from the Other Side.** Houghton Mifflin, 1991. ISBN 0-395-53808-4. 186p. 10 and up.

Fourteen-year-old Marek and his stepfather wade through the Warsaw sewers to bring food to Jews beseiged in the ghetto during World War II. Marek takes further risks by hiding Pan Jozek, a young man who has escaped from the ghetto. The two young men return to fight in the horrifying uprising, and the story culminates with Marek's escape. This extraordinarily moving book, an actual account translated from Hebrew, is written in a dispassionate tone that intensifies the emotional reality. *Mildred L. Batchelder Award, 1992.*

Language and Reading

Language is at the center of human existence. Without language there is no human society, no medicine, no politics, no war. It is at the root of our existence. Our language permits us to think, to understand complicated things, the nuances of our existence. . . . [W]riters assist children in learning how to manipulate language.

James Collier, "Profile: James and Christopher
Collier—More Than Just a Good Read," *Language Arts*

9 Language and Reading

Easy-Reading Books

9.1   Ahlberg, Allan. **The Black Cat. Dinosaur Dreams. Mystery Tour. The Pet Shop.** Illustrated by André Amstutz. Greenwillow Books, 1990. 32p. 4–8 (est.). Fiction.

The Funnybones Easy Reading series cleverly follows the adventures of a big skeleton, a little skeleton, and a dog skeleton, who make up the trio called Funnybones. The three skeletons sled in the snow, are chased by dinosaurs in their dreams, uncover several mysteries by shining a light on some suspicious objects, and swap a parrot for a hippopotamus.

9.2   Anholt, Catherine. **Good Days, Bad Days.** Illustrated by Catherine Anholt. G. P. Putnam's Sons, 1990. ISBN 0-399-22283-9. 26p. 2–6 (est.). Fiction.

With minimal text, Catherine Anholt celebrates ordinary family activities through her lively illustrations, tracing the days—good, bad, sunny, sad, snowy, fun—of a family's life together. Illustrations show a family at play on "healthy days," but Mom ironing and Dad vacuuming on "home days." The color-patch pen-and-ink drawings filled in with bright watercolors are true to children's days, and are sure to stimulate comparisons.

9.3   Barton, Byron. **Bones, Bones, Dinosaur Bones.** Illustrated by Byron Barton. Thomas Y. Crowell, 1990. ISBN 0-690-04827-0. 32p. 3–6 (est.). Fiction.

Six small paleontologists, painted with bold lines and crayon-box colors, set out to look for the bones of dinosaurs. Young dinosaur lovers will be able to read almost instantly the minimal text, cued by full-page pictures: "We find them," reads one page; "We dig them up," reads the next. From discovery to shipment to the National History Museum, the steps are clear. Best of all is the reassembly. A "dry bones" rhythm follows attachment of claw bones to foot bones to leg bones, and so on. *Outstanding Science Trade Books, 1990.*

9.4   Barton, Byron. **Dinosaurs, Dinosaurs.** Illustrated by Byron Barton. Thomas Y. Crowell, 1989. ISBN 0-690-04768-1. 31p. 3–6. Fiction.

"A long time ago there were dinosaurs!" Through simple text and brightly colored illustrations, Byron Barton takes young children on a short tour through prehistoric times when dinosaurs big and small, horned and spiked, fierce and scared, roamed the earth.

9.5 Florian, Douglas. **At the Zoo.** Illustrated by Douglas Florian. Greenwillow Books, 1992. ISBN 0-688-09629-8. 32p. 3–5 (est.). Fiction.

Only two words of text appear on each double-page spread of this rhythmic text recounting animals and activities at the zoo, such as "Zoo guide" on one, "Camel ride" on another. Large, simple drawings are flatly childlike, achieved with colored pencil and strong sepia outlines.

9.6 Ginsburg, Mirra. **Asleep, Asleep.** Illustrated by Nancy Tafuri. Greenwillow Books, 1992. ISBN 0-688-09154-7. 24p. 2–6 (est.). Fiction.

The author/illustrator team of Mirra Ginsburg and Nancy Tafuri, inspired by a verse by A. Vvedensky, produce a gentle lullaby text that rhythmically asks if nature's creatures are asleep. The answer for each simple question (such as "And the bees?") is always the same: "Asleep." At last, the cuddled child is told: "Only you and the wind are awake." Bordered art picks up the quiet nighttime colors of nature at rest.

9.7 Guy, Ginger Foglesong. **Black Crow, Black Crow.** Illustrated by Nancy Winslow Parker. Greenwillow Books, 1991. ISBN 0-688-08957-7. 24p. 4 and up. Fiction.

In the spirit of Bill Martin's *Brown Bear, Brown Bear, What Did You See?*, this book uses rhythmic language to tell the story of a busy mother crow who wakes, feeds, and plays with her children, until finally, back in their nest at the end of a busy day, she sings her brood to sleep. Flat, oversized images in pastel colors, bold type, and repetitive text combine to create a readable and useful book for young children.

9.8 Hoban, Julia. **Buzby.** Illustrated by John Himmelman. Harper and Row, 1990. ISBN 0-06-022398-7. 64p. 5–8(est.). Fiction.

Buzby the cat is grown, and he's ready to get a job. He has all the right qualifications—he's a good mouser, he's clean, and he's polite. When he gets work as a hotel busboy, he finds himself doing all the wrong things. But as Buzby and the others discover, he is good at making the guests feel at home, and so he is given the appropriate job of hotel cat. Ink and watercolor illustrations complement this I Can Read Book about a cat who finds his place in the world.

9.9   King, Bob. **Sitting on the Farm.** Illustrated by Bill Slavin. Orchard Books, 1991. ISBN 0-531-08585-6. 32p. 3–6. Fiction.

"Sitting on the farm, happy as can be, / I had a little bug on my knee." To get rid of the bug, the farm child invites a frog to lunch. But when the frog arrives, it's "MUNCH! MUNCH! MUNCH!" on the lunch. So the girl invites a snake to get rid of the frog. The predictable story line with accumulating lunch guests can be sung in repetitive verse. Words and music appear at the end of the book.

9.10 LeTord, Bijou. **A Brown Cow.** Illustrated by Bijou LeTord. Little, Brown, 1989. ISBN 0-316-52166-3. 29p. 4–7 (est.). Fiction.

In simple, warm text, a little girl describes the "little brown cow with no spots on her back that lives in my backyard." When they are inside the house, the child and her cat admire the cow from a window, which is, in turn, framed by the artist in an ink and watercolor border. In childlike, minimalist style, the art matches the winsome language: "I know she likes trees and the sky. I see her look up and *moo, moo.*"

9.11 Lewis, Thomas P. **Frida's Office Day.** Illustrated by Doug Cushman. Harper and Row, 1989. ISBN 0-06-023844-5. 64p. 5–8 (est.). Fiction.

Frida Cat looks forward to a day with her father at his office. After the train ride to the city, Frida takes phone messages, delivers mail, and enjoys using the copy machine at the office of Flying Cat Airline. Lunch and a movie complete a special day. This I Can Read Book features large print and bright pictures.

9.12 Marshall, James. **Fox Outfoxed.** Illustrated by James Marshall. Dial Books for Young Readers, 1992. ISBN 0-8037-1037-2. 48p. 6–8 (est.). Fiction.

In three chapter-length stories, Fox is outfoxed by his own foibles. First, he convinces little sister Louise to provide some extra engine power for his vehicle so that he can win the Big Race. Next, Fox is tricked out of his ten favorite comic books by foxy Lulu. Finally, Louise turns the tables when Fox and his friends park her on a bench so that they can trick-or-treat without her.

Fox is perfectly smug, perplexed, and discombobulated as the funny situations shift in this Easy-to-Read Book.

9.13   Marshall, James. **Rats on the Roof, and Other Stories.** Illustrated by James Marshall. Dial Books for Young Readers, 1991. ISBN 0-8037-0835-1. 79p. 6–10. Fiction.

The animal characters in these seven fable-like tales for young readers reflect both James Marshall's droll humor at its best and sufficient cleverness to wiggle out of various scrapes. Mrs. Goose manages not to be Christmas dinner for a couple of wolves passing themselves off as canaries. Two sheep who cannot read warning signs nearly end up in a wolf's pot, but eventually bore the wolf to sleep with their bland conversation. Black-and-white drawings offer perplexed, and sometimes thwarted, characters.

9.14   Oxenbury, Helen. **Pippo Gets Lost. Tom and Pippo and the Dog. Tom and Pippo in the Snow. Tom and Pippo Make a Friend.** Illustrated by Helen Oxenbury. Macmillan/Aladdin Books, 1989. 11p. 3–5. Fiction.

Tom and his toy monkey Pippo go sledding, make a new friend, get separated, and play with a dog in four of twelve brief adventures written by Helen Oxenbury, a well-known writer of books for the very young. Pippo Books have a simple, clear text, sturdy pages, and reassuring black-and-white and watercolor illustrations.

9.15   Paterson, Katherine. **The Smallest Cow in the World.** Illustrated by Jane Clark Brown. HarperCollins, 1991. ISBN 0-06-024691-X. 64p. 5–8 (est.). Fiction.

Marvin's favorite cow at Brock's Dairy Farm, where his dad works, is Rosie. To Marvin, she is the most wonderful cow in the world. But when Mr. Brock sells his farm and Rosie, Marvin's family must move. Marvin is heartbroken. To cope, he creates an imaginary tiny Rosie who does naughty things in the family. Marvin's parents are models of understanding, and his sister helps to reassure as well. A child's feelings of frustration and separation reach across the format of this I Can Read Book.

9.16   Rose, Agatha. **Hide and Seek in the Yellow House.** Illustrated by Kate Spohn. Viking Penguin, 1992. ISBN 0-670-84383-0. 26p. 4–8 (est.). Fiction.

"In the yellow house, Mother Cat is searching for her kitten. . . ." As the kitten plays a game of hide-and-seek, young listeners will play along. Because the text is so simple and the art so inviting, young listeners will soon become young "readers" with this one. The repetitive text commands engagement: "Now he isn't there!" Kate Spohn's brush gives stylized texture and pattern to walls and rugs in the yellow house.

9.17   Stadler, John. **Cat Is Back at Bat.** Illustrated by John Stadler. Dutton Children's Books, 1991. ISBN 0-525-44762-8. 30p. 3–7. Fiction.

Fourteen verses about unusual animal behaviors give readers an opportunity to learn about rhythm and rhyme, as well as a chance to use their imaginations. Sentences such as "A goat in a coat sails a boat" and "A big pig wears a wig" are illustrated with watercolor and ink drawings that take the plight of each animal as seriously as possible. After reading this book, children will want to write and illustrate their own silly sentences.

9.18   Van Leeuwen, Jean. **Oliver Pig at School.** Illustrated by Ann Schweninger. Dial Books for Young Readers, 1990. ISBN 0-8037-0813-0. 48p. 4–8. Fiction.

Whimsically depicted in colored pencil and watercolor washes in this Easty-to-Read Book, Oliver Pig puts up a brave front as he says good-bye to his toys and his parents and heads for school. School itself is a bit scary, though manageable—until mischief-maker Bernard gets Oliver into trouble. But the two pigs end up friends, and when Oliver returns home from his first day at school, he reports happily to his family that "school is fun."

9.19   Weiss, Nicki. **Dog, Boy, Cap, Skate. Sun, Sand, Sea, Sail.** Illustrated by Nicki Weiss. Greenwillow Books, 1989. 32p. 2–6 (est.). Fiction.

Two books by Nicki Weiss demonstrate how much story can be conveyed with so few words. Across each spread, only four words march, each matched with the object or action directly above it. As a child and his dog prepare to go outdoors, Mom hands over the cap and skates. The text? "Dog / Boy / Cap / Skate." The next page rhymes with the first, thus a family's day at the beach means "Sun / Sand / Sea / Sail" as well as "Umbrella / Towel / Shovel / Pail."

9.20 Wiseman, B. **Morris and Boris at the Circus.** Illustrated by B. Wiseman. Harper and Row/Harper Trophy Books, 1990. ISBN 0-06-444143-1. 64p. 4–8. Fiction.

Morris and Boris, entertaining and goofy as ever, approach the circus in their own predictable styles. Morris, the eternally optimistic moose, is ready to accept every challenge in the ring. Boris the bear is more cautious. When Boris explains that the circus tent is called the Big Top, Morris cheerfully surmises that the elephant's rear must be the Big Bottom. Even the caged lions chuckle at Morris as the action skips from page to page in this I Can Read Book.

9.21 Ziefert, Harriet. **Who Can Boo the Loudest?** Illustrated by Claire Schumacher. Harper and Row, 1990. ISBN 0-06-026899-9. 32p. 3–6 (est.). Fiction.

When two ghosts meet in the moonlight, they disagree over who can boo louder. To settle the matter, they engage in a booing contest, agreeing that the winner will be the ghost who can scare the moon. Even though both ghosts huff and puff and shake their sheets, neither can scare the moon by itself. Perhaps if they worked together? Cartoon illustrations provide simple accompaniment for an easy-to-read, repetitive text.

Jokes, Riddles, and Puns

9.22 Beisner, Monika. **Catch That Cat! A Picture Book of Rhymes and Puzzles.** Illustrated by Monika Beisner. Farrar, Straus and Giroux, 1990. ISBN 0-374-31226-5. 28p. 4–8 (est.). Nonfiction.

Hidden calicoes, vain tabbies, and mysterious Siamese frolic on the pages of this collection of cat verses, riddles, games, and puzzles. Jewel-toned paintings with the feel of tapestries add to the complexity and detail of a book that will invite a variety of responses from cat fanciers of all ages.

9.23 Bierhorst, John, editor. **Lightning inside You, and Other Native American Riddles.** Illustrated by Louise Brierley. William Morrow, 1992. ISBN 0-688-09582-8. 104p. 6 and up (est.). Nonfiction.

"Riddling, like fever, is contagious." Native Americans caught riddling fever long ago, but not until now have their riddles been gathered and widely circulated. Many of the riddles have several possible answers, but only one Native American one, thus these puzzles indirectly provide a glimpse into Native

American culture. The location and tribal origin of each riddle is meticulously attributed, supplemented by instructive beginning notes and endnotes. Black-and-white pastel drawings are sprinkled throughout.

9.24   Calmenson, Stephanie. **What Am I? Very First Riddles.** Illustrated by Karen Gundersheimer. Harper and Row, 1989. ISBN 0-06-020998-4. 32p. 4–7. Nonfiction.

Here are riddles for children who are just beginning riddling—puzzles that don't depend upon wordplay or pun—as well as a book for emerging readers. Each rhyming riddle appears on a page of its own, sprinkled with small children offering clues, and ends with a boldfaced question: "What Am I?" "I'm sweet and cold, so take a lick. But watch me melt if you're not quick!" Turn the page for a full-color picture answer with the word beneath.

9.25   Gomi, Taro. **Who Ate It? Who Hid It?** Illustrated by Taro Gomi. Millbrook Press, 1991. 22p. 2–6 (est.) Fiction.

In a pair of simple, riddle picture books, children search the artwork to answer Who ate it? or Who hid it? At first glance, it seems almost impossible for readers of the first book to know which of four innocent-appearing Holsteins ate the fried eggs. At second glance, young children will discover the yellow yolks in the middle of one Holstein's white markings. Readers of the second book will need to rely on picture play to determine which giraffe hid the birthday candles. There they are, looking like a pair of giraffe horns! Other familiar objects are camouflaged in the artwork in this simple, riddle picture book.

9.26   Gordon, Jeffie Ross. **Hide and Shriek: Riddles about Ghosts and Goblins.** Walton, Rick, and Ann Walton. **Ho Ho Ho! Riddles about Santa Claus.** Illustrated by Susan Slattery Burke. Lerner, 1991. 32p. 6–10. Nonfiction.

Know what goes, "Ho, ho, ho OOPS"? It's Santa Claus falling out of his sled. Know how the reindeer can tell that Santa has fallen out? "They feel a rein drop." Could you have guessed that "Elves" Presley is Santa's favorite singer? Santa Claus groaners fill *Ho, Ho, Ho!*, while *Hide and Shriek* maintains the pattern, but changes the source for the puns: "Who is the most famous French skeleton?" "Napoleon Bone-aparte," of course. Susan Slattery Burke's two-color illustrations keep the spirits light in these You Must Be Joking Riddle Books.

A.

B.

C.

A. *Black and White* by David Macaulay (see 9.45). **B.** *Bones, Bones, Dinosaur Bones* by Byron Barton (see 9.3). **C.** *Baby-O* by Nancy White Carlstrom; illustrated by Suçie Stevenson (see 9.36).

A.

B.

C.

A. *Asleep, Asleep* by Mirra Ginsburg; illustrated by Nancy Tafuri (see 9.6).
B. *Lightning inside You and Other Native American Riddles* edited by John Bierhorst; illustrated by Louise Brierley (see 9.23). **C.** *We're Going on a Bear Hunt* by Michael Rosen; illustrated by Helen Oxenbury (see 9.50).

9.27 Hall, Katy, and Lisa Eisenberg. **Spacey Riddles.** Illustrated by Simms Taback. Dial Books for Young Readers, 1992. ISBN 0-8037-0815-7. 48p. 4–8. Nonfiction.

What is the astronaut's favorite meal? Launch! Why couldn't the astronaut land on the moon? Because it was already full! Here are forty-two riddles with space as their theme in an easy-to-read format. Clues are generous (and humorously misleading) in these full-color illustrations of space travelers, heavenly bodies, and aliens.

9.28 Koontz, Robin Michal. **I See Something You Don't See: A Riddle-me Picture Book.** Illustrated by Robin Michal Koontz. Cobblehill Books, 1992. ISBN 0-525-65077-6. 32p. 4–8 (est.). Nonfiction.

Clues to thirteen rhyming "riddle-me-rees" can be found in the pictures that accompany the riddles. From morning wake-up to tuck-in time, two smiling children participate in ordinary family events that become the fodder for riddle clues. For example, toothbrushing time: "When you look at my face it's easy to see, you're looking at you when you're looking at me." The accompanying illustration shows the children looking in a mirror. Line drawings done in sunny pastel shades make the answers achievable by the youngest children.

9.29 Livingston, Myra Cohn. **My Head Is Red, and Other Riddle Rhymes.** Illustrated by Tere LoPrete. Holiday House, 1990. ISBN 0-8234-0806-X. 32p. 6–9. Nonfiction.

"My head is red. My back is white. You'll find me near the candlelight. But once I make a shining flame, I never, ever look the same." Turn the pages upside down to discover the answers to this and twenty-six other rhyming, readable riddles. Bold abstract illustrations give visual clues to the shapes and the colors of the answer.

9.30 Maestro, Giulio. **Riddle Roundup: A Wild Bunch to Beef Up Your Word Power.** Illustrated by Giulio Maestro. Clarion Books, 1989. ISBN 0-89919-508-3. 64p. 7–10 (est.). Nonfiction.

"Why did the runner put a net over her head? She wanted to catch her breath." "What happened when the pink flower grew? The rose rose rose." The sixty-two riddles in this collection are based on different kinds of wordplay, including puns, homonyms, and homographs. Each riddle is separated from its answer by a full-page, two-color illustration.

9.31 Marzollo, Jean. **I Spy: A Book of Picture Riddles.** Photographs by Walter Wick. Scholastic/Cartwheel Books, 1992. ISBN 0-590-45087-5. 32p. 2–7 (est.). Nonfiction.

Thirteen double-page picture riddles are created by pairing boldly colored photographs of collections of related objects—such as beach items or old toys—with a rhyming text, which begins with the words "I spy . . . " and then names items to be located. For example, the riddle in the nature collection begins: "I spy an arrowhead, a little white goose, / A horse's shadow, a snake on the loose. . . . " The author closes with "Extra Credit Riddles" and an invitation for children to write their own picture riddles.

9.32 Nims, Bonnie Larkin. **Where Is the Bear at School?** Illustrated by Madelaine Gill. Albert Whitman, 1989. ISBN 0-8075-8935-7. 24p. 2–6. Fiction.

At school, children are busy hanging up their coats, listening to a story, painting pictures, and playing on the playground. But within the bustle of classroom activity, there's a teddy bear loose. Readers are invited through rhyming text and repetitive refrain to find the bear hiding on each page: "But I am looking for a bear. Can you show me—where is the bear?" No matter where bear hides, he does what the children do. The watercolor paintings are of multicultural children thoroughly engaged with school.

9.33 Stevenson, James. **Quick! Turn the Page!** Illustrated by James Stevenson. Greenwillow Books, 1990. ISBN 0-688-09309-4. 32p. 4–7 (est.). Fiction.

Here's an innovative way in which readers can help characters out of scrapes just by turning the page. If Sarah is sick of winter, turn the page and give her spring. If Arthur can't get to the movies until his room is cleaned, turn the page and it's clean as a bean. But if you ignore the warning and turn the last page, it's "the end." As always, young readers will find James Stevenson's illustrations and text simple and appealing.

9.34 Yektai, Niki. **What's Silly?** Illustrated by Susannah Ryan. Clarion Books, 1989. ISBN 0-89919-746-9. 32p. 2–8 (est.). Fiction.

In a book suited for interaction with the youngest of listeners, the children's task is always the same: find what's silly in the pictures. Cartoon-like illustrations provide the kind of silliness that makes three- and four-year-old children scream with delight: Mother lathers up to shave her face. Daughter wears her skirt on her head, then swings from an upside-down tree. There's even a toilet in the living room. No bother, though, if the answer eludes—just turn the page to set everything right.

Language Play

9.35 Baer, Gene. **Thump, Thump, Rat-a-Tat-Tat.** Illustrated by Lois Ehlert. Harper and Row/Charlotte Zolotow Books, 1989. ISBN 0-06-020362-5. 30p. 2–7. Fiction.

On the opening spread, the marching band unloads from the bus with the rat-a-tat-tat of snare drums, the thump, thump of bass drums, and the warmup sounds of chirping horns. Marching boldly toward the reader, band and text enlarge to fill the pages. Flags, plumes, "piping flutes," and "flashing brass" are vibrant cut-paper against Lois Ehlert's bold background colors. Text and art are perfect complements: the rhythmic cadence of the ono-matopoeic text thunders past and then fades.

9.36 Carlstrom, Nancy White. **Baby-O.** Illustrated by Suçie Stevenson. Little, Brown, 1992. ISBN 0-316-12851-1. 32p. 3–6 (est.). Fiction.

All the generations of an island family (from Baby-O to Granny-O) board a jitney to take their wares to market. Festive Caribbean colors are a perfect match for the cadence of the text, its singsong rhythms punctuated by onomatopoeic refrains. As Baby-O chases the chickens in the garden patch, "Sing a song of Baby-O, / Sing it soft, now, sing it slow. / Chucka Chucka." Mama-O's cloth goes "Wusha Wusha" in the big tin tub, and Papa-O's fishnets "dippa dippa" off the sandy shores.

9.37 Catalanotto, Peter. **Mr. Mumble.** Illustrated by Peter Catalanotto. Orchard Books/Richard Jackson Books, 1990. ISBN 0-531-08480-9. 32p. 4–7. Fiction.

Mr. Mumble wakes up with a cough one Saturday morning, and as he sets out on a shopping trip, he discovers how much a little cough can interfere with a person's routine. At the bakery he asks for a dozen bagels; what he gets is a dozing beagle. At the fruit stand, a request for a pound of pears gets Mr. Mumble a panda bear. And a mention to the tailor of a light tan coat lands Mr. Mumble a white goat. Peter Catalanotto's book is chock-full of wonderful language play.

9.38   Cauley, Lorinda Bryan. **Clap Your Hands.** Illustrated by Lorinda Bryan Cauley. G. P. Putnam's Sons, 1992. ISBN 0-399-22118-2. 32p. 3–6. Fiction.

"Reach for the sky, wiggle your toes. Stick out your tongue and touch your nose." Smiling animals and children in a frenzy of activity spill across double-page spreads in this spirited book for which participation is a must. Colorful illustrations capture the happy expressions of the playmates as they jump and twirl and finally wave "Bye-bye!"

9.39   Falwell, Cathryn. **Clowning Around.** Illustrated by Cathryn Falwell. Orchard Books, 1991. ISBN 0-531-08552-X. 32p. 3–6. Fiction.

A red and white polka-dot clown juggles and rearranges oversize letters against stark white backgrounds to make words and fun for the youngest readers. As he pushes, pulls, reshapes, and moves letters and their parts, the art magically follows, taking shape and then transforming to match the print. Beginners may want to try juggling and "clowning around" on paper with some letters of their own.

9.40   Florian, Douglas. **A Beach Day.** Illustrated by Douglas Florian. Greenwillow Books, 1990. ISBN 0-688-09105-9. 32p. 3 and up. Fiction.

"Feet splash / Waves crash / Kites sail / Sand pail." With rhyming, minimalist text, a family's day at the beach is revealed through gestural bold line drawings in crayon, colored pencils, and watercolors in sunny hues of yellow and gold. When the day draws to a close, the foursome enjoys a shimmering fireworks display. The last page lists and illustrates several shells that can be found on coastal beaches.

9.41   Fox, Mem. **Shoes from Grandpa.** Illustrated by Patricia Mullins. Orchard Books, 1992. ISBN 0-531-08448-5. 32p. 3–6 (est.). Fiction.

In cumulative fashion, Jessie is clothed by all the members of her family. First, Grandpa gets shoes for Jessie. Then Dad decides, "I'll buy you some socks from the local shops, / to go with the shoes from Grandpa." Next, it's Mom who buys Jessie a skirt "that won't show the dirt, / to go with the socks from the local shops," and on and on until Jessie asks politely for just "some jeans." Torn paper and fabric scraps give the large-scale illustrations pleasing textures.

9.42 Gordon, Jeffie Ross. **Six Sleepy Sheep.** Illustrated by John O'Brien. Caroline House, 1991. ISBN 1-878093-06-1. 32p. 2–6. Fiction.

In a curly iron bed, six sleepy sheep slumber on six soft pillows—until one sheep snores and the whole crew is awake. In alliterative prose, the sleepy sheep try to regain repose through slurping celery soup, telling spooky stories, singing silly songs, and sipping simmered milk until, one by one, they snooze. At last, when all six are asleep, one snores. . . . Sheep made curly and textured with fine pen lines are distinguishable by human accoutrements—necktie, eyeglasses, slippers, or a nightcap.

9.43 Heller, Ruth. **Merry-Go-Round: A Book about Nouns.** Illustrated by Ruth Heller. Grosset and Dunlap, 1990. ISBN 0-448-40085-5. 46p. 6 and up. Nonfiction.

Ruth Heller adds another title to her series on language in this rhyming, color-rich tribute to nouns. Opening with every schoolchild's definition, "Nouns name a person, place or thing," the artist wraps a green-scaled, fuschia-tongued dragon around birches, through which a determined maiden trots, and the text labels: "a *damsel,* a *forest,* a *dragon,* . . . a *king.*" Children meet nouns common and proper, abstract and concrete, compound and collective, singular and plural, all accompanied by dramatic designs.

9.44 Hilton, Nette. **Prince Lachlan.** Illustrated by Ann James. Orchard Books, 1990. ISBN 0-531-08463-9. 32p. 3–6 (est.). Fiction.

In kilt and a jaunty tam-o'-shanter, Prince Lachlan announces his comings and goings about the castle with sounds like "smash," "crash," and "thud." "Prince Lachlan is home," his mother understates. "I know," sighs his laconic father, the king. Nothing in the castle is quite safe from the Prince's energy. But this irritation becomes an asset when the Great One threatens the kingdom—and Prince Lachlan sets off to "see about that." Repetitive phrases and onomatopoeia add to the appeal.

9.45 Macaulay, David. **Black and White.** Illustrated by David Macaulay. Houghton Mifflin, 1990. ISBN 0-395-552151-3. 32p. All ages (est.). Fiction.

Not without warning, readers are faced with double-page spreads divided into four seemingly dissimilar segments. How do they proceed? Once through the book in conventional fashion? Four times through, reading corresponding quadrants? Or should readers visit and revisit, each time shuffling and reshuffling these elements: a boy returning by train to his parents, a row of newspaper-reading commuters, a pair of wacky parents, and a herd of Holstein cows. David Macaulay leaves it to readers to decide if he has written four stories or one. *Caldecott Medal, 1991.*

9.46   MacCarthy, Patricia. **Herds of Words.** Illustrated by Patricia MacCarthy. Dial Books for Young Readers, 1991. ISBN 0-8037-0892-0. 32p. 3–6. Nonfiction.

In batik paintings on silk, groups and families of "things" are gathered into scenes and labeled with their collective nouns. Near a bright blue watering hole, a *stand* of flamingos, a *bask* of crocodiles, and a *clutch* of eggs share a habitat; under a galaxy of stars, a *coven* of witches stirs the brew, while a *parliament* of owls keeps watch. Such unusual nomenclature as a *wedge* of swans, a *leap* of leopards, and an *exaltation* of larks fills the pages.

9.47   McMillan, Bruce. **One Sun: A Book of Terse Verse. Play Day: A Book of Terse Verse.** Photographs by Bruce McMillan. Holiday House, 1990. 32p. 4–6 (est.). Nonfiction.

Terse verse is an adjective-noun combination that rhymes. Bruce McMillan's two books of terse verse are inspired by the seashore and backyard, with full-page color photographs of such verses as "sand hand," "wet pet," "fun run," and "fat bat." Warm skin shades of photogenic children and royal blues and brilliant greens of sky, water, and grass are set opposite the boldly outlined words. In classrooms in which teachers cover the words, children use the book as puzzles to be solved. Best fest!

9.48   Merriam, Eve. **Fighting Words.** Illustrated by David Small. Morrow Junior Books, 1992. ISBN 0-688-09677-8. 32p. 5 and up. Fiction.

In her author's note, Eve Merriam acknowledges that all the fighting words in her book "live happily, harmoniously together in the *Oxford English Dictionary* and in *Webster's Unabridged.*" Within the story, the fighting words are hurled and blasted and growled and howled between two friends, who admire each other so much that it calls for a fight. Fighting words appear in giant type (*Lummox, Ignoramus, Ninny, Lout*) while the children clamor over and through their remarkably undersized world to be friends again.

9.49 Most, Bernard. **Zoodles.** Illustrated by Bernard Most. Harcourt Brace Jovanovich, 1992. ISBN 0-15-299969-8. 32p. 3–8. Nonfiction.

"What do you call a kangaroo that wakes you up every day?" Answer: "A kangarooster!" In this animal riddle book, Bernard Most creates name-blended imaginary beasts. Unlike other imaginary animal books, however, Most doesn't produce a new body design merging the two animals. Instead, he lets each animal retain its recognizable shape and form on the answer page. As with the author/illustrator's dinosaur books, these animal drawings are large, simple, and cheerful.

9.50 Rosen, Michael, reteller. **We're Going on a Bear Hunt.** Illustrated by Helen Oxenbury. Margaret K. McElderry Books, 1989. ISBN 0-689-50476-4. 32p. 4–8. Fiction.

On expansive pages, alternately black-and-white and color, a father and four children set forth on the traditional bear hunt, complete with its predictable challenges of long grass, deep river, oozy mud, and dark forest—all of which must be negotiated: "We can't go over it. / We can't go under it. / Oh, no! / We've got to go through it!" Most fun of all are the full-color sound pages, on which "splash splosh" the river, "squelch squerch" the mud, and "swishy swashy" the grass. *Boston Globe–Horn Book Honor Book, 1990.*

9.51 Shaw, Nancy. **Sheep in a Shop.** Illustrated by Margot Apple. Houghton Mifflin, 1991. ISBN 0-395-53681-2. 32p. 2–5. Fiction.

It's a rollicking shopping trip with five comical sheep. The goal: to find the perfect birthday present for a friend. These enthusiastic customers try on jackets, play with rackets, fly planes, try trains, and dismantle a display of beach balls along the way. Rhyming text and colored-pencil drawings that offer just the right sheepish expressions are a perfect combination for a successful read. Nancy Shaw's *Sheep in a Jeep* and *Sheep on a Ship* add more sheep adventures.

9.52 Shaw, Nancy. **Sheep on a Ship.** Illustrated by Margot Apple. Houghton Mifflin, 1989. ISBN 0-395-48160-0. 26p. 2–6 (est.). Fiction.

The silly sheep from Nancy Shaw's *Sheep in a Jeep* and *Sheep in a Shop* are having another tongue-tripping adventure. This time, in rhyming text, they are pirates on a deep-sea trip. When a storm arises, they are comically unprepared: "Waves slosh.

Sheep slip. Decks tip. Sheep slide. Sheep trip. Sheep collide." Colored pencil drawings add action to the storm and mild desperation to their sheep-overboard faces.

9.53   Shaw, Nancy. **Sheep Out to Eat.** Illustrated by Margot Apple. Houghton Mifflin, 1992. ISBN 0-395-61128-8. 32p. 4–8 (est.).

Dining out for tea is a disaster for the sheep whose rhyming adventures have populated *Sheep in a Jeep* and *Sheep in a Shop*. This time, they can't read the menus, so they neither know what to order nor how to eat it. They add sugar, salt, and mustard to their lovely spinach custard. Adding pepper to their teacakes is even worse. Sneezes turn the teashop upside down. Ejected, they find the lawn is just what sheep need to munch for lunch.

9.54   Steig, Jeanne. **Alpha Beta Chowder.** Illustrated by William Steig. HarperCollins, 1992. ISBN 0-06-205007-9. 32p. 4–10 (est.). Fiction.

A collaboration of Steigs has cooked up an alphabet chowder of twenty-six rhymes and seasoned them with spirited, witty characters. For the letter *H*, there is the "Heebie-Jeebies," which is what a harpy with the hiccups hurls upon the hag who hexes her. In alliterative verse with the bite of Ogden Nash or the sting of Roald Dahl, Jeanne Steig succeeds with such unexpected subjects as "Ken, the killer kangaroo," and Daphne, who dresses divinely.

9.55   Ziefert, Harriet. **Parade.** Illustrated by Saul Mandel. Bantam/Little Rooster Books, 1990. ISBN 0-553-05862-2. 32p. 2–6 (est.). Fiction.

"A parade! A parade! I know a parade by the sound of the drum. A-rum-a-tee-tum! A-rum-a-tee-tum!" In rhythmic, easy-to-read text that evokes a cadence, Harriet Ziefert describes a circus parade as it marches jauntily down the street, accompanied by clowns and elephants, jugglers and twirlers, and popcorn and candy. Saul Mandel's loose, cartoon-like drawings complement the action-packed event.

Poetry

"I," says the poem matter-of-factly,
"I am a cloud,
I am a tree,

I am a city,
I am the sea,

I am a golden
mystery."

But, *adds the poem silently,*
I cannot speak until you come.
Reader, come, come with me.

Eve Merriam, *It Doesn't Always
Have to Rhyme*

10 Poetry

Anthologies

10.1 Bennett, Jill, compiler. **The Animal Fair.** Illustrated by Susie Jenkin-Pearce. Viking Penguin, 1990. ISBN 0-670-82691-X. 32p. 2–7.

This collection of twenty-two rhymes in celebration of animals includes works by Aileen Fisher, Langston Hughes, and Eleanor Farjeon, as well as humorous verse by anonymous poets, such as the title poem, "Animal Fair." Watercolor and ink combine on generously spaced page layouts to achieve a whimsy that sits lightly with the verse.

10.2 **Big Bear's Treasury: A Children's Anthology.** Candlewick Press, 1992. ISBN 1-56402-113-0. 80p. 4–8 (est.).

Dozens of poems and very short stories to match every mood are woven together with excerpts from well-known fairy tales and nonsense rhymes in this second volume of Big Bear's favorites. The anthology is enriched by the inclusion of original illustrations and features works by Anthony Browne, Charlotte Voake, Helen Oxenbury, and Jan Ormerod. The pages take only minutes to read aloud, but are distinctive and sufficiently illustrated for the youngest to find and "read" alone.

10.3 Booth, David, compiler. **Voices on the Wind: Poems for All Seasons.** Illustrated by Michèle Lemieux. Morrow Junior Books, 1990. ISBN 0-688-09555-0. 48p. All ages.

Poems from favorite poets celebrating the sights and sounds of the seasons are combined with artistic impressions of the poems' moods. Included are Mary Ann Hoberman's "Spiders," Robert Louis Stevenson's "Autumn Fires," Beatrix Potter's "Fishes Come Bite!" and William Blake's "The Lamb."

10.4 Bruchac, Joseph, and Jonathan London. **Thirteen Moons on Turtle's Back: A Native American Year of Moons.** Illustrated by Thomas Locker. Philomel Books, 1992. ISBN 0-399-22141-7. 28p. All ages.

Many North American Indian tribes used the scales of the turtle's shell to represent the "months" of the year. From traditions of the Sioux, Lakota, and Cherokee, to name a few, this collection of seasonal poems represents an anthology of native beliefs. Each "moon" includes both a legend and a dramatic, brilliantly hued oil painting. Together, they provide a unique orientation to time, the Earth, and humanity's role within each.

10.5 **Cameo Cats.** Illustrated by Isabelle Brent. Little, Brown, 1992. ISBN 0-316-10836-7. 22p. 6 and up (est.).

This ornate anthology features bordered mosaics in royal colors and snippets from literature celebrating felines. Contributors range from Edward Lear to Chaucer to Mother Goose. The cameo portraits represent cats of various types and in varying poses. "Even the smallest of the felines is a masterpiece," said Da Vinci, and this tiny jewel of a book demonstrates that mastery.

10.6 Cassedy, Sylvia, and Kunihiro Suetake, translators. **Red Dragonfly on My Shoulder.** Illustrated by Molly Bang. HarperCollins, 1992. ISBN 0-06-022625-0. 32p. 6–10 (est.).

Turn the collection sideways to read, scroll-like, these thirteen haiku, the ancient Japanese form of poetry. The translations offer inspired images, but Molly Bang's clever and playful collages demand close attention as well. Throughout, she uses common materials—from a yam to a crab leg—in inspired ways. Jet-black crickets constructed of safety pins, screws, wires, and hairpins climb blades of grass toward a golden cricket to accompany the lines "Above the chorus, / listen! A single cricket / shakes a golden bell."

10.7 Cole, Joanna, and Stephanie Calmenson, compilers. **The Eentsy, Weentsy Spider: Fingerplays and Action Rhymes.** Illustrated by Alan Tiegreen. Morrow Junior Books, 1991. ISBN 0-688-09439-2. 64p. 3 and up.

This cheery collection of action rhymes brings together some of the most popular rhymes ("This Old Man," "I'm a Little Teapot") as well as less familiar pieces. "How-to" illustrations demonstrate how to act out the rhymes, gesture by gesture. An index to first lines, bibliography, and some musical arrangements are also included.

10.8 Cole, Joanna, and Stephanie Calmenson, compilers. **Miss Mary Mack, and Other Children's Street Rhymes.** Illustrated by Alan Tiegreen. Morrow Junior Books, 1990. ISBN 0-688-08330-7. 64p. 7 and up.

Joanna Cole and Stephanie Calmenson have collected five chapters of rhymes for street games and jumping rope—not the rhymes read to kids in school or at home, but those that children experience while playing independently. Topical chapters include "Hand-Clapping," "Ball-Bouncing," and "Teases and Comebacks," with introductory paragraphs instructing readers on hand-clapping and ball-bouncing techniques. The compilers go to the line in this collection and include street rhymes to which some parents might object, but which kids often chant among themselves.

10.9   Cole, William, compiler. **A Zooful of Animals.** Illustrated by Lynn Munsinger. Houghton Mifflin, 1992. ISBN 0-395-52278-1. 88p. 4–9.

A trip to the zoo is the organizing theme for this wide-ranging collection of whimsical poetry. Humorous poems and illustrations are gracefully balanced and vividly formatted. Both famous poets (such as John Ciardi, Rudyard Kipling, and Carolyn Wells) and little-known authors contribute poems about the funny, wry, and often-touching plights of a variety of animals. Personified inhabitants of this eccentric world range from a lonely platypus to a dancing giraffe. Comical paintings are carefully drawn, colorful, and engaging.

10.10   Daniel, Mark, compiler. **A Child's Treasury of Seaside Verse.** Dial Books for Young Readers, 1991. ISBN 0-8037-0889-0. 130p. All ages.

In this collection of verses inspired by the sea, works by nineteenth-century and early twentieth-century British and American poets predominate. Accompanying poems by Byron, Whitman, Longfellow, Rossetti, Poe, and Dickinson are full-color reproductions of oil paintings from the Edwardian and Victorian eras, as well as black-and-white prints.

10.11   Demi, compiler. **In the Eyes of the Cat: Japanese Poetry for All Seasons.** Illustrated by Demi. Henry Holt, 1992. ISBN 0-8050-1955-3. 77p. All ages (est.).

Classic Japanese poetry is organized around the seasons of the year, with animals and their activities depicted in ink and watercolor paintings which capture both the subject and the mood of each poem. This collection exemplifies simple, elegant imagery for students of all ages—from a mother hen at a pond pecking her image into bits to the monkey in winter who wants a warm snowsuit.

10.12   Frank, Josette, compiler. **Snow toward Evening: A Year in a River Valley.** Illustrated by Thomas Locker. Dial Books, 1990. ISBN 0-8037-0811-4. 32p. 5 and up (est.).

The rich combination of poems and paintings makes *Snow toward Evening* a picture book to be appreciated by readers of all ages. Poets such as Langston Hughes, William Wordsworth, and John Updike describe the diversity of the seasons. Thomas Locker's lush, detailed oil paintings of the Hudson River Valley allow the reader to experience the grandeur of nature. Teachers could use the book to introduce younger children to close observation and reflection on the seasons, or older readers to the exquisite imagery of language.

10.13   Goldstein, Bobbye S., compiler. **Inner Chimes: Poems on Poetry.** Illustrated by Jane Breskin Zalben. Boyds Mills Press/Wordsong, 1992. ISBN 1-56397-040-6. 24p. All ages.

Delicate and engaging illustrations help word lovers of all ages to enjoy again the familiar works of Eleanor Farjeon ("Poetry"), Eve Merriam ("Inside a Poem"), and Beatrice Schenk de Regniers ("Keep a Poem in Your Pocket") in this twenty-poem collection which celebrates the wonder of poetry. Young poets will be reminded of the nature of poetry ("It doesn't always have to rhyme") and the comforts and challenges of writing it ("Where do you get the idea for a poem?").

10.14   Goldstein, Bobbye S., compiler. **What's on the Menu?** Illustrated by Chris L. Demarest. Viking Penguin, 1992. ISBN 0-670-83031-3. 32p. 3–8.

From animal crackers to chocolate cake, Italian noodles to codfish, Bobbye Goldstein gathers poems with food as their subject and organizes them into a day's bill of fare. For the opening section titled "From Sleepyhead to Breakfast Spread," there is "Breakfast Talk" by Bobbi Katz, John Ciardi's "Mummy Slept Late . . . ," and Karla Kuskin's "The Meal." Throughout the day, readers are offered tastes of the works of Eve Merriam, Arnold Adoff, X. J. Kennedy, Aileen Fisher, Jack Prelutsky, and Ogden Nash. Watercolor washes over ink-line cartoons make for simple, cheery pages.

10.15   Harvey, Anne, compiler. **Shades of Green.** Illustrated by John Lawrence. Greenwillow Books, 1992. ISBN 0-688-10890-3. 192p. 12 and up.

Selecting works by Walt Whitman, William Blake, and Chaucer, Anne Harvey shows a historical concern about the environment in this collection of poems celebrating nature. Grouped into ten chapters ranging from "A Green Hope" through "So They Are Felled" to "For Those Born Later," the cumulative message of this anthology is that humanity should look upon itself as one with, not superior to, the natural world.

10.16   Hopkins, Lee Bennett, compiler. **Good Books, Good Times!** Illustrated by Harvey Stevenson. Harper and Row/Charlotte Zolotow Books, 1990. ISBN 0-06-022528-9. 32p. 5–8.

For book fans of all stripes, for teachers and librarians who wish to grow book lovers, and for the sheer joy of reading about reading, Lee Bennett Hopkins has selected fourteen celebratory poems, and Harvey Stevenson has painted readers' worlds to accompany each. For Arnold Lobel's "Books to the Ceiling," a child sits atop a mile-high stack wearing the beard he'll have before he reads them all. Poets such as Aileen Fisher, X. J. Kennedy, Jack Prelutsky, and David McCord share their imaginations and sunny reading days.

10.17   Hopkins, Lee Bennett, compiler. **Happy Birthday.** Illustrated by Hilary Knight. Simon and Schuster Books for Young Readers, 1991. ISBN 0-671-70973-9. 30p. 5–9 (est.).

This collection of sixteen birthday poems is cleverly arranged and illustrated to follow a birthday boy awakening on "A Special Day" (by Sandra Liatsos) to the tucked-in star blessing of William Shakespeare. Along the way, the preparation, festivities, and traditions are exuberantly engaged in by children. Poets include Myra Cohn Livingston, Rose Fyleman, Aileen Fisher, Beatrice Schenk de Regniers, and Dr. Seuss.

10.18   Hopkins, Lee Bennett, compiler. **On the Farm.** Illustrated by Laurel Molk. Little, Brown, 1991. ISBN 0-316-37274-9. 32p. 4–10 (est.).

Superimposed on homey illustrations in colors of the seasons are sixteen poems by a roster of award-winning poets. Subjects for Aileen Fisher, Valerie Worth, David McCord, Lilian Moore, William Carlos Williams, and others include farm animals (cows, foals, pigs, roosters), farm activities (berry picking, haying), and farm equipment (wheelbarrow, lawn mower).

10.19   Hopkins, Lee Bennett, compiler. **Questions.** Illustrated by Carolyn Croll. HarperCollins/Charlotte Zolotow Books, 1992. ISBN 0-06-022413-4. 64p. 4–7 (est.).

In sections titled "Who?" "What?" "Where?" "When?" "How?" and "Why?" Lee Bennett Hopkins collects poetry and simple rhymes that ask questions. Poets Eve Merriam, Karla Kuskin, Aileen Fisher, Sandra Liatsos, Dorothy Aldis, Leland Jacobs, and Hopkins himself are represented. Best of all, young readers (and questioners) can manage for themselves the poems in this I Can Read Book. From Margaret Wise Brown, Hopkins selected "The Secret Song": "Who saw the petals / drop from the rose? / I, said the spider, / But nobody knows." Carolyn Croll's illustrations are rounded forms in warm colors.

10.20   Hopkins, Lee Bennett, compiler. **Side by Side: Poems to Read Together.** Illustrated by Hilary Knight. Simon and Schuster Books for Young Readers, 1991. ISBN 0-671-73622-1. 96p. 4 and up.

Favorite poems, classic and contemporary, are spread across oversize pages and encircled by jubilant children and animals. Poems with a similar setting or theme are illustrated within a single double-page spread. For example, "The Picnic," "Munching Peaches," "Seaweed," and "Sea Wave" are all illustrated by a sandy beach scene with playful splashers. Hilary Knight's watercolors are muted, but her subjects are consistently joyous and animated.

10.21   Hopkins, Lee Bennett, compiler. **To the Zoo: Animal Poems.** Illustrated by John Wallner. Little, Brown, 1992. ISBN 0-316-37273-0. 32p. 4–9 (est.).

Here is a collection of poems, short and long, in testimony to the zoo and its inhabitants. Included are works by Myra Cohn Livingston, Dorothy Aldis, Beatrice Schenk de Regniers, Maxine Kumin, and Lee Bennett Hopkins himself. Tribute is offered to zebras, camels, hippos, and monkeys. The dappled paintings give texture to the animals, depth to the pages, and bring light to the faces of the children.

10.22   **I Love You: Verses and Sweet Sayings. Nursery Poems and Prayers. Nursery Songs and Lullabies.** Illustrated by Bessie Pease Gutman. Grosset and Dunlap, 1990–91. 30p. All ages.

Full-page reproductions of Bessie Pease Gutmann's rosy early twentieth-century paintings of babies and toddlers grace these nostalgic anthologies. *Songs and Lullabies* prints musical arrangements for each of its tunes, including "Where is Thumbkin?" and "The Mulberry Bush." *Verses and Sweet Sayings* features poems about friendship and love. *Poems and Prayers* collects traditional nursery rhymes ("One, Two, Buckle My Shoe") as well as other cherished verses.

10.23   Kennedy, X. J., and Dorothy M. Kennedy, compilers. **Talking like the Rain: A First Book of Poems.** Illustrated by Jane Dyer. Little, Brown, 1992. ISBN 0-316-48889-5. 95p. All ages.

Luminescent watercolors reflect the varied tones of favorite poems, old and new. Works of Christina Rossetti, Edward Lear, Robert Frost, and Robert Louis Stevenson are set beside those of Myra Cohn Livingston, David McCord, Dennis Lee, and Karla Kuskin. Poems are gathered into sections of play, family, magic and wonder, and calendars and clocks. The compilers link the inspiration for their title to Isak Dinesen, who wrote of young field workers who, enchanted with the sound of rhymes, begged Dinesen to "speak like the rain."

10.24   Larrick, Nancy, compiler. **Mice Are Nice.** Illustrated by Ed Young. Philomel Books, 1990. ISBN 0-399-21495-X. 45p. All ages.

"Mice are whiskers, mice like rice, mice are tiny, mice are nice." In gathering this collection of poems about mice by such renowned poets as John Ciardi, A. A. Milne, Patricia Hubbell, and others, Nancy Larrick has captured the innocence and playfulness of these tiny creatures. Ed Young's full-page, dark-toned charcoal and pastel sketches illustrate the celebrated verses and help to convey the mysterious nature of these gentle friends.

10.25   Larrick, Nancy, compiler. **The Night of the Whippoorwill.** Illustrated by David Ray. Philomel Books, 1992. ISBN 0-399-21874-2. 71p. All ages.

In her foreword to *The Night of the Whippoorwill*, Nancy Larrick writes that "Through the ages, musicians, poets, and storytellers have been caught up in . . . nighttime magic." These thirty-four selections from both ancient and modern poets were collected in tribute to the night and its continuing enchantment. Each is accompanied by the night colors of David Ray's acrylic paintings. Included are selections from Langston Hughes, David McCord, Jane Yolen, Carl Sandburg, and Patricia Hubbell, as well as from Hopi and Papago Indians, Estonians, and Society Islanders.

10.26 Larrick, Nancy, compiler. **To the Moon and Back: A Collection of Poems.** Illustrated by Catharine O'Neill. Delacorte Press, 1991. ISBN 0-385-30159-6. 84p. 6–9.

Forty-eight English and American poets and sixty-six poems are represented in this collection that covers topics, ideas, and moods that range "to the moon and back." Title credit belongs to Rowena Bennett's "From the Witch of Willowby Wood." Nancy Larrick's organizational sections include "I'll Tell You a Story," "To the Edge of the Dashing Sea," "Casting Their Nets for Stars," "How Nice to Be a Speckled Frog," "Someone Small but a Piece of It All," and others.

10.27 Larrick, Nancy, and Wendy Lamb, editors. **To Ride a Butterfly: Original Pictures, Stories, Poems, and Songs for Children by Fifty-two Distinguished Authors and Illustrators.** Bantam Doubleday Dell, 1991. ISBN 0-440-50402-3. 96p. All ages.

To celebrate the twenty-fifth anniversary of Reading Is Fundamental, fifty-two highly regarded authors and illustrators of books for children contributed original drawings, paintings, photographs, stories, poems, songs, and nonfiction to this magnificent full-color collection. Joining in as donors were suppliers of materials (paper and cartons) and services (printers, binders, separators, strippers, typesetters). The purchase of this book means a contribution to RIF, a fifty-state nonprofit organization devoted to bringing books to children.

10.28 Livingston, Myra Cohn, compiler. **Dog Poems.** Illustrated by Leslie Morrill. Holiday House, 1990. ISBN 0-8234-0776-4. 32p. 5–12 (est.).

Fourteen poems are collected here for all dog-loving readers. Poems range in scope from Ann Whitford Paul's description of the "Newborn Puppy" to John Ciardi's loving account of his "Dollar Dog" to Beverly McLoughland's playful look at the always-brave "Chihuahua." This varied group of traditional and contemporary poems is illustrated with pencil sketches.

10.29 Livingston, Myra Cohn, compiler. **If You Ever Meet a Whale.** Illustrated by Leonard Everett Fisher. Holiday House, 1992. ISBN 0-8234-0940-6. 32p. 6–10 (est.).

If you ever meet a whale outside of its ocean home, try to arrange to meet the whales in this volume, experiencing them through the poetry of John Ciardi, X. J. Kennedy, or Elizabeth Coatsworth, as well as through poetry by Native Americans and Greenland Inuits. The poetry itself ranges from the wrenching pain of a harpooned whale in its last confused moments of life to the lighthearted anonymous title poem. Leonard Everett Fisher's paintings are equal to the range of feelings.

10.30 Livingston, Myra Cohn, compiler. **Poems for Grandmothers.** Illustrated by Patricia Cullen-Clark. Holiday House, 1990. ISBN 0-8234-0830-2. 32p. 5–8.

Grandmothers across time and representing all kinds of life-styles—from those who work at the department store to those who wear wool shawls and rock in a chair—are celebrated by poets such as David McCord, X. J. Kennedy, Lucille Clifton, and Valerie Worth. Black-and-white pencil drawings find a child's link to each grandmother.

10.31 Livingston, Myra Cohn, compiler. **A Time to Talk: Poems of Friendship.** Margaret K. McElderry Books, 1992. ISBN 0-689-50558-2. 115p. 12 and up.

The title of this collection is taken from Robert Frost's "Time to Talk," a poem of testimony to leaving work undone to walk to the stone wall "for a friendly visit." Five sections divide the poetry into "Friends in Company," "Strange Friends," "False Friends," "Lost Friends," and "Friends Remembered." Among the poets whose works are included are Paul Lawrence Dunbar, e. e. cummings, Gwendolyn Brooks, Bertolt Brecht, Christina Rossetti, and Emily Dickinson.

10.32 Marzollo, Jean, adapter. **The Teddy Bear Book.** Illustrated by Ann Schweninger. Dial Books for Young Readers, 1989. ISBN 0-8037-0633-2. 32p. 2–7.

For those who love their teddies, here is a collection of jump-rope jingles, songs, and traditional rhymes adapted to yield a teddy bear flair. In "Eenie, meenie, minie, mo," it's a teddy, not a tiger, that gets caught by the toe. In "Down by the Station," teddy bears are all in a row. Other rhymes have teddy where it has always been—in bear hunts and in jumping rhymes turning around and touching the ground. Illustrations are bear-filled and sunny.

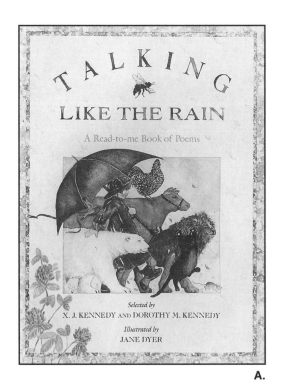

A.

B.

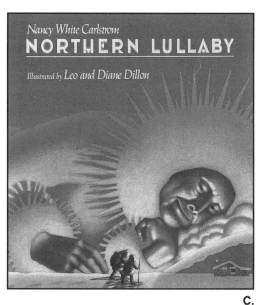

C.

D.

A. *Talking Like the Rain: A First Book of Poems* selected by X. J. Kennedy and Dorothy M. Kennedy; illustrated by Jane Dyer (see 10.23). **B.** *Bizarre Birds & Beasts: Animal Verses* by James Marsh (see 10.65). **C.** *Northern Lullaby* by Nancy White Carlstrom; illustrated by Leo and Diane Dillon (see 10.82). **D.** *Neighborhood Odes* by Gary Soto; illustrated by David Diaz (see 10.76).

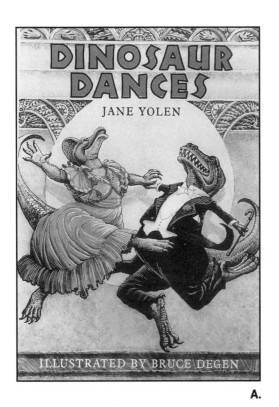

A.

B.

C.

A. *Dinosaur Dances* by Jane Yolen; illustrated by Bruce Degen (see 10.80). **B.** *hist whist* by e. e. cummings; illustrated by Deborah Kogan Ray (see 10.85). **C.** *The Animal That Drank Up Sound* by William Stafford; illustrated by Debra Frasier (see 10.102).

10.33 Milnes, Gerald, compiler. **Granny Will Your Dog Bite, and Other Mountain Rhymes.** Illustrated by Kimberly Bulcken Root. Alfred A. Knopf/Borzoi Books, 1990. ISBN 0-394-94749-5. 45p. 4–10.

Every nation must pass on its traditional art to its children, and this collection of Appalachian folk poetry does exactly that. The pages include riddles, spelling rhymes, nonsense rhymes, and stories; rhyme, dialect, and humor combine to make them irresistable introductions to a culture. Full-color Rockwell-like illustrations of mountain life help explain and dramatize the language. A foot-tapping audio tape is available.

10.34 Moore, Lilian, compiler. **Sunflakes: Poems for Children.** Illustrated by Jan Ormerod. Clarion Books, 1992. ISBN 0-395-58833-2. 96p. All ages.

Lilian Moore believes that poems in the lives of young children can help them "to stay in touch with the poets they . . . are." Primarily for this audience she has drawn together forty poems for sharing and enjoying, for remembering sensory pleasures, for comforting, for playing with ideas and language, and for stretching the imagination. Jan Ormerod's gently washed sketches edge works by Valerie Worth, Eve Merriam, David McCord, Karla Kuskin, Mary Ann Hoberman, John Ciardi, Jack Prelutsky, and others.

10.35 Nye, Naomi Shihab, compiler. **This Same Sky: A Collection of Poems from around the World.** Four Winds Press, 1992. ISBN 0-02-768440-7. 212p. All ages (est.).

Naomi Shihab Nye has collected poems from all around the world that are "accessible to younger readers." Poets from Mexico, Paraguay, Kuwait, Syria, El Salvador, Bangladesh, and sixty-two other countries are grouped in three sections labeled "Dreams and Dreamers," "Families," and "Human Mysteries." A noted poet herself, Nye believes that "those of us living in the United States suffer from a particular literary provinciality, imagining ourselves to be the primary readers and writers of the planet." The voices of similar struggles attest to our connections to those in foreign lands.

10.36 Osborne, Mary Pope, compiler. **Bears, Bears, Bears: A Treasury of Stories, Songs, and Poems about Bears.** Illustrated by Karen Lee Schmidt. Silver Press, 1990. ISBN 0-671-69631-9. 96p. 3–7.

Bears, bears everywhere star in a bear revue of poems, legends, fables, rhymes, and songs. Included are excerpts from Maurice Sendak's *Little Bear* and from A. A. Milne's *Winnie-the-Pooh*. Arnold Lobel's "The Bear and the Crow" from his *Fables* is here, as well as poems by Jane Yolen, Margaret Wise Brown, Ogden Nash, and Dennis Lee. Folktales and fables are included from the Inuit, Native Americans, and the American South. Bear tales are also translated from the Norse and German.

10.37   Prelutsky, Jack, compiler. **Poems of A. Nonny Mouse.** Illustrated by Henrik Drescher. Alfred A. Knopf/Borzoi Books, 1989. ISBN 0-394-98711-X. 44p. 5–9 (est.).

Thanks to an unexpected letter from a rodent poet, Ms. A. Nonny Mouse, Jack Prelutsky has been able to correct the typographical errors that, over the years, credited Ms. Mouse's many poems to "Anonymous." With her works now (at last) collected in a book of her own, Ms. Mouse invited Mr. Prelutsky to tuck in a few of his own poems as well, which he did, anonymously of course. Funny, bouncing rhymes abound with zany color illustrations to boot.

10.38   Rosen, Michael, editor. **Home.** HarperCollins/Charlotte Zolotow Books, 1992. ISBN 0-06-021789-8. 32p. 6–12 (est.).

In support of Share Our Strength, an organization to aid the homeless, Michael Rosen has gathered the contributions of thirteen authors and seventeen illustrators who, in turn, waived their royalties in support of hunger relief. The pieces explore the theme of home as a special place of belonging from the vantage points of varying genres, cultures, and art styles. For Fritz Brandenberg and Aliki, home is "My Bed" and all the roles that a child plays out there. Also included are works by Karla Kuskin and Myra Cohn Livingston and artwork by Leo and Diane Dillon and Jerry Pinkney.

10.39   Rosen, Michael, compiler. **Itsy-Bitsy Beasties: Poems from around the World.** Illustrated by Alan Baker. Carolrhoda Books, 1992. ISBN 0-87614-747-3. 32p. 5–8.

From the playground version of "Little Miss Muffet" (in which Miss Muffet eats the spider) to Lilian Moore's "Hey Bug!" to Japanese and aboriginal poems, Michael Rosen has produced a collection of tributes to nature's smallest creatures—bees and fleas, worms and wasps. Some of the poems are humorous, some are thoughtful, but each is very short, easy to read, and accompanied by Alan Baker's sharp-line, realistic interpretations of the subjects.

10.40 Schwartz, Alvin, compiler. **And the Green Grass Grew All Around: Folk Poetry from Everyone.** Illustrated by Sue Truesdell. HarperCollins, 1992. ISBN 0-06-022758-3. 195p. All ages.

On the cover flap of Alvin Schwartz's collection, folk poetry is equated with "autograph and street rhymes, parodies, riddles, and nonsense"—the verse of ordinary people that begs to be chanted, sung, shared, and created. Here, three hundred rarely written-down verses that children teach children are collected along with source information. Among the sections are "People," "Food," "School," "Teases and Taunts," and "Wishes and Warnings." Remember "Liar, liar, pants on fire?" In a classroom library, this book will never get reshelved.

10.41 Schwartz, Alvin, compiler. **I Saw You in the Bathtub, and Other Folk Rhymes.** Illustrated by Syd Hoff. Harper and Row, 1989. ISBN 0-06-025299-5. 64p. 5–8 (est.).

Children's humorist Alvin Schwartz has gathered forty folk rhymes (jingles, jump-rope rhymes, and even playground taunts) from eleven states and three countries into an I Can Read Book; for example: "Tattle tale, ginger ale, Stick your head in a garbage pail." Each rhyme, illustrated with Syd Hoff's familiar artwork, covers only one or two pages and offers beginners predictable print. The real appeal, however, is the element of silly humor in each rhyme, which is bound to entertain children.

10.42 Whipple, Laura, compiler. **Eric Carle's Dragons Dragons, and Other Creatures That Never Were.** Illustrated by Eric Carle. Philomel Books, 1991. ISBN 0-399-22105-0. 69p. 5–9 (est.).

If you were asked to choose only one illustrator to produce a picture poetry book of dragons and other imaginary beasts, you might say without hesitation, "Eric Carle!" Imagine a wildly sprawling, clawing Chinese dragon that requires two fold-out pages just to contain it. Imagine Pegasus, Anansi, and centaurs, or a unicorn, griffin, and phoenix from Carle's unbridled fancy. Included are poems about fantasy creatures by such poets as Karla Kuskin, Rainer Maria Rilke, Paul Fleischman, and Myra Cohn Livingston in this companion book to Carle's *Animals Animals*. Bring out the paint and colored tissue, because both books beg for response.

Collections by a Single Poet

10.43   Adoff, Arnold. **Chocolate Dreams.** Illustrated by Turi MacCombie. Lothrop, Lee and Shepard Books, 1989. ISBN 0-688-06823-5. 63p. 8–12 (est.).

Chocolate chip cookies, hot chocolate stew, macaroni and chocolate, sweet milk-chocolate-covered cherries, and a steamy cup of hot chocolate with melting marshmallows are all inspirations for these forty-eight original poems. Wordplay, story poems, and even labels for chocolate products are included in this temptingly illustrated anthology for chocolate devotees. The poet warns, "We will be watching very lovingly to make sure no one licks any of these pages, bites the binding, or chews the covers of this chocolate book."

10.44   Barker, Cicely Mary. **A Treasury of Flower Fairies.** Illustrated by Cicely Mary Barker. Federick Warne, 1991. ISBN 0-7232-3796-4. 126p. All ages.

This handsome volume, collected from Cicely Mary Barker's many flower fairy books, gives the reader an introduction to the grace of her illustrations and the charming poetry that she created to share her love of wildflowers. The poems combine fanciful fairy songs and accurate descriptions of each flower, including occasional warnings not to eat them. The illustrations are enlarged and reprinted from her original watercolors begun in 1923 in which she faithfully depicts each flower and the fairy who sings its song.

10.45   Bryan, Ashley. **Sing to the Sun.** Illustrated by Ashley Bryan. HarperCollins, 1992. ISBN 0-06-020833-3. 32p. All ages (est.).

Twenty-three original poems "sing to the sun" in the rhythms and voice of the Caribbean, accompanied by the poet/illustrator's patterns of shapes and colors in primitive representations of the songs. There's the swooshing poem of "The Hurricane": "I blow as I wish / I wish / I wish / I crush and / I splash and / I rush and / I swish." Then at last: "Ah, *now* the wind listens / It brushes my hair / Chases clouds slowly / Sings in my ear, *'Whooree, whooree!'* " Ashley Bryan invites participation in nature and family.

10.46   Ciardi, John. **The Hopeful Trout, and Other Limericks.** Illustrated by Susan Meddaugh. Houghton Mifflin, 1989. ISBN 0-395-43606-0. 52p. 6 and up.

Lively limericks by John Ciardi, winner of the 1982 NCTE Award for Excellence in Poetry for Children, are arranged by topic headings such as "It Came from Outer Space" and "Sometimes Even Parents Win." The rhymes are funny, silly yet clever, and many recount full narrative stories in the course of their five short lines about such characters as the silly old skinflint named Quince. Susan Meddaugh's quirky pen-and-ink illustrations add depth to the text, sometimes leading the reader down unexpected paths of interpretation.

10.47   de Gasztold, Carmen Bernos (translated by Rumer Godden). **Prayers from the Ark: Selected Poems.** Illustrated by Barry Moser. Viking Penguin, 1992. ISBN 0-670-84496-9. 32p. 8 and up (est.).

First published within a French abbey, the manuscript from which these prayers were selected was discovered by Rumer Godden, who translated them because she believed in their economy, sense, and truthfulness. Godden explains in the foreword to these thirteen prayers of the ark animals that they are not wishes, pleas, or cries, but rather convey acceptance of one's state. Noah's pensive prayer is to reach the shore of "Your covenant." The pig harrumphs that he won't thank them "for fattening me up to make bacon." Barry Moser's paintings are luminous portraits of each supplicant.

10.48   de la Mare, Walter. **Peacock Pie: A Book of Rhymes.** Illustrated by Louise Brierley. Henry Holt, 1989. ISBN 0-8050-1124-2. 111p. 5 and up (est.).

First published in 1913, this collection offers ninety-two rhymed poems, interspersed with softly shadowed black-and-white etchings and pastel color plates prepared for this edition. Although young readers may not understand some of the vocabulary (*darnel, fray, dree, cullie*), they will still delight in the rhymes and rhythms of Walter de la Mare's verse. The poems, ranging in length from eight lines to five pages, touch on such varied topics as castle thieves, mistletoe, ships, mad princes, witches, and fairies.

10.49   Dickinson, Emily (selected by Karen Ackerman). **A Brighter Garden.** Illustrated by Tasha Tudor. Philomel Books, 1990. ISBN 0-399-21490-9. 63p. 6–12 (est.).

To commemorate the one-hundredth anniversary of the first publication of Emily Dickinson's poetry, Karen Ackerman has

selected twenty-three poems that revel in the relationships between human beings and their natural world. In her introduction, Ackerman writes that Emily Dickinson "intended to touch
the child within us all . . . because she believed . . . that the child
who sees each season of the year as a new and uncomplicated
miracle never really grows old." Tasha Tudor's cameo-shaped
watercolors exquisitely capture Dickinson's garden world.

10.50   Fisher, Aileen. **Always Wondering: Some Favorite Poems of
Aileen Fisher.** Illustrated by Joan Sandin. HarperCollins/Char-
lotte Zolotow Books, 1991. ISBN 0-06-022858-X. 86p. 7–12.

This collection of poems by Aileen Fisher, winner of the 1978
NCTE Award for Excellence in Poetry for Children, has been
selected by the poet herself. Four sections organize the book:
"Think About People," "Suddenly," "Such Things as These,"
and "Whoever Planned the World." Fisher's love of nature and
keenly observant eye are evident throughout. Joan Sandin's
black-and-white illustrations announce the units.

10.51   Fleischman, Paul. **Joyful Noise: Poems for Two Voices.** Illustrated by Eric Beddows. Harper and Row/Charlotte Zolotow
Books, 1988. ISBN 0-06-021853-3. 46p. All ages.

In the manner of his *I Am Phoenix: Poems for Two Voices,* Paul
Fleischman presents fourteen poems intended to be read aloud
by two readers (or two groups of readers), with one reader's text
appearing in a left column and the other's on the right. The
joyful noises are those of insects: grasshoppers, fireflies, wasps,
beetles, and more. Black-and-white drawings of musical critters
show hints of realism. *Boston Globe–Horn Book Honor Book, 1988;
Newbery Medal, 1989.*

10.52   Greenfield, Eloise. **Night on Neighborhood Street.** Illustrated
by Jan Spivey Gilchrist. Dial Books for Young Readers, 1991.
ISBN 0-8037-0778-9. 32p. 6 and up (est.).

The strengths and fears of the African Americans living on
Neighborhood Street are explored through this collection of poems by award-winning author Eloise Greenfield: Karen is sung
to sleep by her older sister while Mama works a late-night job;
the Robinsons have "fambly time"; and little Darnell listens
anxiously to night noises. Jan Spivey Gilchrist's gouache paintings lend a warm, hazy character to the city sights at nighttime.
Coretta Scott King Honor Book (Writing), 1992.

10.53   Hague, Kathleen. **Bear Hugs.** Illustrated by Michael Hague.
Henry Holt, 1989. ISBN 0-8050-0512-9. 28p. 2–7.

"I like to talk to teddy bears; / They always have the time / To listen till I'm really through / With stories that are mine." This warm and fuzzy set of nine teddy bear poems identifies some of the enchanting virtues of everyone's favorite friend. Big ones, small ones, old ones, sleepy-eyed ones—teddy bears are always there for a big bear hug. Michael Hague's charming illustrations contain lots of details and a folk-art-stenciled border on every page.

10.54 Heide, Florence Parry. **Grim and Ghastly Goings-on.** Illustrated by Victoria Chess. Lothrop, Lee and Shepard Books, 1992. ISBN 0-688-08322-6. 32p. 6–12 (est.).

Twenty-one "grim and ghastly" monster poems are moderated by illustrations of children who are only mildly frightened and by comic monsters. A funny twist on motherhood is offered by "Monster Mothers," who brag about their babies in strange ways: "Mine is ugly." / "Mine is mean." / "Mine is turning nice and green." A poem reminiscent of Shel Silverstein's poetry is "Before You Fix Your Next Peanut Butter Sandwich—Read This," while a highly original fear is reflected in "Beware of Rubber Bands."

10.55 Hoberman, Mary Ann. **A Fine Fat Pig, and Other Animal Poems.** Illustrated by Malcah Zeldis. HarperCollins, 1991. ISBN 0-06-022426-6. 28p. 6–11 (est.).

"So many kinds of animals / So many shapes and sizes / So many funny spots and dots / So many strange disguises." Bold folk-art paintings created by the highly acclaimed Malcah Zeldis colorfully complement Mary Ann Hoberman's fourteen witty and rhythmic animal verses. The music and ingenuity of the poems and illustrations are certain to enlist close observations and, perhaps, to inspire some well-chosen animal descriptors and interpretations from young language (and art) lovers.

10.56 Kennedy, X. J. **The Beasts of Bethlehem.** Illustrated by Michael McCurdy. Margaret K. McElderry Books, 1992. ISBN 0-689-50561-2. 39p. 6 and up.

All creatures great and small in attendance within the humble stable at the birth of Jesus gain voice through X. J. Kennedy's concise poems. Each, in its turn, responds to the birth, bids the babe welcome, and lives in momentary truce. This sentiment from the cow: "To warm Him in his stall, / I breathe my clover breath." The bat's simple gift is a promise to hunt the mosquitoes in the mows. Illustrations are scratchboard and colored pencils, achieving dark backgrounds for moonlit celebrants.

10.57   Kennedy, X. J. **Ghastlies, Goops and Pincushions.** Illustrated by Ron Barrett. Margaret K. McElderry Books, 1989. ISBN 0-689-50477-2. 57p. 8–12 (est.).

A collection of nonsense rhymes from the pen of X. J. Kennedy could be just the ticket for teasing a reluctant reader, the right ingredient for the bulletin board, or the invitation to extend to the young writer. No topic is too outlandish to be turned into verse: Guinevere Ghastly baby-sits her brother by tying him to a parking meter and feeding him dimes; a pincushion is stuffed with pins for rolling or bowling. While Kennedy plays with language, Ron Barrett offers Dr. Seuss-like black-and-white drawings.

10.58   Kuskin, Karla. **Soap Soup, and Other Verses.** Illustrated by Karla Kuskin. HarperCollins/Charlotte Zolotow Books, 1992. ISBN 0-06-023572-1. 63p. 5–8 (est.).

Karla Kuskin, winner of the NCTE Award for Excellence in Poetry for Children in 1979, doubles as illustrator for this collection of easy-reading poems that explore everyday wonders of our world: "In winter there is too much ice; / In summer, ice is very nice." Happy, childlike drawings with an adult's eye for detail make vibrant use of color in this I Can Read Book.

10.59   Lear, Edward. **Of Pelicans and Pussycats: Poems and Limericks.** Illustrated by Jill Newton. Dial Books for Young Readers, 1990. ISBN 0-8037-0728-2. 32p. 6–10 (est.).

This collection of Edward Lear's nonsense poetry is filled with clever ink and watercolor illustrations, executed in an appealing flat, primitive style. The oversize pages are colorfully bordered and the poems surrounded by madcap scenes and creatures—birds in a beard, the Quangle Wangle, chorusing pelicans, and, of course, an owl and a pussycat. Thirteen poems are included, both long and short, in a setting sure to add to the glee of those who enter Lear's Moppsikon Floppsikon world.

10.60   Lewis, J. Patrick. **A Hippopotamusn't, and Other Animal Verses.** Illustrated by Victoria Chess. Dial Books for Young Readers, 1990. ISBN 0-8037-0519-0. 40p. 3–8.

"A hippopotamusn't sit on lawn chairs, stools, and rockers. A hippopotamusn't yawn directly under tightrope walkers." J.

Patrick Lewis's animal verses are lighthearted, playful experiments with language and provide fresh ways of seeing the natural world. Here are poems of luggage-beaked pelicans, a song of the snake, rules for following a fellow-phant in an elephant parade, and speculation over whether a boy oyster is a "boyster." Victoria Chess interprets the poems with ink, colored pencils, tempera paint, and wit.

10.61　Little, Jean. **Hey World, Here I Am!** Illustrated by Sue Truesdell. Harper and Row, 1989. ISBN 0-06-024006-7. 89p. 8–12.

Kate Bloomfield, a precocious character from Jean Little's *Look through My Window* and *Kate*, muses about school, family, writing, friendship, and the world in this lively volume of poems, essays, and vignettes. Sometimes humorous, such as "Today," the school poem about potential, and sometimes poignant, such as "Mrs. Thurstone," the story of Kate's ninety-year-old friend, this collection praises life and change. Black-and-white drawings illustrate each selection. *Notable 1989 Children's Trade Books in the Field of Social Studies.*

10.62　Livingston, Myra Cohn. **Light and Shadow.** Photographs by Barbara Rogasky. Holiday House, 1992. ISBN 0-8234-0931-7. 32p. 6–10 (est.).

Poet and photographer work as one to produce fourteen extraordinary examples of the play of light and shadow through the day, heralded both in color photography and metaphoric language. The photographer, for example, catches the light through beads of water on the outline of a grape leaf, and the poet describes "a shiny necklace of / dew drops." Light and shadow are in constant play off oceans, carnival mirrors, and campfires, but these artists help us to see the "silver pathways" across our days.

10.63　Livingston, Myra Cohn. **Remembering, and Other Poems.** Margaret K. McElderry Books, 1989. ISBN 0-689-50489-6. 54p. 5 and up.

The forty-five poems comprising this slim book all focus upon childhood memories and emotions. From popcorn to poison ivy, Christmas trees to coyotes, ladybugs to Lincoln, poet Myra Cohn Livingston reveals universal truths about life in her sometimes light, sometimes serious poems.

10.64　Mado, Michio (translated by the Empress Michiko of Japan). **The Animals: Selected Poems.** Illustrated by Mitsumasa Anno.

Margaret K. McElderry Books, 1992. ISBN 0-689-50574-4. 48p. 6 and up (est.).

Michio Mado, considered by some to be the foremost contemporary Japanese children's poet, presents this collection on facing pages, first in Japanese and then in English. Twenty poems that reflect the poet's unabashed joy in his universe are printed on taupe pages, edged in white, with an intricate cut-paper lower border of delicately intertwined animal shapes. Translated by the Empress Michiko, the poems are simple and concise, whether considering the sleep of butterflies or reflecting on a zebra's self-made cage.

10.65   Marsh, James. **Bizarre Birds and Beasts.** Illustrated by James Marsh. Dial Books, 1991. ISBN 0-8037-1046-1. 30p. 7–11 (est.).

Readers must be prepared to pay attention to detail in James Marsh's elaborate illustrations; otherwise, they will miss some fun. From the dust jacket, where the wise owl's eyeglasses actually spell "hoot," to the string of pearls of the "jewelled parrot," the bizarre beasts and birds are a visual treat as well as some poetic fun. A thematic concluding poem, "Future Ark," reminds readers of the precarious state of the world's wildlife. *Notable 1991 Children's Trade Books in the Field of Social Studies.*

10.66   Merriam, Eve. **A Poem for a Pickle: Funnybone Verse.** Illustrated by Sheila Hamanaka. Morrow Junior Books, 1989. ISBN 0-688-08138-X. 34p. 4–8 (est.).

This poetry collection by the late Eve Merriam ranges in subject from spectacles to junk to a talking dog, and each is offered to "tickle the funnybone." Included are poems that play with language; for example, there is naming play—of apples (Jonathan, Macintosh, Granny Smith) and of boats (liner, schooner, cutter, cruiser), as well as play with the music of language—of rain, of dance, and of the city. Colored pencil drawings lend a light and airy touch.

10.67   Merriam, Eve. **The Singing Green: New and Selected Poems for All Seasons.** Illustrated by Kathleen Collins Howell. Morrow Junior Books, 1992. ISBN 0-688-11025-8. 102p. 6–12 (est.).

Some of Eve Merriam's poems in *The Singing Green* have an unwritten melody; others march, hum, or dance. In all, her characteristic sensitivity to the natural world, her poet's eye, and her ear for language have produced a collection of out-of-print verses and new favorites with something for every classroom.

Within the section labeled "Sallies and Saunters," there is the "chime-in-able" "A Vote for Vanilla": "Vanilla, vanilla, vanilla for me, that's the flavor I savor particularly."

10.68 Moore, Lilian. **Adam Mouse's Book of Poems.** Illustrated by Kathleen Garry McCord. Atheneum/Jean Karl Books, 1992. ISBN 0-689-31765-4. 53p. 6 and up (est.).

In this third book of poetry, some of Adam Mouse's earlier works—poems of reflection on the country and the city—are reprinted along with new ones. Adam's quiet observations of nature ponder "Turtle Time," the "cold gold glow" of fireflies, the moment before a baby wren takes flight, and the silence of the garden as it grows. Kathleen Garry McCord's black-and-white drawings edge the pages.

10.69 Moss, Jeff. **The Butterfly Jar.** Illustrated by Chris Demarest. Bantam Books, 1989. ISBN 0-553-05704-9. 115p. 7 and up (est.).

The lively poems in this collection offer witty, sometimes silly, portraits of kids' lives, most often from a child's perspective. As in the "butterfly jar" image that opens the collection, Jeff Moss opens the jar of his imagination to let ideas take flight. Chris Demarest's ink drawings, improvisational and informal, suit the whimsy of the poems—from "ice cream pain" to disgusting "Mr. Bogardus," who "talks while he's chewing his meatballs."

10.70 Prelutsky, Jack. **Beneath a Blue Umbrella.** Illustrated by Garth Williams. Greenwillow Books, 1990. ISBN 0-688-06429-9. 64p. All ages (est.).

From a hippo that swallows melons beneath a blue umbrella to four goats that swallow coats on a boat, a colorful cast of characters comes to life in Jack Prelutsky's lively and humorous poems. Garth Williams's brightly colored, full-page illustrations beautifully embellish the rhyming and lyrical language found in the poetry. This collection is an appropriate companion to Prelutsky and Williams's earlier collaboration, *Ride a Purple Pelican.*

10.71 Prelutsky, Jack. **Something BIG Has Been Here.** Illustrated by James Stevenson. Greenwillow Books, 1990. ISBN 0-688-06434-5. 160p. 5 and up.

The lively poems juxtapose sane ideas to produce ridiculous ones, and introduce improbable creatures and people involved in absurd activities. Black-and-white line drawings illustrate such silly subjects as a tough grandmother carrying her grandson, who in turn is carrying an elephant, in "Super Samson Simpson." Jack Prelutsky chooses words which match the action and enchant the poetic ear.

10.72   Ryder, Joanne. **Mockingbird Morning.** Illustrated by Dennis Nolan. Four Winds Press, 1989. ISBN 0-02-777961-0. 32p. 6–9 (est.).

In praise of a summer day, a mockingbird sings outside a child's window, "borrowing his song from a hundred different birds, calling . . . in a hundred different ways." Out goes the child into the scents and tastes and textures of the day, exploring nature's offerings, touching, observing closely, and wondering. Joanne Ryder's poetry is lyrical and evocative, while Dennis Nolan's paintings catch the sunlight and capture the child's feelings of appreciation of a turtle's shell, a brown goose feather, dragonfly wings, and the slow mystery of cloud shapes.

10.73   Rylant, Cynthia. **Soda Jerk.** Illustrated by Peter Catalanotto. Orchard Books/Richard Jackson Books, 1990. ISBN 0-531-08464-7. 48p. 12 and up.

Twenty-eight poems contemplate the world through the eyes of an earnest boy who serves up the cheeseburgers and sodas at Maywell's Drugstore. Although worried that he'll be mired in Cheston, West Virginia, forever ("we've never learned a thing about making dreams come true"), the soda jerk secretly dreams of becoming an actor. These reflective, insightful poems about small-town life and a boy's growing restlessness with it are periodically interrupted with kaleidoscopic watercolors in mottled hues depicting the scenes at Maywell's.

10.74   Seabrooke, Brenda. **Judy Scuppernong.** Illustrated by Ted Lewin. Cobblehill Books, 1990. ISBN 0-525-65038-5. 64p. 10 and up.

Life seems simpler in a Georgia childhood of the 1950s. Girls had time to hang from their knees to contemplate important things and to ponder a strong, self-aware new girl whom they call Judy Scuppernong. In a revelation of character through unrhymed poetry, Judy's life is unveiled through three friends' observations and accounts until she is no longer larger-than-life, and no longer so enviable. Ted Lewin's watercolors, reproduced in black-and-white, are barefoot, soda-fountain-days cool.

10.75   Singer, Marilyn. **Turtle in July.** Illustrated by Jerry Pinkney. Macmillan, 1989. ISBN 0-02-782881-6. 29p. All ages.

In this collection of sixteen poems, the twelve months of the year and the four seasons are celebrated. Speaking in first person, nature's creatures, including a deer, a barn owl, a cow, and a bullhead, praise their special time of year. Jerry Pinkney's full-page watercolor, pen, and pencil portrait-like paintings of each animal complement the varied songs of the animals. *Notable Children's Trade Books in Science, 1989.*

10.76 Soto, Gary. **Neighborhood Odes.** Illustrated by David Diaz. Harcourt Brace Jovanovich, 1992. ISBN 0-15-256879-4. 80p. 8–12.

This collection of twenty-one odes celebrates the delights of children eating snow cones, romping with puppies, and picnicking with family in neighborhood parks. Though focusing specifically on his own Hispanic neighborhood in Los Angeles, Gary Soto's poems will remind readers of the sights and sounds of their own childhoods. David Diaz's black-and-white woodblock illustrations capture Soto's images in the straightforward manner of the children who speak through his poems. A glossary translates Spanish words and phrases.

10.77 Steele, Mary Q. **Anna's Garden Songs.** Illustrated by Lena Anderson. Greenwillow Books, 1989. ISBN 0-688-08218-1. 31p. 4–7 (est.).

Anna, a bespectacled towhead, has written fourteen poems in appreciation of the beet, potato, rhubarb, radish, and other plants in her garden. On each two-page spread, the text appears along with a full-page watercolor illustration of the plant. The verse is light to match: "I do not think I'll eat / This beet. / Too much of it is red, / Too much of it is head."

10.78 Wilson, Sarah. **June Is a Tune That Jumps on a Stair.** Illustrated by Sarah Wilson. Simon and Schuster Books for Young Readers, 1992. ISBN 0-671-73919-0. 32p. 4–7 (est.).

Thirty-one poems for young children are illustrated with rounded, cheery figures and smiling pets. Topics include pretending, spiders, the rabbit in the moon, toothpaste wiggles, playing, and friends. Bound to be a child's favorite is "In and out / the back door. SLAM! / In and out / again. BAM BAM!"

10.79 Yolen, Jane. **Bird Watch: A Book of Poetry.** Illustrated by Ted Lewin. Philomel Books, 1990. ISBN 0-399-21616-X. 38p. All ages.

Jane Yolen's reflections, born of keen observations of fourteen species of birds from cardinals to kildeer, are beautifully woven into a book of poetry that highlights each species' unique characteristics and fosters an appreciation for them all. Realistic watercolor washes use closeups and unusual perspectives to capture the spirit of each poem. The final page contains additional factual information about the habits and habitats of each species. *Outstanding Science Trade Books for Children in 1990; ALA Notable Children's Books, 1991.*

10.80   Yolen, Jane. **Dinosaur Dances.** Illustrated by Bruce Degen. G. P. Putnam's Sons, 1990. ISBN 0-399-21629-4. 39p. 7–11.

The rhythms of waltzes, tangos, and reels lift the feet of the dancing dinosaurs in this collection of seventeen poems. Ms. Allosaurus hulas off the Richter scale. Vain Tyrannosaurus, in white suit and gold chains, glides onto the floor. Courting pterodactyls dance on the wing. Only homely Brontosaurus is a wallflower. The last poem, "And After," assures that when the dancing is through and the footprints are washed away, memories of the music and the steps will be felt in the bones of the children—who will also dance.

Individual Poems

10.81   Allingham, William. **The Fairies.** Illustrated by Michael Hague. Henry Holt, 1989. ISBN 0-8050-1003-3. 32p. 4–8 (est.).

Under moss-covered roots and in a red-capped mushroom, bramble-bush world, the wee folk from an 1850s Irish poem are reawakened in Michael Hague's newly illustrated edition. By today's standards, the wee folks' mischief seems severe—stealing little Bridget from her bed and keeping her "for seven long years" until she died of sorrow. Hague must have been discomfited, too, because the endpiece illustration shows an awakening Bridget—not dead, just sleeping.

10.82   Carlstrom, Nancy White. **Northern Lullaby.** Illustrated by Leo and Diane Dillon. Philomel Books, 1992. ISBN 0-399-21806-8. 32p. 3–8.

"Goodnight Papa Star / Goodnight Mama Moon / Bending your silver arms down / through the darkness." A snug snow-covered cabin nestles against the winter night, forming the backdrop for this Alaskan lullaby. Good-night wishes are chanted to Grandpa Mountain, Grandma River, Great Moose Uncle, Auntie Willow, and Cousin Beaver, as stylized human-faced winter inhabitants register sweet repose. At last, Mama Moon and Papa

Star, in native costumes, spread the soft, majestic quilt of night-time stillness.

10.83   Carryl, Charles E. **The Walloping Window-Blind.** Illustrated by Ted Rand. Arcade, 1992. ISBN 1-55970-154-4. 32p. 5–8 (est.).

Christopher Award-winner Ted Rand confesses that he always felt Charles Carryl's rollicking poem would make a wonderful children's book. This nonsensical sailor's chant of the brave crew of the ship the *Walloping Window-Blind* was originally published in 1885 as a part of a larger work; it was later adapted as a song (music and lyrics are included in this version). Crisp in black-and-white, sailors and ship roll and pitch with the waves beneath the Union Jack in paintings that offer just the right perspectives on the quirky antics.

10.84   Coltman, Paul. **Witch Watch.** Illustrated by Gillian McClure. Farrar, Straus and Giroux, 1989. ISBN 0-374-38461-4. 30p. 6–10 (est.).

A suspicious boy observes a lonely old woman with a black cat, sure that she is a witch. In a colloquial British dialect, the child describes being pulled into the "witch's house" to help with the chores. On each spread, verse is illustrated with paintings, edged with eerie shapes, that reflect both the boy's fears as well as the innocent reality of the two at work gathering sticks, sweeping the chickens off the porch, and feeding the pig.

10.85   cummings, e. e. **hist whist.** Illustrated by Deborah Kogan Ray. Crown, 1989. ISBN 0-517-57258-3. 32p. 5 and up (est.).

When little ghost-things tiptoe, twinkle-toe out under the moon-lit sky, they are joined by twitchy witches, tingling goblins, and little itchy mousies. The precise word choice of e. e. cummings is given misty, murky interpretation through Deborah Kogan Ray's illustrations. All perception of threat comes to an end, however, when tiny trick-or-treaters gleefully unmask on Halloween.

10.86   Edwards, Roland. **Tigers.** Illustrated by Judith Riches. Tambourine Books, 1992. ISBN 0-688-11686-8. 32p. 3–8 (est.).

Watercolor illustrations almost overwhelm this rhyming tale of imaginary tigers roaming the house at night and talking in "whispered roars." Striped in a joyful array of unlikely colors, the tigers prowl and gambol in nooks and corners so that the child, hearing nighttime creaks, can picture them at play and can sleep without nightmares.

10.87   Farjeon, Eleanor. **Cats Sleep Anywhere.** Illustrated by Mary Price Jenkins. J. B. Lippincott, 1990. ISBN 0-397-32464-2. 23p. 4–7.

Cats sleep on tables, chairs, and tops of pianos—"they don't care, cats sleep anywhere." Eleanor Farjeon's simple verse about the unique sleeping habits of felines is humorously reinterpreted and made predictable for young readers by Welsh artist Mary Price Jenkins. Her full-color illustrations depict cats in a variety of reposes—in drawers, shoes, laps, boxes, garbage cans, and even on the toilet seat!

10.88   Field, Eugene. **The Gingham Dog and the Calico Cat.** Illustrated by Janet Street. Philomel Books, 1990. ISBN 0-399-22151-4. 32p. 4–8.

Janet Street's illustrations for Eugene Field's well-known poem place the dueling pair in an antique shop with price tags affixed to their ears. Narrated by a wise old bear, the poem's nonsensical characters (the Chinese plate and the old Dutch clock) take on new purpose as items for sale that are observing the gingham/calico war. The melee of fighting animals and flying fabric contrasts with the staid shop scenes.

10.89   Field, Rachel. **A Road Might Lead to Anywhere.** Illustrated by Giles Laroche. Little, Brown, 1990. ISBN 0-316-28178-6. 32p. 4–8.

Rachel Field's poem is the inspiration for paper-sculpture illustrations that draw the reader into the pages' depths. On a country porch swing, a young girl nods off while reading. In her "daydream," she follows a winding pathway across the pages and, with two companions she meets along the way, visits harbor towns, treasure caves, and foreign shores before the road leads her back home again. The illustrator's technique will invite children to try their own paper sculpture or three-dimensional collage.

10.90   Lear, Edward. **The Jumblies.** Illustrated by Ted Rand. G. P. Putnam's Sons, 1989. ISBN 0-399-216324. 32p. 3–8.

Not just "The Owl and the Pussycat" went to sea. Edward Lear's imagination also launched "The Jumblies" on a voyage; their sail was pea-green, and their boat a sieve: "Far and few, far and few, / Are the lands where the Jumblies live: / Their heads are green,

A.

B.

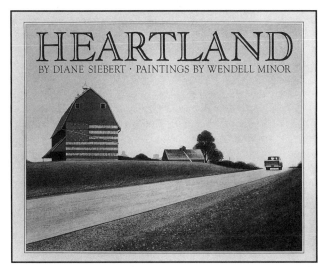

C.

A. *Thirteen Moons on Turtle's Back: A Native American Year of Moons* by Joseph Bruchac and Jonathan London; illustrated by Thomas Locker (see 10.4). **B.** *Eric Carle's Dragons, Dragons & Other Creatures That Never Were* compiled by Laura Whipple (see 10.42). **C.** *Heartland* by Diane Siebert; illustrated by Wendell Minor (see 10.99).

A.

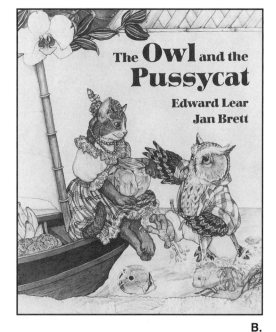

B.

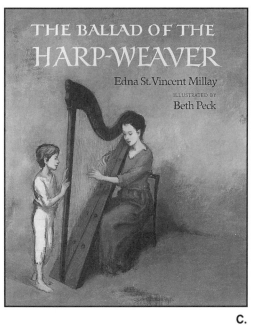

C.

D.

A. *Paul Revere's Ride* by Henry Wadsworth Longfellow; illustrated by Ted Rand (see 10.94). **B.** *The Owl and the Pussycat* by Edward Lear; illustrated by Jan Brett (see 10.91). **C.** *The Ballad of the Harp-Weaver* by Edna St. Vincent Millay; illustrated by Beth Peck (see 10.97). **D.** *Poems of A. Nonny Mouse* selected by Jack Prelutsky; illustrated by Henrik Drescher (see 10.37).

and their hands are blue; / And they went to sea in a sieve." Ted Rand's sieve is a tea strainer, and the Jumblies are jolly, tumbling characters with curling-toed slippers whose "souvenirs" bear a closer look.

10.91 Lear, Edward. **The Owl and the Pussycat.** Illustrated by Jan Brett. G. P. Putnam's Sons, 1991. ISBN 0-399-21925-0. 28p. 4–8 (est.).

In this newly illustrated edition, the Owl woos and weds the Pussycat in a jewel-tone Caribbean setting. Jan Brett's hallmark bordered spreads are lavish with tropical flowers, woven rattans, and an intricately detailed sea floor. As the couple sails their richly laden vessel to "the land where the bong tree grows," a second love story—this one of fish—unfolds in the illustrations beneath the crystal sea.

10.92 Lear, Edward. **The Owl and the Pussycat.** Illustrated by Helen Cooper. Dial Books for Young Readers, 1991. ISBN 0-8037-1044-5. 20p. 3–6 (est.).

In a tiny version that is only four inches high, the feathered owl and his gray ladylove sail across delicate endpapers to the land where the bong-tree grows. Each illustration and verse are encased in patterned borders that reflect an element of the poem. Each miniature painting is perfectly detailed.

10.93 Lear, Edward. **The Owl and the Pussy-Cat.** Illustrated by Louise Voce. Lothrop, Lee and Shepard Books, 1991. ISBN 0-688-09537-2. 32p. 3 and up.

In stylized illustrations reminiscent of *New Yorker* cartoons, saucer-eyed Owl and Pussy-cat undertake yet another voyage. Never, however, has their boat been more "pea-green" and never have they looked more pleased to be in one another's company—they're downright dotty over one another. Thick rope sets Edward Lear's verses apart from Louise Voce's watercolor paintings. The wealth of reissues of this work provide plenty of opportunity for comparison. For example, Jan Brett's lavish illustrations markedly contrast with the simplicity of Voce's scenes.

10.94 Longfellow, Henry Wadsworth. **Paul Revere's Ride.** Illustrated by Ted Rand. Dutton Children's Books, 1990. ISBN 0-525-44610-9. 40p. 5–9.

"Listen my children and you shall hear...." Longfellow's 1861 epic-length poem has helped countless schoolchildren recall the significance of April 18, 1775, and Paul Revere's frenzied ride through Boston and the nearby countryside to announce the route that the British troops were taking to the American arsenal at Concord. With watercolors evocative of the intensity of the historical moment, Ted Rand interprets the poem in paintings that are also likely to endure—capturing the splashes of light from moon, candles, and window lanterns against the dark night's journey. *Teacher's Choices for 1991.*

10.95 Lyon, George Ella. **Together.** Illustrated by Vera Rosenberry. Orchard Books, 1989. ISBN 0-531-08431-0. 32p. 4–6.

"Let's put our heads together and dream the same dream" is the repeated refrain as two best friends build a house, crank ice cream, sail, fish, and eat a giant sundae together. Sunny watercolor illustrations bordered in warm shades spreading across the pages bring the actions (and imaginations) of this cross-cultural pair to life. The text is rhyming, lyrical, and appropriate for young readers.

10.96 Marshak, Samuel (translated by Richard Pevear). **The Pup Grew Up!** Illustrated by Vladimir Radunsky. Henry Holt, 1989. ISBN 0-8050-0952-3. 32p. 4–8.

The pan is the same, as are the divan, the basin, the box with three locks, and the valise. But at the end of a train trip a woman's Pekingese pup is now a Great Dane. Could it be that the pup grew up? American children will delight in this hilarious, boldly illustrated, new translation of a 1926 poem by best-loved Russian children's author Samuel Marshak.

10.97 Millay, Edna St. Vincent. **The Ballad of the Harp-Weaver.** Illustrated by Beth Peck. Philomel Books, 1991. ISBN 0-399-21611-1. 32p. 5 and up.

Edna St. Vincent Millay dedicated this poem to her mother at the turn of the century, yet the theme and expression are just as effective today. A destitute mother is driven to burn furniture in order to heat her home against the harsh winter. In final desperation, she weaves warm clothing for her son from an old "harp with a woman's head / Nobody will buy." Beth Peck's loose, yet intimate, illustrations are painted in warm colors, adding an eerie, mystical glow to the poem.

10.98 Nash, Ogden. **The Adventures of Isabel.** Illustrated by James Marshall. Little, Brown/Joy Street Books, 1991. ISBN 0-316-59874-7. 32p. 4–8.

When Ogden Nash created Isabel, he gave her spunk and derring-do. As interpreted by James Marshall's artistry, Isabel has pluck and savvy—a girl with puffy red hair, bright nail polish, glasses, and a pink bow that stands straight up. She's a match for a hungry bear, a gruesome witch, a wicked giant, and even a bad dream. So, read along: "Whenever you meet a bugaboo, / Remember what Isabel used to do. / Don't scream when the bugaboo says, "Boo!" / Just look it in the eye and say, 'Boo to you!' "

10.99 Siebert, Diane. **Heartland.** Illustrated by Wendell Minor. Thomas Y. Crowell, 1989. ISBN 0-690-04732-0. 27p. All ages.

In a poetic tribute to the Midwest region of the United States, vibrant illustrations reveal the beauty of patchwork-quilt fields, the strength of sun-lined faces of farmers, the pleasures of the seasons, and the awe-inspiring brushes with nature. The repetition of the phrase "I am the Heartland" throughout the poem rumbles with pride and trembles with feeling. Adults and children who savor the landscapes of the Midwest will enjoy the similarly lyrical *Mojave,* also by Diane Siebert and Wendell Minor.

10.100 Siebert, Diane. **Sierra.** Illustrated by Wendell Minor. HarperCollins, 1991. ISBN 0-06-021640-9. 26p. 6–12 (est.).

Formed millions of years ago, the Sierra Nevadas stand "like a sentinel" to America's western frontier. The natural history of these magnificent mountains is told through Diane Siebert's lyrical, rhyming text and Wendell Minor's animal portraits and haunting landscapes. Another in a series celebrating the beauty of North America, this book parallels Siebert's *Mojave* and *Heartland* in style. *Notable 1991 Children's Trade Books in the Field of Social Studies.*

10.101 Siebert, Diane. **Train Song.** Illustrated by Mike Wimmer. Thomas Y. Crowell, 1990. ISBN 0-690-04728-2. 32p. 3–7.

Mesmerizing text subconsciously evokes the constant rhythm of a train moving along a track, while stunning, mixed-medium illustrations allow the reader to watch a train journey from unique perspectives. Together, text and illustrations take the reader along on a transcontinental ride. *Notable 1990 Children's Trade Books in the Field of Social Studies.*

10.102 Stafford, William. **The Animal That Drank Up Sound.** Illustrated by Debra Frasier. Harcourt Brace Jovanovich, 1992. ISBN 0-15-203563-X. 32p. 3–8 (est.).

William Stafford's 1964 story poem captures the deep, empty silence and solitude of northern winters. A shadowy bear drinks up all sound from the lake where echoes gather, from the rustling leaves and grasses, and from the whole world, until it lies silent, disregarded by sun and warmth. But deep in the ground, a cricket wakes to make a soft, hopeful sound. Debra Frasier's wide, dramatic landscapes are flour-paste paper collages, painted with thick acrylics and then wiped off to achieve textured stripes.

10.103 Stevenson, Robert Louis. **My Shadow.** Illustrated by Ted Rand. G. P. Putnam's Sons, 1990. ISBN 0-399-22216-2. 32p. 4–8 (est.).

Robert Louis Stevenson's poem of wonder at one's own shadow is beautifully elaborated by Ted Rand's paintings of children from around the world blowing bubbles, swinging on an old tire swing, dancing, and playing with kites, all accompanied by their shadows.

10.104 Titherington, Jeanne. **A Child's Prayer.** Illustrated by Jeanne Titherington. Greenwillow Books, 1989. ISBN 0-688-08318-8. 19p. 2–6 (est.).

A young boy kneels at bedtime to say his evening prayer, surrounded by four plush friends: lion, cow, clown, and eagle. As the child recites the simple rhyming prayer, he acts out each verse with his toys. When the prayer is concluded, the boy's father gives him a big hug and tucks him into bed. Soft colored pencil illustrations enhance the warmth and tenderness of the text.

10.105 Treece, Henry. **The Magic Wood.** Illustrated by Barry Moser. HarperCollins/Willa Perlman Books, 1992. ISBN 0-06-020803-1. 32p. 4–8 (est.).

Henry Treece's Halloween poem, first published in 1945, is one with evocative language and images: "The wood is full of shining eyes, / The wood is full of creeping feet." Barry Moser's foliage is shadow black against a jade-deep night, executed in ink and transparent watercolor on glossy handmade paper, with flecks of starlight, moonlight, and "shining eyes." And just when things are the spookiest comes the reassurance: "And found myself safe on my father's land."

10.106 Turner, Ann. **Rainflowers.** Illustrated by Robert J. Blake. HarperCollins/Charlotte Zolotow Books, 1992. ISBN 0-06-026042-4. 32p. 3–8 (est.).

As the corn stalks dried and the pumpkins ripened on the vine, "a thunderstorm swept the field." Jagged streaks of lightning and long drops of cold rain send "mice chittering to their grass nests," "birds skittering to the line of trees," and "woodchucks lumbering to their deep, dry holes." As winds bend the grasses and tear leaves from the trees, animals seek shelter until, at last, the sun bursts through. A lyrical, quiet mood offsets the violent storm.

10.107 Turner, Ethel. **Walking to School.** Illustrated by Peter Gouldthorpe. Orchard Books, 1989. ISBN 0-531-08399-3. 32p. 4–7.

Ethel Turner, a nineteenth-century Australian poet, wrote "Walking to School" when her own five-year-old son left for school for the very first time. Now a full-length picture book, the poem's lines and verses are set against the perceived threats and challenges of a solitary walk to school (fighting boys, trampling cows, and plunging, rearing horses), which nearly burst from the pages. Peter Gouldthorpe used black crayons and watercolors to give his illustrations "the soft, grainy look of old photographs."

10.108 Whitman, Walt. **I Hear America Singing.** Illustrated by Robert Sabuda. Philomel Books, 1991. ISBN 0-399-21808-4. 32p. 4–8.

One of America's most celebrated poets, Walt Whitman traveled across America to preserve America—the rich, the poor, the women, children, and minorities. In a newly illustrated version of this best-known poem from *Leaves of Grass*, Whitman's eloquence is captured by Robert Sabuda's textured linoleum cuts. Historical, cultural, and geographical details of the poem sing to the child of this country's diversity and richness.

10.109 Whittier, John Greenleaf. **Barbara Frietchie.** Illustrated by Nancy Winslow Parker. Greenwillow Books, 1992. ISBN 0-688-09830-4. 32p. 6 and up.

Over 130 years ago in Maryland, as the story goes, ninety-five-year-old Barbara Frietchie, a brave Union loyalist, waved her flag from the attic window toward General Stonewall Jackson, who was riding through town with his Confederate troops. Her courage was preserved in John Greenleaf Whittier's famous poem. Now, Nancy Winslow Parker's fresh, simple illustrations for the poem are accompanied by maps, period flags, historical notes, and biographical sketches, providing a text for appreciation and scrutiny.

Poetry Writing

10.110 Livingston, Myra Cohn. **Poem-Making: Ways to Begin Writing Poetry.** HarperCollins/Charlotte Zolotow Books, 1991. ISBN 0-06-024020-2. 162p. 9–12 (est.).

Myra Cohn Livingston shares her observant eye and love of language with those who would "experience the joy of making a poem." Across short, readable chapters overflowing with poetic examples of her points, she introduces the voices of poetry, its sounds and rhymes, rhythms and metrics, its figures of speech, and its forms. Although the text is aimed toward children and will find an audience in intermediate-grade writing centers, teachers will also find it a valuable reference for their own libraries.

Sciences and Mathematics

A good book on the seashore should move the reader to go out and examine . . . the wonderful life at the edge of the sea. An astronomy book should turn the reader's eye to the sky. . . . A good nature book should stimulate a young person to hear, see, smell, and taste things—to use all . . . senses to observe.

Millicent Selsam, "Writing about Science for Children," in *A Critical Approach to Children's Literature*

11 Sciences and Mathematics

Aeronautics and Space

11.1 Asimov, Isaac. **The Asteroids. Space Garbage.** Dell/Yearling Books, 1991. 30p. 7–12 (est.).

Isaac Asimov's Library of the Universe series introduces young readers to space with excellent graphics, readable text, and a wealth of information. Asimov's narrative ranges from the informative ("Ceres is the largest asteroid") to the speculative ("We may some day use black holes for trash disposal!"). Helping to keep the pace quick and the contents lively are maps and photographs. Special sections include a glossary, reference lists, and boxes of fascinating facts.

11.2 Branley, Franklyn M. **Shooting Stars.** Illustrated by Holly Keller. Thomas Y. Crowell, 1989. ISBN 0-690-04703-7. 32p. 4–6.

Look up at the sky at night and you might see a shooting star. Look through the pages of this addition to the Let's-Read-and-Find-Out Science Books series, and you'll find information about the origin and travels of meteors and what happens when they land on Earth. Colorful illustrations, detailed diagrams, and authentic photographs support this easy-to-understand introduction to shooting stars.

11.3 Branley, Franklyn M. **Superstar: The Supernova of 1987.** Illustrations by True Kelley. Thomas Y. Crowell, 1990. ISBN 0-690-04841-6. 58p. 8–12.

Supernovas, explains author Franklyn Branley in clear prose, are not really "new" stars, but rather stars new to star observers because they suddenly become very bright. The brightest such supernova in the past 383 years was spotted in 1987 and prompted intense studies and new support for scientific theories. It also inspired this explanatory look by Branley at why stars explode, historical sightings of "guest stars," and the hypothesized life of a supernova.

11.4 Embury, Barbara, with Thomas D. Couch. **The Dream Is Alive: A Flight of Discovery aboard the Space Shuttle.** Harper and

Row/Somerville House Books, 1990. ISBN 0-06-021814-2. 64p. 6 and up.

Those fortunate enough to have seen the IMAX film *The Dream Is Alive* will be gratified that some of its most spectacular images of space-shuttle flight are reprinted in this oversize photo-information book, supplemented with archival photographs from the Smithsonian. The clearly written, nontechnical text follows three shuttle flights through preparations, blastoff, a day in space, and scientific experimentation. A brief but straightforward explanation of the *Challenger* tragedy includes a tribute from the crew of *Discovery*, promising that "your dreams are still alive. . . . "

11.5 Harris, Alan, and Paul Weissman. **The Great Voyager Adventure: A Guided Tour through the Solar System.** Julian Messner, 1990. ISBN 0-671-72538-6. 80p. 10 and up.

The billion-dollar, twelve-year Voyager mission was a bold and daring plan to send an unmanned space vehicle to explore the far reaches of our solar system. Specifically, it was designed to take closeup pictures of distant planets and to transmit them back to Earth. An information-packed text, tables, diagrams, index, glossary, and photos taken on Earth, as well as those beamed to Earth from Jupiter, Saturn, Uranus, and Neptune, combine to introduce readers to the "final frontier." *Outstanding Science Trade Books for Children in 1990.*

11.6 Jones, Brian. **Space: A Three-Dimensional Journey.** Illustrated by Richard Clifton-Dey. Dial Books for Young Readers, 1991. ISBN 0-8037-0759-2. 14p. 7–12.

With dramatic paintings and NASA photographs as backdrops for its paper engineering, this pop-up book presents a spacecraft tour of the solar system. Each two-page presentation has a fold-out simulation of the ship's operating panels, with screens giving information and views of the focus planet. Pop-ups include the spacecraft itself, lunar and planetary volcanoes, and the craft in orbit around Uranus.

11.7 Kelch, Joseph W. **Small Worlds: Exploring the 60 Moons of Our Solar System.** Julian Messner, 1990. ISBN 0-671-70014-6. 160p. 11 and up.

Seven chapters about the moons of individual planets are preceded by general information on moons (finding them, measuring them, their movement and phases, eclipses) and followed by a chapter on other small worlds, asteroids, and comets. Included is information on manned and unmanned space exploration. Helping young readers become familiar with space concepts and terminology are tables, diagrams, black-and-white photographs throughout, an eight-page center insert of color photos of lunar surfaces, a concluding checklist summarizing essential facts about all sixty moons, and an index. *Outstanding Science Trade Books for Children in 1990.*

11.8 Lauber, Patricia. **Seeing Earth from Space.** Orchard Books, 1990. ISBN 0-531-08502-3. 80p. 10 and up.

With sixty full-color photographs, this portrait series presents with powerful immediacy one of the profound achievements of the twentieth century: viewing Earth from outer space. Stunning whole-planet views in blue and swirling white are balanced by shots of familiar geographies, such as the brown snaking Mississippi Delta, Hawaiian volcanoes, and Montreal in fall color. Other photographs reveal pollution, vast hurricanes, even the calving of an iceberg twice the size of Rhode Island. The clear, informative text explains remote sensing and interprets the images.

11.9 Maurer, Richard. **Junk in Space.** Simon and Schuster Books for Young Readers/NOVABOOKS, 1989. ISBN 0-671-67768-3. 48p. 10–12.

The title of this superbly written and profusely illustrated book belies its scope. In pursuing the origin and nature of space debris, ranging from mislaid cameras and tools to abandoned satellites and moon vehicles, author Richard Maurer gives accurate and dramatic explanations of the basic phenomena of space travel: satellite technology, the physics of gravity, orbital mechanics, solar distances, and others. He includes detailed information on Soviet space achievements and dramatizes his topic by regular comparisons to voyages of discovery during the 1500s. This is a relatively technical presentation of a body of knowledge which is becoming progressively more important to human destiny.

11.10 Simon, Seymour. **Galaxies.** Mulberry Books, 1991. ISBN 0-688-10992-6. 32p. 6–11 (est.).

Alive with historical details as well as current data, *Galaxies* presents a fascinating narrative, elaborating both on the vastness of the universe and on specific galaxies. Photographs, taken through telescopes and from satellites, give readers a realistic glimpse into an astronomer's world. Although reading the book from cover to cover might be stimulating for avid space enthusiasts, the book could also be satisfying if read in sections.

11.11 Simon, Seymour. **Mercury. Venus.** Morrow Junior Books, 1992. 32p. 5 and up.

In the latest contributions to his planetary series, Seymour Simon provides up-to-date information for each of the sun's closest neighbors. Each planet is introduced with geologic information, findings from space probes, and interesting numerical facts—temperature, length of orbit, and time of rotation. Limited text per page and a highly readable style make complex information manageable for young readers. Stunning color photographs, as well as images from satellites and remote sensing instruments, contribute to these remarkable books.

11.12 Simon, Seymour. **Our Solar System.** Morrow Junior Books, 1992. ISBN 0-688-09993-9. 72p. 5 and up.

This companion volume to Seymour Simon's planetary series explains the birth and evolution of our solar system, as well as current knowledge of its elements. Endpapers provide accessible comparative planetary data, along with scaled pictures. Asteroids, moons, comets, and meteors are discussed and illustrated with satellite photography, photocomposites, and computer-reduced graphic data.

11.13 Simon, Seymour. **Space Worlds: A Dictionary.** Illustrated by Randy Chewning. HarperCollins, 1991. ISBN 0-06-022533-5. 48p. 7–11 (est.).

The epitome of a reference work for any outer-space buff, this illustrated dictionary by well-known nonfiction author Seymour Simon defines terms customarily used when discussing astronomy. From *Apollo Program* to *Johannes Kepler* to *quasar* to *zero gravity*, words and concepts are clearly defined and illustrated with vivid watercolor drawings. Airbrushed backgrounds create an incandescent glow in this comprehensive description of our solar system.

11.14 Sullivan, George. **The Day We Walked on the Moon: A Photo-History of Space Exploration.** Scholastic, 1990. ISBN 0-590-43632-5. 72p. 8 and up.

Vivid color photographs, newspaper reproductions, and clear informative text make for a fine introduction to the highlights and setbacks of the space program, from the moon walk to planetary probes. Author George Sullivan also includes speculation on the future of the space program and a helpful appendix of significant space events.

11.15   Verba, Joan Marie. **Voyager: Exploring the Outer Planets.** Lerner, 1991. ISBN 0-8225-1597-0. 64p. 11 and up.

This account of the Voyager space probes presents photos, maps, diagrams, a glossary, an index, and detailed prose in an account of planning, communicating, and discovery. Highlights include information about the braided Jovian rings, the "family picture" of the planets of our system, Saturn's rings, and closeups of many planetary moons.

Animal Kingdom

Animal Behaviors

11.16   Arnosky, Jim. **Come Out, Muskrats.** Illustrated by Jim Arnosky. Mulberry Books, 1991. ISBN 0-688-10490-8. 32p. 4–8.

It's late afternoon; the cove is still—"Come out, muskrats, come out." As nighttime approaches and turns into dawn, playful muskrats swim and dive in the pond's shallow waters. In this sensitive portrait, Jim Arnosky captures the simplicity of nature and explains what muskrats do in their daily lives. Full-page earth-toned sketches invite readers to view closeup the wonders of life in a pond.

11.17   Arnosky, Jim. **Otters under Water.** Illustrated by Jim Arnosky. G. P. Putnam's Sons, 1992. ISBN 0-399-22339-8. 28p. 3–6.

Jim Arnosky, known as a careful observer of the way in which animals behave in their natural environments, turns his talents to two otter pups as they hunt, feed, and explore their underwater world. Minimal text superimposed upon earth-tone spreads helps readers to feel the warm sunlight and escape beneath sparkling water.

11.18   **Awesome Animal Actions. Baffling Bird Behavior. Freaky Fish Facts. Incredible Insect Instincts.** Illustrated by Paul Mirocha. HarperCollins/HarperFestival Books, 1992. 10p. 5–9.

Surprising facts of nature are illustrated with pop-up, movable parts in these Amazing Nature Pop-up Books. Each book offers five unusual creatures that engage in some truly "baffling," "freaky," or "incredibly awesome" behaviors. For example, a male gaff-topsail catfish protects both eggs and baby fish in its mouth, and when the young fish mature, he spits them out. A doodlebug worm, camouflaged as a piece of sod, pulls its victim into its pit. Each of the creatures moves to demonstrate its unusual behavior.

11.19 Barkan, Joanne. **Creatures That Glow.** Doubleday, 1991. ISBN 0-385-41979-1. 29p. 7–11.

A number of creatures—from fireflies to deep-sea fish to glow-worms—produce their own light, or are bioluminescent. This book explains bioluminescence and then describes a variety of animals that glow in the dark. Unusual full-color photographs are treated with a substance that produces glow-in-the-dark effects. Children will enjoy the novelty of reading about the creatures and thus exposing the photographs to light, and then turning off the lights and watching the creatures glow.

11.20 Batten, Mary. **Nature's Tricksters: Animals and Plants That Aren't What They Seem.** Illustrated by Lois Lovejoy. Sierra Club Books and Little, Brown, 1992. ISBN 0-316-08371-2. 54p. 8–12 (est.).

Nature's disguises help plants and animals survive by deceiving competitors, pollinators, predators, and prey. In an informational book chock-full of natural deceptions, readers will learn about animals that look poisonous when they're not, those that mimic more ferocious species, and harmless species that have adopted scary features or traits. Chapters address aggressive mimicry (when predators trick their prey by looking harmless), animals that mimic plants, plants that mimic animals, males that mimic females, and "Camouflage: The Big Cover Up."

11.21 Berman, Ruth. **American Bison.** Photographs by Cheryl Walsh Bellville. Carolrhoda Books, 1992. ISBN 0-87614-697-3. 48p. 7–10.

The American bison in history, especially its importance to the Plains Indians, is linked with its significance today. Full-color photographs help describe the animal's zoological place, social and survival behaviors, and its territorial range before widespread slaughter by early settlers. Information about the American Bison Society, an organization committed to preserving the animal, helps to make this an upbeat account of the bisons' reappearance on the landscape. A range map, glossary, and index complement this entry in the Nature Watch series.

11.22   Bird, E. J. **How Do Bears Sleep?** Illustrated by E. J. Bird. Carolrhoda Books, 1990. ISBN 0-87614-384-2. 25p. 4–8.

Just how do bears sleep? Do they sleep on their bellies or flat on their backs? Do they have scary dreams and wake up with a roar? The question posed in the title leads to humorous speculations about what bears do during their long winter hibernation. Rhyming text and funny bear drawings engage the reader and can serve to motivate more serious research on the topic of hibernation.

11.23   Clarke, Barry. **Amazing Frogs and Toads.** Parsons, Alexandra. **Amazing Birds. Amazing Cats. Amazing Mammals. Amazing Poisonous Animals. Amazing Snakes. Amazing Spiders.** Smith, Trevor. **Amazing Lizards.** Photographs by Jerry Young. Alfred A. Knopf/Borzoi Books, 1990. 32p. 4 and up (est.).

Amazing! The horned toad will squirt blood from its eyelids when it is attacked. Some male frogs turn blue to attract females. In these Eyewitness Juniors books, the wondrous animal kingdom is presented in a unique format, combining photographs and illustrations with stories, legends, and "fun facts" in easy-to-understand language about the various members of each animal group.

11.24   Cossi, Olga. **Harp Seals.** Carolrhoda Books, 1991. ISBN 0-87614-437-7. 48p. 7–12.

A generous endowment of glossy closeup photographs reveals every facet of a harp seal's life. From white coat to beater to bedlamer to adult, the harp seal grows, learns, migrates, mates, and works at surviving its unfriendly environment and enemies. The author provides a well-researched, clearly understandable text, complete with glossary and index. Although recommended for second through fifth grades, this Nature Watch Book appeals to all ages as it underscores the plight of a now-protected species.

11.25   Dewey, Jennifer Owings. **Animal Architecture.** Illustrated by Jennifer Owings Dewey. Orchard Books, 1991. ISBN 0-531-08530-9. 72p. 8–11.

The author reminds readers in her introduction that thousands of animals create dwellings for themselves, working as "masons, carpenters, weavers, carvers, diggers, and structural engineers." Whether using jaws, legs, beaks, teeth, or claws, they build homes, traps, or storage rooms as ways of adapting their environments. Included in this text are full-page, detailed pencil drawings of the structures of insects, birds, and mammals, as well as the large, clearly written text that explains the feats.

11.26 Dewey, Jennifer. **Can You Find Me? A Book about Animal Camouflage.** Illustrated by Jennifer Dewey. Scholastic Hardcover Books, 1989. ISBN 0-590-41552-2. 40p. 4–7.

Sea animals, insects, spiders, birds, and mammals are different in many ways, but all share some common needs, such as finding food and avoiding attack. One of the ways in which animals meet these needs is through the use of camouflage. Simple but descriptive text explains the remarkable ways in which animals camouflage themselves. Accompanying illustrations require careful attention to distinguish the camouflaged creatures, effectively demonstrating nature's protection. *Notable Children's Trade Books in Science, 1989.*

11.27 Dorros, Arthur. **Animal Tracks.** Illustrated by Arthur Dorros. Scholastic Hardcover Books, 1991. ISBN 0-590-43367-9. 40p. 3–7.

Soft mud by a stream can silently tell a story through the tracks that animals leave behind. Each animal that comes to feed at this stream is briefly discussed and its tracks identified. The reader may notice another pair of tracks, whose imprinter is revealed on the following page. Double-page watercolor illustrations, accented in pen-and-ink, provide an array of details to discover. The last page tells how to make plaster casts of animal (and human) tracks.

11.28 Epstein, Sam, and Beryl Epstein. **Bugs for Dinner? The Eating Habits of Neighborhood Creatures.** Illustrated by Walter Gaffney-Kessell. Macmillan, 1989. ISBN 0-02-733501-1. 48p. 7–12 (est.).

Have you ever wondered what kinds of animals live in a vacant lot or what they do to get food without themselves being eaten? The Epsteins address the surprising ways in which creatures in the neighborhood obtain and eat their dinners. Among the city creatures whose diets and eating habits are full of surprises are honeybees, earthworms, ants, spiders, birds, and butterflies. Black-and-white drawings accompany carefully detailed descriptions. Readers should also see the Epsteins' *What's for Lunch? The Eating Habits of Seashore Creatures.*

11.29 George, Jean Craighead. **The Moon of the Chickarees. The Moon of the Fox Pups. The Moon of the Salamanders.** Illustrated by Norman Adams; Don Rodell; Marlene Hill Werner. HarperCollins, 1992. 48p. 8–12 (est.).

In honor of the thirteen new or full moons that occur each year, Jean Craighead George identifies thirteen animals that "do wondrous things" in their phases of the moon. Originally published in the 1960s, these books have been lavishly reillustrated by wildlife artists, each presenting their subjects both evocatively and in exacting detail. In March, on the evening of the first spring rain, the salamanders emerge and return to the water. In April, the chickaree's shrill voice defends her young red squirrels, and in June, fox pups venture from their den.

11.30 Johnson, Rebecca L. **The Secret Language: Pheromones in the Animal World.** Lerner, 1989. ISBN 0-8225-1586-5. 60p. 10 and up.

Pheromones, the communication chemicals of living things, are explained in this clearly formatted book. The first chapters explain the types and methods of sending and receiving pheromone messages. An extensive chapter on honey bee society is followed by an explanation of how studying animal pheromones can be applied to humans. Although long sentences and paragraphs may intimidate the young reader, a table of contents, glossary, and index will help. Closeup color photographs and diagrams, comparable to those in *National Geographic,* entice all ages. *Notable Children's Trade Books in Science, 1989.*

11.31 Jones, Frances. **Nature's Deadly Creatures: A Pop-up Exploration.** Illustrated by Andrew Robinson and Tony Smith. Dial Books for Young Readers, 1992. ISBN 0-8037-1342-8. 14p. 8 and up.

Six of nature's most venomous creatures pop from the pages in deadly detail and elaborate engineering. In addition to the perfectly executed animals, the six spreads present interesting facts about the dangers and habits of the black widow, the Gila monster, the blow fish, the scorpion, the king cobra, and the blue-ringed octopus, as well as their role in the balance of life. By opening a flap, readers can uncover crisp photos and illustrations of the creature at work.

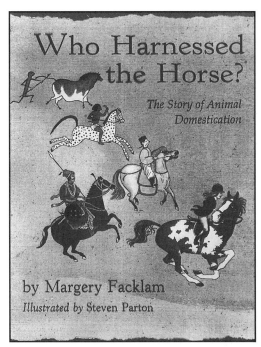

A.

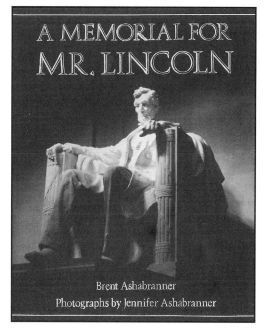

B.

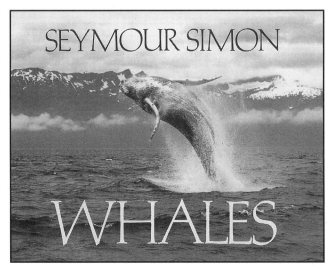

C.

A. *Who Harnessed the Horse? The Story of Animal Domestication* by Margery Facklam; illustrated by Steven Parton (see 11.47).   **B.** *A Memorial for Mr. Lincoln* by Brent Ashabranner; photographs by Jennifer Ashabranner (see 12.60).   **C.** *Whales* by Seymour Simon (see 11.65).

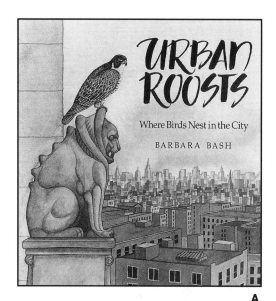

A.

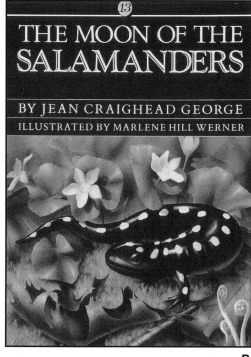

B.

C.

A. *Urban Roosts: Where Birds Nest in the City* by Barbara Bash (see 11.38). **B.** *The Moon of the Salamanders* by Jean Craighead George; illustrated by Marlene Hill Werner (see 11.29). **C.** *The Dream Is Alive: A Flight of Discovery aboard the Space Shuttle* by Barbara Embury, with Thomas D. Crouch (see 11.4).

11.32 Machotka, Hana. **Breathtaking Noses.** Photographs by Hana Machotka. Morrow Junior Books, 1992. ISBN 0-688-09527-5. 32p. 4–9 (est.).

A fish uses it for smelling underwater, a pig uses it to uncover tasty morsels from the dirt, and an elephant can uproot a tree with it. The noses of eight different animals—from a walrus to a snake—are illustrated with "breathtaking" closeup color photographs showing their wide variety of shapes and sizes. Entertaining descriptions reveal in large-print text how each animal's nose is particularly adapted for its survival.

11.33 Pringle, Laurence. **Bearman: Exploring the World of Black Bears.** Photographs by Lynn Rogers. Charles Scribner's Sons, 1989. ISBN 0-684-190945-X. 42p. 7–9 (est.).

Tracking and observing black bears in the Superior National Forest in Minnesota is the work of wildlife biologist Lynn Rogers. For over twenty years Rogers has entered dens to check sleeping bears; on foot and by airplane he has followed bears for long periods, gaining new understanding of their habits and life cycle. Readers gain new respect for bears by reading about the work of a dedicated bearman and by inspecting the color photographs. Sources for further reading and an index enhance the usefulness of the book.

11.34 Riha, Susanne. **Animals in Winter.** Illustrated by Susanne Riha. Carolrhoda Books, 1989. ISBN 0-87614-355-9. 32p. 6–10.

The author describes how different animals (such as the marmot, bat, garden snail, badger, hazel mouse, and hedgehog) prepare for winter, including the suspended state of hibernation, which is nature's way of ensuring survival when food and water are scarce. All of the animals described are European species, although related species are found in North America. The text is supplemented with detailed color drawings, useful for science lessons.

11.35 Royston, Angela. **Chick. Duck. Frog. Kitten. Puppy. Rabbit.** Photographs by Jane Burton; Kim Taylor; Barrie Watts. Lodestar Books, 1991–92. 21p. 3–7 (est.).

Told in first person and in simple language, each sturdy book in the See How They Grow series traces the development of a single species from birth (or before) to early maturity. Artistically and instructively arranged color photographs show life's milestones in breathtaking detail, while border drawings at top and bottom feature a developmental continuum. In the end, each book photographically summarizes the animals growth in a "See How I Grew" double-page spread.

11.36   Selsam, Millicent E., and Joyce Hunt. **A First Look at Bats.** Illustrated by Harriett Springer. Walker, 1991. ISBN 0-8027-8136-5. 32p. 6–9.

Settle into your bat-chair and learn bat-facts from the scientist/teacher author team of Millicent Selsam and Joyce Hunt. Myths connected with this misunderstood mammal are exploded as readers learn basic information about where bats are found, what they eat, and how to tell them apart. Detailed black-and-white pencil drawings help to embellish the uncomplicated text in this excellent resource for younger readers.

11.37   Selsam, Millicent, and Joyce Hunt. **Keep Looking!** Illustrated by Normand Chartier. Macmillan, 1989. ISBN 0-02-781840-3. 32p. 5–8.

From a distance, the wood-frame farmhouse and surrounding yard in the opening wintry scene look deserted, but if the reader will "sit quietly, wait patiently, and keep looking," a secret world will appear. Millicent Selsam and Joyce Hunt help children use their senses to learn how animals—from skunks and chickadees to ants and snakes to bats and raccoons—live and survive in the cold. Double-page illustrations in earth-toned watercolors help to set the quiet, peaceful mood of a woodland winter.

Birds

11.38   Bash, Barbara. **Urban Roosts: Where Birds Nest in the City.** Illustrated by Barbara Bash. Sierra Club Books and Little, Brown, 1990. ISBN 0-316-08306-2. 32p. 6–8 (est.).

Where the natural habitats of birds have been destroyed, adapters have managed to thrive in the city. Barbara Bash documents their urban roosts, sometimes from a bird's eye view. To a pigeon, for example, skyscrapers and city streets may be like cliffs and canyon floors. To a house finch, a streetlight cavity provides shelter. Bash turns urban eyes upward, informing young readers of the habits of city dwellers—sparrows, owls, swallows, swifts, wrens, nighthawks, crows, and falcons.

11.39 Brown, Mary Barrett. **Wings along the Waterway.** Illustrated by Mary Barrett Brown. Orchard Books, 1992. ISBN 0-531-08581-3. 80p. 8–11.

Mary Barrett Brown presents an Audubon-like picture book of birds that seek their shelter and food from the water and its environment. A description of habits and habitats of twenty-one birds of the marshes, wetlands, and lagoons is accompanied by oversize watercolor paintings and smaller studies that offer magnificent color and texture. The text provides interesting details of bird behaviors—nesting, raising young, and preserving the species.

11.40 Gibbons, Gail. **The Puffins Are Back!** Illustrated by Gail Gibbons. HarperCollins, 1991. ISBN 0-06-021604-2. 32p. 8–11.

Watercolors, pens, and black ink serve as Gail Gibbons's media to capture the Atlantic puffins as they make their yearly pilgrimage to the coast of Maine to lay eggs and raise their young. Descriptions of puffins' behaviors are balanced with explanations of how scientists observe and learn from these behaviors. The text chronicles the efforts of scientists from the National Audubon Society to preserve and reinforce the endangered colony. Tones of blue, green, and brown establish the puffins' habitat.

11.41 Goldin, Augusta. **Ducks Don't Get Wet, rev. ed.** Illustrated by Leonard Kessler. Thomas Y. Crowell, 1989. ISBN 0-690-04782-7. 32p. 4–8.

Although ducks go in and out of the water, dive in ponds for food, and fly south in the rain, they don't get wet. The four-color illustrations help to support the description of ducks' behaviors and characteristics. Easy-to-do experiments, detailed and illustrated in the text, explain a duck's waterproof nature and could be used as a way to extend this Let's-Read-and-Find-Out Book in the classroom.

11.42 Hirschi, Ron. **The Mountain Bluebird.** Photographs by Galen Burrell. Cobblehill Books, 1989. ISBN 0-525-65010-5. 48p. 7–11 (est.).

In his introduction, author Ron Hirschi explains that blue is a symbol of hope and happiness in many cultures. This account of the mountain bluebird brings to life a natural world that fills the reader with wonder. The author details every aspect of the life of the mountain bluebird—the raising of the young, feeding, predators, nesting patterns, and its migration from high in the Rocky Mountains to deep in Texas. The text is accompanied by color photographs of the bird in its natural habitat and by a glossary, index, and appendix titled "What Can You Do to Help Bluebirds?"

11.43   Horton, Tom. **Swanfall: Journey of the Tundra Swans.** Photographs by David Harp. Walker, 1991. ISBN 0-8027-8107-1. 48p. 7–10.

Tundra swans, the dominant species in North America, migrate yearly from the Arctic to the Blackwater National Wildlife Refuge in the Chesapeake Bay. Stunning color photographs record the journey, capturing the pristine beauty of the world's largest waterfowl. *Swanfall* is a coined word, used to describe the sighting of the arriving flock. Tom Horton's well-crafted prose is filled with information.

11.44   Ryder, Joanne. **Dancers in the Garden.** Illustrated by Judith Lopez. Sierra Club Books for Children, 1992. ISBN 0-87156-578-1. 30p. 6 and up (est.).

In testimony to the hummingbird, Joanne Ryder and Judith Lopez have created an information book with its text reminiscent of the cadences of haiku, and have set the book within a graceful Japanese-like garden, complete with arching bridge and gingko trees. The hummingbird's daily activities—waking, feeding, bathing, guarding its territory, and attracting a mate—are treated with graceful prose and watercolors.

11.45   Sattler, Helen Roney. **The Book of Eagles.** Illustrated by Jean Day Zallinger. Lothrop, Lee and Shepard Books, 1989. ISBN 0-688-07022-1. 64p. 8–12.

In a magnificently illustrated text, Helen Roney Sattler offers readers the natural history of eagles, including their physical characteristics, behavior, and life cycle. The African fish eagle, the bald eagle, the booted eagle, and the harpy eagle are among the many individual species discussed. Shaded maps show the eagles' habitats. Closeup drawings allow inspection of feet, talons, and eyes. A bibliography is also included.

11.46   Vernon, Adele. **The Hoiho: New Zealand's Yellow-Eyed Penguin.** Photographs by Dean Schneider. G. P. Putnam's Sons, 1991. ISBN 0-399-21686-3. 44p. 8–12.

In the forests of New Zealand live the hoihos, yellow-eyed penguins named by the Maori for their distinctive calls. This well-researched book presents information about hoiho characteristics, day-to-day life, and New Zealand's efforts to save them from extinction. Full-color photographs beautifully document the habitat and lifestyle of the world's rarest penguins.

Domesticated Animals

11.47 Facklam, Margery. **Who Harnessed the Horse? The Story of Animal Domestication.** Illustrated by Steven Parton. Little, Brown, 1992. ISBN 0-316-27381-3. 160p. 9 and up (est.).

Margery Facklam describes the varying ways in which animals have been domesticated to work for humans. Through anecdotes, descriptive narrative, and black-and-white drawings, readers will learn how different breeds of horses, cows, and cats developed to fill people's specific needs, as well as how domestication has changed these animals. This historical account offers a global perspective on human relationships with animals. A glossary and index will help readers find specific points within the uninterrupted narrative.

11.48 Hirschi, Ron. **What Is a Horse? Where Do Horses Live?** Photographs by Linda Quartman Younker and Ron Hirschi. Walker, 1989. 32p. 5–9.

Young horse lovers will be enchanted by both panoramic and closeup photographs of their favorite animal at work and at play, domesticated and wild, in this two-book photo essay. Brief text offers descriptive and identifying information overlaid on breathtaking views of where horses live, what they do, and what care they need. Each book ends with a short afterword that includes additional notes either about the sites of the photographs or in testimony to horses as companions.

11.49 Saville, Lynne. **Horses in the Circus Ring.** Photographs by Lynne Saville. E. P. Dutton, 1989. ISBN 0-525-44417-3. 32p. 5–9.

Action photographs of circuses in five countries illustrate in full color the nature of training and performing with horses. The accompanying text describes various acts, from solo to team performances and includes stunt riding and comedy acts. Animal training is described sensitively, but without sentiment.

Insects and Spiders

11.50   Goor, Ron, and Nancy Goor. **Insect Metamorphosis: From Egg to Adult.** Photographs by Ron Goor. Atheneum, 1990. ISBN 0-689-31445-0. 26p. 7–11.

Metamorphosis is the unique way that some insects grow and change from egg to adult. Closeup, full-color photographs of a variety of insects—butterflies, mosquitoes, wasps, and others—along with a simple and clear text explain the stages of egg, larva, and pupa. Additional photographs and descriptions feature incomplete metamorphosis, where insects do not undergo radical changes in appearance from one stage to the next. *Boston Globe–Horn Book Honor Book, 1990.*

11.51   Hopf, Alice L. **Spiders.** Photographs by Ann Moreton. Cobblehill Books, 1990. ISBN 0-525-65017-2. 64p. 5 and up.

Do you think that if you've seen one spider you've seen 'em all? Do you believe that spiders are insects? After sixty-four pages of engaging text, splashed with full-color closeup photographs, readers will know not only that spiders come in 35,000 varieties and that they are classified as Arachnida, but also that some spiders jump, some fish, and others spit. *Outstanding Science Trade Books for Children in 1990.*

11.52   McLaughlin, Molly. **Dragonflies.** Walker, 1989. ISBN 0-8027-6847-4. 32p. 6–10 (est.).

Through clear, descriptive text and closeup color photographs, readers are introduced to fascinating information about dragonflies and their close relatives, damselflies. Readers can learn that dragonflies lived on Earth before dinosaurs and that there are over 4,000 species of these helpful insects. How they find food, escape danger, adapt, lay eggs, and undergo metamorphosis makes for high-interest reading. *Notable Children's Trade Books in Science, 1989.*

11.53   Pringle, Laurence. **Killer Bees, rev. ed.** Morrow Junior Books, 1990. ISBN 0-688-09524-0. 64p. 8 and up.

"They're here!" In the fall of 1990, killer bees, descendents of bees from Africa, crossed from Mexico into the United States near Brownsville, Texas. Laurence Pringle brings a rational, objective approach to the description of the invasion and includes maps and black-and-white photos. Originally issued in 1986, the first two chapters of the text have changed little, describing why these African bees behave as they do, and their effect in Central and South America. New information deals with the northward movement of the bees and their likely impact in the United States. A glossary, guidelines for safety, and suggestions for further reading are included.

11.54 Souza, D. M. **Insects around the House. Insects in the Garden. What Bit Me?** Carolrhoda Books, 1991. 40p. 6–9.

The life cycles and habits of such insects as the termite, housefly, and cockroach are described in detail against closeup color photographs. The Creatures All Around Us series looks at insects around the house and garden, including ones that bite and ones that are beneficial to humans, as well as looking at arachnids. In an easy-to-read format, children are introduced to fascinating facts. Critical terms appear in boldface, and there are charts, glossaries, and indexes to help young researchers.

Ocean Life

11.55 Bendick, Jeanne. **Exploring an Ocean Tide Pool.** Illustrated by Todd Telander. Henry Holt/Redfeather Books, 1992. ISBN 0-8050-2043-8. 56p. 7–10 (est.).

Jeanne Bendick's voice is personal and close as she guides young readers to notice the life in the neighborhood of a tidal pool. In a chapter book that fits small hands, readers are introduced to the plants and animals in a small home linked to a larger ecosystem. Full-page color photographs and closeup black-and-white diagrams inform readers about mollusks, crustaceans, fish, and Cnidaria.

11.56 Cousteau Society. **Dolphins. Penguins. Seals. Turtles.** Photographs by the Cousteau Society. Simon and Schuster/Little Simon Books, 1991–92. 16p. 3–7 (est.).

Full-page colorful, closeup photographs bring the young reader into the world of four ocean-dwelling animals—the sea turtle, the dolphin, the penguin, and the seal. Each of the books in the Ocean Animals series begins with a fact sheet revealing the weight, lifespan, food, and reproductive cycle of the animal. Then, in a single line of text per page, interesting information appears in clear, simple language, such as dolphins "are among the fastest swimmers in the oceans" and "Penguins are most unusual birds. They can't fly because their wings are too small."

11.57   Gibbons, Gail. **Sharks.** Illustrated by Gail Gibbons. Holiday House, 1992. ISBN 0-8234-0960-0. 32p. 6–9 (est.).

In an information book that many beginning readers will manage for themselves, Gail Gibbons provides comprehensive information about sharks. Pages with minimal text give children what they like best—basic facts and large, clear labels. For example, mako sharks can swim forty-three miles per hour, and out of the 350 kinds of sharks, only thirty species have been known to attack people. The color illustrations show sharks in fluid movement with text overlaid on the blue-green ocean.

11.58   Gibbons, Gail. **Whales.** Illustrated by Gail Gibbons. Holiday House, 1991. ISBN 0-8234-0900-7. 30p. 6–10.

Whales are the largest and most wondrous creatures of the sea. This informative book introduces readers to different kinds of whales, explains their natural history, and describes how they struggle to survive today. Sea-shaded watercolor paintings illustrate the easy-to-understand text. Detailed information about individual whales, labeled diagrams, phonetic pronounciations, maps, and a list of interesting facts about whales provide young "whale watchers" with a fascinating look at the ocean's most graceful inhabitant.

11.59   Grover, Wayne. **Dolphin Adventure: A True Story.** Illustrated by Jim Fowler. Greenwillow Books, 1990. ISBN 0-688-09442-2. 48p. 8 and up.

Eight short chapters recount the extraordinary events of a day that Wayne Grover, an accomplished scuba diver, spent diving off the Florida coast. On his second dive, a family of three dolphins approached him. One was injured. Sensing that the dolphins were seeking assistance, Grover successfully removed a fishing hook from the baby's back. The smell of blood attracted sharks, but they were fended off by the mother and father dolphin. Black-and-white pencil illustrations appear on almost every page.

11.60   Johnson, Rebecca L. **The Great Barrier Reef: A Living Laboratory.** Lerner, 1992. ISBN 0-8225-1596-2. 64p. 5 and up.

One of the best-known barrier reefs in the world now comes to life through color photographs. The young reader is introduced to plants and creatures inside and around the barrier reef, including giant clams, fish of all kinds, sizes, and shapes, sea turtles, and coral animals.

11.61 Lauber, Patricia. **An Octopus Is Amazing.** Illustrated by Holly Keller. Thomas Y. Crowell/Let's-Read-and-Find-Out Science Books, 1990. ISBN 0-690-04801-7. 32p. 6–10.

What has a bag-shaped body, lives in the sea, and can change colors in a flash? The amazing octopus! In this Let's-Read-and-Find-Out Book, Patricia Lauber introduces readers to one of the sea's most intelligent creatures and describes its characteristics and life cycle. Full-page watercolor paintings make explicit the easy-to-understand text. A full-color, labeled chart offers readers further information about several of the world's most common octopuses.

11.62 Maestro, Betsy. **A Sea Full of Sharks.** Illustrated by Giulio Maestro. Scholastic Hardcover Books, 1990. ISBN 0-590-43100-5. 32p. 4–7.

Sharks both scare us and fascinate us. Although live sharks are difficult to study, scientists are aware that there are about 350 different species of sharks, ranging in size from six inches to more than fifty feet long. Shark facts are related in clear and simple language in a book that encourages respect for these sometimes dangerous, yet important, creatures of the deep.

11.63 Mallory, Kenneth, and Andrea Conley. **Rescue of the Stranded Whales.** Simon and Schuster Books for Young Readers and New England Aquarium, 1989. ISBN 0-671-67122-7. 64p. 5–10.

Kenneth Mallory and Andrea Conley give a fascinating account of a close encounter with whales—a successful rescue of three young pilot whales stranded on a Cape Cod beach. The well-written narrative describes scientists' attempts to move the whales to the New England Aquarium and eventually return them to the sea. Full-page color photographs add to the drama of the real-life story. *Notable Children's Trade Books in Science, 1989.*

11.64 McDonald, Megan. **Is This a House for Hermit Crab?** Illustrated by S. D. Schindler. Orchard Books/Richard Jackson Books, 1990. ISBN 0-531-08455-8. 32p. 3–6.

Hermit Crab searches for a new home: "He stepped along the shore, by the sea, in the sand . . . scritch-scratch, scritch-scratch." But finding a home safe from the pricklepine fish is not easy. A rock is too heavy, a rusty can too noisy, a piece of driftwood too dark, and a sand pail too deep—until, at last, Hermit Crab finds the safety of a snail's empty shell. S. D. Schindler's textured pastels add sandy, shimmery beaches and seas to a read-it-again text. *IRA Children's Book Award, 1991.*

11.65 Simon, Seymour. **Whales.** Thomas Y. Crowell, 1989. ISBN 0-690-04758-4. 35p. 4–8.

Dramatic color photographs and simple text describe the physical characteristics and habits of various species of whales. Seymour Simon, an acclaimed science writer for children, explains the dangers of the possible extinction of these giant creatures of the sea.

11.66 Waters, John F. **Watching Whales.** Cobblehill Books, 1991. ISBN 0-525-65072-5. 42p. 8 and up.

John Waters inspects and explains the relationship among boat owners, scientists, and whale watchers in the Cape Cod area. By following a fifth-grade class as it prepares for a whale watch, readers also gain general information about East Coast whales, such as the minke, the finback, and the humpback. Color photographs record whales breaching, spouting, and feeding. An appendix offers information on other opportunities for whale watching as well how to adopt a whale.

11.67 White, Sandra Verrill, and Michael Filisky. **Sterling: The Rescue of a Baby Harbor Seal.** Crown/New England Aquarium Books, 1989. ISBN 0-517-57112-9. 29p. 6–10 (est.).

Sterling, an orphaned harbor seal pup, is rescued by workers from the New England Aquarium. As she learns how to catch fish and swim, specialists monitor her progress and prepare her for a return to the ocean. Over sixty full-color photographs feature Sterling and other seals in their natural environment and in temporary captivity. *Notable Children's Trade Books in Science, 1989.*

Pets

11.68 Ashabranner, Brent. **Crazy about German Shepherds.** Photographs by Jennifer Ashabranner. Cobblehill Books, 1990. ISBN 0-525-65032-6. 81p. 10 and up.

Peggy O'Callaghan's dream took shape when she temporarily adopted a lost German shepherd. Peggy then bought her own German shepherd puppy and worked hard to learn all she could about dog care before opening her own kennel in the northern Virginia foothills of the Blue Ridge Mountains. Black-and-white photographs sensitively capture the four canine stars of Peggy's domain: Dare, Zoe, Freesia, and Coyote. Readers will find this both an informative and heartwarming account of a dog-lover's career.

11.69   Hirschi, Ron. **What Is a Cat? Where Do Cats Live?** Photographs by Linda Quartman Younker. Walker, 1991. 32p. 5–9.

Cats are fun-loving kittens, lap-warming pals, and sunbathing nappers. *What Is a Cat?* explains the distinctive markings, habits, and moods of domesticated felines and provides readers with useful information about cat care. *Where Do Cats Live?* presents a scenic look at the habitats of both wild and domestic cats. Full-color photographs in both easy-to-read information books capture the independence and interdependence of cats.

Reptiles and Amphibians

11.70   Bare, Colleen Stanley. **Never Kiss an Alligator!** Photographs by Colleen Stanley Bare. Cobblehill Books, 1989. ISBN 0-525-65003-2. 28p. 4–8.

At least one stunning closeup color photograph of an alligator adorns each page of this entertaining and informative book. In one to four sentences of pithy text per page we learn about these ancient reptiles: their food, their habitat, their size, their young, and how they differ from crocodiles. Alligators' greatest enemy is man, so the author's closing words implore readers to "watch, study, admire and to preserve, protect, and respect" these ancient creatures. *Notable Children's Trade Books in Science, 1989.*

11.71   Lavies, Bianca. **Lily Pad Pond.** Photographs by Bianca Lavies. E. P. Dutton, 1989. ISBN 0-525-44483-1. 28p. 3–8.

Life in a woodland pond is captured in full-page photographs which center on a tadpole's development into a bullfrog. A dramatic sequence of photos shows the young frog capturing a dragonfly. The text is clearly written, flush with interesting detail, and varied in style: "After a year of eating pond ooze and plant material, she is plump." Bianca Lavies includes a list of the featured pond inhabitants and the amount of enlargement of each photo to give readers an indication of actual size.

11.72   Parker, Nancy Winslow, and Joan Richards Wright. **Frogs, Toads, Lizards, and Salamanders.** Illustrated by Nancy Winslow

Parker. Greenwillow Books, 1990. ISBN 0-688-08681-0. 48p. 6 and up.

Introduced through amusing couplets, various water, land, and desert creatures are the subjects in this fact-filled companion to Nancy Winslow Parker and Joan Richards Wright's earlier collaboration, *Bugs*. The easy-to-understand text includes information on physical characteristics, habits, and natural environments of sixteen reptiles and amphibians found in the United States. Clearly labeled scientific drawings and diagrams enrich full-color, stylized illustrations. Glossaries, maps, and charts included at the back of the book will help teachers and young herpetologists alike.

11.73 Simon, Seymour. **Snakes.** HarperCollins, 1992. ISBN 0-06-022530-0. 32p. 5–12.

Snakes opens with a dramatic double-page color photograph of six baby snakes simultaneously hatching. This remarkable shot sets the stage for the impressive photos to come: a yellow rat snake swallows its prey; a copperhead's forked tongue shoots out; and a sidewinder makes its ladder-rung tracks across the sand. The narrative facing the full-page photos helps children to identify the snakes and to understand more about snakes' habitats, behaviors, and value.

11.74 Ziter, Cary B. **When Turtles Come to Town.** Photographs by Chuck Bigger. Franklin Watts/First Books, 1989. ISBN 0-531-10691-8. 64p. 8–10.

Every summer, sea turtles come ashore to lay their eggs on sandy Atlantic beaches of the Southeast United States. Many people are now involved in saving these creatures after years of slaughter by humans. Young Claire and Jesse, accompanied by their father, meet experts devoted to preserving the sea turtle. The children learn about turtle birth and growth, the hunting and poaching of turtles, their history, and the preservation of these reptiles. Numerous color photographs add information and drama.

Wild Animals

11.75 Arnold, Caroline. **Cheetah. Flamingo. Hippo. Orangutan. Snake. Wild Goat.** Photographs by Richard Hewett. Morrow Junior Books, 1989–91. 48p. 7 and up.

Vividly illustrated with full-color photographs on every page, this captivating Animal Favorites series does not patronize young readers with its wide variety of information—including height, weight, reproduction, hunting habits, and survival. Each book begins by introducing a specific zoo resident. Responsibilities involved in keeping the animal in captivity are explained before the discussion broadens to include information about that animal species' life in the wild. *Notable Children's Trade Books in Science, 1989 (Cheetah).*

11.76 Arnosky, Jim. **Crinkleroot's Book of Animal Tracking, rev. ed.** Illustrated by Jim Arnosky. Bradbury Press, 1989. ISBN 0-02-705851-4. 48p. 7–11.

Crinkleroot, a hilarious woodsman born in a tree and raised by bees, tells readers how to track and trail wild animals. He explains how to identify animals from their tracks, how and where animal tracks are found, what the animals eat, and where they drink. Detailed drawings accompany the text and aid the reader in identifying the homes and tracks of beavers, otters, raccoons, rabbits, bobcats, a red fox, and others.

11.77 Halton, Cheryl M. **Those Amazing Bats.** Dillon Press, 1991. ISBN 0-87518-458-8. 96p. 9 and up.

Striking a balance between technical information and a fascinating adventure story, Cheryl Halton describes the intricacies of the biology, behavior, and mythology of bats. Color photos accompany chapters on bat species, the raising of young, echolocation, bats in science, bats' roles in the environment, and dangers facing bats. Appendixes describe procedures for building a bat house and list endangered or threatened species.

11.78 Johnston, Ginny, and Judy Cutchins. **Windows on Wildlife.** Morrow Junior Books, 1990. ISBN 0-688-07873-7. 48p. 7 and up.

Ginny Johnston and Judy Cutchins describe how scientists and exhibit specialists have designed and built six natural-habitat enclosures across the country in which people can view animals and conduct research on animal behavior. These habitats include a forest for gorillas, an icy home for penguins, an indoor jungle, a hippoquarium, an aviary for tropical birds, and an aquarium for giant kelp. Color photographs, a glossary, an index, and an informative text sensitize readers to the need to preserve wild animals and their natural habitats from human encroachment. *Outstanding Science Trade Books for Children in 1990.*

11.79 Kitchen, Bert. **Gorilla/Chinchilla, and Other Animal Rhymes.** Illustrated by Bert Kitchen. Dial Books, 1990. ISBN 0-8037-0771-1. 32p. All ages.

It may not be often that a Hog hangs out with a Frog, a Hippopotamus befriends a Duck-billed Platypus, or a Beagle plays fetch with an Eagle, but strange things happen when animals are grouped in rhyming pairs. A short verse about each animal pair appears on one page, with a realistic, intricately detailed drawing of the subjects in full-color on the facing page, providing a unique way to explore the diversity of the animal kingdom.

11.80 Ryden, Hope. **Your Cat's Wild Cousins.** Photographs by Hope Ryden. Lodestar Books, 1991. ISBN 0-525-67354-7. 47p. 8–12 (est.).

Although cats appear to be domesticated, they have a wild side and a wild set of cousins. Using her own cat, Lily, for comparison, naturalist Hope Ryden helps readers notice and understand the similarities and differences between domesticated and wild cats. Beautiful full-color photographs capture Lily and eighteen of her wild cat cousins in their natural habitats and provide a closeup look at their behaviors. Graphically rendered catpaws signal information bullets about each wild cat, inviting cat enthusiasts to learn more about these incredible felines.

11.81 Sattler, Helen Roney. **Giraffes, the Sentinels of the Savannas.** Illustrated by Christopher Santoro. Lothrop, Lee and Shepard Books, 1989. ISBN 0-688-08285-8. 80p. 8 and up.

While scientists don't know exactly how intelligent the tallest animal in the world is, it is known that once, when a male giraffe was making unwanted advances toward a female giraffe at the Manchester, England, zoo, the female lured the male into a stall, backed out, and closed the door after her. This award-winning book affectionately describes the natural history of giraffes traced from twenty million years ago, as well as the animals' present-day habits, habitat, and chances of future survival. The well-written text is supplemented by intricate pencil drawings. *Outstanding Science Trade Books for Children in 1990; ALA Notable Children's Books, 1991.*

11.82 Simon, Seymour. **Big Cats.** HarperCollins, 1991. ISBN 0-06-021647-6. 40p. 5–8 (est.).

"The Big Cats," according to Seymour Simon, are those that can roar: the lion, tiger, leopard, and jaguar. In this photo essay that demonstrates the grace and power of the animals, three other cats are included as well—the puma, cheetah, and snow leopard. Readable text describes habitats, behaviors, and threats to their continued existence.

11.83　Stirling, Ian. **Bears.** Photographs by Aubrey Lang. Sierra Club Books for Children, 1992. ISBN 0-87156-574-9. 64p. 10 and up (est.).

Polar bears can hibernate when food is unavailable; on some Alaskan trails, each grizzly that passes steps in the same footprints. With fascinating tidbits like these, full-color photographs of bears in their natural habitats, and lively drawings, this book in the Sierra Club Wildlife Library is a masterful introduction to an animal that has captivated humans for millennia. Chapters focus on species evolution, cub life, adult behavior, diet, communication, hibernation, and the outlook for bears in today's world.

11.84　Yoshida, Toshi. **Elephant Crossing.** Illustrated by Toshi Yoshida. Philomel Books, 1989. ISBN 0-399-21745-2. 32p. 5–9.

As the herd of elephants crosses the plain on its way to the forest where green leaves are plentiful, it is suddenly confronted by three young lions out hunting. When the leader of the herd boldly charges, the lions retreat. Yet there are some dangers that even fully grown elephants cannot guard against. Through a flashback, the reader learns of the dangers of the African plain, including a time when the elephant herd encountered a swarm of desert grasshoppers that destroyed every source of food in its path. Panoramic colored-pencil spreads reveal the vastness of this wildlife habitat.

11.85　Yoshida, Toshi. **Young Lions.** Illustrated by Toshi Yoshida. Philomel Books, 1989. ISBN 0-399-21546-8. 32p. 6–10.

On the African plain three young lions leave their sleeping mother to go on their first hunt. They encounter many of the animals that live on the great African plain—a group of zebras, a herd of impalas, cheetahs running at lightning speed, a herd of gnus, and a leopard feeding high in a tree. Unsuccessful, the young lions return to their pride. Readers will also enjoy Toshi Yoshida's *Elephant Crossing,* with its similar colored-pencil vistas of the African plain.

Archeology

11.86   Giblin, James Cross. **The Riddle of the Rosetta Stone: Key to Ancient Egypt.** Thomas Y. Crowell, 1990. ISBN 0-690-04799-1. 85p. 8–13.

With the discovery in 1799 of the Rosetta Stone, historians believed that they would finally unlock the secrets of ancient Egypt. But deciphering the writing on the stone became a riddle that stumped scholars for years. James Cross Giblin's book traces the history of how this riddle was solved, explaining how the symbols and their meanings were finally matched. Illustrated with authentic black-and-white photographs and explanatory hieroglyphics, this book provides both readers and young researchers with a fascinating look at the key that revealed the history of an ancient civilization.

11.87   Lasky, Kathryn. **Traces of Life: The Origins of Humankind.** Illustrated by Whitney Powell. Morrow Junior Books, 1989. ISBN 0-688-07237-2. 128p. 10 and up (est.).

"Time can become unimaginable." And so, Kathryn Lasky's opening chapter sets time—all five billion years of Earth—into a single day, and ticks off the hours to trace life on Earth from bacteria's arrival at dawn to humankind's entrance at 11:59 p.m. Documenting like a scientist, building intrigue like a mystery writer, and never losing her storyteller's stance, Lasky describes the work of paleoanthropologists, specialists in the fossil remains of our early ancestors. Pages are replete with labeled black-and-white sketches, maps, diagrams, and photographs.

Conservation and Ecology

11.88   Arnosky, Jim. **In the Forest: A Portfolio of Paintings.** Illustrated by Jim Arnosky. Lothrop, Lee and Shepard Books, 1989. ISBN 0-688-09138-5. 32p. 6 and up (est.).

"This book is a little bit of forest you can hold, composed of paintings done outdoors, printed on paper made from forest trees, and bound together by two seasons." Thus ends Jim Arnosky's introduction to eleven full-page impressionistic paintings in six colors of oil on canvas. Opposite the paintings are detailed captions in which the artist describes each forest setting and his experiences while painting it.

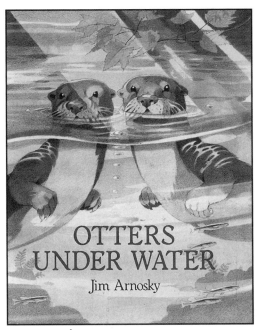

A.

B.

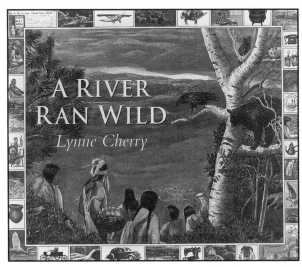

C.

A. *Otters under Water* by Jim Arnosky (see 11.17). **B.** *Visual Magic* by David Thomson (see 11.125). **C.** *A River Ran Wild: An Environmental History* by Lynne Cherry (see 11.91).

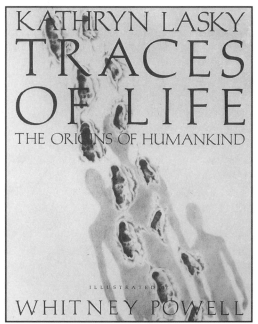

A.

B.

C.

A. *Brother Eagle, Sister Sky: A Message from Chief Seattle* paintings by Susan Jeffers (see 11.92). **B.** *Traces of Life: The Origins of Humankind* by Kathryn Lasky; illustrated by Whitney Powell (see 11.87). **C.** *Surtsey: The Newest Place on Earth* by Kathryn Lasky; photographs by Christopher G. Knight (see 11.99).

11.89 Arnosky, Jim. **Near the Sea: A Portfolio of Paintings.** Illustrated by Jim Arnosky. Lothrop, Lee and Shepard Books, 1990. ISBN 0-688-09327-2. 32p. 6 and up (est.).

In full-page oil paintings on canvas, Jim Arnosky leads an intimate tour of a Maine island's seascapes and landscapes, conveying the texture of rocky island coasts, lobster boats, clapboard houses, tall grasses, and shifting tides. Simple paragraphs explain the settings and the feelings that the artist experienced as he worked: "The ocean owns two-thirds of this round earth and would have the rest inch by inch." Using only six colors, Arnosky explains, he economized on weight as he hiked to his vantage points.

11.90 Brown, Laurie Krasny, and Marc Brown. **Dinosaurs to the Rescue! A Guide to Protecting Our Planet.** Illustrated by Marc Brown. Little, Brown/Joy Street Books, 1992. ISBN 0-316-11087-6. 32p. 6–10 (est.).

Wise dinosaurs demonstrate some tested rules for keeping planet Earth green. One "sloposaurus" is the exception, a crabby dinosaur who violates the book's three guidelines: "Use less," "Use things again," and "Give something back to the earth." The unabashed messages are illustrated in cartoon style with genial dinosaurs preserving resources, recycling in various ways, and enhancing the environment.

11.91 Cherry, Lynne. **A River Ran Wild: An Environmental History.** Illustrated by Lynne Cherry. Harcourt Brace Jovanovich/Gulliver Green Books, 1992. ISBN 0-15-200542-0. 40p. 6–10.

Beginning with a tribe of Native Americans whose chief named it Nash-a-way—"River with the Pebbled Bottom"—through the logging by early European settlers and the development of the plastics and paper industries, the Nashua River has been an important life source to many generations of people in Massachusetts and New Hampshire. When industrial pollution nearly killed the river, citizens organized to clean up and save the Nashua. Earth-toned, colored-pencil, and watercolor drawings depict this remarkable environmental story, and a detailed border provides historical supplements to the text.

11.92 Chief Seattle. **Brother Eagle, Sister Sky: A Message from Chief Seattle.** Illustrated by Susan Jeffers. Dial Books, 1991. ISBN 0-8037-0963-3. 32p. 6 and up.

The eloquent text of this book is attributed to Chief Seattle, peaceful leader of the Suquamish Indian nation in the Northwest over a century ago, and is adapted and vivified through Susan Jeffers's magnificent artwork. Chief Seattle's message is one of life in harmony with mother earth, brother rivers, and sister flowers, reminding today's land dwellers that Earth does not belong to us—rather, we belong to Earth. In double-page spreads, Jeffers's fine line illustrations with ink and dyes are beautifully detailed representations of Native Americans of long ago.

11.93   Cone, Molly. **Come Back, Salmon: How a Group of Dedicated Kids Adopted Pigeon Creek and Brought It Back to Life.** Photographs by Sidnee Wheelwright. Sierra Club Books for Children, 1992. ISBN 0-87156-572-2. 48p. 7–10 (est.).

Pigeon Creek flows from Everett, Washington, past Jackson Elementary School, to Puget Sound. Students had seen mud and trash in the creek, but never fish—until they cleaned and stocked it with salmon raised from eggs in a classroom aquarium. Crisp, color photos record the ugly—evidence of human thoughtlessness—and the beautiful—students on an instructive and rewarding mission and mature salmon that returned to their former home. Readers, upon learning that "kids can make a difference," may be inspired to initiate local environmental projects. *NCTE Orbis Pictus Honor Book, 1992.*

11.94   Dolan, Edward F. **Our Poisoned Sky.** Cobblehill Books, 1991. ISBN 0-525-65056-3. 111p. 10 and up.

In this well-researched book, both the complex problem of air pollution and viable solutions to it are enumerated and discussed. The numerous definitions, subheadings, diagrams, and photographs, as well as a clearly readable text, make the book a useful research text for middle- to upper-level students. Timely topics include acid rain, industrial air pollution, ozone depletion, and the greenhouse effect. Ten practical solutions are outlined in the last chapter.

11.95   Dorros, Arthur. **Rain Forest Secrets.** Illustrated by Arthur Dorros. Scholastic Hardcover Books, 1990. ISBN 0-590-43369-5. 40p. 6–9.

Arthur Dorros introduces readers to the vegetation and animals of rain forests around the world and explains the dangers facing these important ecosystems. Colorful full-page illustrations and labeled drawings support the informative text and help to explain the complicated and integrated life system of a rain forest. The list of organizations dedicated to saving the world's rain forests and the author's personal note provide readers with sources and a stimulus to learn more about these fascinating and endangered ecosystems.

11.96 Elkington, John, Julia Hailes, Douglas Hill, and Joel Makower. **Going Green: A Kid's Handbook to Saving the Planet.** Illustrated by Tony Ross. Viking Penguin/Tilden Press Books, 1990. ISBN 0-670-83611-7. 96p. 8 and up.

Can one person play a role in saving the Earth? Four lively and logically sequenced sections demonstrate that the answer is a most emphatic "Yes." The high-energy text, complemented by action-packed, cartoon-style drawings, informs readers about such environmental issues as the greenhouse effect, depletion of the ozone layer, acid rain, trash, and air and water pollution. The book teaches readers how to conduct a "green audit" of their homes, schools, and communities and alphabetically lists actions that the reader can take. A bibliography and a list of organizations concerned about the environment provide additional information. *Notable 1990 Children's Trade Books in the Field of Social Studies.*

11.97 Gibbons, Gail. **Recycle! A Handbook for Kids.** Illustrated by Gail Gibbons. Little, Brown, 1992. ISBN 0-316-30971-0. 32p. 5–10 (est.).

With distinct, colorful graphics and up-to-the-minute explanatory text, Gail Gibbons shows how paper, glass, cans, plastic, and styrofoam are recycled, thus reducing the amount of waste in our landfills. The lively pen-and-ink and watercolor drawings often contain labels and supplementary information about the recycling procedures. Gibbons concludes her narration with alarming facts about the trash problem and what we can do to curb it.

11.98 Hirschi, Ron. **Fall. Spring. Summer. Winter.** Photographs by Thomas D. Mangelsen. Cobblehill Books, 1990–91. 32p. 3–8 (est.).

In a photographic tribute to the seasons designed especially for young readers, the team of Ron Hirschi and Thomas Mangelsen has produced four books whose brief text and striking photographs invite close looks at living things in natural habitats and encourage appreciation of nature's changes. Out-of-doors throughout the year, the photographer of these Wildlife Seasons Books catches spring flowers peeking through snow, baby birds begging for food, salmon spawning in river gravel, and coyotes with thick warm coats.

11.99 Lasky, Kathryn. **Surtsey: The Newest Place on Earth.** Photographs by Christopher G. Knight. Hyperion Books for Children, 1992. ISBN 1-56282-301-9. 64p. 8–12.

Surtsey is an old story about the life of a young island. Rising from the sea in 1963 in the violence of a volcanic eruption, this island off the coast of Iceland has served as a laboratory for scientists documenting the arrival of life on its shores. An information-packed text, dramatic color photographs, and chapter-opening quotes from *The Prose Edda*—a thirteenth-century collection of Viking poetry, Scandinavian myths, and stories of Norse gods—juxtapose distant past and present.

11.100 Lauber, Patricia. **Summer of Fire: Yellowstone 1988.** Orchard Books, 1991. ISBN 0-531-08543-0. 64p. 9 and up (est.).

In the hot, dry summer of 1988, forest fires raged through Yellowstone Park. After intense lightning storms started the series of fires, they spread rapidly, and summer rains did not come. Patricia Lauber takes a careful look at those fires, considering their effects on the park and its inhabitants. Dramatic color photographs of the fires, as well as contrasting photographs of spruce, fir, and meadows, demonstrate effectively how old growth made way for new. A glossary and index are included.

11.101 Pringle, Laurence. **Living Treasure: Saving Earth's Threatened Biodiversity.** Illustrated by Irene Brady. Morrow Junior Books, 1991. ISBN 0-688-07710-2. 64p. 8 and up.

Scientists and lay people are amazed by the biological diversity of organisms on the planet Earth. Laurence Pringle considers how and why there is such a variety of living things, discussing how species develop over time, describing the past based partly on fossils, and enlisting the help of people around the world to save the Earth's living treasure—its biological diversity.

11.102 Siy, Alexandra. **Ancient Forests. Arctic National Wildlife Refuge. Hawaiian Islands. Native Grasslands.** Dillon Press, 1991. 70–80p. 9 and up.

Each volume in the Circle of Life series examines a separate environment, presenting it through clear text and beautiful, full-color photographs. Each book also includes a "Facts" section, activity pages, a list of appropriate environmental organizations, a glossary, and an index. Emphasis is placed on understanding and conserving each environment.

11.103 Wood, A. J. **Look Again! The Second Ultimate Spot-the-Difference Book.** Illustrated by April Wilson. Dial Books for Young Readers, 1992. ISBN 0-8037-0958-7. 36p. All ages.

In an introduction to global biomes, flora and fauna from Australia's shore, the Central African jungles, the Himalayas, polar regions, and other distinctive ecological regions compete for space on extravagantly colored spreads. Each pair of paintings details a dozen or more differences begging to be noticed. A multipurpose book that is intriguing to look at and that reveals the beauty and variety of nature, *Look Again!* follows the format of its predecessor, *Look!*, in providing supportive notes for lessons in natural history.

Earth Science, Meteorology, and Oceanography

11.104 Ballard, Robert D., with Rick Archbold. **The Lost Wreck of the Isis.** Illustrated by Wesley Lowe and Ken Marschall. Scholastic/Madison Press Books, 1990. ISBN 0-590-43852-2. 64p. 8–12.

Led by Dr. Robert Ballard, the discoverer of the wreck of the *Titanic,* underwater explorers search for a sunken ship over 1,600 years old. Both the discovery of this Roman treasure on the floor of the Mediterranean Sea and the technology that enabled Ballard to locate the *Isis* are described. Full-color photos, graphics, and drawings clarify the text. *Outstanding Science Trade Books for Children in 1990.*

11.105 Branley, Franklyn M. **Earthquakes.** Illustrated by Richard Rosenblum. Thomas Y. Crowell, 1990. ISBN 0-690-04663-4. 32p. 6–10.

In another title in the Let's-Read-and-Find-Out Science Books series, Franklyn Branley explains the causes of earthquakes, identifies danger zones, and describes the destruction that can result. In addition, information about preparation for and safety during an earthquake is presented. Colorful maps, diagrams, and illustrations help to explain the clear and accurate text.

11.106 Branley, Franklyn M. **Mysteries of Planet Earth.** Illustrated by Sally J. Bensusen. Lodestar Books, 1989. ISBN 0-525-67278-8. 63p. 10 and up.

In the sixth book of the Mysteries of the Universe series, Franklyn Branley poses and responds to questions regarding the Earth's origins, oceans, rotation, life forms, plate movements, and destiny. The book's format is one that lends itself to being read cover to cover or to being used as a well-indexed reference. Both black-and-white diagrams and photography enhance the text.

11.107 Cobb, Vicki. **This Place Is Dry.** Illustrated by Barbara Lavallee. Walker, 1989. ISBN 0-8027-6855-5. 32p. 7–9.

Can you imagine living in a place where the temperature can reach 130 degrees Fahrenheit and where cacti can grow as tall as three-story buildings? Well, Gila monsters, jaguars, and Tohono O'Odham Indians can because they live on Arizona's Sonora Desert. Full-color illustrations complement a fact-filled text about the land, people, and animals that flourish in a desert. Three additional books complete the Imagine Living Here series: *This Place Is High, This Place Is Cold,* and *This Place Is Wet.*

11.108 DeWitt, Lynda. **What Will the Weather Be?** Illustrated by Carolyn Croll. HarperCollins, 1991. ISBN 0-06-021597-6. 32p. 6–10.

What will the weather be tomorrow? Readers of this book in the Let's-Read-and-Find-Out Science Books series are introduced to the basics of weather forecasting, including the main characteristics of weather (temperature, humidity, wind speed and direction, and air pressure) and how meteorologists rely on instruments and scientific information to make their forecasts. Labeled diagrams and character dialogue support the informative text. A good companion book is Gail Gibbons's *Weather Words and What They Mean.*

11.109 Dorros, Arthur. **Feel the Wind.** Illustrated by Arthur Dorros. Thomas Y. Crowell, 1989. ISBN 0-690-04741-X. 32p. 4–8.

"See it, hear it, feel the wind." This Let's-Read-and-Find-Out Science Book invites children to use their senses to explore the wind, including its properties and its effects on our lives and on the environment. Simple definitions are supported by stylized illustrations. Experiments are presented that use children's bikes, toy boats, kites, and gliders to extend understanding. A brief history of wind power and directions for making a homemade weather vane are also included. *Notable Children's Trade Books in Science, 1989.*

11.110 Dorros, Arthur. **Follow the Water from Brook to Ocean.** Illustrated by Arthur Dorros. HarperCollins, 1991. ISBN 0-06-021599-2. 32p. 6–10.

Water is always moving downhill to the ocean, traveling from brooks to streams to rivers to the sea. Readers of this Let's-Read-and-Find-Out Science Book can also take the journey and learn more about how water changes the Earth's surface, how water is used, and why clean water is important. Key land features and relevant terms are explained as readers follow the water on its journey. Earth-toned watercolor drawings support the text.

11.111 Gibbons, Gail. **Weather Words and What They Mean.** Illustrated by Gail Gibbons. Holiday House, 1990. ISBN 0-8234-0805-1. 30p. 5–8 (est.).

Moisture, temperature, and air pressure are just a few of the concepts clearly explained in Gail Gibbons's easy-to-understand text for young children. Full-color illustrations, complete with labeled drawings and cartoon-dialogue inserts, help to define the meaning of commonly used weather words. The list of interesting weather facts included at the end of the book may be used as a model to spark children's interest in producing their own "weather almanac."

11.112 Goodman, Billy. **Natural Wonders and Disasters.** Wu, Norbert. **Life in the Oceans.** Little, Brown, 1991. 96p. 8–12.

Each of these oversized science books in the Planet Earth series, with handsome color photographs and lucid, informative prose, is written by a specialist who addresses natural history topics. The information is accurate, direct, and accessible. Although photographs will draw readers in, heightened interest in the subject matter will do the rest.

11.113 Lauber, Patricia. **How We Learned the Earth Is Round.** Illustrated by Megan Lloyd. Thomas Y. Crowell, 1990. ISBN 0-690-04862-9. 32p. 6–10.

Patricia Lauber presents a historical account of how the ancient Greeks and later explorers learned about the shape of our planet in this Let's-Read-and-Find-Out Science Book. Flat-Earth theories gave way to a belief in a round Earth, which was proven by the voyages of Columbus and Magellan. Animated ink-and-watercolor line drawings, along with diagrams, satellite photographs, and simple experiments, explain and support the clear and accurate text. *Notable 1990 Children's Trade Books in the Field of Social Studies.*

11.114 Peters, Lisa Westberg. **Water's Way.** Illustrated by Ted Rand. Little, Brown/Arcade, 1991. ISBN 1-55970-062-9. 32p. 4–8 (est.).

"Water has a way of changing." Lisa Westberg Peters's simple text makes the changes comprehensible—from fog, rain, and snow to puddles, creeks, and seas—while Ted Rand's watercolors amplify the explanations and testify to the beauty of water's forms. A square inset on each spread sets windows of Tony's house against outside changes. Inside, there is steam from the soup, moisture on the bathroom window, and a puddle on the sill. Outside, at last, there is snow for Tony's sled.

11.115 Simon, Seymour. **Deserts.** Morrow Junior Books, 1990. ISBN 0-688-07416-2. 32p. 6–10 (est.).

Seymour Simon once explained that he tries to write just as he speaks, ever mindful of the effect of his words on young readers. In *Deserts*, he once again achieves readable prose that both intrigues and informs. Crisp color photographs, outline maps, and graphs are offered to help young reader-researchers respond to the beauty and life forms of deserts, locate North American deserts, and understand their landscapes and variations. World map endpapers depict locations and relative sizes of world deserts.

11.116 Simon, Seymour. **Earthquakes.** Morrow Junior Books, 1991. ISBN 0-688-09634-4. 32p. 5 and up.

Leave it to Seymour Simon to draw in young readers with a "cool" fact in the first paragraph. This time, they'll learn that there are a million earthquakes each year, even though most are too small to be noticed. With diagrams, coded maps, and full-color photographs of earthquake damage, Simon explains the cause of quakes, ways to measure their strength, and their devastating power.

11.117 Simon, Seymour. **Oceans.** Morrow Junior Books, 1990. ISBN 0-688-09453-8. 32p. 5 and up.

In clear, concise text, Seymour Simon explains how the Earth's 70 percent liquid surface makes it "different from any other planet or moon in our solar system." The magnificence of our world's oceans is captured in full-page photographs and explained with computer-generated maps. Readers will not only learn about currents, tides, and how oceans affect weather patterns, but they may also develop a deeper interest and respect for the seas through this readable book.

Energy

11.118 Asimov, Isaac. **How Did We Find Out about Lasers?** Illustrated by Erika Kors. Walker, 1990. ISBN 0-8027-6936-5. 64p. 10–12 (est.).

Lasers, a term coined from Lightwave Amplification by Stimulated Emission of Radiation, are explained in Isaac Asimov's clear prose, beginning with chapters that explain light waves, light as a form of energy, and masers. The story of the discoveries that led to scientists' production of a coherent, monochromatic light—a laser—is illustrated with diagrams and sketches. A final chapter addresses the uses of lasers, and a topical index ensures the book's value as a reference. *Outstanding Science Trade Books for Children in 1990.*

11.119 Asimov, Isaac. **How Did We Find Out about Microwaves?** Illustrated by Erika Kors. Walker, 1989. ISBN 0-8027-6838-5. 64p. 10 and up.

This thirty-second book in the How Did We Find Out series reveals the history of research on light and microwaves. Since Dutch scientist Christian Huygens first theorized that light was composed of waves, others have learned how to measure the waves, how we see light and color, the relationship between sound waves and light waves, how to measure radiation in microwaves, and how to use microwaves to learn about the universe. Black-and-white illustrations and diagrams, plus an index, add interest and usefulness to the text.

11.120 Berger, Melvin. **Switch On, Switch Off.** Illustrated by Carol Croll. Thomas Y. Crowell, 1989. ISBN 0-690-04786-X. 32p. 5–8.

In this Let's-Read-and-Find-Out Science Book, two children explore the seeming magic of electricity. After constructing a simple magnet and wire generator, the children visit a real generator. They follow its coil pathway, first to their home and then to their own light switch and lamp. Along the way such concepts as atoms, electrons, and circuits are introduced simply and with clear diagrams. *Notable Children's Trade Books in Science, 1989.*

General Science Concepts

11.121 Cobb, Vicki. **For Your Own Protection: Stories Science Photos Tell. Fun and Games: Stories Science Photos Tell. Natural Wonders: Stories Science Photos Tell.** Lothrop, Lee and Shepard Books, 1989–91. 32p. 8 and up.

Three books explore science concepts, giving new perspectives on everyday objects and activities through magnified or highly detailed color photographs. *Fun and Games* exhibits a bouncing ball and popping popcorn. *Natural Wonders* looks at a magnified insect eye and falling cat, and *For Your Own Protection* reveals enlarged plaque bacteria, a dust mite, and a sneeze. Vicki Cobb's text explains the photos with understandable language and interesting details. Glossaries and indexes help to extend the fun of learning about science.

11.122 Eldin, Peter. **Troll's Student Handbook.** Troll Associates, 1992. ISBN 0-8167-2525-X. 192p. 10 and up (est.).

Easy to tuck into a backpack, this eclectic little handbook supplies information on such diverse topics as how to cope with bad-tasting medicine, plant a pineapple, and repair a puncture. General subject areas include Science and Technology, History and Customs, and Sports and Hobbies. Appendixes (labeled *datafiles*) supply concise information on the arts, sports, and geography. All in all, this may be considered a high-level, portable "trivial pursuit."

11.123 Gallant, Roy A. **Before the Sun Dies: The Story of Evolution.** Macmillan, 1989. ISBN 0-02-735771-6. 190p. 11 and up.

Professor Roy Gallant, award-winning author of over seventy science books for children, tackles the cosmic puzzle of how Earth and its inhabitants came to be. In addition to the ever-popular dinosaurs, the author explores topics such as the Big Bang theory, fossil formation, genetic mutation, climatic changes, and human evolution. Black-and-white photos, maps, diagrams, a glossary, and an index provide additional useful information in this provocative reference text. *Notable Children's Trade Books in Science, 1989.*

11.124 Richards, Roy. **101 Science Tricks: Fun Experiments with Everyday Materials.** Illustrated by Alex Pang. Sterling, 1991. ISBN 0-8069-8388-4. 104p. 7–12.

While learning how to make paper boats, mathematical magic squares, or curves from circles, children are able to discover the fun in science. "Tricks" are divided into projects exploring looking, moving, and paper. Each section includes introductory remarks for kids and closing notes for parents and teachers, explaining each experiment's concepts. Full-page color illustrations and clear instructions assist children in completing these harmless experiments independently.

11.125 Thomson, David. **Visual Magic.** Illustrated by David Thomson. Dial Books, 1991. ISBN 0-8037-1118-2. 57p. 5–10.

With lines straight and curved, with images for repositioning, with colors for fixed stares, and with hidden pictures, visual magic occurs to fool the eye and puzzle the brain. The thirty "magical" events include explanations as well, so readers will learn of their optic blind spot, of after-images, and of their brain's efforts to make sense of things. Packed into the back of the book is a pair of 3-D glasses that make some of the images emerge and others reveal their secrets.

11.126 White, Laurence B., Jr., and Ray Broekel. **Shazam! Simple Science Magic.** Illustrated by Meyer Seltzer. Albert Whitman, 1991. ISBN 0-8075-7332-9. 48p. 8–12.

Section titles such as "How to Hypnotize a Potato" or "The Uncanny Can That Can" will entice young readers to investigate nineteen simple science "tricks." Humorous illustrations in simple black line, highlighted with orange, add appeal and clarity. Directions are given in short paragraphs rather than prescriptive "steps," and each bit of magic is explained scientifically in a highly readable style. Overall, this lively text would become a popular addition to any elementary or middle school library.

Geography

11.127 Leedy, Loreen. **Blast Off to Earth! A Look at Geography.** Illustrated by Loreen Leedy. Holiday House, 1992. ISBN 0-8234-0973-2. 32p. 7–10 (est.).

Aliens with the appearance of colorful trash cans and vacuum cleaner parts visit the Earth with their leader, Mr. Quark, who knows a great deal about the planet's geographic features. On screens and maps, Mr. Quark informs his listeners of land masses, poles, and the equator. As their ship zips around the Earth, he points out the people, animal life, and land features, punctuated with simple maps keyed to the continents' terrains. Conversation, light-hearted and brief, is in speech balloons.

Human Body, Health, and Development

11.128 Aliki. **I'm Growing!** Illustrated by Aliki. HarperCollins, 1992. ISBN 0-06-020245-9. 32p. 3–7 (est.).

Using primary-level language, a young boy describes how he has grown, from babyhood to the present. The reader learns basic information about nutrition and discovers that organs, bones, and muscles stop growing at a certain age, while hair and nails never stop growing. Aliki's trademark ink-and-watercolor drawings in bright, bold colors depict multiethnic children in this Let's-Read-and-Find-Out Science Book.

11.129 Aliki. **My Feet. My Hands.** Illustrated by Aliki. Thomas Y. Crowell, 1990. 32p. 3–6.

These two science picture books in the Let's-Read-and-Find-Out Science Books series present easy-to-understand information about hands and feet. Colorful full-page drawings support the simple and informative text and show how children of all nationalities use their hands and feet to explore and understand their world. *Outstanding Science Trade Books for Children in 1990.*

11.130 Brown, Laurie Krasny, and Marc Brown. **Dinosaurs Alive and Well! A Guide to Good Health.** Illustrated by Laurie Krasny Brown and Marc Brown. Little, Brown/Joy Street Books, 1990. ISBN 0-316-10998-3. 32p. 4–8 (est.).

A bouncy family of pale green dinosaurs demonstrates how a reader can care for himself or herself to become "the healthiest, happiest person you can be." Sections offer helpful advice on foods to choose and avoid, selecting appropriate clothing, and washing up from head to tail. These dinosaurs exercise their bodies and their minds, and even learn how to identify and deal with feelings, to take breaks, and to relax.

11.131 Bruun, Ruth Dowling, and Bertel Bruun. **The Brain: What It Is, What It Does.** Illustrated by Peter Bruun. Greenwillow Books, 1989. ISBN 0-688-08454-0. 64p. 8 and up.

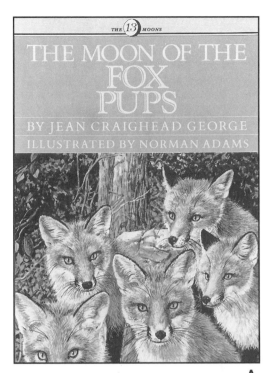

A.

B.

C.

D.

A. *The Moon of the Fox Pups* by Jean Craighead George; illustrated by Norman Adams (see 11.29).   **B.** *Nature's Tricksters: Animals and Plants That Aren't What They Seem* by Mary Batten; illustrated by Lois Lovejoy (see 11.20).   **C.** *Our Solar System* by Seymour Simon (see 11.12).   **D.** *Dinosaurs Alive and Well! A Guide to Good Health* by Laurie Krasny Brown and Marc Brown (see 11.130).

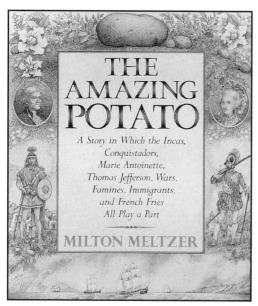

A.

B.

C.

A. *The Amazing Potato: A Story in Which the Incas, Conquistadors, Marie Antoinette, Thomas Jefferson, Wars, Famines, Immigrants, and French Fries All Play a Part* by Milton Meltzer (see 11.148). **B.** *Come Back, Salmon: How a Group of Dedicated Kids Adopted Pigeon Creek and Brought It Back to Life* by Molly Cone; photographs by Sidnee Wheelwright (see 11.93). **C.** *Recycle! A Handbook for Kids* by Gail Gibbons (see 11.97).

The Bruuns—neurologist Bertel, psychiatrist Ruth, and their artist son Peter—collaborate on this Read-Alone Book introducing readers to the human brain. Stylized orange-and-black line drawings accompany a spare text in eight chapters to describe the composition of the brain, to compare the brains of different animals, and to explain thinking, learning, intelligence, feelings, and sleep. *Notable Children's Trade Books in Science, 1989.*

11.132 Dahl, Tessa. **Babies, Babies, Babies.** Illustrated by Siobhan Dodds. Viking Penguin, 1990. ISBN 0-670-83921-3. 28p. 2–6.

Sam and Sophie's mother is expecting a new baby, and they have lots of questions. How long before our baby is born? How many babies will we have? Do all babies grow in tummies? Young children's questions about new babies are answered and supplemented with information about other kinds of babies: most people have only one baby, but dogs have one to twenty, and fish have hundreds. Charming watercolors depict the many types of babies in our world.

11.133 Dinner, Sherry H. **Nothing to Be Ashamed Of: Growing Up with Mental Illness in Your Family.** Lothrop, Lee and Shepard Books, 1989. ISBN 0-688-08482-6. 197p. 10 and up.

Author Sherry Dinner, a child psychologist specializing in mental illness, offers important information on such topics as depression, eating disorders, Alzheimer's disease, schizophrenia, and posttraumatic stress disorder. This guide also defines mental illness, discusses typical reactions of people living with a mentally ill person, explains the role of mental health professionals, and offers youngsters helpful advice concerning aid and support for this difficult family situation.

11.134 Drimmer, Frederick. **Born Different: Amazing Stories of Very Special People.** Bantam Skylark Books, 1991. ISBN 0-553-15897-X. 173p. 10–12.

These accounts of "special people"—Tom Thumb, the Elephant Man, the Siamese twins, and others—are informative and compassionate. The author combines a clear style, deep sensitivity, and much detail and anecdote to bring these unique and difficult lives to the page. Readers will begin to see people with physical disabilities as fully human individuals, even as magnificent examples of the human spirit. Photographs and drawings, as well as medical explanations of the various conditions, round out this excellent presentation.

11.135 Haldane, Suzanne. **Helping Hands: How Monkeys Assist People Who Are Disabled.** Photographs by Suzanne Haldane. Dutton Children's Books, 1991. ISBN 0-525-44723-7. 42p. 8 and up (est.).

Greg, a teenager with quadraplegia, is disabled from a diving accident. His friend Willie, a female capuchin monkey, has been trained to help with the simple tasks that Greg's paralyzed hands cannot manage. Black-and-white photographs show how Greg and Willie work together. The book demonstrates how carefully trained animals can be invaluable to people with disabilities, allowing them a measure of independence, and another friend. *Notable 1991 Children's Trade Books in the Field of Social Studies; Outstanding Science Trade Books for Children in 1991.*

11.136 Hausherr, Rosmarie. **Children and the AIDS Virus: A Book for Children, Parents, and Teachers.** Photographs by Rosmarie Hausherr. Clarion Books, 1989. ISBN 0-89919-834-1. 48p. 5–10.

In this timely book, Rosmarie Hausherr explains in clear language how the human immune system works, what the AIDS virus is, and how people get infected with the AIDS virus. Two children with AIDS are featured in this book: five-year-old Jonathan, who contracted AIDS through a blood transfusion, and ten-year-old Celeste, who was born with AIDS. Split text offers larger print for children, while adults read background information in smaller print. An appendix includes resources, hotlines, and a bibliography for further reading.

11.137 Hyde, Margaret O., and Elizabeth H. Forsyth. **Medical Dilemmas.** G. P. Putnam's Sons, 1990. ISBN 0-399-21902-1. 112p. 12 and up.

With many recent medical innovations intended to heal and to prolong life have come agonizing life-and-death questions needing a response from the medical and legal communities as well as from patients, their families, and the public. Issues related to research on animals, gene therapy, transplants, AIDS, the right to die, and premature, severely ill, and hi-tech babies are analyzed without illustrations, but with suggestions for further reading and an index. *Outstanding Science Trade Books for Children in 1990.*

11.138 Peters, David. **From the Beginning: The Story of Human Evolution.** Illustrated by David Peters. Morrow Junior Books, 1991. ISBN 0-688-09476-7. 128p. 8 and up.

A compendium of fascinating information with readable text, crisp illustrations, and a well-organized layout should help readers and young researchers through the fascinating and complex topic of evolution. Line drawings and charts present animals, molecules, and more abstract materials within insets highlighting evolutionary changes such as "The Development of the Eye" or "The Amniote Family Tree." The text ranges from the Big Bang to contemporary humans, and is followed by fascinating appendixes—one, for example, on the evolution of the face.

Machines

11.139 Horvatic, Anne. **Simple Machines.** Photographs by Stephen Bruner. E. P. Dutton, 1989. ISBN 0-525-44492-0. 30p. 7–10.

Clear and simple definitions and explanations make this book a valuable resource for any elementary unit on simple machines. The text is amplified with black-and-white closeup photographs of examples of each machine in its functional roles—lever, wheel, inclined plane, screw, and wedge.

Mathematics

11.140 Anno, Mitsumasa. **Anno's Math Games II.** Illustrated by Mitsumasa Anno. Philomel Books, 1989. ISBN 0-399-21615-4. 102p. 5–9.

Anno's engaging watercolors provide an added element of fun for these math puzzles, which are divided into sections focusing on skill development in basic arithmetic, comparison, grouping, symbolism, and volume. These games can be played in the classroom. For example, the arithmetic section is based on a magic box, operated by two elves, which changes objects put into it. The reader must then figure out how the objects have changed. *Notable Children's Trade Books in Science, 1989.*

11.141 Schwartz, David M. **If You Made a Million.** Illustrated by Steven Kellogg. Lothrop, Lee and Shepard Books, 1989. ISBN 0-688-07018-3. 40p. 6–10.

With Mathematical Magician as guide, readers explore the world of money, learning about such things as monetary equivalences, saving, spending, banking, and borrowing. David Schwartz's text keeps the child central to the earning process and involved with the sizes of various amounts of cash. Real currency is pictured so that children can make value comparisons. Steven Kellogg's detailed illustrations ensure that this journey into the world of finance is a lively one. *Notable 1989 Children's Trade Books in the Field of Social Studies.*

Plants

11.142 Burns, Diane L. **Sugaring Season: Making Maple Syrup.** Photographs by Cheryl Walsh Bellville. Carolrhoda Books, 1990. ISBN 0-876614-422-9. 48p. 6–11.

As the days fluctuate between winter and spring, the sugaring season begins. In this well-organized book, Diane Burns explains how modern-day sugar bush owners/producers mix tradition and technology to bring maple syrup to breakfast tables. Full-color photographs, diagrams, and maps support the easy-to-understand text and help to illustrate each step in the making of maple syrup.

11.143 Coldrey, Jennifer. **Strawberry.** Photographs by George Bernard. Silver Burdett Press/Stopwatch Books, 1989. ISBN 0-382-09801-3. 25p. 3–6.

The growth cycle of strawberries is described in simple text and with lush color photographs and line drawings. The last double-page spread of six photographs provides an informal review: "Do you remember how a strawberry plant grows?" First published in London, the book was adapted for publication in the United States. The brief index provides a list of important words.

11.144 Gibbons, Gail. **From Seed to Plant.** Illustrated by Gail Gibbons. Holiday House, 1991. ISBN 0-8234-0872-8. 32p. 4–8.

As in her other information books, Gail Gibbons's explanations of processes are straightforward and attractively illustrated. Each page concisely explains one stage in the growth of a plant, accompanied by a colorful illustration or diagram; parts of the plant are clearly labeled. The book's colorful layout perfectly amplifies the simple text. The inclusion of a plant-growing project at the end of the book makes it an especially useful addition to a classroom collection.

11.145 Hindley, Judy. **The Tree.** Illustrated by Alison Wisenfeld. Clarkson N. Potter, 1990. ISBN 0-517-57630-9. 32p. 6–10 (est.).

Twelve special trees are introduced through poetic phrases and lyrical informational text, edged with pale watercolor leaves, figures, and tree shapes. Readers are introduced to the tree's history and lore, significance, utility, and appearance, both in winter and summer. For the beech, "The Gold and Silver Tree": "big as a castle / cool as a cave / calm as a church / green as a wave."

11.146 Jaspersohn, William. **Cranberries.** Photographs by William Jaspersohn. Houghton Mifflin, 1991. ISBN 0-395-52098-3. 32p. 7–10.

Did you know that the Pilgrims thought that the cranberry flower resembled the head of a crane, so they originally called this native American fruit a "crane-berry"? Interesting cranberry trivia is included in this description of a year-long cycle of how cranberries are grown, harvested, and distributed from June to June. Plainly written text and bordered, brightly colored photographs clearly explain the somewhat complicated process of cranberry farming.

11.147 King, Elizabeth. **The Pumpkin Patch.** Photographs by Elizabeth King. Dutton Children's Books, 1990. ISBN 0-525-44640-0. 32p. 4–8.

When October days are crisp and cool, and wind rustles the cornstalks, pumpkins are ready to be picked. But the work of raising pumpkins began back in July when the farmer prepared the soil for the seeds, and that is where Elizabeth King begins her photographic essay on pumpkin farming. From seed to glowing jack-o'-lantern, the camera's eye and nontechnical, informative text record the planting, tending, and harvesting of the pumpkin patch.

11.148 Meltzer, Milton. **The Amazing Potato: A Story in Which the Incas, Conquistadors, Marie Antoinette, Thomas Jefferson, Wars, Famines, Immigrants, and French Fries All Play a Part.** HarperCollins, 1992. ISBN 0-06-020807-4. 117p. 8–12.

Nine chapters, plus bibliography and index, tell a potato story best described by the book's lengthy subtitle, which emphasizes the potato's long and important history. Anything readers could possibly want to know about a potato can be found in an informative text, in tidbit-filled fact boxes, in captioned diagrams, and in black-and-white photographic reproductions.

11.149 Robbins, Ken. **A Flower Grows.** Illustrated by Ken Robbins. Dial Books, 1990. ISBN 0-8037-0764-9. 32p. All ages.

The opening spread of *A Flower Grows* is a straight-down perspective on a flowerpot, with the trumpet blossoms of an amaryllis in full bloom, forming a wreath-like pattern of pink-tipped flowers. The book itself is a stunning portrayal of the growth of an amaryllis bulb, described in simple text and rendered in water-based dyes applied to black-and-white photographs. "Sometimes beauty comes from the most unexpected places," the book begins, and then sets out to prove it.

11.150 Wexler, Jerome. **Wonderful Pussy Willows.** Photographs by Jerome Wexler. Dutton Children's Books, 1992. ISBN 0-525-44867-5. 32p. 6 and up (est.).

In tribute to "wonderful pussy willows," Jerome Wexler's photographic essay on their life cycle offers both description and spectacular color microphotographic vantages. Relative of the weeping willow and with buds as soft as cat's fur, this springtime plant, Wexler speculates, came naturally by its name. Through text which encourages observation and hypotheses, young readers can inspect for changes as the plants pollinate and mature; children are even encouraged to root and transplant their own pussy willows.

Prehistoric Life

11.151 Aliki. **Fossils Tell of Long Ago, rev. ed.** Illustrated by Aliki. Thomas Y. Crowell, 1990. ISBN 0-690-04829-7. 32p. 5–10.

A big fish dies, and with time its bones turn to stone—the fish has become a fossil. This Let's-Read-and-Find-Out Science Book explains how fossils are formed and how they "tell of long ago." Detailed, color-rich drawings illustrate the informative and easy-to-read text. Cartoon-like conversations between budding paleontologists provide readers with additional information. This updated edition is a fine companion to Aliki's other dinosaur-focused books, *Digging Up Dinosaurs* and *Dinosaurs Are Different. Outstanding Science Trade Books for Children in 1990.*

11.152 Branley, Franklyn. **What Happened to the Dinosaurs?** Illustrated by Marc Simont. Thomas Y. Crowell, 1989. ISBN 0-690-04749-5. 32p. 5–10.

What happened to the dinosaurs? No one really knows for sure. This addition to the Let's-Read-and-Find-Out Science Books series presents several current theories and their explanations of dinosaur extinction. Supported with full-color illustrations, the text is both clear and challenging. In a classroom study of dinosaurs, this book will help children to think carefully about the mystery of their disappearance. *Notable Children's Trade Books in Science, 1989.*

11.153 Lasky, Kathryn. **Dinosaur Dig.** Photographs by Christopher G. Knight. Morrow Junior Books, 1990. ISBN 0-688-08575-X. 64p. 8 and up (est.).

Through color photographs and a detailed chronology, readers join a New England family's preparations for a trip to the Badlands of Montana, where they and other families join a paleontologist, a geologist, and their student team. All smell dirt, bag dirt, slosh sifting boxes, pick, trowel, and scrape. They endure heat, rattlesnakes, dirt, and the absence of conveniences for the satisfaction of teamwork and the thrill of being the first to view dinosaur bones that are 67 million years old. *Outstanding Science Trade Books for Children in 1990.*

11.154 Lauber, Patricia. **The News about Dinosaurs.** Bradbury Press, 1989. ISBN 0-02-754520-2. 48p. 8–12.

New discoveries that supersede previous scientific theories about dinosaurs are presented in a series of statements that contrast older with more recent theories. The conversational style of the text and the varied colorful illustrations by five artists answer some questions and raise others. A guide to pronunciation and an index assist the reader.

11.155 Most, Bernard. **The Littlest Dinosaurs.** Illustrated by Bernard Most. Harcourt Brace Jovanovich, 1989. ISBN 0-15-248125-7. 32p. 4–7.

Through fact and fancy, simple text, and colorful drawings, Bernard Most once again relates information about the smaller dinosaurs (those fourteen feet and shorter) in the style of his *Dinosaur Cousins?* and *If the Dinosaurs Came Back.* His lighthearted manner is sure to appeal to the youngest of dinosaur lovers and could offer creative extension of dinosaur study in the classroom.

11.156 Peters, David. **A Gallery of Dinosaurs and Other Early Reptiles.** Illustrated by David Peters. Alfred A. Knopf/Borzoi Books, 1989. ISBN 0-394-99982-7. 64p. 8–12.

Although this oversized book includes much technical information, its most outstanding feature is David Peters's realistic paintings of dinosaurs and reptiles in actual proportion to children playing on or around the giants. It's hard to imagine a more stimulating and immediate presentation of the size and beauty of these ancient creatures. The foldout pages are particularly dramatic—the seismosaurus, for example, stretches to over four feet. An introduction, evolutionary chart, and short sections on individual species are included. *Notable Children's Trade Books in Science, 1989.*

11.157 Sattler, Helen Roney. **The New Illustrated Dinosaur Dictionary, rev. ed.** Illustrated by Joyce Powzyk. Lothrop, Lee and Shepard Books, 1990. ISBN 0-688-08462-1. 352p. 7 and up.

In the foreword to the revised edition of this reference book, Yale paleontologist John H. Ostrom writes that of the approximately 350 different kinds of dinosaurs included in this volume, "almost one hundred were discovered and named in just the last twenty years." Fifty new additions are included in this alphabetical listing, as well as classifications of dinosaurs by size, weight, and era. Black-and-white illustrations, pronunciations, descriptions, related terms, charts, references, and discovery sites contribute to the comprehensiveness of the book.

11.158 Simon, Seymour. **New Questions and Answers about Dinosaurs.** Illustrated by Jennifer Dewey. Morrow Junior Books, 1990. ISBN 0-688-08196-7. 48p. 6 and up (est.).

In an organization scheme that will serve classroom research as well as individual "reports," twenty-two interesting questions about dinosaurs are posed, one for each spread, and are accompanied by straightforward text and large, color illustrations. Questions deal with statistics ("Which dinosaur was the longest?" "biggest?" "smallest?" "largest meat-eater?" "had the most teeth?"), with issues ("Why did the dinosaurs become extinct?" "How smart were the dinosaurs?"), and childlike curiosity ("What color were the dinosaurs?").

11.159 Whitfield, Philip. **Macmillan Children's Guide to Dinosaurs and Other Prehistoric Animals.** Macmillan, 1992. ISBN 0-02-762362-9. 96p. 6–12 (est.).

Zoologist Philip Whitfield increases the classroom value of this dinosaur reference text by incorporating several useful features.

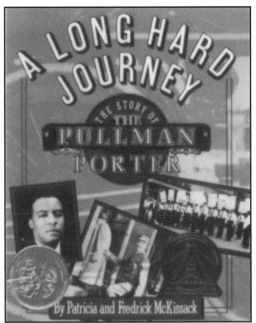

A.

B.

C.

A. *A Long Hard Journey: The Story of the Pullman Porter* by Patricia and Frederick McKissak (see 12.70). **B.** *Exploring an Ocean Tide Pool* by Jeanne Bendick; illustrated by Todd Telander (see 11.55). **C.** *Gorilla/Chinchilla, and Other Animal Rhymes* by Bert Kitchen (see 11.79).

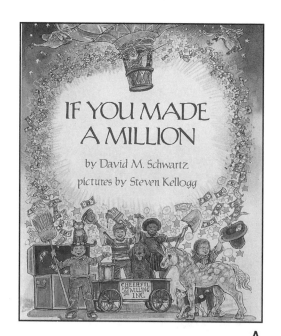

A.

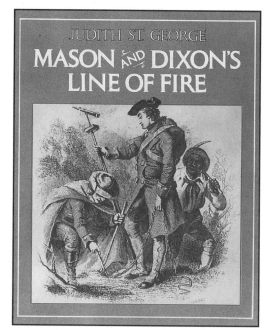

B.

C.

A. *If You Made a Million* by David Schwartz; illustrated by Steven Kellogg (see 11.141).
B. *Mason and Dixon's Line of Fire* by Judith St. George (see 12.74).   **C.** *Dinosaur Dig* by Kathryn Lasky; photographs by Christopher G. Knight (see 11.153).

Recurring graphic aids fix and describe each geologic period, and "to-scale" silhouettes permit comparison of human and dinosaur sizes. Chronologically organized, each section opens with a color spread of the era's inhabitants and environment and presents dinosaur information by location. Featured dinosaurs (approximately 125) are profiled with notecard-brief information that is both clearly and interestingly written.

Social Studies

Can such books written for young people flower into thought? Yes, if you bore into the subject with an eye sharpened by the need to see beyond fact to value and meaning. If you look for particulars that universalize experience and make it memorable. If you are concerned not with "covering a subject" as the curriculum-constructor thinks of it, but with discovering something meaningful in it and finding the language to bring the reader to the same moment of recognition.

Milton Meltzer, "Beyond Fact," in *Beyond Fact: Nonfiction for Children and Young People*

12 Social Studies

Careers

12.1 Ancona, George (text by Joan Anderson). **The American Family Farm: A Photo Essay by George Ancona.** Photographs by George Ancona. Harcourt Brace Jovanovich, 1989. ISBN 0-15-203025-5. 92p. 9–12 (est.).

With the American family farm in jeopardy—and removed from most children's urban lifestyles—this photo essay is a timely and valuable work. It focuses on three farms in different states (Massachusetts, Georgia, and Iowa) and emphasizes practical operations and the values of family members involved. Some technical and economic aspects of farming are included, but quite palatably. The outstanding and numerous black-and-white photographs complete this portrait of a unique and increasingly rare way of life.

12.2 Gibbons, Gail. **Marge's Diner.** Illustrated by Gail Gibbons. Thomas Y. Crowell, 1989. ISBN 0-690-04606-5. 28p. 6–10.

Marge's Diner is a special place that all kinds of folks visit each day, including truck drivers, a vacationing family, Mike the policeman, a gang of construction workers, and the high school crowd. And little wonder it's such a popular place: Marge's Diner is cozy and friendly, and the food is great. But the success of this diner didn't occur by happenstance. Teamwork, long hours, and attention to detail make Marge's Diner the place it is. *Notable 1989 Children's Trade Books in the Field of Social Sciences.*

12.3 Johnson, Jean. **Librarians A to Z.** Photographs by Jean Johnson. Walker, 1988. ISBN 0-8027-6842-3. 44p. 5–8.

One of the titles in the Community Helpers series, *Librarians A to Z* is an informative guide to library facilities, equipment, and activities, as well as to the duties performed by librarians. Organized by letters of the alphabet, the book describes library-related terms such as *exhibits, recordings,* and *weeding* in simple language, accompanied by large black-and-white photographs. The postscript to the book gives more detailed information about types of library jobs in denser text using a more sophisticated vocabulary.

Communication

12.4 Ancona, George, and Mary Beth. **Handtalk Zoo.** Photographs by George Ancona. Four Winds Press, 1989. ISBN 0-02-700801-0. 32p. 5–10 (est.).

George Ancona's bright, full-color photographs follow a group of five children and Mary Beth on a field trip to the zoo, as they identify the animals by both signing and fingerspelling. In a companion book to *Handtalk* and *Handtalk Birthday*, Ancona captures children being children, talking about animals with their hands. Signing is demonstrated by facial expressions and blurred hand motions; closeup black-and-white insets focus only on children's hands in linear fingerspelling arrays of each animal's name.

12.5 Leedy, Loreen. **Messages in the Mailbox: How to Write a Letter.** Illustrated by Loreen Leedy. Holiday House, 1991. ISBN 0-8234-0889-2. 32p. 7–10 (est.).

Mrs. Gator's motley class of animals and children complain that they don't get any mail. When Mrs. Gator suggests that the children write a few letters, the book's format unfolds in response, stuffed with model letters. There are samples of friendly letters, invitations, thank-you notes, get-well cards, letters of sympathy and congratulations, business letters, form letters, and even love letters, many with labeled parts and friendly speech balloons. There is so much good information that the book may become a permanent addition to classroom writing centers.

12.6 **My First 100 Words in Spanish and English.** Simon and Schuster Books for Young Readers, 1992. ISBN 0-671-74965-X. 12p. 6–10 (est.).

This bilingual vocabulary book offers successive pages of tidy boxes, each containing an object and captioned by words in English. The Spanish translation appears when a tab is pulled. Each of the five left-hand pages is a contextualized scene (such as a farm, store); objects can be searched for on right-hand pages and then identified in both languages.

12.7 Rankin, Lauren. **The Handmade Alphabet.** Illustrated by Lauren Rankin. Dial Books, 1991. ISBN 0-8037-0975-7. 28p. 5 and up (est.).

A single hand positioned on each page demonstrates how American Sign Language can render sophisticated messages as well as bread-and-butter communication. Without contrivance, the signed letters are humorously integrated with an object beginning with each respective letter, such as the *I* reaching up to an icicle, and the *J* dipping into a jelly jar. Colored pencil on charcoal paper results in a soft, tranquil effect.

12.8   Schwartz, Perry. **How to Make Your Own Video.** Lerner, 1991. ISBN 0-8225-2301-9. 72p. 10 and up.

Through skillful text and both color and black-and-white photographs, a video producer, director, and writer introduce the art of home video production. Perry Schwartz insists that young camera operators "have something to say" and "see the way the camera sees." The book's ten chapters provide guidance with camera selection, as well as help with lighting, composition, storyline, and editing. Text is balanced with ample illustrations, making for inviting page layouts. Both a glossary and index are included.

Community Life

12.9   Ashabranner, Brent. **Born to the Land: An American Portrait.** Photographs by Paul Conklin. G. P. Putnam's Sons, 1989. ISBN 0-399-21716-9. 129p. 10 and up.

Born to the Land offers an informative, realistic portrait of the ranching, farming, and small-town families of Luna County, New Mexico. Award-winning author Brent Ashabranner discusses the hardships these hardy people endure daily: drought, low crop prices, expensive fuels and feed, and too few hands to help with the labor. Nevertheless, the community also has its share of fun times: county fairs, potluck dinners, and firehall dances. Black-and-white photos, an index, and bibliography supplement the text. *Notable 1989 Children's Trade Books in the Field of Social Studies.*

12.10   Curtis, Patricia. **Dogs on the Case: Search Dogs Who Help Save Lives and Enforce the Law.** Photographs by David Cupp. Lodestar Books, 1989. ISBN 0-525-67274-5. 128p. 10 and up.

No one knows if any survivors exist below a mountain of fresh snow deposited by an avalanche—no one except Bridget, a German shepherd search dog. Five days later, Bridget signals the exact location of one girl, who miraculously survives her ordeal.

This is just one of Patricia Curtis's fascinating stories of search dogs, dogs that are highly trained to use their sense of scent to save lives and enforce laws. Upper-level elementary students and their teachers will appreciate not only the stories contained in this book but also the booklist and directory of search-and-rescue organizations found at the end.

12.11 Graff, Nancy Price. **The Call of the Running Tide: A Portrait of an Island Family.** Photographs by Richard Howard. Little, Brown, 1992. ISBN 0-316-32278-4. 78p. 8–12.

The combination of quiet, eloquent black-and-white photographs and supple, flowing prose make this portrait of a Maine lobstering family a model of its kind. The author follows the Joyces through a full year of their challenging traditional life, describing the difficulties as well as the rewards of fishing and island living. The beauty of the Gulf of Maine, and the dangers of its weather, are powerfully evoked, and the family's deep satisfaction with this life shines through.

12.12 Huff, Barbara A. **Greening the City Streets: The Story of Community Gardens.** Photographs by Peter Ziebel. Clarion Books, 1990. ISBN 0-89919-741-8. 61p. 8–12.

The Sixth Street and Avenue B Garden is one of forty community gardens on Manhattan's Lower East Side. It serves as a case study of a special urban landscape feature where flowers and vegetables are tended in four-by-eight-foot plots. Community gardens have a historical as well as a functional and aesthetic tale to tell, and here the story is told engagingly with color photographs that emphasize the importance and beauty of such unlikely growing spots and the involvement of young people.

12.13 Kendall, Russ. **Eskimo Boy: Life in an Inupiaq Eskimo Village.** Photographs by Russ Kendall. Scholastic Hardcover Books, 1992. ISBN 0-590-43695-3. 40p. 5–8.

This informative photographic essay introduces Norman Kokeok, a young Inupiaq Eskimo who lives on an Alaskan island where hunting and fishing are for survival. Readers meet Norman's family and neighbors, and follow their daily routines through the changing seasons. For example, Norman must take a plane to the dentist and travel locally by snow machine. He learns traditional crafts and the Inupiaq language in his first-grade classroom. Simple text and an afterword offering more detailed information round out a useful and enjoyable book.

12.14 Thomson, Peggy. **City Kids in China.** Photographs by Paul S. Conklin. HarperCollins, 1991. ISBN 0-06-21655-7. 114p. 8–12.

Changsa is a typical city—to the Chinese. But the commonplace there holds an exotic fascination for onlookers. Familiar physical barriers are absent in streets, where barbers, food vendors, and repair people ply their trades. Readers meet Chinese children who struggle with homework, stage a puppet show, enjoy television, visit a traditional doctor, and cycle through perilous crowds. Despite different lifestyles, city kids in China are universal in their vitality and sense of fun. Black-and-white photographs, index, and boxed vignettes complement an informative text.

12.15 Tresselt, Alvin. **Wake Up, City! Wake Up, Farm!** Illustrated by Carolyn Ewing. Lothrop, Lee and Shepard Books, 1990–91. 32p. 3 and up.

Alvin Tresselt, 1947 Caldecott winner, originally published these two companion books about the early morning in 1957. Here they are reissued, with revised text and new illustrations. On the farm, a rooster signals the break of day, which sets the pigs oinking, the ducks quacking, and the pigeons cooing. In contrast, first to wake in the city are a lonely alley cat and two patrolling police officers, but soon activity abounds. Graceful, double-page watercolor paintings support the gentle narrative.

12.16 Van Rynbach, Iris. **Everything from a Nail to a Coffin.** Illustrated by Iris Van Rynbach. Orchard Books, 1991. ISBN 0-531-08541-4. 48p. 7–9.

From the actual town records and accounts of Glastonbury, Connecticut, Iris Van Rynbach has constructed the story of a community as it revolves around a one-hundred-year-old store—a place where customers once could find anything "from a nail to a coffin." From general store to pharmacy, from hardware to groceries, the building changes over time in ownership, facades, and wares. Sun-faded, old-fashioned watercolor paintings show the changes brought by time and events.

Crafts and Hobbies

12.17 Aytüre-Scheele, Zülal (translated by Elisabeth E. Reinersmann). **Beautiful Origami.** Photographs by Gerhard Burrock. Sterling, 1990. ISBN 0-8069-7381-1. 80p. 5–9.

Because its origami figures are so beautiful and its photographed settings for them so colorful and lifelike, this how-to book will attract young readers. The thirty-three folded-paper figures are mostly animals and are organized in groups ("The Sky," "The Meadow," "The Fantasy World"). Both the written directions and the accompanying closeup photographs are simple and clear, and the tasks are broken into the smallest possible steps. A companion book, *Great Origami,* is also available to help children master this traditional Japanese art of paper folding.

12.18 Churchill, E. Richard. **Terrific Paper Toys.** Illustrated by James Michaels. Sterling, 1991. ISBN 0-8069-7496-6. 128p. 8–12 (est.).

With instructions for twenty-four paper toys, this collection of do-it-yourself fun provides a rich source of activities for kids. Categories include headgear, animals, buildings, toys that move, decorations, and inflatable or air-driven toys. The easily followed directions are accompanied by black-and-white illustrations of good size and clarity. Inked cartoon characters provide commentary on the products and procedures.

12.19 Corwin, Judith Hoffman. **The Home. The School.** Illustrated by Judith Hoffman Corwin. Franklin Watts, 1989. 48p. 5–9.

The Colonial American Crafts series about family life in colonial America is for adults and children to share. Almost everything used during this period was handmade, and cooperation at home, at school, and at work was essential. The hows and whys of activities like brewing ink and cutting quill pens are illustrated in black-and-white with red highlights.

12.20 Emberley, Ed. **Ed Emberley's Thumbprint Drawing Box.** Illustrated by Ed Emberley. Little, Brown, 1992. ISBN 0-316-23648-9. 64p. 4–6 (est.).

Complete with drawing paper, ink pad, and two how-to-draw books, this guide for young artists has instant hands-on appeal. The books offer simple directions for over one hundred drawings. With each, the child starts with a thumbprint and then adds simple lines, following step-by-step models. *Thumb Puns* has visual jokes ("Thumbrellas," "Thumbingbirds," and "Thumbderclouds"). *Bugs 'n' Beasts* includes dinosaurs, mammals, and insects. Clear directions and instant creations combine to provide young readers with successful experiences with thumb craft.

12.21   Hawcock, David. **Paper Warplanes.** Illustrated by David Haw-cock. David and Charles, 1989. ISBN 0-7153-9366-9. 80p. 7–13 (est.).

Here, along with patterns, pictures, and assembly instructions, are the brief histories of some of the world's most famous war-planes, from the *Sopwith Camel* to the F-111. Gridded and num-bered patterns to scale will help with the enlarging, transfer, and assembly of these paper planes; full-color photographs show the products complete with paint and trim. Some of the twelve planes have movable parts, such as propellers and wheels; all but the helicopter are designed to glide.

12.22   Johnson, Neil. **Fire and Silk: Flying in a Hot Air Balloon.** Pho-tographs by Neil Johnson. Little, Brown/Joy Street Books, 1991. ISBN 0-316-46959-9. 32p. 4–8.

Fire and Silk takes readers on a hot-air balloon trip through words and pictures. Color photographs follow the trip from start to finish, while the text addresses how balloons stay aloft, how they are steered, and how fast they move. Perspectives from both the basket and from the ground crew in its chase vehicle make the photo essay as informative as it is visually pleasing.

12.23   Lewis, Brenda Ralph. **Stamps! A Young Collector's Guide.** Lodestar Books, 1991. ISBN 0-525-67341-5. 96p. 5–9.

Through full-color photographs and diagrams with detailed captions and through an informative text, readers can learn about a world without stamps, early stamps, what stamps to collect, stamp stories, famous collectors, how stamps are made, stamp forgers, stamp clubs, famous stamps, collecting tools, tak-ing care of stamps, and much more. *Stamps!* may make readers not only experts but collectors as well.

12.24   Morgan, Terri, and Shmuel Thaler. **Photography: Take Your Best Shot.** Photographs by Terri Morgan and Shmuel Thaler. Lerner, 1991. ISBN 0-8225-2302-7. 72p. 10 and up.

In a book designed to improve photographs taken by young readers, separate chapters address the camera itself, peripheral equipment, composition, lighting, action shots, portraits, and even how to photograph animals. Relative advantages of black-and-white versus color photographs are briefly addressed, as well as information on developing and displaying finished works. The large-format text is amply illustrated with exem-plary photos, and a glossary defines terms used in the text.

Because the information flow is rapid and concepts are dense, the book seems best suited for the photographer with at least some experience.

12.25 Paul, Ann Whitford. **Eight Hands Round: A Patchwork Alphabet.** Illustrated by Jeanette Winter. HarperCollins, 1991. ISBN 0-06-024704-5. 27p. 4–8 (est.).

Early American patchwork quilt patterns from Anvil to Zigzag form an alphabetic sequence. On the top third of each page, whimsical folk-art illustrations depict the origin of the quilt pattern. The middle portion of the page is a paragraph of text that describes the activity or occupational origin of the pattern. The lower third of each page is illustrated by two colorful designs—one of a single quilt block and the second of an entire quilt. *Notable 1991 Children's Trade Books in the Field of Social Studies.*

12.26 Tofts, Hannah (written and edited by Diane James). **The Paint Book. The Paper Book. The Print Book. The 3-D Paper Book.** Photographs by Jon Barnes. Simon and Schuster Books for Young Readers, 1990. 32p. 6 and up.

Need a craft idea? This splendid four-book set describes "fun things to make and do" with print, paint, paper, and 3-D paper. Each book in the Color Craft series begins with information about supplies and equipment to be gathered in preparation for working with the medium—and then the creative ideas commence: print with raw vegetables, paint a window, make torn-paper flowers or papier mâché bowls, build a cardboard sculpture. Well-organized, plainly written text unites with bold and colorful full-page photographs to make methods for creation clear.

12.27 Walter, F. Virginia. **Fun with Paper Bags and Cardboard Tubes.** Photographs by Walter Kaiser. Sterling/Tamos Books, 1992. ISBN 1-895569-08-7. 79p. 6 and up (est.).

What can you make from used brown paper bags and cardboard tubes? A pan pipe, a frog headdress, and a horn of plenty are just a few of the more than seventy-five craft items featured in this book. Step-by-step drawings and detailed instructions accompany photographs of finished products. Paper projects are divided into three categories: toys and games, costumes and masks, and special events (holidays). It's time to start collecting.

Ethnic, Racial, and Religious Groups

12.28 Aaseng, Nathan. **Navajo Code Talkers.** Walker, 1992. ISBN 0-8027-8182-9. 114p. 10 and up.

Nathan Aaseng's fascinating, carefully documented book reveals the critical role that Navajo Indians played as secret-code makers, senders, and decoders during World War II. Although Japanese and American military personnel were able to decipher each other's secret messages fairly easily, only one code proved unbreakable—the one developed by the Navajos and based on their extraordinarily complex language of tones, inflections, and vocabulary. The book also describes the many cultural differences and accommodations that the Navajos and their fellow marines experienced as they battled the Japanese.

12.29 Adler, David A. **We Remember the Holocaust.** Henry Holt, 1989. ISBN 0-8050-0434-3. 148p. 11 and up.

Award-winning author David Adler once again focuses on Jewish history, this time chronicling the horrors experienced by Jews during the Nazi regime (1933–45). The book is especially poignant since most of the information is revealed through the voices of actual survivors of the Holocaust. Topics include Hitler's rise to power, Kristallnacht, concentration-camp ordeals, and the psychological trauma endured by survivors today. Supplementing the text are black-and-white photos, maps, a chronology, a glossary, an index, and a list of suggested readings. *Notable 1989 Children's Trade Books in the Field of Social Studies.*

12.30 Ammon, Richard. **Growing Up Amish.** Atheneum, 1989. ISBN 0-689-31387-X. 93p. 8–13 (est.).

Richard Ammon, Pennsylvania Dutch himself, delightfully depicts one year in the life of Anna, a young Amish girl. To supplement his informative prose, Ammon includes black-and-white photos, maps, Amish recipes, German nursery rhymes and prayers, descriptions of children's games, and a helpful bibliography of further recommended reading. The book also debunks several common myths about the Amish (that they paint hex signs on barns, never wear bright clothing, and never use telephones).

12.31 Ashabranner, Brent. **An Ancient Heritage: The Arab-American Minority.** Photographs by Paul S. Conklin. HarperCollins, 1991. ISBN 0-06-020048-0. 148p. 9 and up.

A.

B.

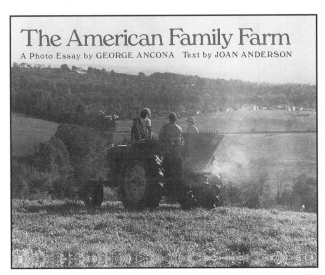

C.

A. *An Ancient Heritage: The Arab-American Minority* by Brent Ashabranner; photographs by Paul S. Conklin (see 12.31). **B.** *Noah's Ark* illustrated by Isabelle Brent (see 12.103). **C.** *The American Family Farm: A Photo Essay by George Ancona* text by Joan Anderson (see 12.1).

A.

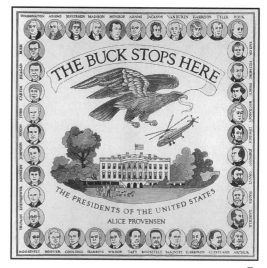

B.

C.

D.

A. *Fiesta! Mexico's Great Celebrations* by Elizabeth Silverthorne; illustrated by Jan Davey Ellis (see 12.43). **B.** *The Buck Stops Here: The Presidents of the United States* by Alice Provensen (see 12.54). **C.** *Fire and Silk: Flying in a Hot Air Balloon* by Neil Johnson (see 12.22). **D.** *American Politics: How It Really Works* by Milton Meltzer (see 12.53).

Award-winning author Brent Ashabranner offers a revealing portrait of one of America's least-known (and perhaps most misunderstood) minorities: Arab Americans. The book examines such diverse issues as Arab history; the generational differences and commonalities existing among Arab Americans today; and the group's political, cultural, and religious concerns (the need for a Palestinian homeland, immigration quotas, dealing with prejudice and misconceptions, and occasional rejection of the group's cultural heritage by their children). Black-and-white photos add interest and information.

12.32 Bolick, Nancy O'Keefe, and Sallie G. Randolph. **Shaker Inventions.** Illustrated by Melissa Francisco. Walker, 1990. ISBN 0-8027-6934-9. 96p. 12 and up.

In colonial America and throughout the nineteenth century, a religious community called Shakers, distinguished by their purity of spirit and industriousness, invented or improved many labor-saving devices. From their efficient laundry system to their pharmacies, seed gardens, food preparation techniques, agricultural tools, and business sense, the contributions of Shaker societies are described. Black-ink illustrations show the simplicity and utility of their inventions.

12.33 Carter, Alden R. **The Shoshoni.** Doherty, Craig A., and Katherine M. Doherty. **The Apaches and Navajos. The Iroquois.** Franklin Watts, 1989. 64p. 9–11.

In the First Books series about Native Americans, the authors skillfully compress into relatively few pages satisfying portraits of tribal life, including history, hunting and gathering, religion, culture, customs, games, and art, as well as contact with the advancing world. Compelling illustrations and photographs detail clothing, behavior, and artifacts of remarkable peoples.

12.34 Faber, Doris. **The Amish.** Illustrated by Michael E. Erkel. Doubleday, 1991. ISBN 0-385-26131-4. 45p. 7–11.

With historical quilts on the endpapers and an index, this large-format book features earthy double-page spreads and inset boxed text. The Amish come to life through descriptions of their history, their everyday life, and the tensions between modern and traditional ways. *Notable 1991 Children's Trade Books in the Field of Social Studies.*

12.35   Freedman, Russell. **An Indian Winter.** Illustrated by Karl Bodmer. Holiday House, 1992. ISBN 0-8234-0930-9. 88p. 8 and up (est.).

Between 1833 and 1834, German Prinz von Maximilian Wied, his servant, and Swiss artist Karl Bodmer wintered with the Mandan Indians in what is now North Dakota. The highly educated and well-traveled prince kept a journal while the artist painted the peoples and the vistas, the dances, and the customs. Russell Freedman tells their story clearly, quoting from the journal and offering the artist's views to amplify the perspectives of the two European observers.

12.36   Geography Department, Lerner Publications. **Estonia. Latvia. Lithuania. Russia.** Lerner, 1992. 56p. 8–12 (est.).

The Then and Now series gathers a store of information on Eastern European countries and presents it colorfully and attractively, with artwork supplementing excellent photographs. Describing first the land and people, the pages then trace each country's history, and, finally, suggest likely directions of change. Maps are simple, but clear and useful, and features such as fact boxes, a glossary, and translations round out these introductory materials.

12.37   Hoyt-Goldsmith, Diane. **Arctic Hunter.** Photographs by Lawrence Migdale. Holiday House, 1992. ISBN 0-8234-0972-4. 32p. 7–11 (est.).

Ten-year-old Reggie lives in Alaska, above the Arctic Circle. He becomes a proud Inupiaq hunter when he kills his first seal—with rifle and harpoon, a metaphor for the two worlds that he straddles. Photographs reveal how each member of the community plays a designated role in harvesting the bounty of the sea. Sections address games, customs, chores, and changes. A glossary and an index are included.

12.38   Hoyt-Goldsmith, Diane. **Pueblo Storyteller.** Photographs by Lawrence Migdale. Holiday House, 1991. ISBN 0-8234-0864-7. 28p. 6–12 (est.).

April, a Cochiti Indian who lives with her grandparents in the Cochiti Pueblo near Santa Fe, New Mexico, invites the reader to learn about her culture, traditions, and everyday family life. Captioned color photographs, a glossary, an index, and an engaging text introduce adobe construction, bread baking, pottery making, native dancing, and the telling of legends which keep the Cochiti past alive. *Notable 1991 Children's Trade Books in the Field of Social Studies.*

12.39   Keegan, Marcia. **Pueblo Boy: Growing Up in Two Worlds.** Photographs by Marcia Keegan. Cobblehill Books, 1991. ISBN 0-525-65060-1. 44p. 6 and up (est.).

Ten-year-old Timmy, whose family is very involved with the traditional Pueblo Indian arts, lives in the San Ildefonso Pueblo of New Mexico, not far from Santa Fe. With more than fifty color photographs depicting his life, Timmy invites readers to his home and school to meet the people closest in his life and to see him take part in the ceremonies of his heritage. Curious boys and girls will learn much about another way of life. *Notable 1991 Children's Trade Books in the Field of Social Studies.*

12.40   Morris, Ann. **When Will the Fighting Stop? A Child's View of Jerusalem.** Photographs by Lilly Rivlin. Atheneum, 1990. ISBN 0-689-31508-2. 52p. 8–12.

Mishkin is a Jewish boy who loves his hometown, the city of Jerusalem, where his family has lived for generations. He wanders past the ancient holy places, through the *souk*, and weaves across the streets where some people are friendly and others resent him. Refreshed by a cool drink offered by an old Arab, he wonders how long the threat of fighting will continue. The attitudes and atmosphere of the city are presented in black-and-white photographs.

12.41   Pitkänen, Matti A., with Reijo Härkönen. **The Children of Egypt.** Pitkänen, Matti A., with Ritva Lehtinen and Kari E. Nurmi. **Grandchildren of the Incas.** Photographs by Matti A. Pitkänen. Carolrhoda Books, 1991. 32p. 8–11.

Children don't see the same world that adults see. For many youngsters in Egypt and Peru, two countries chosen for the World's Children series, daily life means work rather than the schoolroom. Lake Titicaca is a glorious backdrop for the *Grandchildren of the Incas.* The ancient Incan civilization is compared to the lifestyle of their descendents, the Quechua Indians of Peru, who share space with llamas and wear handwoven clothes to protect against the elements. In Egypt, children's lives blend ancient and modern. Throughout both books, the brilliant sun illuminates poverty as well as beauty in the numerous four-color photographs.

12.42 Regguinti, Gordon. **The Sacred Harvest: Ojibway Wild Rice Gathering.** Photographs by Dale Kakkak. Lerner, 1992. ISBN 0-8225-2650-6. 48p. 8–12.

Eleven-year-old Glen is a regular American kid from Minnesota, but he is also an Ojibway Indian, privileged to harvest the *mahnomin*, the wild rice that is a sacred food of his people. Boating along river channels with his father to gather the rice, Glen also learns how to parch and winnow it and learns that some of the rice will be kept and the rest sold. Photographs, maps, drawings, and text tell the Ojibway story—their legacy, migration, and respect for nature. The book is a valuable cultural cameo.

12.43 Silverthorne, Elizabeth. **Fiesta! Mexico's Great Celebrations.** Illustrated by Jan Davey Ellis. Millbrook Press, 1992. ISBN 1-56294-055-4. 64p. 8–12.

Both the great and small fiestas of Mexico are described, beginning with the historical background that sets the stage for the blending of cultures, making these festivals unique. The author organizes the presentation into religious fiestas, patriotic fiestas, and the local, personal, and national celebrations that are too numerous to count. Included are easy-to-follow directions for making piñatas, God's Eye ornaments, clay pottery, and masks, as well as recipes for tasty fiesta dishes—tacos, enchiladas, guacamole, and hot chocolate.

12.44 Trimble, Stephen. **The Village of Blue Stone.** Illustrated by Jennifer Owings Dewey and Deborah Reade. Macmillan, 1990. ISBN 0-02-789501-7. 58p. 6–12 (est.).

In 1888, ruins of a highly civilized people, the Anasazi, were discovered by cowboys in New Mexico. In this well-researched information book, a year in the life of the Anasazi people circa 1100 is re-created. Detailed maps, labeled drawings, and black-and-white sketches help to explain the customs and ceremonies of these ancestors of today's Pueblo Indian people. Additional information, including a list of Anasazi ruins to visit, sources of technical information, related children's books, and a glossary, helps to make this book an in-depth resource for investigators.

Food, Clothing, and Shelter

12.45 Gibbons, Gail. **How a House Is Built.** Illustrated by Gail Gibbons. Holiday House, 1990. ISBN 0-8234-0841-8. 30p. 6–8 (est.).

From the architect to the landscaper, many people work together to build a house. Gail Gibbons introduces those workers and describes integrated stages involved in their tasks. Colorful labeled drawings help to explain the informative text. An illustrated list of simple shelters of the past included at the end of the book might encourage children to begin their own research on how houses are built in different parts of the world.

12.46 Isaacson, Philip M. **Round Buildings, Square Buildings, and Buildings That Wiggle like a Fish.** Photographs by Philip M. Isaacson. Alfred A. Knopf, 1988. ISBN 0-394-99382-9. 121p. 10 and up.

Using an array of black-and-white and color photographs, this book explores the amazing world of architecture and the ways in which we perceive a building when we look at it. From the Taj Mahal in India to simple churches in rural Florida, and including bridges, terminals, and lighthouses, this book emphasizes all the little things that go together to make up a beautiful work of architecture: building materials, color, ornamentation, landscaping, shapes, pathways, and much more. The photographs highlight these wondrous features, bringing out the beauty of buildings all over the world. *Boston Globe–Horn Book Honor Book, 1989.*

12.47 Sherrow, Victoria. **Huskings, Quiltings, and Barn Raisings: Work-Play Parties in Early America.** Illustrated by Laura LoTurco. Walker, 1992. ISBN 0-8027-8188-8. 77p. 10 and up.

When colonists first established life in the American wilderness, they had to build homes, grow food, and make their own clothes. To construct the barns and clear the land, to spin and weave the cloth for clothes, to replace what nature destroyed, or to welcome newcomers, the settlers worked together and played together. Black-and-white illustrations help to explain the details of these community efforts.

Geography

12.48 Brownstone, David M., and Irene M. Franck. **Natural Wonders of America.** Atheneum, 1989. ISBN 0-689-31430-2. 56p. 8–12 (est.).

From Acadia National Park to Yosemite, readers can visit forty-two of North America's scenic wonders. Each site is represented with a full-color photograph, offered as a taste rather than a full treatment. The camera's eye takes a panoramic view of Pike's

Peak and a closeup of a petrified trunk in the Petrified Forest. Both cultural geography and natural history are the subjects of brief passages. The wonders are arranged alphabetically, and an index is included.

12.49   Kandoian, Ellen. **Is Anybody Up?** Illustrated by Ellen Kandoian. G. P. Putnam's Sons, 1989. ISBN 0-399-21749-5. 32p. 4–8.

When Molly wakes early on a Saturday morning, she wonders, "Is anybody up?" The answer reflects the book's basic concept: far to the north and south along Molly's meridian, people with different customs share the same breakfast time. From an Inuit woman of Baffin Bay preparing griddlecakes to a Haitian child eating peanut butter and bananas to a Peruvian boy munching roasted corn, people in different communities begin their day when Molly does. Watercolor illustrations are sketchy washes in pale shades.

12.50   Margolies, Barbara A. **Rehema's Journey: A Visit in Tanzania.** Photographs by Barbara A. Margolies. Scholastic Hardcover Books, 1990. ISBN 0-590-42846-2. 32p. 5–9.

Nine-year-old Rehema is taken by her father to visit Tanzania's magnificent national game park, the Ngorongoro Crater, to see wild animals in their natural environment. It is her first trip down from her home in the Pare Mountains. Through color photographs, readers share Rehema's adventure, seeing people, scenery, and the culture of traditional and modern Tanzania. *Notable 1990 Children's Trade Books in the Field of Social Studies.*

12.51   Munro, Roxie. **The Inside-Outside Book of London. The Inside-Outside Book of Paris.** Illustrated by Roxie Munro. E. P. Dutton, 1989–92. 46p. All ages.

Two additions to the Inside-Out series follow the same format as their predecessors. Each site is introduced with a sprawling double-page spread, followed by an inside view of the same site. Inside the Tower of London, readers peek at armor. In St. Paul's Cathedral, the view is from the rotunda. The tour of Paris includes explanatory text in addition to labels. From a panorama of the Tuileries, the artist climbs aboard the carousel. The depiction of L'Arc de Triomphe includes a view from its observation deck. *Notable 1989 Children's Trade Books in the Field of Social Studies.*

Government

12.52 Ashabranner, Melissa, and Brent Ashabranner. **Counting America: The Story of the United States Census.** G. P. Putnam's Sons, 1989. ISBN 0-399-21747-9. 92p. 10 and up.

Here is an informative, yet interesting, account of the United States Decennial Census. The purposes, the history, and a sequential account of the actual census taking are described in detail. The text aptly ends with a summary of how census information is used by virtually every segment of society. Numerous black-and-white photographs amplify the text, and a three-page glossary clarifies the sometimes difficult vocabulary. *Notable 1989 Children's Trade Books in the Field of Social Studies.*

12.53 Meltzer, Milton. **American Politics: How It Really Works.** Illustrated by David Small. Morrow Junior Books, 1989. ISBN 0-688-07494-4. 185p. 11 and up.

Milton Meltzer, award-winning historian and author of over seventy books for young people, analyzes the complex political processes at work each day in the United States. Topics covered in this highly readable reference text include America's development of a two-party system, politicians' relationships with lobbyists and the press, the presidential election process, and the balance of powers among the three branches of the government. Enhancing the text are black-and-white sketches, a bibliography, and an index.

12.54 Provensen, Alice. **The Buck Stops Here: The Presidents of the United States.** Illustrated by Alice Provensen. Harper and Row, 1990. ISBN 0-06-024787-8. 42p. 9–12.

From the first president to the forty-first, George Washington to George Bush, each U.S. president and the significant events of his term of office are effectively pulled together in a unified design accompanied by rhyming couplets in this oversize picture book. Caldecott award-winning artist Alice Provensen skillfully weaves information through newspaper heads, banners, placards, stamps, and portraits to produce a source for quickly placing U.S. presidents in a historical context. *Notable 1990 Children's Trade Books in the Field of Social Studies.*

12.55 St. George, Judith. **The White House: Cornerstone of a Nation.** G. P. Putnam's Sons, 1990. ISBN 0-399-22186-7. 160p. 10 and up.

Judith St. George chronicles the events and changes in the structure that has housed leaders of the United States across two centuries. With intriguing detail and the right dosage of contemporary quotes, and with black-and-white photographs and through reproductions, she manages rich detail and intimate insights within ten themes. Chapters address the White House in times of mourning, through rebuilding, as host to greats and to common people, and even as portrayed through mass media. A listing of presidents, a bibliography, and an index are included.

12.56   Waters, Kate. **The Story of the White House.** Scholastic Hardcover Books, 1991. ISBN 0-590-43335-0. 40p. 5–8.

In 1800, when President John Adams moved into his new home, called the President's Palace or the President's House, it was the largest residence in young America. Not until after the first structure burned in the War of 1812 and was rebuilt and repainted did the president's home become known as the White House. In this photo-essay account of the history of Washington and its most famous house, color photographs and renderings dominate the brief, accessible text and pleasingly designed pages.

History

United States

12.57   Alter, Judith. **Growing Up in the Old West.** Franklin Watts/First Books, 1989. ISBN 0-531-10746-9. 64p. 8–12.

In straightforward prose, author Judith Alter describes an American frontier childhood—its homelife, chores, recreation, schooling, and its threats and dangers. Color illustrations and black-and-white photographs amplify the text. Alter includes a bibliography and a complete index.

12.58   Anderson, Joan. **Spanish Pioneers of the Southwest.** Photographs by George Ancona. Lodestar Books, 1989. ISBN 0-525-67264-8. 58p. 10–12 (est.).

This weaving of black-and-white photography, historical reenactment, and a child's perspective depicts a Spanish settlement in present-day New Mexico twenty years before the Pilgrims landed at Plymouth Rock. In portraying the whole of community life—the dangers, isolation, interdependence, joy, pride, and religiosity of frontier living—the text is clear, detailed, child-oriented, and historically accurate. *Notable 1989 Children's Trade Books in the Field of Social Studies.*

12.59   Ashabranner, Brent. **A Grateful Nation: The Story of Arlington National Cemetery.** Photographs by Jennifer Ashabranner. G. P. Putnam's Sons, 1990. ISBN 0-399-22188-3. 117p. 10 and up.

This book presents the history of Arlington National Cemetery from its beginning as land surrounding the Washington-Custis family mansion through its conversion to a Union burial ground during the Civil War to its current status as our country's most famous cemetery. Almost half of the book is devoted to black-and-white photographs (such as the Tomb of the Unknown Soldier, famous graves, and park monuments). A general information guide, bibiliography, and index supplement this well-written, carefully researched text.

12.60   Ashabranner, Brent. **A Memorial for Mr. Lincoln.** Photographs by Jennifer Ashabranner. G. P. Putnam's Sons, 1992. ISBN 0-399-22273-1. 113p. 10 and up (est.).

Brent Ashabranner's historical account of the Lincoln Memorial offers a brief history of the man and his times, but it primarily addresses the history of the monument itself, including the proposals and aborted plans, evolution of the design, selection of the site, and influences on the architect, Henry Bacon, and sculptor, Daniel Chester French. Both text and black-and-white photographs attest to the effect of the memorial on its multitude of visitors, young and old.

12.61   Blumberg, Rhoda. **The Great American Gold Rush.** Bradbury Press, 1989. ISBN 0-02-711681-6. 135p. 10 and up (est.).

This engaging, detailed account of the 1848–52 California gold rush strikes an effective balance between anecdotes and the larger historical forces at play. With its wealth of historical illustrations—cartoons, posters, sketches, and photographs—these lost times and forgotten people live again. Chapters focus on routes to the gold fields, life in the mining camps, law and violence, and the end of the rush. Endnotes, a bibliography, and an index are included.

12.62   Chang, Ina. **A Separate Battle: Women and the Civil War.** Lodestar Books, 1991. ISBN 0-525-67365-2. 91p. 12 and up (est.).

As overworked nurses, heartbroken mothers, and courageous liberators, as teachers, laborers, and volunteers, and even as spies and soldiers, American women participated fully in the Civil War. In this volume of the *Young Readers' History of the Civil War* series, Ina Chang details the experiences of these women—black and white, Southern and Northern, famous and obscure—in special insets and with anecdotes, quotations, and well-researched historical background. Photographs and illustrations further emphasize war's profound effect on individual lives, even those far from battle.

12.63   Devaney, John. **America Goes to War: 1941. America Fights the Tide: 1942. America on the Attack: 1943.** Walker, 1991. 188p. 12 and up.

This series, which will total five volumes, takes the reader through America's World War II years, 1941–45. John Devaney explores each year through a series of short, daily descriptions and firsthand accounts of the lives of those affected by the war (soldiers, world leaders, teenagers, pilots, wives, sailors). Each book offers a preface summarizing prior events and a closing note introducing the next book in the series. In addition, each text is accompanied by informative photos, maps, and a reference section.

12.64   Fleming, Thomas. **Behind the Headlines: The Story of American Newspapers.** Walker, 1989. ISBN 0-8027-6891-1. 144p. 9–12 (est.).

With its emphasis on captivating anecdotes, adventure, and the evolution of real freedom of the press, this history of American journalism is irresistible. Chapters are developed chronologically, with each presenting technical matters in fascinating form. From coverage of the American Revolution to yellow journalism to modern investigative and war reporting, Thomas Fleming shows the courage and drive for free expression behind journalistic success—and the personal stories that go with it. Though in places it is a bit overheroic, this book in the American History Series for Young People is consistently stirring. *Notable 1989 Children's Trade Books in the Field of Social Studies.*

12.65   Gibbons, Gail. **Beacons of Light: Lighthouses.** Illustrated by Gail Gibbons. Morrow Junior Books, 1990. ISBN 0-688-07380-8. 32p. 6 and up.

History comes alive in Gail Gibbons's intriguing look at the structure and function of lighthouses. Labeled diagrams help to explain various lighting systems developed and used throughout the years. Bright watercolor illustrations, enriched with detailed drawings of various lighthouses found in the United States, complement the simple but fact-filled text. *Notable 1990 Children's Trade Books in the Field of Social Studies.*

12.66 Hamanaka, Sheila. **The Journey: Japanese Americans, Racism, and Renewal.** Illustrated by Sheila Hamanaka. Orchard Books, 1990. ISBN 0-531-08449-3. 40p. 10 and up.

To commemorate and to remember a time of great injustice in United States history, Sheila Hamanaka painted a five-panel dramatic mural depicting the internment of 120,000 Americans of Japanese ancestry during World War II, including members of her own family. This picture book was inspired by that mural; its panels are reproduced and accompanied by Hamanaka's descriptions of the indignity and degradation afforded people, including orphaned children, who had committed no crime. Government officials, including President Franklin Roosevelt, are indicted.

12.67 Hoig, Stan. **A Capital for the Nation.** Cobblehill Books, 1990. ISBN 0-525-65034-2. 132p. 8 and up.

To Stan Hoig, Washington, D.C., is much more than memorials, statues, parks, and symbols. Rather, it means history, leaders, change, and a reminder of our national unity. The dream of the temperamental French architect L'Enfant for a city with broad, tree-lined avenues and impressive structures was destined to unfold slowly for a young, impoverished nation. In chapters illustrated with early drawings, maps, and photographs, Hoig relates anecdotes and stories of the Capitol, the White House, the Washington Monument, and more.

12.68 Hoobler, Dorothy, and Thomas Hoobler. **Vietnam: Why We Fought—An Illustrated History.** Alfred A. Knopf/Borzoi Books, 1990. ISBN 0-394-81943-8. 189p. 10 and up (est.).

This meticulous, dramatic, and analytical history of the war in Vietnam is wholly appropriate for young readers. Dozens of haunting black-and-white photographs and numerous anecdotes bring harrowing events to life. The text, supplemented by maps, glossary, bibliography, and index, captures the many different points of view about the war and informs the reader about

Vietnamese history and culture. *Notable 1990 Children's Trade Books in the Field of Social Studies.*

12.69 King, John. **The Gulf War.** Dillon Press, 1991. ISBN 0-87518-514-2. 48p. 10 and up.

With lucid prose and instructive illustrations, maps, and photographs, this work is an engrossing presentation of the Persian Gulf War. John King sates, but doesn't overwhelm, the young reader's curiosity with a combination of facts and personal accounts of the war. Chapters include the Kuwait invasion; the historical, economic, political, and cultural background of the region; and the war and its aftermath. A glossary, a chronology, an index, and suggestions for further reading round out the book.

12.70 McKissack, Patricia, and Frederick McKissack. **A Long Hard Journey: The Story of the Pullman Porter.** Walker, 1989. ISBN 0-8027-6885-7. 144p. 12 and up.

This volume in the American History Series for Young People chronicles the first black-controlled union. As younger, more educated African American men joined the ranks of Pullman porters aboard the trains, new thinking about dehumanizing working conditions began to replace traditional ideas. Beginning in the mid 1860s, ex-slaves hired as "travelin' men" had endured long hours, hard work, low wages, separation from families, humiliation, and no channels to redress their grievances. Although forced to go underground, the Brotherhood of Sleeping Car Porters was organized, and the long, hard journey for justice, dignity, and labor rights was begun. *Notable 1989 Children's Trade Books in the Field of Social Studies; Jane Addams Award, 1990; Coretta Scott King Award (Writing), 1990.*

12.71 Myers, Walter Dean. **Now Is Your Time! The African-American Struggle for Freedom.** HarperCollins, 1991. ISBN 0-06-024371-6. 292p. 10 and up (est.).

Walter Dean Myers claims ancestry and heritage from that African who was "worked and beaten, humiliated and subjected to the will of people willing to exploit. . . ." In a carefully researched treatise illustrated with black-and-white photographs and reproductions, Myers traces the history of African Americans' struggles, from the capture of Africans in 1619 for slavery in America through contemporary civil rights. The history is "story-like," covering African Americans from Fula prince Abd al-Rahman Ibrahima, brought to Mississipi in 1788 as a slave, to Martin Luther King, Jr., and includes episodes from Myers's own family history. *ALA Notable Children's Books, 1991; Coretta Scott King Award (Writing), 1992.*

12.72 Rappaport, Doreen. **Escape from Slavery: Five Journeys to Freedom.** Illustrated by Charles Lilly. HarperCollins, 1991. ISBN 0-06-021632-8. 118p. 10 and up.

These five stories of African American slaves who reached freedom before the Civil War also address how freed slaves, antislavery activists, and abolitionists engaged in dangerous work on the Underground Railroad. The line drawings complement the text and help to convey the tension and courage inherent in each of the five journeys to freedom. *Notable 1991 Children's Trade Books in the Field of Social Studies.*

12.73 Ray, Delia. **Behind the Blue and Gray: The Soldier's Life in the Civil War.** Lodestar Books, 1991. ISBN 0-525-67333-4. 102p. 10 and up (est.).

Following *A Nation Torn: The Story of How the Civil War Began,* this second volume in the three-volume Young Readers' History of the Civil War chronicles raw recruits, harsh battles, joyless victories, and crushing defeats, as well as camp life, shortages, prisons, filth, pastimes, and hospitals—all from the perspectives of the soldiers themselves. In their own words, drawn from letters, diaries, and secondary collections, the soldiers prove poignant, courageous, boyish, hopeful, and despairing. Illustrated with photographs, drawings, and paintings, Delia Ray's work provides a sympathetic, but not antiseptic, account of the Civil War.

12.74 St. George, Judith. **Mason and Dixon's Line of Fire.** G. P. Putnam's Sons, 1991. ISBN 0-399-22240-5. 119p. 10 and up.

With a historical perspective, Judith St. George tells the story of the English surveyors Charles Mason and Jeremiah Dixon, who in the 1760s plotted the historic boundary which bears their names. The disputed border between Maryland and Pennsylvania has witnessed quarrels, massacres, rebellions, natural disasters, and wars. Well-known figures and thousands of nameless Americans have left their imprint on the line which has become a symbolic landmark of the country's survival.

12.75   Siegel, Beatrice. **George and Martha Washington at Home in New York.** Illustrated by Frank Aloise. Four Winds Press, 1989. ISBN 0-02-782721-6. 74p. 9–12 (est.).

New York City, the first federal capital of a new nation, received George Washington for his inauguration in April 1789, and for sixteen months served as the Washingtons' home. At a time in which Martha Washington thought her service to the country had come to an end, their lives became even more demanding. Against the changes in one bustling city, with its poverty, diverse population, and political divisions, Beatrice Siegel makes clear the demands of the presidency on the modest Washingtons.

12.76   Waters, Kate. **Sarah Morton's Day: A Day in the Life of a Pilgrim Girl.** Photographs by Russ Kendall. Scholastic Hardcover Books, 1989. ISBN 0-590-4263-6. 32p. 4–8.

Narrated in the language of the day by Sarah Morton, who was nine years old in 1627, this color photo-essay is set at the fully restored Plimoth Plantation in Massachusetts. With time suspended, visitors can interact with seventeenth-century Americans as they go about their daily lives. Reenactments in the book focus on clothing, food preparation, and schooling, and are rounded out with informative endnotes. *Notable 1989 Children's Trade Books in the Field of Social Studies.*

World

12.77   Andronik, Catherine M. **Quest for a King: Searching for the Real King Arthur.** Atheneum, 1989. ISBN 0-689-31411-6. 120p. 10 and up (est.).

Though tales of King Arthur have been told through the ages, questions about their authenticity remain. In this well-researched book, Catherine Andronik investigates historical evidence and examines theories surrounding this hero of the Middle Ages. Black-and-white photographs, labeled maps, manuscripts, and drawings support an intriguing look at history and legend. Additional references at the end of the book will help those who wish to continue their own research on this "once and future king."

12.78   Beattie, Owen, and John Geiger, with Shelley Tanaka. **Buried in Ice.** Scholastic/Madison Press Books, 1992. ISBN 0-590-43848-4. 64p. 8–12.

In 1845, Sir John Franklin, together with the crews of two ships, sailed off to chart the Northwestern Passage. But not one of the crew returned. The mystery of the disappearance of Sir John and his men continued for more than 140 years. Now readers can follow anthropologist Owen Beattie as he races against the on-coming winter to unravel clues, gained partly by exhuming and examining the nearly perfectly preserved remains of a sailor on the expedition. Color illustrations and photographs help to tell the historical tale as well as document the recent one.

12.79   Clements, Gillian. **The Truth about Castles.** Illustrated by Gillian Clements. Carolrhoda Books, 1990. ISBN 0-87614-401-6. 40p. 7–11.

Prospective readers probably think that all castles look like the one at Disneyland, but this unique and understandable book demonstrates that this is not the case. Elaborate illustrations, jam-packed with action, and boxed explanations do most of the work. History, traditions, necessary preparations for feasts and wars, as well as the roles and hierarchies of the people who lived in castles, are fully explored through the simple text and detailed drawings and diagrams.

12.80   Columbus, Christopher (selected by Steve Lowe). **The Log of Christopher Columbus: The First Voyage: Spring, Summer and Fall, 1492.** Illustrated by Robert Sabuda. Philomel Books, 1992. ISBN 0-399-22139-5. 32p. 4 and up.

Details of a thirty-five day voyage that occurred five centuries ago are available to today's children because copies of Columbus's daily log still exist. Steve Lowe's excerpts from that log are short enough to sustain the interest of young children. Neatly bordered by bold-line frames, the excerpts are surrounded by double-page, full-color linoleum-cut illustrations that represent the voyage from varying perspectives, including a gull's-eye view of one ship under full sail.

12.81   Giblin, James Cross. **The Truth about Unicorns.** Illustrated by Michael McDermott. HarperCollins, 1991. ISBN 0-06-022479-7. 104p. 9–12.

Detailed black-and-white illustrations, photographs, and full-color prints add to the fascinating blend of fantasy and reality surrounding the lore of the unicorn across time and cultures. This account not only summarizes information about the variety of forms that the beast has taken, but it also provides the unicorn's 2,500-year history through art, literature, and even scientific explanations. Perhaps the most fascinating explanation is the story of the unicorn told through seven medieval tapestries.

12.82   James, Simon. **Ancient Rome.** Wood, Tim. **The Aztecs.** Viking Penguin, 1992. 48p. 8 and up (est.).

Two ancient civilizations come to life with peel-away acetates that allow young readers to look inside a Roman townhouse or bath, or to lift away the exterior of an Aztec temple or home. In addition to see-through scenes, the books offer a broad range of general information, easily retrievable through an organization that places one major heading on each double-page spread (such as "Trade and Transport") and then presents information with subtopics and informative paintings.

12.83   Jurmain, Suzanne. **Once Upon a Horse: A History of Horses—And How They Shaped Our History.** Lothrop, Lee and Shepard Books, 1989. ISBN 0-688-05550-8. 176p. 10 and up (est.).

"Once upon a time there were no horses." So begins Suzanne Jurmain's chronicle of the history and importance of horses and their relationships to people for the past 6,000 years. Chapters offer accounts, evidence, anecdotes, and artistic representations of horses in war and as servants, messengers, travelers, game players, and friends. Black-and-white reproductions of horses on coins, as stone reliefs, and in woodcuts, tapestries, paintings, and photographs support the text, as do the extensive notes and source bibliography. *Notable 1989 Children's Trade Books in the Field of Social Studies.*

12.84   Katz, William Loren, and Marc Crawford. **The Lincoln Brigade: A Picture History.** Atheneum, 1989. ISBN 0-689-31408-X. 81p. 12 and up (est.).

During the Spanish Civil War (1936–39), 2,800 Americans and thousands of volunteers from fifty-two other countries responded to a plea for help from a weakened Spanish democracy. Dedicated to the American volunteers who were traditionally called the "Lincoln Brigade," this photo history provides an account of that eclectic and largely untrained army which fought bravely and with many casualties to save Spain from military takeover. Accompanying the text are both historical and fifty-year reunion photos of the veterans, as well as personal letters and first-person accounts. *Notable 1989 Children's Trade Books in the Field of Social Studies.*

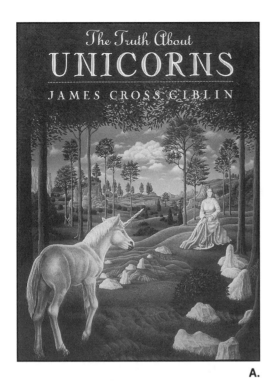

A.

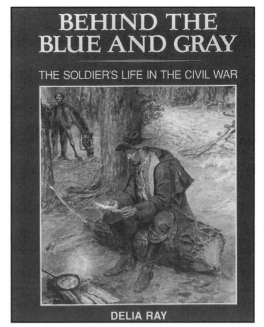

B.

C.

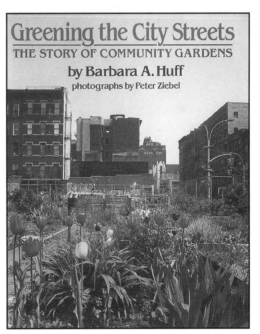

D.

A. *The Truth about Unicorns* by James Cross Giblin; illustrated by Michael McDermott (see 12.81). **B.** *Behind the Blue and Gray: The Soldier's Life in the Civil War* by Delia Ray (see 12.73). **C.** *Fun with Paper Bags and Cardboard Tubes* by F. Virginia Walter (see 12.27). **D.** *Greening the City Streets: The Story of Community Gardens* by Barbara A. Huff; photographs by Peter Ziebel (see 12.12).

A.

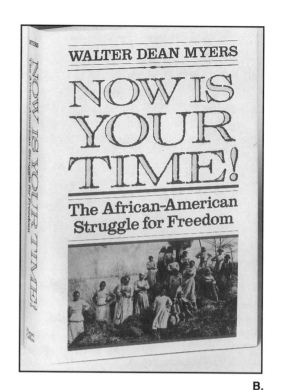

B.

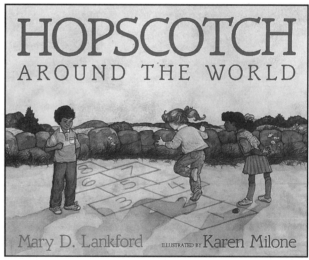

C.

A. *Who Discovered America? Mysteries and Puzzles of the New World* by Patricia Lauber; illustrated by Mike Eagle (see 12.85). **B.** *Now Is Your Time! The African-American Struggle for Freedom* by Walter Dean Myers (see 12.71). **C.** *Hopscotch around the World* by Mary D. Lankford; illustrated by Karen Milone (see 12.116).

12.85 Lauber, Patricia. **Who Discovered America? Mysteries and Puzzles of the New World, rev. ed.** Illustrated by Mike Eagle. HarperCollins, 1992. ISBN 0-06-023729-5. 79p. 6–10 (est.).

When Columbus's ships reached a "new world," he found it already populated. Patricia Lauber asks readers to consider the origin of the peoples whom Columbus found, as well as to probe history's shrouded evidence for even earlier indications of exploration or settlement of the Americas. Drawing from archeological findings, sagas, and ancient history manuscripts, she poses hypotheses and offers support to account for voyagers from Japan and northern Europe, as well as land trekkers from Siberia. Chapters are short, intriguing, and accompanied by maps and watercolors.

12.86 Leroi-Gourhan, André (translated by Claire Jacobson). **The Hunters of Prehistory.** Atheneum, 1989. ISBN 0-689-31293-8. 158p. 10 and up (est.).

How did people live in the time of the reindeer hunters, between ten and thirty thousand years ago, and why should we care today? Archeologist André Leroi-Gourhan introduces young readers to the excitement and, above all, the hard work that such exploration involves. The demanding content and the French perspective require an inquisitive, adept reader. Illustrations are black-and-white charts, drawings, and photographs. *Notable 1989 Children's Trade Books in the Field of Social Studies.*

12.87 Littlewood, Valerie. **Scarecrow!** Illustrated by Valerie Littlewood. Dutton Children's Books, 1992. ISBN 0-525-44948-5. 32p. 6–10 (est.).

In salute to the three-thousand-year-old scarecrow, Valerie Littlewood traces the history and variations of this protector of crops, a servant as ancient as the practice of farming. Each spread offers a new topic (including "Myths and Legends" and "Clappers and Callers"), as well as paintings and ink drawings to amplify the text. Although the most common image of the scarecrow is a straw-stuffed dummy, across history dead birds, shiny objects, smoky fires, and live people have served field duty.

12.88 Maestro, Betsy. **The Discovery of the Americas. The Discovery of the Americas Activities Book.** Illustrated by Giulio Maestro. Lothrop, Lee and Shepard Books, 1991–92. 48p. 6–10.

Columbus's "discovery" is put in perspective; he is regarded as only one of a number of explorers and nomadic people who journeyed to and/or settled in the Americas. From the last Ice Age thousands of years ago to the Vikings, Columbus, Vespucci, and Magellan, the past is clearly chronicled through text, descriptive maps, and lush, watercolor-and-ink illustrations. The companion ninety-six-page activities book provides "a hands-on cross-curriculum approach" in forty-three text-extending activities. *Notable 1991 Children's Trade Books in the Field of Social Studies.*

12.89   Marrin, Albert. **Inca and Spaniard: Pizarro and the Conquest of Peru.** Atheneum, 1989. ISBN 0-689-31481-7. 211p. 12 and up.

Here is the story of how a few ill-equipped but very determined Spaniards toppled the Inca Empire of Peru in less than a year, aided by an Incan civil war and arrogant, uncomprehending Incan leadership. Albert Marrin's very readable text is dramatic without being sensational, detailed but never dull. The strengths and weaknesses of both cultures and their principal players are fairly and nonjudgmentally depicted. This is first-rate history for a young audience, complete with index and selected bibliography.

12.90   Marzollo, Jean. **In 1492.** Illustrated by Steve Björkman. Scholastic Hardcover Books, 1991. ISBN 0-590-44413-1. 32p. 3–6 (est.).

School children still chant, "In fourteen hundred ninety-two, Columbus sailed the ocean blue." Jean Marzollo picked up the couplet pattern from there and spun it out into a rhyming story of the famous voyage and landing. Both the brevity of the rhyme and its sea-splashed watercolors are inviting to the youngest readers and listeners. Issues surrounding Columbus's voyage are gently alluded to: "The first Americans? No, not quite. But Columbus was brave and he was bright."

12.91   Osband, Gillian. **Castles.** Illustrated by Robert Andrew. Orchard Books, 1991. ISBN 0-531-05949-9. 14p. 8–10 (est.).

Replete with material on medieval life, including technical terms and intriguing details, this pop-up book focuses on the development of castles, chivalry, and tournaments. Two large scenes—one of a great hall and its interior, the other of a castle besieged—allow inspection for detail and scale. Punch-out paper-doll knights and a gallery of famous castles are also included.

12.92 Roop, Peter, and Connie Roop, editors. **I, Columbus: My Journal—1492–3.** Illustrated by Peter E. Hanson. Walker, 1990. ISBN 0-8027-6978-0. 59p. 9–12.

Excerpts from Columbus's journal recount his travails, as well as his keen observations, of his voyage in search of the Indies. The journal follows the first voyage from its beginning in August of 1492 until the return to Spain in 1493. Crew unrest, natural wonders, and awe-filled descriptions make the brief entries readable and engaging. Full-color endpapers track the voyage, and watercolor sketches add detail to the pages. *Notable 1992 Children's Trade Books in the Field of Social Studies.*

12.93 Smith, Howard E., Jr. **All about Arrowheads and Spear Points.** Illustrated by Jennifer Owings Dewey. Henry Holt, 1989. ISBN 0-8050-0892-6. 56p. 9 and up (est.).

Howard Smith's narrative focuses on the discovery of arrowheads and spear points in North America and then links the objects with ancient cultures and lifestyles. Readers are guided through the story of early toolmaking and the gradual improvements in materials and techniques over time. Black-and-white drawings offer closeup views of the varying types of points, and maps locate their discovery sites.

12.94 Warren, James A. **Portrait of a Tragedy: America and the Vietnam War.** Photographs by James A. Warren. Lothrop, Lee and Shepard Books, 1990. ISBN 0-688-07454-5. 206p. 10 and up.

James Warren traces twenty-five years of military action in Vietnam, from French domination to U.S. intervention to the fall of Saigon. The author makes a concerted effort to depict objectively and dispassionately the major issues, controversies, and historical events underpinning the Vietnam conflict, such as the geographical importance of Vietnam in international politics, the role of the Vietcong, reasons for the war's unpopularity at home, and the ramifications of America's defeat. Complementing the text are informative maps, black-and-white photos, a glossary, index, and a list of further readings. *Notable 1990 Children's Trade Books in the Field of Social Studies.*

12.95 Weil, Lisl. **Let's Go to the Library.** Illustrated by Lisl Weil. Holiday House, 1990. ISBN 0-8234-0829-9. 32p. 6–10 (est.).

From a historical perspective, libraries are explored as places in which books have been kept through the ages. But readers also gain information on how libraries function today, the people who work in them, their organization, and different kinds of libraries. Cartoon-like tinted illustrations interpret the easy-to-read but conceptually loaded text.

12.96   Wulffson, Don L. **Amazing True Stories.** Illustrated by John R. Jones. Cobblehill Books, 1991. ISBN 0-525-65070-9. 128p. 8 and up.

Classified by subject, these enticingly brief true stories are indeed amazing. Numbering more than fifty, the tales relate such mysteries as a human radio, a vanishing farmer who leaves only his voice behind, and a dog sentenced to life in prison. Sure to entertain, this book will also motivate reluctant readers. Black-and-white drawings complement every third story.

12.97   Wulffson, Don L. **More Incredible True Adventures.** Cobblehill Books, 1989. ISBN 0-525-65000-8. 108p. 8 and up.

Large print and compelling chapter titles lure readers into these bizarre tales of adventure, danger, disaster, and heroism. One tale follows a "tunnel rat" into a Vietcong underground; another graphically describes a grizzly attack on two teens. Each story is accompanied by black-and-white photographs. The subject matter, the characters' conversation, and relatively short paragraphs may also serve to entice reticent middle-grade readers.

Human Relationships

12.98   Aliki. **Manners.** Illustrated by Aliki. Greenwillow Books, 1990. ISBN 0-688-09199-7. 32p. 5 and up.

On the cover a small bird chirps, "Some people have them. Some people don't." Throughout, cartoon vignettes illustrate the point well, gently instructing the niceties of saying "please," turning down food without the comment "yuk," and admitting "I'm sorry." Lessons in manners are embedded in sleep-over behavior and telephone talk. With good humor, Aliki offers ample evidence that good manners preserve feelings and friendships.

12.99   Hyde, Margaret O. **Peace and Friendship/Mir i druzhba: Russian and American Teens Meet.** Cobblehill Books, 1992. ISBN 0-525-65107-1. 92p. 10 and up (est.).

How do students get to know their peers in other lands? Exchange programs can pave the way. When teenagers from the United States and the former Soviet Union got together, they recognized shared values and interests, ranging from environmentalism to pop music. Besides recalling Samantha Smith's bequest and recounting the experiences of individual teens, the book provides information on numerous exchange programs and addresses for inquiries.

12.100 LeShan, Eda. **What Makes You So Special?** Dial Books for Young Readers, 1992. ISBN 0-8037-1155-7. 145p. 10 and up (est.).

As young people mature, they often wish to be "like everyone else." Author Eda LeShan, an educator and family counselor, explains to readers why it is their fate to become someone special. From heredity and our earliest experiences to the relationships that we have with family and friends, she traces the influences which shape our individuality. Illustrated with the stories of real people, this text acts as a guide to self-awareness. A list of additional sources suggests further reading.

Religion

12.101 Eisler, Colin, compiler and editor. **David's Songs: His Psalms and Their Story.** Illustrated by Jerry Pinkney. Dial Books, 1992. ISBN 0-8037-1059-3. 58p. 8 and up (est.).

In the preface to this book, Colin Eisler describes the Psalms as the self-portrait of David: "as fresh today as when first sung over three thousand years ago, set to David's now long-lost music." In a simplified version designed to appeal to younger readers or listeners, Eisler gives brief interpretation to each selected Psalm attributed to David. Jerry Pinkney's full-page watercolors are reverent, dappled compositions from intriguing perspectives.

12.102 Gellman, Marc. **Does God Have a Big Toe? Stories about Stories in the Bible.** Illustrated by Oscar de Mejo. Harper and Row, 1989. ISBN 0-06-022433-9. 88p. All ages.

"The one best way to understand a story in the Bible is to make up another story about it"—so Rabbi Marc Gellman explains his collection of stories from Genesis, Exodus, and Numbers, retold in a voice that seems both deep and affable. "Is the world finished now?" the angels ask God. "And God answered, 'Nope.'" The book's title stems from the story of the Tower of Babel and a little girl's question that prompted its construction. Oscar de Mejo's primitive paintings illuminate the text.

12.103 Noah's Ark. Illustrated by Isabelle Brent. Little, Brown, 1992. ISBN 0-316-10837-5. 32p. 4–8.

This favorite Bible story is simply and poetically told, using the Revised English Bible: "This is the story of Noah. Noah was a righteous man, the one blameless man of his time." Illuminated by highly detailed animal portraits in gilded frames, the text is set opposite magnificent paintings, reminiscent of Persian manuscripts. Each painting is framed with precise geometric patterns accented with gold leaf.

12.104 Noah's Ark. Illustrated by Jane Ray. Dutton Children's Books, 1990. ISBN 0-525-44653-2. 32p. All ages.

On the Earth, people and animals were not at peace with one another, and it grieved God. In a flat, primitive style, illustrator Jane Ray has populated the Earth with creatures and other growing things, but also with pollution, destruction, and conflict. The text, spread between the paintings and a border motif, is taken directly from the Book of Genesis, the Authorized King James Version.

12.105 Stoddard, Sandol, compiler. **Prayers, Praises, and Thanksgivings.** Illustrated by Rachel Isadora. Dial Books, 1992. ISBN 0-8037-0421-6. 152p. 8 and up (est.).

From all around the world, Sandol Stoddard has gathered devotions and arranged them into three sections akin to the supplicant's developing awareness. "Beginnings" offers children's prayers in praise of God and creation; "Reaching Out" are prayers of reflection and self-awareness; and "The Great Journey" offers the searching prayers for truth in the midst of suffering. The collection is far-ranging, with contributions from Dag Hammarskjöld, Mohammed, the Psalms, Mahatma Gandhi, Christina Rossetti, and St. Francis of Assisi. Rachel Isadora's vivid illustrations are in pencil, ink, and watercolor.

12.106 Strom, Yale. **A Tree Still Stands: Jewish Youth in Eastern Europe Today.** Photographs by Yale Strom. Philomel Books, 1990. ISBN 0-399-22154-9. 110p. 8 and up.

Throughout Eastern Europe, Judaism is enjoying a reflowering. Children learn, often from their grandparents, about the practices and traditions destroyed during the Holocaust. Yale Strom traveled through the region where important Jewish communities once thrived, interviewing and photographing articulate children, often offspring of the intelligensia. He records their accounts of Jewish social and learning opportunities, their hopes for the future, and their fears of renewed anti-Semitism.

Social Issues and Family Relationships

12.107 Greenspun, Adele Aron. **Daddies.** Photographs by Adele Aron Greenspun. Philomel Books, 1991. ISBN 0-399-22259-6. 32p. All ages.

As we learn from the sparse text in this black-and-white photographic essay celebrating the relationship between fathers and their children, "Daddies . . . share feelings, read stories," but they "need hugs and kisses, smiles and tickles," too. By including all races in her photographs, Adele Aron Greenspun shows that the powerful link between "daddies" and their children is universal.

12.108 Meltzer, Milton. **Crime in America.** Morrow Junior Books, 1990. ISBN 0-688-08513-X. 158p. 12 and up.

Milton Meltzer, an award-winning historian and biographer, investigates the many facets of crime in America, such as the Mob, our imperfect court system, physical and sexual abuse of children and adults, white-collar crime, and substance abuse and addiction. To personalize the shocking statistics, Meltzer uses actual case histories to illustrate the problems inherent in our legal system. He concludes his text on a positive note by offering suggestions for increasing justice in America. A glossary and index are included.

12.109 Pringle, Laurence. **The Animal Rights Controversy.** Harcourt Brace Jovanovich, 1989. ISBN 0-15-203559-1. 103p. 9 and up (est.).

The philosophical and historical background of the animal rights movement and the controversy about animal rights are explored in this work by renowned wildlife biologist and author Laurence Pringle. Issues include whether human beings have a moral obligation to respect the ecological needs of animals and whether it is morally justifiable for human beings to use animals as food and as subjects for research which will benefit human beings. Photographs, a bibliography, and an index accompany this balanced treatment of a controversial movement.

12.110 Rosenberg, Maxine B. **Growing Up Adopted.** Bradbury Press, 1989. ISBN 0-02-777912-2. 107p. 10 and up (est.).

This companion to *Not My Family* offers revealing information gleaned from author Maxine Rosenberg's interviews with fourteen adoptees of all ages. She presents both a wide variety of adoptive situations and the adoptees' differing reactions. For example, she interviewed children who have been removed from abusive biological parents, children adopted at birth, and adopted children from different countries and ethnic backgrounds. The book is an invaluable guide for adoptees, their families, and friends.

12.111 Seixas, Judith S. **Living with a Parent Who Takes Drugs.** Greenwillow Books, 1989. ISBN 0-688-08627-6. 102p. 9 and up (est.).

Judith Seixas, author of several books on alcoholism and drugs, uses fictional case studies to provide helpful information to children and teens living with parents who abuse drugs. Sympathetic yet frank, she describes typical adult addictive behaviors and suggests coping strategies for young people. Other topics discussed include types of drugs and addiction, treatment and recovery programs, and children's rights and responsibilities.

Sports and Games

12.112 Boyd, Brendan, and Robert Garrett. **Hoops: Behind the Scenes with the Boston Celtics.** Photographs by Henry Horenstein. Little, Brown/Pond Press Books, 1989. ISBN 0-316-37319-2. 128p. 8 and up (est.).

Touted as neither a history of the team nor an analysis of a season, *Hoops* is rather a photograph album of the players, support squad, and coaches of the Boston Celtics. The authors' focus is athletic team as family. Brief chapters address scouting, drafting, practice, equipment, training and conditioning, and basketball strategies. Full-page black-and-white photos accompany informative descriptions of game days and road trips and contrast a rookie with a veteran.

12.113 Egan, Terry, Stan Friedmann, and Mike Levine. **The Macmillan Book of Baseball Stories.** Macmillan, 1992. ISBN 0-02-733280-2. 127p. 8 and up (est.).

Nineteen short stories about baseball's greats are told in an oversize book with wide margins and large print and accompanied by black-and-white photographs. In the introduction,

Tommy John writes that these are glimpses of people, "decent human beings with problems just like anyone else," who just happen to play baseball. In "Papi and Robertito," Roberto Clemente, Jr., recalls his father's humanity. Sandy Koufax's bravery gives a young boy courage in "Koufax and the Kid." Other greats include Ted Williams, Ernie Banks, and Roger Maris.

12.114 Hollander, Phyllis, and Zander Hollander. **More Amazing But True Sports Stories.** Scholastic/Associated Features books, 1990. ISBN 0-590-43876-X. 129p. 8–12 (est.).

Young sports fans will be attracted to this collection of quips, incidents, and ironies from successful figues in all major sports. There are stories of the one-handed professional pitcher, the first goalie to score in the NHL, and the mother who joined her son in pummeling his opponent during a boxing match. Black-and-white-photographs accompany the text.

12.115 Isberg, Emily. **Peak Performance: Sports, Science, and the Body in Action.** Simon and Schuster Books for Young Readers/NOVABOOKS, 1989. ISBN 0-671-67750-0. 48p. 8 and up (est.).

Sure to appeal to young people and their coaches, *Peak Performance* focuses on human physiology as it relates to sports and athletes. Through drawings, color photographs, and text, Emily Isberg shows how athletes' injuries can result from improper technique or exercise and describes medical and therapeutic methods that have been developed to overcome injuries. She explains how computer analysis of a sport is helping athletes to improve their performance and tells how psychologists are encouraging athletes to use visualization to reach "peak performance."

12.116 Lankford, Mary D. **Hopscotch around the World.** Illustrated by Karen Milone. Morrow Junior Books, 1992. ISBN 0-688-08420-6. 48p. 8 and up.

This unique book describes ways in which the common elements of the hopscotch game (a thrown object, a pattern through which players must hop without touching the lines) vary in nineteen countries around the world. A brief narrative describes the game in countries as diverse as China, Bolivia, and the United States, followed by thorough directions and a drawing of the game's hopping pattern, which includes labels naming the parts of the pattern. A full-page, full-color illustration featuring native children playing their variant of hopscotch faces each description.

12.117 Ritter, Lawrence S. **The Story of Baseball, rev. ed.** William Morrow, 1990. ISBN 0-688-09056-7. 206p. 10–12 (est.).

Numerous black-and-white photographs, charming anecdotes, and technical knowledge combine in an entertaining, newly revised introduction to America's national sport. Covering both famous players and baseball techniques, Lawrence Ritter's clear and lively writing should draw in young fans. Topics include everything from Jackie Robinson's breaking the color barrier to quips by old-timers like Honus Wagner and Yogi Berra.

12.118 Schmidt, Diane. **I Am a Jesse White Tumbler.** Photographs by Diane Schmidt. Albert Whitman, 1990. ISBN 0-8075-3444-7. 40p. 7–10 (est.).

Eighth-grader Kenyon Conner is a member of the Jesse White Tumbling Team, a program that provides inner-city Chicago children with challenges and training to become tumblers. Narrated by Kenyon, the photo essay underscores anti-drug and anti-gang messages as it follows the children through their routines and performances, emphasizing the hard work, dedication, and self-esteem of the young tumblers.

12.119 Schulman, L. M., compiler. **The Random House Book of Sports Stories.** Illustrated by Thomas B. Allen. Random House, 1990. ISBN 0-394-92874-1. 248p. 6 and up (est.).

In short stories about football, baseball, boxing, horse racing, and hunting, various authors celebrate human endeavor through sports competition. "Tennis" by Judie Angell is a moving story of love and competition between father and son. Other authors included in the collection are Ernest Hemingway, Ring Lardner, Jack London, and John Updike.

12.120 Winfield, Dave, with Eric Swenson. **The Complete Baseball Player.** Illustrated by Bob Cram. Avon Books, 1990. ISBN 0-380-75830-X. 212p. 7–12 (est.).

Readers who want to know "How to Hit, Field, Catch, Pitch, Steal, Slide, Bunt, Pivot, and even Coach" can use this guide as a reference or for cover-to-cover reading. Chapters on attitude, fitness, equipment, and skills are dotted with black-and-white photographs, cartoons, diagrams, and tips from baseball greats.

Transportation

12.121 Baer, Edith. **This Is the Way We Go to School: A Book about Children around the World.** Illustrated by Steven Björkman. Scholastic Hardcover Books, 1990. ISBN 0-590-43161-7. 40p. 3–7.

All over the world, children go to school. Edith Baer and Steven Björkman team up to show that whether in Hawaii, Illinois, India, Mexico, Canada, Siberia, or anywhere, children get to school in a host of ways. In Venice, "Bianca, Beppo, Benedetto ride aboard the vaporetto." In Norway, "Bundled up against the breeze, Niels and Solveig go on skis." Appendixes help children identify the countries of the schoolchildren of the world, as well as locate their homelands on a map.

12.122 Blanchard, Anne. **Navigation: A 3-Dimensional Exploration.** Illustrated by Irvine Peacock. Orchard Books, 1992. ISBN 0-531-05455-1. 12p. 7–11.

Words are an awkward medium to explain how navigation instruments work. Although this sophisticated pop-up book may not survive a classroom, it shows how trade winds, stars, and sea currents help navigators. They are guided further by the compass, sextant, and chronometer, as well as the lighthouse, radio beacons, and navigation satellites. Several of the three-dimensional colored cardboard "instruments" can be manipulated.

12.123 Brown, Laurie Krasny, and Marc Brown. **Dinosaurs Travel: A Guide for Families on the Go.** Illustrated by Marc Brown. Little, Brown/Joy Street Books, 1988. ISBN 0-316-11253-4. 32p. 4–8.

With just the right blend of humor and practical information, the Browns provide a book for young children who may be getting ready "to travel around the world, or around the block." The travel advice is arranged by chapters, and the action follows a dinosaur family as they pack, explore their options for transportation, eat and sleep away from home, and return again. The paperback edition also features two pullout postcards illustrated by Marc Brown.

12.124 Burleigh, Robert. **Flight: The Journey of Charles Lindbergh.** Illustrated by Mike Wimmer. Philomel Books, 1991. ISBN 0-399-22272-6. 28p. 5 and up.

In 1927, when he was just twenty-five years old, Charles Lindbergh stayed awake for sixty hours (flying for thirty-three of them) to become the first person to cross the Atlantic Ocean in an airplane. This book takes the reader along on Lindbergh's historic trip through the immediacy of both terse, lyrical prose and dramatic perspectives in the double-page, impressionist illustrations. *Notable 1991 Children's Trade Books in the Field of Social Studies.*

12.125 Fisher, Leonard Everett. **Tracks across America: The Story of the American Railroad, 1825–1900.** Holiday House, 1992. ISBN 0-8234-0945-7. 192p. 9 and up (est.).

Leonard Everett Fisher's chronicle of the railroad in the nineteenth century follows several themes. Chapters address westward expansion, the railroad in the Civil War, Native American resistance, train robbers, robber barons, and railroad disasters. In a unifying narrative, the railroad is linked with the transformation of the United States from an agricultural country into a mighty industrial nation and is "closely linked with American economic and political history." The volume is meticulously researched and accompanied by drawings, maps, photographs, and portraits, as well as an index and selected bibliography.

12.126 Gibbons, Gail. **The Great St. Lawrence Seaway.** Illustrated by Gail Gibbons. Morrow Junior Books, 1992. ISBN 0-688-06985-1. 40p. 6 and up.

From its discovery by western explorers in 1535 to the present day, the St. Lawrence Seaway has been the site of great courage and innovation. Today the "tallest water staircase in the world" makes it possible for ships to travel from the Atlantic Ocean to the upper Great Lakes—2,400 miles. Gail Gibbons's characteristic pen-and-ink drawings filled in with watercolor washes assist readers in interpreting the process involved in a ship's passage through the seaway's complicated lock system.

12.127 Lindblom, Steven. **Fly the Hot Ones.** Houghton Mifflin, 1991. ISBN 0-395-51075-9. 102p. 9 and up.

Fixed-wing airplanes are described extensively, beginning with the standard Piper J-3 cub single-engine airplane to the world's finest jet fighter, the F-16 Fighting Falcon. Altogether eight "of the radical extremes of flying" are illustrated with both color and black-and-white photos.

12.128 McVey, Vicki. **The Sierra Club Wayfinding Book.** Illustrated by Martha Weston. Sierra Club Books/Little, Brown, 1989. ISBN 0-316-56340-4. 88p. 9–12.

Readers interested in travel, hiking, or orienteering will find this book a valuable source of information. Chapters focus on gathering information, "wayfinding" systems from many cultures, maps, city navigation, and instructions on what to do when lost. Each chapter also includes games and exercises—from advice about the compass to games involving stargazing and scavenger hunts.

12.129 Moseley, Keith. **Steam Locomotives: A Three-Dimensional Book.** Illustrated by Brian Bartle and Brian Watson. Orchard Books, 1989. ISBN 0-531-05844-1. 12p. All ages (est.).

Magnificent steam locomotives pop from the pages of this book through the wonders of complex paper engineering. The accompanying text is dense, but clearly written, presenting a historical look at steam locomotives across 150 years. Both European and American locomotives are included.

12.130 Robbins, Ken. **Boats.** Photographs by Ken Robbins. Scholastic Hardcover Books, 1989. ISBN 0-590-41157-8. 32p. 3–8.

Ken Robbins's *Boats* is a well-written, aesthetically pleasing information book for younger readers. Tinted black-and-white photographs extend a simple text that explains the history, features, and functions of seventeen kinds of boats—boats that range from large to small, complex to simple, unusual to familiar.

12.131 Robbins, Ken. **Bridges.** Photographs by Ken Robbins. Dial Books, 1991. ISBN 0-8037-0930-7. 32p. 4–7 (est.).

Hand-tinted photographs accompany an informative text about twelve different types of bridges. From the simplest bridge, a log across a creek, to one of the most complex, a truss bridge, Ken Robbins elaborates on the design and construction in a clear and simple way. "But bridges are more than just practical structures. They are monuments to craft and imagination, to technology and beauty, and to our need to reach beyond the boundaries of nature."

Traditional Literature

. . . stories lean on stories,
lives lean on lives.

Folklore can talk in
the modern tongue,
and the child,
given the chance,
can bridge the centuries.

Jane Yolen, "How
Basic Is SHAZAM?"
Language Arts

13 Traditional Literature

Fables

13.1 Anno, Mitsumasa, reteller. **Anno's Aesop: A Book of Fables by Aesop and Mr. Fox.** Illustrated by Mitsumasa Anno. Orchard Books, 1989. ISBN 0-531-08374-8. 64p. 4–12 (est.).

When Freddy Fox finds a copy of *Aesop's Fables*, he begs his father to read the stories. However, his father only pretends to read them, offering instead his own stories. Included in this volume are the original Aesop's fables as well as Mr. Fox's versions of each one, which are often, in classic Anno fashion, puzzles of some sort. Each picture does double duty, serving to illustrate both the original fable and Mr. Fox's story.

13.2 Clark, Margaret, reteller. **The Best of Aesop's Fables.** Illustrated by Charlotte Voake. Little, Brown/Joy Street Books, 1990. ISBN 0-316-14499-1. 61p. 4–10 (est.).

All the favorite Aesop fables gather here, but two things are very different. First, the voice of the narrator is immediate and contemporary. Second, no moral appears in scrolling print at the fable's end. Morals, explains Margaret Clark in her introduction, are "best left unsaid. If children understand and enjoy the stories as we have presented them, they will certainly appreciate the morals behind them." Charlotte Voake's lively art adds wit and action to these twenty-seven large-print retellings.

13.3 Craig, Helen, reteller. **The Town Mouse and the Country Mouse.** Illustrated by Helen Craig. Candlewick Press, 1992. ISBN 1-56402-102-5. 32p. 4–8 (est.).

In a contemporary version of an ancient fable, the town mouse, Tyler, is dismayed by the absence of night life and the "boring food" of his country sojourn. When his country cousin, Charlie, visits Tyler "to see how exciting life can be," the city doesn't really get equal treatment. Its turmoil, trash, and traffic are enough to make almost anyone long for one of Charlie's country sunsets. Helen Craig's watercolor and ink mouse-hole details—from tiny teapots to oil lamps and wing chairs—are charming.

13.4 Gatti, Anne, reteller. **Aesop's Fables.** Illustrations by Safaya Salter. Harcourt Brace Jovanovich/Gulliver Books, 1992. ISBN 0-15-200350-9. 80p. 6 and up.

Retellings of fifty-eight fables by the ancient Greek writer Aesop are newly and distinctively illustrated. Detailed borders frame the subjects, rendered as flat and exotic as Persian manuscripts. From the story of the rooster whose unhappy fate teaches that pride goes before a fall to a contest between the north wind and the sun that reveals the power of persuasion, these tales, both familiar and less well known, make animals and nature the engaging reminders of piquant and direct moral lessons.

13.5 Kherdian, David, reteller. **Feathers and Tails: Animal Fables from around the World.** Illustrated by Nonny Hogrogian. Philomel Books, 1992. ISBN 0-399-21876-9. 96p. 6 and up (est.).

Nonny Hogrogian has produced spirited illustrations for twenty-one fables, framing both characters and texts with broad, color rectangles. At times, tails and paws escape the frames, giving a three-dimensional quality to the pages. Reteller David Kherdian explains that although the stories came from all parts of the Earth—from India, Africa, Armenia, and Europe and including Inuit and Native American tales—"they are almost certainly drawn from a single source, the Bidpai Fables," which traveled east to Persia and then on to Greece. Today's children will discover that such stories preserve the truth and lore of people everywhere.

13.6 McDonald, Suse, and Bill Oakes, retellers. **Once Upon Another: The Tortoise and the Hare.** Illustrated by Suse MacDonald and Bill Oakes. Dial Books for Young Readers, 1990. ISBN 0-8037-0787-8. 32p. 5–8.

In a book that can be read front-to-back, then upside down and back again, two favorite fables are told with abstract collages for illustrations. Turn the book one way and imagine a tortoise and a hare in brightly colored torn-paper blobs. But when the book is turned over and read the other way, the same torn-paper shapes represent the huge orange lion and the tiny mouse who saves him. The textured, representative art may spark some children's own imaginative efforts.

13.7 Paxton, Tom, reteller. **Androcles and the Lion, and Other Aesop's Fables.** Illustrated by Robert Rayevsky. Morrow Junior Books, 1991. ISBN 0-688-09683-2. 40p. 4 and up.

"Androcles and the Lion" and nine other fables are recast in rhyme and given energy by Robert Rayevsky's designs, using two styles and two techniques—some on rough-textured paper and some on smooth watercolor paper. Colored inks, acrylics, and pencils are alternated with pen, ink, and watercolors to depict fables that are set in ancient Greece, medieval times, and even Central Park. Included are "The Man, the Boy, and the Donkey" and "The King of the Barnyard."

13.8 Paxton, Tom, reteller. **Belling the Cat, and Other Aesop's Fables.** Illustrated by Robert Rayevsky. Morrow Junior Books, 1990. ISBN 0-688-08159-2. 40p. 4 and up (est.).

Folksinger Tom Paxton, in this sequel to his *Aesop's Fables,* retells ten more tales in verse, including "Town Mouse and Country Mouse," "The Crow and the Pitcher," "Honesty Is the Best Policy," and "The Milkmaid and Her Pail." Russian artist Robert Rayevsky's watercolors, in framed double-page spreads, are pleasingly comical and delightfully expressive. *Notable 1990 Children's Trade Books in the Field of Social Studies.*

13.9 Wallis, Diz, reteller. **Something Nasty in the Cabbages.** Illustrated by Diz Wallis. Boyds Mills Press/Caroline House, 1991. ISBN 1-878093-10-X. 24p. All ages.

"There was once, not so very long ago, a farm that was owned by Constant and his wife. Here they are, looking cross." So begins the artist's retelling of the twelfth-century tale of Chantecler, the glorious cockerel whose pride was almost his downfall. Having learned the difficult lesson of ignoring flattery used to deceive, Chantecler barely escapes wily Reynard the Fox. Classic paintings on creamy paper are handsomely detailed; frames can't contain the flurry of feathers and fur.

13.10 Watts, Bernadette, reteller. **The Wind and the Sun: An Aesop Fable.** Illustrated by Bernadette Watts. North-South Books, 1992. ISBN 1-55858-163-4. 32p. 5–8.

In a quarrel between Sun and Wind as to which is stronger, each agrees that whoever can force the removal of the cloak from a man who travels below them will be winner of the contest. Although Wind's ferocity cannot meet the challenge, Sun's warmth causes the man to remove his cloak, teaching that "it is easier to influence by warmth than by force." Sunny illustrations are textured and shaded with crayon-like strokes.

13.11 Young, Ed. **Seven Blind Mice.** Illustrated by Ed Young. Philomel Books, 1992. ISBN 0-399-22261-8. 38p. 4–7.

Just as blind men explore various parts of an elephant only to draw different conclusions in the Indian fable "The Blind Men and the Elephant," so do Ed Young's seven blind mice try to make sense of the beast. The mice are crayon-bright, vividly contrasting with the black backgrounds of the pages. Never has the elephant looked so huge or so mysterious as when it is viewed through its elephant elements. In an interesting twist, White Mouse, the last to venture forth, finds each mouse's guess to be somewhat right, but knows true "wisdom comes from seeing the whole." *Boston Globe–Horn Book Picture Book Award, 1992; Caldecott Honor Book, 1993.*

Folk Songs and Ballads

13.12 Bryan, Ashley, compiler. **All Night, All Day: A Child's First Book of African-American Spirituals.** Illustrated by Ashley Bryan. Atheneum, 1991. ISBN 0-689-31662-3. 48p. 4–10.

Bright, two-page watercolor paintings capture the excitement and energy of African American spirituals, including such popular pieces as "When the Saints Go Marching In" and "He's Got the Whole World in His Hands." Each of the rainbow-like illustrations is a companion piece to the words and music—for both piano and guitar—for the twenty songs from the Civil War era to the present. *Coretta Scott King Honor Book (Illustration), 1992.*

13.13 Burgie, Irving. **Caribbean Carnival: Songs of the West Indies.** Illustrated by Frané Lessac. Tambourine Books, 1992. ISBN 0-688-10780-X. 32p. 6 and up.

If just the thought of "Day-o, day-o / Daylight come and me wan' go home" sets your fingers snapping and your toes tapping to the calypso beat, this collection of original Irving Burgie works and other Caribbean folk songs is for you. Primitive island paintings of brilliantly colored flowers, fruits, birds, and sea are set opposite piano and guitar arrangements for the thirteen songs—from the familiar "Michael Row the Boat" and "Yellow Bird" to the less familiar "Judy Drowned-ed."

13.14 **The Friendly Beasts: A Traditional Christmas Carol.** Illustrated by Sarah Chamberlain. Dutton Children's Books, 1991. ISBN 0-525-44773-3. 32p. 3–7 (est.).

In this traditional carol, animals of the stable sing their lullabies of gifts to the infant Jesus on the first Christmas: "'I,' said the cow, all white and red, 'I gave Him my manger for his bed.'" Large-scale illustrations are multicolor linoleum-block prints that are highlighted with pastels.

13.15   Hart, Jane, compiler. **Singing Bee! A Collection of Favorite Children's Songs.** Illustrated by Anita Lobel. Lothrop, Lee and Shepard Books, 1989. ISBN 0-688-41975-5. 160p. 4 and up (est.).

This collection of 125 children's songs is organized into lullabies, finger plays, counting songs, rounds, and dances. Indexes offer the songs by subject/theme and by titles. In an author's note, Jane Hart explains that the piano accompaniments are arranged in lower keys for singing and include guitar chords. Anita Lobel's illustrations, alternately full-color and black-and-white, are rendered in eighteenth-century little theater sets and costumes. "The characters," Lobel writes, "fell into place as principals, chorus, and stage assistants."

13.16   **I Know an Old Lady Who Swallowed a Fly.** Illustrated by Glen Rounds. Holiday House, 1990. ISBN 0-8234-0814-0. 29p. 4–7.

Youngsters will delight in this rendition of a traditional folk song. The funny old lady still swallows some most peculiar things (a fly, a spider, a bird, a cat, a dog, a goat, and a horse), but this time each object takes up a full page—in Glen Rounds's unconventional primitive closeup illustrations of animals from different perspectives.

13.17   Manson, Christopher, reteller. **A Farmyard Song: An Old Rhyme.** Illustrated by Christopher Manson. North-South Books, 1992. ISBN 1-55858-170-7. 32p. 2–6.

As the farmer tells it, he is pleased with all his animals, and likes to repeat their voices: "I had a cat and the cat pleased me, / I fed my cat by yonder tree; / Cat goes fiddle-i-fee." One by one, depicted in nineteenth-century-style hand-colored woodcuts, the farmer feeds each of the animals. Stenciled borders encase both the illustrations and the verses. At last, the animals reprise their performances, with the reader/listener invited to produce the sounds.

13.18   McNally, Darcie, adapter. **In a Cabin in a Wood.** Illustrated by Robin Michal Koontz. Cobblehill Books, 1991. ISBN 0-525-65035-0. 32p. 4–8.

It's the same little cabin of camp-song fame adapted into a cumulative tale. To the snug, snow-covered cabin of an affable artist comes the original rabbit seeking refuge from the hunter. But the rabbit is soon followed by a family of possums, a raccoon, a beaver, and even a moose until the little cabin overflows with animal chaos. Artist and rabbit conspire to disguise the lop-eared bunny as a skunk; as the interlopers flee, the wildlife photographer "hunter" snaps pictures. Safely, the rabbit/skunk abides.

13.19 Metropolitan Museum of Art, in association with the Buffalo Bill Historical Center. **Songs of the Wild West.** Metropolitan Museum of Art and Simon and Schuster Books for Young Readers, 1991. ISBN 0-671-74775-4. 128p. 10 and up.

This historical and musical tribute to the Old West combines the music of the frontier and informed commentary by Alan Axelrod with paintings, sketches, and photographs from the Metropolitan Museum of Art and the Buffalo Bill Historical Center in Cody, Wyoming. The songs are arranged simply, and the book closes with guitar chords and an index. Together, the songs reflect a cultural range of cowboys, pioneers, and miners.

13.20 Moser, Barry, reteller. **Polly Vaughn: A Traditional British Ballad.** Illustrated by Barry Moser. Little, Brown, 1992. ISBN 0-316-58541-6. 28p. 10–12 (est.).

"Polly Vaughn," a traditional English ballad, is a folk tragedy of love and wrongful death. Barry Moser's version transports the story to America, maintaining both the dark mood of the events and the bright goodness of the main characters—two young lovers reunited after death. Moser gives Appalachian charm to the characters' voices and achieves haunting realism with dramatic transparent watercolors.

13.21 Raffi. **Baby Beluga.** Illustrated by Ashley Wolff. Crown, 1990. ISBN 0-517-57840-9. 30p. 4–8.

Baby Beluga, "a little white whale on the go," lives a happy and protected life in the cold Arctic waters. Raffi's popular song, a tribute to one of the world's endangered creatures of the sea, describes Baby Beluga's activities and interactions with other marine life. Full-page illustrations, rich in Arctic landscapes and wildlife, complement the simple, lyrical text of this Raffi Songs to Read book.

13.22   Raffi. **Tingalayo.** Illustrated by Kate Duke. Crown, 1989. ISBN 0-517-56926-4. 32p. 5–8.

Tired and bored with his work, Tingalayo the donkey slips away from his master and heads to the town carnival. Befriended by a little girl, Tingalayo joins in the fun by dancing, singing, swimming, and water skiing. But when he hears his master call, "Come, little donkey, come," the fun-loving donkey returns home. Cartoon-like tropical pastel washes help bring this traditional Caribbean folk song to life. Words and music are included in this Raffi Songs to Read book so that readers can join in the singing.

13.23   Richardson, Jean. **Stephen's Feast.** Illustrated by Alice Englander. Little, Brown, 1991. ISBN 0-316-74435-2. 24p. 4–8.

It is the time of the Feast of St. Stephen's, and Stephen, the youngest page at the court of King Wenceslas, plans to celebrate the holiday within the warm and festive Great Hall. But King Wenceslas summons Stephen to accompany him through a snowstorm to take food to a peasant family. As Stephen participates in this mission of good will, he learns about the true meaning of the season. Snowy scenes contrast with glowing firesides in Alice Englander's illustrations of this adaptation of a classic carol, which is reprinted on the endpapers.

13.24   Rosen, Michael, reteller. **Little Rabbit Foo Foo.** Illustrated by Arthur Robins. Simon and Schuster Books for Young Readers, 1990. ISBN 0-671-70968-2. 26p. 4–8 (est.).

A new generation of children will sing along with little Rabbit Foo Foo as he hops merrily through the forest, nonchalantly bopping field mice, goblins, and even tigers on the head, despite the admonitions of the Good Fairy: "Little Rabbit Foo Foo, I don't like your attitude . . . I'm going to give you two more chances to change, and if you don't, I'm going to turn you into a goon." Unabashedly, goofy Rabbit Foo Foo persists until his punishment is delivered and the moral pronounced: "Hare today, goon tomorrow."

13.25   Simon, Paul. **At the Zoo.** Illustrated by Valérie Michaut. Doubleday/Bryon Preiss Books, 1991. ISBN 0-385-41906-6. 32p. 4–7 (est.).

Paul Simon's lyrics from his 1960s song "At the Zoo" are fleshed into a complete story by Valérie Michaut's detail-packed illustrations. Animal-loving children notice in the newspaper that the zoo's polar bear is lonely. Packing a stuffed bear to give to a real bear, they set off on the crosstown bus (piloted by a monkey) for a trip to the imaginative zoo, run by the animals. Without close inspection, funny sequences will be missed. Even Simon himself is playing a guitar on a park bench.

13.26 Slavin, Bill. **The Cat Came Back: A Traditional Song.** Illustrated by Bill Slavin. Albert Whitman, 1992. ISBN 0-8075-1097-1. 32p. 6–11.

Even if you can't remember the New Christy Minstrels' folk song, you may remember other renditions of this tongue-in-cheek, outrageous account of attempts to discourage a cat from coming home. Mr. Johnson is vexed by his cat's slovenly habits, so he sends him off on an ocean liner, in a hot-air balloon, and even on a train heading west, but, as always, "the cat came back." Cat fanciers may be put off by the thesis, but this cool-dude cat is indefatigable, even returning by taxi.

13.27 Sweet, Melissa, adapter. **Fiddle-I-Fee: A Farmyard Song for the Very Young.** Illustrated by Melissa Sweet. Little, Brown/Joy Street Books, 1992. ISBN 0-316-82516-6. 32p. 3–6 (est.).

An old song makes for a lovely sing-along picture book. "I had a cat and the cat pleased me, I fed my cat under yonder tree; Cat went fiddle-i-fee." True to the original, the young farmer also has a duck, a goose, a dog, a sheep, a pig, a goat, and a cow—and each of their sounds is repeated in cumulative fashion as they trail behind the youngster to a picnic. Both the words and music for the song are included.

13.28 Watson, Wendy. **Frog Went a-Courting.** Illustrated by Wendy Watson. Lothrop, Lee and Shepard Books, 1990. ISBN 0-688-06540-6. 32p. 4–7.

The folk-song account of the courtship and wedding of Frog and Miss Mouse involves lots of little creatures—from a seed-tick to Missus Snake—and ends with a disruption of the wedding festivities by an old bobcat. Readers will have to look closely to spot all the details as the village creatures prepare to celebrate the nuptials. Tiny, busy pen-and-ink scenes and characters in pastel greens and blues depict each verse with meticulous detail.

13.29 Westcott, Nadine Bernard, adapter. **Skip to My Lou.** Illustrated by Nadine Bernard Westcott. Little, Brown/Joy Street Books, 1989. ISBN 0-316-93137-3. 128p. 3–7 (est.).

This is "Skip to My Lou" like you've never danced it. Left in charge of a spit-spot farm by the farmer and his wife, a young boy has a kind of *Cat in the Hat* experience with the farm animals. Cats in the buttermilk (lapping contentedly), pigs in the parlor (eating buttermilk pancakes prepared by cows in the kitchen), roosters in the pantry, and sheep in the bathtub make quite a hullabaloo. Chorus, music, and frenetic-pace illustrations are included.

Folktales and Fairy Tales

13.30 Aardema, Verna. **Anansi Finds a Fool: An Ashanti Tale.** Illustrated by Bryna Waldman. Dial Books for Young Readers, 1992. ISBN 0-8037-1165-4. 32p. 6–10 (est.).

From West African oral tradition, Anansi the trickster seeks someone to become his fishing partner—a partner foolish enough to do all the work. Although his best friend Bonsu agrees, Bonsu tricks the trickster, assuring Anansi that the work must be divided: one partner must build the trap, while the other must feel the weariness. Anansi is convinced that feeling weary is the harder job, so he sets to work, aptly illustrating the lesson: "When you dig a hole for someone else, you will fall into it yourself."

13.31 Afanasyev, Alexander Nikolayevich (retold by Lenny Hort). **The Fool and the Fish: A Tale from Russia.** Illustrated by Gennady Spirin. Dial Books, 1990. ISBN 0-8037-0861-0. 22p. 4–8.

Ivan, the lazy fool, reluctantly hauls two pails to an icy stream to draw water for his brothers' wives. Instead, he pulls out a king-size fish, who tells Ivan that if he spares its life, the fish will grant every wish that Ivan makes. This retold Russian folktale of Ivan's magical fate is presented to the reader with finely detailed, earth-toned illustrations that contain stocky peasants and elaborately accessorized nobility.

13.32 Aksakov, Sergei (translated by Isadora Levin). **The Scarlet Flower: A Russian Folk Tale.** Illustrated by Boris Diodorov. Harcourt Brace Jovanovich, 1989. ISBN 0-15-270487-6. 32p. 4–8.

A wealthy merchant asks his daughters what gift they would like him to bring from his travels. The youngest, his favorite, who remains nameless throughout the story, requests only a scarlet flower. In fairy-tale tradition, the simple request turns out to be the most complicated. A monstrous figure demands the merchant's daughter in return for his trespassing and taking the flower. Extravagantly illustrated by Russian artist Boris Diodorov to match the mood and scenes, this version of "Beauty and the Beast" follows the well-known course.

13.33   Andersen, Hans Christian (retold by Riki Levinson). **The Emperor's New Clothes.** Illustrated by Robert Byrd. Dutton Children's Books, 1991. ISBN 0-525-44611-7. 38p. 4–8 (est.).

In this retelling of Hans Christian Andersen's tale, the vain emperor is a lion, surrounded by animal sycophants. The scurrilous tailors—foxy foxes—bewilder the court as they gleefully play their trick. Andersen's sense of fun remains intact, and the illustrations, intricately detailed with castle finery, add further zest to the glorious deception.

13.34   Andersen, Hans Christian. **The Little Mermaid.** Illustrated by Katie Thamer Treherne. Harcourt Brace Jovanovich, 1989. ISBN 0-15-246320-8. 42p. 5–8 (est.).

True to Andersen's original text, this book offers a sadder, gorier version of the tale than the popular Disney film. Here, the little mermaid painfully and pitifully loses her voice and tail in order to have a chance at becoming the prince's bride. At story's end, she does not marry the prince, but she does discover upon her death that she has earned a soul for herself. The striking, vibrantly hued watercolors make for pleasurable viewing, despite the tragic ending. *Redbook Children's Picture Book Award.*

13.35   Andersen, Hans Christian. **The Nightingale.** Illustrated by Alison Claire Darke. Doubleday, 1989. ISBN 0-385-26082-2. 24p. 5–8.

Exquisitely detailed watercolors enhance this newly illustrated version of Hans Christian Andersen's beloved story of a nightingale caged to sing for the emperor. But when the emperor receives a jeweled clockwork nightingale as a gift, everyone agrees that the model sings just as beguilingly as the real nightingale. Yet it is only the song of a live nightingale that can revive a dying Emperor. In this timeless tale, readers are reminded of the futility of capturing nature's wonders or re-creating its perfection.

13.36   Andersen, Hans Christian (retold by Neil Philip). **The Snow Queen: A Story in Seven Parts.** Illustrated by Sally Holmes. Lothrop, Lee and Shepard Books/Albion Books, 1989. ISBN 0-688-09048-6. 64p. All ages.

Kay and Gerda's childhood happiness is destroyed when the Snow Queen cruelly destroys their friendship. In this new translation, blessed by the luminous beauty of Sally Holmes's illustrations, the story of Kay's disappearance and Gerda's search for him weaves the same magical spell. Creature, countryside, and character are portrayed with equal grace in both full-page paintings and cameos tucked within the text.

13.37 Andersen, Hans Christian (translated by Naomi Lewis). **The Steadfast Tin Soldier.** Illustrated by P. J. Lynch. Harcourt Brace Jovanovich/Gulliver Books, 1992. ISBN 0-15-200599-4. 32p. All ages.

The toys in the nursery are new editions of today's antiques, and a freckled-face registers delight. Throughout P. J. Lynch's version, the visual perspectives shift dramatically. Readers get a table-top view of the toys, a bird's-eye view of the sidewalk as the soldier plummets to the street, and a commodore's perspective as the paper boat rushes through the rat-infested sewer. Each double-page painting insets the text into a total design; single-page paintings are framed opposite bordered text. Translator Naomi Lewis has compiled several collections of Hans Christian Andersen's stories.

13.38 Andersen, Hans Christian (retold by Tor Seidler). **The Steadfast Tin Soldier.** Illustrated by Fred Marcellino. HarperCollins/Michael di Capua Books, 1992. ISBN 0-06-205001-X. 32p. 4–8 (est.).

Fred Marcellino offers rare perspectives on Tor Seidler's smooth retelling of the tale of steadfast love. The paper's texture, visible through the paint, gives a soft inner light and antique feel to the nineteenth-century Christmas celebrants. The tin soldiers themselves are, as Andersen may have intended, rendered flat. After all, "they had all been made out of the same old tin spoon." Given that the soldier's love was made of paper, and that his perilous voyage was on a paper boat, the interpretation seems apt as well as beautiful.

13.39 Andersen, Hans Christian (adapted by Deborah Hahn). **The Swineherd: Narrated by Himself and Acted by His Favorite Friends and Relatives.** Illustrated by Deborah Hahn. Lothrop, Lee and Shepard Books, 1991. ISBN 0-688-10053-8. 32p. 5–8 (est.).

In Deborah Hahn's version, Hans Christian Andersen himself narrates the tale, writing all night to fashion a play with parts for everyone. As in the original tale, a prince discovers that his beloved princess is too foolish to understand true beauty, and so, disguised as a swineherd, he attracts the princess with worldly baubles, only to abandon her. Dissatisfied with the play's ending, the pig characters clamor for a new, happier resolution. Simple line drawings are softly washed and then overwritten with swirls of dialogue.

13.40 Andersen, Hans Christian. **Thumbelina.** Illustrated by Alison Claire Darke. Doubleday, 1991. ISBN 0-385-41404-8. 26p. 5–8.

Thumbelina's world is beautifully rendered in this version of the famous Andersen fairy tale. Detailed watercolor illustrations capture both the world of small animals and the feelings and mannerisms of the diminuitive characters. The mole in his dark velvety jacket looks as stodgy as any country squire, and the swallow's feathers—as Thumbelina mounts his back—seem soft as any linen. The text is rhythmic and full of feeling. A tale so well loved deserves this kind of quality, full-color presentation.

13.41 Andersen, Hans Christian (retold by Deborah Hautzig). **Thumbelina.** Illustrated by Kaarina Kaila. Alfred A. Knopf/Borzoi Books, 1990. ISBN 0-679-90667-3. 32p. 6–10 (est.).

Kaarina Kaila's Thumbelina is wispy soft and inhabits pages reminiscent of a Victorian garden book, bordered with leaves and blossoms. Thumbelina's kind soul makes her no match for the threats of toads, the insults of insects, or the wishes of moles. Rescued by a swallow whose life she once saved, the thumb-sized woman-child is transported to a southern garden where she becomes the Queen of Flowers. Throughout, flora and fauna are gracefully rendered in delicate watercolors.

13.42 Andersen, Hans Christian (retold by James Riordan). **Thumbelina.** Illustrated by Wayne Anderson. G. P. Putnam's Sons, 1991. ISBN 0-399-21756-8. 32p. 4–8.

Hans Christian Andersen's tiny Thumbelina encounters many adventures as she thwarts the efforts of the ugly toad and the heartless mole to marry her. Not until the beautiful swallow, whom she saved from freezing to death, returns does she find happiness. Each tiny butterfly wing and droplet of water is represented in portrayals remarkable for their color, texture, and depth.

13.43 Andersen, Hans Christian (retold by Troy Howell). **The Ugly Duckling.** Illustrated by Troy Howell. G. P. Putnam's Sons, 1990. ISBN 0-339-22158-1. 38p. All ages.

In his retelling of Andersen's classic tale, Troy Howell recounts the scorn, pain, and ultimate fulfillment experienced by the ugly little "duckling" who eventually develops into a graceful swan. Although the abuse and isolation that the young swan suffers may upset very young readers, the retelling is true to its happy ending. Howell's lovely full-page illustrations offer bucolic scenes in muted greens, rich browns, and deep oranges, often washed with a delicate golden haze.

13.44   Arnold, Caroline. **The Terrible Hodag.** Illustrated by Lambert Davis. Harcourt Brace Jovanovich, 1989. ISBN 0-15-284750-2. 29p. 4–8 (est.).

In this American folktale, the boss man refuses to pay Ole Swenson and the other lumberjacks unless they cut lumber stands of such size that the men must work day and night. Yet none of the men dares work at night, for that is when the mythical giant Hodag goes out into the forest, a beast that stands forty feet tall, with glowing eyes, the feet of a bear, the tail of an alligator, and the head of an ox. Ole Swenson must find a way to save his friends' wages. In the process, he learns a subtle lesson about the deception of appearances, and what "beasts" are really like. Northern landscapes painted in a surreal style are coolly serene.

13.45   Arnold, Tedd. **Ollie Forgot.** Illustrated by Tedd Arnold. Dial Books for Young Readers/Pied Piper Books, 1991. ISBN 0-8037-0985-4. 32p. 4–8 (est.).

In this version of a noodlehead tale, Ollie's poor memory causes him to forget his mother's market list. Instead, poor Ollie remembers only the last words he hears. Along his route, Ollie's responses to others (delivered in rhyming lines) are always inappropriate. So he is chased, taunted, and berated all the way to market, where a fortuitous set of circumstances turns the last words to his mother's original market list. Tedd Arnold's figures are short, round peasants rendered in color pencils and watercolor washes.

13.46   Barton, Byron. **The Three Bears.** Illustrated by Byron Barton. HarperCollins, 1991. ISBN 0-06-020424-9. 32p. 3–6 (est.).

Broad strokes of acrylic paint in blazing, basic colors depict two-dimensional bears and their nemesis, Goldilocks. The bold and childlike repackaging of this classic story includes simple illustrations and minimal text.

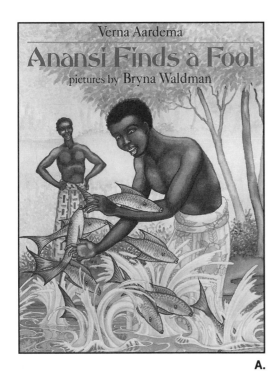

A.

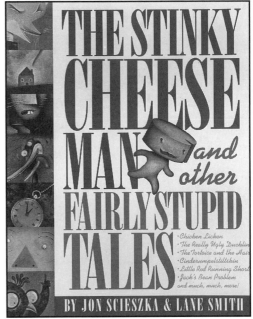

B.

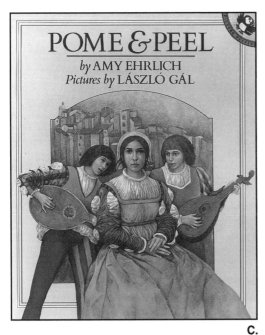

C.

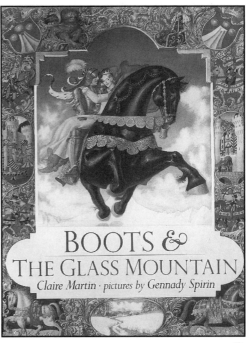

D.

A. *Anansi Finds a Fool: An Ashanti Tale* by Verna Aardema; illustrated by Bryna Waldman (see 13.30). **B.** *The Stinky Cheese Man and Other Fairly Stupid Tales* by Jon Scieszka and Lane Smith (see 13.129). **C.** *Pome & Peel: A Venetian Tale* by Amy Ehrlich; illustrated by László Gál (see 13.72). **D.** *Boots & the Glass Mountain* by Claire Martin; illustrated by Gennady Spirin (see 13.104).

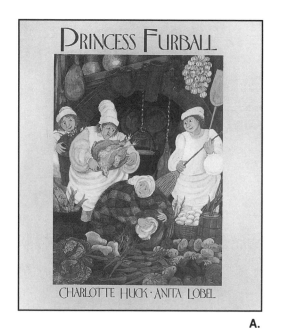

A.

B.

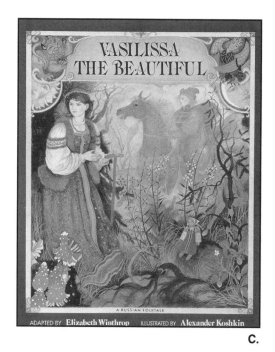

C.

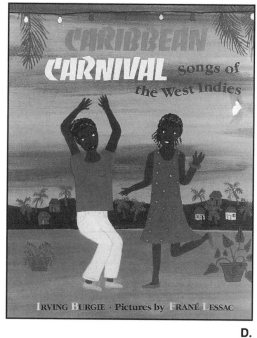

D.

A. *Princess Furball* retold by Charlotte Huck; illustrated by Anita Lobel (see 13.86). **B.** *Melisande* by E. Nesbit; illustrated by P. J. Lynch (see 13.113). **C.** *Vasilissa the Beautiful: A Russian Folktale* adapted by Elizabeth Winthrop; illustrated by Alexander Koshkin (see 13.145). **D.** *Caribbean Carnival: Songs of the West Indies* by Irving Burgie; illustrated by Frané Lessac (see 13.13).

13.47 Brett, Jan, reteller. **Beauty and the Beast.** Illustrated by Jan Brett. Clarion Books. ISBN 0-89919-497-4. 28p. 6–12.

In her research for this retelling, Jan Brett found the 1910 version by Sir Arthur Quiller-Couch especially helpful. Against airbrushed backgrounds and in her trademark frames, she retells this classic fairy tale with rich prose and captivating illustrations filled with color and romantic detail. For example, message-woven tapestries on the castle walls reveal story events.

13.48 Brett, Jan, adapter. **The Mitten: A Ukrainian Folktale.** Illustrated by Jan Brett. G. P. Putnam's Sons, 1989. ISBN 0-399-21920-X. 28p. 4–8.

In this retelling of a Ukrainian folktale, Nicki goes out to play and drops one of his new white mittens in the snow. One-by-one, the forest animals find the forgotten mitten and snuggle inside. The mitten stretches and stretches until a tiny mouse's whiskers bring about a sneeze and a hilarious climax. Each softly colored double-page illustration permits the reader to view a snowy world through three wood-framed windows, bordered with folk-art motifs.

13.49 Brooke, William J. **A Telling of the Tales: Five Stories.** Illustrated by Richard Egielski. Harper and Row, 1990. ISBN 0-06-020689-6. 132p. 8–13.

This collection of five nontraditional retellings of traditional tales presents versions of "Sleeping Beauty," "Cinderella," "Paul Bunyan," "John Henry," and "Jack and the Beanstalk." In William Brooke's rendition, when Sleeping Beauty is awakened by the prince's kiss, she demands some identification and scolds him for his bold advances. Cinderella teaches a prince a few things about dreams and love, and Paul Bunyan, the logger, meets Johnny Appleseed, the environmentalist. The final tale is a poignant tribute to the tellers of tales across generations.

13.50 Brooke, William J. **Untold Tales.** HarperCollins, 1992. ISBN 0-06-020272-6. 165p. 10 and up.

Following his *A Telling of the Tales,* William Brooke once again demonstrates his talent for sophisticated humor in these retellings of "The Frog Prince," "Snow White," "Beauty and the Beast," and "Sleeping Beauty." The volume closes with a contemporary twist, entitled "A Tale Untold," in which Brooke cleverly writes himself—with the help of his word processor—into a confusing and delightful mix of all the tales.

13.51   Brothers Grimm (translated by Elizabeth D. Crawford). **Hansel and Gretel.** Illustrated by Lisbeth Zwerger. Scholastic/Blue Ribbon Books, 1991. ISBN 0-590-44459-X. 32p. 5 and up (est.).

Imagine Hansel and Gretel with golden yellow hair, innocent in peasant dress, and with brown tones of cottage and forest floor ready to engulf them. Then you will see them as portrayed by Austrian artist Lisbeth Zwerger, winner of the 1990 Hans Christian Andersen Award, in this melodic retelling of a best-loved German tale of child abuse, retribution, and forgiveness.

13.52   Brothers Grimm (translated and adapted by Anthea Bell). **Jack in Luck.** Illustrated by Eve Tharlet. Picture Book Studio/Michael Neugebauer Books, 1992. ISBN 0-88708-249-1. 32p. 4–8 (est.).

In a noodlehead story with a message, simple Jack leaves his master after seven years of work and asks for his wages in gold. Because the gold is too heavy to carry, Jack trades it for a horse. Trades continue predictably as Jack exchanges the horse for a cow, the cow for a pig, the pig for a sheep, the sheep for a goose, and the goose for a whetstone. When the stone falls into a well, Jack rejoices. Freed of burdens, he happily races home. Illustrations offer a bird's-eye perspective on gnomish, rounded forms.

13.53   Brothers Grimm (retold by Alison Sage). **Rumpelstiltskin.** Illustrated by Gennady Spirin. Dial Books for Young Readers, 1990. ISBN 0-8037-0908-0. 32p. 6 and up (est.).

Gennady Spirin has produced magnificent scenes, festooned castles, and glorious sixteenth-century costumes to accompany the tale of the braggart miller, his hapless daughter, the greedy king, and the strange little man who could spin straw into gold. The characters are clearly drawn, the tale fast-paced. In discussion, children may decide that the king and the miller deserved a bit of Rumpelstiltskin's punishment for their cavalier and threatening treatment of the future queen.

13.54   Bryan, Ashley, reteller. **Turtle Knows Your Name.** Illustrated by Ashley Bryan. Atheneum/Jean Karl Books, 1989. ISBN 0-689-31578-3. 32p. 3–7.

"Once there was a little boy and he had a very long name. His name was UPSILIMANA TUMPALERADO." And, at first, his name was very difficult for him to remember. But his patient Granny taught him, and when he could say his name, he and Granny danced the name dance by the sea within earshot of

Turtle. Ashley Bryant's musical voice and hot colors retell this West Indies story of the importance of names and of those who remember them.

13.55   Burkert, Nancy Ekholm. **Valentine and Orson.** Illustrated by Nancy Ekholm Burkert. Farrar, Straus and Giroux/Floyd Yearout Books, 1989. ISBN 0-374-38078-3. 44p. 10–12 (est.).

This ambitious and ornate medieval story from France is somewhat demanding in its plot complications but worth the effort to read. Twin princes are separated at birth, one to lead a knight's life, the other to be suckled by a bear. They meet years later as enemies, become friends, and together seek to discover their true identities. The story is told in verse as a folk play narrated by a Muslim dwarf and is accompanied by magnificent color-pencil drawings that present the actions as a village play. This historical literature could inspire student drama. *Notable 1989 Children's Trade Books in the Field of Social Studies; Boston Globe–Horn Book Award for Creative Excellence, 1990.*

13.56   Butler, Stephen. **Henny Penny.** Illustrated by Stephen Butler. Tambourine Books, 1991. ISBN 0-688-09922-X. 32p. 3–6 (est.).

Stephen Butler adds a new twist to the ending of the tale of Henny Penny and her pals: instead of being eaten by the fox, Henny Penny wakes to find it was all a bad dream. However, when an acorn hits the foolish chicken on the head as she wanders outdoors after her nap, she nonetheless jumps to her familiar conclusion. Big and bold illustrations in crayon-box colors create a naive spirit for this traditional folktale.

13.57   Calmenson, Stephanie. **The Principal's New Clothes.** Illustrated by Denise Brunkus. Scholastic Hardcover Books, 1989. ISBN 0-590-41822-X. 40p. 6–9.

Mr. Bundy, the principal of P.S. 88, is the sharpest dresser in town. So when two tricksters offer to make him a one-of-a-kind suit that will be invisible to anyone who is "no good at his job or just plain stupid," Mr. Bundy readily accepts the offer. In this modern-day version of the Hans Christian Andersen fairy tale, all the members of the school community insist that the principal's new clothes are truly magnificent, until a kindergartner finally speaks the truth.

13.58   Carey, Valerie Scho, adapter. **Quail Song: A Pueblo Indian Tale.** Illustrated by Ivan Barnett. G. P. Putnam's Sons/Whitebird Books, 1990. ISBN 0-399-21936-6. 32p. 4–8.

It is Quail's distress and not her song that makes her cry, "Ki-ruu, ki-ruu!" But Coyote is not satisfied with that explanation and insists that Quail teach him her song. Time and again, through comedic mishaps, Coyote drops the song and must return to relearn it. Time and again, Quail insists that it is not a song, until, at last, she is forced to trick the old trickster, Coyote. Ivan Barnett's illustrations are collages of oxidized and painted metal in colors of the Southwest.

13.59   Cech, John. **First Snow, Magic Snow.** Illustrated by Sharon McGinley-Nally. Four Winds Press, 1992. ISBN 0-02-717971-0. 32p. 6–9 (est.).

Inspired by the traditional Russian tale "The Snow Maiden," John Cech retells the story of a woodsman and his wife who desperately want a child. From the first magic snow of the season, he shapes a snow child who comes alive in his arms. In the spring, little Snowflake disappears, and her distraught parents search for her. Against icy blue backgrounds, the illustrations tell of a happy reunion, painted with liquid watercolors, inks, and acrylics, full of folk patterns and stylized motifs.

13.60   Chorao, Kay. **The Child's Fairy Tale Book.** Illustrated by Kay Chorao. Dutton Children's Books, 1990. ISBN 0-525-44630-3. 64p. 4–8 (est.).

Five tales, three old favorites ("Snow White and the Seven Dwarfs," "Rapunzel," and "Cinderella") and two less well known, are surrounded by Kay Chorao's delicate, glowing paintings. "Muchie Lal" is an East Indian tale that combines motifs of transformation and a wicked stepmother. "The Ants That Pushed on the Sky" is a Pueblo tale of cooperation and triumph over evil.

13.61   **Cinderella, and Other Tales from Perrault.** Illustrated by Michael Hague. Henry Holt, 1989. ISBN 0-8050-1004-1. 80p. All ages (est.).

Seven tales from Charles Perrault, ranging from the classic "Sleeping Beauty" and "Cinderella" to the less-familiar "Riquet with the Tuft," are accompanied by one or two full-page watercolor paintings and border motifs. Michael Hague describes his technique as working from small sketches to larger drawings, using models to create lifelike poses. Eventually, pencil outlines are inked, shaded, and color washed. The writing style is embellished, the print is much tinier than might be expected, and Little Red Riding Hood is *not* saved by the woodcutter.

13.62 Claverie, Jean, reteller. **The Three Little Pigs.** Illustrated by Jean Claverie. North-South Books, 1989. ISBN 1-55858-004-2. 23p. 3–10 (est.).

As Jean Claverie's French folktale of three little pigs unfolds, teachers and students alike will be struck by the similarities to the American version. The whimsical pastel illustrations and some smaller selected pencil drawings entice the reader to move through this predictable storyline. Claverie concludes with the pigs enlarging their brick home so that even their mother can live with them.

13.63 Cole, Joanna. **It's Too Noisy!** Illustrated by Kate Duke. Thomas Y. Crowell, 1989. ISBN 0-069-04737-1. 28p. 4–8.

Joanna Cole retells the traditional Jewish folktale which teaches that troubles are relative. When a farmer consults the Wise Man for a solution to the problem of his noisy, family-filled house, the Wise Man repeatedly advises that more and more animals be brought in until the cacophony is tremendous—clucking and crowing, oinking and baaing, braying and mooing. When the animals are finally removed, the relative quiet "was as quiet as quiet can be." Large, colorful, cartoon-like illustrations accompany the text.

13.64 Compton, Patricia A., reteller. **The Terrible EEK: A Japanese Tale.** Illustrated by Sheila Hamanaka. Simon and Schuster Books for Young Readers, 1991. ISBN 0-671-73737-6. 26p. 6–10.

One stormy night a father tells his son about the things that he fears—a thief, a wolf, and a leak in the roof. Hovering close by the house, a thief and a wolf hear the father's words and become frightened by the unknown and terrible "leak." What follows is a series of mishaps and misunderstandings in which a tiger, a wolf, a monkey, and a thief frighten each other with a terrible "EEK!" Dark-toned oil paintings illustrate this retelling of an old Japanese tale filled with humor and misadventure.

13.65 Croll, Carolyn, adapter. **The Little Snowgirl: An Old Russian Tale.** Illustrated by Carolyn Croll. G. P. Putnam's Sons/White-bird Books, 1989. ISBN 0-399-21691-X. 28p. 4–8.

Carolyn Croll's moving adaptation of a Russian Christmas folktale depicts the transforming power of love. Pavel, the wood cutter, and his wife, Caterina, want a child of their own. Watching children build snowmen gives Pavel the idea to shape a daughter of snow. Magically, the beautiful snowgirl comes to life but can eat only ice and must live outdoors. Distressed to leave their child outside on Christmas Eve, the couple carry her sleeping form to the fireside where, while they sleep, Babouschka, the old woman who grants children their dearest wishes, makes the snowgirl a real child. Vivid colors and Russian folk-art details rendered in the style of Tomie dePaola's rounded forms lend authenticity. *Notable 1989 Children's Trade Books in the Field of Social Studies.*

13.66   Croll, Carolyn, adapter. **The Three Brothers: A German Folktale.** Illustrated by Carolyn Croll. G. P. Putnam's Sons/Whitebird books, 1991. ISBN 0-399-22195-6. 28p. 4–8.

An old farmer has three sons—Gideon cares for the animals, Simon plows the fields, and Amos, the youngest, washes clothes and makes candles. However, when the farmer decides to leave his farm to the son who can "fill up the old barn before the day is done," Amos uses the knowledge that he has gained from his mundane tasks to cleverly outwit his older brothers. Carolyn Croll was inspired by Pennsylvania Dutch wood paintings, costumes, and quilts in creating her distinctive folk-art illustrations for this German folktale.

13.67   deChristopher, Marlowe. **Greencoat and the Swanboy.** Illustrated by Marlowe deChristopher. Philomel Books, 1991. ISBN 0-399-22165-4. 28p. 4 and up.

Leading a simple life, Baptiste the swanherd contentedly watches his flocks and plays his reed pipe. But then an old man dressed in a green coat steals the swans when Baptiste refuses to give up the gold band he wears. In his efforts to reclaim his swans, Baptiste discovers the meaning of the gold band and fulfills his destiny as prince of the land. Full-page, romantic nineteenth-century oil paintings illustrate this magical tale from France.

13.68   Demi. **The Magic Boat.** Illustrated by Demi. Henry Holt, 1990. ISBN 0-8050-1141-2. 32p. 5 and up (est.).

When young Chang saves an old man from drowning, the boy is rewarded with a magical boat that can change in size. A terrible flood strikes, and Chang bravely uses the boat to save his mother and his white cat, an ant, a queen bee, and a crane.

But when the evil Ying witnesses the boat's magical powers, he steals the boat from Chang and takes it to the corrupt Emperor. With the help of his rescued friends, Chang sets out to retrieve the boat. Demi's delicate, gold-highlighted illustrations depict Oriental scenes.

13.69   dePaola, Tomie. **Tony's Bread: An Italian Folktale.** Illustrated by Tomie dePaola. G. P. Putnam's Sons/Whitebird Books, 1989. ISBN 0-399-21693-6. 28p. 4–6.

In this retelling of an Italian folktale, Tomie dePaola accounts for how the sweet Italian bread in a flower-pot shape came to be called *panettone*, or Tony's bread. Tony dreams of being the most famous baker in Northern Italy, but has to be content making simple bread. His daughter, Serafina, has everything she could want except a husband, because Tony thinks that no suitor is good enough for her. But when Angelo, a wealthy nobleman from Milano, falls in love with Serafina, Angelo helps Tony make panettone—and win Serafina. *Notable 1989 Children's Trade Books in the Field of Social Studies.*

13.70   Deuchar, Ian. **The Prince and the Mermaid.** Illustrated by Ian Deuchar. Dial Books for Young Readers, 1989. ISBN 0-8037-0638-3. 32p. 4–8.

A mermaid longs to talk with a handsome prince, but to do so she must invoke an ancient spell to turn herself into a human. When the prince falls in love with her, she asks him to promise that he will not ask where she comes from or goes to at each full moon. A jealous woman convinces the prince to break his promise, resulting in sadness to the whole kingdom. The dark blues, cool browns, and deep purples depicting the mermaid, the prince, and the jealous woman in the full-page oil paintings evoke the somber mood of this medieval French folktale.

13.71   Ehlert, Lois (translated by Amy Prince). **Moon Rope: A Peruvian Folktale/Un lazo a la luna: Una leyenda Peruana.** Illustrated by Lois Ehlert. Harcourt Brace Jovanovich, 1992. ISBN 0-15-255343-6. 32p. 4–8.

In both English and Spanish text, *Moon Rope* tells of adventurous Fox, who talks his timid friend, Mole, into climbing to the moon together using a grass rope. With "all the creatures" watching, Mole slips, falls, and is caught by a passing bird, which is so embarrassing that he now comes out only at night. However, Fox's triumphant face can still be seen in the sky on full-moon nights. Peruvian-influenced illustrations include Lois Ehlert's characteristically bright colors, particularly the shiny silver moon.

13.72 Ehrlich, Amy, reteller. **Pome and Peel: A Venetian Tale.** Illustrated by László Gál. Dial Books for Young Readers, 1990. ISBN 0-8037-0288-4. 32p. 4–8.

An enchanted apple causes both a wealthy woman and her maid to give birth to sons. The two young men, Pome and Peel, are raised as brothers, and both fall in love with the beautiful daughter of a wizard. When she leaves her father to marry Pome, the wizard places three curses on her. Peel, in an act of brotherly love, sacrifices himself to save her. Recognizing Peel's love and loyalty, the daughter induces the wizard to break his destructive spell. Watercolor paintings add a rich warmth to the story.

13.73 Eisen, Armand, editor. **A Treasury of Children's Literature.** Houghton Mifflin/Ariel Books, 1992. ISBN 0-395-53349-X. 304p. All ages.

Within this compendium of thirty children's classics are traditional tales, fables from Aesop, selections from Mother Goose, excerpts from such children's classics as *Wind in the Willows* and *Peter Pan*, poems from Robert Louis Stevenson, American tall tales, and Hans Christian Andersen's fairy tales. The treasury is handsomely and generously illustrated with more than 225 oil paintings from sixteen artists.

13.74 Geras, Adèle. **My Grandmother's Stories: A Collection of Jewish Folk Tales.** Illustrated by Jael Jordan. Alfred A. Knopf/Borzoi Books, 1990. ISBN 0-679-90910-9. 96p. 8–12 (est.).

A sensual description of the rooms, closets, and cupboards of Grandmother's house winds its way through this collection of ten Jewish folktales. While chopping apples and nuts in the fragrant kitchen, Grandmother tells the story of selfish Bavsi, who would not share his wealth of food with his starving neighbors. While watching her granddaughter try on high-heeled shoes from the vast collection stacked neatly on the bedroom shelves, Grandmother remembers the foolish Chief Sage of mythical Chelm who wears golden shoes on his hands. The stories are ideally suited for reading aloud or retelling. *Notable 1990 Children's Trade Books in the Field of Social Studies.*

13.75 Gerson, Mary-Joan, reteller. **Why the Sky Is Far Away: A Nigerian Folktale.** Illustrated by Carla Golembe. Little, Brown/Joy Street Books, 1992. ISBN 0-316-30852-8. 32p. 4–8 (est.).

Long ago, a low and deliciously edible sky supplied all food; people had but to reach for a piece of it. But because of their greed and waste, the sky threatened to move far away. The lesson is clear: "Perhaps through your own labor you will learn not to waste the gifts of nature." The vivid, stylized scenes of the Nigerian folktale are rendered with monotypes, a technique using oil-based inks on plexiglass, which are then transferred to paper by means of an etching press.

13.76 **Goldilocks and the Three Bears: A Peek-through-the-Window Book.** Illustrated by Penny Ives. G. P. Putnam's Sons, 1992. ISBN 0-399-22121-2. 26p. 3–6.

To enliven this retelling, Penny Ives has spiced her cheery colored pencil and washed illustrations with cutout windows leading from one page to the next. As the bears eat breakfast, only the reader will spy Goldilocks through the window—effectively threading the narrative. The cutouts work both ways: on the next page, the same cutout window reveals porridge on the stove inside the house.

13.77 Goode, Diane, compiler. **Diane Goode's Book of Silly Stories and Songs.** Illustrated by Diane Goode. Dutton Children's Books, 1992. ISBN 0-525-44967-1. 64p. All ages.

From all over the world come stories of foolishness, of sillies, and of noodleheads. Diane Goode has illustrated a representative collection of these tales and songs ranging from Jamaica to Iran. Readers familiar with "The Three Sillies" will recognize the Italian version, "Sweet Giongio." Other familiar favorites are an African Anansi tale and the Norwegian story of the husband who minds the house. Each selection has its own detailed borders, its own opening letter that winds about a story character, and its own beguiling set of sillies.

13.78 Greaves, Margaret, reteller. **Tattercoats.** Illustrated by Margaret Chamberlain. Clarkson N. Potter, 1990. ISBN 0-517-58026-8. 23p. 5–10.

Living with her morose grandfather, lovely and kind Tattercoats is forced to wear rags and beg for food. When the king announces that his son is to choose a bride, all the kingdom readies for the festivities—all except Tattercoats. Out for a walk, Tattercoats meets a handsome lord on his way to the palace. Enchanted by Tattercoats, the "lord" makes her promise to join him there at midnight. Children may enjoy comparing this English tale of "Cinderella" with other versions. Fanciful cartoon-like drawings dance across the pages.

13.79   Greene, Carol. **The Old Ladies Who Liked Cats.** Illustrated by Loretta Krupinski. HarperCollins, 1991. ISBN 0-06-022105-4. 28p. 6–10 (est.).

When the mayor of a small island decrees that all cats must stay in at night, life on the island is turned upside-down and a once safe and tranquil lifestyle becomes anything but peaceful. But the old ladies who liked cats know what to do. They let the felines out, the mutual needs among creatures are once again met, and life returns to normal. Full-page gouache and colored-pencil illustrations enhance this humorous ecological folktale inspired by Charles Darwin. *Notable 1991 Children's Trade Books in the Field of Social Studies.*

13.80   Gregory, Valiska. **Through the Mickle Woods.** Illustrated by Barry Moser. Little, Brown, 1992. ISBN 0-316-32779-4. 24p. 8 and up.

In solitude, a lonely king mourns his wife's death, but to honor her last wish he reluctantly follows a young guide, Michael, into the deep woods to find the magic bear. The great bear tells the travelers three stories—tales deep and mysterious, but full of renewal. And in the morning the king leads young Michael home, having found the courage and joy to go on living. Barry Moser's frosty watercolor, ink, and gouache illustrations contribute to a poignant story about surviving the loss of a loved one.

13.81   Haley, Gail E., reteller. **Puss in Boots.** Illustrated by Gail E. Haley. Dutton Children's Books, 1991. ISBN 0-525-44740-7. 32p. 4 and up (est.).

The youngest son of a miller is willed only a cat, but the cat is so clever that it ensures its young master's fortune. Gail Haley used her own cat as a model for Puss, and her energetic illustrations are boldly outlined interpretations of the French court. Costumed Puss, in the most swashbuckling scenes, is clad in purple cape, a green-plumed purple hat, and a golden sword. When the action is at its peak, the paintings escape their frames.

13.82 Haley, Gail E. **Sea Tale.** Illustrated by Gail E. Haley. E. P. Dutton, 1990. ISBN 0-525-44567-6. 32p. 5–8 (est.).

Tom O'Shaunessy grew up by the sea, where his toy boats and sand castles were the stuff of dreams. But adult life as a sailor is even more magical than his childhood imagination allowed. A story of love for a mermaid and the promise of a lock of her hair to a mysterious old woman is brought to life by Caldecott-medalist Gail Haley in her nautical linoleum-cut illustrations.

13.83 Harris, Joel Chandler (adapted by Van Dyke Parks). **Jump On Over! The Adventures of Brer Rabbit and His Family.** Illustrated by Barry Moser. Harcourt Brace Jovanovich, 1989. ISBN 0-15-241354-5. 48p. All ages.

Adapted for children, these Brer Rabbit tales from the American South have lost none of their sauciness, humor, or African American dialect. Many tales in this third volume, despite the fame of creator Joel Chandler Harris, will be unfamiliar to the general reader, which makes for some fine surprises. Watercolor illustrations of the animal characters pursuing human activities are painted to perfection. *Notable 1989 Children's Trade Books in the Field of Social Studies.*

13.84 Haviland, Virginia, reteller. **The Talking Pot: A Danish Folktale.** Illustrated by Melissa Sweet. Little, Brown/Joy Street Books, 1990. ISBN 0-316-35060-5. 30p. 4–8.

When a poor man sells his only cow for a three-legged pot, his wife scolds him for his foolishness. But when the pot comes alive, it skips to the rich man's house, returning with food and riches and changing the poor family's fortunes forever. Detailed with Danish style and tradition, full-page watercolors help tell this humorous folktale about a mischievous talking pot. In the classroom or at home, children can make Baked Danish Apple Pudding by following the recipe included at the end of this Danish folktale.

13.85 Hodges, Margaret, compiler and reteller. **Hauntings: Ghosts and Ghouls from around the World.** Illustrated by David Wenzel. Little, Brown, 1991. ISBN 0-316-36796-6. 123p. 8–12.

In a collection of sixteen ghost stories from every continent, a boy is recruited and flown by a stork to save a lost city, a corpse searches in vain for the missing lid to its coffin, and the ghost of Joe Magarac saves a steamer from colliding with a barge. Dramatic full-page illustrations in black-and-white help to create a mood of magic and foreboding.

13.86   Huck, Charlotte, reteller. **Princess Furball.** Illustrated by Anita Lobel. Greenwillow Books, 1989. ISBN 0-688-07838-9. 35p. 4–6 (est.).

In this charming English variant of the "Cinderella" theme, elegantly illustrated by Anita Lobel, a greedy king betrothes his only daughter to an ogre for fifty wagons of silver. Clothed in a coat of a thousand furs, the princess runs away and is found by hunters, who name her Furball. She takes up the guise of a servant to a cook by day but attends balls in her own finery at night. The king is smitten by her, and Furball cleverly reveals her identity without the help of a fairy godmother.

13.87   Hunter, C. W., reteller. **The Green Gourd: A North Carolina Folktale.** Illustrated by Tony Griego. G. P. Putnam's Sons/Whitebird Books, 1992. ISBN 0-399-22278-2. 32p. 4–8.

In North Carolina, the saying goes, "Never pull a green gourd afore it's ripe, or it'll witch ye sure." But a saucy old woman needs a drinking gourd for herself, and so she pays that saying no mind at all. In the dialect of the hills of North Carolina, and in cumulative pattern, the yarn unfolds as the gourd first "fumps" the old woman and then her would-be rescuers. Only the cleverness and courage of a small boy are a match for the gourd's wily green nature.

13.88   Isadora, Rachel, adapter. **The Princess and the Frog.** Illustrated by Rachel Isadora. Greenwillow Books, 1989. ISBN 0-688-06374-8. 29p. 4–7.

Rachel Isadora has given an almost Victorian cast to her illustrations for this retelling of the German folktale "The Frog King and Iron Heinrich" by the Brothers Grimm. The princess is garden-party prim in puffed sleeves and straw hat, and the frog a gentleman model of despair, then hope, as he seeks his transformation through acceptance by the princess. Inked silhouettes adorn the text page, while the opposing page is an edge-to-edge, translucent watercolor.

13.89   Jacobs, Joseph, compiler and editor. **Tattercoats.** Illustrated by Margot Tomes. G. P. Putnam's Sons, 1989. ISBN 0-399-21584-0. 26p. 5–9.

Using a palette of rich shades of brown, Margot Tomes interprets this English Cinderella-like folktale of ragged Tattercoats, her bitter grandfather, and her magical, gooseherd friend, against medieval castles and village streets. Rejected by her grandfather, growing up neglected and unloved, Tattercoats chances to meet the king's son on her way to town. It is her friend, the gooseherd, who assumes the role of fairy godmother in this retelling.

13.90 Johnston, Tony, adapter. **The Badger and the Magic Fan: A Japanese Folktale.** Illustrated by Tomie dePaola. G .P. Putnam's Sons/Whitebird Books, 1990. ISBN 0-399-21945-5. 28p. 4–8 (est.).

In this adaptation of a Japanese folktale, an impish badger steals a magic fan from the *tengu* (goblin children) and makes a beautiful girl's nose grow. Many try to shrink it, but only the badger succeeds. Her grateful father prepares a wedding feast, but when the badger overeats and falls asleep, the tengu appear and make the badger's nose reach the sky. The badger's fate is depicted in brilliantly colored, flowing line illustrations by Tomie dePaola.

13.91 Johnston, Tony. **The Cowboy and the Black-Eyed Pea.** Illustrated by Warren Ludwig. G. P. Putnam's Sons, 1992. ISBN 0-399-22330-4. 32p. 4–8.

In a Texas version of "The Princess and the Pea," beautiful Farethee Well is advised by her dying father to give her hand in marriage to only a *real* cowboy—instead of one who loves her solely for her longhorn herd. Suitors come from hither and yon to court her, so Farethee Well must devise a test for a real cowboy. She puts a black-eyed pea beneath each suitor's saddle blanket, since only a real cowboy would be sorely troubled by a pea. Illustrations are the colors of the plains.

13.92 Karlin, Barbara, reteller. **Cinderella.** Illustrated by James Marshall. Little, Brown, 1989. ISBN 0-316-54654-2. 32p. 5–8 (est.).

Although the text of this English folktale keeps a straight face, James Marshall's illustrations are out of control. Cinderella, barefooted, with lolling tongue, struggles under chores and dust. Her father is a caricature of Marshall himself, but the stepfamily spoofs painted, pinched, plumed, and bedecked feminine pulchritude. When Cinderella is sent to fetch two lizards, the poor girl carries them at arm's length, grimacing hysterically. Generous and forgiving, this Cinderella finds lords of the court for her stepsisters to wed, and moves the fairy god-mother into the castle.

13.93 Kellogg, Steven, reteller. **Jack and the Beanstalk.** Illustrated by Steven Kellogg. Morrow Junior Books, 1991. ISBN 0-688-10251-4. 48p. All ages.

From the first endpaper in which a hapless pirate crew is sunk by a hoary ogre riding a hurricane, readers know how Jack's nemesis comes by his treasures. Steven Kellogg's retelling of this favorite English tale is salted with the language of Joseph Jacobs's 1889 version, but the wit and energy are Kellogg's own. Both ogre and wife are frightfully hilarious, and new discoveries in the art are possible with each rereading.

13.94 Kimmel, Eric A. **Bearhead: A Russian Folktale.** Illustrated by Charles Mikolaycak. Holiday House, 1991. ISBN 0-8234-0902-3. 26p. 4–8 (est.).

Bearhead's doltish efforts seem sure to lead to disaster, but the gentle foundling, with the body of a man and the head of a bear, always manages to triumph. In this adaptation of a classic Russian folktale, Bearhead fearlessly tackles his job at the palace of a wicked witch, Madame Hexaba, and naively manages to outwit her. The vivid watercolor and colored-pencil illustrations are filled with character and gusto.

13.95 Kimmel, Eric A., reteller. **Boots and His Brothers: A Norwegian Tale.** Illustrated by Kimberly Bulcken Root. Holiday House, 1992. ISBN 0-8234-0886-8. 32p. 6–10 (est.).

Eric Kimmel's version of *Boots and His Brothers* is a storyteller's version in unadorned text that nevertheless evokes rich visual images. Three brothers—"Peter, who was rough and rude," "Paul, who was rude and rough," and Boots, who was neither—set out to seek their fortunes. Only Boots is kind to a beggar woman, and it is from her that his good fortune and magic stem. The illustrations are darkly expressive, making for a good contrast with Claire Martin's golden *Boots and the Glass Mountain*.

13.96 Kimmel, Eric A., reteller. **Nanny Goat and the Seven Little Kids.** Illustrated by Janet Stevens. Holiday House, 1990. ISBN 0-8234-0789-6. 28p. 5–9.

A thoroughly modern version of the Brothers Grimm tale means the seven little kids own skateboards, Walkmen, and tricycles, and wear, variantly, rompers, diapers, and jams. But Nanny Goat is as caring and cautioning as ever when she must leave her kids home alone, and the eye-patched wolf (whose T-shirt reads "Big and Bad") is every bit as devious as his predecessors. In charcoal swirls of unkempt fur and energy, he bursts through the borders of the fun-filled illustrations and nearly off the pages before he gets his just desserts.

13.97 Kirstein, Lincoln, reteller. **Puss in Boots.** Illustrated by Alain Vaës. Little, Brown, 1992. ISBN 0-316-89506-7. 32p. 3–7 (est.).

Lincoln Kirstein's retelling of this old French tale of loyal, clever Puss and his lucky master is accompanied by paintings worthy of the marquis' ancestral hall. Polished boots, gleaming marble, lace-edged velvets, rich tapestries, and gold filigree in the Versailles-like settings contrast with the rustic scenes of country peasant life. Puss, looking very much a cat despite his boots, outwits an ogre, tricks a king, marries off his master, and ensures golden boots for himself.

13.98 Krensky, Stephen. **The Missing Mother Goose.** Illustrated by Chris Demarest. Doubleday, 1991. ISBN 0-385-26274-4. 48p. 5–8.

Stephen Krensky fleshes out the stories that lie behind the nonsense in Mother Goose rhymes, providing background and filling the gaps. If the nonsensical has not been made totally sensical, it is at least made entertaining and fun. Included are expanded versions of "Old King Cole," "Jack Be Nimble," "Little Miss Muffet," and four others. Miss Muffet's tale seems the most plausible of all: despising curds and whey, she seizes the opportunity provided by a passing spider, feigns fear, and dumps her bowl. Colorful, cartoon drawings accompany the retellings.

13.99 Langley, Jonathan, reteller. **Rumpelstiltskin.** Illustrated by Jonathan Langley. HarperCollins, 1992. ISBN 0-06-020199-1. 32p. 4–8 (est.).

Jonathan Langley gives his retelling of this popular tale a queen named Ruby, a leprechaun-like Rumpelstiltskin, and a bit of poetic justice. For readers who can never understand why the miller's daughter could possibly marry a king who has threatened to feed her to the Royal Crocodiles, there is a somewhat-welcome twist when the king himself falls into the crocodile pool. Illustrations are cheery and tongue-in-cheek, as is this version of the text. Notice the female messenger who overhears the name and saves the royal offspring.

13.100   Lester, Julius. **Further Tales of Uncle Remus: The Misadventures of Brer Rabbit, Brer Fox, Brer Wolf, the Doodang, and Other Creatures.** Illustrated by Jerry Pinkney. Dial Books, 1990. ISBN 0-8037-0611-1. 160p. All ages.

Julius Lester's retellings of thirty-three Uncle Remus classics have humor, grit, and authenticity. The tales are told in an African American dialect; the language is direct, rolling, and spiced with modern allusions. Jerry Pinkney's illustrations for these tales of predation and trickery are so well crafted and detailed that the human behaviors of the animals ring true.

13.101   Lester, Julius. **How Many Spots Does a Leopard Have? and Other Tales.** Illustrated by David Shannon. Scholastic Hardcover Books, 1989. ISBN 0-590-41973-0. 72p. 5–8.

Julius Lester offers readers a varied and unusual collection of twelve folktales based on African and Jewish stories, explaining such diverse occurrences as why dogs chase cats and why monkeys live in trees. Lester has crafted these retellings with care, altering or combining stories to make them more effective for American readers. David Shannon's richly colored paintings match the tone of the stories, varying from reverent to humorous to bizarre to melancholy. The lush cover illustration recalls images of Kipling's *Just So Stories.* Author's notes explain the origins of the tales.

13.102   Ludwig, Warren, adapter. **Old Noah's Elephants: An Israeli Folktale.** Illustrated by Warren Ludwig. G. P. Putnam's Sons/Whitebird Books, 1991. ISBN 0-399-22256-1. 28p. 4–8.

In this adaptation of an Israeli folktale, Noah is frustrated when he can't stop the elephants from guzzling the food supply. Eventually, their combined weight tilts the ark. With God's help, Noah finds an outrageous solution, setting all the animals in action on one colorful page after another, until the mouse scares the elephants in opposite directions. Clear, vivid pictures reflect the humor of the situation.

13.103   Marshall, James, reteller. **Hansel and Gretel.** Illustrated by James Marshall. Dial Books for Young Readers, 1990. ISBN 0-8037-0828-9. 32p. 4–8.

James Marshall's retelling of this Brothers Grimm tale is a blend of pathos and humor, of modernisms ("The horrid witch roasted to a regular crisp") and classic fare ("Nibble, nibble, little mousie . . . "), of the fear of abandonment and the courage of

B.

A.

C.

A. *The Rainbow People* by Laurence Yep; illustrated by David Weisner (see 13.150).
B. *Beauty and the Beast* retold and illustrated by Jan Brett (see 13.47).   **C.** *Elfwyn's Saga* told and illustrated by David Wisniewski (see 13.147).

A.

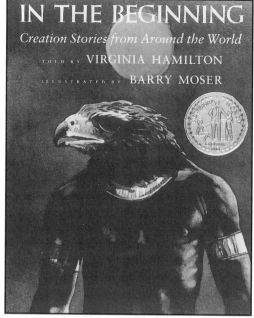

B.

C.

D.

A. *The Samurai's Daughter: A Japanese Legend* retold by Robert D. San Souci; illustrated by Stephen T. Johnson (see 13.122). **B.** *In the Beginning: Creation Stories from Around the World* by Virginia Hamilton; illustrated by Barry Moser (see 13.166). **C.** *Sundiata: Lion King of Mali* retold and illustrated by David Wisniewski (see 13.188). **D.** *Moon Rope: A Peruvian Folktale* by Lois Ehlert (see 13.71).

circumstances. Avoiding the term *wicked stepmother*, Marshall refers to the first villainess as simply the woodcutter's wife, while the witch is a Viola Swamp look-alike, festooned in yards of red. The dialogue begs to be read aloud.

13.104 Martin, Claire, reteller. **Boots and the Glass Mountain.** Illustrated by Gennady Spirin. Dial Books, 1992. ISBN 0-8037-1111-5. 32p. 6–10 (est.).

In a beautifully designed edition, gold-toned medieval tapestries hang suspended from wooden frames, retelling a Norwegian tale of knights, kings, and fair maidens. Brave Boots, youngest of a farmer's three sons, is able, with the aid of a gift from his dying mother, to protect his father's crops from troll magic and to tame three noble crop-munching steeds. The steeds, in turn, help Boots to climb the perilous glass mountain and claim the hand of the princess.

13.105 Mayer, Marianna. **The Prince and the Princess: A Bohemian Fairy Tale.** Illustrated by Jacqueline Rogers. Bantam Skylark Books, 1989. ISBN 0-553-05843-6. 64p. 8–12 (est.).

A brave prince knows his heart belongs to the princess in his dreams. But alas! She and her castle are the victims of a cruel sorcerer who has turned them all to stone. Setting out to rescue the princess, the prince meets a trio of super-hero misfits—Tall, Large, and Sure-eyes. With their allegiance and their particular gifts, the prince foils the sorcerer and rescues the princess, thus demonstrating the advantage of the "misfits'" different abilities. Castle, dragon, and villain are fairy-tale true in vibrant paintings.

13.106 Mayer, Marianna, reteller. **Twelve Dancing Princesses.** Illustrated by K. Y. Craft. Morrow Junior Books, 1989. ISBN 0-688-02026-7. 38p. 8–12 (est.).

In this classic Brothers Grimm tale, the satin dancing slippers of twelve enchanted princesses mysteriously wear out each night as the princesses "sleep." Suitor after suitor attempts to solve the mystery and thereby claim the hand of a princess, but each vanishes in the night. The simple gardener, Peter, gains the gift of invisibility with the aid of a fairy-godmother character, and that gift, along with true love, breaks the spell. Elegantly decorated borders, illuminations, and radiant period paintings lend formality to the book's design. *Notable 1989 Children's Trade Books in the Field of Social Studies.*

13.107 McAllister, Angela. **The Enchanted Flute.** Illustrated by Margaret Chamberlain. Delacorte Press, 1991. ISBN 0-385-30327-0. 26p. 4–8 (est.).

Queen Pernickety is even fussier than her name. She has to have the best of everything and wants no competitors. When the goldsmith makes a flute with magical powers as a gift for the princess, the queen learns her lessons the hard way. Busy, bright, and boisterous illustrations dazzle the eye and add flourish to a humorous tale.

13.108 McDermott, Gerald. **Zomo the Rabbit: A Trickster Tale from West Africa.** Illustrated by Gerald McDermott. Harcourt Brace Jovanovich, 1992. ISBN 0-15-299967-1. 32p. 4–8.

Through the oral traditions of West African folklore come the tales of tricksters who triumph over larger powers through wit and guile. Graphic artist Gerald McDermott renders one of these tricksters, Zomo the Rabbit in an African dashiki, bouncing across brilliant pages filled with fiery sun colors and geometric images and performing tasks of courage given by the Sky God in exchange for the wisdom that Zomo seeks. Children may enjoy comparing Zomo with Brer Rabbit or Anansi tales.

13.109 Miller, Moira. **The Moon Dragon.** Illustrated by Ian Deuchar. Dial Books for Young Readers, 1989. ISBN 0-8037-0566-2. 28p. 4–8.

Ling Po is so boastful that he makes fun of others' efforts to fly kites, claiming that he can build a kite that can fly to the moon. When his latest boast spreads through the village and to the emperor, he is forced to fulfill his promise. Full-page, evocative paintings express the feelings of Ling Po and the villagers as the story develops in an unexpected way.

13.110 Montresor, Beni. **The Witches of Venice.** Illustrated by Beni Montresor. Doubleday, 1989. ISBN 0-385-26-355-4. 32p. 3–8.

A magical plant turns into a small boy after the sun warms it. However, kept alone in a garden and ostracized by the king, the flower-plant boy is lonely. When he hears that the Witches of Venice have imprisoned a flower-plant girl, he escapes from the locked kitchen garden, hidden in a magic pigeon. Flat, scratchy watercolor and ink drawings depict the flower-plant boy's encounters with dragons, ogres, and finally a ballroom full of witches to find and rescue his new friend.

13.111 Morgan, Pierr. **The Turnip: An Old Russian Folktale.** Illustrated by Pierr Morgan. Philomel Books, 1990. ISBN 0-399-22229-4. 29p. 4–8.

A large purple turnip is ready to be harvested, but Farmer Dedoushka finds that he can't pull it out of the ground. One by one, other members of the family come to help until, finally, a tiny field mouse provides the extra "muscle" that extricates the giant turnip. In this retelling, the cast of characters reflects the traditions of Old Russia in both name and dress. Full-page resist illustrations, created with gouache and India ink, bring this traditional folktale to life once again.

13.112 Morris, Ann, reteller. **The Cinderella Rebus Book.** Illustrated by Ljiljana Rylands. Orchard Books, 1989. ISBN 0-531-08361-6. 32p. 4–8.

The enjoyment of this version of "Cinderella" lies less with the familiarity of the French folktale and more with Ljiljana Rylands's tiny, precise, and whimsical rebus drawings. Children may want to try their hand at creating their own "rebus words" for other folktales. This edition, billed for beginners, could be an interesting variation for the classroom teacher who collects versions of this tale.

13.113 Nesbit, E. **Melisande.** Illustrated by P. J. Lynch. Harcourt Brace Jovanovich, 1989. ISBN 0-15-253164-5. 41p. 6–10 (est.).

Cursed at her christening by an evil fairy, Melisande grows up beautiful but bald. When granted one wish, she asks for golden hair that grows an inch a day. The princess is then plagued with problems of a wish fulfilled, but these are resolved through the determination of a dashing prince. The complex plot of this hundred-year-old fairy tale is complemented by expressive depictions of Melisande and her uncontrollable hair.

13.114 Ormerod, Jan, and David Lloyd, retellers. **The Frog Prince.** Illustrated by Jan Ormerod. Lothrop, Lee and Shepard Books, 1990. ISBN 0-688-09569-0. 32p. 5–8.

In this enchanting Brothers Grimm tale, a princess, held to her promise, helps to transform a frog into a handsome prince. Jan Ormerod frames text and art into pleasing pages with understated colors and flowing lines, giving life, and even humor, to the court in this classic happily-ever-after fairy tale.

13.115 Page, P. K., reteller. **The Traveling Musicians of Bremen.** Illustrated by Kady MacDonald Denton. Little, Brown/Joy Street Books, 1992. ISBN 0-316-68836-3. 32p. 3–10 (est.).

Obsolescence is still a theme, but P. K. Page sets this retelling of the Brothers Grimm tale in the present, where, quite naturally, it's a new red truck that makes a donkey no longer needed. Runaway Donkey meets a "down in the mouth" dog, a ragtag cat, and a rooster in danger of the chopping block. Together, they discover robbers in the woods. But these robbers are also modern-day characters—males and females, some a bit punk. Children may enjoy comparing the dialogue in this version with other retellings.

13.116 Perrault, Charles. **Puss in Boots.** Illustrated by Fred Marcellino. Farrar, Straus and Giroux, 1990. ISBN 0-374-36158-4. 32p. 6 and up (est.).

The intrepid Puss, who makes his poverty-stricken master wealthy through his own cunning, is content to play a supporting role in Fred Marcellino's period paintings. In scenes of hazy summer days, of rounded peasants and cobblestone streets, and of vain royals and courtly scenes, Marcellino interprets the cat as cat-sized, yet his crafty plans are delivered with humor, spirit, and innovative perspectives. Spread the dust jacket out for a dashing Puss à la musketeer in plumed red hat and frill. *ALA Notable Children's Book, 1991; Caldecott Honor Book, 1991.*

13.117 Rappaport, Doreen, reteller. **The Journey of Meng: A Chinese Legend.** Illustrated by Yang Ming-Yi. Dial Books for Young Readers, 1991. ISBN 0-8037-0896-3. 30p. 4–10 (est.).

When the emperor presses Meng's scholar-husband into service building the Great Wall, Meng travels into the bitter North to help him. Magic aids her in her travels, but she finds her husband already dead. Her attempt to bury him awakens the wrath of the emperor, whose hatred and lust she ultimately defeats. This tale of a woman's strength and the power of freedom over tyrannical might presents scenes of traditional China depicted with ink-line detail and watercolor-wash backgrounds. *Notable 1991 Children's Trade Books in the Field of Social Studies.*

13.118 Rayevsky, Inna, reteller. **The Talking Tree: An Old Italian Tale.** Illustrated by Robert Rayevsky. G. P. Putnam's Sons, 1990. ISBN 0-399-21631-6. 30p. 4–8.

Long ago, a king who collects rare and beautiful things is told of an amazing Talking Tree. He resolves to add it to his collection, only to discover that the tree is actually a beautiful princess under the spell of a wicked witch. To save the princess, the king must confront an ogre, battle the witch, and break the magic spell. Period illustrations add bold color and humor to this Italian folktale.

13.119 Rounds, Glen. **Three Little Pigs and the Big Bad Wolf.** Illustrated by Glen Rounds. Holiday House, 1992. ISBN 0-8234-0923-6. 32p. 3–8 (est.).

Created with thick, scratchy pen outlines, scribbly crayon bodies, and the tiniest of legs, the little pigs meet the scrawny big bad wolf in Glen Rounds's version with some variants: First, these pigs don't buy their building materials; they adapt ramshackle heaps. Even the brick house is an abandoned structure to be claimed. Second, there are definitely piggies for lunch, and a wolf for dinner. Bold text varies in size so the reader will know just how loudly to interpret the action.

13.120 Sanfield, Steve. **The Adventures of High John the Conqueror.** Illustrated by John Ward. Orchard Books/Richard Jackson Books, 1989. ISBN 0-531-08407-8. 107p. 8 and up.

Steve Sanfield compares High John, a nineteenth-century trickster hero of African Americans, to Brer Rabbit, who could outfox Brer Fox, a symbol of witless power. In these sixteen retellings of High John legends, John's triumphs prove consistently funny and audacious. From predicting the future to proving that his master's walking stick has three "ends," John's stories reflect an inextinguishable human spirit. Black-and-white drawings accompany the tales.

13.121 San Souci, Robert D. **The Boy and the Ghost.** Illustrated by J. Brian Pinkney. Simon and Schuster Books for Young Readers, 1989. ISBN 0-671-67176-6. 32p. 6–10 (est.).

Thomas is one of seven children born to a hard-working but poor African American family. To contribute to the family income, Thomas goes out into the world and shows kindness to a stranger who leads him to a house with a hidden treasure and a frightening ghost. Courageous and kind, Thomas succeeds in making friends with the ghost and returning to his family with the treasure. Double-page watercolored pencil drawings bring alive this provocative folktale.

13.122 San Souci, Robert D., reteller. **The Samurai's Daughter: A Japanese Legend.** Illustrated by Stephen T. Johnson. Dial Books for Young Readers, 1992. ISBN 0-8037-1136-0. 32p. 6–10 (est.).

Robert San Souci retells a medieval Japanese folktale of a samurai's beautiful and courageous daughter, Tokoyo, who was trained in the ways of a samurai warrior herself. Pastel paintings give a quiet radiance as the young noblewoman also learns the trade of the *amas*, the women divers who harvest shellfish. When her loyal father is banished by the ruler whom he served, Tokoyo sets out to rescue him, battling a sea serpent and eventually reversing the curse on the ruler through her courage, discipline, and skills.

13.123 San Souci, Robert D., reteller. **The Six Swans.** Illustrated by Daniel San Souci. Simon and Schuster Books for Young Readers, 1988. ISBN 0-671-65848-4. 32p. 4–8.

Bewitched by a sorceress, six brothers are turned into swans in this retelling of a German folktale. Their only chance for rescue lies with their sister, who must neither talk nor laugh for six years. In addition, she must sew a shirt of rare dew-flowers for each brother. Ultimately evil is vanquished, and the brothers happily revert to their human form. Colors in Daniel San Souci's full-page, watercolor illustrations are especially striking: deep cobalt blues, bright kelly greens, vibrant golds, and rich russets provide a visual feast for all ages.

13.124 San Souci, Robert D., reteller. **The Tsar's Promise: A Russian Tale.** Illustrated by Lauren Mills. Philomel Books, 1992. ISBN 0-399-21581-6. 32p. 4 and up.

Long ago, a tsar, captured by a demon, barters for his freedom by promising that which awaits him at home. Sadly, while the tsar is away, the tsaritsa gives birth to a son. When the demon finally claims his prize, young Ivan relies on the magic of a beautiful, enchanted maiden to perform tasks to ensure his escape from the demon. An unusual combination of magic, cunning, and religion combine for a happy ending. Lauren Mills's watercolors are handsome, bordered scenes and portraits for this retelling of a Russian folktale from Andrew Lang's *Green Fairy Book*.

13.125 San Souci, Robert D., reteller. **The White Cat: An Old French Fairy Tale.** Illustrated by Gennady Spirin. Orchard Books, 1990. ISBN 0-531-08409-4. 32p. 4–8.

On a journey to fulfill his father's requests, a young prince meets the beautiful White Cat, whose magical powers aid the prince in his quest. When the White Cat is threatened by an evil dwarf-wizard, the prince uses his courage and love to destroy the beast, an act which later changes the White Cat into a lovely woman. Finely detailed medieval-style paintings by Gennady Spirin distinguish Robert San Souci's version of this old French tale.

13.126 Scheffler, Ursel (translated by Amy Gelman). **The Giant Apple.** Illustrated by Silke Brix-Henker. Carolrhoda Books, 1990. ISBN 0-87614-413-X. 26p. 6–10 (est.).

The farmers of Beet Valley always win the grand prize for vegetables at the Harvest Festival. But the mayor of the neighboring town of Appleville has a plan: Appleville citizens will work together to grow the biggest apple of all time, no matter what the sacrifices. However, their award-winning efforts lead to neglected crops and a lack of food, and Appleville learns an important lesson about single-mindedness. Full-page watercolor paintings illustrate this cautionary tale from Germany. Children may note and want to talk about the environmental issues that are raised.

13.127 Schwartz, Alvin, compiler and reteller. **Scary Stories 3: More Tales to Chill Your Bones.** Illustrated by Stephen Gammell. HarperCollins, 1991. ISBN 0-06-021795-2. 115p. 9 and up.

In the tradition of *Scary Stories to Tell in the Dark* and *More Scary Stories to Tell in the Dark*, this third volume recounts tales of mystery and unexplained events collected from folklore. The stories are reminiscent of those that kids have always told around campfires or at slumber parties about moving objects, the reappearance of the dead, or witch's spells. Stephen Gammell's drawings are appropriately eerie. The "Notes and Sources" section gives the background of each of the over eighty stories as well as suggestions for further reading.

13.128 Schwartz, Howard, and Barbara Rush, compilers and retellers. **The Diamond Tree: Jewish Tales from around the World.** Illustrated by Uri Shulevitz. HarperCollins, 1991. ISBN 0-06-025243-X. 120p. 8 and up (est.).

The richness of Jewish storytelling shines through a collection of fifteen stories in this brightly illustrated volume. Each story is told in plain language at a brisk pace, its origins are identified, and it is further glossed in a "Sources and Commentary" section at the end of the book. The collection's title comes from a Moroccan tale in which gentle Nissim discovers that what looks to be a tree full of diamonds is actually a tree of enchanted children who can be rescued by foiling their enchantress.

13.129 Scieszka, Jon. **The Stinky Cheese Man and Other Fairly Stupid Tales.** Illustrated by Lane Smith. Viking Penguin, 1992. ISBN 0-670-84487-X. 32p. All ages.

Jon Scieszka explodes the format of the traditional picture book in these tales. Reviewers have used terms like *zany* and *madcap* in reference to this collection of revisionist fairy tales with titles like "The Really Ugly Duckling" and "The Princess and the Bowling Ball." Narrator Jack (of beanstalk fame) and an obnoxious Little Red Hen even bring the book's format features to a conscious level, with typeface, endpapers, and page layouts maximized in this riotous retelling. *Caldecott Honor Book, 1993.*

13.130 Stanley, Diane. **Fortune.** Illustrated by Diane Stanley. Morrow Junior Books, 1990. ISBN 0-688-07211-9. 32p. 6 and up.

Omar, a poor Persian boy, seeks riches in order to marry Sunny, the clever girl from a neighboring farm. In a folk narrative illustrated with Persian miniatures, Omar's quest leads him to a dancing tiger, which he names Fortune. When the tiger's talents make Omar rich, he sets his sights on a grander bride—a princess. Through a magical twist of events, Omar not only finds a princess but serves as the unwitting instrument of her reunion with her true prince. The wiser Omar returns to his faithful Sunny.

13.131 Stevens, Janet, reteller. **The Bremen Town Musicians.** Illustrated by Janet Stevens. Holiday House, 1992. ISBN 0-8234-0939-2. 32p. 4–8 (est.).

Although there is undoubtedly competition for the scuzziest, scraggliest animals in the various versions of the Brothers Grimm tale about the Bremen Town band, Janet Stevens's entry is certainly a contender. Her cat is reminiscent of Berkeley Breathed's Bill the Cat, her donkey is a gangly mass of matted hair and missing teeth, her dog is a woeful skin-and-bones hound, and her flat-combed chicken is molting. But together, and in a ferocious hullabaloo, they successfully drive off an equally bedraggled gang of robbers.

13.132 Stewig, John Warren, reteller. **Stone Soup.** Illustrated by Margot Tomes. Holiday House, 1991. ISBN 0-8234-0863-9. 32p. 4–8.

A specialist in period drawings, Margaret Tomes offers plenty to dwell on in John Warren Stewig's version of this French tale of resourcefulness. Readers more familiar with soldiers in the lead roles may be surprised to find a girl, Grethel, as the protagonist. Famished and unable to procure even a heel of bread from excuse-laden villagers, Grethel finds a smooth stone and hatches the soup-from-a-stone plot. Villagers contribute cabbages, potatoes, carrots, and even a shank of beef for the best stone soup ever.

13.133 Tadjo, Véronique, reteller. **Lord of the Dance: An African Retelling.** Illustrated by Véronique Tadjo. J. B. Lippincott, 1989. ISBN 0-397-32352-2. 26p. 5–9.

The Senufo people are farmers who live in the Ivory Coast of West Africa and who believe in invisible spirits hidden in nature. During ceremonies the spirits are represented by sacred wooden masks. The "Lord of the Dance" is a mask's song, which conveys the beliefs that guide Senufo tradition and modern life. It is based on an English hymn and features the regular beat of African drums: "Tom-tom-tom-tom-tom." Senufo art has been replicated in style, but not in medium, with bright colors replacing brown vegetable ink. An endnote explains the role of masks in Senufo culture. *Notable 1989 Children's Trade Books in the Field of Social Studies.*

13.134 Tejima. **Ho-Limlim: A Rabbit Tale from Japan.** Illustrated by Tejima. Philomel Books, 1990. ISBN 0-399-22156-5. 32p. 4–8 (est.).

Woodcuts shaded with the tones of Hokkaido, the northernmost island of Japan and home of the Ainu people, provide the setting for this ancient Ainu tale of an aging rabbit who journeys from his home to see the world a final time before recognizing fully that his eyes are bad enough to play tricks on him and that he should stay near home. "Ho-limlim" is the light running sound of the rabbit, bounding as he did in his youth, across the fields toward the sea.

13.135 Thomson, Peggy, reteller. **The Brave Little Tailor.** Illustrated by James Warhola. Simon and Schuster Books for Young Readers, 1992. ISBN 0-671-73736-8. 32p. 6–10 (est.).

In a busy medieval village, a little tailor swats some flies buzzing about his jam pot, killing seven of them in one blow. Proud of his strength, he embroiders *seven at one blow* on a cloth, which he then stitches into a vest, announcing his accomplishment to the whole world. Advertising, of course, pays. With a bit of bravado, some trickery, and a lot of braggadocio, the plain little tailor in this German folktale conquers a giant, marries a princess, and improves his lot.

13.136 Torre, Betty L., reteller. **The Luminous Pearl: A Chinese Folktale.** Illustrated by Carol Inouye. Orchard Books, 1990. ISBN 0-531-08490-6. 32p. 4–8.

Although the Dragon King offers likely suitors for his daughter, because she wants a mate who is honest and brave, she therefore finds reasons to reject each suitor. So a clever test of honesty and bravery is devised by the king's counselors. Through the use of realistic detail, Carol Inouye's illustrations paint a vivid portrait of the undersea world that two brothers experience in their quest to prove their honesty and bravery by finding the luminous pearl in this Chinese folktale.

13.137 Vá, Leong (translated by James Anderson). **A Letter to the King.** Illustrated by Leong Vá. HarperCollins, 1991. ISBN 0-06-020070-7. 32p. 5–8.

When a Chinese physician is sentenced to jail because of the death of an influential patient, he bemoans his bad fortune of having only daughters and no sons to rescue him. Desperate, youngest daughter Ti Ying writes and delivers a letter to the king. Moved by the letter's poignancy, the king releases her father, who gratefully acknowledges the value of daughters. In this two-hundred-year-old true story, childlike Chinese murals are banded with Chinese characters that also tell the tale.

13.138 Voake, Charlotte, compiler. **The Three Little Pigs, and Other Favourite Nursery Stories.** Illustrated by Charlotte Voake. Candlewick Press, 1992. ISBN 1-56402-118-1. 92p. 3–7 (est.).

Ten fairy tales, ranging from the familiar ("Red Riding Hood," "The Three Bears") to the not-so-familiar ("Lazy Jack," "Mr. Vinegar"), have been brought together in an anthology specially designed for young children. The simple text, printed in bold type, is supplemented with lively watercolor and ink illustrations.

13.139 Volkmer, Jane Anne, reteller (translated by Lori Ann Schatschneider). **Song of the Chirimia: A Guatemalan Folktale/La Musica de la Chirimia: Folklore Guatemalteco.** Illustrated by Jane Anne Volkmer. Carolrhoda Books, 1990. ISBN 0-87614-423-7. 37p. 4–9.

Only one suitor, Black Feather, catches the eye of the Princess Moonlight, daughter of King Clear Sky. But to wed the princess, Black Feather must learn to sing like the birds. Aided by the Great Spirit, Black Feather finds an instrument—the chirimia—that joins the harmony of voice and song to produce the music that wins his beloved. Illustrated with folk-art drawings of characters modeled after ancient Mayan stone carvings, this Guatemalan folktale, told in both English and Spanish, explains the origin of the chirimia.

13.140 Wahl, Jan. **Little Eight John.** Illustrated by Wil Clay. Lodestar Books, 1992. ISBN 0-525-67367-9. 32p. 5–8.

Little Eight John was a boy as mean as mean there was. Why, whatever his mama told him, he did just the opposite: "Don't kick at the toad frogs," his mother told him, "or you'll bring bad luck on us." But Little Eight John did just that. In a tale packed full of North Carolina folk superstitions, this African American boy changes his ways when "Old Raw Head Bloody Bones" shows up in his dreams. Wil Clay's acrylics offer a lush countryside and warm family relationships.

13.141 Wells, Rosemary. **The Little Lame Prince.** Illustrated by Rosemary Wells. Dial Books for Young Readers, 1990. ISBN 0-8037-0789-4. 32p. 4–8.

Rosemary Wells creates an interesting array of memorable characters in her adaptation of a classic tale by Dinah Maria Mulock Craik about the courageous young prince who must rescue his kingdom from the clutches of his evil uncle. With the help of a magical cape from his tiny fairy godmother, the little lame prince becomes a king. Wells tells her story by use of unique animal characters, such as a pig for Prince Francisco, that humorously embody the qualities of good and evil. Spanish names and phrases, along with watercolor paintings, add to this timeless tale.

13.142 Wilde, Oscar. **The Happy Prince.** Illustrated by Ed Young. Simon and Schuster Books for Young Readers, 1989. ISBN 0-671-67754-3. 32p. 6–8.

High atop a pedestal rests a gilded statue of a prince. Once complacent about pleasures in his life, the prince now views for the first time the suffering of the people whom he ruled. Moved by what he sees, he persuades a migrating swallow to serve as his messenger and to deliver his golden, jeweled exterior to the needy. The multiperspective paintings of Caldecott-winner Ed Young give sweeping overviews and intimate closeups. Texture, light, and shades work together to give impressions of sun-kissed days and chilling cold.

13.143 Willard, Nancy, reteller. **Beauty and the Beast.** Illustrated by Barry Moser. Harcourt Brace Jovanovich, 1992. ISBN 0-15-206052-9. 80p. All ages.

Against satiny, cream-colored paper, Barry Moser's dark wood-cuts give a Gothic flavor to this favorite French tale, even though Nancy Willard's version is set in nineteenth-century New York City and the Hudson River Valley. When Beauty's father is saved by an enchanted Beast, it is Beauty, whose values and resource-fulness are so different from those of her haughty sisters, who offers her own life in repayment. Willard's well-researched story is fresh, beautifully descriptive, and complete with well-developed characters.

13.144 Windham, Sophie. **Read Me a Story: A Child's Book of Favorite Tales.** Illustrated by Sophie Windham. Scholastic Hardcover Books, 1991. ISBN 0-590-44950-8. 96p. 3–8.

This collection of well-known tales, with its large print, simple wording, and warm, full-colored illustrations, is appropriate for lap-time reading. Fifteen stories are included, none of them longer than five or ten minutes in the reading, and most are well-loved tales (such as "The Gingerbread Boy," "Little Red Riding Hood," and "The Ugly Duckling"). From full-page to small cameos, Sophie Windham's illustrations are like folk-art tapestries.

13.145 Winthrop, Elizabeth, adapter. **Vasilissa the Beautiful: A Russian Folktale.** Illustrated by Alexander Koshkin. HarperCollins, 1991. ISBN 0-06-021663-8. 38p. 6–11 (est.).

A best-loved tale of Russia that combines motifs from "Cinderella" and "Hansel and Gretel" is represented with a cross-cultural blend of talents. Elizabeth Winthrop, an American writer, and Alexander Koshkin, a contemporary Russian artist, collaborated to retell the story of the beautiful heroine, her wicked stepmother, two jealous stepsisters, and the magical talisman doll that guides and protects her from the witch, Baba Yaga. Seventeenth-century costumes and settings are richly depicted in double-page paintings that alternate with text.

13.146 Wise, William, reteller. **The Black Falcon: A Tale from the *Decameron*.** Illustrated by Gillian Barlow. Philomel Books, 1990. ISBN 0-399-21676-6. 32p. 5 and up.

The Black Falcon is adapted from a fourteenth-century tale from the *Decameron*, written by Giovanni Boccaccio, the "first great writer of prose in a modern language." It tells of Federigo, the poor but honorable knight who values his only possession, a black peregrine falcon, above all else. When he sacrifices that falcon for love of the beautiful Lady Elena, the knight's decision should prompt good discussion even 650 years later. Gillian Barlow's watercolors are glowing expressions of medieval life. Hillside Italian villas and the accoutrements of plain and sumptuous living are perfect accompaniment to the story.

13.147 Wisniewski, David. **Elfwyn's Saga.** Illustrated by David Wisniewski. Lothrop, Lee and Shepard Books, 1990. ISBN 0-688-09590-9. 32p. 6–9 (est.).

Being cursed by Gorm the Grim means that Anlaf Haraldsson's daughter is born blind and that her family receives a menacing gift. Readers will be charmed not only by a blind daughter who has vision, but by the dramatic, intricate, multilayered cut-paper illustrations. A concluding author's note explains Viking-era references in this good-versus-evil tale based on Icelandic history and legend. *Notable 1990 Children's Trade Books in the Field of Social Studies.*

13.148 Wolkstein, Diane, reteller. **Oom Razoom; or, Go I Know Not Where, Bring Back I Know Not What: A Russian Tale.** Illustrated by Dennis McDermott. Morrow Junior Books, 1991. ISBN 0-688-09417-1. 32p. 4–8 (est.).

In the voice of the storyteller, Diane Wolkstein tells of the amiable Russian archer, Alexis, whose beautiful, wise, and magical wife, Olga, was the envy of the wicked king. Banished by the king to "Go I Know Not Where" and to "Bring Back I Know Not What," Alexis carefully follows Olga's instructions. In traditional storytelling form, the narrator directly addresses the reader: "Was his journey long? Was it short?" Fur hats, rich fabrics, and onion domes give the art a blend of Russian fancy and authenticity to this Russian folktale.

13.149 Yeats, W. B. (compiled by Neil Philip). **Fairy Tales of Ireland.** Illustrated by P. J. Lynch. Delacorte Press, 1990. ISBN 0-385-30249-5. 154p. 10–12 (est.).

Neil Philip's selection of stories from Yeats's two-volume collection of authentic Irish tales offers a broad spectrum of magical beings, foolish mistakes, and fearsome trials. Both silhouettes and pen-and-ink illustrations set the old-fashioned, hearty Irish mood. Yeats's ear for poetry and dialect was superb, so the read-aloud sound is lilting. But it is the fairy lore and the elemental power of the stories themselves that will capture children most completely.

13.150 Yep, Laurence. **The Rainbow People.** Illustrated by David Wiesner. Harper and Row, 1989. ISBN 0-06-026761-7. 194p. 10 and up (est.).

Originally passed down from generation to generation by word of mouth, these twenty Chinese folktales artfully reveal the wisdom of the ages on such topics as fools, love, tricksters, virtues, and vices. For the nineteenth-century Chinese immigrants who settled in America, the familiar stories of magic lands, mountain spirits, and canny dragons offered both solace and entertainment. Discriminating readers will reap similar benefits from these imaginative tales of ancient China. *Boston Globe–Horn Book Honor Book, 1989; Notable 1989 Children's Trade Books in the Field of Social Studies.*

13.151 Yep, Laurence. **Tongues of Jade.** Illustrated by David Wiesner. HarperCollins, 1991. ISBN 0-06-022471-1. 194p. 10 and up (est.).

In presenting seventeen traditional Chinese folktales brought to America by Chinese immigrants and collected by Chinese scholars, Laurence Yep explains that "every storyteller speaks with a tongue of jade, preserving an entire time period." These introspective tales lend insight to Chinese tradition and culture: the stories of magic and family ties always contain a lesson about respect, courage, patience, or some other virtuous quality. Black-and-white watercolor illustrations preview each narrative.

13.152 Young, Ed, translator. **Lon Po Po: A Red-Riding Hood Story from China.** Illustrated by Ed Young. Philomel Books, 1989. ISBN 0-399-21619-7. 32p. 5–9.

It's hard to imagine a better example of the power of language and illustrations in combination. This award-winning picture book belongs in every library. The Chinese version of the "Red Riding Hood" story is powerful in itself, but Ed Young's colorful impressionistic paintings make it even stronger. As translator of the 1000-year-old tale, Young writes sparingly and rhythmically, and allows the Chinese flavor to come through clearly. Children will be mesmerized—first with fear, then with relief. *School Library Journal's Best Books, 1989; Boston Globe–Horn Book Picture Book Award, 1990; Caldecott Medal, 1990; Horn Book Fanfare, 1990.*

13.153 Zimmerman, H. Werner. **Henny Penny.** Illustrated by H. Werner Zimmerman. Scholastic Hardcover Books, 1989. ISBN 0-590-42390-8. 28p. 4–8.

Werner Zimmerman's retelling of this folktale includes all the expected events. Henny Penny's snap decision to rush and tell the king that the sky is falling once again proves to be fatal. As usual, Foxy Loxy convinces Henny Penny and her friends to follow his shortcut to the castle. Henny Penny, Cocky Locky, Ducky Lucky, Goosey Loosey, and Turkey Lurkey soon become dinner for the fox. Humorous, action-packed illustrations from a variety of visual perspectives add to the enjoyment of this tale.

13.154 Zwerger, Lisbeth, compiler (translated by Anthea Bell). **Hans Christian Andersen Fairy Tales.** Illustrated by Lisbeth Zwerger. Picture Book Studio/Michael Neugebauer Books, 1991. ISBN 0-88708-182-7. 32p. 4 and up (est.).

In a tall book (measuring nearly fourteen inches) that allows for abundant white space top and bottom, fifteen full-color paintings accompany eight Hans Christian Andersen tales: "The Sandman," "The Emperor's New Clothes," "The Princess and the Pea," "The Tinderbox," "The Rose Tree Regiment," "The Naughty Boy," "The Jumpers," and "The Little Match Girl." Austrian artist Lisbeth Zwerger, winner of the Hans Christian Andersen Medal, is internationally known for her illustrations of numerous other Andersen stories, as well as for illustrating Aesop's fables and tales from the Brothers Grimm.

Myths and Legends

13.155 Alexander, Ellen. **Llama and the Great Flood: A Folktale from Peru.** Illustrated by Ellen Alexander. Thomas Y. Crowell, 1989. ISBN 0-690-04729-0. 39p. 5–10.

From the high mountains of Peru comes this ancient Andean myth of how a wise llama saves its family from the great flood and helps to bring about the rebirth of a new world. The watercolor illustrations, in light earth tones detailed in ink, help to convey the Andean culture and its respect for nature. Information about the origin of this myth is included in both the introduction and epilogue.

13.156 Anderson, David A./Sankofa. **The Origin of Life on Earth: An African Creation Myth.** Illustrated by Kathleen Atkins Wilson. Sights Productions, 1991. ISBN 0-9629978-5-4. 31p. 3 and up (est.).

Colorful, interpretive, full-page illustrations help to retell the creation myth from Yoruba, an ancient West African culture that once thrived where Nigeria and Benin are today. Long ago, says the myth, all life was in the sky; below was only water. And it was there that Obatala wanted to create the Earth and humans. This traditional folktale captures all the wonder of that ancient time and culture. *Coretta Scott King Award (Illustration), 1993.*

13.157 Belting, Natalia M. **Moon Was Tired of Walking on Air.** Illustrated by Will Hillenbrand. Houghton Mifflin, 1992. ISBN 0-395-53806-8. 48p. 5–10 (est.).

In this collection of fourteen Native American creation myths from South America, Natalia Belting has compiled tales of sun and moon, seasons and weather, man and animals. Stylized paintings evoke images of pre-Columbian art; the language of the storyteller is equally unadorned. The dark earth tones enhance the swirling and disturbing images, interpreting a mystical past. A map locating the origin of various myths makes for a cross-curricular connection.

13.158 Fisher, Leonard Everett. **Cyclops.** Illustrated by Leonard Everett Fisher. Holiday House, 1991. ISBN 0-8234-0891-4. 32p. 7–11.

Odysseus and his Greek ship are blown off course by the gods, so they seek refuge on an island. There, they are victimized by an evil, one-eyed monster, Polyphemus. Odysseus' escape from the cyclops involves extensive violence as well as wit. With proper introduction, this richly illustrated, simply told version can serve children as a preview to the heroic adventure in Homer's epic poem *The Odyssey.* Leonard Everett Fisher's paintings give massive proportions and threatening moods to the island giant.

13.159 Fisher, Leonard Everett. **Jason and the Golden Fleece.** Illustrated by Leonard Everett Fisher. Holiday House, 1990. ISBN 0-8234-0794-2. 30p. 6–10 (est.).

A.

B.

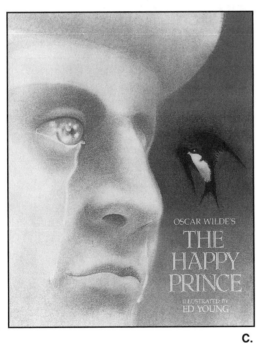

C.

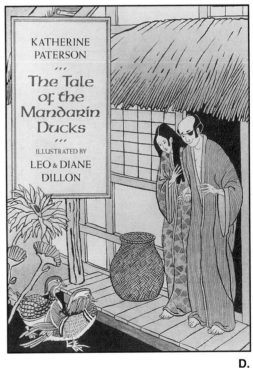

D.

A. *Beauty and the Beast* retold by Nancy Willard; illustrated by Barry Moser (see 13.143). **B.** *Seven Blind Mice* by Ed Young (see 13.11). **C.** *The Happy Prince* by Oscar Wilde; illustrated by Ed Young (see 13.142). **D.** *The Tale of the Mandarin Ducks* by Katherine Paterson; illustrated by Leo and Diane Dillon (see 6.182).

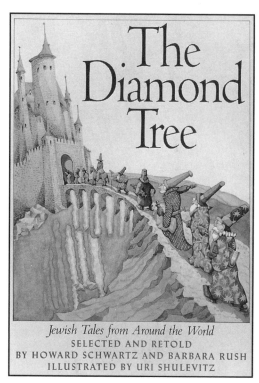

A.

B.

C.

A. *The Diamond Tree: Jewish Tales from around the World* retold by Howard Schwartz and Barbara Rush; illustrated by Uri Shulevitz (see 13.128). **B.** *Ho-Limlim: A Rabbit Tale from Japan* by Tejima (see 13.134). **C.** *Zomo the Rabbit: A Trickster Tale from West Africa* by Gerald McDermott (see 13.108).

In order to return his deposed father to the throne, Jason sets sail on the *Argo* to bring back the golden fleece, which is guarded by a sleepless dragon. Although judiciously retold by Leonard Everett Fisher, the story ends tragically. Adults should be aware of the murder and violence in the tale of Jason and his crew of the Argonauts. But if properly introduced, the tale could serve as a wonderful introduction to Greek mythology for young students.

13.160 Flora. **Feathers like a Rainbow: An Amazon Indian Tale.** Illustrated by Flora. Harper and Row, 1989. ISBN 0-06-021838-X. 22p. 4–8.

Long ago, birds of the Amazon River Valley were much alike—all but hummingbirds had dark feathers. But Jacamin, the gray-winged trumpeter, was not satisfied with his dark feathers and wanted colorful feathers as "beautiful as the rainbow." So Jacamin's mother stole Hummingbird's bowl of colors. Quickly, the other birds bathed themselves in the bright colors, leaving Jacamin with only a dot of purple for his breast feathers, the coloring that all gray-winged trumpeters wear today. Flora's retelling of this Amazon Indian tale is enriched with her bold and exotic illustrations. For a comparison of lavish bird colors, teachers may choose Lois Ehlert's *Feathers for Lunch* as a companion book. *Notable 1989 Children's Trade Books in the Field of Social Studies.*

13.161 Goble, Paul. **Crow Chief: A Plains Indian Story.** Illustrated by Paul Goble. Orchard Books, 1992. ISBN 0-531-08547-3. 32p. 4–7.

Because the white-feathered Crow Chief always warns the buffalo when human hunters approach, the people go hungry. But the magical Falling Star arrives with a plan to silence the raucous bird, and in the end, the people are well fed and the crow has turned black. Paul Goble's intricate illustrations, with power, quiet dignity, and Native American motifs, aptly interpret this pourquoi tale.

13.162 Goble, Paul, reteller. **Iktomi and the Berries: A Plains Indian Story.** Illustrated by Paul Goble. Orchard Books/Richard Jackson Books, 1989. ISBN 0-531-08419-1. 32p. 5–8.

Paul Goble's second tale about Iktomi ("eek-toe-me"), the Plains Indian trickster, is a truly interactive reading experience. Alongside the humorous story of Iktomi's disastrous hunting trip, Goble provides sample responses (set apart by italic lettering) that listeners might inject if the story were being told by a traditional storyteller. Goble's distinctive India ink and watercolor illustrations meld ancient lore into a contemporary, nearly timeless depiction. Teachers might find the book a useful way to introduce Native American storytelling, as well as a means for introducing tricksters as they are represented in literature across cultures.

13.163 Goble, Paul, reteller. **Iktomi and the Ducks: A Plains Indian Story.** Illustrated by Paul Goble. Orchard Books/Richard Jackson Books, 1990. ISBN 0-531-08483-3. 32p. 3–6.

Iktomi the trickster is up to more antics, this time tricking the ducks in the pond so that they can be his roast duck dinner. But the trees and the wind take revenge. While the trees hold Iktomi captive, a coyote gobbles his dinner and plans a trick of his own. In the tradition of Native American storytelling, Goble invites audience participation by screening and italicizing the typeface to indicate logical points for verbal response or reflection on the events.

13.164 Goble, Paul. **Love Flute.** Illustrated by Paul Goble. Bradbury Press, 1992. ISBN 0-02-736261-2. 32p. 6–10 (est.).

According to legend, the Elk People gave their flute to man so that he, like the magnificent bull elk, could attract the woman whom he loved by expressing the divine mystery and beauty of love. In Paul Goble's tale, a young warrior, too shy to tell a beautiful girl that he loves her, is given a flute with which he speaks directly to her heart. Beside detailed paintings of Plains Indians, Goble has carefully sketched authentic love flutes on each page.

13.165 Hamilton, Virginia. **The Dark Way: Stories from the Spirit World.** Illustrated by Lambert Davis. Harcourt Brace Jovanovich, 1990. ISBN 0-15-222340-1. 154p. 8 and up.

In Virginia Hamilton's retelling of myths, legends, and folktales depicting "the spirit world," the award-winning author introduces young readers to stories scary and funny, tricksters wily and stupid, and monsters ferocious and pitiable. Cultures represented in this collection include those of Japan, India, Africa, America, and Ireland. Hamilton concludes each story with a brief "comment" in which she explains the tale's origin, provides additional background information, or describes central motifs. Lambert Davis's vivid acrylics chillingly bring the monsters to life.

13.166 Hamilton, Virginia. **In the Beginning: Creation Stories from around the World.** Illustrated by Barry Moser. Harcourt Brace Jovanovich, 1988. ISBN 0-15-238740-4. 163p. 10 and up.

Hans Christian Andersen-medalist Virginia Hamilton has collected twenty-five creation myths that Barry Moser has enriched with forty-two striking watercolor paintings. Through these myths readers learn how the beginning of humankind has been explained in cultures as diverse as Greece, Iceland, India, Micronesia, Nigeria, Guatemala, and America. Author comments at the end of each story, telling its origin and interpretation, along with an instructive preface, epilogue, and reading list, make this a valuable addition to any collection of children's literature. *ALA Best Book for Young Adults, 1989; ALA Notable Book, 1989; Newbery Honor Book, 1989.*

13.167 Hawkes, Kevin. **His Royal Buckliness.** Illustrated by Kevin Hawkes. Lothrop, Lee and Shepard Books, 1992. ISBN 0-688-11063-0. 32p. 4–8 (est.).

When the giants steal Lord Buckley and carry him off to their frozen lands, they treat him gingerly, but he grows cranky and sends a message to a warmer place. There, loyal Sir Joshua and Sir Jake pack a red-checked bundle and set off to the rescue. Across sparkling snows they reach his Royal Buckliness with "a bag of bullfrogs croaking," bringing spring to the frozen lakeland and setting the giants' kilts to dancing. Illustrations are Scottish plaids, powdery snows, and dusty blues.

13.168 Hodges, Margaret, reteller. **The Kitchen Knight: A Tale of King Arthur.** Illustrated by Trina Schart Hyman. Holiday House, 1990. ISBN 0-8234-0787-X. 32p. 6–10 (est.).

Drawing from Sir Thomas Malory's version of the ancient legends of King Arthur and his knights, as well as from a manuscript discovered in the twentieth century, Margaret Hodges retells "The Tale of Sir Gareth of Orkney," nephew of King Arthur. Gareth, who does not identify himself as the king's kin, works modestly in the kitchen, readying himself for knightly charges, such as battle with the fierce Red Knight and rescue of the fair Linesse. Trina Schart Hyman's paintings are bordered court scenes and medieval pageantry, with text and cameo portraits inset.

13.169 Lattimore, Deborah Nourse. **Why There Is No Arguing in Heaven: A Mayan Myth.** Illustrated by Deborah Nourse Lattimore. Harper and Row, 1989. ISBN 0-06-023718-X. 30p. 8–12 (est.).

Like Deborah Nourse Lattimore's *The Flame of Peace,* this work is a sumptuously illustrated retelling of a Mayan myth. The Creator God challenges other gods to create worshipful beings, but only the Maize God succeeds—creating men and women who kneel before the gods with "voices like the song of a turtle dove." Darkly lush color illustrations are dynamic renderings of Mayan sculptural forms; endpapers, with their carving-to-text translations, make an ancient foreign culture more accessible for North American readers. *Notable 1989 Children's Trade Books in the Field of Social Studies.*

13.170 MacGill-Callahan, Sheila. **And Still the Turtle Watched.** Illustrated by Barry Moser. Dial Books for Young Readers, 1991. ISBN 0-8037-0932-3. 32p. All ages.

Long ago, a turtle was carved into a rock overlooking a river to watch over the Delaware peoples. As the years go by, the Delaware disappear, but the turtle keeps watch as generations of humans slowly make the water brown, the skies heavy, and finally deface the turtle itself. When a kind man recognizes the turtle's importance, he cleans it for display at a botanical garden. Naturalistic watercolor illustrations depict the world's changes as seen by the vigilant turtle.

13.171 Manson, Christopher, reteller. **The Tale of the Marvellous Blue Mouse.** Illustrated by Christopher Manson. Henry Holt, 1992. ISBN 0-8050-1622-8. 32p. 6–10 (est.).

A 1,100-year-old tale is given new audiences through Christopher Manson's retelling in an illuminated text which simulates an ancient manuscript. The legend tells of Charlemagne's appointed Lord Mayor, a man so greedy and so foolish that his town falls into poverty and ruin while he collects expensive baubles for himself. But Charlemagne's faithful friend Isaac teaches the Lord Mayor a lesson using only an ordinary house mouse, some blue paint, a few extraordinary spices, and a keen wit.

13.172 Martin, Claire. **The Race of the Golden Apples.** Illustrated by Leo and Diane Dillon. Dial Books for Young Readers, 1991. ISBN 0-8037-0249-3. 27p. 4–8.

This retelling of the Greek myth of Atalanta is highlighted by Leo and Diane Dillon's full-color paintings reminiscent of medieval tapestries. The plot and its layers of meaning have contemporary resonance: The princess Atalanta is adopted by Diana, the goddess of the hunt, and grows up in the forest, hating the human race for its ravages and her father's misogynistic cruelty. But Atalanta must learn to live among her kind and accept her own humanity, and so she agrees to marry the suitor who can outrun her.

13.173 Martin, Rafe. **The Rough-Face Girl.** Illustrated by David Shannon. G. P. Putnam's Sons, 1992. ISBN 0-399-21859-9. 32p. 4–8.

In this Algonquin "Cinderella" story, a girl whose face is scarred by her work over the fire is reviled by her tribe. In the largest tent in the village lives the rich, powerful (and supposedly handsome) Invisible Being. The villagers know that only the woman who can see him will marry him. Although many women try, it is the Rough-Face Girl who, seeing beauty in earth and skies, also sees his face. Paintings cast a quiet, reflective mood for this dramatic retelling.

13.174 McAllister, Angela. **When the Ark Was Full.** Illustrated by Michaela Bloomfield. Dutton Children's Books, 1990. ISBN 0-525-44616-8. 32p. 4–7.

Long ago, whales lived on land and spent their days pretending to be hills and eating unpleasant people. In those days, whales hated water. Then came the flood, and, although Mr. Noah was kind, his ark was full. It was then that whales accidently discovered their love of the sea. In this humorous pourquoi tale, Walt and Wisteria Whale, in lavender tints against the blues and greens of skies, storms, and water, look first doleful, then woeful, and, at last, gleeful.

13.175 McCaughrean, Geraldine. **Saint George and the Dragon.** Illustrated by Nicki Palin. Doubleday, 1989. ISBN 0-385-26529-8. 32p. 5–8.

Unity of word and picture make this a unique and effective retelling of the legend of St. George, patron saint of England. The illustrations, dominated by shades of orange and suggestive of Renaissance art, are placed border to border and are stunningly realistic. Attention to detail—the begrimed lace folds of the endangered princess's bodice, for example—makes them mesmerizing. The text, too, is superb, a stately, resonant narrative in which the combined sounds of words lend strong emotion to the plot. A legend retold with such vigor and grace will attract young readers.

13.176 Osborne, Mary Pope, reteller. **Favorite Greek Myths.** Illustrated by Troy Howell. Scholastic Hardcover Books, 1989. ISBN 0-590-41338-4. 96p. 7–11.

Using their Roman names, the author retells twelve Greek myths (including the story of King Midas) in a style which humanizes the characters and their stories. Relatively short paragraphs and generous conversation balance the use of vivid vocabulary and syntax. The first appendix identifies significant Greek gods, goddesses, mortals, and locations. A second appendix acknowledges creators of myths in this and other collections. Each myth is accompanied by a full-page muted color illustration.

13.177 Osofsky, Audrey. **Dreamcatcher.** Illustrated by Ed Young. Orchard Books, 1992. ISBN 0-531-08588-0. 32p. 4–7.

"In the land of the Ojibway in a time long ago a baby sleeps, dreaming." Ed Young's dream-soft paintings, bordered with embroidered flowers, accompany the lullaby sounds of Audrey Osofsky's poetic text. Inspired by a dreamcatcher she spotted in a museum, Osofsky researched the Ojibway culture to discover the function of this web-like net, stitched onto a willow hoop, and hung above the cradleboard to capture bad dreams that attempt to invade the baby's sleep. Baby's waking and sleeping day is lovingly represented.

13.178 Quayle, Eric, compiler. **The Shining Princess, and Other Japanese Legends.** Illustrated by Michael Foreman. Arcade, 1989. ISBN 1-55970-039-4. 111p. 8 and up.

After researching Japanese legends and listening to his Japanese wife tell bedtime stories to their children, Eric Quayle compiled his ten favorite tales of the Orient. Readers will be intrigued by the cultural differences, such as samurai warriors, diets of rice-balls and seaweed, and wood-and-paper houses. Children may also be surprised at the many folk-tradition similarities. Princesses, knights, magicians, ogres, and treasure chests abound. Michael Foreman's detailed watercolors (ranging from delicate pastels to shadowy, gray-brown tones) reflect the action and emotions of each story.

13.179 Rodanas, Kristina, reteller. **Dragonfly's Tale.** Illustrated by Kristina Rodanas. Clarion Books, 1991. ISBN 0-395-57003-4. 31p. 6–12 (est.).

Once the Ashiwi people offended the spirits of the corn by wasting their food. But a young brother and sister, with the help of a magical dragonfly, restored the good fortune of the people. Based on a traditional Zuni folktale, *Dragonfly's Tale* reflects the values of kindness to others and respect for nature's gifts. The rounded forms of the humans and the blending of adobe-muted tones with deep purple hues soften the landscapes of the Southwest.

13.180 Scott, Bill, reteller. **Many Kinds of Magic: Tales of Mystery, Myth, and Enchantment.** Illustrated by Lisa Herriman. Viking Penguin, 1990. ISBN 0-670-82971-4. 256p. All ages.

This hefty collection of seventeen folktales from around the world focuses on magic under the guise of pure fun. The direct and clever writing of these versions of traditional tales heightens the appeal. The stories are from Australia, Japan, Wales, Central Europe, China, North America, and South America. Several miniature black-and-white illustrations decorate each title page.

13.181 Sloat, Teri, reteller. **The Eye of the Needle.** Illustrated by Teri Sloat. Dutton Children's Books, 1990. ISBN 0-525-44623-0. 32p. 4–8.

This predictable story is based on an actual Yupik Inuit tale. Text and colored-pencil illustrations present genuine aspects of traditional life. But children will probably most enjoy the protagonist, Amik, a young boy sent out to hunt. In his innocent self-centered hunger, Amik forgets his grandmother's needs and eats all he catches, each prey bigger than before. Only his grandmother's magic—and wise acceptance—can eventually solve the problem.

13.182 Small, Terry. **The Legend of William Tell.** Illustrated by Terry Small. Bantam/Little Rooster Books, 1991. ISBN 0-553-07031-2. 32p. 4–8.

When Gessler the Black, an Austrian lord, occupied the Swiss lands, silent revolution smoldered among the abused peoples. It was William Tell whose marksmanship and personal courage inspired the villagers to overthrow the tyrant. The legend of the Swiss woodsman, who was called upon to shoot an apple from his own son's head, is smoothly told in elaborately framed verses and illustrated by colorful scenes of mountains, villages, and horses in full trappings.

13.183 Te Kanawa, Kiri. **Land of the Long White Cloud: Maori Myths, Tales and Legends.** Illustrated by Michael Foreman. Little, Brown/Arcade, 1989. ISBN 1-55970-046-7. 119p. 9 and up (est.).

In this anthology Kiri Te Kanawa, renowned opera singer of Maori descent, recounts nineteen myths and legends of her native New Zealand. The short tales (two to seven pages in length) include stories of trickster gods, young love, scary monsters, daring adventures, underworld spirits, and the creation of lands and species. Award-winning illustrator Michael Foreman complements the text with vibrant, rainbow-hued watercolors. *Notable 1990 Children's Trade Books in the Field of Social Studies.*

13.184 Van Laan, Nancy. **Rainbow Crow: A Lenape Tale.** Illustrated by Beatriz Vidal. Alfred A. Knopf/Borzoi Books, 1989. ISBN 0-394-99577-5. 32p. 5–10.

This Lenape Indian tale from the American Northeast relates how Rainbow Crow, with beautiful feathers and melodic song, offers to fly to the Great Spirit to seek protection for the animals from snow and wind. Crow receives a stick of fire to warm the Earth, but the fire blackens its feathers and dries up its song. Although it has saved the animals, Crow has lost its beauty. The Great Spirit's final reward to Crow is a wonderful secret for readers to share. Watercolor illustrations are memorable for their portrayal of woodlands, animals, sky, and fire.

13.185 Wetterer, Margaret K. **The Boy Who Knew the Language of the Birds.** Illustrated by Beth Wright. Carolrhoda Books, 1991. ISBN 0-87614-652-3. 48p. 7–9.

In magical, long-ago Ireland, young Colum understood the language of birds and gained fame for telling their stories. Summoned to entertain the king and queen, Colum learns that two young princes have been snatched from the castle. Accidentally transformed into a dog, Colum risks his life to save the third newborn prince from the Fairy Queen. Although he manages to save the princes, he loses all magic, becoming a boy again. Granite-like frames lend substance to the tale.

13.186 Williams, Marcia. **Greek Myths for Young Children.** Illustrated by Marcia Williams. Candlewick Press, 1992. ISBN 1-56402-115-7. 32p. 6–10 (est.).

Eight Greek myths are retold through comic-strip-like illustrations, accompanied by minimal text and spread across oversize pages. Characters offer observations and even flip commentary in conversational balloons. For example, when a dull-looking Prometheus breaks off a piece of the blazing sun to bring fire to Earth, one blue-cold person approves: "Three cheers for old asbestos fingers." Children may be more receptive than their teachers to the irreverence. Pages are bordered with colorful, themed motifs.

13.187 Wilson, Barbara Ker, reteller. **The Turtle and the Island: A Folktale from Papua New Guinea.** Illustrated by Frané Lessac. J. B. Lippincott, 1990. ISBN 0-397-32439-1. 24p. 6–10 (est.).

Long, long ago, a mother sea turtle, tired of spending all her time swimming in the Pacific Ocean, builds a huge island from rocks and sand. Afterward, she dives back into the sea and brings to her new home a man who lives in an undersea cave and a woman who lives alone on an adjacent island. In time, the island is filled with many people who grow crops and fish along the seashore, and soon the island becomes known as New Guinea. Brightly colored folk-art illustrations help to retell this legend of the origin of a special island in the Pacific Ocean.

13.188 Wisniewski, David. **Sundiata: Lion King of Mali.** Illustrated by David Wisniewski. Clarion Books, 1992. ISBN 0-395-61302-7. 32p. 6–10 (est.).

Long ago in Mali, West Africa, there lived a Lion King, Sundiata, "who overcame all things to walk with greatness." His story is told by a *griot*, a keeper of the oral tradition. As a child, Sundiata could neither speak nor walk. Exiled by one of his father's wives to ensure the rule of her own son, Sundiata grew wise and strong, returning eventually to save his people from tyranny. Illustrations are intricately textured cut-paper collages, with all the colors of sunshine, plains, and glorious African textiles.

Tall Tales

13.189 Kellogg, Steven, reteller. **Mike Fink: A Tall Tale.** Illustrated by Steven Kellogg. Morrow Junior Books, 1992. ISBN 0-688-07004-3. 48p. 3 and up.

To accompany his retellings of the tales of Johnny Appleseed, Pecos Bill, and Paul Bunyan, Steven Kellogg offers the tale of Mike Fink, legendary keelboat operator and frontiersman. By wrestling bears, Mike Fink grows to be the strongest man on the Mississippi River, but like John Henry, he eventually has to compete with machinery—steamboats. Amidst all the blowing and clanging and belching, Kellogg pulls off a satisfying ending. The artwork is as energetic, detailed, and humorous as Kellogg fans have come to expect.

13.190 Kesey, Ken. **Little Tricker the Squirrel Meets Big Double the Bear.** Illustrated by Barry Moser. Viking Penguin, 1990. ISBN 0-670-81136-X. 32p. All ages.

Best known for his novels *One Flew Over the Cuckoo's Nest* and *Sometimes a Great Notion,* Ken Kesey retells a tale that his grandmother told him about Big Double, the grizzly bear who threatened the animals in Topple's Bottom. The story has a homespun flavor that draws on traditional trickster tales. Little Tricker the squirrel, who had been "lazing in the highest hole in his cottonwood high rise," uses his wits to save the animals. Comical, watercolor illustrations enliven the story.

13.191 Manes, Stephen. **Some of the Adventures of Rhode Island Red.** Illustrated by William Joyce. J. B. Lippincott, 1990. ISBN 0-397-32348-4. 117p. 8–12.

Did you say that you know of Paul Bunyan and Pecos Bill, but have never heard tell of a Rhode Island hero about the size of a grade A egg? Discovered in a hen's nest, with carrot-colored hair, denim overalls, and an indefatigable spirit, Red is tough enough to handle henhouse foxes, bullies of all shapes, and even wily politicians. As told by a Rhode Island farmer who has reason to know, the legend is illustrated by the artist of *George Shrinks.*

Prizes and Lists

Among the countless ways of honoring children's books, the following serve as noteworthy examples of awards and recognitions. Excluded are dozens of popular awards granted at the local, state, and regional levels; most international awards; and awards given for a body of work rather than for a specific title. Most books named here were published between 1988 and 1992, though an award may have been conferred in 1993. This section closes with descriptions of some popular booklists.

Jane Addams Award

Given annually to a children's book that most effectively promotes peace, social justice, world community, or equality of sexes and of all races, the Jane Addams Award was established in 1953. It is given by the Women's International League for Peace and Freedom and by the Jane Addams Peace Association.

1988 Gordon, Sheila. *Waiting for the Rain: A Novel of South Africa.* Orchard Books.

1989 Hamilton, Virginia. *Anthony Burns: The Defeat and Triumph of a Fugitive Slave.* Alfred A. Knopf.

1990 McKissack, Patricia, and Frederick McKissack. *A Long Hard Journey: The Story of the Pullman Porter.* Walker and Company.

1991 Durell, Ann, and Marilyn Sachs, eds. *The Big Book for Peace.* Dutton Children's Books.

1992 Buss, Fran L. *January of the Sparrows.* Edited by Daisy Cubias. Dutton Children's Books.

Mildred L. Batchelder Award

Given annually (unless no book is deemed worthy) to a United States publisher, the Batchelder Award honors the most outstanding book originally published in a language other than English or a country other than the United States. Established in 1968, it is given by the Association for Library Service to Children of the American Library Association.

1988 Margaret K. McElderry Books—*If You Didn't Have Me* by Ulf Nilsson. Translated from the Swedish by Lone Thygesen-Blecher and George Blecher.

1989   Lothrop, Lee & Shepard Books—*Crutches* by Peter Härtling. Translated from the German by Elizabeth D. Crawford.

1990   Dutton—*Buster's World* by Bjarne Reuter. Translated from the Danish by Anthea Bell.

1991   Dutton Children's Books—*A Hand Full of Stars* by Rafik Schami. Translated from the German by Rika Lesser.

1992   Houghton Mifflin—*The Man from the Other Side* by Uri Orlev. Translated from the Hebrew by Hillel Halkin.

Boston Globe–Horn Book Award

Given annually since 1967 by *The Boston Globe* and *The Horn Book Magazine*, these awards are conferred in three categories: outstanding fiction or poetry, outstanding nonfiction, and outstanding picture book.

1988   **Fiction Award**

Taylor, Mildred D. *The Friendship.* Dial Books.

Fiction Honor Books

Doherty, Berlie. *Granny Was a Buffer Girl.* Orchard Books.

Fleischman, Paul. *Joyful Noise: Poems for Two Voices.* Illustrated by Eric Beddows. HarperCollins/Charlotte Zolotow Books.

Mahy, Margaret. *Memory.* Margaret K. McElderry Books.

Nonfiction Award

Hamilton, Virginia. *Anthony Burns: The Defeat and Triumph of a Fugitive Slave.* Alfred A. Knopf.

Nonfiction Honor Books

Chiasson, John. *African Journey.* Bradbury Press.

Little, Jean. *Little by Little: A Writer's Education.* Viking Kestrel.

Picture Book Award

Snyder, Dianne. *The Boy of the Three-Year Nap.* Illustrated by Allen Say. Houghton Mifflin.

Picture Book Honor Books

Baker, Jeannie. *Where the Forest Meets the Sea.* Illustrated by the author. Greenwillow Books.

Williams, Vera B. *Stringbean's Trip to the Shining Sea.* Illustrated by Jennifer Williams and the author. Greenwillow Books.

1989   **Fiction Award**

Fox, Paula. *The Village by the Sea.* Orchard Books/Watts.

Fiction Honor Books

Dickinson, Peter. *Eva.* Delacorte Press.

Mayne, William. *Gideon Ahoy!* Delacorte Press.

Nonfiction Award

Macaulay, David. *The Way Things Work.* Houghton Mifflin.

Nonfiction Honor Books

Isaacson, Philip M. *Round Buildings, Square Buildings, and Buildings That Wiggle like a Fish.* Photographs by the author. Alfred A. Knopf.

Yep, Laurence. *The Rainbow People.* Illustrated by David Wiesner. HarperCollins.

Picture Book Award

Wells, Rosemary. *Shy Charles.* Illustrated by the author. Dial Books.

Picture Book Honor Books

Cooney, Barbara. *Island Boy.* Illustrated by the author. Viking Kestrel.

Vivas, Julie. *The Nativity.* Illustrated by Julia Vivas. Gulliver/Harcourt.

1990 Fiction Award

Spinelli, Jerry. *Maniac Magee.* Little, Brown.

Fiction Honor Books

Conrad, Pam. *Stonewords: A Ghost Story.* HarperCollins.

Fleischman, Paul. *Saturnalia.* HarperCollins/Charlotte Zolotow Books.

Nonfiction Award

Fritz, Jean. *The Great Little Madison.* Putnam.

Nonfiction Honor Books

Goor, Ron, and Nancy Goor. *Insect Metamorphosis: From Egg to Adult.* Photographs by Ron Goor. Atheneum.

Hoban, Tana. *Shadows and Reflections.* Photographs by the author. Greenwillow Books.

Picture Book Award

Young, Ed. *Lon Po Po: A Red Riding Hood Story from China.* Illustrated by the author. Philomel Books.

Picture Book Honor Books

Martin, Bill, Jr., and John Archambault. *Chicka Chicka Boom Boom.* Illustrated by Lois Ehlert. Simon & Schuster.

Rosen, Michael. *We're Going on a Bear Hunt.* Illustrated by Helen Oxenbury. Margaret K. McElderry Books.

Award for Creative Excellence

Burkert, Nancy Ekholm. *Valentine and Orson.* Illustrated by the author. Farrar, Straus & Giroux/Floyd Yearout Books.

1991   **Fiction Award**

Avi. *The True Confessions of Charlotte Doyle.* Orchard Books.

Nonfiction Award

Rylant, Cynthia. *Appalachia: The Voices of Sleeping Birds.* Illustrated by Barry Moser. Harcourt Brace Jovanovich.

Picture Book Award

Paterson, Katherine. *The Tale of the Mandarin Ducks.* Illustrated by Leo and Diane Dillon. Lodestar Books.

1992   **Fiction Award**

Rylant, Cynthia. *Missing May.* Orchard Books.

Nonfiction Award

Cummings, Pat (ed.). *Talking with Artists.* Bradbury Press.

Picture Book Award

Young, Ed. *Seven Blind Mice.* Illustrated by the author. Philomel Books.

Randolph Caldecott Medal

Given annually since 1938, the Caldecott Medal honors the illustrator of the most distinguished American picture book published in the United States in the preceding year. Illustrators of winning books and of honor books must be citizens or residents of the United States. This award is conferred by the Association for Library Service to Children of the American Library Association.

1988   **Medal**

Yolen, Jane. *Owl Moon.* Illustrated by John Schoenherr. Philomel Books.

Honor Book

Steptoe, John. *Mufaro's Beautiful Daughters: An African Tale.* Illustrated by the author. William Morrow.

1989   **Medal**

Ackerman, Karen. *Song and Dance Man.* Illustrated by Stephen Gammell. Alfred A. Knopf.

Honor Books

Marshall, James. *Goldilocks and the Three Bears.* Illustrated by the author. Dial Books for Young Readers.

McKissack, Patricia. *Mirandy and Brother Wind.* Illustrated by Jerry Pinkney. Alfred A. Knopf.

Snyder, Dianne. *The Boy of the Three-Year Nap.* Illustrated by Allen Say. Houghton Mifflin.

Wiesner, David. *Free Fall.* Illustrated by the author. Lothrop, Lee & Shepard Books.

1990 **Medal**

Young, Ed. *Lon Po Po: A Red Riding Hood Story from China.* Illustrated by the author. Philomel Books.

Honor Books

Ehlert, Lois. *Color Zoo.* Illustrated by the author. Lippincott.

Kimmel, Eric A. *Hershel and the Hanukkah Goblins.* Illustrated by Trina Schart Hyman. Holiday House.

Peet, William. *Bill Peet: An Autobiography.* Illustrated by the author. Houghton Mifflin.

1991 **Medal**

Macaulay, David. *Black and White.* Illustrated by the author. Houghton Mifflin.

Honor Books

Perrault, Charles. *Puss in Boots.* Illustrated by Fred Marcellino. Farrar, Straus & Giroux.

Williams, Vera B. *"More, More, More," Said the Baby: Three Love Stories.* Illustrated by the author. Greenwillow Books.

1992 **Medal**

Wiesner, David. *Tuesday.* Illustrated by the author. Clarion Books.

Honor Book

Ringgold, Faith. *Tar Beach.* Illustrated by the author. Crown Publishers.

1993 **Medal**

McCully, Emily Arnold. *Mirette on the High Wire.* Illustrated by the author. Putnam.

Honor Books

Scieszka, John. *The Stinky Cheese Man and Other Fairly Stupid Tales.* Illustrated by Lane Smith. Viking.

Williams, Sherley Anne. *Working Cotton.* Illustrated by Carole Byard. Harcourt Brace Jovanovich.

Young, Ed. *Seven Blind Mice.* Illustrated by the author. Philomel Books.

International Reading Association Children's Book Award

Given annually since 1975, this award honors the first or second book of an author, from any country, who shows unusual promise.

1988   Baker, Leslie. *Third Story Cat.* Illustrated by the author. Little, Brown.

Pullman, Philip. *Ruby in the Smoke.* Alfred A. Knopf.

1989   Polacco, Patricia. *Rechenka's Eggs.* Illustrated by the author. Philomel Books.

Wolff, Virginia Euwer. *Probably Still Nick Swansen.* Henry Holt.

1990   Crew, Linda. *Children of the River.* Delacorte Press.

Smucker, Anna Egan. *No Star Nights.* Illustrated by Steve Johnson. Alfred A. Knopf.

1991   Conlon-McKenna, Mariata. *Under the Hawthorn Tree.* Illustrated by Donald Teskey. Holiday House.

McDonald, Megan. *Is This a House for Hermit Crab?* Illustrated by S. D. Schindler. Orchard Books.

1992   Grossman, Virginia. *Ten Little Rabbits.* Illustrated by Sylvia Long. Chronicle Books.

Kass, Pnina. *Five Words.* Cricket Magazine.

Mikaelsen, Ben. *Rescue Josh McGuire.* Hyperion Books.

1993   Hesse, Karen. *Letters from Rifka.* Henry Holt.

Wood, Douglas. *Old Turtle.* Illustrated by Cheng-Khee Chee. Pfeifer-Hamilton.

Coretta Scott King Award

These writing and illustration awards and honor designations have been given annually since 1969 to black authors and illustrators for books that are outstanding inspirational and educational contributions to literature for children and young people. They are given by the Social Responsibilities Round Table of the American Library Association.

1988   **Writing Award**

Taylor, Mildred D. *The Friendship.* Dial Books for Young Readers.

Writing Honor Books

De Veaux, Alexis. *An Enchanted Hair Tale.* Illustrated by Cheryl Hanna. Harper & Row.

Lester, Julius. *The Tales of Uncle Remus: The Adventures of Brer Rabbit.* Dial Books for Young Readers.

Illustration Award

Steptoe, John. *Mufaro's Beautiful Daughters: An African Tale.* Illustrated by the author. Lothrop, Lee & Shepard Books.

Illustration Honor Books

Bryan, Ashley. *What a Morning: The Christmas Story in Black Spirituals.* Illustrated by the author. Macmillan.

Rohmer, Harriet. *Invisible Hunters.* Illustrated by Joe Fam. Children's Press.

1989 **Writing Award**

Myers, Walter Dean. *Fallen Angels.* Scholastic.

Writing Honor Books

Berry, James. *A Thief in the Village, and Other Stories.* Orchard Books.

Hamilton, Virginia. *Anthony Burns: The Defeat and Triumph of a Fugitive Slave.* Alfred A. Knopf.

Illustration Award

McKissack, Patricia. *Mirandy and Brother Wind.* Illustrated by Jerry Pinkney. Alfred A. Knopf.

Illustration Honor Book

Greenfield, Eloise. *Under the Sunday Tree.* Illustrated by Amos Ferguson. Harper & Row.

1990 **Writing Award**

McKissack, Patricia, and Frederick McKissack. *A Long Hard Journey: The Story of the Pullman Porter.* Walker and Company.

Illustration Award

Greenfield, Eloise. *Nathaniel Talking.* Illustrated by Jan Spivey Gilchrist. Black Butterfly Children's Press.

1991 **Writing Award**

Taylor, Mildred. *The Road to Memphis.* Dial Books.

Writing Honor Book

Haskins, James. *Black Dance in America: A History through Its People.* Thomas Y. Crowell.

Illustration Award

Price, Leontyne. *Aïda.* Illustrated by Leo and Diane Dillon. Harcourt/Gulliver Books.

Illustration Honor Book

Johnson, Angela. *When I Am Old with You.* Illustrated by David Soman. Orchard Books/Jackson.

1992 **Writing Award**

Myers, Walter Dean. *Now Is Your Time! The African-American Struggle for Freedom.* HarperCollins.

Writing Honor Book

Greenfield, Eloise. *Night on Neighborhood Street.* Illustrated by Jan Spivey Gilchrist. Dial Books.

Illustration Award

Ringgold, Faith. *Tar Beach.* Illustrated by the author. Crown Publishers.

Illustration Honor Book

Bryan, Ashley. *All Night, All Day: A Child's First Book of African American Spirituals.* Illustrated by the author. Atheneum.

1993 **Writing Award**

McKissack, Patricia C. *The Dark-Thirty: Southern Tales of the Supernatural.* Illustrated by Brian Pinkney. Alfred A. Knopf.

Illustration Award

Anderson, David A. *The Origin of Life on Earth: An African Creation Myth.* Illustrated by Kathleen Atkins Wilson. Sight Productions.

John Newbery Medal

The Newbery Medal, and honor book designations, have been given annually since 1922 to the authors of the most distinguished contributions to children's literature published in the United States during the preceding year. The authors must be citizens or residents of the United States. The award is given by the Association for Library Service to Children of the American Library Association.

1988 **Medal**

Freedman, Russell. *Lincoln: A Photobiography.* Clarion Books.

Honor Books

Mazer, Norma Fox. *After the Rain.* William Morrow.

Paulsen, Gary. *Hatchet.* Bradbury Press.

1989 **Medal**

Fleischman, Paul. *Joyful Noise: Poems for Two Voices.* Illustrated by Eric Beddows. HarperCollins/Charlotte Zolotow Books.

Honor Books

Hamilton, Virginia. *In the Beginning: Creation Stories from Around the World.* Illustrated by Barry Moser. Harcourt Brace Jovanovich.

Myers, Walter Dean. *Scorpions.* Harper & Row.

1990 **Medal**

Lowry, Lois. *Number the Stars.* Houghton Mifflin.

Honor Books

Lisle, Janet Taylor. *Afternoon of the Elves.* Orchard Books.

Paulsen, Gary. *The Winter Room.* Orchard Books.

Staples, Suzanne Fisher. *Shabanu: Daughter of Wind.* Alfred A. Knopf.

1991 **Medal**

Spinelli, Jerry. *Maniac Magee.* Little, Brown.

Honor Book

Avi. *The True Confessions of Charlotte Doyle.* Orchard Books.

1992 **Medal**

Naylor, Phyllis Reynolds. *Shiloh.* Atheneum.

Honor Books

Avi. *Nothing but the Truth: A Documentary Novel.* Orchard Books.

Freedman, Russell. *The Wright Brothers: How They Invented the Airplane.* Illustrated by Wilbur and Orville Wright. Holiday House.

1993 **Medal**

Rylant, Cynthia. *Missing May.* Orchard Books.

Honor Books

Brooks, Bruce. *What Hearts.* HarperCollins.

McKissack, Patricia C. *The Dark-Thirty: Southern Tales of the Supernatural.* Illustrated by Brian Pinkney. Alfred A. Knopf.

Myers, Walter Dean. *Somewhere in the Darkness.* Scholastic.

Scott O'Dell Award for Historical Fiction

Established in 1981, the Scott O'Dell Award is given to a distinguished work of historical fiction for children or young adults. The author must be a citizen or resident of the United States, the work must be written in English and published in the United States, and the story must be set in the New World (North, South, or Central America). The award is given annually (if a worthy book has been published) by the Advisory Committee of the Bulletin of the Center for Children's Books.

1988   Beatty, Patricia. *Chaley Skedaddle.* William Morrow.

1989   De Jenkins, Lyll B. *The Honorable Prison.* Lodestar Books.

1990   Reeder, Carolyn. *Shades of Gray.* Macmillan.

1991   Van Raven, Pieter. *Time of Troubles.* Macmillan.

1992   Hahn, Mary Downing. *Stepping on the Cracks.* Clarion Books.

1993   Dorris, Michael. *Morning Girl.* Hyperion Books.

Booklists

American Library Association Notable Children's Books

The Notable Children's Book Committee of the Association for Library Service to Children, a division of the American Library Association, selects notable books each year on the basis of literary quality, originality of text and illustrations, design, format, subject matter of interest and value to children, and likelihood of acceptance by children. The complete list of Notable Children's Books appears yearly in the March 15 issue of *Booklist,* a journal published by the American Library Association.

International Reading Association Children's Choices

The Children's Choices Committee of the International Reading Association–Children's Book Council Joint Committee selects a group of children's books each year to be presented to children for their consideration and vote. The list comprises those books receiving the highest number of children's votes. The complete list of Children's Choices appears yearly in the November issue of *The Reading Teacher,* a journal published by the International Reading Association. Single copies are available at no charge by sending a stamped (4 oz.), self-addressed 9 x 15 envelope to The International Reading Association, 800 Barksdale Road, P.O. Box 8139, Newark, DE 19714-8139.

Notable Children's Trade Books in the Field of Social Studies

The Book Review Subcommittee of the National Council of the Social Studies–Children's Book Council Joint Committee selects books published in the United States each year that (1) are written primarily for children in grades K–8; (2) emphasize human relations; (3) present an original theme or a fresh slant on a traditional topic; (4) are highly readable; and, when appropriate, (5) include maps and illustrations. The complete list of these notable books appears yearly in the April/May issue of *Social Education*, the journal of the National Council for the Social Studies. Single copies are available at no charge by sending a stamped (3 oz.), self-addressed 6 x 9 envelope to the Children's Book Council, 568 Broadway, Suite 404, New York, NY 10012.

Outstanding Science Trade Books for Children

The Book Review Committee of the National Science Teachers Association, in cooperation with the Children's Book Council, selects books each year that (1) are readable; (2) contain information consistent with current scientific knowledge; (3) are pleasing in format and illustrations; and (4) are nonsexist, nonracist, and nonviolent. The complete list of these outstanding books appears yearly in the March issue of *Science and Children*, the journal of the National Science Teachers Association. Single copies are available at no charge by sending a stamped (3 oz.), self-addressed 6 x 9 envelope to the Children's Book Council, 568 Broadway, Suite 404, New York, NY 10012.

Lists and descriptions of other awards, prizes, and booklists can be located at the front of recent editions of *Children's Books in Print*, an annual publication of R. R. Bowker.

Directory of Publishers

Arcade. Division of Little, Brown. Orders to: 200 West Street, Waltham, MA 02254. 800-343-9204.

Atheneum. Division of Macmillan. Orders to: 100 Front Street, Riverside, NJ 08075. 800-257-5755.

Atheneum/Jean Karl Books. See Atheneum.

Avon Books. Orders to: P.O. Box 767, Dresden, TN 38225. 800-762-0779.

Avon/Flare Books. Imprint of Avon. See Avon Books.

Bantam Books. Division of Bantam Doubleday Dell, 666 Fifth Avenue, New York, NY 10103. 800-223-6834.

Bantam/Little Rooster Books. See Bantam Books.

Bantam/Skylark Books. See Bantam Books.

Boyds Mills Press. Division of Highlights Company. Distributed by St. Martin's Press, 175 Fifth Avenue, New York, NY 10010. 800-221-7945.

Boyds Mills Press/Bell Books. See Boyds Mills Press.

Boyds Mills Press/Caroline House. See Boyds Mills Press.

Boyds Mills Press/Wordsong. See Boyds Mills Press.

Bradbury Press. Imprint of Macmillan. Orders to: 100 Front Street, Riverside, NJ 08075. 800-257-5755.

Candlewick Press. Distributed by Penguin USA. Orders to: 120 Woodbine Street, Bergenfield, NJ 07621. 800-526-0275.

Candlewick Press/Toddler Books. See Candlewick Press.

Carolrhoda Books. 241 First Avenue, N., Minneapolis, MN 55401. 800-328-4929.

Children's Book Press. Distributed by Raintree Publications, 310 W. Wisconsin Avenue, Mezzanine Level, Milwaukee, WI 53203. 800-558-7264.

Chronicle Books. Division of Chronicle Publishing, 275 Fifth Street, San Francisco, CA 94103. 800-722-6657 (800-445-7577 in California).

Clarion Books. Division of Houghton Mifflin. Orders to: Wayside Road, Burlington, MA 01803. 800-225-3362. Call for school ordering information.

Cobblehill Books. Division of Penguin USA. Orders to: 120 Woodbine Street, Bergenfield, NJ 07621. 800-526-0275.

Thomas Y. Crowell. Distributed by HarperCollins. Orders to: 1000 Keystone Industrial Park, Scranton, PA 18512. 800-242-7737.

Crown. Division of Random House. Orders to: 400 Hahn Road, Westminster, MD 21157. 800-733-3000.

Crown/New England Aquarium Books. See Crown.

David and Charles. Brunel House, Forde Close, Newton Abbot, Devon, England, TQ12 4PU. 011-44-06-266-1121.

Delacorte Press. Division of Bantam Doubleday Dell. Orders to: 666 Fifth Avenue, New York, NY 10103. 800-223-6834.

Dell. Division of Bantam Doubleday Dell, 666 Fifth Avenue, New York, NY 10103. 800-223-6834.

Dell/Yearling Books. See Dell.

Dell/Young Yearling Books. See Dell.

Dial Books. Division of Penguin USA. Orders to: 120 Woodbine Street, Bergenfield, NJ 07621. 800-526-0275.

Dial Books for Young Readers. See Dial Books.

Dillon Press. Imprint of Macmillan. Orders to: 100 Front Street, Riverside, NH 08705. 800-257-5755.

Doubleday. Division of Bantam Doubleday Dell, 666 Fifth Avenue, New York, NY 10103. 800-223-6834.

Doubleday Books for Young Readers. See Doubleday.

Doubleday/Bryon Preiss Books. See Doubleday.

E. P. Dutton. Division of Penguin USA. Orders to: 120 Woodbine Street, Bergenfield, NJ 07621. 800-526-0275.

Dutton Children's Books. See E. P. Dutton.

Farrar, Straus and Giroux. 390 Murray Hill Parkway, East Rutherford, NJ 07073. ATTN: Dept. B. 800-631-8571.

Farrar, Straus and Giroux/Michael di Capua Books. See Farrar, Straus and Giroux.

Farrar, Straus and Giroux/Sunburst Books. See Farrar, Straus and Giroux.

Farrar, Straus and Giroux/Floyd Yearout Books. See Farrar, Straus and Giroux.

Fawcett Book Group. Division of Ballantine Books. Orders to: 400 Hahn Road, Westminster, MD 21157. 800-733-3000.

Fawcett Juniper Books. See Fawcett Books.

Four Winds Press. Orders to: 100 Front Street, Riverside, NJ 08705. 800-257-5755.

Greenwillow Books. Division of William Morrow. Orders to: 39 Plymouth Street, Fairfield, NJ 07004. 800-843-9389.

Greenwillow Books/Beech Tree Books. See Greenwillow Books.

Grosset and Dunlap. Imprint of Putnam Publishing Group. Orders to: 390 Murray Hill Parkway, East Rutherford, NJ 07073. 800-631-8571.

Harcourt Brace Jovanovich. 6277 Sea Harbor Drive, Orlando, FL 32887. 800-225-5425.

Harcourt Brace Jovanovich/Gulliver Books. See Harcourt Brace Jovanovich.

Harcourt Brace Jovanovich/Gulliver Green Books. See Harcourt Brace Jovanovich.

Harcourt Brace Jovanovich/HBJ Contemporary Classics. See Harcourt Brace Jovanovich.

Harper and Row. Division of HarperCollins. Orders to: 1000 Keystone Industrial Park, Scranton, PA 18512. 800-242-7737.

Harper and Row/Harper Trophy Books. See Harper and Row.

Harper and Row/Somerville House Books. See Harper and Row.

Harper and Row/Charlotte Zolotow Books. See Harper and Row.

HarperCollins. Orders to: 1000 Keystone Industrial Park, Scranton, PA 18512. 800-242-7737.

HarperCollins/Michael di Capua Books. See HarperCollins.

HarperCollins/Laura Geringer Books. See HarperCollins.

HarperCollins/Harper Trophy Books. See HarperCollins.

HarperCollins/Charlotte Zolotow Books. See HarperCollins.

HarperKeypoint/Charlotte Zolotow Books. See HarperCollins.

Holiday House. 425 Madison Avenue, New York, NY 10017. 212-688-0085.

Henry Holt. Orders to: 4375 W. 1980 S., Salt Lake City, UT 84104. 800-488-5233.

Henry Holt/Bill Martin Books. See Henry Holt.

Henry Holt/Redfeather Books. See Henry Holt.

Houghton Mifflin. Orders to: Wayside Road, Burlington, MA 01803. 800-225-3362.

Houghton Mifflin/Ariel Books. See Houghton Mifflin.

Hyperion Books for Children. Imprint of Walt Disney Publishing Group. Distributed by Little, Brown. Orders to: 200 West Street, Waltham, MA 02254. 800-343-9204.

Alfred A. Knopf. Subsidiary of Random House. Orders to: 400 Hahn Road, Westminster, MD 21157. 800-733-3000.

Alfred A. Knopf/Borzoi Books. See Alfred A. Knopf.

Alfred A. Knopf/Dragonfly Books. See Alfred A. Knopf.

Lerner Publications. 241 First Avenue, N., Minneapolis, MN 55401. 800-328-4929.

J. B. Lippincott. J. B. Lippincott Junior Books, 227 E. Washington Square, Philadelphia, PA 19106-3780. 800-638-3030.

Little, Brown. Division of Time Warner Publishing. Orders to: 200 West Street, Waltham, MA 02254. 800-343-9204.

Little, Brown/Joy Street Books. See Little, Brown.

Little, Brown/Pond Press Books. See Little, Brown.

Little, Brown/Springboard Books. See Little, Brown.

Lodestar Books. Affiliate of Dutton Children's Books, a division of Penguin Books. Orders to: Penguin USA, 120 Woodbine Street, Bergenfield, NJ 07621. 800-526-0275.

Lothrop, Lee and Shepard Books. Division of William Morrow. Orders to: 39 Plymouth Street, Fairfield, NJ 07004. 800-843-9389.

Lothrop, Lee and Shepard Books/Albion Books. See Lothrop, Lee and Shepard Books.

Macmillan. Orders to: 100 Front Street, Riverside, NJ 08075. 800-257-5755.

Macmillan/Aladdin Books. See Macmillan.

Margaret K. McElderry Books. Division of Macmillan Children's Books Group. See Macmillan.

Julian Messner. Division of Silver Burdett Press. Orders to: P.O. Box 1226, Westwood, NJ 07675-1226. 800-843-3464.

Metropolitan Museum of Art. Orders to: Special Services Office, Flushing, NY 11381. 718-326-7050.

Millbrook Press. 2 Old New Milford Road, Brookfield, CT 06804. 203-740-2220.

Morrow Junior Books. Orders to: 39 Plymouth Street, Fairfield, NJ 07004. 800-843-9389.

Morrow Junior Books/Seashore Books. See Morrow Junior Books.

Mulberry Books. See Morrow Junior Books.

Museum of Modern Art. See Delacorte Press.

North-South Books. Orders to: 1133 Broadway, Suite 1016, New York, NY 10010. 800-282-8257.

Orchard Books. Division of Franklin Watts. 387 Park Avenue, S., New York, NY 10016. 800-672-6672.

Orchard Books/Richard Jackson Books. See Orchard Books.

Pfeifer-Hamilton. Imprint of Whole Person Press. Orders to: P.O. Box 3151, Duluth, MN 55803. 800-247-6789.

Philomel Books. Imprint of the Putnam Publishing Group. Orders to: 390 Murray Hill Parkway, East Rutherford, NJ 07073. 800-631-8571.

Picture Book Studio/Michael Neugebauer Books. Orders to: Simon and Schuster Children's Books, 200 Old Tappan Road, Old Tappan, NJ 07675. 800-223-2336.

Pippin Press. 229 East 85th Street, Gracie Station Box 92, New York, NY 10028. 212-288-4920.

Pocket Books. Division of Simon and Schuster. Orders to: 200 Old Tappan Road, Old Tappan, NJ 07675. 800-223-2336.

Pocket Books/Minstrel Books. See Pocket Books.

Clarkson N. Potter. Distributed by the Putnam Publishing Group. Orders to: 390 Murray Hill Parkway, East Rutherford, NJ 07073. 800-631-8571.

Putnam and Grosset. See G. P. Putnam's Sons.

G. P. Putnam's Sons. Imprint of the Putnam Publishing Group. Orders to: 390 Murray Hill Parkway, East Rutherford, NJ 07073. 800-631-8571.

G. P. Putnam's Sons/Sandcastle Books. See G. P. Putnam's Sons.

G. P. Putnam's Sons/Whitebird Books. See G. P. Putnam's Sons.

Random House. Orders to: 400 Hahn Road, Westminster, MD 21157. 800-733-3000.

Random House/Just Right Books. See Random House.

Random House/Dorling Kindersley Books. See Random House.

R & S Books. Distributed by Farrar, Straus and Giroux, ATTN: Dept. B. 390 Murray Hill Parkway, East Rutherford, NJ 07073. 800-631-8571.

Scholastic. Orders to: 2931 E. McCarty Street, Jefferson City, MO 65102. 800-325-6149.

Scholastic Hardcover Books. See Scholastic.

Scholastic Hardcover Books/Byron Preiss–New China Pictures Books. See Scholastic.

Scholastic/Associated Features Books. See Scholastic.

Scholastic/Blue Ribbon Books. See Scholastic.

Scholastic/Cartwheel Books. See Scholastic.

Scholastic/Lucas Evans Books. See Scholastic.

Scholastic/Madison Press Books. See Scholastic.

Charles Scribner's Sons. Division of Macmillan. Orders to: 100 Front Street, Riverside, NJ 08075. 800-257-5755.

Charles Scribner's Sons/Books for Young Readers. See Charles Scribner's Sons.

Sierra Club Books for Children. Distributed by Random House. Orders to: 400 Hahn Road, Westminster, MD 21157. 800-733-3000.

Sights Productions. P.O. Box 101, Mt. Airy, MD 21771. 410-795-4582.

Silver Burdett Press. Subsidiary of Simon and Schuster. Orders to: P.O. Box 1226, Westwood, NJ 07675-1226. 800-843-3464.

Silver Burdett Press/Stopwatch Books. See Silver Burdett Press.

Silver Press. See Silver Burdett Press.

Simon and Schuster. Orders to: 200 Old Tappan Road, Old Tappan, NJ 07675. 800-223-2336.

Simon and Schuster Books for Young Readers. See Simon and Schuster.

Simon and Schuster Books for Young Readers/NOVABOOKS. See Simon and Schuster.

Simon and Schuster/Green Tiger Press. See Simon and Schuster.

Tambourine Books. Division of William Morrow and Company. Orders to: 39 Plymouth Street, Fairfield, NJ 07004. 800-843-9389.

Troll Associates. Subsidiary of Educational Reading Services, 100 Corporate Drive, Mahwah, NJ 07430. 800-526-5289.

Viking Penguin. Division of Penguin USA. Orders to: 120 Woodbine Street, Bergenfield, NJ 07621. 800-526-0275.

Viking Penguin/Vanessa Hamilton Books. See Viking Penguin.

Viking Penguin/Puffin Books. See Viking Penguin.

Viking Penguin/Tilden Press Books. See Viking Penguin.

Walker and Company. Division of Walker Publishing, 720 Fifth Avenue, New York, NY 10019. 800-289-2553.

Frederick Warne. Division of Viking Penguin. Orders to: Penguin USA, 120 Woodbine Street, Bergenfield, NJ 07621.

Warner Books. 1271 Sixth Avenue, New York, NY 10010. 212-484-2900.

Franklin Watts. Subsidiary of Grolier. Orders to: 5450 N. Cumberland Avenue, Chicago, IL 60656. 800-672-6672.

Franklin Watts/First Books. See Franklin Watts.

Albert Whitman and Company. 6340 Oakton Street, Morton Grove, IL 60053. 800-155-7675.

Author Index

Illustrator Index

Subject Index

Title Index

Photo Credits

We wish to thank the following publishers for their gracious permission to reprint the photographs of book covers that appear on our photo pages.

Ballantine
The Vandemark Mummy by Cynthia Voigt. Copyright © 1991 by Cynthia Voigt. Cover photo used with permission.

Candlewick Press
South and North, East and West: The Oxfam Book of Children's Stories edited by Michael Rosen; illustrated by various artists.

Carolrhoda Books
Jump at de Sun: The Story of Zora Neale Hurston by A. P. Porter. Cover photograph: Zora Neale Hurston's graduation from Morgan Academy, courtesy of The Maitland Art Center; Cover illustration: painting of Eatonville by Jules Andre Smith.

Clarion Books, an imprint of Houghton Mifflin Company
Beauty and the Beast retold and illustrated by Jan Brett. Jacket illustration © 1989 by Jan Brett, Clarion Books.
Greening the City Streets: The Story of Community Gardens by Barbara A. Huff; photographs by Peter Ziebel. Jacket photograph © 1990 by Peter Ziebel, Clarion Books.
How Many Days to America? A Thanksgiving Story by Eve Bunting; illustrated by Beth Peck. Jacket illustration © 1988 by Beth Peck, Clarion Books.
June 29, 1999 by David Wiesner. Jacket illustration © 1992 by David Wiesner, Clarion Books.
Our Teacher's Having a Baby by Eve Bunting; illustrated by Diane de Groat. Jacket illustration © 1991 by Diane de Groat, Clarion Books.
Stepping on Cracks by Mary Downing Hahn. Jacket illustration © 1991 by Diane de Groat, Clarion Books.
Sundiata: Lion King of Mali by David Wisniewski. Jacket illustration © 1992 by David Wisniewski, Clarion Books.
Tuesday by David Wiesner. Jacket illustration © 1991 by David Wiesner, Clarion Books.
The Wall by Eve Bunting; illustrated by Ronald Himler. Jacket illustration © 1990 by Ronald Himler, Clarion Books.

Harcourt, Brace & Company
Aïda told by Leontyne Price; illustrated by Leo and Diane Dillon. Used by permission of Harcourt Brace & Company.
The American Family Farm: A Photo Essay by George Ancona text by Joan Anderson. Used by permission of Harcourt Brace & Company.
The Animal that Drank Up Sound by William Stafford; illustrated by Debra Frasier. Used by permission of Harcourt Brace & Company.
Appalachia: The Voices of Sleeping Birds by Cynthia Rylant and Barry Moser. Used by permission of Harcourt Brace & Company.
Beauty and the Beast told by Nancy Willard; illustrated by Barry Moser. Used by permission of Harcourt Brace & Company.

Drylongso by Virginia Hamilton; illustrated by Jerry Pinkney. Used by permission of Harcourt Brace & Company.
Eating the Alphabet: Fruits and Vegetables from A to Z by Lois Ehlert. Used by permission of Harcourt Brace & Company.
Encounter by Jane Yolen; illustrated by David Shannon. Used by permission of Harcourt Brace & Company.
I Went Walking by Sue Williams; illustrated by Julie Vivas. Used by permission of Harcourt Brace & Company.
In the Beginning: Creation Stories from around the World told by Virginia Hamilton; illustrated by Barry Moser. Used by permission of Harcourt Brace & Company.
The Lady Who Put Salt in Her Coffee by Lucretia Hale; adapted and illustrated by Amy Schwartz. Used by permission of Harcourt Brace & Company.
Little Penguin's Tale by Audrey Wood. Used by permission of Harcourt Brace & Company.
Melisande by E. Nesbit; illustrated by P. J. Lynch. Used by permission of Harcourt Brace & Company.
Moon Rope by Lois Ehlert. Used by permission of Harcourt Brace & Company.
Neighborhood Odes by Gary Soto; illustrated by David Diaz. Used by permission of Harcourt Brace & Company.
Nurse Lugton's Curtain by Virginia Woolf; illustrated by Julie Vivas. Used by permission of Harcourt Brace & Company.
Piggins and the Royal Wedding by Jane Yolen; illustrated by Jane Dyer. Used by permission of Harcourt Brace & Company.
Pish, Posh, Said Hieronymus Bosch by Nancy Willard; illustrated by Leo and Diane Dillon. Used by permission of Harcourt Brace & Company.
A River Ran Wild by Lynne Cherry. Used by permission of Harcourt Brace & Company.
The Steadfast Tin Soldier by Hans Christian Andersen; illustrated by P. J. Lynch. Used by permission of Harcourt Brace & Company.
Teammates by Peter Golenbock; illustrated by Paul Bacon. Used by permission of Harcourt Brace & Company.
Who Is the Beast? by Keith Baker. Used by permission of Harcourt Brace & Company.
You Silly Goose by Ellen Stoll Walsh. Used by permission of Harcourt Brace & Company.
Zomo the Rabbit: A Trickster Tale from West Africa by Gerald McDermott. Used by permission of Harcourt Brace & Company.

HarperCollins Children's Books
The Amazing Potato: A Story in Which the Incas, Conquistadors, Marie Antoinette, Thomas Jefferson, Wars, Famines, Immigrants, and French Fries All Play a Part by Milton Meltzer. Jacket ill. © by Laszlo Kubinyi for *The Amazing Potato* by Milton Meltzer.
An American Heritage: The Arab-American Minority by Brent Ashabranner; photographs by Paul S. Conklin. Jacket photography © by Paul S. Conklin for *An Ancient Heritage* by Brent Ashabranner.
Bones, Bones, Dinosaur Bones by Byron Barton. Jacket ill. © 1990 by Byron Barton for *Bones, Bones, Dinosaur Bones.*
The Buck Stops Here: The Presidents of the United States by Alice Provensen. Jacket ill. © 1990 by Alice Provensen from *The Buck Stops Here.*
Color Farm by Lois Ehlert. Jacket ill. © 1990 by Lois Ehlert from *Color Farm.*
The Diamond Tree: Jewish Tales from Around the World by Howard Schwartz and Barbara Rush; illustrated by Uri Shulevitz. Jacket ill. © 1991 by Uri Shulevitz for *The Diamond Tree* by Howard Schwartz & Barbara Rush.

The Dream Is Alive by Barbara Embury and Thomas D. Crouch.

The Folks in the Valley: A Pennsylvania Dutch ABC by Jim Aylesworth; illustrated by Stefano Vitale. Jacket ill. © 1992 by Stefano Vitale for *The Folks in the Valley* by Jim Aylesworth.

Go Fish by Mary Stoltz; illustrated by Pat Cummings. Jacket ill. © 1991 by Pat Cummings for *Go Fish* by Mary Stoltz.

Heartland by Diane Siebert; illustrated by Wendell Minor. Jacket ill. © 1989 by Wendell Minor for *Heartland* by Diane Siebert.

If You Give a Moose a Muffin by Laura Joffe Numeroff; illustrated by Felicia Bond. Jacket ill. © 1991 by Felicia Bond for *If You Give a Moose a Muffin* by Laura Joffe Numeroff.

The King's Day: Louis XIV of France by Aliki. Jacket ill. © 1989 by Aliki from *The King's Day*.

The Moon of the Fox Pups by Jean Craighead George; illustrated by Norman Adams. Jacket ill. © 1992 by Norman Adams for *The Moon of the Fox Pups* by Jean Craighead George.

The Moon of the Salamanders by Jean Craighead George; illustrated by Marlene Hill Werner. Jacket ill. © 1992 by Marlene Hill Werner for *The Moon of the Salamanders* by Jean Craighead George.

Now Is Your Time! The African-American Struggle for Freedom. Used with permission.

Poem-Making by Myra Cohn Livingston. Jacket ill. © 1991 by Lisa Desimini for *Poem-Making* by Myra Cohn Livingston.

Prairie Visions: The Life and Times of Solomon Butcher by Pam Conrad. Jacket design by David Saylor.

Shadow-Play by Paul Fleischman; illustrated by Eric Beddows. Jacket ill. © 1990 by Eric Beddows for *Shadow Play* by Paul Fleischman.

Townsend's Warbler by Paul Fleischman. Jacket ill. © 1992 by Vincent Nasta for *Townsend's Warbler* by Paul Fleischman.

The Truth About Unicorns by James Cross Giblin. Jacket ill. © 1991 by Michael McDermott for *The Truth About Unicorns* by James Cross Giblin.

The Tub People by Pam Conrad; illustrated by Richard Eglieski. Jacket ill. © 1989 by Richard Eglieski for *The Tub People* by Pam Conrad.

Whales by Seymour Simon. Photo on jacket ©1989 by Ocean Images, Inc. and Al Gidding.

What Hearts by Bruce Brooks. Jacket ill. © 1992 by Lambert Davis for *What Hearts* by Bruce Brooks.

Who Discovered America? Mysteries and Puzzles of the New World by Patricia Lauber; illustrated by Mike Eagle. Jacket ill. © 1992 by Mike Eagle for *Who Discovered America?* by Patricia Lauber.

Willie's Not the Hugging Kind by Joyce Durham Barrett; illustrated by Pat Cummings. Jacket ill. © 1989 by Pat Cummings for *Willie's Not the Hugging Kind* by Joyce Durham Barrett.

The Year of the Panda by Miriam Schlein; illustrated by Kam Mak. Jacket ill. © 1990 by Kam Mak for *The Year of the Panda* by Miriam Schlein.

Young Joan by Barbara Dana. Jacket ill. © 1991 by Viqui Maggio for *Young Joan* by Barbara Dana.

Henry Holt and Company, Inc.

Exploring an Ocean Tide Pool by Jeanne Bendick; illustrated by Todd Telander. Henry Holt and Company, copyright 1992.

Lunch by Denise Fleming. Henry Holt and Company, copyright 1993.

Old Black Fly by Jim Aylesworth; illustrated by Stephen Gammell. Henry Holt and Company, copyright 1992.

Train Leaves the Station by Eve Merriam; illustrated by Dale Gottlieb. Henry Holt and Company, copyright 1993.

Houghton Mifflin Company
Anastasia at this Address by Lois Lowry. © 1991 by Lois Lowry with permission of Houghton Mifflin Company.
Bill Peet: An Autobiography by Bill Peet. © 1989 by Bill Peet with permission of Houghton Mifflin Company.
Black and White by David Macaulay. © 1990 by David Macaulay with permission of Houghton Mifflin Company.
Number the Stars by Lois Lowry. © 1989 by Lois Lowry with permission of Houghton Mifflin Company.
Oink by Arthur Geisert. © 1991 by Arthur Geisert with permission of Houghton Mifflin Company.
The Widow's Broom by Chris Van Allsburg. © 1992 by Chris Van Allsburg with permission of Houghton Mifflin Company.

Hyperion Books for Children
Goodnight to Annie: An Alphabet Lullaby by Eve Merriam; illustrated by Carol Schwartz. Used with permission.
Morning Girl by Michael Dorris. Used with permission.
Surtsey: The Newest Place on Earth by Kathryn Lasky; photographs by Christopher G. Knight. Used with permission.

Little, Brown
The Antique Store Cat by Leslie Baker. Copyright 1992 by Leslie Baker.
Antler, Bear, Canoe: A Northwoods Alphabet Year by Betsy Bowen. Copyright 1991 by Betsy Bowen.
Baby-O by Nancy White Carlstrom; illustrated by Sucie Stevenson. Text copyright 1992 by Nancy White Carlstrom; illustrations copyright 1992 by Sucie Stevenson.
Celia's Island Journal by Celia Thaxter; adapted and illustrated by Loretta Krupinski. Copyright 1992 by Loretta Krupinski.
Cockatoos by Quentin Blake. Copyright 1992 by Quentin Blake.
Dinosaurs Alive and Well! A Guide to Good Health by Laurie Krasny Brown; illustrated by Marc Brown. Copyright 1990 by Laurie Krasny Brown and Marc Brown.
Fire and Silk: Flying in a Hot Air Balloon by Neil Johnson. Copyright 1991 by Neil Johnson.
The Jolly Christmas Postman by Janet and Allan Ahlberg. Copyright 1991 by Allan Ahlberg and Janet Ahlberg.
The Lemonade Babysitter by Karen Waggoner; illustrated by Dorothy Donohue. Text copyright 1992 by Karen Waggoner; Illustrations copyright 1992 by Dorothy Donohue.
Noah's Ark illustrated by Isabelle Brent. Illustration copyright 1992 by Isabelle Brent.
The Pop-Up, Pull-Tab, Playtime House That Jack Built by Nadine Bernard Westcott. Copyright 1991 by Intervisual Communications, Inc.; illustrations copyright 1991 by Nadine Bernard Westcott.
The Rag Coat by Lauren Mills. Copyright 1991 by Lauren Mills.
A Real Nice Clambake by Oscar Hammerstein II; illustrated by Nadine Bernard Westcott. Text copyright 1945 by Williamson Music, Inc.; illustration copyright 1992 by Nadine Bernard Westcott.
Recycle: A Handbook for Kids by Gail Gibbons. Copyright 1992 by Gail Gibbons.

Talking Like the Rain: A Read-to-me Book of Poems selected by X. J. Kennedy and Dorothy M. Kennedy; illustrated by Jane Dyer. Text copyright 1992 by X. J. and Dorothy Kennedy, Ltd.; illustrations copyright 1992 by Jane Dyer.

Who Harnessed the Horse? The Story of Animal Domestication by Margery Facklam; illustrated by Steven Parton. Text copyright 1992 by Margery Facklam; illustrations copyright 1992 by Steven Parton.

Macmillan Publishing Company

Amy Elizabeth Explores Bloomingdale's written and illustrated by E. L. Konigsburg. Published by Atheneum, an imprint of the Macmillan Publishing Company.

Beyond the Ridge written and illustrated by Paul Goble. Published by Bradbury Press, an imprint of the Macmillan Publishing Company.

Big Pumpkin by Erica Silverman; illustrated by S. D. Schindler. Published by Macmillan, an imprint of the Macmillan Publishing Company.

A Birthday Basket for Tía by Pat Mora; illustrated by Cecily Lang. Published by Macmillan, an imprint of the Macmillan Publishing Company.

The Exiles by Hilary McKay. Published by McElderry, an imprint of the Macmillan Publishing Company.

Grasshopper Summer by Ann Turner. Published by Macmillan, an imprint of the Macmillan Publishing Company.

Katie's Trunk by Ann Turner; illustrated by Ron Himler. Published by Macmillan, an imprint of the Macmillan Publishing Company.

The Moon Lady by Amy Tan; illustrated by Gretchen Schields. Published by Macmillan, an imprint of the Macmillan Publishing Company.

Tehanu: The Last Book of Earthsea by Ursula K. Le Guin. Published by Atheneum, an imprint of the Macmillan Publishing Company.

Three Young Pilgrims by Cheryl Harness. Published by Bradbury Press, an imprint of the Macmillan Publishing Company.

We're Going on a Bear Hunt by Michael Rosen; illustrated by Helen Oxbury. Published by McElderry, an imprint of the Macmillan Publishing Company.

Millbrook Press

Fiesta: Mexico's Great Celebrations by Elizabeth Silverthorne; illustrated by Jan Davey Ellis. Used by permission of The Millbrook Press Inc.

William Morrow & Company

Aardvarks, Disembark! by Ann Jonas from Greenwillow Books: a division of William Morrow & Company.

Alison's Zinnia by Anita Lobel from Greenwillow Books: a division of William Morrow & Company.

American Politics: How It Really Works by Milton Meltzer from Morrow Junior Books: a division of William Morrow & Company.

Asleep, Asleep by Mirra Ginsburg; illustrated by Nancy Tafuri, from Greenwillow Books: a division of William Morrow & Company.

Bard of Avon: The Story of William Shakespeare by Diane Stanley and Peter Vennema; illustrated by Diane Stanley, from Morrow Junior Books: a division of William Morrow & Company.

Caribbean Carnival: Songs of the West Indies by Irving Burgie; illustrated by Frané Lessac, from Tambourine Books: a division of William Morrow & Company.

Dinosaur Dig by Kathryn Lasky; photographs by Christopher G. Knight, from Morrow Junior Books: a division of William Morrow & Company.

Each Orange Had 8 Slices: A Counting Book by Paul Giganti, Jr.; illustrated by Donald Crews, from Greenwillow Books: a division of William Morrow & Company.

Elfwyn's Saga story and illustrations by David Wisniewski, from Lothrop, Lee & Shepard: a division of William Morrow & Company.

Greedyanna by Frank Remkiewics, from Lothrop, Lee & Shepard Books: a division of William Morrow & Company.

Hopscotch around the World by Mary D. Lankford; illustrated by Karen Milone, from Morrow Junior Books: a division of William Morrow & Company.

I Spy: An Alphabet in Art devised and selected by Lucy Micklethwait, from Greenwillow Books: a division of William Morrow & Company.

If You Made a Million by David M. Schwartz; illustrated by Steven Kellogg, from Lothrop, Lee, & Shepard Books: a division of William Morrow & Company.

Lightning Inside You edited by John Bierhorst; illustrated by Louise Brierley. Published by Morrow Junior Books: a division of William Morrow & Company.

Little Mouse's Painting by Diane Wolkstein; illustrated by Maryjane Begin, from Morrow Junior Books: a division of William Morrow & Company.

Loop the Loop by Barbara Dugan; illustrated by James Stevenson, from Greenwillow Books: a division of William Morrow & Company.

An Ocean World by Peter Sis, from Greenwillow Books: a division of William Morrow & Company.

Our Solar System by Seymour Simon, from Morrow Junior Books: a division of William Morrow & Company.

Princess Furball by Charlotte Huck; illustrated by Anita Lobel, from Greenwillow Books: a division of William Morrow & Company.

The Rainbabies by Laura Krauss Melmed; illustrated by Jim LaMarche, published by Lothrop, Lee & Shepard Books: a division of William Morrow & Company.

The Rainbow People by Laurence Yep, from Morrow Junior Books: a division of William Morrow & Company.

The Star Fisher by Laurence Yep, from Morrow Junior Books: a division of William Morrow & Company.

The 13th Clue by Ann Jonas, from Greenwillow Books: a division of William Morrow & Company.

Traces of Life: The Origins of Humankind by Kathryn Lasky; illustrated by Whitney Powell, from Morrow Junior Books: a division of William Morrow & Company.

Twinkle, Twinkle, Little Star illustrated by Michael Hague, from Morrow Junior Books: a division of William Morrow & Company.

Up North at the Cabin by Marsha Wilson Chall; illustrated by Steve Johns, published by Lothrop, Lee & Shepard Books: a division of William Morrow and Company.

Words of Stone by Kevin Henkes, from Greenwillow Books: a division of William Morrow & Company.

Penguin USA

has granted permission to use photo images of covers of the following titles:

Abuela by Arthur Dorros; illustrated by Elisa Kleven.

Amazing Grace by Mary Hoffman; illustrated by Caroline Binch.

Anansi Finds a Fool by Verna Aardema; illustrated by Bryna Walman.

Behind the Blue and Gray: The Soldier's Life in the Civil War by Delia Ray.

Benjamin's Barn by Reeve Lindbergh; illustrated by Susan Jeffers.

The Big Book of Peace by various artists and writers.

Bizarre Birds and Beasts: Animal Verses by James Marsh.

Boots and the Glass Mountain by Claire Martin; illustrated by Gennady Spirin.

Brother Eagle, Sister Sky illustrated by Susan Jeffers.

The Day the Goose Got Loose by Reeve Lindbergh; illustrated by Steven Kellogg.
The Fortune Tellers by Lloyd Alexander; illustrated by Trina Schart Hyman.
Fox Outfoxed by James Marshall.
Fudge-a-mania by Judy Blume.
Gorilla/Chinchilla by Bert Kitchen.
The Horrendous Hullabaloo by Margaret Mahy; illustrated by Patricia MacCarthy.
A Little Excitement by Marc Harshman; illustrated by Ted Rand.
Lyddie by Katherine Paterson.
The Jedera Adventure by Lloyd Alexander.
The Man Who Kept His Heart in a Bucket by Sonia Levitin; illustrated by Jerry Pinkney.
Matthew and Tilly by Rebecca C. Jones; illustrated by Beth Peck.
Max's Chocolate Chicken by Rosemary Wells.
Mississippi Bridge by Mildred D. Taylor; illustrated by Max Ginsburg.
Mother Goose's Words of Wit and Wisdom: A Book of Months by Tedd Arnold.
The Minpins by Roald Dahl; illustrated by Patrick Benson.
A Nice Walk in the Jungle by Nan Bodsworth.
Ocean Parade: A Counting Book by Patricia MacCarthy.
Paul Revere's Ride by Henry Wadsworth Longfellow; illustrated by Ted Rand.
Pome & Peel by Amy Ehrlich; illustrated by László Gál.
The Remarkable Journey of Prince Jen by Lloyd Alexander.
The Road to Memphis by Mildred D. Taylor.
Rosa Parks: My Story by Rosa Parks with Jim Haskins.
Ryan White: My Own Story by Ryan White and Ann Marie Cunningham.
The Samurai's Daughter by Robert D. San Souci; illustrated by Stephen T. Johnson.
The Stinky Cheese Man and Other Fairly Stupid Tales by Jon Scieszka and Lane Smith.
The Tale of the Mandarin Ducks by Katherine Paterson; illustrated by Leo and Diane Dillon.
Treasure Island by Robert Louis Stevenson; illustrated by Robert Ingpen.
The Trolley to Yesterday by John Bellairs.
Visual Magic by David Thomson.
Weird Parents by Audrey Wood.
When You Were Just a Little Girl by B. G. Hennessy; illustrated by Jeanne Arnold.

Putnam & Grosset Group
The Ballad of the Harp-Weaver by Edna St. Vincent Millay; illustrated by Beth Peck. Reprinted by permission of Philomel Books.
Bully for You, Teddy Roosevelt by Jean Fritz; illustrated by Mike Wimmer. Reprinted by permission of G. P. Putnam's Sons.
Chicken Sunday by Patricia Polacco. Reprinted by permission of Philomel Books.
Dear Dr. Bell . . . Your friend, Helen Keller by Judith St. George. Reprinted by permission of G. P. Putnam's Sons.
Dinosaur Dances by Jane Yolen; illustrated by Bruce Degen. Reprinted by permission of G. P. Putnam's Sons.
Eric Carle's Dragons Dragons and Other Creatures that Never Were. Reprinted by permission of Philomel Books.
Finding Foxes by Allison Blyler; illustrated by Robert J. Blake. Reprinted by permission of Philomel Books.
Handel and the Famous Sword Swallower of Halle by Bryna Stevens; illustrated by Ruth Tietjen Councell. Reprinted by permission of Philomel Books.
Ho-Limlim: A Rabbit Tale from Japan by Tejima. Reprinted by permission of Philomel Books.

Laura Charlotte by Kathryn O. Galbraith; illustrated by Floyd Cooper. Reprinted by permission of Philomel Books.
The Leaving by Budge Wilson. Reprinted by permission of Philomel Books.
Mariel of Redwall by Brian Jacques. Reprinted by permission of Philomel Books.
Mason and Dixon's Line of Fire by Judith St. George. Reprinted by permission of G. P. Putnam's Sons.
A Memorial for Mr. Lincoln by Brent Ashabranner; photographs by Jennifer Ashabranner. Reprinted by permission of G. P. Putnam's Sons.
Michelangelo's World by Piero Ventura. Reprinted by permission of G. P. Putnam's Sons.
Mirette on the High Wire by Emily Arnold McCully. Reprinted by permission of G. P. Putnam's Sons.
Nate the Great and the Stolen Base by Marjorie Weinman Sharmat; illustrated by Marc Simont. Reprinted by permission of G. P. Putnam's Sons.
Northern Lullaby by Nancy White Carlstrom; illustrated by Leo and Diane Dillon. Reprinted by permission of Philomel Books.
Otters Under Water by Jim Arnosky. Reprinted by permission of G. P. Putnam's Sons.
The Owl and the Pussycat by Edward Lear; illustrated by Jan Brett. Reprinted by permission of G. P. Putnam's Sons.
Picnic at Mudsock Meadow by Patricia Polacco. Reprinted by permission of G. P. Putnam's Sons.
Seven Blind Mice by Ed Young. Reprinted by permission of Philomel Books.
Thirteen Moons on Turtle's Back: A Native American Year of Moons by Joseph Bruchac and Jonathan London; illustrated by Thomas Locker. Reprinted by permission of Philomel Books.
The Trouble with Trolls by Jan Brett. Reprinted by permission of G. P. Putnam's Sons.
Will's Mammoth by Rafe Martin; illustrated by Stephen Gammell. Reprinted by permission of G. P. Putnam's Sons.

Random House
The Dark Thirty: Southern Tales of the Supernatural by Patricia C. McKissack; illustrated by Brian Pinkney. Illustrations copyright © 1992 by Brian Pinkney.
The High Rise Glorious Skittle Skat Roarious Sky Pie Angel Food Cake by Nancy Willard; illustrated by Richard Jesse Watson. Illustrations copyright © 1990 by Richard Jesse Watson.
hist whist by e. e. cummings; illustrated by Deborah Kogan Ray. Illustrations copyright © 1989 by Deborah Kogan Ray.
No Star Nights by Anna Egan Smucker; illustrated by Steve Johnson. Illustrations copyright © 1989 by Steve Johnson.
Piggies by Audrey and Don Wood. Illustration copyright © 1991 by Don Wood.
Poems by A. Nonny Mouse selected by Jack Prelutsky; illustrated by Henrik Drescher. Illustrations copyright 1989 by Henrik Drescher.
Tar Beach by Faith Ringgold. Illustrations copyright © 1991 by Faith Ringgold.
Tillie and the Wall by Leo Lionni. Illustrations copyright © 1989 by Leo Lionni.

Sierra Club Books for Children
Come Back, Salmon: How a Group of Dedicated Kids Adopted Pigeon Creek and Brought It Back to Life by Molly Cone; photographs by Sidnee Wheelwright. Cover photograph © Sidnee Wheelwright from *Come Back, Salmon* written by Molly Cone and published by Sierra Club Books for Children.

Nature's Tricksters: Animals and Plants that Aren't What They Seem by Mary Batten; illustrated by Lois Lovejoy. Illustration copyright © 1992 by Lois Lovejoy from *Nature's Tricksters*, written by Mary Batten and published by Sierra Club Books for Children.

Urban Roosts: Where Birds Nest in the City by Barbara Bash. Illustration copyright © 1990 by Barbara Bash from her book *Urban Roosts*, published by Sierra Club Books for Children.

Simon & Schuster

Chicka Chicka Boom Boom by Bill Martin Jr. and John Archambault; illustrated by Lois Ehlert. Copyright © by Lois Ehlert, reprinted by arrangement with Simon & Schuster.

Frog Odyssey by Juliet and Charles Snape. Copyright © 1991 by Juliet and Charles Snape, reprinted by arrangement with Simon & Schuster.

The Grandpa Days by Joan W. Blos; illustrated by Emily Arnold McCully. Copyright © 1989 by Emily Arnold McCully, reprinted by arrangement with Simon & Schuster.

The Happy Prince by Oscar Wilde; illustrated by Ed Young. Copyright © 1989 by Ed Young, reprinted by arrangement with Simon & Schuster.

What Comes in 2's 3's and 4's? by Suzanne Aker; illustrated by Bernie Karlin. Copyright © 1990 by Bernie Karlin, reprinted by arrangement with Simon & Schuster.

The Wise Woman and Her Secret by Eve Merriam; illustrated by Linda Graves. Copyright © 1991 by Linda Graves, reprinted by arrangement with Simon & Schuster.

Sterling

Fun with Paper Bags & Cardboard Tubes by F. Virginia Walter. Used by permission of Sterling Publishing Co., Inc., 387 Park Ave. S., New York, NY 10016 from *Fun with Paper Bags & Cardboard Tubes* by F. Virginia Walter, © 1992 by F. Virginia Walter.

Walker & Company

A Long Hard Journey: The Story of the Pullman Porter by Patricia and Frederick Mekissak. Jacket photos courtesy of A. Philip Randolph Institute, World Arts Foundation, Inc. and A. Philip Randolph Institute. Jacket design by Michael Chesworth.

Editors

Julie M. Jensen is professor of Language and Literacy Studies, a division of the Department of Curriculum and Instruction at The University of Texas at Austin. She is a graduate of the University of Minnesota and a former teacher in the Minneapolis Public Schools. Long active in the Council and its affiliates, Jensen was president of both NCTE (1988) and of its Central Texas Council. She has served NCTE's publication program as a member of the Editorial Board, as well as editor of the elementary section journal, *Language Arts* (1976–1983), and several NCTE titles, including *Measures for Research and Evaluation in the English Language Arts* (two volumes with William Fagan and Charles Cooper) and *Composing and Comprehending.*

Nancy Roser is professor of Language and Literacy Studies in the Department of Curriculum and Instruction at The University of Texas at Austin. She teaches both graduate and undergraduate courses in language arts and reading. Her research interests include the use of trade literature within elementary classrooms.